Christmas 25

Aunty Marlene,
For your collection is a book about the city & hope you will have plenty of opportunity to get to know.

love

Done with Slavery

Studies on the History of Quebec
Études d'histoire du Québec
MAGDA FAHRNI and JARRETT RUDY Series Editors/Directeurs de la collection

1 *Habitants and Merchants in Seventeenth-Century Montreal*
Louise Dechêne

2 *Crofters and Habitants*
Settler Society, Economy, and Culture in a Quebec Township, 1848–1881
J.I. Little

3 *The Christie Seigneuries*
Estate Management and Settlement in the Upper Richelieu Valley, 1760–1859
Francoise Noël

4 *La Prairie en Nouvelle-France, 1647–1760*
Louis Lavallée

5 *The Politics of Codification*
The Lower Canadian Civil Code of 1866
Brian Young

6 *Arvida au Saguenay*
Naissance d'une ville industrielle
José E. Igartua

7 *State and Society in Transition*
The Politics of Institutional Reform in the Eastern Townships, 1838–1852
J.I. Little

8 *Vingt ans après, Habitants et marchands*
Lectures de l'histoire des xviie et xviiie siècles canadiens
Habitants et marchands, Twenty Years Later
Reading the History of Seventeenth- and Eighteenth-Century Canada
Edited by Sylvie Dépatie, Catherine Desbarats, Danielle Gauvreau, Mario Lalancette, Thomas Wien

9 *Les récoltes des forêts publiques au Québec et en Ontario, 1840–1900*
Guy Gaudreau

10 *Carabins ou activistes? L'idéalisme et la radicalisation de la pensée étudiante à l'Université de Montréal au temps du duplessisme*
Nicole Neatby

11 *Families in Transition*
Industry and Population in Nineteenth-Century Saint-Hyacinthe
Peter Gossage

12 *The Metamorphoses of Landscape and Community in Early Quebec*
Colin M. Coates

13 *Amassing Power*
J.B. Duke and the Saguenay River, 1897–1927
David Perera Massell

14 *Making Public Pasts*
The Contested Terrain of Montreal's Public Memories, 1891–1930
Alan Gordon

15 *A Meeting of the People*
School Boards and Protestant Communities in Quebec, 1801–1998
Roderick MacLeod and Mary Anne Poutanen

16 *A History for the Future*
Rewriting Memory and Identity in Quebec
Jocelyn Létourneau

17 *C'était du spectacle !*
L'histoire des artistes transsexuelles à Montréal, 1955–1985
Viviane Namaste

18 *The Freedom to Smoke*
Tobacco Consumption and Identity
Jarrett Rudy

19 *Vie et mort du couple en Nouvelle-France*
Québec et Louisbourg au XVIIIe siècle
Josette Brun

20 *Fous, prodigues, et ivrognes*
Familles et déviance à Montréal au XIXe Siècle
Thierry Nootens

21 *Done with Slavery*
The Black Fact in Montreal, 1760–1840
Frank Mackey

DONE WITH SLAVERY

The Black Fact in Montreal

1760–1840

Frank Mackey

MCGILL-QUEEN'S UNIVERSITY PRESS
MONTREAL & KINGSTON · LONDON · ITHACA

© McGill-Queen's University Press 2010

ISBN 978-0-7735-3578-7

Legal deposit first quarter 2010
Bibliothèque nationale du Québec

Printed in Canada on acid-free paper that is 100% ancient forest free
(100% post-consumer recycled), processed chlorine free.

This book has been published with the help of a grant from the Canadian Federation for the Humanities and Social Sciences, through the Aid to Scholarly Publications Programme, using funds provided by the Social Sciences and Humanities Research Council of Canada.

McGill-Queen's University Press acknowledges the support of the Canada Council for the Arts for our publishing program. We also acknowledge the financial support of the Government of Canada through the Book Publishing Industry Development Program (BPIDP) for our publishing activities.

Library and Archives Canada Cataloguing in Publication

Mackey, Frank
Done with slavery : the Black fact in Montreal, 1760–1840 / Frank Mackey.

(Studies on the history of Quebec ; 21)
Includes bibliographical references and index.
ISBN 978-0-7735-3578-7

1. Blacks–Québec (Province)–Montréal–History. 2. Slavery–Québec (Province)–Montréal–History. 3. Blacks–Québec (Province)–Montréal–Social conditions. 4. Québec (Province)–History–1763–1791. 5. Québec (Province)–History–1791–1841. I. Title. II. Series: Studies on the history of Quebec ; 21

FC2947.9.B6M33 2010   971.4'2800496   C2009-904007-7

This book was designed and typeset by studio oneonone in Times 10.2/12.5

To Nicholas Dorais,

blessed with every gift

CONTENTS

Acknowledgments | ix
Introduction | 3

1 What slavery? | 15
2 There ought to be a law | 36
3 Still counting | 79
4 "Things as they were" | 108
5 Deer out of a cage | 136
6 On steamboats | 164
7 Jacks of all trades | 183
8 Political colours | 218
9 The colour of justice | 236
10 Shoulder to shoulder, arm in arm | 266
11 One thousand characters in search of an author or two | 292

Appendices
I Newspaper notices
   A. Slave sales and fugitives | 307
   B. Miscellaneous notices referring to blacks | 340
   C. Three earliest advertisements by blacks | 344
II Slavery in the judges' eyes | 345
III Spoils of war | 381
IV The King v. Alexander Grant, George Nixon and Moses Powell Wormley | 408

Abbreviations | 417
Notes | 419
Sources | 553
Information on illustrations | 577
Index | 581

ACKNOWLEDGMENTS

In researching and writing this book, I have accumulated debts of gratitude so numerous that I must list them only selectively here. Thanks, then, to the staff of the Bibliothèque et Archives nationales du Québec in Montreal for their advice and help in locating documents. Thanks to the staff at Library and Archives Canada, who were invariably helpful, and particularly to Patricia Kennedy for her interest, enthusiasm, and practical advice, and to Stephen Salmon for providing access to the Molson Papers at a time when conservation work was keeping them out of general circulation. Thanks to Soeur Nicole Bussières, archivist of the Soeurs Hospitalières de Saint-Joseph, for providing access to the old admission records of the Hôtel-Dieu in Montreal, which proved to be invaluable in establishing the identities of many black figures. Thanks to Myriam Cloutier of Mount Royal Commemorative Services for her help in consulting the records of Montreal's old Protestant burial grounds. And thanks to Ann Carroll for everything – an ear, a hand, wise counsel, and infinite patience.

Done with Slavery

Introduction

Outside of specialized works devoted to "black history," blacks are largely absent from Canada's historical literature. It is not that they have been airbrushed out of the grand panorama: they were never included to begin with. This state of affairs obscures the fact that "black history" is "white history" – what usually passes for history *tout court* – and the sooner this is recognized the better. We cannot know who we are without knowing who we were, and we in Canada – whatever our origins or skin tone – will never know that without understanding the black experience and what it tells us about the Eurocentric culture that has dominated our history. But we cannot begin to restore the missing black element to its rightful place without first establishing who the blacks were who have been left out.

The researching and writing of works that do not specifically focus on blacks pose enough of a challenge that most authors do not devote the considerable time that would be needed to ascertain whether blacks were involved and, if so, precisely who they were. Consider, for example, a pair of probing articles on master-servant relations in early nineteenth-century Montreal, published a few years ago in a reputable law journal. The articles named the parties in many court cases. None was identified as black, yet one of the prosecutions cited, the June 1835 case of *Alexander Grant v. Alexander McPherson*, was brought by a black master against his white apprentice. This would have been worth noting, particularly in view of the current belief that slavery had been abolished by the British parliament less than a year before. But, since the records on which the study was based do not identify the parties by race, how could the author have known that Alexander Grant, for one, was black? It would have required prolonged research into the identities of the parties to all the cited cases to determine whether any were black. Who has the time or the inclination to conduct such side-investigations when the focus of the study lies elsewhere?[1]

Similarly, in glancing at the population's makeup, writers tend to rely on published census reports rather than undertake a laborious scrutiny of the manuscript returns. But see what results if, for example, we consult the census of 1861, the first for which there is a complete set of returns for Montreal that name not just the heads of households but, at least theoretically, all the inhabitants. A careful study of the returns shows that at least 150 blacks lived in the city; the official report says there were fewer than 50. Appendix I of the report, a tabulation of the population by origin, counts 46 "Colored Persons" at Montreal, and 190 in all of Quebec. There are said to be 18 in St-Jacques Ward, 12 in St-Laurent, 11 in St-Antoine, and 5 in Ste-Anne. In Appendix 5, a breakdown of the province's population by age, the "Colored Persons," now termed "Negroes," are said to total 163, yet if we tot up the report's figures for each locality, we find that they add up to 180. Forty-eight "Negroes" are said to be living at Montreal – 18 in St-Jacques Ward and 12 in St-Laurent, as in Appendix I, but also 13 in St-Louis, 4 in the Centre Ward, one in the East Ward – and none in St-Antoine and Ste-Anne. Clearly, the returns contain mistakes in the enumeration of blacks, but these are, in the main, explicable. The report, on the other hand, is a baffling work of fiction where blacks are concerned.[2]

All of which is to say that the work of identifying who the blacks were presents untold difficulties and must be carried out by researchers for whom this is the primary concern. This would give specialists in other areas of historical investigation tools to work with in beginning the integration of blacks into studies from which they have been routinely left out. This book was written partly in that spirit. Its main purpose is to begin to place black Montrealers of the years 1760–1840 on the historical map so that their presence can no longer be overlooked in works dealing with that time and place. My chief approach in this study has been to scour archival sources to uncover names and tease out whatever details may be found of individual black lives. Close observation is the order of the day rather than analysis of the relative importance of the contributions made by blacks in one field or another.

Throughout this project I have been dogged by the thought that otherwise good people owned slaves. This is no revelation, but the idea rankled and took the form of a syllogism: good people owned slaves; but truly good people do not own slaves, therefore those who did own slaves were not truly good. An equally nagging question followed: Is it wise to judge the people of more than two hundred years ago by today's standards and to strip all those who abetted slavery of any claim to our esteem? That would mean arraigning virtually the entire society of the day, men and women from every walk of life. Should we now denounce them all, and scrap the monuments raised to them over the years, in bronze and stone, prose and verse? Should we, for instance, change the name of McGill University because the man whose name it enshrines was

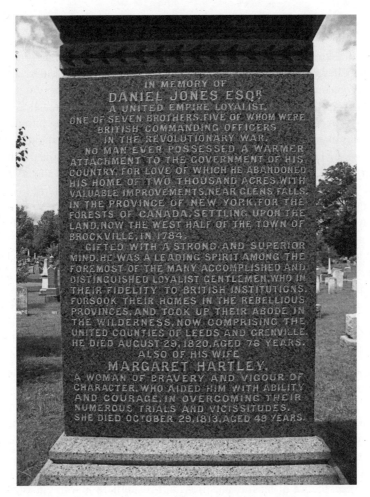

The merits of Loyalist Daniel Jones, sometime Montrealer and occasional slave trader, are carved in stone at the Oakland Cemetery in Brockville, Ont.

a slave-owner and occasional dealer in slaves? Given Daniel Jones' slave-trading activities in Quebec, should we not place a fig leaf over the adulatory inscription on the memorial stone to this one-time Montrealer and Loyalist founder of Brockville, Ontario? (See photograph above) Perhaps, but that would mean covering up even more of the truth rather than living with it. Besides, regard for our own posthumous reputations might make us hesitate to pronounce a blanket, retroactive condemnation. James McGill, Daniel Jones, and their contemporaries could live with slavery; we recoil at this, but future generations may be equally appalled by some of our present-day attitudes and practices. And yet, a re-evaluation would not be amiss. History is constantly toppling statues and rehabilitating villains. We cannot simply let the abettors of slavery off the hook.[3]

Should there be skeptics or kind souls at this late date who cannot bring themselves to believe that people of all stripes – Christians and Jews, French- and English-speaking, male and female, high and low – once engaged in slavery in Quebec, let them skip directly to Appendix I and there begin by reading and digesting the notices of the sales and escapes of black slaves. These make for a chilling introduction to a historical truth too readily ignored or obfuscated. Never mind arguing that there were more slave-owners among one group than another, that those of a given religious persuasion, language, or culture were more "racist" than another, that slavery in Quebec was mild because it was not murderous, or that is was an anomaly of no consequence, given that slaves were relatively few. Virtually everyone, "good" and "bad," was complicit, whether by active involvement, tacit acceptance, tolerance, indifference, or blindness. Until the 1780s, there seems to have been a general acceptance, even among blacks who chafed at their own enslavement, that slavery in some form, like poverty and war, would always exist. The poor bemoaned their lot and aspired to escape poverty, but without any illusions that poverty itself would disappear; slaves aspired to be free without necessarily expecting that freedom would be universal.

The inescapable truth is that people once accepted slavery as part of the natural order of society. The difference between their attitudes and ours is like night and day, and darkness did fall remarkably quickly on the whole sorry chapter. Within a generation of slavery's passing, its existence was generally forgotten – so much so that, by 1840, the grown children of a one-time Montreal slave would deny that she had been any such thing: slavery, they argued, had never been a fact of life in Canada. Some were inclined to agree, while others disputed the claim. Recent immigrants from overseas – one-fifth of Montreal's population in 1831 – would have had no idea that slavery ever existed in Quebec.

This book – a source book, progress report, and goad to further research – begins with slavery, the lot of most blacks in Montreal until 1800. Straying occasionally from that commercial beehive to Quebec, the seaport and political and administrative capital, and out to the countryside and points beyond, it spans the first eighty years of the British regime in colonial Quebec, roughly the last forty years of slavery and the first forty years without. A period of transition for blacks in Quebec, it was also one of flux abroad and at home, an age of wars and earth-shaking revolutions, notably in Britain's American colonies, in France, and in Haiti, and a time when, as a result of the Seven Years War, French-Catholic Quebec had to come to terms with British rule, including sudden bursts of a multiculturalism fed by American, English, German, Irish, and Scottish immigrants,who brought with them their own customs, religious beliefs and languages, along with competing notions of what the laws were, what they should be, and who should make them. This strained process culminated in the Rebellions of 1837–38, followed by the legislative union of Lower and Upper Canada, imposed by Britain for purposes of administrative efficiency and to give the combined English-speaking white population of the two colonies the upper hand in the political and legislative arenas. It was a second British Conquest, or a stab at one; as if to underscore this, the union came into effect on 10 February 1841, the anniversary of the Treaty of Paris by which France had ceded its North American colonies to England in 1763.

The end of slavery in Quebec was, in part, an indirect consequence of Britain's military capture of New France in 1760 and its retention of that war prize at the signing of the peace in 1763. This is not to resurrect the old idea of a "providential" Conquest or to argue that a British victory was indispensable to slavery's end. What with the propagation of revolutionary ideals of freedom and equality in the late eighteenth century, slavery might have come to a similar end had Quebec remained a French possession or thrown in its lot with the rebellious American colonies. We will never know. As it happened, neither revolutionary ardour nor anti-slavery zeal brought the issue to a head, but rather local circumstances engendered by the Conquest. The transition to British rule led to unease and perplexity about, and ultimately to a denial of, the legality of slavery as it had been practised in Quebec since the early 1600s and, more particularly, as it had been sanctioned by the decree of a French colonial official. Under new British management, it was all the easier for the new men in power to jettison a law that was not British; even those who clung to the old French laws as a bulwark against cultural annihilation were not about to fly to the barricades in defence of an old edict that touched few of them directly and counted for nothing in the struggle for survival of the *Canadiens* as a people.

The first task, then, in probing the black fact, is to undertake a racial recognizance: we have to pinpoint who was black. Everything hinges on this. This kind of census-taking at a distance is not as simple as it might appear; professionals and amateurs have tried their hand at it with mixed results. It is dismaying, for instance, to find historians turning a "Panise" (or Panis, from Pawnee, the name of a western Indian nation that became a generic French term for aboriginal slaves), clearly identified as such in the one source that speaks of her, into a black woman, or to see Irish-born slave-owner Patrick Langan, an officer of the British Indian Department, turned into a Mohawk.[4] Such confusions – there are more than enough – may be understandable in older studies, undertaken when archival materials were less accessible, but their perpetuation today leads one to question the authors' familiarity with characters and context, and to doubt the soundness of their analyses. The accumulation of such mistakes from one publication to another distorts our understanding not just of the players but of the play and the stage on which it was performed. If professionals can so easily err in identifying who was black, it is a sure sign that this most essential task is also one of the slipperiest.

And just who was "black"? The answer can be deceptively simple: whoever looked black was black. The determination was made wholly by sight, not by any pretended science or by law. There was no legal definition of blackness, and no fine line was drawn between light- and dark-skinned blacks. Indeed, strictly speaking, the laws did not distinguish between black and white. A person of mixed race was sometimes termed a mulatto (*mulâtre*), sometimes a *métis* (meaning simply mixed-race), to the point where it can be impossible to tell whether the person referred to was of white and black background or part aboriginal. A "mulatto" one moment could be a *nègre* the next, or both at once. The fugitive slave Bell, for example, was a "mulatto negress" in a notice of her flight published at Quebec in 1778; twenty years later, Lydia, a runaway at Montreal, was termed "a Negro Woman ... partly of the mulatto colour."[5] "Passing" for white was not an issue: if one looked white, one was. There was no "one drop rule," no instance recorded of a person, white in appearance, being "suspected" of having black blood. No one indulged in such hair-splitting of racial pedigrees.

Just as blacks were identified by eye, the names of the many who could not write were known by ear – and were recorded by French- and English-speaking scribes in wildly varying forms. Thus Caesar Hunkings, a free black labourer, possibly from New Hampshire, was at times simply César, or Caesar Hernking, César Angune and, at his death, Scishahungken.[6] The same was true for illiterate whites of course, but in the case of slaves names could be particularly confusing. A slave might be known by just a first name, in constant mutation – Geneviève might be Jenny or Jane in English, retranslated as Jeanne or Marie Jeanne or simply Marie – and surnames, when they existed, could change with successive masters. Similarly, ages were estimated with wild imprecision by eye: the same person might be said to be thirty-five one year and still thirty-five, or younger, ten years later – or, if she looked very old, to be 106 at her death![7]

As imprecise as this identification by eye and ear certainly was, we today are all the more blind and deaf. Our senses cannot tell us who was black then. We cannot see the subjects of our inquiry, since with one or two possible exceptions we have no portraits of the black Montrealers of the day, aside from hazy images conjured up from the physical descriptions found in fugitive-slave notices or elsewhere. We cannot hear them speak their names and judge for ourselves how we should write them, but must often make some arbitrary decision to choose one form – and stick with it, at the risk of being wrong. We must trust to old written records to tell us who was black and how their names sounded. This is not entirely to our disadvantage: documentary records can reveal information that was not available to observers of the day. How, for instance, were people of the late eighteenth century to tell whether a black "servant" was slave or free? We scarcely picture the question being put as a matter of course to the blacks themselves: there were no Southern-style slave patrols, no routine quizzings of blacks or requirements to exhibit a pass.[8] And it would have been considered impudent to inquire of a master or mistress whether the liveried black in his or her household was bought or hired. We can find answers to some of these questions today by prying into records once accessible only to a few.

But these records are not always explicit in telling us who was black. For those known to be slaves, the problem is circumscribed: the slave is either black or aboriginal, and from one source or another it can often be puzzled out which. Outside of slavery, without a clear statement that a person is black, racial identification can be perplexing. We look to the family, friends, and associates of that person to provide a key. But even the most intimate acquaintances and relations of blacks are not exclusively black. One might suppose, for example, that Fleure Deniger, as her name was sometimes written, was black.[9] Her husband, John Trim, a former slave, was the leading black figure in Montreal in his day. She was his second wife; his first, a former slave like him, was a native of Africa. Deniger (*duh-nee-jay*) is a French name, but as slaves often bore the names of their masters, "Fleure Deniger" might plausibly be a name picked up in bondage, or a Canadianized form of a name that conveyed an evocation of Africa: Flower of the Niger. But Fleure Deniger was in fact a white French Canadian, and her name contained no allusion whatever to the great river of west Africa. Such interracial marriages were not as rare as we might think, and whatever descendants of Quebec's black slaves may still be living in the province today are whites and, in most cases, probably unaware of their black ancestry. (This question of self-identification could have a bearing on any collective claim to reparations for slavery. The fact of intermarriage is also a factor to keep in mind with respect to any supposed "exodus" of blacks from Canada to the United States after the abolition of slavery there in 1865: would a mixed-race couple – say a French Canadian married to a Jamaican – have rushed across the border to live in a country where, in most states, interracial unions were illegal?)

In Quebec's black past, little is as it seems on the surface. We must look beneath, immersing ourselves in the sources, and hope that an enigmatic or misleading reference in one will find its explanation or rectification in another. For example, the earliest information found in Montreal about John Trim has him as a free black man buying a property in 1796. He was relatively well off, we might think, but where had he sprung from? The records of a notary who practised at Quebec, 300 kilometres to the east, show that Trim had been a slave until 1793 – not so well off. The notarized document of manumission does not call him John Trim: the slave's name is simply Trim. Can we prove that Trim was John Trim? Only to the extent that at the time of his manumission, Trim, the black slave, was a resident of Montreal, that there was no other Montrealer of the time, black or white, named Trim, and that, within three years of being freed, John Trim began to leave his mark at Montreal. The time fits, the name fits, and they fit no one else. We might even see a sort of negative evidence of John Trim's slave past in the fact that later records of his life are silent about it: none hints at his origins, place of his birth, parentage, or the life he led before surfacing as a free man. The same is true of distiller Caesar Johonnot, who seems without doubt to have been Caesar, the slave of Boston distiller Zachary Johonnot, although none of the many documents concerning him at Montreal speaks of his origins or of a slave past. Connecting the dots in these cases, as in so many others, is essential, even if it means courting error.

Although this work contains elements of the history of slavery in Quebec, it is not a comprehensive treatment of the subject. That would have required going back to the early days of New France and encompassing the enslavement of North American Indians, who, in the territory covered by the modern province of Quebec, constituted a much greater proportion of enslaved people than did blacks. A study of the two forms of slavery, like historian Marcel Trudel's of half a century ago, has its place, as would separate examinations of the one or the other. The subject of this book, however, is the history of blacks at Montreal – not the history of slavery, but the progress of that drawn-out moment when black slavery waxed, then suddenly waned, and what followed.

Certainly, others have looked into black slavery in Quebec. Among the early investigators whose works still merit attention are Jacques Viger and Louis-Hippolyte LaFontaine, who first brought that buried historical fact to public attention in their 1859 documentary compilation, *De l'esclavage en Canada;* the Reverend Thomas Watson Smith of Nova Scotia in the 1890s; and the more probing and prolific Justice William Renwick Riddell of Ontario in the first third of the twentieth century, who both mined the archives and unearthed much valuable information, seeking to determine colonial slavery's scope and reach. But they stopped there. No one has looked closely at slavery's end *and* its aftermath, which is what this book sets out to do.

The confusion surrounding the question of when and how slavery ended is evidence of the scant attention the subject has received. One of the most persistent myths in this regard has Chief Justice William Osgoode simultaneously abolishing and not abolishing slavery in Lower Canada in 1803. At this writing, an online document entitled "The Underground Railroad Years: Canada in an International Arena," part of the government of Canada's Digital Collections, states: "In a key 1803 case, William Osgoode, Chief Justice of Lower Canada ... ruled that slavery was incompatible with British law. ... slavery was not officially abolished, but his ruling set free 300 Blacks." Daniel Hill's *The Freedom-Seekers*, published in 1981 and republished in 1992, says much the same thing: "In 1803 [Osgoode] handed down the historic decision that slavery was inconsistent with British law. While this judgment did not legally abolish slavery, it set free the 300 slaves in Lower Canada." In their 1996 work, *Towards Freedom,* Alexander and Glaze wrote: "In 1803, William Osgoode, then Chief Justice of Lower Canada, ruled that slavery was incompatible with British law. ... The hypocrisy of slavery 'under the law' had been exposed. Though not officially abolishing slavery, the ruling set free the 300 slaves of Lower Canada." Dorothy Williams's 1997 historical account of blacks in Montreal, *The Road to Now,* tersely restates the point: "Then in Montreal in 1803, Chief Justice Osgood ruled that 'slavery was incompatible with the laws of the country.'"[10] Although these works treat Osgoode's ruling as momentous, none ventures to state the nature of the case before him, the names of the parties, the precise date of his ruling, or how such a far-reaching decision by the chief justice of the colony freed the slaves yet failed to abolish slavery. The truth is, there was no such Osgoode ruling: Osgoode had left the country in 1801 and officially resigned as chief justice in 1802. If we believe with any degree of sincerity that slavery was a crime against humanity, how is it that we have treated the eradication of this great evil so carelessly?

If more evidence were needed of our poor grasp of the end of slavery, we have only to consider that, until 2006, not a word had ever been written about the first abolition bill debated by Canada's lawmakers at Quebec in 1787, before the division of the colony into Lower and Upper Canada.[11] That such a capital fact should have escaped the notice of historians for 220 years is one powerful indication that all has not been said about the history of blacks. More evidence of the gaps in our knowledge is found in Robin Winks' standard reference, *The Blacks in Canada,* now nearly forty years old. It contains virtually no information about blacks in Quebec through the first eighty-odd years of the nineteenth century, a rather glaring omission considering that Montreal was then the largest city in British North America. The "Canada" of Winks's title brings to mind Metternich's famous dictum about Italy, before its unification into one kingdom in 1861, as being a mere "geographical expression." The eighty-year gap in Winks's study is the product of a common view of "Canada" as a rather elastic geographical expression.

What do we mean by "Canada"? During the period covered by this study there was no country of that name, and no Canadian nation (at least, not as we now understand the term), and the inhabitants of colonial New Brunswick, Newfoundland, Nova Scotia, and Prince Edward Island certainly did not think of themselves as Canadian. Canada was a colony, then a pair of colonies, up the St Lawrence. The label "Canadian" referred to a person of French descent born in New France or the territory of colonial Quebec, and the development of a collective self-consciousness in the early nineteenth century did give rise to the idea of a *nation canadienne,* today redefined and renamed *nation québécoise.* But that is not what we have in mind today when we speak of the Canadian people.

As concerns blacks, can we even speak of "Canadian" slavery? Black slavery, with its record of human drama, corrosive social effects, and everlasting scars, played a central role in the formation and growth of the United States. We can speak of "American" slavery: it was present in one form or another in all thirteen colonies that united to form that country in the last quarter of the eighteenth century, and it remained an important and ever more divisive fact of national life until well after the Civil War of 1861–65. Slavery holds no such place in the national life of Canada, a country formed after slavery had ended. Certainly, black slavery had been practised, under the French and the British in those eastern colonies that, between 1867 and 1873, became the Canadian provinces of New Brunswick, Nova Scotia, Ontario, Prince Edward Island, and Quebec. A few black slaves were found in Newfoundland, which did not join Canada until 1949, and in the hands of missionaries, soldiers, fur traders, and Indians, who wandered the expanse of territory extending from present-day northern Quebec and Ontario to British Columbia and Yukon – a vast area that was, for practically two hundred years from 1670, entrusted by a British royal charter to the care of the Hudson's Bay Company. But these territories did not constitute a Canada-in-waiting; if anything, the tendency in slavery's time was more toward splintering than toward unification. As France's North American empire crumbled through the eighteenth century, French Acadia, Île Royale, and Île St-Jean fell to the British to become Nova Scotia, Cape Breton, and Prince Edward Island. New France, or Canada, stretching from the Gulf of St Lawrence to the Mississippi River, followed in 1760, to become known after 1774 as the Province of Quebec, but still widely called "Canada." Britain then lost its American colonies in the American War of Independence. In the process, the Province of Quebec was amputated, losing its southwestern extremities, where it touched on the former French possession of Louisiana, in Spanish hands since 1762. When the American colonists revolted, they made efforts to rally Nova Scotia and Quebec to the cause; to that end, American forces occupied Quebec in 1775-76, so that it might have ended up a state of the union. In the end, the influx of refugees from the American war into Nova Scotia led to the breakup of that colony in 1784, part of it being lopped off to form the Loyalist haven of New Brunswick. In the Province of Quebec, where the Loyalists were settled mostly on land grants along the upper St Lawrence and on the Great Lakes, the formal separation took place seven years later. In 1791, the eastern, more settled part, French and Catholic at heart, became the colony of Lower Canada (Quebec); the western part, Upper Canada (Ontario), was to be the home of Loyalists, British at heart, Protestant for the most part, and American by experience.

Too often, those who write on the black past overlay the map of modern Canada on these atomized colonial elements and unite them, creating a "Canadian" figment. To speak of a "Canadian" slavery or a "Canadian" racism at that time suggests a homogeneity, or at least a close association, that did not exist. (As anachronisms go, we could just as well extend the discussion of "American" slavery to include Hawaii and Alaska, Puerto Rico, and the Panama Canal Zone.) Conjuring up this fictional "Canada," one can easily zero in on the black experience in some colony or other in British North America and present it as the "Canadian" reality. By the same token, one can ignore developments in Quebec for eighty years, papering them over with a picture of the "Canadian" scene drawn from the experiences of blacks in Nova Scotia and in Upper Canada (or Canada West, as Ontario was officially called for most of that time). Engaging in this kind of slippage, an argument might be made that because the black populations in those two areas were considerably larger than Quebec's, it is fitting that we should concentrate our attention on them. But, besides the fact that Nova Scotia was not part of Canada for most of that time – and at no time in the period covered by this book – this kind of justification by numbers is hazardous. It is precisely what led writers of former times to gloss over black slavery: the number of slaves was so comparatively slight that the historical fact of slavery was not worth mentioning.

The fact is that the course and practice of slavery were not uniform in all the North American colonies, or at all times, nor was the experience of "freedom" everywhere the same. We cannot, under the guise of examining "Canadian" slavery, illustrate its character in New France by drawing on incidents from, say, British New Brunswick, which was another place, of another time and culture, and under different management, so to speak; nor can we create a picture of the experience of blacks in Lower Canada by drawing inferences from what black life was like in Upper Canada or Prince Edward Island (or, worse, from what it was in colonies or countries beyond these). There were similarities, of course, but there were also significant differences. Hence this book: not a comparative study of black life in the various colonies that later formed Canada, or even in different cities in Quebec, but an exploration of facets of black life at Montreal.

INTRODUCTION

Missouri may seem like an unlikely starting point for this study, but four related freedom suits filed by slaves in the courts of St Louis in the mid-nineteenth century offer a unique window on slavery as it had been practised in Quebec, specifically at Montreal, and also on its legal foundations. This is the subject of the first chapter. The legality of slavery is further considered in the second chapter, which, through an examination of slave cases in the courts of Montreal and of the abortive efforts to legislate a more or less gradual abolition, challenges the conventional view that Britain "officially" put an end to slavery in Quebec in 1834.

Chapter 3 deals with the size of the slave population, notably the difficulties of identifying the slaves and establishing an accurate count. Marcel Trudel deserves much credit for being the first to have attempted this necessary, painstaking work. His enumeration of all slaves in French Canada, Indian as well as black, over two hundred years, periodically updated since 1960, has served as a statistical reference for questions such as the average price of slaves and slave mortality. But, for various reasons, there are such flaws in his enumeration of black slaves that it cannot stand.

Chapter 4 looks more closely at some traits of slavery as it was practised in and around Montreal, and chapter 5 focuses on the passage from slavery to freedom. For some black Montrealers, a significant feature of this transition was the acquisition of landed property. The subsequent two chapters deal with the occupations of free blacks, the first focusing on their work on the earliest steamboats, one of the principal sources of employment for blacks, and the second surveying the range of other jobs at which they were employed. Chapter 8 is concerned with the participation of blacks in politics in the 1820s and 1830s, the earliest period for which we have records of their involvement, and chapter 9 considers their treatment by the criminal justice system. Chapter 10 focuses on apprenticeships and interracial marriage as two areas that brought blacks and whites closer together than was common in the general population. The final chapter takes stock of the condition of blacks around 1840, and gives some indication of what the future would bring.

Throughout, I have been concerned to stay as close as possible to individual black figures through whatever concrete details that can be ascertained about them from the archival record. I also quote at length from documents of the period, especially in the appendices, so that readers may see for themselves how rich these materials are and judge whether the conclusions that I have drawn are warranted. Appendix I gives the text of all the newspaper notices I have found concerning black slaves in Quebec, as well as other notices pertaining to, or placed by, blacks from 1764 to 1830. In Appendix II will be found the opinions of three nineteenth-century Montreal judges on the legal foundations of slavery as practised in Quebec. Appendix III, concerning blacks who arrived in the province around the time of the American War of Independence, also reproduces various period documents. Appendix IV consists of a record of the trial in 1836 of three black Montrealers on a charge of riot, stemming from the presence in the city of a visitor from North Carolina, a former resident of Montreal, whose "servant" was thought to be a slave.

If I have been so bold as to contest the findings of others, it is because there seemed no other way to convey the necessary message that the accretion of errors is leading the history of blacks in Quebec in directions that are unsupported by the evidence, and that we had better check our sources and bearings before going on. No writer has gone so far as to repeat the patently false claim made by historian Benjamin Sulte a century ago that Quebec adopted a law to end slavery in 1833, and that "Le parlement de Londres imita sa colonie" (the British parliament followed suit).[12] But, given the few works published on blacks in Quebec, it it regrettable that the latest, sociologist Daniel Gay's *Les Noirs du Québec 1629–1900,* abounds in such egregious errors and distortions of simple facts as to render its historical profile of the black population (chapters 1–4) utterly unreliable. Here are a few characteristic examples. A sad story of interracial love, said to have unfolded in a Montreal suburb, is cited in support of the contention that such unions were discouraged in Quebec (p. 37). The story, in fact, is drawn from a snippet of foreign news published in the *Quebec Herald* of 4 February 1790 about events that had occurred in a suburb of London, not Montreal. As an illustration of do-or-die slave resistance in Quebec, Gay cites a plot by the slaves to rise on 24 June 1731 and massacre all the French inhabitants; after word of the conspiracy leaked out, ten or twelve of the ringleaders were hanged (p. 127). No such conspiracy, with such a gruesome end, was ever hatched in Quebec: the source for this tale, a footnote in Sulte's *Histoire des Canadiens-français*, refers to events that occurred in Louisiana.[13] An incident of urban violence that occurred in August 1860 in the east-side Ste-Marie suburb of Montreal is said to have taken place more than 300 kilometres away, in rural L'Ange-Gardien, east of Quebec. It is cited as hinting at how unfair and racially biased the courts could be. As Gay tells it, a band of young whites were accused of harassing Archibald Brown, a black teenager, who, in self-defence, struck one of his tormentors with a knife; for this, Brown was sentenced to an unspecified term at hard labour in the Quebec Jail (p. 154). In fact, the accused was Brown. Charged with assault for stabbing a Joseph Souligny, he pleaded guilty in the Montreal Court of Weekly Sessions on 5 September. Considering that he had been provoked and that he had spent two weeks in pre-trial detention, Magistrate Charles J. Coursol sentenced him to only eight days' imprisonment after warning him not to carry dangerous weapons. "Mr Coursol also admonished Soligny [*sic*] and some of his witnesses against a repetition of such conduct. Nobody should be insulted either on account of creed or color," the judge was reported as saying. Revealing as the case may be, it does not support the suggestion of racial prejudice on the part of the judiciary.[14]

Some readers may question the facts and interpretations presented here. Fair enough. History is a cold case – colder than most, where blacks are concerned – that needs constant reopening. One lesson that I have learned in preparing this work is that once we have sifted through the evidence, the best course to follow would be to start over, on the principle that "If I had known then what I know now …". But after plowing through more than a century's worth of assorted records – page by page in the case of Montreal newspapers, church, cemetery, hospital and jail records, censuses and poll books; deed by deed in notarial archives; file by file in court papers – I count on others to carry on, if only to cast a fresh eye on the same material.

ONE

What Slavery?

"A Constant Reader" in 1847 happened upon a copy of a Quebec newspaper from eighty years before, and an advertisement in its pages caught his eye. He wrote to the editor of the Quebec *Morning Chronicle*, inviting him to reprint the 1767 text for the benefit of anyone who "may feel interested in looking upon 'things as they were,' and contrasting them with 'things as they are.'" The item was brief. "To be sold," it said, "A healthy Negro boy, about 15 years of age, well qualified to wait on a Gentleman, as a body servant. For further particulars enquire of the Printers."[1] Without further explanation, this was little more than a curiosity, giving mid-nineteenth-century readers no idea of how extensive the practice of buying and selling "negroes" had been. Still, the fact that black slavery had shown its face in Quebec would have come as news to many: slavery was seen as an American problem.

Coincidentally, the historical fact of slavery in Quebec was then a small part of that American problem, and it is to the proceedings in an American court that we must turn for a rare insight into slavery as it was practised and viewed in Quebec, as we are invited to do in the foreword to *De l'esclavage en Canada*, published in 1859, the first attempt at a historical exploration of slavery in Quebec. This slim collection of historical documents was compiled by Jacques Viger, the first mayor of Montreal, and completed after his death by Chief Justice Sir Louis-Hippolyte LaFontaine, a former prime minister of the united Province of Canada. "We hasten to publish it," the newly founded Société d'histoire de Montréal declared, "because this question of slavery in Canada, highly important in itself, is currently being debated in the state of Missouri where it will determine the outcome of interesting trials among our neighbours."[2]

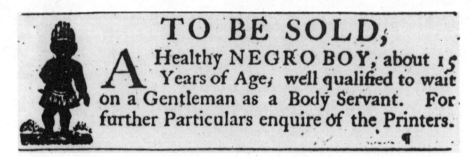

Slavery in Quebec? This advertisement from a 1767 issue of the *Quebec Gazette* caught the attention of a nineteenth-century reader, who shared his find with the public.

The question that by then had exercised the courts of St Louis for almost twenty years was fundamental: Had slavery existed in Canada? Viger's opening words in *De l'esclavage* raised the question and answered it categorically: "Did slavery exist in Canada? Yes, slavery existed in Canada." But when it came to the legal foundation of slavery, he was not so sure. "It will perhaps be said that it existed outside the law [*par abus*]," he wrote, "nevertheless, it always existed in fact, under French rule as under the rule of England."[3] By Canada, Viger and the Missouri courts meant what is now called Quebec, and indeed most of the documents that Viger compiled pertained to Montreal. Is it conceivable that slavery was practised there, outside the law, for two centuries?

Viger had more than the Missouri courts in mind when he affirmed the existence of slavery. He also sought to convince his fellow Quebecers, most of whom had forgotten, or perhaps never known, "things as they were," and to challenge the view propounded a decade earlier by historian François-Xavier Garneau. In his *Histoire du Canada*, published between 1845 and 1849, Garneau claimed that the government of France had kept Canada free of the scourge of slavery. This would have made New France an oddity, since every European power that had once colonized the Atlantic edge of the New World – Denmark, England, France, Holland, Portugal, Spain and Sweden – had introduced black slavery in its overseas domains. Later editions of Garneau's work acknowledged that at least a few slaves had found their way into the colony, and that officials had laid down certain rules on the subject, but still portrayed slavery as an insignificant element in the life of the colony. At the time of the British conquest, the number of slaves in New France had supposedly amounted to no more than a handful; this number had increased slightly under the British, but only for an instant, before dwindling away to nothing.[4] Historians and others ever since have disparaged these views. But Garneau was not alone in his day in minimizing the scope of slavery in Quebec's past, or denying it altogether. As early as 1790, when slaves walked the streets of Montreal, a free-thinking correspondent who signed himself "Un Canadien" had written to the *Montreal Gazette:* "The mild and peaceable government which we enjoy is founded on principles of liberty and excludes all sorts of slavery."⁵ The French scholar Isidore Lebrun had asserted in a book-length study of the Canadas published in 1833 that "Jamais l'esclavage n'a souillé les Canadas" – slavery never tarnished the Canadas.⁶ Four American slaves would claim as much in the courts of Missouri in the mid-nineteenth century.

THE CHILDREN OF ROSE

The argument that slavery was unknown in Canada was brought before the Circuit Court of St Louis by the four adult children of a black woman called Rose. All advanced the same claim, beginning with Pierre in 1840, followed by Charlotte in 1843 (on behalf of her four children as well as herself), and Louis Chouteau and Michel Paul in 1844. They had inherited their slave status from their mother, but she had been wrongfully held as a slave, they said: Rose was in fact a free woman because she had been born in 1768 at Montreal, where slavery was not recognized.⁷ According to their version of their mother's odyssey, fur-trader John Stock had taken Rose in 1791 from Montreal to the western posts, first to Michilimackinac (Mackinac Island, Michigan), then still in British hands, the hinterland hub of Montreal's fur trade, where several witnesses reported having seen her at work as a cook for Étienne Campion, a Montreal merchant. She had then accompanied Stock to his trading post on the upper Mississippi River at Prairie du Chien in present-day Wisconsin, where he held her as a slave.⁸ At Stock's death in 1793 or 1794, Andrew Todd, nephew of Montreal fur-trade merchant Isaac Todd, had taken Rose to St Louis, then in Spanish hands, where he had sold her on 28 October 1795 to the Reverend Pierre Joseph Didier, the parish priest. A copy of this deed of sale was filed with the court, the first hard evidence submitted concerning Rose. On 8 August 1798, Didier had sold her, along with her then two infant sons, Benoît and Toussaint, to the prominent New Orleans–born merchant and public official Auguste Chouteau, one of the founders of St Louis in 1764. This sales contract was also entered in evidence. Rose and Auguste Chouteau were in their graves by the time her children joined battle – Michel Paul with Gabriel Paul, the man to whom he had been sold after Chouteau's death; the three others with Chouteau's heirs, first with his widow, Thérèse Cerré, and, after her death, with her son, Gabriel Sylvestre Chouteau.⁹

Since the key argument was the same in all the cases, the lawyers for the contending parties agreed by 1849 that the evidence in one would serve for all.¹⁰ Charlotte finally carried the day in December 1862, after much disagreement between the Circuit Court in St Louis and the Missouri Supreme Court over the issue of whether the existence of slavery in Canada should be left to the determination of the jury as a question of fact or settled by the judges as a point of law. Her victory came as the Civil War raged, a few days before the coming into force of Abraham Lincoln's Emancipation Proclamation, and despite the notorious 1857 decision by the US Supreme Court in the contemporaneous Missouri case of the slave Dred Scott, that blacks had no rights that whites were bound to respect.¹¹

More important for our purposes than the decisions of the Missouri courts was the evidence presented to them about slavery in Quebec. The testimony came from former Quebecers, people who had left the colony years before and whose memories of persons, events, and conditions there were enlightening, if sometimes clouded by age, time, and distance. On two occasions, in 1846 and 1859, the Circuit Court of St Louis empowered commissioners at Montreal to gather evidence on the matter. The witnesses examined before these rogatory commissions included four whites who recalled the slaves whom their parents and acquaintances had kept, and, most notably, three prominent Montreal jurists who delivered their opinions on what the legal status of slavery had been.[12]

THE TESTIMONY IN ST LOUIS

"There were no slaves in Canada, they generally hired white persons," Romain Dufresne said under oath. Born at Quebec around 1770, he had lived there until 1793, when he had moved to St Louis. "There was no other slavery there than the slavery of white people being hired to others," he said. "If slavery had existed there I should have known it."[13] Paschal Léon Cerré, brother-in-law of Auguste Chouteau, was of a similar opinion. Born at Montreal in 1773, Cerré had joined his father, Gabriel Cerré, a prominent St Louis merchant and owner of a considerable number of slaves, in the territory of Upper Louisiana at the age of four, and then returned to Montreal, where he had lived from 1781 to 1787. He had lived there again from 1791 to 1794 before returning to the shores of the Mississippi for good. "Did not know of the existence of slavery in Canada, did not see any person held as a slave there," he said at seventy-two, his words recorded in note form; "never heard of a slave being held there, if it was as general there as here would have known it, if it was the custom would have known it." He recalled having travelled with his father, a native of what is now the Côte-St-Paul district of Montreal, from St Louis to Canada with a retinue of slaves. His father had parked the slaves at the border – "did not take the Negroes into Canada for fear they would become free." But, on other occasions, he acknowledged, his father had taken slaves across the border, and once, at St Louis, Gabriel Cerré had given a slave girl to his daughter, Marie-Anne, to take back to Canada. Marie-Anne Cerré was married in 1781 to Pierre-Louis Panet, a lawyer and notary who would later serve as a judge of the Montreal Court of King's Bench. Whether the girl she took back to Canada had been treated as a slave there, Paschal Cerré did not know. By 1794, the girl was no longer with his sister, he said.[14]

There was more in this vein from witnesses who testified in support of Rose's children. Pierre Larivière had lived at Montreal until the age of twenty or twenty-one, leaving for St Louis around 1805: "Don't know of any persons held as slaves there, has no knowledge of any such thing, he never heard any such thing spoken of there, if it had existed he should have known it, as he went around the town frequently & was for sometime a servant himself. Knew negroes who were voyagers & who

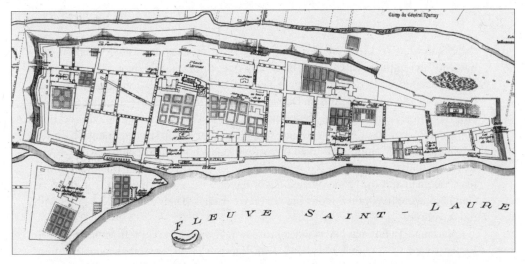

The walled city of Montreal as it was in 1761.

said they were free, nobody pretended to claim them."[15] Michel Fontaine (or Fortin), aged sixty-nine, born at Quebec, had lived there seventeen years, and six years at or near Montreal, working as a sailor on the St Lawrence River. He, too, had never heard of slavery, but noted, "When I say that there was no slavery in Canada, I mean that I never knew any."[16] Peter Payant, who had lived the first fourteen years of his life "about 3 leagues south of Montreal" and was apprenticed to a blacksmith from the age of seven, testified that he had never seen a black person until he moved to St Louis in 1784.[17] Michel Marly claimed in 1845, when he was seventy-three years old, that although he had left his native Montreal at age ten, "if slavery had been there he had knowledge enough to have known it, but never heard tell of any." Again called to testify in 1847, Marly spoke of how rare it had been to see blacks at Montreal during his childhood: "I saw 2 negros in Montreal. We were at work in the field and saw those 2 Negros coming & thought it was the devil & away we went."[18] One can easily picture young Africans or Indians of the Americas fleeing in the same way at their first sight of whites.

The witnesses for Chouteau told a different story. "At the time I left Canada and previous thereto, there were in that province negroes and mulattoes who were known and held as slaves," said Pierre Ménard of Kaskasia, across the Mississippi in Illinois. Ménard, who served as the first lieutenant-governor of the state of Illinois from 1818 to 1822, was born at St-Antoine on the Richelieu River in October 1766 and had left Quebec at the age of nineteen. In his brief deposition, he spoke only in generalities, naming no slaves or slave-owners, but affirming slavery's existence and pointing to one of its basic traits. The slaves in Quebec were domestics: "They were generally employed about the house, and treated in the same manner as the house slaves in the slave states of the United States."[19]

Other witnesses made similar references to the status of Quebec slaves; one of them, Antoine Smith, observed that as domestic servants "Negroes were better dressed there than whites." Born outside Montreal in 1771 but a resident of the town for seventeen years until he was twenty or twenty-one, Smith had known of eight slaves. Four had belonged to Colonel Daniel Claus and three to Colonel John Campbell, both top-ranking officers in the Indian Department,[20] and there was also a mulatto slave of "Mr St George," i.e., Georges Hyppolite Le Compte Dupré, a merchant and one-time inspector of police at Montreal who was elected to the first parliament of Lower Canada in 1792.[21] Smith had lived opposite Claus's house and claimed to have visited there daily for ten or twelve years. Claus's slaves were "4 men, one of them was his coachman and the others waited about the house ... The slaves of Col. Closs & Campbell wore livery on Sunday but not on week days. Their clothes were faced with red & yellow."[22]

Marianne Tison, née Normandeau *dit* Deslauriers, who had left Montreal for St Louis around 1789 with her husband, Jean-Baptiste Tison,[23] and their three children, also claimed to have known Claus and Campbell and their slaves. Not that she had had any close contact with the masters – "I had no personal acquaintance with either Col. Closs or Col. Campbell, he kept his rank and we kept ours. I never spoke to either of them" – but for four or five years she had worked as an apprentice to a tailor who made the slaves' clothes every spring and fall. "Clause's slaves were clad in blue and yellow livery, and Campbell's in blue & red. They were not dressed richly, but neatly." Where Smith had identified Claus's slaves as four males, she spoke of a mother and father and an unspecified number of children. "The Colonels treated their slaves as slaves usually are treated, they were well maintained & taken care of, and better treated than they are in Missouri," she observed on one occasion. On another, she said that their masters "took same care of them as if they were white" and that, like white servants, in their off hours the slaves "visited & went where they chose ... There is a great difference between slaves in Canada & here." She had never heard of the slaves being whipped. As to how she knew that they were slaves, she offered the confusing explanation that "no body ever spoke of it, it was a matter not mentioned, always understood they were slaves, they were always spoken of as slaves."[24]

Tison was the one witness to place Rose at Montreal. In the winter before she left for St Louis, she said, her uncle, baker Joseph Berlinguet, had bought Rose, then somewhere between seventeen and twenty years old, in the marketplace in exchange for a valuable horse.[25] While Rose's children understood that their mother had been born at Montreal, Tison claimed that "Americans brought her to Montreal." Yet Rose spoke French, which suggests an origin other than American. Rose was the only black person whom Tison remembered seeing at Montreal, other than the slaves of Claus and Campbell. If black slaves had been relatively few, it was because "people preferred to be waited on by people of their own color," she said[26] – an observation that, if not simply a projection of Tison's own bias, implied that colour prejudice might have operated at cross-purposes, fostering black slavery on the one hand while impeding it on the other. Some opposition to slavery could spring not from altruism but from the same racial antipathy as slavery itself: slavery was objectionable not because it degraded blacks but because it required their presence, which was otherwise

The marketplace depicted in this 1790 sketch is where baker Joseph Berlinguet bought the slave Rose in exchange for a horse in 1789.

unwanted. Although any opposition to slavery, whatever the motive, was a blow against the practice, anti-slavery based on a view of blacks as undesirable did nothing to promote their rights. The exploiter of black slaves would disappear with slavery; the excluder, who refused to be served by any but whites, would live on.

THE TESTIMONY IN MONTREAL

Tison had heard of Panis, or Indian slaves, in Montreal but she had never seen one. Adélaïde Chaboillez, daughter of fur trader Charles Chaboillez and his wife, Marguerite Larchevêque *dit* La Promenade, had known such slaves at home as a girl. Called to testify at Montreal on behalf of Chouteau in April 1846, the sixty-three-year-old widow of Surveyor-General Joseph Bouchette said: "I have a distinct recollection that during my Youth up to the Year 1795 or 6 there were several Slaves owned by my Mother, who resided in Montreal in this Province." Four were Panis, including a woman (bought from fur trader Edward Pollard) and her daughter, and three – Hanover, Jack and Louison – were black males. Louison had been emancipated, Chaboillez recalled, and she believed that several of the others had also been freed at her mother's death in 1798. Judging by the record of his death in July 1800, Hanover, or François Anovre, as he was called then, was not among the freed; he was identified as a roughly fifty-year-old "Nègre appartenant à M Charles Chaboiller Voyageur" (Negro belonging to Mr Charles Chaboillez, fur trader). Of Jack, we know that he was held by the Chaboillez family as far back as 1780, when he was admitted to hospital under the name Jacques.[27] Montreal resident Marie Angélique Bouchette, Chaboillez's Quebec-born sister-in-law, also had a "very clear recollection" of slavery. "Many of our friends in Quebec were slave holders," she said, "and about the year 1790 I remember that my father [Jean-Baptiste Bouchette] sold a slave called Caesar, at public auction, at Quebec."[28]

The appearance of these two witnesses before the commission, and their willingness to speak candidly about slavery, no doubt owed something to the fact that Robert Shore Milnes Bouchette, the son of the one and nephew of the other, had been retained as the Montreal counsel for Chouteau. He had not needed to look far afield for eyewitnesses to slavery. Did he ever consider producing a former Canadian slave, or children of slaves, before the commission? As conclusive as the testimony of such black survivors might have been, it would have been difficult to procure. Locating a former slave in Montreal would have been a problem: the very few still living did not trumpet their slave background. Would they have been willing to revisit the past in this way, or would they have considered it painful and humiliating to have their servile origins held up before strangers for no better reason than to confirm a historical fact that should have been beyond dispute and that they themselves had striven to put behind them? Had the circumstances of the case been explained to them, it might also have struck them as perverse that their personal stories of bondage, or those of their parents, were to be used to tighten the bonds of living slaves. We have to wonder whether this dilemma troubled Jacques Viger. Intent on proving the historical fact of slavery, and on communicating his findings to men of the law at St Louis concerned in the cases of Rose's children, he had to have known that he was supplying ammunition to the upholders of American slavery.[29]

Charles William Grant, Baron de Longueuil, born in 1782, was another witness for Chouteau before the commission in 1846 who remembered slavery as being alive and well at Quebec during his boyhood. His family had owned two black slaves, Fanny and Williams, as well as a Panis called Thomas. A neighbour, Charles-Louis Tarieu de Lanaudière, seigneur of Ste-Anne-de-la-Pérade, also had a slave, Grant said, referring perhaps to Geneviève, the twenty-seven-year-old de Lanaudière slave identified as a native of Montreal when she was hospitalized at the Hôtel-Dieu at Quebec in the fall of 1794, but as New York–born when she was registered as a patient at the hospital two years later. As far as Grant could recall, Chief Justice William Smith, who died in December 1793, had owned two slaves.[30]

Montreal lawyer Janvier Domptail Lacroix, seigneur of Blainville, remembered slavery as persisting until the turn of the century. His father, Joseph-Hubert Lacroix, had owned a young female slave who had died around 1790–91, he said.[31] As a law student articling at Montreal under Solicitor-General Louis Charles Foucher, Lacroix had had personal knowledge of Foucher's purchase of a mulatto slave in 1793. This slave, Jean Louis, was advertised for sale in February that year by Jean-Baptiste Routier, a maker of starch and hair powder. Unnamed in the newspaper notice, Jean Louis was identified as a "bon Perruquier pour homme & pour femme, & bon Cuisinier" (a good wigmaker for men and women, and a good cook), about twenty-two years old. Foucher had bought Jean Louis that March for 1,300 livres. Jean Louis had been one of several slaves whom Routier had brought back to Lower Canada in 1792 after spending twenty-eight years abroad, mostly in St-Domingue (Haiti). He had bought Jean Louis and Jean Louis's mother there in 1778. Leaving the Caribbean island in 1790, Routier had moved to Philadelphia, and then returned to Canada in July 1792 with, besides his own family and Jean Louis, a black woman and her three children, the oldest about seven years old, and a sixteen-year-old Carib Indian. According to Lacroix, Foucher kept Jean Louis until 1799, when he emancipated him. Lacroix recalled the names of several other Montreal slave-owners: fur-trade merchants James McGill, John Gregory (who owned three slaves, according to Lacroix) and Joseph Howard, as well as Marguerite Larchevêque *dit* La Promenade and a Pierre Dumignault. He also remembered that, in 1795 or 1796, Gabriel Cerré of St Louis had turned up at Montreal with six slaves for sale, but finding no one prepared to meet his prices, he had left, taking his slaves with him.[32]

To Adélaïde Chaboillez, "at that time the holding & having slaves in Montreal was never objected to or considered illegal, but seemed on the contrary to be perfectly sanctioned by the usage of the Country." The same was true at Quebec, Marie Angélique Bouchette said: "[T]he ownership ... of slaves ... was a pretty general thing and spoken of as a matter of course. I have no knowledge that the right to hold slaves was ever questioned in Quebec or elsewhere in Canada at that time." Charles William Grant also had "no knowledge of the question of the legality of slavery in Canada ever being raised in a court of law in this country." But he had left for Europe in 1794, when he was twelve, and had not returned until 1801. Something had happened in his absence: on his return, his family's three slaves were gone. Lacroix, the lawyer, was slightly more aware. "It is only in 1799 or 1800 that some doubt arose and that a slave claimed by his master was set free by one of the law courts in Montreal," he said. "I am under the impression that this ruling was based on some act of the British Parliament, but I do not know which one and I am not familiar with the details of this case."[33]

From this limited survey of white witnesses, we can at least see that there were black slaves in Quebec at the end of the eighteenth century. They worked as domestics, some in livery, and were treated much the same as white servants. Physical brutality was not a hallmark of their treatment, it seems. Their presence was not obvious to all, suggesting that they were few in number, but it was no secret: Rose was sold in the marketplace at Montreal, and Caesar at public auction at Quebec. In fact, the sales of Caesar and of Jean Louis, like that of the "healthy Negro boy" mentioned at the head of this chapter, were advertised in the newspapers, meaning that a literate minority had access to details on the workings of slavery – notices of slave sales and escapes – of which the general populace may have been unaware. The slave-owners included a solicitor-general and a chief justice, two veteran military officers in charge of the Indian Department, as well as prominent merchants, many of them engaged in the fur trade, and other members of the elite, as well as the baker Berlinguet, who had bought Rose, and the starch-maker Routier, who had returned to Quebec in 1792 with several slaves in tow. If some expatriates at St Louis had been oblivious to slavery, perhaps it was because there had been nothing out of the ordinary about its practice – it had been, as Marie Angélique Bouchette termed it, a "pretty general thing and spoken of as a matter of course." Other than lawyer Lacroix, those who, as children, had known slaves in their own homes were oblivious to the legal contests that had spelled the end of slavery.

ENTER THE JURISTS

In 1846, James Reid, retired chief justice of the Montreal Court of King's Bench, and Samuel Gale, a judge of that same court since 1834 (styled Court of Queen's Bench after Victoria's accession in 1837), were examined on behalf of the slave Pierre. Superior Court Justice William Badgley, a former member of parliament and attorney-general, and the first dean of the McGill University law faculty (1853–55), testified in 1859 as a witness for Charlotte. All three gave it as their opinion that no law had ever properly established slavery in the colony.[34]

True, the three judges acknowledged, Intendant Jacques Raudot, as the official in charge of the civil administration of New France, had issued an ordinance on 13 April 1709 affirming the colonists' right to buy and own blacks and Panis as slaves. It was also true that one of his successors, Intendant Gilles Hocquart had decreed on 1 September 1736 that the only valid way for an owner to emancipate his slave was by deed passed before a notary.[35] And, yes, on the surrender of New France to the British at Montreal on 8 September 1760, the 47th article of capitulation had stated that, other than those slaves whom the French had captured from the British, "The negroes and panis of both sexes shall remain, in their quality of slaves, in the possession of the French and Canadians to whom they belong; they shall be at liberty to keep them in their service in the colony, or to sell them; and they may also continue to bring them up in the Roman religion."[36] The British parliament itself had adopted a law in 1790 that permitted settlers from the United States to import their "negroes" free of duty into the British colonies.[37]

The judges knew of these official pronouncements, but they held that, in both France and England, the public law was so fundamentally inimical to slavery that the practice could not have been introduced into the colony by such incidental means; it had to have been sanctioned by positive law, such as France's *Code noir* of March 1685, the royal edict that had established and regulated slavery in the French West Indies, and its variant of March 1724, which had done the same for the French colony of Louisiana. No such "Black Code" or fundamental law on slavery was ever drafted for, or registered in, New France,[38] they said, and in the absence of such legislative

Judge James Reid (1769–1848)

Judge Samuel Gale (1783–1865)

Judge William Badgley (1801–1888)

expression of the royal will, no colonial official had possessed the power to legalize slavery, as Raudot had professed to do with his irregular ordinance in 1709. As Reid put it, "The establishment of Slavery was an act of high authority in any Legislature, and more especially in such a subordinate Legislature as that vested in an Intendant in Canada, and my opinion is, that Mr Raudot had no more power to establish Slavery in the Colony, than he had to establish torture or death for any new offence occurring there without the consent and authority of the King."[39] The laws of France had applied in the colony until the formal cession of New France to the British Crown in 1763 and the Royal Proclamation of October that year had established the laws of England (French civil law returning under the *Quebec Act* of 1774), assuring to all subjects equal protection and rights as British subjects.

If blacks in Canada benefited from the same rights as whites from 1763 – a debatable proposition – this was more than could be said of blacks in Britain itself. Although no positive law established slavery in England, many West Indian masters were in the habit of taking their slaves there with them. By some estimates, there could have been as many as 15,000 black slaves or "near slaves" in Britain on 22 June 1772, the date when Lord Mansfield, chief justice of England's Court of King's Bench, handed down his judgment in the epochal case of James Somerset. Somerset, purchased in Virginia, had accompanied his master, Charles Stewart of Boston, to England in 1769 and subsequently deserted Stewart's service. In 1771, Stewart had had him abducted and placed on board a ship for Jamaica, where he was to be sold. Mansfield ruled that Stewart had no right to forcibly ship Somerset out of the kingdom. This decision was widely reported to have entirely abolished slavery in England; some went so far as to suggest that Mansfield had rendered it illegal in the colonies.[40] Mansfield himself insisted that he had gone no farther than to rule "that the Master had no right to compel the slave to go into a foreign country," but in giving the reasons for his decision, he had laid down principles that were to weigh heavily in colonies or countries, including the United States, whose legal systems were based on English common law.[41] "So high an act of dominion" as that to which Stewart pretended over his slave, "must derive its authority, if any such it has, from the law of the kingdom where executed," he said.

> The power of a master over his servant is different in all countries, more or less limited or extensive, the exercise of it therefore must always be regulated by the laws of the place where exercised. The state of slavery is of such a nature, that it is incapable of being introduced by courts of justice upon mere reasoning, or inferences from any principles natural or political; it must take its rise from positive law; the origin of it can in no country or age be traced back to any other source. ... Tracing the subject to natural principles, the claim of slavery can never be supported.[42]

The idea that slavery could exist only by positive law, and that such law did not extend beyond the territorial jurisdiction of those who had adopted it, resonated in the argument raised by Rose's children and in the opinions of the three Montreal judges who were called upon to clarify what had been the legal basis of slavery in Canada.

Only Badgley, testifying thirteen years after Reid and Gale, appears to have been made aware of correspondence between colonial officials and the French government, by which in 1689 the Sun King, Louis XIV, had authorized settlers in Canada to try their hand at importing from the West Indies freshly landed African slaves to satisfy the demand for cheap labour. Rather than explore this royal nod, Badgley played down its significance. He had seen this correspondence, or extracts of it, in the hands of "a Collector of old colonial records," he said, but he could not verify its authenticity. Besides, the comment that he had seen came not from the king himself but from the secretary of state, and its thrust "was simply, that the King made no particular objection" to the proposed slave-importing scheme. As Badgley correctly pointed out, the scheme had come to nothing.[43]

None of the judges had seen or heard of the king's mandate of 1 May 1689 to the colonial authorities, in which he was "pleased to tell them that he consents" to the importation of slaves.[44] Even so, the extract of the response from the secretary of state was more supportive than Badgley allowed. "Sa Majesté trouve bon que les habitants du Canada y fassent venir des nègres pour faire leur culture," it said, which might fairly be translated: "His Majesty deems it well and good that the inhabitants of Canada should cause negroes to be brought there to labour on their farms."[45] The king's one reservation was that black slaves from the tropics might not survive the cold climate of Canada, and that settlers should therefore refrain from investing too heavily in a slave-importing experiment lest it ruin them and thereby damage the colony's economy. Even though no slave ship ever materialized, and even if there was no formal royal edict establishing slavery, the fact is that the king had assented to the introduction of black slaves into the colony. The person who had communicated that extract and other papers to Badgley was the recently deceased Jacques Viger, who perhaps deserved more credit than Badgley allowed in passing him off as a nameless collector of unauthenticated historical documents.[46]

If the king's approval, formal or informal, was necessary for the legal establishment of slavery in New France, it was largely irrelevant to the situation on the ground. Slavery, at least on a limited scale, had been practised in Quebec without benefit of a royal nod for sixty years before 1689. The first known black slave, Olivier Le Jeune, had arrived in Quebec in 1628. In other words, legal niceties mattered little in practice: in the colonial world, whether ruled by a chartered company, as New France had been until 1663, or by the Crown, whites acted as though they were naturally entitled to enslave blacks and Indians. By all accounts, Panis far outnumbered black slaves in New France, and while Louis XIV in 1689 had assented to the importation of *nègres,* he had said nothing of Indian slavery, a practice rooted as much in aboriginal culture as in European racial attitudes, and that had become common well before Raudot gave it his stamp of approval in 1709. Indeed, as the text of his ordinance shows, Raudot promulgated it precisely because some colonists were inducing Panis to desert their masters on the grounds that, since there was no slavery in France, there could be none in New France. Raudot countered that New France had to be considered on the same footing as the French West Indies, and that Panis were as important to New France as black slaves were to those other colonies.

Badgley held that the public law of France at the time did not recognize slavery in France or in French Canada. Raudot's ordinance of 1709 "was a nullity," never sanctioned by the king, and an "abusive servitude" had existed in New France "simply by the abuse of power, in those who held the Panis and Negroes, and from the fear of the penalty imposed upon 'ceux qui les débauchent' " (those who encourage them to desert). That is, the abuse went uncontested because any opponents of slavery were cowed by the hardships and costs that they feared they would incur in challenging the slave-owners, and by the penalty of fifty livres that Raudot's ordinance imposed on anyone who incited slaves to leave their masters.[47]

To all three judges, even if there had been some royal approval of slavery, it would have been immaterial from 1763 onward, because any such sanction would have lapsed with the formal cession of the colony to the British Crown. It appears that much the same idea had been expressed by the first lieutenant-governor of Upper Canada, John Graves Simcoe. "In January, 1793, some gentlemen of the settlement informed me that it was the intention of the Governor to liberate the negroes," a visiting Englishman wrote of Simcoe's plans to abolish slavery in that new colony. "They said, that, the Governor contended that, by the introduction of the English Constitution, slavery was necessarily done away in the colony, as it could not subsist in England. An opinion of this kind, coming from an authority that could enforce it, you may well suppose, excited both surprise and consternation."[48] Elements of the opinions expressed by the nineteenth-century Montreal judges were therefore not new; they had been raised by Simcoe in 1793. In fact, men in positions of power in Quebec had voiced similar views by 1785, as we shall see in the next chapter.

THE ONUS ON THE SLAVES

While denying slavery a legal foundation, Reid, Gale, and Badgley recognized that a species of de facto slavery had existed in New France, and for some time under British rule. They showed little awareness, however, of how widely accepted the practice had been. They seem to have been unaware that, in the 1730s, the colonial government itself, on instructions from Paris, had gone shopping for a slave in Martinique to be the colony's public executioner. The government had even played at matchmaking, importing a black female slave who was intended to be the hangman's wife.[49] The last governor of New France, Pierre Rigaud de Vaudreuil-Cavagnial, marquis de Vaudreuil, as well as the first British governor of the conquered colony, General James Murray, and General Thomas Gage, the military governor of Montreal after the Conquest, had each owned at least one slave.[50] In 1778, Lieutenant-Governor Hector-Theophilus Cramahé had bought a fifteen-year-old mulatto girl, whom he had sold the following year.[51] Loyalists had made no secret of bringing their slaves into Canada at the time of the American War of Independence, and British raiding parties had carried back to Montreal and sold many slaves who had been seized in upstate New York and elsewhere. In the 1780s, Edward William Gray, the sheriff of the Montreal District, had owned at least one slave, sold another at public auction and, for several years, as the executor of an estate, kept one whose ownership and status were in dispute.[52] Judges and magistrates had owned slaves, not to mention Solicitor-General Foucher and Chief Justice Smith, president of the Legislative Council. When the elections to the first parliament of Lower Canada were held in 1792, at least eighteen of its fifty seats went to men who owned, or had owned, slaves.[53] Under the circumstances, residents of the colony might have assumed that slavery was legal under the king of England as of France. Everyone acted as if it were so.

Yet Reid, who had become a resident of Montreal when black slavery was "a matter of course" and who had been admitted to the bar there in 1794, seemed to have been as oblivious to it as some of the expatriates at St Louis. He had known no slave-owners in Canada, he said.[54] He believed that the British law of 1790 encouraging Americans to immigrate with their black slaves had been meant to help populate the area that soon became Upper Canada, and that it was an exceptional measure – the only one that officially sanctioned slavery in any part of Canada. The door that it opened to slavery was soon shut by Upper Canada's Act of 1793, which prohibited the further introduction of slaves, he said. "There would not seem to have been any need of such an act in Lower Canada, as slavery was never known to exist there [by law] under any period of the British Government. The immigrants who brought slaves with them under the British Statute 30 George III, ch. 27 [the 1790 law], appear to have gone to Upper Canada, where the means of settlement were principally provided."[55] As to whether the legality of slavery had ever been tested in the courts, he had no first-hand knowledge of this and was only slightly better informed than Janvier Domptail Lacroix about that one case in 1800: "I am informed that a case was determined in the Court of King's Bench at Montreal, and that by the Judgment of that Court of the eighteenth of February 1800, one *Robin* alias* *Robert,* who had been arrested as a slave for leaving his Master, was brought before the Court on a writ of *Habeas corpus,* and discharged, on the ground that no slavery existed in Canada."[56] That case had received no publicity in the press, and, clearly, Robin's victory had created no stir in the tiny legal fraternity of Montreal in 1800, at least not enough to impress itself on Reid's memory.

Gale, born in British Florida in 1783 but raised from infancy in Quebec, considered, as did Badgley, that de facto slavery had endured because of the failure of the slaves to challenge it. "The agency of the Courts of Justice of course would not be exercised between individual and individual, unless demanded," he said,

---

*This term is used to give the different names recorded for a black person. It does not mean that blacks themselves used different names, but simply that the records identify the same person under different names, or different spellings of the same name.

and it is therefore most likely that there were instances of persons called slaves, who continued to remain as such ... long after the conquest of Canada, and while it continued one Province. Such voluntary acquiescence in servitude might be owing to various motives, – such as affection or ignorance of their rights – or fear. But no legal inference could be drawn from the exercise of such assumed ownership on the one hand, while no objection was raised on the other.[57]

Since the division of the old Province of Quebec into Lower and Upper Canada in 1791, Gale said, he had never heard of persons in Lower Canada being held in slavery if they had challenged their enslavement in court. Unlike Reid, Gale at least recalled having known slaves:

I knew two or three individuals when a child who were held, as I understood from themselves and others, as slaves, but who were induced to apply to the Courts of justice to be declared free, and, as I also understood, were so declared. One of these, as nearly as I recollect, was called Phillis,[58] and lived at Sorel in this district; and there was also another, whose name I cannot call to mind. These things are however, as I believe, fifty years bygone or more, – and I do not now recollect having myself seen any more recent instances of persons residing in Lower Canada who were held as slaves.[59]

Badgley, the most studied of the three in his answers, had examined the records of the civil courts from 1761 to beyond 1802 and found only six slave cases. The earliest was a judgment of 18 March 1788 in the Court of Common Pleas ordering tailor Donald Fisher and his wife to turn over to shopkeeper Mary Jacobs, née Martin, or her representative the two female slaves for which she had paid, or else to refund her £50. (If the law did not recognize slavery, the court certainly knew a slave sale.) The last was the decision of 18 February 1800 in the habeas corpus application by Robin, alias Robert. Badgley observed that "no case can be found of record in the archives of the Courts, under the British or French rule, in which involuntary servitude has been judicially sustained, or in which application for freedom has been judicially denied."[60]

Was that so? Under the French, in separate cases in 1733 and 1740, the question of whether baptism made Panis free was argued in the courts and decided in the negative.[61] Under the British, on 27 September 1763, merchant Charles Rhéaume had asked the Chambre des milices, the civil court in Montreal under British military rule (1760–64), to order the return of Marie *dite* Manon, identified as a "panis esclave" belonging to the estate of his late mother, Thérèse Catin. Rhéaume's brother-in-law, Daniel Robertson, who seems to have hired the woman, said he would readily comply if she were, in fact, a slave. The court ordered him to do so. That same day, Manon, designated a "negresse" – the word "panise" was crossed out in the court record – asked the court to order Rhéaume to grant her the freedom that she had been promised by her late master, Catin's second husband, Charles Ruette d'Auteuil de Monceaux. The court turned her down. Nothing daunted, she addressed herself to the court of appeal, in the person of Gage, the governor of Montreal. It seems that Ruette d'Auteuil had promised that Manon would go free after he and his wife had died. Catin had vowed to honour his promise, Manon argued, and had she changed her mind, she would have said so in her will. On 15 October, Gage ruled in her favour, declaring that since Rhéaume had adduced no proof that the promise had been revoked, Manon must go free.[62]

In 1762–63, before the same court, André, the black slave of fur-trade merchant Gershon Levy, was engaged in a struggle to establish his claim to freedom. He applied to the court in July 1762, insisting that Levy had no right to keep him because his former owner, a man named Best, had bought him for a term of only four years, which had now expired. Levy countered that he had bought André in good faith and that André could not prove his allegation. The court invited André to produce witnesses or documents to substantiate his claim; in the meantime, he was to remain with Levy. He still had not provided the necessary evidence by the following spring, when Levy sought to sell him outside the court's jurisdiction. As a result, in May, André petitioned the court, which ordered Levy not to dispose of his slave who, "from the proofs he has submitted appears to have presumption in his favour."[63]

The ultimate outcome of André's suit is unknown,[64] but it is clear from his case and that of Manon that, from the early days of British rule, although the courts were prepared to entertain applications from slaves who challenged their master's title and to free those who could back their claims, they assumed the legitimacy of slavery. They wanted proof that petitioning slaves were entitled to their freedom. Freedom was in the gift of the masters or the courts, not the intrinsic right of people like Manon and André. As we shall see in the next chapter, it was not until 1794, when a runaway New York slave known as Diah (alias Dick) was arrested at the behest of his master, that a Montreal tribunal held that the law did not recognize slavery. It must be acknowledged, however, that the question of slavery's legality does not seem to have been tested in the courts of British Quebec before that time. Manon and André did not challenge the practice of slavery, only their own continued enslavement.

Besides contending that slaves had only to apply to the courts to gain their freedom, Badgley also questioned whether their servitude constituted slavery in any true sense. In his view, the slave contracts that he had examined, spanning the years 1780 to 1792, lacked "the ingredients of slavery." That is, although persons were sold for a period of service – in some cases for life, in others for less – "in no case [did] it interfere with the acquisitions of the purchased persons, or stipulate regulations over his wife and children."[65] Anyone looking through the records of slavery in Quebec must acknowledge that its practice did, generally, lack the harsher features that we associate with slave systems elsewhere. But if buying and selling humans in the manner of livestock or real property did not constitute slavery, what was it? The sales contracts called it slavery, the masters understood it to be slavery, and the slaves knew it as such, regardless of which "ingredients" may have been lacking to satisfy a textbook definition. Without knowing which and how many contracts Badgley examined, and whether these were representative, it is difficult to understand exactly what he was driving at. Many slaves were single persons, without "acquisitions." The question of interfering with their effects or regulating their wives and children did not arise. Since slaves could not marry without the consent of their owners, their owners could easily withhold approval, or impose whatever conditions they pleased without setting them down in writing. As to a female slave, her children, whether legitimate or born out of wedlock, belonged to her master; an ancient rule, rooted in Roman law, dictated that children follow the condition of the mother. There was no need to spell this out in a contract: it went without saying.

ROOM FOR DOUBT

The opinions of Reid, Gale, and Badgley on the legality of slavery had their weaknesses, owing largely to their incomplete access to the historical record. But what matters is their interpretation of the law, not our thoughts on the correctness of their views. They believed that the law did not authorize slavery. None of them ever had to rule in a slave case, but their views help us understand the rulings of the judges who did. This is particularly true of Reid, the oldest of the three. Admitted to the bar in 1794, he had been appointed to the bench in 1807; his colleagues then had included the three judges who had sat together in 1800 on the important case of Robin, mentioned earlier: Montreal district Chief Justice James Monk, whom he would succeed in 1825; Isaac Ogden, a New Jersey Loyalist; and Pierre-Louis Panet, the brother-in-law of Auguste Chouteau and Paschal Léon Cerré. By the 1840s, those men had disappeared from the scene,[66] and we have only sketchy accounts of the judicial decisions they had rendered, with little information on how they arrived at them. If Reid considered, as did Simcoe and his legal advisers in Upper Canada in 1793, that the practice of slavery had no proper foundation in law, no doubt others had shared that opinion. It was not a unanimous view, but by 1794 it had led Montreal magistrates to rule that Diah, claimed by an American as a runaway slave, was no slave under the law of Canada.

Specialists in legal history today might dispute the idea that slavery had existed in a virtual legal vacuum from beginning to end. However much Reid and company might have considered it abusive or *ultra vires,* Raudot's ordinance of 1709, sanctioning the ownership of black and Indian slaves, had never been formally challenged in the colony or disallowed by the Crown in the fifty-one years before New France fell to the British. Still, the absence of laws regulating the practice of slavery is notable. There was no fundamental law on slavery beyond Raudot's ordinance. Other than this, and Hocquart's ordinance of 1736 on the proper manumission of slaves, anyone in Reid's day would have found little more on the subject among the recorded laws of New France than a few rules emanating from France, generally in response to incidents or conditions in the French West Indies. By a royal declaration of December 1721, for example, registered by the *Conseil supérieur* at Quebec on 5 October 1722, emancipated minors in the French possessions were barred until the age of twenty-five from disposing of the *nègres* who cultivated their lands – a situation that prevailed in the Caribbean but not in Canada. A royal edict of October 1727, registered at Quebec on 17 September 1728, prohibited the import or export of *nègres* between the colonies of France and the territories of a foreign power. A ruling of the King's *Conseil d'état* in 1745, registered at Quebec on 19 July 1748, stipulated that *nègres* who escaped from enemy colonies to any French colony were deemed the property of the Crown.[67] In all these cases, the term *nègres* was a synonym for "slaves." None of these rules had applied in Quebec after the Conquest, if even before. As Badgley rightly noted, in New France, "no authentic documents can be found in her archives or records which regulate the mode, or period or effect of servitude, the extent of the Master's power, the period of the enforced subjection or any of its incidents or consequences, either affecting the purchased person himself, or his offspring, or any Act of Police, justice or administration connected with slavery."[68]

Under the British, the practice of freeing slaves by means of notarized deeds continued; whether this was considered a legal requirement, or simply the best way to proceed both for slave and master was never tested. Beyond this the law was mum – with one slight exception, of which neither Badgley nor the other two judges seemed to be aware. Over a period of almost twenty years after the institution of civil government in 1764, the magistrates of Montreal, as the administrators of the city's affairs, adopted general "regulations of the police" (the equivalent of today's municipal bylaws), which explicitly recognized slavery when it came to the rules governing taverns. In an "Order agst. harbouring servants" of 10 April 1766, for example, keepers of taverns, alehouses and inns were forbidden to "receive, harbour, or entertain, any bond, or servant slaves, drinking, gaming, or loitering in their houses under the penalty of five pounds currency."[69] This rule was renewed and expanded at the end of 1767:

> WHEREAS It was Ordered by His Majesty's Justices of the Peace at a General Quarter Sessions of the Peace held at Montreal the 10th day of April 1766, That no Tavern keepers, Alehouse or Inn keepers in the District or Suburbs of the City of Montreal Should receive harbour or Entertain any Bond or Servants Slaves Drinking gaming or Loitering in their Houses under the Penalty of five pounds Lawfull money of Quebec to be received by Summons Process or Execution and whereas Complaints hath been made this Day to the Above mentioned Justices notwithstanding the aforesaid Order that Several Tavern and Alehouse keepers in this City Still Continue receiving and Entertaining as well bond Servants as free Servants to the great hurt and Damage of their Masters and Also that Several Tavern and Alehouse keepers in this City do frequently harbour and Entertain Private Soldiers Drinking at Night and after dark to the Injury of the Public and hurt and Injury of his Majesty's Troops in General, It is therefore this Day Ordered that the said former Order of Sessions be hereby

renewed and is hereby renew'd Accordingly in Every Particular thereof against all or any Tavern or Alehouse keepers or retailers of Liquors in this City or District who shall harbour or Entertain all or any bond or free Servant or Servants Slave or Slaves or that shall harbour or Entertain any Private Soldiers in this City Drinking and Loitering in their Houses after dark or Night fall, and that all such Tavern and Alehouse keepers So entertaining and harbouring Such Servants and Soldiers in manner as herein before mentioned, Shall in addition to the Punishment or fine mentioned in Such former Order be Subject to the Loss of his her or their Licence or Licences on proof being made of the charge.[70]

A slimmed-down version of this regulation, adopted in May 1777, had a different thrust. It applied only to slaves, not to servants or soldiers. It also did not expressly prohibit the serving of alcohol to slaves, but simply forbade "tavern keepers and others" to let "negro and Panis slaves congregate" on their premises on pain of a fine of ten shillings for a first offence, and £1 for repeat offences. The measure seems to have been concerned less with dissipation than with the desire to prevent slaves from assembling. This regulation, with its sharply reduced penalty, remained in force until 1781, when a new version once more prohibited the sale of liquor to slaves and servants, who were not to be allowed to drink in taverns and alehouses "without an order from their Masters." The penalty for infractions was ten shillings.[71] These successive regulations never prescribed penalties for the found-ins, only for the tavern keepers. The rule of 1781 was renewed for one year in April 1782. From 1783, the regulations made no more mention of slaves.[72] It is curious that the sole rule explicitly applicable to slaves was allowed to lapse at the close of the American War of Independence, given that the number of black slaves had swelled during the war with the coming of the Loyalists. If the magistrates saw fit to dispense with such a rule, it may be that the presence of slaves in taverns was not deemed such a problem as to require special regulation. It may also hint at some dawning uneasiness on the question of slavery.

A BRITISH COLOURING

We do not know why lawyers for the slave plaintiffs in the Missouri cases chose to call Reid, Gale, and Badgley as witnesses.[73] Given the research that he had done on the subject of slavery to complete Viger's work, Sir Louis-Hippolyte LaFontaine might have been the perfect witness in 1859, if not for the plaintiffs, then for Chouteau. But he did not appear; it may be that he was ill, or that it was considered unseemly for a sitting chief justice to appear as a witness in such a proceeding. As all three judges examined were members of the English-speaking elite, a pro-British bias may have coloured their responses. There was a John Bullish tinge to Badgley's reply to the question of whether blacks had possessed the right to vote, testify in courts, and sit on juries: "Since the establishment of the British dominion in Canada, negroes have enjoyed the same Civil rights as other natural born, or naturalized, subjects of the Crown in the Colony, without any disqualification whatever by reason of their complexion."[74] This was true on paper, but it did not reflect the everyday reality; no one could deny that de facto discrimination had long kept blacks off juries.[75] As a slave-born American expatriate and contemporary of Badgley concluded after a couple of years in Canada: "And here is the grand difference betwixt Yankee and Canadian Negro-hate – the former is sanctioned by the laws and the courts, the latter is *not*."[76] To be pro-British in Canada at this time also implied a certain degree of smugness in regard to the Americans, and to this, too, the judges may not have been immune. If the United States was far ahead of Canada in terms of population, material progress, and social and economic dynamism, Canadians could take solace in the moral certainty that they were free of the taint of slavery. Americans were mired in it. From the Missouri Compromise of 1820 on, growing anti-slavery pressure and hardening slave-state resistance led to a succession of political crises in the United States and mounting fears for the integrity of the union. Between the testimony of Reid and Gale in 1846 and that of Badgley in 1859, the Fugitive Slave Act of September 1850, adopted in the United States as part of the "Great Compromise" meant to soothe Northern and Southern feelings on the issue of slavery, had spurred an exodus of American blacks, slave and free, to Queen Victoria's dominions, sealing Canada's reputation in the popular mind as the land of refuge. Under the circumstances, to persuade the doubting Thomases on a Missouri jury that, not so long ago, Canada had been a land of slavery would have been a challenge. Gabriel Chouteau's lawyers were unable to make that case. Many Canadians too – the young, or the immigrants who had arrived in successive waves since the War of 1812 – would have been skeptical, if not incredulous.

In discussing slavery and its legality, neither Reid, Gale, nor Badgley made the slightest allusion to the British Abolition Act of 1833. Neither did Viger and LaFontaine, for that matter. This legislation is often touted as having put an "official" end to slavery in Quebec. Had that been the case, it would have been passing strange for the judges to ignore it altogether, or for the French scholar Isidore Lebrun to assert, in the very year that the law was passed, that Canada had never known slavery. Bouchette, the Montreal counsel for Gabriel Chouteau, surely would have made the point in 1846, and the Missouri courts would have given short shrift to the central argument presented by Rose's children. If one effect of the British law had been to put an official end to slavery in Quebec, then there could be no doubt that slavery had enjoyed recognition up to that point. Indeed, the memory of slavery's legal existence would have been too fresh in the 1840s for any dispute to arise. The anonymous correspondent of the Quebec *Morning Chronicle* in 1847 would not have had to reach back eighty years for evidence of "things as they were," and Viger and LaFontaine in the 1850s would not have had to look back more than half a century for proofs that slavery had existed.

TWO

THERE OUGHT TO BE A LAW

A plaque donated in 2004 by the Quebec government to the City of Montreal honouring the memory of Marie Josèphe Angélique, the black slave of New France who was hanged for arson at Montreal in 1734, reminded us that black slavery had endured in Quebec until 1833.[1] Few might quarrel with the tribute, but the reminder was misguided. Twelve black Montrealers of 1833, and the experience of many others before them, tell us as much.

The mention of 1833 in the text of the plaque referred to the legislation adopted that year by the British parliament to abolish colonial slavery. In late July 1833, Alexander Grant, a scourer (clothes-cleaner) and hairdresser from New York, three years resident in Montreal, convened a meeting of the city's "Coloured brethren" at his home at 80 St-Paul Street to discuss this legislation in the works. Eleven men showed up. Composed of working men, immigrants from the West Indies, the United States and other parts, most of them illiterate and with no political clout, Grant's small band could not hope to influence the debate that was nearing its end across the Atlantic (the British House of Commons would pass the bill three days later). Even had they been men of stature, with the ear of government, no word of their deliberations could have reached London in time. Yet they met and, for what it was worth, made their sentiments known in a press release:[2]

> At a meeting of the Coloured brethren, inhabitants of the city of Montreal, convened on Tuesday the 23rd of July, at the residence of Mr Alexander Grant, *St Paul Street.*
> *Resolved unanimously,*

Governor-General Michaëlle Jean, a native of Haiti, accompanied by Mayor Gérald Tremblay, laid a floral tribute by a plaque in Old Montreal honouring the memory of the slave Marie Josèphe Angélique in April 2006. The plaque was stolen a few weeks later.

    1st. – That as British subjects we duly appreciate the blessings of the constitution under which we have the happiness to live – a constitution which will ever be dear to our hearts – a constitution, which the march of *chastened* intellect has stamped with its highest approbation, and which is the envy and admiration of the civilized world.

    2nd. – That as men and as christians, we must naturally feel anxious that the sacred blessings we enjoy, should be extended to the habitable globe; consequently we are *peculiarly* anxious that our brethren of the "BRITISH WEST INDIA COLONIES," should fully participate in the glorious privileges we are so justly proud of.

    3rd. – We, therefore, contemplate with *intense anxiety,* the progress of the bill which His Majesty's Ministers have introduced into Parliament, for the "TOTAL ABOLITION" of slavery in the West Indies; and we wish it complete success, conceiving it to be the harbinger of *light* and *life* and *liberty,* to all of our fellow brethren and subjects; and we hereby most respectfully tender to His Majesty's Ministers, and to all the friends of humanity, our heartfelt acknowledgments for their benevolent and God like exertions.

A. Grant,	Thomas H. Smith,
G. Grant,	Louis Greene,
P. Dogo,	Anthony Ingston,
A. Low,	Jacob Abadillard,
Gerard Banks,	John Broome,
John Russell,	Joseph Shaw.[3]

In the worldwide saga of slavery and abolition, this statement is of little moment, but it constitutes a milestone in the history of blacks in Quebec. A manifesto of sorts, it marked the first occasion on which a group of blacks spoke as one on a public issue.The literate and articulate Grant, then about thirty-three, was Montreal's first black "activist," the first to rally the "brethren" and to give them a public voice. Their message was clear: they were anxious to see the freedom they knew as British subjects – "the sacred blessings we enjoy," those "glorious privileges we are so justly proud of" – extended to blacks everywhere, notably to the slaves of the British West Indies.[4] What their resolutions implied was that slavery was dead in Lower Canada and had been for some time. The point was made explicitly that same year with respect to all of Britain's North American possessions by William Lyon Mackenzie, the Upper Canadian political misfit who, from his arrival in North America in 1820, made a career of picking every possible nit in a colonial system he deemed corrupt: "Negro slavery is unknown in British America."[5]

To the relief of blacks everywhere, the British bill did pass. On 28 August 1833, King William IV assented to "An Act for the Abolition of Slavery throughout the British Colonies; for Promoting the Industry of the Manumitted Slaves; and for compensating the Persons hitherto entitled to the Services of such Slaves." The law was to take effect one year later, on 1 August 1834.[6] The fact is, although this law cast a wide net it was aimed principally at ending slavery in the British West Indies. That is how it was generally understood by the parliamentarians in London, by the West Indian planters who fought it, by Grant and his friends in Montreal, and, indeed, by black Canadians of later years, who celebrated the First of August as the anniversary of West Indian emancipation.[7] The law had no direct impact in Quebec: it freed no slaves; no blacks entered on the prescribed six-year "apprenticeship" during which freed slaves were to continue serving their masters while preparing for full freedom (this scheme, applied in the West Indies, was aborted in 1838); and of the £20,000,000 in compensation that the law provided for slave-owners divested of their human chattels, not a penny was earmarked for distribution in Quebec or anywhere in North America.[8] When the law came into effect, Grant, as the keynote speaker at the celebration organized by black Montrealers, hailed the 1 August 1834 as "a day which England has decided shall be the auspicious moment which is to give light, life and liberty to 800,000 of our fellow-creatures, namely, to the slaves of the British West India Colonies."[9] Neither in the celebrations of 1834, nor in the communiqué of 1833, was there the least reference to slavery in Quebec or any part of British North America.

Some will counter that, even if there were no slaves, slavery remained legally permissible until 1834, and that it was not "officially" abolished until then. Had colonial lawmakers not declined to legislate an end to slavery when given the chance? The Legislative Assembly of Upper Canada had at least adopted a scheme for gradual abolition in 1793. In terms of ending slavery, however, although the appointed Legislative Council of Quebec missed a golden opportunity in 1787, the elected Legislative Assembly of Lower Canada later accomplished more by doing *nothing* than Upper Canada did by legislating. Upper Canada's gradual-abolition law removed all doubts about the legality of slavery there and gave it legislative sanction, prescribing the rules under which it was to continue. Even as slavery waned in the next few decades, the law remained in force until Britain's emancipation law overrode it. As barrister William Elliot of Upper Canada testified in the Missouri court cases concerning Rose's children, "I am not aware that the right of holding Slaves was ever questioned in any of the Courts of law in Upper Canada. On the Contrary the existence of Slavery was formally recognized by the Legislature of the then Province of Upper Canada, by which an Act was passed in 1793 providing for the gradual abolition of Slavery in that Province."[10] In Lower Canada, slavery was *not* formally recognized by the legislature and it *was* challenged in the courts. The failure to legislate left the practice without any cloak of legality once the courts had stripped it away. To maintain that slavery was still permissible up to the 1830s – that it is conceivable that some slaves were held in bondage until 1 August 1834 – because no statute had put an end to it is to place too much stock in legislation as the determining factor. Slavery had not begun with a law, and it did not end with one, either.

We would have to be naive to think that slavery could have endured in Lower Canada, notably at Montreal, through the first third of the nineteenth century without a voice being raised in dissent or protest – whether it be that of some idealist, an anti-slavery preacher, the press, an opportunistic political gladiator seeking an edge against an opponent, or of a James Reid, chief justice of the Montreal District from 1825, who, as we saw, considered that slavery had no legal basis. To believe that slavery was permissible up to 1834 is also to ignore the forthright view expressed by the Executive Council in 1829 in spurning a request for the extradition of a fugitive slave to Illinois: "The state of slavery is not recognized by the Law of Canada nor does the Law admit that any Man can be the proprietor of another."[11] If the law by then did not admit of slavery, neither did public feeling. In a farewell letter to his congregation in 1828, the Pennsylvania-born Reverend Joseph Christmas, after four years as the first pastor of Montreal's American Presbyterian Church, expressed his conviction that, despite the fact that the sale of liquor was at least as damnable as slavery, intemperance flourished while "he who should now barter in the persons and liberties of his fellow man, would be branded with an infamy – indelible as that of Cain."[12] To this zealous minister of anti-slavery convictions, only twenty-one when he took up his post at Montreal in 1824, the evils that plagued Quebec were liquor and the Roman Catholic Church. To his friend, the English-born Reverend George Bourne, a fiery American abolitionist who served as Congregationalist minister at Quebec at almost the same time, if there was slavery in Quebec it was the thralldom in which the "Romish" church held the people. Out of his experience as a Presbyterian minister in Virginia had come *The Book and Slavery Irreconcilable* (1816), a landmark denunciation of slavery as sin – that is, an affront to God committed by all who abetted slavery, and not, as some Southern defenders of slavery contended, an inherited problem for which they were not to blame. Out of his years in Quebec came a tourist guide, *The Picture of Quebec* (1829), and, after his return to the United States, the anti-Catholic novel *Lorette: The History of Louise, Daughter of a Canadian Nun, Exhibiting the Interior of Female Convents* (1834), a work that can not have been helped by the fact that, as he later acknowledged, "all the influence which could be obtained was formerly urged to procure an entrance for my relative Mr Christmas, and myself into the Nunneries of Montreal and Quebec; but every solicitation for that favor invariably was rejected." He made it his life's work to thunder against his two *bêtes noires* – slavery and the Church of Rome, holding that "Moderation against sin is an absurdity."[13] Had he caught a whiff of slavery in the land where "the whore of Babylon" held sway, the world would have heard about it, we can be sure. We can also be fairly certain that the *Montreal Gazette* would not have ventured to criticize the United States in 1823 for nourishing "slavery – and the worst of slavery – within her own bosom," had slavery persisted in that newspaper's own back yard.[14]

Slavery's day had passed before Christmas's time at Montreal, and Bourne's at Quebec.[15] Can we be more precise? As we saw in the previous chapter, none of the Montreal witnesses in the freedom suits filed by Rose's children made any reference to slavery's existence in Quebec after 1800, when a court had freed the slave Robin.[16] This was the last known case tried in Quebec in which a master sought to reclaim a slave.[17] As Justice Samuel Gale observed in his testimony in 1846, slave cases were then "fifty years bygone or more, – and I do not now recollect having myself seen any more recent instances of persons residing in Lower Canada who were held as slaves." Here are a few more pointed clues: In 1785, Dr Adam Mabane, then a sort of acting chief justice, called for legislation to end slavery in the Province of Quebec, "as doubts may be entertained how far the Law at present permits it [slavery], the Code Noir having never been introduced in Canada by the French Government, but the Practice of importing & selling slaves only authorised by an Ordinance of one of the Intendants till the King's pleasure should be known."[18] In 1787, a representative committee of French- and English-speaking Montreal merchants, including some slave-owners, gave it as their opinion that because slavery contravened the spirit of the British constitution, steps should be taken to stop the introduction of slaves into the province.[19] Once the province was divided into Upper and Lower Canada, the new Legislative Assembly of Lower Canada, in 1793, dealt with the first of several bids by some elected representatives to legislate a gradual end to slavery. The last advertisement for the sale of a slave in Quebec appeared in the *Montreal Gazette* on 29 January 1798. The last notice of a slave escape was published in the same newspaper on 27 August that year. The last known sale of a slave in the colony took place at Montreal on 14 September 1799.[20] For these reasons, Montreal in the late eighteenth century, rather than London in the 1830s, must be the focus of any investigation of slavery's end in Quebec.

MABANE'S ABOLITION BILL

On 29 March 1787, Montreal distiller John Lagord sold Cynda (alias Marie Jeanne, Jenny), a ten-year-old black girl, for 750 livres to Pierre Fafard *dit* Joinville of Île Dupas, off Berthier, on the understanding that Lagord would take her back and refund the purchase money should the Legislative Council or any higher authority adopt a law emancipating slaves.²¹ Lagord and Joinville, the ranking government agent in his area in his capacity as captain of militia, were well informed. The Legislative Council, which met behind closed doors and did not publicize its debates, was considering just such a measure. On 23 January, Adam Mabane had moved for leave to introduce his bill, pursuant to the notice he had given nearly two years earlier. In his notice of 29 April 1785, he had spoken of his intention to bring in a measure that would stop the importing of slaves and provide for the freeing of all slaves in seven years. On 25 January 1787, he tabled the draft "Ordinance to abolish Slavery in the Province of Quebec," which called for an immediate ban on slave imports and the freeing of all slaves within five years.²² The bill contained only two clauses:

> Whereas Slavery is contrary to Religion & is in contradiction to yᵉ Spirit and Liberality of yᵉ Antient Laws and Usages of Canada which are established in the Province by the Statute of the 14th of His Majesty [the Quebec Act of 1774], It is enacted by His Excellency the Governor by and with the Advice and Consent of the legislative Council That every Person or Persons who shall after the Publication of yᵉ present Ordinance be brought or who shall come into this Province, shall be considered as free, and be entitled to claim their Freedom notwithstanding he she or they have been Slaves in the Country where they last resided.
>
> And be it further enacted by the Authority aforesaid that all Slaves who may have been brought or who may have come into this province since the Month of Sept. 1763 as well as those who may have been in it prior to that Period, shall at the Expiration of yᵉ Term of five years from the Publication of this Ordinance be entitled to their freedom and may claim the same.²³

Mabane's bill almost totally disregarded slavery's economic dimension. It did not propose that slave-owners be compensated for the loss of their investment in human property. It did not even offer them the implicit compensation generally found in gradual-abolition measures: the possibility of getting their money's worth out of their investments by keeping and exploiting their slaves for an extended period.²⁴ The grace period was too short: slavery would end in five years. But could the legislators declare slavery offensive to God and man and yet maintain it for a single year, let alone five? Acceptance of the principle surely called for them to put an immediate stop to so vile a practice. Why did Mabane not propose immediate abolition and close the five-year gap between virtue in principle and virtue in deed? Pragmatism, no doubt. Persuading his fellow legislators to approve of abolition would have been difficult enough without insisting that it take place overnight. A good indication of how far interested parties were prepared to go is found in the collective opinion expressed by the men of business who ruled the roost at Montreal at this very time.

To assist Governor Lord Dorchester in framing the legislative program for the session of 1787, a committee of the Legislative Council had written to the magis-

> present Legislature is competent thereto.—
>
> The Prohibition of bringing Slaves into the Province
>
> Slavery being alike contrary to the principles of humanity, and to the spirit of the British constitution; this Committee recommends that means be adopted to prevent the bringing of Slaves into the Province in future, but as to the few negroes or Indian Slaves who are already in servitude they conceive that they ought not in justice or policy to be emancipated into many families, there are of them, who are Valuable as property and Servants, we have frequently seen instances of Slaves being manumitted soon becoming idle and disorderly, and finally a burthen to the public, we would therefore recommend that after years all Infants that are born of Parents who are Slaves be declared free.—

In a report to the Legislative Council in 1787, Montreal merchants and magistrates recommended an immediate end to slave imports and the gradual abolition of slavery.

Legislative Councillor Adam Mabane (ca 1734–1792) was the first Canadian legislator to propose a bill outlawing slavery.

13 Apr 1787

An Ordinance To abolish Slavery in the Province of Quebec.

Whereas Slavery is contrary to Religion & is in contradiction to ye Spirit and Liberality of ye Antient Laws and Usages of Canada which are established in the Province by the Statute of the 14th of His Majesty, It is enacted by His Excellency the Governor by and with the Advice and Consent of the Legislative Council That every Person or Persons who shall after the Publication of ye present Ordinance be brought or who shall come into this Province, shall be considered as free, and be entitled to claim their Freedom notwithstanding he, she or they may have been Slaves in the Country where they last resided

And be it further enacted by the Authority aforesaid that all Slaves who may have been brought or who may have come into this Province since the Month of Sep. 1763, as well as those who may have been in it prior to that Period, shall at the Expiration of ye Term of five Years from the Publication of this Ordinance be entitled to their freedom and may claim the same.

Mabane's bill of 1787 called for an end to slavery within five years.

trates and merchants of Montreal, Quebec, and Trois-Rivières the previous fall, seeking their ideas on the issues of trade and public order. Only the Montrealers, who had hastened to appoint a committee to present their views, adverted to slavery in their report, dated 23 January 1787, the day on which Mabane sought the Council's permission to introduce his draft ordinance. In a section headed "The Prohibition of bringing Slaves into the Province," they acknowledged that slavery was "alike contrary to the principles of humanity, and to the spirit of the British constitution." We would expect this to be followed by a call for immediate abolition, but the committee, reflecting its members' hard-nosed pragmatism, proposed nothing so drastic:

> [T]his Committee recommends that means be adopted to prevent the bringing of Slaves into the Province in future, but as to the few negroes or Indian Slaves who are already in servitude they conceive that they ought not in Justice or Policy to be emancipated into [sic] many families, there are of them who are Valuable as property and Servants, we have frequently seen instances of Slaves being manumitted soon becoming idle and disorderly, and finally a burthen to the public, we would therefore recommend that after [blank] years all Infants that are born of Parents who are slaves be declared free.[25]

Mabane and the Montreal merchants and magistrates were in agreement on the desirability of bringing the business of slavery to a close and, true to their stated principles, they agreed on the idea of immediately stopping the practice of bringing slaves into the province. But principle was then muffled, and Mabane's bill proposed that the intolerable be tolerated for five years, without specifying the reasons for this apparent inconsistency, while the Montrealers, for reasons of public order and to protect the masters' investments in slaves, favoured keeping the current slaves in bondage indefinitely and providing only for their children to go free after several years, the number of which was yet to be determined. Although Mabane's bill remained closer to its statement of principle by providing for a clear and relatively quick end to slavery, it seems that in giving the slave-owners a five-year leeway, he shared some of the same practical concerns as the Montreal merchants. They wanted investors in slave labour to enjoy the full benefits of that labour and said so; he did not say so in his bill, but his proposal would have given slave-owners time to adjust to the new law and to seek to recover their investment by, for instance, selling their slaves abroad.

The Legislative Council voted 13–5 to refer Mabane's bill to a committee. A committee of the whole, which he chaired, took up the measure on 13 April. By a vote of 14–3, the councillors adopted its lofty statement of principle, that slavery was contrary to religion and to the spirit of the laws of Canada. Even slave-owners Sir John Johnson, the Loyalist leader from New York's Mohawk Valley, and Chief Justice William Smith, another Loyalist, formerly chief justice of the colony of New York, voted with the majority. The only opponents were slave-owning Quebec merchant William Grant, Provincial Secretary George Pownall, and Deputy Post Master General Hugh Finlay. But the councillors then voted 14–3 against the first clause of the bill, which provided that all persons entering the province thereafter be recognized as free. Councillor Paul Roch de Saint-Ours valiantly proposed, as a substitute for the rejected clause, that the importing or sale of slaves be forbidden on pain of a fine of £100 per slave, and that any slave brought into Quebec in defiance of the ordinance be acknowledged as free. Five members voted for this strong measure, and twelve against. Debate ended with members approving Johnson's motion to postpone discussion of the matter to the next session. Only one of seventeen councillors present, Gaspard Chaussegros de Léry, voted against delay. Mabane, as chairman, did not vote, since chairmen were called on to do so only in the event of a tie. He did vote on 16 April, however, when the Council itself was called on to declare whether it concurred with the committee's decision. Of the eighteen councillors present, only he, Saint-Ours, and de Léry voted no.[26]

While Mabane's notice of 1785 may have suggested that he viewed an ordinance simply as a legal matter, the defeat of his measure drew from him a statement of personal conviction and impatience. The minutes of the Council recorded his dissent:

> I dissent from the Vote of the L. Council which concurred with the Report of the Committee upon the Bill for abolishing Slavery for the following Reasons
> 1st – Slavery is so repugnant to Humanity that it cannot be too soon abolished by Law in any Country, where it has been either established or tolerated.
> 2dly – because the difficulties (if any ought to have been made to such a Salutary Law), must, as ye Number of Slaves encrease, be augmented by delay.
> 3dly – because the Argument adduced from ye Impolicy of giving Umbrage to ye United States & especially that of Virginia is frivolous in the extreme, when it is considered that several of the United States have already abolished Slavery, tho' more Contiguous to Virginia than this Province is, and that ye large Tract of Indian Country thro' which fugitive slaves must pass before they can reach any part of this Province from Virginia renders it almost impossible for them to attempt an Escape by that way.[27]

From this statement, we understand that a majority of councillors had voiced concern that significant numbers of American slaves would seek refuge in Quebec, and that this would act as an irritant in relations with the United States so soon after the War of Independence. Whether this was just a pretext to avoid the issue, who can say? But note Mabane's first reason for dissenting: slavery was so wicked that it could not be abolished soon enough wherever it had been "established or *tolerated* [emphasis added]." From this, as well as from his notice of 1785, his proposed bill, and the views expressed by the Montreal merchants, it is clear that the question of whether slavery existed in Quebec by law or *par abus* was already a subject of debate. Certainly, when the powerful fur-trade barons and other members of the Montreal elite collectively acknowledged that slavery was "contrary to the principles of humanity, and to the spirit of the British constitution," and the legislators were prepared to recognize that it was "contrary to Religion & is in contradiction to ye Spirit and Liberality of ye Antient Laws and Usages of Canada," the practice was rather shorn of moral and legal justification. Yet, ending it then and there, or even in five years, was deemed impolitic and inconvenient, and that is all that could be said in defence of a practice "so repugnant to Humanity." Under the circumstances, it is surprising that Mabane, who died in 1792, apparently made no further attempt to press the point. The Council did not again take up the question of slavery.

We may well wonder what echoes of these closed-door discussions reached the slaves themselves, and with what effect. They were, after all, the persons most interested, and perhaps even more attuned than the Lagords and Joinvilles of the day to the least sign of change in the wind. It is possible that some slave, or incident connected with slavery, led Mabane to act as he did when he did.[28] It has been suggested that the arrival of free blacks in the British North American colonies upon the conclusion of the American War of Independence awoke slaves in Quebec to the idea that they, too, could be free.[29] But slaves had always been alive to the possibilities of freedom, and the presence of free blacks was nothing new. Indeed, it was the freeing of slaves by no more than a word from their masters that had led Intendant Hocquart to decree in 1736 that all manumissions had to be recorded in a notarized deed. There had been free blacks in Quebec in the days of New France and ever since, and so the arrival of others in the 1780s hardly constituted an eye-opener.[30] If hope now stirred among slaves, it was more likely stoked by rumours and murmurs and fly-on-the-wall reports of conversations concerning Mabane's notice of 1785, his bill of 1787, and attendant discussions; these were the first signs of gaping cracks in the masonry of slavery, the first serious indication that men of power and influence were opposed to the practice. Years later, a claim was even made that, a few months after the defeat of Mabane's bill, some enslaved blacks had received a sympathetic hearing at Montreal from a visiting Prince William Henry (the future King William IV) when they complained to him of their lot.[31]

1798: THE YEAR OF "ESCAPES"

From the political arena, we turn our attention to the slaves themselves. As with most slave-sale advertisements published in Quebec, the last one, of 22 January 1798, named neither the slave nor the seller.[32] "For Sale," it said, "An excellent Negro Wench aged about 30 years, can do all kind of work belonging to a house particularly washing and ironing. She has no fault, and is very honest, sober and industrious. Enquire at the Printing Office."[33] Who was this perfect being – excellent and faultless, yet condemned to slavery – whose owner, from modesty or other motives, chose to remain nameless? It would be idle to attempt an answer if the slave population had numbered in the thousands. The fact that there were never more than a couple of hundred black slaves in all of Quebec at any one time compels us to make the effort, with the prospect of coming away with, at the very least, a plausible hypothesis.

The advertisement tells us that she was black, experienced in housework, and about thirty years old. Because the ages assigned to slaves, especially the foreign born, were usually little more than a guess, she might have been anything from an older-looking twenty-year-old to a younger-looking woman in her forties. Since she was advertised in the *Montreal Gazette,* and the notice was dated at Montreal, it is likely that she lived in town or close by. Even allowing for hyperbole in the statement of her merits, she was probably a trusted servant. Had she been "difficult," word of that would have spread, keeping buyers at bay. Her owner might then have had little choice but to put her up for auction – never the preferred choice, because it fetched lower prices than a private sale and entailed extra costs, such as the auctioneer's fee and, if the auction were to take place in some other locality, might involve paying an agent to escort the slave to market, providing him with a notarized power of attorney authorizing him to sell the slave, transporting, lodging and feeding the slave, and so forth.

As it happens, there was a Montreal slave who fit the profile. Her name was Charlotte. She was African-born, said to be a native of Guinea. From the ages given at her death twenty-five years later – one record said that she was fifty-one, another sixty-one – she would have been between twenty-five and thirty-six years old, or "about 30," in 1798, and she had faithfully served the Cook family for some twenty years – by her account, since the age of twelve. In his will, made out on the Caribbean island of St Vincent in 1777, George Cook, quartermaster sergeant of the 2nd Battalion, 60th (Royal American) Regiment, left Charlotte to his wife, Margaret Rafter, a nurse; and in her will, made out at Antigua in 1779, Rafter left Charlotte to her daughter, Jane Cook, who returned to Canada with Charlotte and members of the regiment after the American War of Independence. Jane Cook had a bastard child by Lieutenant Gabriel Gordon of the 60th; the boy was christened in June 1787 at Quebec, where it is believed that Charlotte was also baptized the following 30 December.[34] It is not known exactly when Jane Cook and Charlotte moved to Montreal; by the mid 1790s, however, Cook had become the paramour there of the prosperous silversmith-turned-fur-trade merchant Dominique Rousseau, by whom she was to have five children between 1796 and 1811.[35]

In February 1798, Charlotte ran out on her mistress. In the absence of any recorded explanation of her motives, we are left to wonder what could have impelled a slave, who had stuck by the Cook family through more than twenty years, to jump ship in the depths of a Montreal winter.[36] It had to have been more than a whim. Fear for her own safety? If Cook had grown abusive and beat her, this might have given Charlotte reason to run for cover, but there is not the slightest hint that this was the case. Separation from a loved one? This is a possibility. The threat of her imminent sale? This seems like the probable cause. Because of the chain of circumstances, the temptation is irresistible to link Charlotte's flight to the advertisement for the sale of the "excellent Negro Wench," published in the *Montreal Gazette* of 22 January and repeated in the next issue of 29 January. Charlotte's flight occurred shortly after that last publication. No further slave sales were advertised in Lower Canada and, search as we might, we find no record of the sale, then or later, of any slave approaching the description given in the advertisement.

A decision by Cook to sell her longtime slave would have been a powerful inducement to Charlotte to run. The two women had shared the highs and lows of life through war and peace, the move to Canada from the Caribbean, and Cook's first pregnancies. Even if there were barriers between them that they could not cross, an attachment would have grown over time: they would have come to depend on each other to play their assigned roles. However unequal their positions, they were, in a way, family. If Cook had decided to sever the link and to sell Charlotte, making her very devotion a selling point, it is easy to see how this would have amounted to a cruel betrayal and desertion in Charlotte's eyes. If her mistress had, in effect, run out on her, why should she sit still and wait for a new master the devil she did not know – to come and collect her? The threat of being sold may have been that much more unbearable if it also meant separation from a lover.

If Cook pushed Charlotte away, John Trim may have done some pulling. Perhaps Charlotte had already been drawn to this enterprising man, whom she was to marry sometime within the next few years. Making her bid for freedom in the depths of winter, she had to have support. She needed shelter. Trim, freed from slavery himself only five years before, already owned a house outside of town; within a few months, he would acquire another in town. He had the means to hire legal help.[37]

When Charlotte was arrested and refused to return to Cook, the magistrates put her in jail. On a writ of habeas corpus she appeared before James Monk, chief justice of the Montreal Court of King's Bench, outside the regular term of the court. He let her go without ordering her to return to her mistress, as a servant bound by contract would have been obliged to do. Interestingly, Monk, trained as a lawyer in Nova Scotia in the 1760s, had travelled to London in 1770, where he was called to the English bar, and then returned to Nova Scotia in 1774. Perhaps he had sat in on the hearings there before Lord Mansfield in 1772 in the case of the slave James Somerset. Even if he was not present in court, he was on the scene, among men of the law, and would have shared in the excitement about this widely publicized case. Monk had been attorney-general of Quebec at the time of Mabane's effort in 1787 to push through his ordinance to abolish slavery. As a law officer of the crown, he doubtless had an eye on Mabane's bill; evidence may yet surface to indicate whether he helped or hindered that measure in any way.[38]

Charlotte's winning bid for freedom emboldened other Montreal slaves, or, as the slave-owners put it in deploring the spirit of insubordination that then arose, "the Negroes in the city and district of Montreal threatened a general revolt."[39] Later that fateful February, Judith, alias Jude, left her master, Loyalist merchant Elias Smith. Caught, jailed, and taken before Monk on 8 March, Judith was freed like Charlotte. Monk seized the occasion to warn masters that he would release all other errant slaves or servants who were held, contrary to an ancient British law, in the common jail rather than in a house of correction.[40] This had never posed a problem before.[41]

and, as Monk well knew, Montreal had no house of correction. In effect, without tackling the problem of slavery itself, his rulings left magistrates "no power to compel absconding Slaves to return to their owner's service, nor the owners any power to enforce obedience, or detain their Slaves, in their Service," those same owners complained.[42] On 1 March, a week before Judith was freed, Manuel Allen deserted the service of Thomas John Sullivan, keeper of Sullivan's Coffee House, who had bought him only the previous summer for £36. In his flight, Allen told an acquaintance "that other Blacks were free and that he wanted to be free also." Like Charlotte and Judith, Allen remained in Montreal; but unlike in their cases, no move was made to arrest him.[43]

Perhaps it was the writing on the wall that had led Loyalist Dr Charles Blake, on 26 February, to file on record with a notary the papers establishing his title to three slaves whom he had bought at Montreal thirteen years earlier.[44] Loyalist farmer James Frazer, who also owned three slaves, expressed the slave-holders' general alarm on 13 March when he pleaded with the acting governor, Robert Prescott, to step in because "the Honorable Court at Montreal, are about Setting all Negroes Free from their Owners."[45] Frazer's fretfulness may have given his own slaves ideas: five months later, they would walk out on him. In the meantime, another slave desertion took place on 8 May. Like Manuel Allen, Augustin claimed that he was no slave "by the laws of this land" when he left the service of merchant Andrew Winklefoss, future seigneur of St-Charles on the Richelieu River. Like Allen, he did not leave Montreal – he went to work for a carpenter in the Récollets Suburb – and no move was made to arrest him. It becomes impossible to speak of these cases as slave "escapes," or of the slaves themselves as "fugitives": they did not head for the hills, but simply walked out on their owners and remained on the spot.

In Allen's case, in the face of his desertion and his insistence that he was no slave, Thomas Sullivan refused to pay the £18 still owing on his purchase. As a result, Allen's previous owners, Jervis George Turner, a soldier in the 2nd Battalion, Royal Canadian Volunteers, and his wife, Mary Blaney, sued Sullivan. But the court ruled against them in February 1799, holding that they had had "no title or right to transfer and sell the property claimed in Manuel, a Negro-man." Their title was indeed nebulous – they claimed to have acquired Allen from Turner's late father, John Turner Sr, who had allegedly bought him from someone called Allen, but there were no deeds to support this. The court ordered them to return to Sullivan the £18 that he had already paid, plus costs, and since they had failed to establish their title to Allen, Allen went free.[46]

A similar dispute over Augustin was not settled until 1802. Montreal fur trader Nicolas Marchesseau claimed to have bought Augustin in 1783 at Cahokia, in the Illinois country of Upper Louisiana, from a Jean Roy *dit* Lapensée. Augustin, then called Auguste, had been about thirteen; he would therefore have been almost thirty years old on 27 January 1798 when Marchesseau's wife, Marie Josephte Gatien, sold him as a "garçon nègre esclave" to Winklefoss, stipulating that Augustin was to go free after seven years. Augustin was not disposed to wait: he left Winklefoss's service on 8 May. Uncertain as to the Marchesseaus' title – they had no document proving their ownership of Augustin – Winklefoss, rather than seek to have his slave arrested, sent a notary to him to protest his desertion and to urge him to return. Augustin refused, claiming that the Marchesseaus had had no right to dispose of him, whereupon Winklefoss sued the Marchesseaus, alleging that Augustin was no slave and demanding the return of the 1,500 livres (£62 10s) that he had paid them. The Court of King's Bench ruled on the case in 1802. Unfortunately, the records of the court for February to October 1802 are missing. From the rulings in other slave cases at this time, however, it is safe to say that Augustin remained a free man and that the lack of a clear title left the Marchesseaus unable to support their claim that Augustin had ever been theirs to sell.[47]

James Frazer had no doubts about his ownership of his slaves, Robin (alias Robert, Bob) and Lydia. When they left his service on 12 August 1798, taking with them the four-year-old Jane, who was probably Lydia's daughter, he offered a $9 reward for their capture and return. This was the last notice published in Lower Canada concerning fugitive slaves.[48] The mere fact that newspapers stopped carrying notices of slave sales and escapes does not constitute conclusive proof that slavery had expired.[49] It does, however, signal the collapse of the local market for slaves, and of the slave-owners' confidence in their right to claim slaves as property and to reclaim those who deserted them. Three more sales were to take place, and at least two more desertions, under circumstances that tend to confirm this.

MASTERS ON A LOSING STREAK

The cases of Charlotte, Judith, and Manuel Allen are relatively well known, and Augustin's much less so, but these were far from the only body blows that slavery suffered in the law courts of Quebec in the 1790s and early 1800s. There were various other judgments to discomfit the slave-owners, and few, if any, to reassure them. The one possible exception was the legal tussle between Mary Martin, known by one of her married names as Mary Jacobs,[50] a dry-goods wholesaler, and merchant tailor Donald Fisher and his wife, Elizabeth, over the sale of two "Negro wenches." The outcome and implications of this case, which predated the slave desertions of 1798 by several years, are far from clear.

On 4 December 1785, Mary Jacobs had paid the Fishers £50 for the sisters Sylvie Jane and Ruth Jane, one of whom was said to be twenty-two years old, the other seven. The deed of sale stated that Donald Fisher had "put the said Mary Jacobs in Due Possession by delivering to her the said Negro Wenches at the sealing and Delivery hereof," but this was a fiction, as subsequent events were to show.[51] On 30 June 1787, Jacobs lent the Fishers £600 in cash and goods to enable them to carry on their business and furnish their tailor's shop, the sum to be repaid within one year. As security, they mortgaged to Jacobs all their shop and household goods, as well as sizeable lots of land which they had recently acquired near present-day Cornwall,

Ontario. On the same day, the Fishers acknowledged before a notary that they were indeed the Donald and Elizabeth Fisher who had executed the deed of sale for Ruth Jane and Sylvie Jane to Jacobs eighteen months earlier.[52] It is difficult to fathom these transactions and the conduct of the parties involved. First, Donald and Elizabeth Fisher sign a false statement that they have delivered two slaves to Mary Jacobs, when they have not. Mary Jacobs, an experienced businesswoman, pays them £50 yet has nothing to show for it. Eighteen months later, still out £50, without her two slaves but with good reason to mistrust the Fishers, as we would think, she lends them £600.

In October 1787, hearing that the Fishers were about to leave the province, Jacobs obtained a writ of attachment against their goods and chattels. The Fishers, along with schoolmaster Finlay Fisher (possibly related to Donald Fisher), signed the inventory of goods under seizure, pledging that they would answer for every item should the court eventually rule against them. Shortly afterward, Mary Jacobs went bankrupt. As agent for the trustees of her bankrupt estate, merchant Rosseter Hoyle demanded in February 1788 that Donald and Elizabeth Fisher hand over the two slaves whom they had sold to Jacobs in 1785, a sale which they had confirmed as recently as the previous 30 June. In the absence of her husband, Elizabeth Fisher replied that "they would not deliver anything to the Trustees of the Estate of the said Mary Jacobs before the Court should have determined in the Month of June next what in Justice they ought and will be obliged to pay or deliver – and as to the two Negro wenches[,] that only one of them was their property[,] Namely the one named Ruth Jane, that the other was the Property of her Brother in the States."[53] In view of Mary Jacobs' writ of attachment, we can understand the Fishers' reluctance to cede any of their assets until the court had settled that case. But the slaves were not among the goods covered by the writ and should not even have been in the Fishers' possession, having already been sold to Jacobs. The claim by Elizabeth Fisher that one of the slaves had not been theirs to sell seems tantamount to an admission of fraud.

Hoyle went to court on 5 March, demanding that the Fishers hand over the two slaves or pay £100 plus interest. The Fishers failed to show up on the two occasions when called on to do so. On 17 March, judgment was given against them by default to deliver the two slaves or refund the £50 that Mary Jacobs had paid for them. This was one of the judgments that Jacques Viger unearthed for his documentary record of slavery and that, as we saw in the last chapter, Judge William Badgley cited in his testimony in a Missouri slave case in 1859. Still, the Fishers disregarded the court ruling, ceding neither the slaves nor the £50. By default again, judgment was given against them in September in Mary Jacobs' suit to recover her £600. In the meantime, Donald Fisher absconded to New York State.[54]

Back in business in February 1792, Jacobs discovered that one of the slaves, now called Jenny, whom she had bought from the Fishers, was living at the home of schoolmaster Finlay Fisher. She secured a warrant for Jenny's arrest from magistrate Thomas McCord, one of the committee of Montreal merchants and magistrates who had signed the report to the Legislative Council in 1787 acknowledging the inhumanity of slavery. Jacobs sent the law after Jenny, but Fisher fought off the constable, brandishing a shovel and threatening to kill him if he tried to remove Jenny from the house. About two months later, the same constable spotted Jenny in the street. He seized her and took her before McCord at the courthouse. McCord sent the constable to fetch Mary Jacobs' husband. In the constable's absence, Fisher slipped into the courthouse and spirited Jenny away. That May, an exasperated Mary Jacobs sued Finlay Fisher for £100 in the Court of Common Pleas, claiming that, "in defiance of the Law and in contempt of public Justice [he] has ... aided, abetted and protected the said slave, and illegally & unwarrantably did openly take her to his house and there secured the said slave contemptuously threatening the officer if he persisted in doing his duty."[55]

The case was tried one year later. The constable who had been sent packing by schoolmaster Fisher testified that the latter had told him that Jenny did not belong to Mary Jacobs, but that "she belonged to him[,] Fisher." The same witness stated that he had "often Seen the Said Negro Wench Since he apprehended her, Sometimes at the Said Fisher's house in Town, and Sometimes at Mrs Donald Fisher in the St Lawrence Suburbs." On 31 May 1793, the court delivered its verdict, rejecting Mary Jacobs' £100 suit, with costs assessed against her, on the ground that her "declaration is insufficient to support the present action."[56] Five years earlier, the same court had ruled that Jacobs was entitled to the two slaves whom she had bought or to a refund of the £50 that she had paid for them. Now, it turned her away empty-handed. It is all thoroughly perplexing – the persistent snubbing of the law by Donald and Elizabeth Fisher, the imprudence shown by Mary Jacobs in her dealings with them, the illegal obstruction and criminal threats made by Finlay Fisher to an officer of the law in the exercise of his duty, and the final judicial rebuff to Jacobs' claim to ownership of a slave that she had paid for. If nothing else, the case gives us a strong, early indication that the courts of the 1790s offered no rubber stamp when it came to claiming ownership of slaves.

It does seem that this case concerned competing claims to the ownership of a slave, but Fisher's extraordinary conduct suggests another possible construction. His hotheaded exertions to hold on to Jenny – his threat to kill a constable, his taking her from the courthouse where she was detained under a legal warrant – go well beyond the efforts that any other Montreal slave-owners are known to have made to retain or regain their slave property, so much so that we are tempted to see in his behaviour a sign that he was not clinging to Jenny as a piece of property, but to prevent her being re-enslaved. His removing her from the courthouse after her arrest does have about it something of the air of a "slave rescue" of the sort that abolitionists elsewhere would stage in the next century to save fugitive American slaves from re-enslavement.[57] In this regard, it is interesting that, in her complaint against Fisher, Mary Jacobs charged that he had "aided, abetted and protected the said slave." This may have been no more than a formulaic way of accusing Fisher of complicity in an offence – or perhaps Fisher had truly "protected" Jenny. It may also be significant that in the course of the trial, when Jacobs' lawyer demanded that Fisher produce Jenny in court, Fisher's lawyer, James Walker, countered "that he is not in possession of the Wench ... nor does he Conceive Such request to be regular in as much as he knows of no other mode of bringing parties or persons before a Court of Justice, than by the Kings Writ duly executed."[58] Was this to say that to Fisher's lawyer, at least, Jenny was a "person" to be summoned like any other, not a piece of evidence that a witness could be ordered to produce? In the end, it seems that Jenny did not appear in court, by summons or otherwise, before the judges quashed Jacobs' suit. What we know of schoolmaster Fisher's conduct here is puzzling. If he went to the lengths that he did to defend his property in Jenny as a slave, he was a dangerous lawbreaker. If he sought to protect Jenny from slavery, he would rank as the only white Montrealer of his day known to have flouted the law so brazenly in the anti-slavery cause.

There is one more piece to this puzzle. On 23 February 1799, Jenny Jacobs, "Negro woman (the property of Mrs. Jacobs of the Quebec Suburbs, Montreal)," died at the reputed age of thirty-six.[59] Her stated age jibes with that of the twenty-two-year-old slave sold to Mary Jacobs by Donald and Elizabeth Fisher in 1785. It would seem that between 1793 and 1799 Mary Jacobs did get her hands on Jenny – unless this was another Jenny. This is not impossible. Merchant Samuel Jacobs, the brother of Mary Jacobs' second husband, Phillip Jacobs, had bought a very young "Negro Girl" called Jenny from Hyam Myers of New York City in 1761.[60] Jenny appears to have remained with the Jacobs family after Samuel Jacobs' death in 1786; she was perhaps the unnamed black slave woman who then passed from his daughter Marianne to his widow, Marie Josette Audet *dit* Lapointe, and from her in 1790 to her other daughter, Marie Geneviève Jacobs, wife of Joseph Vignau of Boucherville.[61] If the age of thirty-six given for Jenny Jacobs at her death was only approximate, then she might have been not the Jenny withheld from Mary Jacobs by Finlay Fisher, but the Jenny who had been a slave of the Jacobs family from her infancy.

A more straightforward case concerned Diah, a slave of Nathaniel Platt of Plattsburgh, New York. In September 1794, Diah had fled to Montreal, then on to Rivière du Chêne (St-Eustache), where he found refuge. Platt sent a man after him. To facilitate proceedings, the slave-hunter, farmer Eden Johnston (or Johnson) bought Diah from Platt – he paid £80 New York currency, the equivalent of about £50 Quebec currency – which allowed him to claim Diah as his own, with a bill of sale to prove his ownership. Johnston secured a warrant from magistrate McCord and had Diah arrested and taken to jail in Montreal. Diah appeared before the Court of Quarter Sessions on 14 October, when a bench of four magistrates, including McCord, ruled that "slavery was not known by the Laws of England and therefore discharged the negro man."[62] Such was the magistrates' opinion as reported in a newspaper, the only account we have of the outcome. No high judicial authority had yet expressed itself so trenchantly on the subject. Although this low-court ruling established no binding precedent, it was, if accurately reported, a rather stunning verdict, all the more so since McCord's three fellow magistrates – Dr Charles Blake, James Finlay, and Alexander Henry the elder – were current or former slave-owners.[63] It might be argued that the decision was wrongheaded, insofar as property and civil rights were supposed to be governed by French civil law, not by the law of England, but apparently Eden Johnston did not contest the magistrates' ruling.

The case of Catherine Coll was not so quickly settled. On the evening of 5 November 1791, only three weeks after she had married Jacob Smith, tailor Peter McFarlane barged into their home, dragged her away and, soon afterward, sent her "up the country."[64] He had every right to do so, he claimed, because she was his, bought and paid for: he filed in court a deed of 29 May 1790 by which he had bought the mulatto "Kate" or "Katy" from baker Andrew Mabon of St-Jean[65] for £30, and a receipt showing that Mabon had bought her in 1786 from Joseph Barney of Richmond, New Hampshire. McFarlane also claimed that Smith's and Coll's marriage was bogus, since the Presbyterian pastor John Young had united them at his home without benefit of either a marriage licence or publication of banns, as required by law. Smith sued for £2,000, rubbing in the indecency of McFarlane's conduct by suggesting that, for all that he knew, McFarlane had stolen his wife "with an intent to ravish debauch and carnally know her." McFarlane's lawyer hastened to have that imputation stricken from the record as itself "altogether scandalous and indecent." In November 1792, the Court of Common Pleas ruled in Smith's favour, and a jury awarded him £100 in damages. Procedural irregularities led the Appeal Court to overturn that award in July 1793 and to send the case back to the Court of King's Bench (the Common Pleas being about to be dissolved in a judicial reorganization). By the time a new trial began in 1795, two of the judges had felt obliged to declare an interest. James Monk, appointed to the court as chief justice of the Montreal District in August 1794, acknowledged that he had acted as counsel to slave-owner McFarlane before the Court of Appeal, while James Walker, named to the court in December 1794, had been Jacob Smith's lawyer from the outset (and Finlay Fisher's in 1793). In 1796, Smith, who had by then moved to Quebec with his restored wife, finally won damages of £20 7s 3d, which he was still trying to collect in 1801. Here was another instance where strong evidence of slave ownership was dismissed by the courts.[66]

THE LAST THREE SALES

Suffering setback after setback, the slave-owners knew that the wind was blowing against them. It was in this context that the last three slave sales took place in Lower Canada.

Antoine Smart, *nègre esclave*, about twenty-eight years old, went from being the slave of one man to slave of a corporation, so to speak, on 4 May 1798 when merchant Charles Lusignan sold him to the North West Company for 1,500 livres. John Gregory, a partner in the Montreal-based fur-trade concern, acted for the company in this transaction.[67] We do not know where Antoine Smart ended up, but given slavery's precarious status in Lower Canada by then, and Upper Canada's ban on the introduction of new slaves, he may have been destined for service beyond those territories – out West perhaps, where the company was seeking a practical all-British overland route to the Pacific, or aboard the ships that the company dispatched to China that year in search of new markets to offset the risks and losses incurred in shipping furs to England, five years into a long war with France.

Of Sylvie we know slightly more. Daniel Jones, a Connecticut-born Loyalist from Fort Edward, New York, and one of the founders of present-day Brockville, Ontario, bought her at some unspecified date and place in New York state, probably around Albany, where he purchased other slaves at other times. She was about fifteen years old when he sold her on 28 July 1794 to merchant Nicolas Berthelet of Longue-Pointe, at the eastern tip of Montreal Island, for £32. She had survived smallpox, which may have reassured Berthelet as to the state of her health, but unlike Jane Cook's Charlotte, Sylvie was trouble, as we can tell from the way Berthelet got rid of her and from the way that her cash value plummeted. One year after he bought her, Berthelet shipped Sylvie to Quebec auctioneer John William Woolsey with instructions to dispose of her by private sale or public auction, whichever seemed best. Woolsey sold her at auction for £25 on 7 September 1795 to his brother-in-law, Pierre Guerout, a Quebec merchant, seigneur of St-Denis on the Richelieu River and a member of the Assembly for Richelieu County. Only two months later, Guerout resold her, through Woolsey again, to Quebec shipbuilder Patrick Beatson for £22 10s. Sylvie's value had dropped by a third in little more than a year. Beatson kept her for almost four years before selling her, on 17 June 1799, for £35 – 56 per cent more than he had paid. He managed this by selling her, not to a local purchaser – no one was buying – but to a ship captain, who could carry her off to some foreign market where, being only twenty "or thereabouts," with years of service left in her, Sylvie would no doubt fetch a good price.[68]

Three months later, Thomas was also exported – to the United States. He is believed to have been the boy Thomas, born on 2 January 1790 and identified then as a *Neigre inconnu* (unknown negro, i.e., born of parents unknown, a way of identifying a foundling or bastard child). In fact, he was the son of slaves of Colonel John Campbell, superintendent of the Indian Department, and his wife, Marie Anne de Lacorne St-Luc. Sometime before he died in June 1795, Campbell had made a gift of Thomas to Marguerite Boucher de Boucherville, widow of his late father-in-law, Luc de Lacorne St-Luc. On 14 September 1799, she sold the nine-year-old boy for £25 to trader Joseph Campeau of Detroit. The deed of sale stipulated that Campeau was to treat Thomas well and raise him as a Roman Catholic, provisions commonly found in deeds for the apprenticeship of minors. That was followed by a promise of freedom that was next to meaningless: Thomas was to remain Campeau's slave until he reached the age of twenty-one, at which point he was to go free – unless Campeau wished to keep him enslaved indefinitely, "if such a thing were possible."[69]

Anything was possible. After all, the Northwest Ordinance, adopted by the Continental Congress of the United States in 1787, had outlawed slavery in the unorganized American territory north of the Ohio River and east of the Mississippi (the territory that is now Illinois, Indiana, Michigan, eastern Minnesota, Ohio and Wisconsin). Detroit lay within that territory, which did not stop Campeau from buying

Thomas. It is true that Britain had not surrendered that post to the United States until July 1796, but from that time the ordinance applied. Under the terms of Jay's Treaty, by which Britain ceded Detroit and other posts in American territory, Campeau could claim the right to hold on to the slaves that he owned, but he had no right to import more. Yet, as an oldtime Detroiter later noted of the ordinance: "Notwithstanding this wise provision our ancestors paid but little attention to it, for whenever a spruce negro was brought by the Indians he was sure to find a purchaser at a reasonable price. Most every prominent man in those days had a slave or two, especially merchants trading with the Indians."[70] Indians or no, the sale of Thomas to Campeau in 1799 suggests that the law was easily skirted. It is also evidence, as in Sylvie's case, and probably Antoine Smart's as well, that a few Lower Canadian slave-owners hastened to dump their slaves off-stage as the curtain fell.

In this regard, a slightly earlier Montreal slave transaction involving a resident of Detroit is also interesting. On 31 August 1797, Detroit trader Jacques Lasselle paid 100 dollars to his uncle, Montreal merchant and real estate mogul Pierre Berthelet, himself a former Detroiter and older brother of the Nicolas Berthelet who had purchased the troublesome Sylvie, to buy the freedom of Sarah, a woman in her late forties who had been in Berthelet's possession for two years. According to the deed of emancipation, Sarah was to be "free and enjoy all the rights of a free person and to do with herself as she pleases." But there was a catch: to reimburse Lasselle, Sarah "willingly" bound herself to him as a servant for eight years. For every day accounted wasted or lost by her fault, a week was to be tacked on to her eight years of servitude. Because of a host of factors – among them, the kinship of buyer and seller, the illegality of slavery in Detroit, its uncertain future in Lower Canada, Sarah's relatively advanced age, the power of her new master to extend her term of service indefinitely on the pretext of days lost, and the probability that she would die in harness,– this smacks of slave dumping dressed up as a manumission, debt bondage disguised as freedom. Berthelet, for a good price, got rid of an aged slave and an asset who, in Montreal, would soon lose her cash value; and Lasselle could slip a seasoned slave in all but name into Detroit without fear of contestation. Sarah, too, was perhaps not displeased at the prospect of returning to the Michigan Territory, where she had lived before Berthelet bought her. Perhaps Lasselle could not sell Sarah since, technically, she was free, but her freedom was rather limited: she was free to grow old and die in his service.[71]

ROBIN AND FRANK: TWO LAST FLIGHTS

The slave Frank, who may have been at one time Sarah's mate, deserted the service of his master on 1 June 1799. Three months earlier, Robin had done the same. These were the last two slave desertions that were the subjects of legal contests in Lower Canada.

Back in Frazer's hands after his flight of August 1798, Robin had absconded again on 17 March 1799, only one month after the court ruling that had confirmed Manuel

Place d'Armes, by the old church of Notre-Dame. New Jersey Loyalist James Frazer found his fugitive slave Robin working at a tavern here in January 1800. The court ruling of 18 February setting Robin free proved a death blow to slavery.

Allen's freedom. But it was not before January 1800, on discovering that Robin was working at Richard Dillon's tavern in Place d'Armes, that the leery Frazer summoned the law to his aid and had Robin arrested on 31 January. Robin is the last slave known to have been jailed on a charge of desertion. As Charlotte and Judith had done in 1798, he and his lawyer, Alexander Perry, filed for a writ of habeas corpus. The case came up in the February term of the Court of King's Bench before Chief Justice Monk and Justices Pierre-Louis Panet and Isaac Ogden.[72]

Frazer, represented by lawyer James Kerr, submitted all the evidence that he could muster to prove that Robin was his. He had bought Robin, then a boy, on 10 July 1773. At the time, Frazer lived in Essex County, New Jersey. At the outbreak of the Revolution, harassed by rebels for his loyalty to the Crown, and dispossessed, as he claimed, of all but his child slaves Robin and Lydia, he had fled to the safety of the British-held city of New York. He had served in the army during the war, and at its conclusion had secured a pass from a New York magistrate to leave for Nova Scotia with his two slaves. The pass, dated 19 September 1783, was filed in court. Judge Ogden, himself a New Jersey Loyalist who had left New York on the British removal from the city in 1783, authenticated it: he knew the magistrate who had signed it and recognized his signature. In September 1784, Frazer had moved from Nova Scotia to Prince Edward Island. A man who had sailed from Shelburne with Frazer on that trip swore that Robin had accompanied Frazer and had acknowledged himself to be Frazer's slave. Finally, in 1793, Frazer had left Prince Edward Island for Montreal, where he had bought land at St Mary's Current (known in French as Au Pied-du-Courant), on the eastern outskirts of the city, and settled down to farm.[73]

Frazer had chosen to move to Canada in the year when, from January to April, the Legislative Assembly of Lower Canada debated and rejected gradual abolition, and in which Upper Canada's legislature, in July, enacted such a law. Perhaps word of these doings had influenced his choice of the lower colony as a destination. He had certainly been concerned about the status of his slave property. He could have sold his two slaves before moving to Lower Canada, he said, but he had been encouraged to bring them with him by the British law of 1790 that had been designed to incite American subjects to move to British territory. This "Act for encouraging new settlers in His Majesty's colonies and plantations in America," which Canadian slave-owners considered a big gun in their arsenal, provided that

> from and after the first day of *August* one thousand seven hundred and ninety, if any person or persons, being a subject or subjects of the territories or countries belonging to the united states of *America,* shall come from thence, together with his or their family or families, to any of the *Bahama,* or *Bermuda* or *Somers* islands, or to any part of the province of *Quebec,* or of *Nova Scotia,* or any of the territories belonging to his Majesty in *North America,* for the purpose of residing and settling there, it shall be lawful for any such person or persons, having first obtained a licence for that purpose from the governor, or, in his absence, the lieutenant governor of the said islands, colonies, or provinces respectively, to import into the same, in *British* ships owned by his Majesty's subjects, and navigated according to law, any negroes, household furniture, utensils of husbandry, or cloathing, free of duty: provided always, That such household furniture, utensils of husbandry, and cloathing, shall not in the whole exceed the value of fifty pounds for every white person that shall belong to such family; and the value of forty shillings [£2] for every negro brought by such white person.[74]

The law probably accounts for Frazer's claim, in warning all and sundry against abetting his runaway slaves in 1798, that they would be prosecuted "in the highest manner, [as] the said James Frazer hath the Protection of Government for said negroes."[75] In fact, under this law, Frazer did not qualify for a right to duty-free importation of slaves or any other property, since he had not emigrated from American territory after 1 August 1790 but had been living on British soil since 1783. What he undoubtedly meant was that the Act of 1790 had reassured him that slavery was officially sanctioned and that he did not risk losing his slave property on moving to Lower Canada. Indeed, historian Robin Winks went so far as to term this law "the most important legal protection given to slavery by Britain for the northern provinces."[76] Yet, as we shall see, this imperial "protection" had been brushed aside in Upper Canada in 1793.

Besides this claim of government protection, Frazer may well have pleaded with the court, as he had in his petition to Governor Prescott in 1798, that he had been "at

Considerable Expence & Trouble to Bring up and Maintain said Negroes, in expectation of their Assistance in his Old age, and thinks it a great Hardship to be Deprived of them as he has ever Treated them With Tenderness."[77] Unswayed by Frazer's evidence and pleadings, the judges rendered the following decision on 18 February 1800, a year to the day after the decision in the case of Manuel Allen: "It is considered that the said Robin alias Robert be discharged from his confinement under the said warrant." The written record provided no reasons.[78]

As we have seen, Justice James Reid later understood that the court had freed Robin on the grounds that "no slavery existed in Canada," while lawyer Janvier Domptail Lacroix vaguely recollected that the ruling was "based on some act of the British Parliament." The frustrated slave-owners of Montreal cited the specific Act in question in a petition that they presented to the Legislative Assembly in April 1800:

> [I]t was stated in the course of the judgment of the Court that the Act of 37th of His present Majesty [1797], C. 119 had repealed all the laws respecting slavery: but this statute in the humble opinion of the petitioners only goes the length to declare, that slaves shall not in future be assessed for the payment of debts due by their owners; it does not go so far as to divest such owners of their property in their slaves, nor can it be considered as tending to emancipate the slaves in His Majesty's plantations. That so far from this, subsequent Acts still further recognize slavery to exist, and encourage the importation of Negroes from the coast of *Africa*.[79]

Indeed, a British law of 1732, applying to the colonies, had made a master's "Negroes," like his house and lands, liable to seizure by his creditors, but in 1797 that law had been amended to exclude slaves from the categories of seizable real property.[80] For the court to interpret this change as tantamount to the abolition of slavery was such a stretch – when the British Parliament of the day was prepared to go no farther than a lukewarm commitment to the idea of gradually ending the international trade in slaves[81] – that we are tempted to see in it an early instance of the sort of erratic judicial intervention that Harriet Beecher Stowe praised some fifty years later in denouncing American slavery:

> So abhorrent is the slave code to every feeling of humanity, that just as soon as there is any hesitancy in the community about perpetuating the institution of slavery, judges begin to listen to the voice of their more honorable nature, and by favorable interpretations to soften its necessary severities.
>
> Such decisions do not command themselves to the professional admiration of legal gentlemen. But in the workings of the slave system, when the irresponsible power which it guarantees comes to be used by men of the most brutal nature, cases sometimes arise for trial where the consistent exposition of the law involves results so loathsome and frightful, that the judge prefers to be illogical, rather than inhuman. Like a spring outgushing in the desert, some

noble man, now and then, from the fulness of his own better nature, throws out a legal decision, generously inconsistent with every principle and precedent of slave jurisprudence, and we bless God for it.[82]

In Robin's case, as in the earlier cases of Charlotte and Judith, which Monk had decided on his own, we may like to think of the chief justice acting from anti-slavery conviction or out of "the fulness of his own better nature," but it is highly doubtful that he was doing any such thing. Monk was a thoroughgoing man of the law, never known to express anti-slavery sentiments. In 1793, before his appointment to the bench, it will be remembered, he had acted as counsel to tailor Peter McFarlane as the latter sought to establish his claim to ownership of Catherine Coll. As attorney-general, asked to advise Governor Sir Frederick Haldimand on the course to pursue in the case of a country slave who had escaped with the aid of some soldiers in 1778, he never hinted at sympathy for the slave, or at the illegitimacy of slavery.[83] Concerning Monk's attitude to slavery, what is more likely is that, having been appointed to the bench at a time when there was "hesitancy in the community" about perpetuating the practice, and finding himself called upon to rule in cases where slavery was challenged, he concluded as a conscientious professional, that there was no satisfactory law on the books. Adam Mabane had done the same, and so would Justices Reid, Gale, and Badgley when they went looking for the positive law that established slavery. But if the researches of our three mid-nineteenth century judges were historical and academic, Monk was in the thick of it. Slavery existed in fact, if not in law. Like Lord Mansfield in England in the case of Somerset in 1772, he had slaves before him, and masters who had paid good sums for their slaves and who would not take kindly to seeing their investments wiped out by a meddling judge decreeing that what had been "a matter of course" was suddenly illegal. Mansfield, as is well known, tried his best to avoid having to lay down the law on slavery, doing so only after the parties spurned his suggestions that they try to come to a settlement and insisted on the case being carried to judgment. Perhaps Monk did something similar, skirting the issue in the cases of Charlotte and Judith by freeing them on a technicality, before coming to grips with the problem in Robin's case, reading abolition into the British statute of 1797 and crafting a judgment that everyone but a small coterie of frustrated slave-owners was prepared to live with.

On 1 June 1799, well before Robin had been arrested and his case settled, Frank (alias Franc, François) left the service of John Dease of Côte-des-Neiges, a captain in the Indian Department, formerly the deputy Indian Agent at Michilimackinac, and a cousin of Sir John Johnson. In Montreal a little more than two years earlier, Dease had bought Frank, said to be about forty-five, for £50 from Joseph Ainsse, a former Michilimackinac trader and interpreter in the Indian Department. Ainsse had no documented title to his slave, but he promised nevertheless to deliver a proper deed of sale to Dease. In this respect and in several others, Frank's case was more like those of Manuel Allen and Augustin than like that of Robin. Dease did not seek to have Frank arrested; he repeatedly entreated him to return, but Frank "refused, declaring that he

In his capacity as the first chief justice of the Montreal Court of King's Bench, Massachusetts-born James Monk (1745–1826) played a decisive, if puzzling, role in ending slavery.

was not a Slave" and that Ainsse had had no right to sell him. Finally, Dease sued Ainsse in October 1799 for the reimbursement of his £50, claiming that Frank was not a slave. Ainsse countered that Frank was indeed a slave whom he had bought at Michilimackinac in 1788 or 1789 from trader Charles Morrison, who had acted as agent of Alexis Rivard *dit* Maisonville of Detroit.[84] Maisonville, for his part, made a deposition in Detroit on 23 April 1801 that he had acquired Frank from a Colonel Cohran (Cochran?) in the Illinois country, and Sally (Sarah) from a Mrs. Abbott, the wife of a British lieutenant of artillery at Detroit. There had been a written deed, now lost, recording his purchase of Frank, he said, but none concerning Sally. He believed that Cohran had acquired Frank at Philadelphia. Maisonville said that, on his instructions and in his absence, his wife had disposed of his slaves in 1788 or 1789. She had sent Frank and his wife, Sally, in the care of merchant William Macomb to Charles Morrison at Michilimackinac to be sold. Maisonville believed that he had received £200 New York currency from Ainsse for the two of them. In a letter dated 16 October 1789 filed in court, Morrison advised Macomb that "I have sold the two Negros to Mr Joseph Ainsse," Ainsse paying with two promissory notes, one for £100 New York currency, the other for 1,500 livres.

This was all well and good, but hardly conclusive. Other than Morrison's letter concerning two unnamed slaves, there was no written record of any of these sales. Even assuming that Ainsse and Maisonville were being scrupulously honest, their recollections were far from perfect as to dates and sale prices. Maisonville acknowledged that he had formerly traded in slaves – could he be trusted, at the age of seventy-three, to recall faithfully the details of his every transaction? Ainsse, for his part, could not recall whether it was in 1788 or 1789 that he had bought Frank. There seems little doubt that he had bought Sally from Maisonville; at least, when he sold her to Pierre Berthelet in 1795, he declared that he had acquired her in 1788 through Charles Morrison, who had acted as Maisonville's agent. If that were true, Morrison's letter of October 1789 concerning "the two Negros" sold to Ainsse may have referred to slaves other than Frank and Sally, as he would scarcely have waited a year to convey the news of their sale. Besides, deeds survive showing that Ainsse had bought a slave named Frank at Michilimackinac on 8 July 1785, not from Maisonville or his agent, but from merchant George Lyons.[85] This was not mentioned in the court proceedings; we cite the transaction only to show how questionable was the evidence that Ainsse advanced to establish his title. Even the notarized deed of sale by Ainsse to Dease, dated 10 March 1797 – two months after the actual sale – was contentious. Dease alleged that Ainsse had never given him a deed of sale, and that the notary who had drawn up the deed in question had had no authority to do so. Ainsse called the notary to testify that Dease himself had asked him to prepare it. The deed bore Ainsse's signature, but not Dease's.[86]

The ruling on this suit is unknown. Judgment was given on 20 February 1802 but, as we saw in the case of Augustin, the court's records for this year are missing. Coming three years after the decision in the case concerning Manuel Allen, and two years after the ruling on Robin, we can assume that the settlement of the suit concerning Frank confirmed his free status. Still, it would be interesting to know precisely how the court ruled in 1802, how it handled the question of title and of slavery itself, and whether, as in Manuel Allen's case, the judges ordered that the sellers refund the sums they had been paid for the slaves.

The great problem in understanding the court rulings of the day and moving beyond suppositions is that there are no transcripts of the cases and no texts of reasoned judgments on the specific question of the lawfulness of slavery; in fact, there is no record setting out the anti-slavery arguments that were raised in the Quebec courts, beyond the views expressed in the 1780s when Adam Mabane's bill went down to defeat, and the retrospective opinions given by Montreal judges in the mid-nineteenth century on the illegality of slavery. For Charlotte and Judith, no court files have been found. Copies of documents exist for the civil suits concerning Manuel Allen, Augustin, and Frank, but no judgment in the latter two cases, and only a terse one in Allen's. In the case of Robin, from the documents filed in court and from other sources mentioned below, we have some idea of the arguments advanced to justify his slave status, but no idea how his lawyer answered them. Robin's petition for a writ of habeas corpus claimed that he was held in jail illegally. From Frazer's evidence and the outcome of the case, it is clear that the pleadings went beyond the question of illegal detention to the underlying issues of whether Robin was a slave, and by virtue of what law.[87] Yet it is difficult to believe that his lawyer, Alexander Perry, would have mounted a full-bore attack on the practice of slavery. Admitted to the bar at the age of nineteen on 1 June 1797, he was only twenty-one when he took Robin's case. His youth might suggest more idealism and less tolerance of slavery than old-guard practitioners may have shown. But a year earlier, as counsel for Jervis

George Turner and his wife in their suit against Thomas Sullivan, he had argued for their right to sell Manuel Allen. The least that we can say is that young Perry was no anti-slavery crusader.[88]

MASTERS CRY FOR HELP

The slaveholders of Montreal believed that the evidence advanced by Frazer in support of his claim to Robin was "the best which it was possible in any case to produce, and ... the Court in desiring more, have asked what it would be impossible almost ever to obtain, and in this manner have divested all the owners of slaves of any property in them."[89] They refused to accept the court's ruling as the last word on the subject and turned to the Legislative Assembly for help and a clarification of the rules under which slavery was to continue. If the Assembly deemed that gradual abolition was the answer then so be it, they suggested, in the first of two petitions that they submitted; in the meantime, they were entitled to see their property rights respected.

Their first petition, citing the cases of Charlotte and Judith, was presented to the House on 19 April 1799.[90] The second, submitted one year later, on 18 April 1800, cited the case of Frazer's slave, Robin, in stressing the plight of Loyalists, who,

> after exposing their lives in his [the king's] service, and sacrificing almost the whole property they were possessed of in the late calamitous war, came into this Province with their slaves under the sacred promise held out to them in the last mentioned statute [the 1790 "Act for encouraging new settlers"], and from an idea lately gone abroad, that slavery does not exist in this country, have found that their slaves on whom was all their dependance for support, have deserted them, and held them at defiance.[91]

Notary Joseph Papineau, one of the two members of the Assembly for the County of Montreal, who had himself bought a slave in 1792, took charge of presenting both memorials.[92] Both recited the legal underpinnings of slavery in the colony, from the edicts of intendants Raudot and Hocquart, through the articles of capitulation of 1760, to recent British legislation – in effect, all those elements which, as we have seen, were considered by some men of the law then and later as falling short of legitimating slavery. The second petition was drafted by Frazer's Scottish-born, English-trained lawyer, James Kerr,[93] a relative newcomer to Quebec, and because it is so similar to the first, it seems likely that Kerr, who was also a judge of the vice-admiralty court, drafted both. For much the same reason, Judith's master, New York Loyalist Elias Smith, the driving force behind the second petition, was also probably the instigator of the first, or at least one of its chief backers.

In 1800, Smith, the founder of Port Hope, Ontario, where he was soon to move,[94] had an interest in slavery that went well beyond Montreal and the loss of his slave Judith. As a partner with his New York-based son, David, in the American shipping firm

David Smith & Co., it seems that he was engaged, or considering engaging, in the African slave trade. How else are we to read his interest in a recent British law regulating slave ships? As he informed his son on 29 March, that law provided that "no Vessell shall bring from Africa more than one Slave to every Ton the Vessell Measures under the penalty of Confiscation of Vessell and Cargo so that any Vessell of 100 Tons cannot bring more than 100 Slaves [–] this act in Trade I am just informed of."[95] It is unlikely that David Smith & Co. was contemplating carrying shiploads of slaves to Canada, more probably to the United States or to the West Indies, where the company traded.

Two days before writing to his son about the British rules for slave ships, Elias Smith had hastily scribbled a note about the slave-owners' petition to forwarder and slave-owner John Grant at Lachine:

> Mr Kerr has done the Petition and got some Signers already[.] Mr Smith begs Mr Grant to come to Montreal to morrow Morning to get Mr Grants friends to sign the petition[.] no time is to be lost [–] must if Possible have the petition Completed this Week. Mr Papino Leaves this for Quebec to Day or Tomorrow and Mr [Étienne] Guy another Member of the House of Assembly on Monday or Tuesday[.] by this Opportunity E. Smith must try to forward the Petition to Quebec ... the earlier the Petition is laid before the House the better.[96]

To saddler Frederick Petry at Quebec, who was to co-ordinate efforts on the spot and who appears to have acted in the same capacity with regard to the petition of 1799, Smith sent a copy of the new petition, along with instructions to deliver it to Papineau, assuring Petry that he would cover all costs. Smith included a note to Papineau, advising him that Petry would follow his guidance.[97]

ACTION VERSUS INACTION

The petition of 1799 had failed to stir the 50-seat House to action, but this time members approved a motion by Papineau to refer both the old and new petitions to a committee of five, with instructions to report "with all possible diligence." Constituted on a Friday, the committee duly reported the following Monday, 21 April, that there were "reasonable grounds" to adopt a law regulating slavery. Accordingly, on 30 April, committee member James Cuthbert, seigneur of Berthier and member for the County of Warwick since 1796,[98] introduced his measure, "A bill to regulate the condition of Slaves, to limit the term of Slavery, and prevent the further introduction of Slaves in this Province." Second reading, scheduled for 2 May, was delayed until 5 May, when the House sat in committee on the bill. It resumed its work two days later, only to be brought to a standstill for want of a quorum. "What is done about the Slave Bill?" Smith queried Petry on 6 May, anxious for news. The committee convened on 17 May, once again to be stymied for want of a quorum. The session ended on 29 May.

"Nothing was done In the house of Representatives at Quebec Concerning the negro business for want of Sufficient number of Representatives to make a house," Smith informed an Upper Canadian business associate in July. "Suppose it Will be taken up again when the house Meets again."[99]

That summer, notary Papineau hinted at the slave-owners' dejection as he drew up an inventory of the joint property of Michel Eutache Gaspard Alain Chartier de Lotbinière, seigneur of Vaudreuil, a Legislative Councillor and former member of the Assembly, and his recently deceased wife. Papineau priced every item, but pointedly abstained from assigning a value to de Lotbinière's one remaining slave, Louis Joseph *dit* Pompé: "given the want of means in this province for safeguarding this kind of property, it is considered precarious and uncertain," he noted.[100] This about a male slave, about twenty years old, who would have fetched a prime price a few years earlier.

The House met again at the beginning of 1801, and the slave bill was reintroduced on 17 January on a motion by Cuthbert, seconded by Pierre-Louis Panet, the same Judge Panet who had sat on Robin's case in 1800, and now the member for the East Ward of Montreal. Three days later, the bill was set down for second reading on 23 January. On that day, it was referred to a committee of the whole House, which was supposed to sit on it a week later. But the committee did not take up the bill until 9 March when, as the laconic minutes tell us, "[t]he House resolved itself into the said Committee. Mr Speaker left the Chair. Mr Badgeley [Badgley] took the Chair of the Committee. Mr Speaker resumed the Chair." The committee, in short, made no report, and the House did not again take up the bill.[101]

Legislation had been in the wind for some time. As we have seen, the subject had been floated in the mid-1780s, well before the division of the old Province of Quebec, and before the British parliament had adopted a law encouraging Americans to move there with their slaves. Had Adam Mabane's ordinance been adopted, with its promise of freedom for all slaves within five years, slavery would have ended by 1792 before the elected Assemblies of the newly established colonies of Lower and Upper Canada had had a chance to meet. As it was, the Lower Canada Assembly was called on to deal with slavery in its first session, which opened in December 1792. Pierre-Louis Panet introduced the subject on 28 January 1793, obtaining leave to bring in "A bill tending to abolish slavery in the Province of Lower Canada." The deputy clerk of the Assembly, Quebec merchant William Lindsay, may have got wind the previous fall of what was coming: in September, he had consigned his slave, Sylvia, and her daughter, Hannah, to a ship captain with instructions to sell them in Jamaica.[102] The bill, tabled on 2 March, was clearly not a priority for most members. At least eighteen of them owned slaves at one time or another, as we saw in the previous chapter, and we must assume that James Walker, then the lawyer for Jacob Smith and Finlay Fisher, and representative for the County of Montreal with Joseph Papineau, had at least a professional interest in Panet's proposal. But the bill languished until 10 April, when members agreed to give it a second reading the next day. It was 19 April, however, before they got around to doing so, and on Panet proposing that the House sit in committee on the bill the following week, member Pierre Amable De Bonne, a lawyer and soon to be successively a judge of the Court of Common Pleas and of the Court of King's Bench at Quebec, countered with a motion that the bill "remain upon the table." The House agreed, and the bill died.[103]

Ten years later, after the spate of court rulings in slave cases and the abortive legislative efforts of 1800–01, Panet was involved in one last stab at legislation. On 1 March 1803, he seconded James Cuthbert's bid to present "A Bill to remove all doubts relative to Slavery within this Province, and for other purposes." Cuthbert introduced his bill that day. After second reading on 7 March, he proposed that a five-member committee proceed to clause-by-clause study. On 15 March, the Assembly acceded to his request that two more members be named to the committee. The bill never resurfaced.[104]

So ended the grapplings with slavery by an Assembly that showed much more alacrity in adopting a law for the regulation of servants and apprentices than in dealing with slavery.[105] No copies of these slavery bills have yet come to light; we know only their titles. There were no transcripts or reports of the debates, and so we do not know who said what. Judging by their titles, all the bills proposed gradual abolition; out-and-out advocates and opponents of slavery alike, if such there were, might have spurned this half-a-loaf approach. Also, by 1800, in view of the rulings of the courts, many Assembly members probably considered slavery a dead horse. If slaves were free to leave their masters and had no recognized monetary value, what was left of slavery? If the courts had declared slavery incompatible with the laws as they stood, the need for a law saying so was not readily apparent. There were more pressing matters to attend to. If, on the other hand, the Assembly was being called on to overrule the courts, whose interests would that serve?

THE "NOBLE EXAMPLE"

The fact remains that Lower Canada failed to legislate on slavery while Upper Canada did so. How are we to account for this?

The two colonies were markedly different, even if both were formally set up under the Constitutional Act of 1791. Upper Canada was a largely unsettled territory split off from the old Province of Quebec to serve as a haven for Loyalist refugees from the American colonies who, beginning in 1784, built a new society from scratch. Lower Canada had been the heart of New France; it had nearly 200 years of history, a deeply rooted French-speaking population, and established customs and institutions, the British Conquest notwithstanding.

Any suggestion that the gradual-abolition law adopted in Upper Canada in 1793 was the fruit of an abolitionist "movement" in the infant colony would be wide of the mark. There was no movement, nor was the law a demonstration of Loyalist sympathy for the slave, or an expression of the popular will. It was originally a proposal for out-and-out abolition hatched by Lieutenant-Governor John Graves Simcoe, a stoutly anti-slavery military officer, assisted chiefly by two British transplants, Chief Justice William Osgoode and Attorney-General John White.[106] We can easily conceive of the dismay of slave-owning Loyalists when the plan was first mooted. Chased from their homes and despoiled of most of their earthly goods by their American enemies, but now safe in British territory, among friends, and with a government of their own, they found themselves pressed by the Crown to sacrifice yet more: their "Negroes," on whom they counted to clear their lands, work their farms, and care for them as they grew old. They balked. As a contemporary account put it:

> Some, it is said, went into the States to dispose of their slaves, others, took indentures of theirs, securing their services for a certain number of years, without being aware that if those slaves were virtually entitled to freedom, these indentures would be considered as having been obtained by improper coercion, or duress of imprisonment, and, as such, declared invalid. A third party talked of contesting the business by law, but dreaded the expense of a suit, the result of which, if even favorable to them in the first instance, might finally go against them in an appeal to the Governor in Council, where they apprehended the question might have been already prejudged. As to an appeal, in the last resort, to England, expense would, in this case, receive additional force, besides three fourths of the little planters and farmers might be ruined, without the property to be contested, amounting in value to that sum (£500) which would entitle them to carry the cause into England."[107]

Upper Canada's slave-owners were not about to rebel against this spoliation by the king's representative, because they were the king's men, as they had proved at great personal cost in the war. Americans rebelled against constituted authority; Loyalists, by definition, did not. But they went as far as they could in spurning Simcoe's plan for ending slavery then and there, their representatives in the sixteen-seat Assembly enacting a grudging half-measure in which property rights took precedence.

The bill was introduced on 18 June by Loyalist Hazelton Spencer, a member for the Counties of Lennox, Hastings, and Northumberland, and the compromise nature of the measure as ultimately adopted is evident in its preamble, a grand statement of principle qualified by a less grand reference to property rights: "Whereas it is unjust that a people who enjoy freedom by law should encourage the introduction of slaves, and whereas it is highly expedient to abolish slavery in this province, so far as the same may gradually be done without violating private property; be it enacted ... ."[108] As Simcoe reported in summing up the session:

> The greatest resistance was to the Slave Bill, many plausible Arguments of the dearness of Labour and the difficulty of obtaining Servants to cultivate Lands were brought forward.
>
> Some possessed of Negroes knowing that it was very questionable whether any subsisting Law did Authorize Slavery, and having purchased several taken

in War by the Indians at small prices wished to reject the bill entirely, others were desirous to supply themselves by allowing importation for two years. The matter was finally settled by undertaking to secure the property already obtained upon condition that an immediate stop should be put to the importation and that slavery should be gradually abolished.[109]

The law as adopted treated slavery as a social and economic concern, and scouted the moral premise of anti-slavery efforts that slavery was inherently wrong. If trafficking in humans was wrong – offensive to all principles of humanity, religion, the British constitution, and Canadian laws and customs, as members of the old Province of Quebec's elite had acknowledged at the time of Mabane's bill – nothing could justify its continuance. One does not gradually abolish the right to steal. As the Reverend George Bourne was to put it, "gradual emancipation is a virtual recognition of the right, and establishes the rectitude of the practice. If it be just for one moment, it is hallowed forever; and if it be inequitable, not a day should it be tolerated."[110]

In the face of all the doubts about the legality of slavery, the gradual-abolition law of 1793 was permissive: it allowed slavery to continue. "We have made no law to free the Slaves," David William Smith, a member of the Upper Canadian Assembly for Suffolk and Essex Counties and a lieutenant in the 5th Regiment of Foot, wrote to a friend on 25 June. "All those who have been brought into the Province or purchased under any authority legally exercised, are Slaves to all intents & purposes, & are secured as property by a certain act of Parliament."[111] Section 2 of the Act did indeed provide that slaves were to remain so for life. Under Section 3, the children born of slave mothers after the passage of the Act were to remain in the service of their masters until they reached the age of twenty-five. This troubled Smith because the status of the mother, rather than of the father, was to determine the children's fate: "A free man who is married to a Slave, his heir is declared by this act to be a slave. Fye, fye. The Laws of God & man cannot authorize it," he wrote, seemingly unaware that the laws of man did authorize it in most jurisdictions.[112] What these rules meant is that a child born to a slave mother a day before the passage of the law would be condemned to a life of slavery, but a child born one day later would remain in a state of virtual slavery only until the age of twenty-five. If the child born in slavery lived to old age, slavery would conceivably go on into the 1860s or 1870s. If that child was a female, and she gave birth to a child of her own in her late thirties – say, in 1830 – that child would remain in slavery until 1855. To any master who wished to manumit a slave, Section 5 of the Act presented a deterrent in that the master would have to guarantee that no slave whom he freed would become a charge on the public purse.[113] At that rate, slavery might have survived in Upper Canada beyond its abolition in the United States in 1865 had no other factors come into play, including the evolution of public sentiment – part of that being a holier-than-thou attitude that developed in nineteenth-century English Canada in the face of slavery in the American South – and, of course, the British emancipation law of 1833. There were no blacks dancing in the streets of Upper Canada on 9 July 1793.[114]

The one major concession that the legislators made was to agree to stop the importation of new slaves, as Adam Mabane had urged in 1787. Section I of the law provided that any blacks entering the province after its adoption were to be reckoned free. This marked the birth of Upper Canada as a refuge for fugitive American slaves.[115] This provision would have presented no legal difficulty at the time that Mabane raised the idea, but times and the laws had changed. Section I of the Upper Canada bill flew in the face of the British "Act for encouraging new settlers in His Majesty's colonies and plantations in America," the 1790 law that had led James Frazer to believe that he could bring his slaves to Lower Canada from Prince Edward Island without hindrance. How much this clash of colonial bill with imperial law may have troubled the loyal legislators in the Assembly is not known, but the members of the upper house were certainly sensitive to the conflict. They highlighted their concern in the title they gave the bill as it passed through their hands. The Assembly, which dealt with the bill from 18 to 26 June, and again on 2 July on its return from the Legislative Council, consistently referred to it as a measure "to prevent the further introduction of Slaves, and to limit the term of contracts for servitude within this Province," the title which it ultimately bore. In the Council, from 26 June until its adoption there, with amendments, on 1 July, it was given the more unwieldy handle, "A Bill to limit and restrain to a determined period of time the operation of certain parts of an Act passed in the Parliament of Great Britain in the thirtieth year of His Majesty's reign [1790], intituled, 'An Act for encouraging new settlers in His Majesty's colonies and plantations in America,' and to effect and accomplish the gradual suppression and abolition of slavery from this Province."[116]

The bill proposed to do more than "restrain to a determined period" parts of the British law of 1790: it repealed them insofar as they applied to Upper Canada. Where the British law authorized the lieutenant-governor to issue licences allowing American settlers to bring in their slaves free of duty, the Upper Canadian law deprived him of this power and made the issuing of such permits illegal.[117] This colonial blunting of an imperial statute was the work of American Loyalists who acted at the prodding of a Crown representative who was only too happy to be stripped of his power to admit slaves into the province.[118] As Simcoe told both Houses in proroguing the session: "The Act for the gradual abolition of Slavery in this Colony which it has been thought expedient to frame in no respect meets from me a more cheerful concurrence than in that provision which repeals the power heretofore held by the Executive Branch of the Constitution and precludes it from giving sanction to the importation of Slaves."[119]

Lower Canada had neither an anti-slavery governor willing to be hamstrung for the cause, nor did it bear a Loyalist character. In fact, the loyalty of the colony's largely French-speaking population was considered highly doubtful, if not denied outright, by the Anglo-Scottish elite, which sought to stamp the province as indefectibly British, while the majority, resisting with the weight of numbers and the upper hand in the elected Assembly, affirmed its threatened French identity. Each side eyed the other with suspicion, and the onset of war between Britain and revolutionary

France in 1793, which revived fears and rumours of French designs on Canada, did not help to ease tensions. In such a climate, any unbidden move by the Assembly to repeal provisions of a British law and to clip the powers of the governor, as any abolition measure would have entailed, would have been construed by "loyal subjects" as a flagrant act to be resolutely checked.

It never came to that, but we must bear in mind that the legislative inaction in the Lower Canadian Assembly resulted in part from political circumstances that had little to do with members' views on slavery, pro or con. Undoubtedly, some members took little interest in the question, while others who owned slaves would have opposed setting them free; yet others would have foreseen that any abolition law might have set the Assembly on a collision course with the executive. It would be a mistake to construe the repeated attempts in the Assembly over ten years as contests in which slave-owning members fended off bill toting champions of abolition. The calls for legislation, after all, came from the slave-owners, their sympathizers, and those who, apprehending that slavery was doomed, were not so much eager to hasten its end as to ensure that the end would be orderly, causing the least disruption to society and to property rights. Had Lower Canada managed to adopt a law similar to Upper Canada's in the 1790s or later, this would not have constituted a step toward ending slavery but a brake on abolition, a kind of life support for slavery, a positive law reversing a process that had been set in train in the courts. As William R. Riddell, a historian of slavery and judge of the Supreme Court of Ontario, wrote in 1920: "The reason for the failure of these attempts was that any legislation on slavery would in view of the decisions of the courts be reactionary and change for the worse the condition of the slave."[120] At its heart, gradual abolition could have had no purpose but to prolong slavery's existence to safeguard the property rights of slave-owners. In the end, legislative action in Upper Canada left masters there in possession of their slaves, though cutting off any future supply from outside the province and spelling the end of slavery at some unspecified distance down the road. Even this mild measure did not sit well with the people's elected representatives: five years later, with Simcoe gone, Upper Canada's House of Assembly voted 8–4 to overturn the ban on admitting new slaves. The Legislative Council squelched the proposed legislation, which would have negated the abolition provisions of the 1793 law.[121] Legislative inaction in Lower Canada, meanwhile, left masters without a positive law "to remove all doubts," that is, without power over their slaves, and without any affirmation of the legality of slavery in the face of court rulings that denied it. The slave-owners were stumped. After 1803, they abandoned their attempts to turn back the clock.

The year 1803 marks a milestone in the eradication of slavery in Quebec because it witnessed the slave-owners' last stand, and not for the fanciful reason often cited that, in that year, Chief Justice William Osgoode of Lower Canada declared slavery contrary to law. Osgoode, who had taken up his post at Quebec in 1794 after serving two years as chief justice of Upper Canada, no longer held office in 1803. He had, in fact, left the colony two years earlier, never to return, and John Elsmley had been appointed his successor in May 1802. The Osgoode myth was debunked as long ago as 1899, but in the face of its persistence, the old refutation is worth repeating:

> Several writers on that province, apparently following each other, trace it [the end of slavery] back to an adverse decision by Chief-justice Osgoode in 1803, but these are manifestly in error. That gentleman, who had been removed from Upper Canada to Lower Canada, returned to England ... during the summer of 1801, and there resigned his office early in 1802. ... The decision is said to have been rendered at Montreal; it is altogether probable, therefore, that reference is intended to the judgment given at that place about 1799 by Chief-justice Monk.[122]

The Osgoode legend is sometimes tied, thanks to late-nineteenth-century accounts, to the retrospective characterization of the Upper Canadian law of 1793 as a far more cut-and-dried abolition measure than it was, a "noble example"[123] that French Lower Canada chose not to follow. In 1869, for instance, William Canniff wrote in his *History of the Settlement of Upper Canada*:

> When Upper Canada, in 1793, took the lead in the whole of Britain's vast domain in legislating against slavery, Lower Canada continued to regard it without disfavour; and, even in Montreal, endeavoured to fix the chains of bondage more firmly upon the negro. But what the Provincial Legislature did not, although presented with the example set by Upper Canada, was done in a different way by Chief Justice Osgood, who in 1803, at Montreal, declared slavery inconsistent with the laws of the country, and gave freedom to the persons in that condition. And when the British Act of Emancipation was passed, in 1833, setting free the slaves in all parts of the Empire, there was no slaves in Canada, Upper or Lower. Thirty years previous had the evil been crushed in Lower Canada, and forty years before Upper Canada had declared that it was "highly expedient to abolish slavery," and had enacted laws to secure its abolition.[124]

As noted above, adoption of an Upper Canada-style law in Lower Canada would have constituted a regression. In fact, slavery in Upper Canada, sanctioned by the statute of 1793, went on until the 1820s;[125] in Lower Canada, as we have seen, the last sale of a slave took place in 1799 and, without benefit of an abolition law, slavery came to an end by 1803. Riddell went so far as to say that one result of the legislative inaction was "to induce the escape of Negro slaves from Upper Canada where slavery was lawful to Lower Canada."[126] We might say that from 1793 until the extinction of slavery in Lower Canada, the reverse may have also been true: a slave from Montreal, as much as one from the States, might have run to Upper Canada, where slavery was indeed lawful but where every black newcomer was deemed free by law.

Historian Fernand Ouellet noted that the first decade of the nineteenth century saw significant changes in almost every aspect of life in Lower Canada. One of the greatest changes, generally left unmentioned, was that slavery came to an end.[127]

MASTERS, WHO NEEDS THEM?

Master-slave relations in Lower Canada had been turned on their head from the moment that Chief Justice Monk had set Charlotte free in February 1798. Neither this decision nor any of the subsequent high-court rulings in Montreal slave cases was reported in print, but the spoken word had wings – and slaves had legs. They had the power to decide whether they walked or stayed put. The brash, the confident, walked; the more cautious and uncertain, perhaps as incredulous as their masters at the turn of events, chose to wait and see. Child slaves, on their own, may have remained in the dark. The old and ailing may have chosen to stay, finding that freedom came too late. As an old Halifax slave was reputed to have told his master in spurning an offer of freedom: "Master, you eated me when I was meat, and now you must pick me when I'm bone."[128] A few slaves who had come to feel like part of their master's family refused to leave, playing out their lives in "pseudo-slavery" – not slaves, because they were no longer property, nor legally coercible and liable to be sold; not legally servants, either, since they had entered into no contract of service.

We find people who, identified as slaves before this time, turn up as free, with no record of a manumission. It stands to reason: freedom was no longer in the gift of a master. Jean-Baptiste François, a roughly fourteen-year-old slave of the widow of painter François Malepart de Beaucourt in 1796, was the *"Negre libre"* Jean Beaucour *dit* l'Africain when he married in September 1801, and known thereafter by the name of Jean-Baptiste L'Africain. The widowed Phoebe Johnson, a slave of Quebec tavern keeper Pierce Ryan in the 1790s, was a free resident of the St-Laurent Suburb of Montreal by 1801.[129] Sarah, a twenty-five-year-old slave bought by James McGill in 1788, was free in 1802 when, under the name Charlotte Cavilhe, she married Joseph François.[130] Louis Joseph *dit* Pompé, whom we saw as a de Lotbinière slave in August 1800, appears to have gone free within the next three years and to have married a French Canadian in 1809.[131] William, "a Negro belonging to James Dunlop" at his baptism in 1799, was William Wright, a "servant," when he married in 1806, and specifically a hired servant (*engagé*), when his first child was born in 1807.[132] The words "slave" and "*esclave*" fell into disuse in the records, last appearing in the Montreal registers of civil status on 10 September 1796 at the baptism of Marie Julie, the roughly thirty-year-old slave of notary Louis Chaboillez; and in the registers at Quebec on 18 November 1798 at the baptism of Henry Williams, the eighteen-year-old slave of merchant John Young, a member of both the Legislative Assembly and the Executive Council. Outside of those urban centres, the term *esclave* appears to have been used for the last time in the registers of Lower Canada on 16 March 1802, retrospectively, at the burial at St-Antoine of a Panis whose master, Reverend Louis Payet, had died the previous August.[133]

For yet another slight indicator of the great change that took place over six capital years, we might contrast this advertisement placed in a Quebec newspaper in 1803 with the last notices of slave sales and escapes published in 1798: "WANTED a place to attend one or more Ladies to any part of Europe, a woman of colour lately arrived, that can bring an unspotted character from the lady she attended, a line directed to M.A.J. will be attended to if left at the Printing-Office."[134] This "woman of colour" offered her services, instead of having them requisitioned or sold by others. She was the first black in Canada to make use of the press, previously an all-white instrument.

Of course, few black newcomers were as genteel as M.A.J., or prepared to travel to "any part of Europe." That September, the grand jury of the Court of King's Bench at Montreal, in pressing for a proper jail and house of correction to meet the needs of a growing population, observed with alarm "that the number of Vagabonds, as well white *as black* [emphasis added], has increased to a degree that seems to require further Legislative Provision in respect to the prevention of improper and dangerous Characters, coming among us from other Countries, as also the getting rid of those of such Characters who may have introduced themselves already."[135]

Vital statistics tell a tale, both of slavery's passing and of a surge in the size of the city's black population. For one thing, slave-owners were a dying breed by the end of the eighteenth century. At least forty-three were recorded as dying in the 1790s alone, more than in any other decade after 1760.[136] These included Marguerite Larchevêque *dit* La Promenade, whom we saw in the previous chapter as the owner of seven slaves, who died in 1798, as well as such prominent figures as lawyer, notary, and one-time commissioner of police Pierre Mézière, who died in May 1795; Colonel John Campbell, one of the largest slave-owners (see chapter 3), who died a month later; veteran fur trader Étienne Campion and Judge John Fraser, who both died in December of that same year; prominent merchant Jacob Jordan and former inspector of police Georges Hyppolite Le Compte Dupré, both elected to the first Legislative Assembly, who died respectively in February 1796 and November 1797; and General Gabriel Christie, who died in January 1799. This attrition in the ranks of the slave-owners, coupled with the removal of many Loyalists among them to Upper Canada from 1784 on, sapped their collective strength and influence in the district of Montreal at the critical juncture and deprived their petitions of 1799–1800 of much of the weight they might have had.

As for blacks, if we compare the Montreal vital records of 1790–99 with those of 1800–09, we find a total of seventy-five entries pertaining to them in the former ten-year period, and almost twice that number – 148 – in the latter. Of the seventy-five entries of 1790–99, twenty-eight, or more than one third, explicitly identified blacks as slaves, using terms such as "slave of," "property of," or, most often, "negro [or negress] belonging to." Only seven of the 148 entries between 1800 and 1809, or fewer than one twentieth, featured such language: five between 1800 and 1802, one in 1806, and the last in 1808. The twenty-eight explicit slave entries of 1790–99 recorded sixteen deaths and twelve baptisms, including the baptisms of five newborns. The seven entries of the ensuing decade involved no newborns, but four deaths and three adult baptisms, all but one of the latter *in extremis*. What is more, the subject of two of those seven entries, the African-born widow Marie

Louise Jeanne Thomme, an infirm resident of the Grey Nuns' hospice, about sixty years old, was identified at her conditional baptism in the fall of 1801 and at her death the following summer, not as "belonging to," but as "belonging heretofore" ("appartenant ci-devant") to Jean Orillat, a Montreal nabob who had been dead more than twenty years.[137]

The one black "slave" baptized at this time who was not at death's door was a pseudo-slave named Jacques (Jack), a native of Africa, identified at his baptism in 1806 as a roughly forty-year-old "nègre ... appartenant à l'Honorable James McGill." His attachment to prominent merchant and Executive Councillor James McGill and his family was such that he remained with them for twenty-five years after his master's death in December 1813. One apocryphal story had him as a slave – "perhaps the last in the province" – of McGill's stepson, François Desrivières, as late as the mid-1820s. Yet McGill left no slave property in his will, nor did an inventory of his assets at his death list any slaves. Likewise, his widow, Charlotte Guillimin, did not bequeath Jacques as a piece of property in her will, made out in 1818. She did, however, make special provision for him, indicating that he was not a regularly hired servant. As she did with others of her servants, white and black, she left a small sum to "Jack, mon Domestique" but, unlike in the case of her other servants, she requested that her son, François Desrivières, take "Jack" under his wing and keep him in his service until his death. When Jacques died in 1838 at the reputed age of 80 he was still identified ambiguously as "negro of the late Honorable James McGill," but no one would suggest that he was a slave at that late date. Clearly, Jacques, once a slave, had settled in, and the family, out of regard for a faithful servant, a sense of duty, and perhaps plain practicality – good help was hard to find – could not bring themselves to turn him out.[138]

The best-known illustration of this sort of master-slave relationship is found in Philippe Aubert de Gaspé's semi-fictional *Les Anciens Canadiens*. The mulatto slave Lisette was a real person, bought by de Gaspé's grandfather when she was four years old. She was well advanced in years, the slave of de Gaspé's father by the time de Gaspé himself was born in 1786, and she was still living around 1800, a fixture at the family's manor house at St-Jean-Port-Joli, below Quebec. De Gaspé cast her under her real-life name in his historical tale, presenting her as a beloved but headstrong figure who so strained the patience of her master that he had "long ago emancipated her, but she 'had no more use for emancipation than that,' she would say scornfully, snapping her fingers, 'because she had as much of a right as he and all his tribe to go on living in the house where she had been raised.' If her exasperated master threw her out the by the northside door, she would march right back in by the southside and vice-versa."[139]

Another instance of this kind of attachment, from a master's perspective, may be discerned in the will of tailor and businessman Ralph Gray of Quebec and Beauport. In 1807, he left most of his property to a young woman, Anne Ritchie, who had been caring for his ailing wife, on condition that she continue doing so after his death and that she take care of Nero Bartholomy, at present his negro, as a good servant of long standing, until the day of his death, should he wish to remain in the house and at the service of the said Anne Ritchie and continue to work as much as his strength and his age will allow; And in the case that the said Nero Bartholomy should wish or prefer to quit the house and service of the said Anne Ritchie, the said testator ... ordains and intends that the said Nero Bartholomy shall be free and discharged of the slavery to which he is held unto him, his heirs or legatees, and ordains and intends that the said Anne Ritchie or his heirs and legatees pay to the said Nero Bartholomy, in lieu of the care mentioned above, the yearly sum of twelve pounds currency, in four equal payments of three pounds each payable every three months from the day that he quits the service of the said Anne Ritchie [translation].[140]

This curious state of affairs, with Nero Bartholomy "held to slavery" but free to stay or to go, and where a pension would be paid to him if he departed, could scarcely be termed slavery. Where masters had previously disposed of their slaves at will, human decency and a sense of duty now prevented them from casting them off, and it was largely in the power of the slaves to decide, providing they felt fit to survive on their own, whether they would keep their masters. Where masters had once had a claim to the ownership of their slaves, it was now the slaves who had a claim to support from their masters.

From the first decade of the new century, the records of civil status frequently identified black men by their occupations, most commonly as "labourers." This had been a rare occurrence in the previous decade. Other records register the same kind of change in status. Sampson, a black man buried on 26 January 1802 and identified as "the property of Mr Dumont," a tavern-keeper of Pointe-aux-Trembles at the east end of Montreal Island, appears to have been the last slave interred in Montreal's Protestant cemetery.[141] In the admission records of the Hôtel-Dieu, January 1802 also marked a cut-off as the last time that black patients were identified in relation to an owner. From 1803, they were generally identified, when such details were known, by reference to their birthplace and/or by a family relationship such as "son of" or "wife of."[142]

1834 AND ALL THAT

In a brief biographical sketch of James Monk published in the early twentieth century, lawyer Patrick Buchanan glanced at the cases of Charlotte, Judith, and Robin and opined: "It seems clear that the Court was wrong in its judgment and that slavery in law existed in Lower Canada until the Imperial Act of 1833 removed it from all the colonies." His view might have carried more weight had he plumbed the question himself, but he cribbed most of his account of the court rulings on slavery and their consequences from T. Watson Smith's *The Slave in Canada*, published a quarter century before.[143] As we have seen, the ruling in Robin's case was erratic but still dealt a fatal blow to the slave-owners' cause. Riddell, who looked closely into the subject of slavery, considered that

> [t]he effect of the [court] decisions while not technically abolishing slavery rendered it innocuous. The slave could not be compelled to serve longer than he would, and the burden of slavery was rather on the master who must support his slave than on the slave who might leave his master at will. The legislature refusing to interfere, the law of slavery continued in this state until the year 1833 when the Imperial Parliament passed the celebrated act which forever abolished slavery in British Colonies from and after August 1, 1834.[144]

How can we square this idea of slavery remaining "technically" legal until 1834 with the declaration of the Executive Council (including the chief justice of the province, Jonathan Sewell) in 1829 that the law did not recognize slavery, or with the fact that no one in Quebec in 1833–34 viewed the British abolition act as putting an official end to slavery in the province? As early as 1785, Adam Mabane did not consider slavery as solidly established in law, nor did Lieutenant-Governor Simcoe in Upper Canada in 1793 and Chief Justice Monk at Montreal in 1800. Judges Reid, Gale, and Badgley certainly did not consider it lawful right up to the 1830s, nor did Alexander Grant and his acolytes, nor indeed had those slaves from Upper Canada who, according to Riddell, in the wake of the Montreal court rulings against slavery, had fled from Upper Canada, "where slavery was lawful," to Lower Canada, where it was ... technically lawful but inoperative?

The reality is that 1834 was not a pivotal year for blacks in Quebec. As one historian has written: "The memorable first of August, 1834, so longed-for by West Indian slaves, so feared by West Indian planters, had nothing to render it memorable in northern latitudes."[145] There was no change in the status or condition of blacks at Montreal or elsewhere in Lower Canada. If the British law of 1833 had any impact, it was to confirm what was already the rule and to hearten blacks in the knowledge that the worldwide fight against slavery was making progress and that the United States would have to follow Britain's example, sooner or later, to avoid a race war. On the local front, the British law of 1833 and its implementation in 1834 served to reinforce the attachment of blacks to Britain at a time when white political reformers and their numerous followers were turning their backs on Britain and promoting the idea of American-style republican institutions as a panacea for the colony's ills.

The conventional analyses of the end of slavery are based on an ignorance or misunderstanding of historical facts, resulting in part from a lack of access to pertinent documents and a misreading of the legislative record of Lower and Upper Canada. The Upper Canada law, as originally envisaged by Simcoe, was aimed at abolishing slavery; as adopted, its immediate aim was to stave off the moment of abolition. In Lower Canada, the failure to adopt a similar law did not constitute an endorsement of slavery but reflected more or less the opposite: an unwillingness to interfere with its demise, or at the very least an indifference to its passing. The attempts at legislation in 1800, 1801, and 1803 were a form of drawn-out appeal process in which the slave-owners unsuccessfully sought to have their political representatives undo the anti-slavery decisions of the Montreal courts.

A case might be made that, with its total absence of coercion (and political intervention), the manner in which slavery was abolished in Quebec turned out to be one of the most humane and least contentious. If the courts and legislature did not order slave-owners to free their slaves immediately, masters nevertheless were left without the legal power to restrain them or to claim their unpaid labour. At the same time, the slaves were not turfed out all at once to fend for themselves, to find a livelihood, food and shelter, when many of them – young children, the old and feeble – were ill equipped to do so. No provision needed to be made for the public support of penniless and homeless freed slaves, and the authorities also avoided the problem that bedevilled abolition efforts elsewhere, i.e., whether and how to compensate slave-owners for their loss of property. There was no measure condemning those already enslaved to a life of servitude or imposing a disguised form of slavery such as the six-year "apprenticeship" provided for in the British law of 1833, or a prolonged obligatory period of service for the children of slaves, as some gradual-abolition laws decreed.[146] At the political level, as already mentioned, this way of ending slavery by unwritten law, as we might say, precluded the possibility of a clash with British lawmakers or even the eventual disallowance of an abolition measure that would have abrogated the imperial statute of 1790 sanctioning the importation of slaves. Of course, the aggrieved slave-owners could have appealed to a higher judicial authority, but, whether because they estimated that such a move would be too costly or because they recognized the almost certain futility of a strictly legal claim, they did not do so. As much as we today might consider that a law "to remove all doubts" would have made clear exactly when and how slavery ended, masters and slaves quickly grasped the reality: court rulings in the decade up to 1802 and the last legislative gasp on the subject in 1803 meant that slavery was at an end. The courts had said so, and no competent authority ever said otherwise.

By January 1802, Henry McEvoy, a sixteen-year-old slave on the Rivière-des-Hurons, in Sir John Johnson's seigneury of Monnoir, had heard some version of what had passed in the courts. "Wishing to avail himself of the act of parliament that frees and emancipates all slaves in all the lands held by Great Britain," as he declared, he, as a free man, contracted to work as a domestic servant for Loyalists William and Philip Byrne of nearby Chambly, on the west bank of the Richelieu. No such Act of the British parliament would come for almost thirty-two years, but Henry McEvoy believed that it had, as presumably did the notary who drew up his employment contract, the Byrnes who signed it, and perhaps his master as well, since no one hunted down the slave boy or claimed him as property.[147]

To extend slavery's life by thirty years to 1834 is to misread a capital chapter in the history of Quebec. In practical terms, adding three decades to the record of slavery skews any attempt at a slave count and distorts the experience of the black population: we assume that some blacks of the time must have been enslaved when they were not. This false assumption has helped perpetuate the myth of the existence of a slave cemetery at the site of "Nigger Rock" at St-Armand-Ouest, on the Vermont border.[148] Making "slavery in law" end in 1834 also implies ascribing to the imperial parliament the responsibility for an abolition that was made in Quebec, attributing the "official" downfall of slavery to the British abolitionists and politicians who pressed for the Act of 1833, when in fact the artisans of slavery's end in Quebec were neither zealous white abolitionists nor political heroes, but a few Montreal slaves who, in seeking their freedom, put the courts on the spot. There was no Quebec Granville Sharp or Abbé Raynal, no Wilberforce, Buxton, or Clarkson. There was, to be sure, Adam Mabane, who proved ineffectual. Those who brought down slavery were Charlotte, Judith, Manuel Allen, Robin, Augustin, Frank ...

THREE

STILL COUNTING

Charlotte was always Charlotte. Through a few crucial records that mention her name, we know the fate of this African-born slave, whose flight and ensuing release from bondage in February 1798 signalled the beginning of the end of slavery. But what of Judith – the first slave to follow Charlotte's lead with the same result, who was also instrumental in precipitating slavery's downfall? To shine a light on Judith's story is to illustrate how difficult it is to count Quebec's black slaves.

We do know that Charlotte, formerly the slave of Jane Cook, married gardener and provisioner John Trim, an ex-slave who was the leading black figure in Montreal in the first thirty years of the nineteenth century. She lived out her life in a house on St-Augustin (McGill) Street that Trim had bought five months after her release.[1] They lived in relative comfort, and even had a live-in servant in the person of Haitian-born Catherine Guillet, who remained with them for about fifteen years, until 1820.[2] Godmother to two children, Charlotte had no children of her own.[3] In an ironic twist, in 1821, Jane Cook had to rely on Charlotte to establish her own identity. Her sister had died abroad and, without papers to prove her right to her sister's estate, Cook needed someone to vouch that she was indeed the dead woman's only sibling, the legitimate daughter of the same parents, and the only surviving member of the family. What better witness than the family slave?

> Charlotte, a native of Guinea, in Africa, and wife of John Trim of Montreal ... declared, and affirmed upon oath: that from the age of twelve Years, until she had attained the Age of thirty Years, She was in the Service of George Cook, and Margaret Rafter, both of whom are deceased; that the Said George Cook

and Margaret Rafter were considered by every person who Knew them to be lawfully Married, and highly respected as Such by the Officers of His Majesty's Sixtieth Regiment, of which the said George Cook was Quartermaster Serjeant, and the said Margaret Rafter was Nurse in the Hospital, that they had two Daughters named Jean [sic], and Elisabeth, who were considered to be the legitimate Children of the said George Cook, and Margaret Rafter; and were brought up in a decent, and genteel manner, one of whom (Jean Cook) now resides in the City of Montreal.[4]

Charlotte died two years later, on 23 September 1823.[5]

What about Judith (or Jude)? She rates a brief entry in the *Dictionnaire des esclaves et de leurs propriétaires au Canada Français,* the compendious list of black and Indian slaves compiled by historian Marcel Trudel that served as the basis for his seminal study, *L'esclavage au Canada français* (1960). The details on Judith in the *Dictionnaire* are drawn from the slave-owners' petition to the House of Assembly in April 1799: bought for £80 New York currency by merchant Elias Smith at Albany, New York, on 27 January 1795, she ran off in February 1798, was arrested and jailed, then freed on a technicality on 8 March that year when she appeared before Chief Justice Monk of the Court of King's Bench on a writ of habeas corpus.[6] But there was more to her life than that.

To begin with, while she was still a slave, Judith gave birth to a daughter on 29 December 1797. The girl was not yet two months old when Judith deserted Smith's service, only to be arrested and jailed. When the baby was baptized on 4 March 1798, under the name Emilia, she was identified as "Daughter to John Gray a Neogroe the Servant of John Shuter merchant of Montreal & Judith a Neogress the Servant of Elias Smith Merchant of Montreal."[7] Shuter, twenty-three years old, was then, or soon to be, Smith's son-in-law.[8] John Gray was present at Emilia's baptism, but Judith was not: she was not released from jail – and bondage – until four days later. Whether the freedom granted to her extended to her daughter is a mystery, since the slave-holders' petition of 1799, the only surviving account of the case, makes no mention of Emilia. In freeing Judith, Monk had not ruled on her slave status or on the legality of slavery, but on the narrow point that, as a wayward servant, she had been held improperly in jail instead of in a house of correction. On the face of it, this decision, while it resulted in freedom for the mother, did not affect the status of her daughter. It is possible, if unlikely, that Emilia, born a slave, remained with Elias Smith, or with her father, John Gray. There can be no doubt, however, about Judith's son, William Fleming, born on 14 January 1799. Judith was free then, hence her son was born free. At his baptism, William Fleming was identified as the "Son to John Gray a Negroe & Judith a Negress."[9]

The records reveal no more about a woman named Judith or Jude and the slave called John Gray, or about children named Emilia and William Fleming Gray, other than the fact that John Gray served as a witness at the wedding of the enslaved Manuel Allen to a woman identified as Sarah Jackson in October 1797.[10] What happened to the Grays? Did they leave Montreal? Were Judith and John Gray legally married? There is no record of it. Did their children bear the family name Gray, as we might expect? Who was John Gray, anyway? We know that Elias Smith had bought Judith in Albany in 1795, but there is no record of where and when Shuter got his hands on John Gray.

We do know that, on 3 September 1796, Shuter had bought a slave called Jack for £50 from the merchant and notary Jonathan Abraham Gray, brother of Montreal Sheriff Edward William Gray.[11] Jonathan Gray had acquired Jack for an unknown price on 6 June 1795 from Mary Fleming, widow of John Fleming, quartermaster of the 2nd Battalion, 60th Regiment. At the same time that he bought Jack, Shuter entered into a separate agreement with notary Gray, "stipulating for and on behalf of his late Negro Slave named Jack, the said Negro named Jack being also present and Accepting thereof," to emancipate Jack after six and a half years, provided that he behaved well. If he did not, the agreement would be void, and "the said John Shuter then shall be at full Liberty to Sell and dispose of the said Negro named Jack as of his own right and property."[12] If this conditional promise of freedom had been Shuter's idea, he would have had no reason to make it the subject of an agreement with Gray. Once he had bought Jack, he could free him or not, as he pleased. Extracting a pledge from Shuter seems to have been Jack's idea. Indeed, this was an agreement between Jack and Shuter, with Gray acting as Jack's proxy, since slaves had no power to enter into contracts. A contract was an agreement between consenting parties, and a slave's consent was always subject to the imputation that it had been coerced.[13]

Exactly how many slaves did Shuter have? There was John Gray, and Jack, and a third, who crops up in the records on 29 April 1798 in the person of John Fleming, twenty-two years old, "a black man living at Mr Shuter's," who was baptized that day together with twenty-year-old Julia Johnson, "a black woman."[14] The fact that in the one baptism record Fleming was identified by reference to a master – "living at" was here a euphemism for "slave of" – while Julia Johnson was not, suggests that she was free. There are no earlier documents recording the presence of these two in Montreal. Where had they sprung from? We find them even more closely linked at the end of the year when, on 16 December, John Fleming, "a black man ... Servant to Mr Shuter's Merchant," and Julia Johnson, "a black Woman," were married at the Anglican church.[15]

Bearing in mind that slave-owning merchants usually kept no more than one or two slaves at a time, and that slaves often bore the name of their masters, we begin to suspect that Jack, the slave bought by Jonathan Abraham *Gray* from the widow *Fleming* in 1795 and resold to John Shuter in 1796, is the same man as either John *Gray* or John *Fleming* – but which might he be? If Jack were John Gray, this might help to explain why John Gray had not run away with Judith in February 1798. Having drawn Shuter into signing a promise to free him, he might have felt bound to abide by the bargain he had struck, unless he had found conditions intolerable. He had given his word. Besides, his desertion would have voided the agreement: could he run the risk of being caught and re-enslaved, this time with no hope of going free?

However, two events that occurred in 1803–04 cast doubt on the proposition that Jack was John Gray. On 2 November 1803, Jack was formally emancipated after seven years as Shuter's slave. Six months later, John Fleming, still Shuter's slave when last heard of, acquired two adjoining lots in the west-side Ste-Anne Suburb (also called the Fief Nazareth, or Griffintown) under the seigneurial system.[16] This tells us that, by May 1804, John Fleming was free; no one would have granted lands to a slave, since there was no recourse to be had against him for non-fulfillment of terms, bad debts, and so forth. So, if John Fleming had been freed, where is the record of his emancipation? John Fleming was free in the spring of 1804 because he had been emancipated the previous fall – under the name Jack. We find confirmation of his dual identity some years later when he is referred to as the black householder "Jack Shuter, alias John Fleming" of the Ste-Anne Suburb.[17] This would seem to clinch it: Jack was not John Gray but John Fleming, alias Jack Shuter (Shuter).

In that case, we are left with the puzzle of what happened to John Gray, Judith, and their two children. We might hazard that if John Gray and John Fleming were slaves together of John Shuter, then John Gray's son, William Fleming, was named after John Fleming, as a kind of tribute to a companion in bondage. But, on 16 July 1800, when William Flemming (*sic*) was buried, the cemetery records identified him as the "Inft. Son of John Flemming a Black man livg at Mr Shutter [*sic*]."[18] Son of John Gray at his birth, son of John Fleming at his death – evidently, John Gray, John Fleming and Jack were one and the same. John Shuter had owned one adult male slave, not three. William Fleming was not named Gray after his father, and Fleming was not his middle name but his family name.

If John Gray and John Fleming were one, then Judith, his wife, must be Julia Johnson. This explains why Julia Johnson had been a free woman at the time of her baptism in April 1798 and at her wedding in December that year: under her slave name, Judith, she had been freed by the court the previous 8 March. A confirmation of sorts that Judith and Julia are the same person comes years later. On 15 November 1833, a woman identified as thirty-year-old Marie Émilie Smith died at the Hôtel-Dieu. The church record of her burial tells us no more about her than her name and her estimated age. The hospital records, however, make her a "naigresse," born in Montreal to a man identified only as Smith, and a woman called Julie Jacson.[19] The latter name was one variant of the name by which Julia Johnson was known, as we will see later. There is no record of the birth in Montreal in the late 1790s or early 1800s of a black female named Marie Émilie Smith, or Emily Smith, or anything close. There are, in fact, no records of a woman of that name, black or white. There is, however, Emilia, born in slavery at the end of 1797 to Judith and John Gray. The ages are close enough: Marie Émilie Smith is said to be thirty, Emilia would be thirty-five. So the mysterious Marie Émilie Smith is Emilia, bearing in this instance the last name, not of John Gray, but of Elias Smith, who had been her owner – and perhaps more – at the time of her birth.[20]

The 1833 hospital record gives her father's name as Smith. What if that were true – that Elias Smith, or some member of his family, was her biological father, and that

Montreal counted about nine thousand residents in 1803, the year in which slave-owners gave up their efforts to secure a law upholding slavery, and John Fleming gained his freedom.

the baptism record identifying her as the daughter of John Gray was an imposition? When, shortly after Emilia's birth, her mother ran away, might it have been to escape unwanted sexual attentions? As in Charlotte's case, we cannot help but wonder what led Judith, a nursing mother, to run off in the depths of winter. And if Emilia was not John Gray's biological daughter, this might also help to account for his staying put when Emilia's mother escaped. Speculation about Emilia's paternity is fuelled by a curious hospital record of 1813, when Emilia would have been fifteen years old. It so happens that a black girl of fifteen was registered as a patient at the Hôtel-Dieu in February–March that year under the name Emilie Acsite, daughter of Acsite.[21] This fanciful name (pronounced *ak-sit*), neither French nor English, and recorded nowhere else, is an approximation, written by a French-speaking nursing sister as she heard it. It is conceivable that this was a translated, truncated form of Elias Smith (i.e., *-as-Smit*). It may be that the only connection between Emilia and Smith was one of slave to master, and not of blood relation, but the circumstances of her case do lead us to wonder. Besides Smith, she also used the name Fleming. In that second decade of the century, she moved to Quebec, where, as Amelia Fleming (or Amélia Flemming), a "black girl" or "coloured woman," she was jailed twenty-six times between 1815 and 1829, a few times for larceny but mostly for disorderliness.[22]

The variations in the names of the members of this family account for the disappearance of John Gray and Judith from the records after 1799. Husband and wife did not move away from Montreal after gaining their freedom; inhabiting shifting identities, they moved while standing still. They were slaves, and not formally married, when Emilia was born in December 1797; they married a year later, when Judith was free, one month before the birth of their son, William Fleming.

As for John Gray's failure to escape with Judith in early 1798, we have seen possible explanations in the bargain that he had struck with Shuter, his master, and in the hypothesis that he may not have been the biological father of Judith's daughter. Another possibility is suggested by the swift marital breakdown of this couple. John Fleming had three children after 1800: a son named John in 1802, who died in 1803, and was buried under the name William; Moses Alexander, born in 1804 and named, it is believed, after Fleming's friends Moses Meyers and Alexander Valentine; and Thomas, born in July 1807, who died in July 1808. In each case, the mother was identified as Fleming's "wife" Rose or Rosina. Who she was remains a mystery. Later still, Fleming, identified in French as Jacques Flemming, was to have another son, christened Jacques, by yet another "wife," this one called Magdeleine Carmel, alias Magdeleine Thompson.[23] Meanwhile, Julia Johnson took up with cook Joseph Pierson. Their names were linked in October 1803, one month before John Fleming was formally emancipated, when Julia Fleming and Pierson were sponsors together at the baptism of Maria Keeling, a black girl.[24] The following year, Julia Fleming and Pierson were accused of assaulting a black woman, Hanna Caesar, at Pierson's home in the west side St-Joseph (or Récollets) Suburb. Pierson and Julia – her name sometimes recorded as Juliet or July Jackson, and Julia Pearson – had four children: Joseph (d. 1805); James (1808–1809), a second James (1810–1811), and Sarah Anne (b. 1812). The last two were born after Pierson had married Mary Rusk in 1809 (he had two sons at about the same time in 1810, James by Julia Johnson, and Valentine by his wife). All his sons died in infancy; Sarah Anne is also believed to have died young.[25]

Finally, after being estranged for six or seven years, Fleming and Julia Johnson made their separation official in 1809:

On the sixth Day of february of the year one thousand eight hundred & nine ... Personally Appeared John Fleming of said Montreal yeoman, and Julia Jackson his wife, which said John Fleming & Julia Jackson for divers considerations them moving mutually consented and agreed to live separate and apart from this day henceforth and for ever, without the one having any claim or demand whatever against the other or for any one property or effects whatsoever, or for the support or maintenance of one another, hereby formally renouncing to cohabitation with each other and all matrimonial rights and rights whatsoever in future.[26]

Their vicissitudes suggest that the marriage of John Fleming and Julia Johnson was a mistake, and that little more had brought them together than the kinship of their masters and their own shared misery. If we believe the official records, they had a child, Emilia, in December 1797. Within two months, Judith/Julia had run off, but

John had refused to gamble for his freedom. By the time that she, now free, was about to give birth to a son, someone – John Shuter? – had pushed them to regularize their union. John Fleming was not a free agent; he needed his master's consent to marry. So the slave man and the freed slave woman married, and promptly drifted apart.

From this excursion through the records we find that Jack, John Flem(m)ing, John Gray, Jack Shutter and Jacques Flemming were five names for one man. Jude/Judith, Julia Flem(m)ing, Julia/Juliet/July Jacson, Jackson or Johnson, and Julia Pearson were also one person; as were Emilia, Amelia Fleming, Marie Émilie Smith, and Emilie Acsite; and William Fleming, born the son of John Gray, and William Flemming, who died the son of John Flemming. Counting names alone gives us more than a dozen persons, at least five of whom – Jack, John Gray, John Fleming, Judith, and Emilia – would have been slaves. In reality, they were four – a man, a woman, a girl, a boy – three of whom had been slaves, all but free-born William Fleming.

If we refer to Trudel's *Dictionnaire,* we find no mention of "John Gray," or of his and "Judith's" children, Emilia and William Fleming. Although John Fleming and Julia Johnson were baptized together in 1798 at Montreal's Anglican church, the *Dictionnaire* has them baptized separately, John Fleming as a Roman Catholic and Julia Johnson as an Anglican. Overlooking their joint baptism, and ignoring their marriage and their children, the *Dictionnaire* is oblivious to their relationship. Still, it turns two persons into six slaves, with separate entries for Jack, John Fleming, Jacques Fleming, Jude/Judith, Julia Johnson, and Julie Fleming, the latter unaccountably listed among the slaves at Quebec.[27] In light of this examination of Judith's relations, a revised *Dictionnaire* would count three fewer slaves in all – take away one at Quebec, and two at Montreal.[28] But under which of their names should we list them? The preference in the present account for the names John Fleming and Julia Johnson is arbitrary. Moreover, the fact that no death record for them appears to exist under any of their known names leaves open the possibility that they were buried under entirely different names.

For how many other slaves who "vanished" in a like manner under slavery or after slavery's end must this exercise be repeated?

Take Sarah, for instance. She was said to be about twenty-five years old on 25 September 1788, when James McGill bought her from merchant Jean Louis Cavilhe for £56. Perhaps she was meant to assist or succeed McGill's ailing slave, Marie Louise, who, admitted to hospital the previous summer, would re-enter the hospital that November and linger there until her death the following February.[29] We believe Sarah to be the same woman listed under the name Marie-Charles McGill, alias Charlotte, whom the *Dictionnaire* identifies as a Montreal slave, the wife of labourer Joseph-François (no indication of when they married) and mother of two boys – Joseph (no date of birth), who died on 19 March 1805 at the age of eighteen months, and Pierre-Augustin, born on 3 November 1805.[30] In gratuitously hyphenating her husband's name, the *Dictionnaire* turns the surname François into part of a composite first name, Joseph-François. Returning to the hyphenless form of the name, as it was written at the time, makes a difference. Not quite ten years after McGill had

James McGill (1744–1813) signed a report calling for the gradual abolition of slavery in 1787. At the time, he owned a slave called Louise. The next year, he bought Sarah.

bought her, Sarah was identified as thirty-year-old "Charle Marie ... de chez madame mcgille" when she was in hospital for a month in 1798.[31] She was a free woman by 29 November 1802 when, under the name Charlotte Cavilhe, she married widower Joseph Frank, supposedly a native of Jamaica, in an Anglican ceremony. Their son, Joseph, was born one year later, on 10 October 1803; at his Catholic baptism the next day, his parents were identified as Joseph Franclin and Marie Charles Caville. At his death in March 1805, the boy christened Joseph Franclin was identified as Joseph François, son of Joseph François and Marie Charles MacGill. When the couple's second son was born in November 1805, he was christened Pierre Augustin François, son of Joseph François and Charlotte M'ghil. Finally, when the erstwhile Sarah entered the hospital in mid-April 1809, she was the single-named Charlotte, a fortyish "Négresse," wife of Joseph, "negre." She died there on 23 or 24 April. The church record of her burial made no reference to a family name or to a husband.[32] As for the *Dictionnaire*'s slave count, if we allow that Joseph François may have been a slave in Quebec at some time before his marriage,[33] we must strike four from the total: the three women listed as the slave Sarah, as Marie Charles McGill, wife of Joseph François, and as the black woman Charlotte who died in 1809, were one and the same, and her two children were born free.

THE CAMPBELL SLAVES

Such identification exercises are indispensable if we are to arrive at a more or less firm idea of the total number of black slaves, their identities, and their attributes.

These exercises are also crucial in identifying the major slave-owners. Slaveholding merchants and tradesmen held one or two slaves at a time, but a few others, especially large landed proprietors, had considerably more. Loyalist Sir John Johnson, for instance, a major landowner in New York State who was to become an important landed proprietor in Lower and Upper Canada by the end of the century, brought many slaves up from the Mohawk Valley of New York at the time of the American Revolution (see Appendix III). Scottish-born Colonel John Campbell and his Canadian wife, Marie-Anne de Lacorne St-Luc, were also among the biggest slave-owners in Montreal under the British.[34] Their residence stood on St-Paul Street at the corner of Bonsecours in Montreal, but Campbell also owned another house on the market place, a farm at Lachine, and another at Les Cèdres, and was co-owner with Colonel Gabriel Christie of the seigneury of Noyan on the upper Richelieu River.[35] Witnesses in the Missouri freedom suits of Rose's children spoke of Campbell as owning three black slaves in the 1780s, for whom Marianne Tison had cut and sewn suits of blue and red. But the records suggest that the total number of Campbell slaves between 1785 and the end of the century (Campbell himself died on 23 June 1795, at age 64, his wife almost eighteen years later, on 8 March 1813) was much greater than that. Many were children.

François and Jeanne were the key figures in the Campbell slave holdings. They were married at the Anglican church at Montreal on 20 January 1785, the English-language record stating that "Francis & Jane both Slaves to Colonel Campbell were Married at his request."[36] Campbell's request may have stemmed from the fact that Jane was pregnant. While Francis and Jane were identified as slaves at their wedding, no mention was made of their racial or ethnic origins; we might assume that both were black, but the birth record of their daughter Élisabeth that April identified Francis as François, a black man, and Jane as Geneviève, a Panis.[37]

The slight variations in the names should not be surprising, given that names were routinely translated. Not infrequently, for example, the name Jane or Jenny was an English shortening of the French Geneviève, but Jane or Jenny might also be rendered in French as Jeanne. In the present case, to fail to look behind the names and aliases and assume that Jeanne and Geneviève were two different women would lead to a peculiar result: that is, the black slave Francis would have married Jane but fathered his first three children by two other women – and not one by his lawful wife. Indeed, if the children's birth records were taken at face value, Francis would have had a daughter by the Panis Geneviève in April 1785, only three months after marrying Jane, followed by a son called François in April 1786 and a daughter, Marie Anne, in March 1787, both by a black woman named Louise, said to be another Campbell slave.[38] Before reaching for an explanation of François's seeming promiscuity in some supposed African or Afro-Caribbean sexual mores, we would do well to consult the settlement of Campbell's estate of October 1797.[39] Under this agreement, Mrs Campbell's share of her late husband's slaves consisted of "jenny panise," said to be about forty-five years old, and her daughter Marie Anne, aged about nine (she was ten). Indeed, when Marie Anne died in 1799, she was identified as the child of parents named François and Jeanne. Clearly, Marie Anne was the daughter of a black slave and his Indian wife, not the natural daughter of a roving François and a black Louise. The same, we believe, was true of the boy, François, who would thus have been, like his sisters Elisabeth and Marie Anne, the child of a black-and-Indian marriage, not of an extramarital fling between two blacks. Sorting out the names here is not just a game of hide-and-seek: it has moral, social, and ethnocultural implications. As for the name Louise, it may have been derived from one version of François's name, Louis François.

In October 1788, Campbell's black slave Jean François and his "lawful wife," Jeanne Harissone – yet more variants of the names of this pair – had a daughter called Marie Angélique who died in May 1792. She was buried under the name Marie Angélique Louis and identified as the daughter of Louis François and Marie Jaque. In October 1791, Jean François and his "lawful wife," this time called Josephe, had another daughter called Marie Josephe, about whom nothing else is known. Then in November 1794, François and Jeanne, so called, had a son christened François Josué, named apparently after Mrs Campbell's uncle, François Josué de Lacorne Dubreuil. This was the last child of the slave François, who died on 4 May 1795 in the Hôtel-Dieu at the age of about forty-three.[40]

In all, then, François, a black slave, and Jeanne, an Indian slave, appear to have had six children:

Élisabeth: Born on 12 April 1785, she was identified at her baptism the next day as a "neigresse," the daughter of François and his Panis wife, Geneviève, slaves of John Campbell. At her burial at Longue-Pointe on 21 April 1787, the church record identified her as "â partenant â Md. Campbell Lacorne Décédée d'hier chez jean Archambeau Dans La Côte de St Leonard de la paroisse" (belonging to Mrs. Campbell Lacorne, died yesterday at the home of Jean Archambeau on the St-Léonard Road of this parish). The burial record made no mention of her race.[41]

François: At his birth on 5 April 1786, he was identified as the son of François and Louise, "nègres de monsieur Campbell." The "négresse" Marie Elizabeth, who was recorded as his godmother, was a slave of Mrs Campbell's late father, Luc de Lacorne St-Luc, and after the latter's death in 1784, of his widow, Marguerite Boucher de Boucherville. At François's death on 8 October 1797, he was identified as a "nègre appartenant à Madame Campbel."[42]

Marie Anne: She was born on 31 March 1787, her parents identified as François and Louise, "nègres appartenant a Monsieur Cambel." As we saw, she and her mother, identified as "jenny panise," fell to the widowed Mrs Campbell in the 1797 distribution of Campbell's estate. Marie Anne died at the Hôtel-Dieu on 23 June 1799, identified as a twelve-year-old black girl belonging to Mrs Campbell. At her burial, she was identified as the daughter of François, a black man formerly the property of Mrs Campbell ("formerly" meaning that he had died, not that he had been freed, as the *Dictionnaire* surmises), and of his wife, Jeanne.[43]

Marie Angélique: Born on 23 October 1788, she was identified at her baptism the following day as the daughter of Jean François, a black slave of John Campbell, and of his lawful wife, Jeanne Harissone, but at her burial at Longue-Pointe on 29 May 1792, she was Marie Angélique Louis, daughter of Louis François and Marie Jaque. Her age at death was given as three years and seven months.[44]

Marie Josephe: She was born on 19 October 1791. The record of her baptism on 21 October identified her as a "négresse," daughter of the lawful marriage of Jean François and his wife Josephe, but did not identify her or her parents as slaves of Campbell or of anyone else. There appears to be no other trace of her. The sponsors at her baptism, Jean Baptiste Archambault and his wife, Marie Joseph Chartier, were also the sponsors at the baptism of Marie Angélique. Jean Baptiste Archambault was probably the Jean Archambeau (*sic*) in whose house at Longue-Pointe Élisabeth had died in 1787.[45]

François Josué: Born on 20 November 1794, the son of parents identified as François and Jeanne, "Esclaves de Monsieur Cambel." His fate is unknown.[46]

Was this really the extent of the children of the slaves François and Jeanne? Campbell was also recorded as the owner of a married couple named François Xavier and Marie. All that we know of them comes from the record of the birth of a boy called François Xavier on 10 March 1793. At his baptism, he was identified as the son of François Xavier and his lawful wife, Marie, "nègres appartenant à M. Campbele." At his burial at Longue-Pointe the following 10 July, the church record omitted to mention such germane details as the date of his death or the names of his parents; it identified him as François Xavier, four months old, negro born of idol-worshipping parents ("parents idolâtres"). His name, his age, and the fact that other infant slaves of the Campbells were recorded at Longue-Pointe allow us to conclude with some certainty that this boy was the same black François Xavier who had been baptized at Montreal the previous March.[47] The single record of his parents' names, the fact that no marriage record can be found for them, and the boy's birth in March 1793, roughly a year and a half after the birth of François and Jeanne's daughter Marie Josephe and a year and a half before the birth of their son François Josué, mean that he was very probably a son of François and Jeanne, and that the names François Xavier and Marie were simply more aliases for them.

Yet another couple, Jacque and Marguerite, were identified as Campbell slaves. There appears to be no mention of them other than as the parents of a boy, Jacque, born on 26 May 1788, who was identified as the son of Jacque, a "nègre de monsieur Cambell légitimement marié avec Marguerite négresse" (negro of Mr Campbell lawfully wed to Marguerite, negress).[48] The sponsor at the boy's baptism was the same Jean-Baptiste Archambault who was a sponsor at the baptisms of Marie Angélique and Marie Josephe, daughters of François and Jeanne. It seems that Jacque's parents were also the parents of a girl born one year before him, on 21 April 1787. She was christened Marie Marguerite, identified as the child "d'un nègre et d'une négresse esclaves de Messire Cambel Ecuier" (of a negro and negress, slaves of Mr Campbell, Esquire), and buried on 25 May 1791 under the single name Marguerite, "Négresse ... appartenant en qualité d'Esclave au Sieur Campbell Colonel" (negress ... belonging as a slave to Mr Campbell, colonel). Her parents were unnamed at her

Marguerite Boucher de Boucherville, widow of Legislative Councillor Luc de Lacorne St-Luc, was the last person in Quebec to sell a black slave, in 1799. The slave was a nine-year-old boy she had received as a gift.

baptism, as they were at her death. Trudel supposes her to be a daughter of Jean-François and Jeanne – but this would be a biological impossibility, considering that their daughter Marie Anne was born less than one month before her, in March 1787. She would have to have been the daughter of some other woman than Jeanne.[49] Her brother Jacque likewise cannot be a son of François and Jeanne if, as we saw above, their daughter Marie Angélique was born only five months after him, in October 1788. So although it is probable that the couple called François Xavier and Marie were really François and Jeanne, this is impossible in the case of the couple called Jacque and Marguerite.

We know of one more black child born a slave to the Campbells. This is the boy, Thomas, mentioned in the previous chapter as the last slave sold in Quebec. Mrs Campbell's widowed stepmother, Marguerite Boucher de Boucherville, sold him in 1799 to trader Joseph Campeau of Detroit. On that occasion, she declared that Thomas, then nine years old, was a "don que lui en a fait Mons. et Mad. Campbell étant né d'esclaves appartenans au d[it]. S[ieur] Campbell" (a gift to her from Mr and Mrs Campbell, having been born to slaves belonging to the said Mr Campbell).[50] This is the only known case where the Campbells disposed of a slave, by sale or gift. The question is, why Thomas rather than any other of their young slaves? We suspect that the reason Thomas was given away is that, unlike the rest of the slave children belonging to the Campbells, he was a natural child, with no father on hand to support him.

Indeed, Thomas appears to have been born out of wedlock on 2 January 1790. He was identified at his baptism as a "neigre inconnu" (unknown negro, i.e., a bastard child or a foundling).[51] The sponsors at his baptism were the same as those at the baptism of the Campbells' slave François Josué. It is tempting to think that, like François Xavier, the boy named Thomas was perhaps a son of François and Jeanne; he was born more than a year after their daughter Marie Angélique, and almost two years before their next child, Marie Josephe. But as the Campbells had an adult slave named Thomas in their service in the early 1790s, and considering that the first-born sons of other Campbell slaves seem to have been named after their fathers, the boy Thomas born in 1790 was probably the son of the elder Thomas.[52]

This elder Thomas might not actually have belonged to the Campbells. In December 1793, a slave named Thomas, or Tom Grant, arrested for larceny, gave a statement before a magistrate who identified him as "the property of Col. John Campbell." The magistrate had presumed that, because Tom Grant was in Campbell's service and stood accused of thefts from Campbell's house at Lachine, he was Campbell's slave. But Tom Grant corrected him. As a result, his identification, at the head of the deposition, as "property" of Campbell was crossed out, and the word "Servant" substituted, with this clarification inserted: "and as he says the property of Duncan McKillock Lieut. in the 1st Regt. of foot." By Tom Grant's avowal, then, he was in Campbell's service, but the slave of another man.[53]

Tom Grant appears to have been a single man. If he fathered the child Thomas while in the Campbells' service, it was probably with one of the Campbells' female slaves. The mother being one of their slaves, the Campbells would have felt entitled to claim her progeny as their property. The child's birth out of wedlock, coupled with his father's uncertain status – he was in jail in 1793–94, facing a possible death sentence[54] – might well have led the Campbells to conclude that the best course to follow was to dispose of the child. This would explain their decision to give the young boy to Mrs Campbell's stepmother.

This completes the enumeration of the children known to have been born of slaves in John Campbell's service, listed here in chronological order by date of birth (those of whom we are reasonably sure that they were the children of François and Jeanne are marked with an asterisk):

	Name	Birth	Burial	Age at death
*	Élisabeth	12 April 1785	20 April 1787	2 years
*	François	5 April 1786	8 October 1797	11½ months
*	Marie Anne	31 March 1787	23 June 1799	12 years
	Marie Marguerite	21 April 1787	25 May 1791	4 years
	Jacque	26 May 1788	Unknown	—
*	Marie Angélique	23 October 1788	29 May 1792	3½ years
	Thomas	2 January 1790	Unknown	> 9 years
*	Marie Josephe	19 October 1791	Unknown	—
*	François Xavier	10 March 1793	10 July 1793	4 months
*	François Josué	20 November 1794	Unknown	—

For six of the children, the dates of burial are known (the specific date of death is unknown for two, Marie Angélique and François Xavier, but it would have been within a day or two of their burial). From their ages at death, we see that four died before the age of five, and three after age nine. The ages themselves are not particularly revealing of conditions specific to slaves – infant mortality was common among whites as well as free blacks[55] – but age in conjunction with place of death suggests a pattern. The three youngest died at Longue-Pointe. We know that Élisabeth died there, at age two, at the home of Jean Archambeau (Archambault); Marie Angélique, who died at age three and a half, had had Archambault and his wife as sponsors at her baptism. (Marie Josephe had the same sponsors at her baptism, and Jacque had Archambault as his; but we do not know the date of their deaths.) François Xavier, who died at Longue-Pointe at the age of four months, has no discernible link to the Archambaults. All three children were baptized at Montreal, which suggests that their parents were living there. But the fact that they died at Longue-Pointe, at the Archambault home or elsewhere, would suggest that they were separated from their parents at a very tender age. In that case, they must have been entrusted to a wet nurse – with results that, as we see, were far from happy.

Besides these ten children and their parents, the Campbells had other slaves. There were, for instance, "pierre jean et Marie angélique nègres appartenants à Mr jean Campbelle Lieutenant Colonel des troupes de sa majesté" (Pierre Jean and Marie Angélique, negroes belonging to Mr John Campbell, Lieutenant Colonel of His Majesty's forces), baptized on 12 September 1785.[56] The fact that they were baptized together, that no birth date or age was given for either, and that their parents were unnamed suggests that they were not infants, and that they had only recently come into the Campbells' possession, probably together and from the same source. (They may have been slaves of Campbell's father-in-law, Legislative Councillor Luc de Lacorne St-Luc, who had died the previous year.) This Marie Angélique was clearly not the slave of that name born to François and Jeanne in 1788 and who died in 1792. This second Marie Angélique was older; at her death on 8 September 1795, she was said to be about fourteen.[57] Pierre Jean, we believe, was the "john garçon nègre agé d'environ dix sept ans" (John, negro boy, about seventeen years of age) mentioned in the settlement of Campbell's estate in 1797. In that settlement, by which Mrs Campbell retained "jenny panise" and her daughter Marie Anne, John went to Campbell's brother, Duncan, a merchant of Greenock, Scotland, acting for the rest of the family in Scotland and England. If Pierre Jean/John was really about seventeen at the time, he would have been born *circa* 1780. Judging from Marie Angélique's reputed age at her death, she would have been born *circa* 1781. They may have been brother and sister.

"Jenny panise," Marie Anne, and John were the only surviving slaves mentioned in the division of Campbell's assets after his death. All the others had died or been otherwise disposed of by the fall of 1797. This includes a black couple, Cuff and Violetta, who were both identified at one time as having belonged to Mrs Campbell. Violetta was probably the ten-year-old slave girl who had been sold under the name Violet in

Luc de Lacorne St-Luc (ca 1711–1784), warrior, businessman and political figure, owned slaves under the French régime and under the British.

March 1773 to Montreal merchant Joseph Périnault by Nicholas Smith of Kinderhook, New York, for 100 Spanish dollars.[58] She and Cuff may have been the slaves called Catherine and Cuffé who had been ceded by debt-ridden Town Major James Hughes to his creditors in June 1777 and sold that August by merchant Alexander Hay for £60 to fellow merchant John Franks.[59] In May 1793, Campbell accused the "Negroe wench" Violetta of assaulting and threatening him. The court records provide no hint of what bone Violetta had to pick with him.[60] One year earlier, however, a black patient at the Hôtel-Dieu named Vallette had been identified as a "femme négresse appartenant a md cambel" (a negro woman belonging to Mrs Campbell). The same woman, called Vallet, but still identified as a black woman belonging to Mrs Campbell, spent another three weeks in the hospital in January–February 1793.[61] Vallette or Vallet is undoubtedly a French rendering of the English names Violet or Violetta, and here we find her designated a slave of Mrs Campbell only three months before her dust-up with John Campbell. The next two times that "Vallet" turns up in the hospital – in November 1795 and March 1796 – she is no longer identified as belonging to the now-widowed Mrs Campbell, but both times as the forty-eight-year-old wife of "Caufe nègre" (Cuff, a negro).[62] Cuff was a patient at the same hospital in the fall of 1796, when he was identified as Couph, "appartenant autrefois" (formerly belonging) to Mrs Campbell.[63] The implication of this retrospective labelling, with no mention of a current owner, is that not only was Cuff no longer a Campbell slave, he was no longer anyone's slave.

There are grounds for believing that Violetta and Cuff were free by 1794 at the latest. In May of that year, Catherine Vallet was accused by a sergeant of the 60th Regiment of stabbing a soldier, a charge she fought by claiming self-defence. That summer, the grand jury of the Court of Quarter Sessions brought to the attention of the authorities complaints that a Valette, alias Catherine Valette, was among a group of loose women accused of disturbing the peace in the Quebec Suburb. Two innkeepers were said to be supplying the women with liquor, and one of them, James Seabrook, had them at his place every day and lodged them at night.[64] Valette may have been a slave to drink then, but was obviously no longer a slave of Campbell's. At the end of the year, Marie Louise Valette and her husband, identified as Louis Goffre, had a son, who was christened Joseph. At the boy's death in April 1795, his parents were identified as Joseph Caufre and Marie Valette, "negre et negresse."[65] There can be little doubt that the man called Couph, Louis Goffre, and Joseph Caufre was Cuff, and that Vallet/Vallette, or Catherine, Marie, or Marie Louise Valette, was the woman whose name was given in English as Violetta. (From the birth of their son in 1794, however, we do doubt the age of forty-eight assigned to her in the hospital records in 1795–96. If she was, as we believe, the slave girl Violet who was about ten years old in 1777, she would have been about thirty in 1795–96.)

The records offer only a few more glimpses of Violetta. In April 1804, "Violette, a Blackwoman," testified for the prosecution at the trial of a woman accused of petty larceny.[66] And the otherwise routine lease between two white men of a house in the St-Laurent Suburb in 1810 bears this note: "the black man Cuffs wife to occupy a room in the said house until she can provide another place." The house stood next door to the shop of butcher James Seabrook who, as an innkeeper in 1794, had allegedly offered liquor and lodging to Valette and other women.[67] Although the marginal note refers to "Cuffs wife," she seems to have been on her own; it may be that she should more properly have been termed a widow. We know nothing of Cuff's life after the death of his son. Violetta is believed to have been the black woman who died on 14 June 1821, her age overestimated at ninety years, and her name recorded as Catherine Coff.[68]

How many slaves did the Campbells own? There were, to be sure, ten children born to slaves in their possession, and at least two other youngsters, John (or Pierre Jean) and Marie Angélique, who seem to have come into the Campbell's possession after their birth.[69] In addition, we might estimate that there were about twenty adults if we were to accept without question the welter of names assigned in various records to the Campbell slaves. If, on the other hand, we were to take a more careful tack, we might argue that the adults numbered no more than six or seven, including one Panis, making for eighteen or nineteen slaves all told, rather than the total of thirty-two or so at which we would arrive by the looser count. That is a rather large gap.

By any measure, the Campbells were large slave-holders in the context of Quebec slavery. However, without knowing the precise number of slaves that they owned, and in the absence of deeds of purchase or sale for any of their slaves, it is impossible to calculate the value of their slave holdings. The fact that several of their slaves were at different times registered as patients in the hospital, and that in disposing of the boy Thomas they chose to give him to one of their relatives rather than to sell him to an outsider, and that Mrs Campbell paid considerable sums for the burials of the young slaves Marie Angélique in 1795 and François Jr in 1797 – £4 4s 4d and £2 4s 2d respectively[70] – might suggest that John Campbell and his wife showed their slaves some consideration. On the other hand, the deaths of three very young child slaves at Longue-Pointe might point to a more ambivalent attitude – a readiness to pay for the outside care of infant slaves, but perhaps only so that they would not distract the parents from their labours. The separation of such young children from their parents, ending in the death of the children, cannot have been easy for the parents to bear.

The patchy information about them certainly leaves room for error in the enumeration of the Campbell slaves. The reader who takes the trouble to compare the above survey with the twenty-two Campbell slaves listed in Trudel's *Dictionnaire* will note significant differences between the two. Notably, while the present survey concludes that the black slave we call François was married to an Indian slave, Trudel believes that his wife was black, and while François and his wife appear to have had at least six legitimate mixed-race children, and probably seven, Trudel finds that they had two legitimate black children, and that François's other children – one by an Indian woman – were fathered out of wedlock.[71] The concern is not to establish who is right and who is wrong, so much as to point out the difficulties of establishing the identities of black slaves.

PROBLEMS WITH THE *DICTIONNAIRE*

The value of Trudel's work should by no means be denied. He was the first to plough the ground methodically and to unearth a wealth of interesting data. But his list of slaves stands in need of a thorough revision, as would any first attempt to pin down so many figures whom the records identify so confusingly. Revising the *Dictionnaire* is a daunting task, which no one has ventured to undertake, but it will have to be done sooner or later if a full and accurate picture of slavery in Quebec is to emerge.

By a long and patient search, Trudel attempted to track down and count all slaves, Panis and black, in French Canada from the beginning to the end of slavery. His figures, updated from time to time since 1960, have been widely cited. They are the reference for anyone who has ventured to discuss the size and characteristics of Quebec's slave population. He originally found that, over two centuries, a total of 3,604 persons – 2,509 Panis and 1,095 blacks – had been slaves in French Canada, defined as extending from the Atlantic coast to present-day Michigan. By 1990, when he published his *Dictionnaire,* additional research had led him to estimate that the total figure was 4,092 – 2,692 Panis and 1,400 blacks. A revised edition of his 1960 study, *L'esclavage au Canada français,* published in 2004 under the title *Deux siècles d'esclavage au Québec,* with a companion compact disc of the slightly updated *Dictionnaire,* set the total at 4,185, of which 2,683 were Panis and 1,443 black.

At last count, Trudel had located a total of 1,525 slaves in Montreal over 200 years, of whom 518, or slightly more than one-third, were black.[72] Of particular interest to us are the roughly 370 black slaves whom he locates at Montreal from 1760 onward. We believe that perhaps as many as 150 of those, or roughly 40 per cent, were not slaves while in French Canada, or were slaves but not black, or were black slaves counted in Trudel's survey more than once at Montreal, or at Montreal and some other place. On the other hand, about 100 black slaves who show up at Montreal are not listed. If we are correct, any statistical analysis based on such a compilation is vitiated from the outset.

As it turns out, a total figure of 370 to 400 slaves recorded on the island of Montreal under the British regime seems about right, the number in any one year varying between less than twenty and about sixty. These are relatively slight numbers. A census of the Province of Quebec conducted at the end of 1784 tends to support this. Although the province then was divided into two administrative and judicial districts – the district of Montreal, which stretched north from the American border to the limits of settlement and west from the St-Maurice River as far as Detroit; and the district of Quebec, which covered the whole eastern part of the territory to the Gulf of St Lawrence – the census, reverting to the division that had existed before the Conquest and that was to be restored in 1790, sandwiched a third district, that of Trois-Rivières, between the two. The total population of the province was found to be 113,012, of which 304, or 0.27 per cent, were slaves. The majority of slaves – 212 of them – were located in the District of Montreal, representing 0.38 per cent of the district's population of 55,634.[73] Of those 212 slaves, most would have been Panis. But even supposing that half were black, they would have represented only 0.19 per cent of the district's total population. If we were to use that percentage to estimate the number of black slaves in the city and suburbs of Montreal – whose population is thought to have been between 6,000 and 7,500 – this would yield a total of at most fourteen or fifteen black slaves at Montreal. But, of course, the slaves were not evenly distributed through the district. The present count suggests that the number of slaves at Montreal in 1784 might have been slightly fewer than forty, including children.

Trudel well knew the problems that bedevil any attempt to quantify the slave population. First among these is that, where black slaves were concerned, numerous records leave them unnamed; they are simply a "negro" or "negress" or a "black" or "mulatto." Here is the ultimate act of slave resistance: men and women whose identities were often considered beneath notice while they lived defy posthumous identification now that we would very much like to know who they were. Some or all may resurface in another record under a proper name, but who is to say whether Marie or César or Sarah or Thomas is among the anonymous slaves previously counted? And those single-named slaves might show up elsewhere with a family name, so that we may wonder whether John Brown might be one of the unnamed or one of the slaves named John, or Jean, spotted earlier, or someone else entirely. In the 1790s, for example, Reuben Thomas, a free black man, was familiarly known to a black slave of the time as Jupiter: he may have been the Jupiter recorded a decade earlier as a slave of Sir John Johnson.[74] "In the face of such confusion, there is little that we can do,"

Trudel wrote in 1990, referring to the overall picture "so that when we say that the slave population amounted to 4,092, we mean *about 4,000.*"[75]

Add to these difficulties the fact that Trudel did the bulk of his research in the 1950s, the age of pen and pencil, typewriters, and index cards; consulting old church records, which today are available on microfilm at several archive centres and libraries (and tomorrow online), required him to trudge from church to church. Disaster struck after the publication of his study in 1960, when a fire in 1965 destroyed the slave list he had readied for publication. He was not able to reconstruct it until years afterward, when he had retired from teaching.[76] Archival records are much more accessible today, including some that were not available in the 1950s, and the tools and technology of archival research are much improved.

For us, however, a basic flaw in Trudel's slave enumeration is not attributable to problems of access or technology, but flows from its guiding principle that all blacks who crop up in the records must be counted as slaves: even if the records show them to be free, they must be presumed to have been slaves in French Canada at some time. This presumption is based on the saying that, barring proof of manumission, "tout Noir est esclave, quelque part qu'il se trouve" (every black is a slave, wherever he may be found).[77] This adage may have served as a convenient pretext for a governor of New France refusing to send a captured black man back to New England or New York,[78] but it does not yield an enumeration of Canadian slaves after 1760, and particularly after the American War of Independence, that is anywhere near accurate, any more than would the reverse assumption that all blacks were free unless proven otherwise. Thus, the *Dictionnaire* lists as Canadian slaves people like Dublin, one of several blacks captured in a raid on Ballston, New York, in 1780, all of whom were sold at Montreal, according to the commander of the expedition, except for "Dublin who being known to be a freeman was liberated and enlisted in His Majesty's service;"[79] César Jahomet (Caesar Johonnot), a slave in Boston who had been freed there by 1783, and still resolutely free when, three years later, in the earliest record of his presence at Montreal, he prosecuted a soldier for assault; Diah, the fugitive slave from Plattsburgh, New York, who was a free man once he crossed the border in 1794 and was so acknowledged by a Montreal court when his American master came after him (see chapter 2); and Cesar, a "Free Negroe" who moved to Montreal from New London, Connecticut, and bound himself as an indentured servant to Dr John Henry Aussem for ten years from 23 November 1796.[80] It also lists an anonymous old black washerwoman who was reported to have been working at the Montreal jail in December 1838, justifying her inclusion on the grounds that, in her youth at least, she must have been a slave,[81] although there is no compelling reason to suppose that if she had been a slave, it would have been in French Canada. Still more perplexing is the inclusion of Sambo, the coachman of the Roquebrune family at L'Assomption, east of Montreal, in the late nineteenth century, fondly remembered by author Robert de Roquebrune in a memoir that he wrote in the 1940s. Roquebrune, who was born in 1889, wrote that Sambo had been a Virginia slave before the American Civil War (1861–65), then a domestic servant at Boston, before moving to Montreal. Making his way from Montreal to Joliette one winter night, he had stopped for shelter and food at the manor house of L'Assomption, the home of the Roquebrunes, and never left.[82] Sambo, who landed on the Roquebrunes' doorstep at some unspecified year in the second half of the nineteenth century, "does not seem to have been a slave in Canada," says the *Dictionnaire*, yet it still lists him.[83] Listing blacks found in Canada until late into the nineteenth century as sometime slaves in Canada renders meaningless any distinction between freedom and slavery. Leaving aside the Panis, this yields a *Dictionnaire* that is a spotty list of black people rather than what it purports to be, a list of slaves in French Canada.

The conflation of "negro" with "slave" has been a persistent problem. It was a feature of early British and French laws that used the terms *negro* or *nègre* to mean "slave." It has led to popular notions that virtually all blacks in Canada in the nineteenth century were fugitive American slaves. It also accounts, it seems, for the oral traditions of a "slave cemetery" rather than simply a black cemetery at Nigger Rock, or the notion that the early black settlers of Oro Township in Simcoe County, Ontario, were American runaways, as though white Canadians were not prepared to accept that blacks could be of an origin other than American; that, American or not, some were born free; and that some may have had roots in Canada that were as deep as their own, if not deeper. As historian Robin Winks remarked, "One may ask, What is said of the British North American attitude toward Negroes when all were assumed to be fugitives?" While they may have been looked on as heroes to some extent, fugitive slaves were, at another level and by definition, people born into a degraded state who had fled from their problem rather than fight it. A modern-day echo of the age-old problem might be seen in the common assumption that a black resident of Canada must be an immigrant.[84]

Through some confusion that may have occurred in the reconstruction of Trudel's list after the loss by fire of the original, the *Dictionnaire* lists among the slaves at Quebec twenty-one black Montrealers of the early nineteenth century, most of whom were not slaves in Canada and not residents of Quebec.[85] Certainly, some blacks moved from one city to the other, but it is clear from the sources cited or the events in which they were involved that these are Montreal sources and occurrences, confused with Quebec ones. Maria Keeling (or Kellings), for example, the girl at whose Montreal baptism in 1803 Julia Johnson and Joseph Pierson acted as sponsors, is listed as a slave baptized that year at Quebec.[86] Citing a newspaper notice of 1792, the *Dictionnaire* identifies a "mulatto" at Quebec named Eber Wedden, a shoemaker's apprentice about nineteen years old, who deserted his master's service.[87] Ebert Weldin, as his father wrote the name,[88] was not a slave but an apprentice, as the notice stated. He was indentured on 1 May 1789 at age sixteen to a shoemaker of Sault-au-Récollet on the north side of Montreal Island. In the notice of Weldin's escape in company with a white employee, his master offered a $20 reward to whoever "apprehends the above mentioned men, and delivers them at Montreal, or to the Subscriber at Sault au Recollet." Neither a Quebec resident nor a slave, Ebert Weldin was one of four children of James and Anna Weldin of present-day Laval, north of Montreal: if he is to be classed as a slave, what of his parents and siblings? They are not listed in the *Dictionnaire*. In fact, none of them was a slave.[89]

If the *Dictionnaire* falls short in its stated object of enumerating all slaves, it is in some measure because, as in the case of Judith, it fails to meet its other stated goal, too ambitious for one researcher, of providing all the available biographical data about them.[90] To do this would have required more space than the 490 pages allotted to the list – and a lifetime of research. More detailed biographical information, however, would have prevented many duplications and conflations. Thus the *Dictionnaire* lists Jane Cook's Charlotte twice, once under that name, and once as an unnamed black woman freed in 1798.[91] In neither instance is she identified as having become the wife of John Trim. Trim is identified as the husband of Margaret (Plauvier) Moore, who was in fact the wife of his friend Henry Moore.[92] Hilaire Lamour is also listed twice, without any information on his slave past, once as Antoine Lamour, husband of Catherine, and again as Hilaire Lamour, of whom all that is said is that he made his first communion in 1805. "Antoine" Lamour's wife is listed with him as Catherine, who was buried at the Hôpital-Général on 14 August 1811, and also separately as Catherine, a black woman residing at the same hospice and buried the same day.[93] Manuel Allen is also counted twice, once under that name as the father of Jean Édouard Allen, and under the single name Emmanuel as the father of Marie Anne (alias Marie Hélène) Allen.[94] Both children are counted as slaves, but both were born free. A Montreal slave listed under the name Rose is actually three different slaves of that name.[95]

In counting the slaves in such a vast territory as French Canada, we cannot arrive at an estimate of the total by simply totting up the numbers of blacks found in each locality. The numbers would overlap, as we would inevitably find that some resided at one time at, say, Montreal, and at some other time in some other place. Moreover, we would need to identify and subtract those blacks never known to have been enslaved in Canada.

The case of Robert Ashley and his family offers a pertinent illustration. Drawing from a faulty entry in church records, the *Dictionnaire* lists Ashley, who died at Montreal on 22 January 1818 and was buried as "Joseph Astley or Ashley ... an African," as Joseph Ashley, a Montreal slave. He is said to have been the father of a slave woman named Margaret Ashley, who died one month after him. But "Joseph" Ashley is also listed among slaves at Quebec, under the name Robert Ashley.[96] Robert Ashley is identified as a former cabin boy aboard the ship *Athena* (a misreading of *Adeona,* a brig on which Ashley served as steward, not as cabin boy), the husband of Margaret, and father of Elizabeth Ashley, born at Quebec in 1804. The Quebec list contains another duplication in that Ashley's wife is the subject of two entries – one as Margaret, wife of Robert Ashley, and another, under her maiden name of Margaret Pearce, with no indication that she was the Margaret married to Robert Ashley.[97] As for "Joseph" Ashley's daughter Margaret, listed at Montreal without mention of her mother's name, it is clear from the details given about her acting as sponsor at two baptisms at Montreal in 1803 and 1804 (the 1803 baptism, in fact, took place at

Quebec), that this Margaret is a conflation of Ashley's wife, Margaret Pearce, and their daughter, Margaret Ashley, born at Montreal in 1815, who did indeed die there shortly after her father in 1818 – not a slave woman, but a free black girl, just over two years old.[98] The *Dictionnaire* does not mention the Ashleys' two other Montreal-born children, Ann and Thomas,[99] which is just as well since none of the Ashley children was a slave. As for Ashley and his wife, we may speculate that they had been slaves in Canada, but we have no evidence of it.

Jacob Smith and his wife, the mulatto Catherine Coll, who was unsuccessfully claimed as a slave by tailor Peter McFarlane in 1791, are another case in point. They were both free when they moved to Quebec from Montreal in the mid-1790s. They are not listed at both places, as Ashley is, but only at Quebec. On the basis of a misidentification in the records of a Quebec hospital in 1817, in which their family names were switched, the *Dictionnaire* lists them as Jacob Coale, "probably a negro," husband of Catherine Smith, definitely a black woman. This leads to further confusion, because there happened to be an older black slave at Quebec called Catherine Smith. Confounding these two women, the *Dictionnaire* misidentifies Jacob Smith's wife as the Catherine Smith who was baptized at Quebec in 1796 and supposedly identified on that occasion as the forty-six-year-old slave of a saddler named McLane.[100] There is also a problem with the *Dictionnaire*'s identification of Jacob Smith as "probably a negro." We might assume that Smith was black, and his occupations do nothing to suggest otherwise: he worked as a "servant" of Montreal tailor Benaiah Gibb, and after moving to Quebec, he was identified as a "labourer," "seller of cakes," "cakeman," "pastry cook," and "confectioner," the kinds of jobs that some blacks held. But no surviving document yet found identifies him as black; the one distinctive trait mentioned in the records is that he was missing a hand. Several witnesses who testified in his suit against McFarlane identified him by reference to this amputation.[101] He is again the man with one hand in papers of the 1790s relating to his sale to Richard Wragg, a Loyalist blacksmith from Saratoga, New York, of a 200-acre land grant on the Ottawa River that he had received in 1789, probably for military service in the American War of Independence.[102] The absence of any reference to his race suggests that in fact he was white, the default racial identity of the time, never baldly stated. Indeed, the names of the sponsors at the baptisms of his four children suggest that he may have been of German origin or at least that his connections, perhaps through his war service, were mainly German.[103]

As we can see, the difficulties in identifying and counting the slaves go well beyond naming the unnamed. First, we must determine who was black, and then which blacks were slaves. We cannot safely assume that all blacks, especially those who surfaced after the American War of Independence, and more especially after 1800, had at one time been slaves in Canada. Times had changed. In the last quarter of the eighteenth century, the status quo came under serious fire in three great popular upheavals. The revolutions in Britain's American colonies (1775–83), in France (1789–99), and in the French slave colony of St-Domingue (1791–1804) shattered the old order. The first two, insofar as their goal was to establish republican forms of government based on the equality of all, propagated the highly contagious idea that there should be no kings at the top of the social heap and no slaves at the bottom. The French and Americans may not have lived up to those ideals as concerns the bottom ranks of society, but once the genie was out of the bottle there was no stopping it. In St-Domingue, it was the slaves who threw off bondage and colonial exploitation to establish the first independent black republic in the New World. Not all blacks who show up in Quebec in the wake of these momentous events were slaves, nor can we presume that they had formerly been slaves in French Canada. Although the blacks of New France had almost invariably entered the colony as slaves, in the last quarter of the eighteenth century, some blacks entered the successor British colony under their own steam or as members of a military corps. The old saw that every black was a slave, wherever he or she was found, if it ever had validity, no longer held.

Even among the named, the problems of ascertaining who was black, never mind a slave, seem endless. We saw in the first chapter how, in a court case in 1763, Marie *dite* Manon was identified as a "panis esclave" on her first appearance, then as a "négresse." It does seem that she was black, but the original labelling of her as an Indian leaves a lingering doubt. When eleven-year-old Marie Magdelene died at Lachine in April 1767, she was termed a Panis, like her mother, Marie. But her father, who had died a month earlier, was Charles (alias Charlot), "nègre de nation." Was Marie Magdelene really more Indian than black, and deemed so then? If so, are we bound to follow suit and omit her from a count of blacks of that time?[104] Yet the children of the Campbell slaves François, a black man, and Jeanne, a Panis, were considered to be blacks. What about Henry, a "Garçon Nègre Metis" bought at Detroit in 1786 by Victor Baudin *dit* Sansrémission and resold as a slave (with Henry's consent, it was said) for 1,000 livres in March 1787 by the same Baudin, then a Montreal merchant, to François Larocque, merchant of L'Assomption? Did the expression "Nègre Metis" mean that Henry, then said to be about twenty-three, was the son of black and Indian parents, or was "Metis" used in its original sense of mixed race, making him perhaps the child of black and white parents? One way or another, Henry was at least partly black.[105] In the case of Daniel Steel, this is not at all certain. He was a "mulatto" when he was hired as a domestic servant in August 1792 by John Conolly of Lachine, but at his baptism in 1794 he was "a Pawney."[106] The same goes for Charlotte or (Marie Charlotte) Prudhomme, alias Poll McDonald, who seems to have lived by her wits, at Quebec in the early 1790s, then at Montreal for a few years, and back at Quebec by 1800. A Quebec newspaper identified her as a mulatto in 1791; at Montreal, in 1793, she was termed a Panis, apparently not in the sense of an Indian slave but of a free Indian of lowly status. It is tempting to think that she was indeed Indian or Metis, except that in several cases where she was accused of an offence, some black acquaintance – in Montreal, George Baron and Tom, the latter a slave of Judge John Fraser; at Quebec, a woman called Jane – was also allegedly involved.[107] Jean Jacques, a sailor who died at Montreal in 1822 at age twenty-four or thirty-one, depending on

The watercolourist who sketched this Kahnawake Mohawk couple in 1818 gave them black faces. Contemporary documents can sometimes lead us to confuse blacks and Indians.

the source, was said to be a "metis" from the French West Indies; it may be that he was descended from members of some near-extinct nation indigenous to the area, but we suspect that he was, in fact, of mixed black and white parentage.[108]

As difficult as it is to discern the traits of these distant characters when they are standing still, it becomes incalculably more difficult when mobility blurs the picture. Slaves were always on the move, whether physically, nominally, or socially: *physically*, by moving or simply travelling with their masters, by running away or being sold off, or even, in some cases, by banishment; *nominally*, as in the case of "Judith" and "John Gray," or Sarah/Charlotte Cavilhe/Marie Charle McGill by going through name changes that were sometimes their own choice, sometimes imposed by others, sometimes simply a clerical mistake, sometimes the result of taking on a baptismal name or, in the case of women, a married name; *socially*, chiefly by graduating from slavery to freedom. When these three forms of migration are combined, as, say, when a slave goes free, moves to or from Montreal, and is recorded under a different name than formerly it is easy to lose the thread. In an urban centre such as Montreal, the problem of identification can be compounded by the fact that the services, opportunities, and temptations that the city offered – employment, hospitals, churches, courts, lawyers, notaries, taverns, markets, prostitution and other illicit pursuits, detention facilities, etc. – drew many people for more or less extended periods from the surrounding country. Not all blacks, slave or free, who show up in the city are properly Montreal residents. One more problem, as we have seen, is that some records refer to slaves as "servants"; without some other source to clarify their status, or some elucidating circumstance, that status remains a matter of conjecture. And if we cling to the myth that slavery continued until 1834, we will also be tempted to see slaves where there were none.

Of course, the sheer volume of records that must be consulted poses its own problems in ascertaining black identities. There are gaps in these sources – some records are missing and others illegible, whether from the poor quality of the writing or printing, or from deterioration of the paper on which they were written. The gaps invite speculation, but it must be careful. We must beware of jumping to conclusions of the sort that have led to the hasty misidentification of some persons as black simply because they were called L'Africain[109] or Negrié,[110] or some other suggestive name. Trudel warned against this in respect of the Nègre family, a white family of French origin whose descendants lived in the Montreal area at this time.[111]

Such are some of the difficulties involved in identifying black slaves and simply counting heads, never mind analyzing the makeup of the slave population at different periods by age, sex, origin, occupation, religion, life span, sale price, etc. Needless to say, much the same complications arise in seeking to establish the size and characteristics of the black population as a whole, slave and free.

The present study estimates that about 390 blacks in Montreal post-1760 were enslaved in Canada at some time. Given the number of variables, this figure does not diverge significantly from the 370 found in the *Dictionnaire*, but it encompasses many different persons, with different characteristics. While Trudel, concerned with

Quebec, Feb. 1, 1789.

TO BE SOLD,
A Pawney Boy,

ABOUT seventeen years of age, remarkable sober, very healthy and stout, and an excellent servant to attend table. His present master has had him nine years, and has now no further use for him. *Enquire of the Printer.*

FIVE POUNDS Reward.

BROKE out of His Majesty's Goal in this City, on the Evening of the 3d Instant, AUGUSTIN MORAIN, Canadian born, about Twenty-eight Years of Age, five Feet six Inches high, well made, swarthy Complexion, short black Hair, and small black Eyes: Had on a Canadian Fashion brown Frock, Waistcoat and Breeches, Cowskin Indian Shoes, and a red Cloth Huzzar Cap, garnish'd with Martin Skins. Whoever will secure the said Prisoner, in either of His Majesty's Goals at Quebec or Montreal, shall be intitled to the above Reward, and all reasonable Charges, paid by

JOSEPH GRIDLEY, D. P. *Marshal.*

N. B. It is probable the said Prisoner has taken the Road to Sorrel.
QUEBEC, 6th February, 1767.

CINQ LIVRES *de Recompense, Argent courant de cette Province.*

IL s'est échappé de la prison de sa Majesté en cette ville, sur le soir du trois de ce mois, un nommé AUGUSTIN MORIN, natif de Canada, agé d'environ vingt-huit ans, ayant cinq pieds six pouces d'hauteur, bien fait, d'un teint basané, des cheveux noirs courts, et de petits yeux noirs.

Il avoit sur lui un capot brun, à la mode du Canada, veste et culote, des souliers de boeuf du païs, et un casque à la Huzarde de drap rouge, garni de Martre: Toute personne qui remettra le dit prisonnier dans quelque que ce soit des prisons de sa Majesté, à Québec ou à Montréal, sera en droit de recevoir la susdite Récompense, qui lui sera payée par,

JOSEPH GRIDLEY, D. P. *Maréchal.*

N. B. Il y a apparence que ce prisonnier a pris le chemin de Sorrel.

RUN-AWAY, on Thursday Night, the 18th Instant, from Mr. GRANT at St. Roch, a Negro Man, named Dick, about 40 Years of Age, 5 Feet 10 Inches high: Had on a blue short Coat and green Waistcoat; wears a Cap with an old Hat; shaves his Head and takes Scotch Snuff. He carried with him a brown Frock and Scarlet Waistcoat with Gold Basket Buttons, and some Bed-Cloaths. Any Person who apprehends the said Negroe, shall receive FIVE POUNDS Reward, upon restoring him to the Owner. ——— *Quebec, 19th October, 1768.*

IL s'est échappé, Dimanche le soir, de chez Mr. GRANT, à St. Roch, un Négre nommé DICK, âgé d'environ 40 ans, de la taille de 5 pieds dix pouces: Il portoit un court habit rouge et une veste verte; il porte un bonnet avec un vieux chapeau, il a les cheveux rasés, prend du tabac d'Ecosse: Il a emporté avec lui un surtout brun, et une véste écartate, avec des boutons de fil d'or, et quelques fournitures de lit. Toute personne qui arrêtera le dit Négre, aura CINQUE LIVRES de récompense, en le remettant au proprietaire.
Québec, le 19 Octobre, 1768.

50 2   MONTREAL, 20th *Oct.* 1790.

RUN AWAY

From the Subscriber,

A Negro Man named Richard,

About five foot seven inches high, twenty seven years of age, and has a cast in one eye; had on when he went away, a dark brown jacket and long trowsers; whoever will apprehend and return him to the subscriber shall receive two guineas reward and all reasonable expences paid.
Rosseter Hoyle.

4-6 m   QUEBEC, Dec. 14, 1789.

RUN AWAY

From the Subscriber, last spring, a Negro wench named *Ruth*, it is suspected she is about St. John's. If any person will apprehend the said Negro wench and deliver her to Mr. *Fitch*, at St. John's, Mr. *Dillon* at Montreal, or the Subscriber in Quebec, all reasonable expences will be paid, by
JOHN SAUL.

Images of a standing or running figure sometimes illustrated notices about slaves, but they were also used in notices about absconding apprentices and servants, army and ship deserters, and jail breakers – black, Indian or white.

the larger picture, does not provide a detailed statistical breakdown of the Montreal slave population, he does give certain characteristics for both black and Indian slaves in general in French Canada. For example, he estimates the proportion of males to females among black slaves at 57.3 per cent to 42.8 per cent;[112] for Montreal post-1760, the ratio seems to have been more like 53:46. Trudel estimates the average price of black slaves to have been £37 10s (900 livres);[113] based on eighty-seven transactions after 1760 involving sixty-two individual Montreal slaves (some were sold several times) for which a price is given, we find about the same – an average price of £38 10s – the average price for males being slightly more than £42s, and for females, close to £36. Documentary evidence indicates the lowest price paid was £12 10s, three males and two females having sold for that price. This does not take into account the undocumented claim made by a New York State resident that his slave, Pompey, captured by Indians during the War of Independence, had been sold for only eleven dollars, or less than £3.[114] The highest price for both males and females was £100, recorded for one male and one female. In addition to these transactions involving individual slaves, the prices paid in fourteen sales transactions involving groups of two or more slaves are known, but it is generally impossible to give the estimated monetary value for each person. The prices ranged from £35 for a mother and her young son to about £156 for a group consisting of one grown female, two grown males, and a baby boy. Where Trudel estimated the average age at death of black slaves at 25.2 years,[115] it seems in fact to have been 32.35 years for black slaves at Montreal after 1760, males living to an average of 31.9 years and females 32.8. (The life expectancy at birth of the overall population is generally estimated to have been about thirty years.) With regard to infant mortality, of the 113 slaves for whom there is an estimated age at death, thirty-one (fifteen males and sixteen females) died before the age of ten, fourteen of those before they reached the age of one year, and twenty-one before they turned two. As for the provenance of these black slaves, where such is known or might reasonably be supposed, ninety-seven came from the American colonies or the United States, including sixty-nine from New York and seven, possibly eight, from Massachusetts; fifty-three were born in Quebec, thirty-nine of them at Montreal; ten came from the western posts of Detroit and Michilimackinac; nine from the French West Indies, five of them from St-Domingue; at least five came from Africa, via the West Indies or the United States; and two came from Upper Canada.

Of course, these estimates, other than the breakdown by gender, are based on very incomplete information. For these 390 slaves there are records for the sales of only sixty-two (in eighty-seven transactions) mentioning prices in specie; an age at death is recorded for only 113, or fewer than one-third of the total, and those recorded ages are highly unreliable; and some idea of the origins of only 176, or about 45 per cent of the total, survives in the historical record. These figures are offered here not as definitive statements, but as a demonstration of how shaky such analyses are and how far we are from a reliable statistical picture of slavery.

Trudel blazed a trail for those trying to trace the black presence in colonial Canada. Thanks to his labours, the time is past when historians could pretend to offer a serious overview of slavery in one locality or one colony, let alone the whole territory of present-day Canada, by dabbling – the spotting of a slave here, a slave there – or even by studying a single source, however thoroughly. Any worthwhile work must rest on as comprehensive as possible an enumeration and identification of the population of the area under study. It is not a simple task, and anyone who attempts it had better be prepared to spend a great deal of time juggling minutiae. One factor that, in theory at least, places this goal within reach is that we are not dealing with a cast of thousands; in Montreal under British rule, there were at most about 400 black slaves over a period of about forty years. This relatively small number presents a unique opportunity to look at slaves in detail, case by case. It has at times served as a pretext to dismiss slavery as inconsequential. This is to miss the point – that slavery existed at all, that it was a given, and that Quebecers of the day took it in stride.

THREE

"Things As They Were"

For most Canadians, the word *slavery*, thanks to the overwhelming weight of US cultural productions, evokes lurid scenes of black exploitation drawn from the nineteenth-century American South. We think of *Roots* or *Uncle Tom's Cabin,* countless horror-filled slave narratives or television documentaries; we think of slave ships, coffles, chains, droves of black men, women and children living under the lash, labouring under a baking plantation sun; slave drivers, patrols, bloodhounds, lynchings, mutilations, real or imagined slave revolts brutally suppressed, laws forbidding the teaching of reading and writing to slaves and denying blacks any standing in the courts other than as the accused and the presumed guilty. We think, in short, of a world in which the rule of law was designed to effect a perfect imbalance of power – absolute white control and abject black submission. The thought of a twelve-year-old slave girl enrolled in the boarding school of the Ursuline nuns at Quebec in 1772 does not quite fit this picture.[1] It stops us in our tracks.

The mere fact that, as early as the 1830s, the historical fact of slavery in Quebec could have been largely forgotten or denied strongly suggests that the reality of slavery in this northern colony was different from what it was elsewhere in the Americas, notably in the southern United States and the West Indies, not only in terms of scope and duration but also with respect to its societal impact and its legacy. It might help if we think of slavery as a cancer. Elsewhere it metastasized, affecting all facets of colonial or national life; in Quebec, it did not. Elsewhere, it defined societies; in Quebec, it did not. Elsewhere the memory of slavery was never lost; in Quebec it was, and quickly.

One reason is that, as we have seen, slaves in Quebec were few. A black slave girl enrolled in a boarding school in 1772 was surely an exception, but in a sense the situation of every slave in Quebec was *sui generis,* the numbers being so sparse.

Whites were not so numerous, either. A visitor to Quebec in 1817 was astonished to find that the population of its two chief cities was so small. To an American, he wrote, "the smallness of towns so noted, and so long established as Quebec and Montreal, is inconceivable, and scarcely credible ... I could myself with difficulty believe, that the population of the latter is now estimated at but fifteen thousand, of the former at no more than twelve."[2] At the turn of the century, when slavery had died out, the population of Montreal had been about 9,000.[3] The importance and reputation of the city, founded in 1642, clearly rested on factors other than a head count. So it was with slavery: its historical significance far outstrips its demographic weight.

In terms of numbers, black slavery was marginal; to some people, it was invisible. It may even be a stretch to speak of a slave "population." But slavery was a mainstream affair, however slight the number of slaves. Practised by a few, it was accepted by the many as part of the fixed order of a hierarchical society. As Henry Scadding put it more than century ago, slavery "at the beginning was received in Canada, apparently as an inevitable part and parcel of the social arrangements of a colony on this continent."[4] It is difficult for us to leap back more than 200 years and grasp that what is unquestionably evil to us was not so then. It is tempting but simplistic to believe that, had we been alive in the days of slavery, we would have fought it, and that, had we been slaves, we would have resisted our situation spiritedly.

When Royal Navy Captain Henry Byam Martin toured the Canadas in 1832, slavery was a thing of the past there. He went on to the United States, where he sketched this tabletop slave auction in Charleston, South Carolina, in March 1833.

Our modern sensibilities can easily lead us to demonize slave-owners and view them all as Simon Legrees, even though many were the "good people" of the day. This is part of the extraordinary ordinariness of slavery in Quebec. To Adam Mabane, slavery may have been "contrary to religion," but this was certainly not the common view. Thus, the Reverend Jean-Baptiste Curatteau, the Sulpician priest who, in 1767, founded what is today the Collège de Montréal, had his "nègre," roughly sixty years old, whom he bought in 1779 from the estate of fur-trade merchant Ignace Bourassa for 650 livres, and in 1780 the Swiss-born Reverend David Chabrand Delisle, the first civilian Protestant pastor of Montreal, paid £20 for Charles, a black man captured by British raiders in the American War of Independence.[5] With a straight face, the Reverend John Doty, a Loyalist refugee from Schenectady and the Anglican rector of Sorel, could plead with Governor Frederick Haldimand in 1784 for free rations for the black boy he had just purchased "with some difficulty to myself."[6] The nuns of the Congregation of Notre Dame had an old black slave, Étienne Paul, who died in hospital in November 1772 at the reported age of about 70.[7] As James Singer, deputy commissary general at Sorel, prepared to leave the country in April 1784, he gave Dianne, "Négresse de nation," thirty years old and six years his slave, to the Hospitalières de Saint-Joseph, the nursing sisters of the Hôtel-Dieu in Montreal, who, in gratitude for his "generosity and pious charity toward them," promised ever to pray for Singer's long life and prosperity.[8]

The case of the peripatetic Reverend Louis Payet (1749–1801) is instructive. This Montreal-born missionary was stationed at St-Martin on Île Jésus (Laval) in the 1770s, at Detroit from 1781 to 1786, then as *curé* at St-Antoine on the Richelieu River until 1798, and finally at Verchères, where he died on 26 August 1801 at the age of fifty-two. His black slave Catherine, said to be twenty, was baptized at Detroit on 29 November 1785. No sooner was Payet back in Montreal the following summer when Catherine, said to be twenty-four, entered the hospital on 5 August, where she was to remain for 10 days. As late as 22 July, Payet had been at Michilimackinac, where he had baptized the young slave Rosalie Bonga, a future resident of Montreal.[9] Payet must have brought another slave east with him along with Catherine, because that November, a certain François, described as "Nêgre, Esclave, du Curé Payet" of St-Antoine, died there at the reputed age of thirty-one.[10] Less than two months later, Payet, represented by Joseph Filteau, bought the black slave boy Pomp from Samuel Mix of St-Jean for £20. Payet had the boy christened Jean Baptiste *dit* Pompé in 1789, at the same time as his Panis slave, César (christened Antoine). Both boys were said to be about twelve years old.[11] Payet had one more slave whom we know of. This was Rose, who was said to be about thirty years old when Payet bought her from Joseph Lamothe of Montreal, captain in the Indian Department, for 600 livres on 4 March 1795.[12] She had once belonged to William Byrne, who had served as a captain in Sir John Johnson's King's Royal Regiment of New York in the American War of Independence. In July 1793, Byrne had given her and a black boy called Tanno to his adoptive son, Philip, as a wedding present. On 15 June 1794, Philip Byrne sold Rose to Simon Meloche of Lachine for 360 livres. One

Hôtel-Dieu, Montreal, 1829. The nursing sisters of this hospital expressed their eternal gratitude to a military officer who gave them a slave named Dianne in 1786.

month later, Meloche resold Rose for 83½ Spanish dollars to Lamothe, from whom she passed into Payet's hands.[13] Payet kept Rose for eighteen months. On 2 September 1796, he gave boat captain François Bellet Jr of Quebec a power of attorney to sell Rose for the best price he could get. Bellet sold her a week later for 500 livres to merchant Thomas Lée of Quebec.[14]

From Payet's case, we get some idea of the convenience that slavery represented to wandering men of his stamp – the missionaries, military officers, fur traders, and others who went off into the bush or who, because of their occupations, never settled in one place for long. It would have been difficult to find servants willing to engage in hinterland hut-keeping for such men and to shoulder the isolation this entailed, especially in the service of a celibate priest who would brook no frivolity or dissipation. We can scarcely picture white females volunteering for such rugged wilderness service – or society approving of their doing so. Similarly, a man whose posting changed every few years might have found it tiresome to have to look for new servants every time he moved. But, as long as there was slavery, there was no need to hunt for suitable, willing candidates and to negotiate terms of employment. As Payet did with Catherine, or as John Stock did with Rose, one could simply buy servants and take this disposable human property where one pleased, discarding them at will, without regard for their safe return home. Slavery was part and parcel of the great age of wilderness wanderings, and there could well be a link between the passing of that age and the end of slavery in Quebec.

To excuse the conduct of slave-holders by saying that they were simply men and women "of their time" – as has been said, for instance, of James McGill – is to imply that a practice now universally condemned as a crime against humanity was then considered nothing out of the ordinary.[15] Indeed, besides the slaves and slave-owners, slavery enlisted a host of helping hands – the slave-owners' families, the newspaper publishers who printed notices of slave sales and escapes, the notaries who drew up the deeds of sale and the witnesses thereto, the sheriffs, lawyers, bailiffs, couriers and other middlemen, the magistrates who adopted regulations of public order barring "slaves" from taverns, the estate executors, businessmen and auctioneers who handled slave transactions, the priests and ministers who baptized and married them, the whites who served as witnesses at their baptisms and weddings, and even the white wet-nurses to whom some slave newborns appear to have been farmed out. But the owners went farther than most in that they actually acquired slaves. Relatively few did, as the small size of the slave contingent indicates.

LOW VISIBILITY

If a small white population containing few slave-owners made for little demand for slaves, so too did the short growing season and the absence of single-crop production – rice, sugar, cotton, or tobacco – that would have necessitated a constant supply of gang labour. The nearest thing to gang labour in any sense – other than logging bees, the occasional corvée for military transport duty in times of crisis, or the few days each year when seigneurial tenants were called on to labour unpaid at public works – was the fur trade. It was a business that saw brigades of paddlers and pack-haulers – porters, we would call them, were we speaking of Africa, except that these were white – canoeing deep into the hinterland, there to spend the winters in the service of a bwana, or *bourgeois* as he was termed, trading manufactured goods for the pelts harvested by indigenous trappers and hunters. The occasional black slave or free black man was found among these voyageurs, but few masters ensconced along the St Lawrence would have trusted a slave to return after tasting the freedom of the continent – and what slave would have willingly done so? Besides, French-Canadians were predominant in the trade, and anyone who contemplated replacing them with slaves would have been a social engineer of uncommon foolishness, given the extra expense that the rigid supervision of slave crews would have entailed. Canadians would have resisted any attempt to exclude them from this traditional occupation, so much a part of their culture; besides providing a livelihood for many, it offered the footloose and adventurous an escape from the constraints of colonial society.

The limited market for slaves could not justify any organized international slave trading or large-scale importation. Hence there were no squalid slave ships, no slave depots, slave huts, or other physical markers of the slaves' presence. This "slaugh-

HERALD,
Miscellany & Advertiser:

[Num. 22.] THURSDAY, April 22, 1790. [Vol. I.

TO BE SOLD,
A Young Healthy NEGRO WOMAN capable of most kind of business is a good cook and house-maid, understands milking cows and making butter, and of undoubted sobriety and honesty.---For particulars apply to the printer.

22---4 Quebec, April 19, 1790.

On MONDAY next, the 26th inst.
WILL BE SOLD,
BY
Public Auction,
At the MERCHANT'S COFFEE-HOUSE,
THE SCHOONER
ANGELIQUE,
Of the burthen of one hundred and twenty tons, with her sails, tackle, furniture, standing rigging, &c. as she now lays near the Hangard, at the King's Wood-yard.

The schooner was properly sheathed last summer, the standing rigging is new, and the vessel and furniture may be viewed and examined, at any time from this date to the Day of Sale, by applying to Mr. Prejean, at the Canoterie, or to
JOHN JONES,
Auc. & Br.
The Sale to begin at 7 o'clock in the evening.

Benevolent Society,
THE Members are informed, Wednesday the 5th of May next, in the evening, will be the annual meeting: as several members have resolved to meet and dine on said day, in commemoration of the establishment, those who were not present at the last meeting, are informed the dinner will be at the Merchant's Coffee-house, on said day, and those who mean to dine will be kind enough to leave their names at the bar, that the caterer may judge what will be necessary to provide.

By desire of the officers,
WM. MOORE, Steward.

Quebec, April 19, 1790.
Quebec Coffee-house.

THE Subscriber respectfully informs his friends and the public, that he has opened the Quebec Coffee house, formerly kept by the late Mr. Charles Daly, and in the same house, (by the church lower-town), which he has commodiously fitted for the accomodation of gentlemen. He hopes that his exertions to give general satisfaction will meet with the approbation of the public, which he will studiously endeavour to deserve.
ALEX. CAIRNS.

21--- Quebec, April 10, 1790.
SPRUCE BEER,
Alexander & Thomas Wilson,
HAVING ESTABLISHED A
BREWERY,
At St. Roc,
For supplying the Inhabitants with Spruce Beer,
Assure their friends and the public, that the Beer shall always be of such a quality, as to give satisfaction.

21--- Quebec, April 15, 1790.
WM. GEORGE,
RESPECTFULLY informs his Friends and the Public in general, that he continues to supply such as please to favour him with their commands, with the very best
DOUBLE & SINGLE
SPRUCE BEER,
On the most reasonable rates, delivered at any part of the town; And hopes he may be ESTABLISHED by a continuance of their favour.

American Intelligence.

ADDRESS of the SOCIETY of the CINCINNATI in the State of SOUTH-CAROLINA.
VOTED NOVEMBER 17, 1789.
TO GEORGE WASHINGTON, President of the United States.

SIR,

POSSESSED of every feeling that can act on grateful hearts, the Society of the Cincinnati established in the State of South-Carolina, beg leave to congratulate you on the happy occasion which has once again placed you in a situation of rendering general good to their country.

Retired from the busy scenes of life, to reap the rewards of your virtuous acts, and to enjoy the glory you had already obtained, the Society of the Cincinnati received you with exulting happiness; they saw in you the patriot-hero, the friend and saviour of their country; and with hearts filled with gratitude and affection, they invoked the All-wise-Disposer of human events to render that retirement happy.

The period, however, arrived when the abilities of the virtuous patriot were again to be called forth to assume a public character. A general political government was formed, by which the happiness of the country for whose liberty you had fought, was now to be established. To preside at the head of this new government, to establish it with permanency, the people sought, in the Great Washington, the virtues on which they could rely with safety, and from which they might expect to receive every benefit without alloy. They had experienced his abilities, they had experienced his integrity and his inviolable love for his country. Nor did they seek in vain. The same noble spirit which actuated you at the beginning of your late contest with Great-Britain, now operated. You received and obeyed the summons; and although you should make a sacrifice, yet you nobly determined---It was the voice of your country, in whose service every inferior consideration of ease and retirement must give place.

As citizens, we congratulate you, Sir, on this additional proof of your country's confidence. As soldiers who partook with you in many of the dangers and hardships which attended the general army under your command, we beg leave to express our warmest attachment to your person, and sincerely wish for your happiness and honor; and that we may, under your rule, supported by your amiable virtues, happily experience and long enjoy the fruits of a government which has for its basis, the GOOD of the PEOPLE of AMERICA.

By order of the Society,
(Signed) WILLIAM MOULTRIE, President.

Slavery was "a matter of course" in 1790, when advertisements for the sale of spruce beer, a schooner, and a "young healthy negro woman" shared space on a newspaper page.

terhouse" aspect of slavery – the depredations in Africa, the murderous cruelties of the "middle passage," the penning up of landed cargoes of slaves – was out of sight, out of mind. Slavery in Quebec came in a sanitized form – bloodless and divorced from the reality of its origins. There were no slave traders, either, at least not in the sense of persons for whom buying and selling slaves was a full-time occupation. Slave dealers in Quebec were merchants such as James McGill, who occasionally procured or sold slaves to fill an order from far-flung customers, or tradesmen and others such as Loyalist Daniel Jones, who kept a tavern in the marketplace at Montreal during the American Revolutionary War and, later, as a resident of Upper Canada, travelled to Montreal and Quebec to sell slaves bought in New York.[16] The easy inclusion of the occasional slave among articles of trade underscores how matter-of-factly slavery was viewed. Many of those men and women engaged in trade felt no more hesitation in selling a "Negro" than they would have in selling a bolt of cloth or a barrel of pork.

The most active trader in slaves in Montreal was perhaps distiller John Lagord. His known slave dealings occurred between 1786 and 1789. In that four-year period, he is known to have handled the sales of the following black slaves:

- *Prince:* He was said to be about fifty-four in September 1792 when notary Joseph Papineau, shortly after his election to the first parliament of Lower Canada, bought him from tailor Joseph Benoit *dit* L'hyvernois for 300 livres. The deed of sale recorded that L'hyvernois had acquired Prince from Lagord by private deed on 31 May 1787; Lagord himself had acquired Prince from Elisha Yeoman on 18 December 1786; Yeoman had acquired him from Martin McEvoy of St-Jean on 12 December 1786; and McEvoy had acquired him from Elisha Fullman (or Fullam) of Walpole, New Hampshire, on 15 November 1786. That series of sales in a six-month period suggests that Prince was not bought by any one of these men to serve them, but as an article of trade. All these deeds, now lost, were turned over to Papineau when he bought Prince.[17]

- *Bellai:* A fifteen-year-old girl assigned to Lagord by a James Balis on 21 March 1787, probably to satisfy Balis's creditors. On 18 April, Lagord sold her to the Misses Josephte and Amable Pouget of Berthier for 1,400 livres. The witnesses were Philippe Loubet and Louis Olivier, themselves slave-owners. Bellai is believed to be the black woman of about twenty-one who was baptized at Berthier in 1793 under the name Marie Joseph Elizabeth.[18]

- *Cynda:* A ten-year-old girl whom Lagord acquired from Balis at the same time and in the same manner as Bellai. Eight days later, Lagord sold her for 750 livres to Pierre Fafard *dit* Joinville, militia captain of Île Dupas, off Berthier, and his wife, Marguerite Trullier *dit* Lacombe. Joinville and his wife gave Cynda back to Lagord in May or early June 1788 in exchange for another black slave, Marie Bulkley, for whom they paid an extra 200 livres. By the time this exchange was recorded, on 9 June 1788, Lagord had already sold Cynda, identified as "une Négresse nommée Jenny, âgée de onze ans," to Joseph Dufaux, a "Bourgeois" of Montreal, for 900 livres. Lagord had regained possession of Cynda "par échange quil en a fait avec le Sr Louis Olivier de Berthier Suivans Ses lettres de 23 et 28 mai dernier" (by an exchange with Louis Olivier of Berthier, as per his letters of 23 and 28 May last). Olivier was Joinville's son-in-law. When Cynda died on 14 October 1789, her burial record gave her name as Marie-Jeanne, probably a baptismal name which, in everyday use, had become Jenny.[19]

- *Marie Bulkley (Nancy Buckley):* On 18 November 1785, Marie Bulkley bound herself to Elias Hall as a slave for thirty years as a way of paying off a "dette considérable" that she owed him. At some unknown date, possibly in the spring of 1787 (see Nancy below) she became the property of Lagord who, in late May 1788, traded her to Pierre Fafard *dit* Joinville and his wife in exchange for the slave girl Cynda plus 200 livres. The first record of this exchange, on 9 June 1788, makes no mention of the 200 livres, or of Marie Bulkley's 30-year enslavement agreement with Elias Hall. It simply records the trade of Marie Bulkley for Cynda, noting that Joinville and his wife gave up Cynda and were already in possession of Marie Bulkley. That same day, Joinville and his wife gave Marie Bulkley to their daughter, Charlotte Joinville, wife of Louis Olivier. On 9 February 1789, at Olivier's request, Lagord had a deed of sale drawn up mentioning the thirty-year agreement between Marie Bulkley and Elias Hall. The deed stipulated that Lagord had sold Marie Bulkley to Joinville in May 1788 as a slave to serve out what remained of her thirty-year enslavement. Lagord also acknowledged the payment of the 200 livres by Joinville. Olivier, who would be elected to the first Assembly of Lower Canada in 1792 as one of the two members for the County of Warwick, is not known to have owned any other slave at this time; this would mean that Marie Bulkley was the unnamed "négresse appartenante au Sr Louis Olivier" who gave birth to three children, father unknown, between 1792 and 1797. None of the children lived more than three months: Jean Baptiste (b. 10 September 1792, d. 2 October 1792), Geneviève (b. 25 July 1795, buried 24 October 1795), and Charlotte (b. 29 June 1797, d. 31 July 1797). On 13 May 1797, six weeks before the recorded date of birth of the third child, Olivier and his wife officially sold the unexpired portion of Marie Bulkley's thirty-year servitude to a Joseph Gent, a sailor, for 600 livres. Acting for Gent, who was said to be off in London, was his mother, Mary McFarlane (Mary Ann Stewart Walton), wife of tailor Peter McFarlane, formerly the partner of tailor Benaiah Gibb in Montreal. Mary McFarlane declared that she had known Marie Bulkley for several years. At her death on 12 April 1801, at the age of about thirty, so it was said, Marie Bulkley was identified as Nancy Buckley, a mulatto, "late Servant to Mr Gibb." Two free black men, Caesar Hunkings and Charles Falkner, witnessed her burial.[20]

- *Nancy:* She was said to be about twenty-three years old when Lagord sold her to Joseph Dufaux for 1,100 livres in September 1787. The deed did not spell out where Lagord had acquired her; he simply certified that she had been in his service for about six months and that he held a proper title to her, which he turned over to Dufaux. This sale was annulled by mutual consent on 22 July 1788, a month after Lagord had sold Cynda to Dufaux. Nancy was probably the same woman as Marie Bulkley, alias Nancy Buckley.[21]

- *Unnamed "Esclave nègre":* Lagord sold him on 7 September 1787 for a term of nineteen years and nine months to Joseph Poiré, a "navigateur" (pilot) of Pointe

Lévy, opposite Quebec, for 150 Spanish dollars, paid in kind with furs.[22] This sale was undoubtedly connected with the following.

- *Jean (John) Brown:* On 3 November 1787, Lagord sold the services of this "Nègre esclave" to Poiré for a term of nineteen years and six months, also for 150 dollars, the same price that he had charged Poiré for the unnamed male slave that he had sold him two months earlier. On 20 November, Poiré sued Lagord, charging that the slave Lagord had sold him – which one? the slave is not otherwise identified in the surviving documents – was really a free black man and that the sale was therefore fraudulent. Poiré claimed £47 10s in reimbursement and damages. On 3 July 1788, the Court of Common Pleas ordered Lagord to reimburse Poiré £37 10s, with interest payable on that sum from 20 November 1787.[23] Poiré engaged in some slave-trading of his own. On 17 November 1787, two weeks after he had bought Jean Brown from Lagord, he bought another "Nègre Esclave" named Harry, fourteen or fifteen years old, from Montreal merchant Barrak Hays for £25 (Hays had bought Harry in New York City ten years earlier). On 4 December, Poiré sold Harry to trader John Simpson of Quebec for £36, making a quick and tidy profit of £11.[24]

- *Rose:* She was "une jeune fille Nègre de quatorze à quinze ans Nourrice" (a young negro girl of fourteen or fifteen, a wet nurse) on 27 March 1787 when she was sold for £40 by Samuel Mix, trader at St-Jean, to tanner Louis Gauthier of the St-Laurent Suburb of Montreal. If she was a "nourrice" in March 1787, then she was probably the mother of Jean Baptiste, the slave of Gauthier who died on 30 May 1788 at the reported age of one year. At some unknown date, Gauthier sold Rose to Lagord who, in turn, sold her to innkeeper and grocer William Mathews of Sorel and Montreal. Then on 9 November 1791, Mathews sold her to Montreal trader Lambert St-Omer. Rose, then about 19, went for £38 5s at an auction conducted by Jonathan Abraham Gray, brother of Sheriff E.W. Gray.[25]

Handling eight slave sales in four years, Lagord could hardly expect to make a living at this business. Certainly, the profit from a sale could be considerable, as the quick flip of the slave Harry by Joseph Poiré shows,[26] but as Lagord's transactions also demonstrate, occasional setbacks occurred, such as costly lawsuits or the cancellation of a sale.

The small scale of the slave business could not possibly justify the erection of slave pens or other special facilities dedicated to slave trading. However, the absence of plantations and gang labour did not make slavery uneconomical and doom it to extinction. It did make large-scale slave-holding uneconomical, not slavery itself, which could have gone on indefinitely as long as help, principally household help, was needed. Thus, black slaves straggled in singly, in pairs, occasionally in a family or small group, as part of the baggage of military officers, ship captains landing at Quebec, Loyalists, and others who had spent time in the West Indies, the American colonies or other slave societies, as prisoners seized in raids in the American colonies, as purchases made by fur traders and other frontiersmen at various western posts, or as goods bought in New York or New England for personal use or as a speculation. Until the late 1790s, they generally found a buyer when they were offered for sale, if not at Montreal, in the surrounding country or at Quebec. With a few exceptions, Montreal masters owned one or two slaves at a time. These were usually employed in domestic service, or something akin to it – working in inns and taverns, for instance. They were housed not in slave huts but in a room in the master's house – sometimes just a spot on the kitchen floor – or in a shed, a stable, barn, or other outbuilding. In terms of the tasks they performed – cooking, cleaning, washing, waiting on tables, chopping and fetching wood, drawing water, tending to horses, driving coaches, milking cows, running errands, etc. – there was no difference between slaves and servants. The term "servant" was loaded, however, when used to refer to blacks: it was a job title that might denote a hired servant or mask a slave. In the latter case, it was also a euphemism, perhaps betraying some prudishness about calling a slave a slave. This seems to have been the case with Jane Richardson, the widow of Montreal barrack master John Richardson, when she made out her will in 1777. She spoke of her husband, who had died that year, as having left her all that he owned, including "his two Servants"; she, in turn, bequeathed to her daughter, Jane, "my Negro Servants." The Richardson servants clearly were possessions, not hirelings.[27] The lines were also blurred in the case of the boy Guillaume (William), at once a slave and indentured servant. After the death of his owner, retired fur-trade merchant Joseph Howard, Guillaume was bound out by Howard's executors as a servant to merchant Myer Michaels for seven years, from 1 May 1798. He was said to be nine years old.[28] By then, slave property had become highly uncertain and, as in England after the judgment of Lord Mansfield in the Somerset case, some owners sought to hedge their bets by putting their slaves under contract, apparently believing that this might ensure them a legal right to hold their slaves to service, even if their ownership title were questioned or denied.[29]

The distinction between which black was a slave and which was free, if it is made clear in some documents available to us today, would not always have been apparent at the time. This may help to explain Judge James Reid's statement in 1846 that, although he had practised law since the mid-1790s, he had known no one who owned slaves in Quebec. Consider the remarkable freedom of movement afforded the slave Bruce by his master, Colonel Gabriel Christie, in June 1777, when Britain was at war with its American colonies. Christie, who was about to leave for England, then to spend the rest of the war stationed in the West Indies, left Bruce to his own devices:

> The Bearer – Bruce ... being my property, has my Leave and Permission at his own Request to hyer himself to any Master or Mrs. As a Servant or take any other honest and Lawful Way of Employing himself for his own Sole benefit and advantage providing he do not Embark on Board any vessell by Sea or to

go beyond Albany in the Province of New York giving due notice to me or my agent at Montreal from time to time Where he is as often as he Changes places ...

    This Leave to be only during my absence from this Province or the Good behaviour of Said negroe, or till the Same is recal'd verbally or by other notice either from me, My Agent heirs Executors or assigns and no longer, and in no Shape to be construed into any freedom or discharge from Claim or Right or Property of Said Negroe aforesaid.[30]

The permission for Bruce to venture into enemy territory as far as Albany suggests that the capital of New York, where Christie had served during the Seven Years War and where he had married the daughter of a local merchant, was familiar ground to Bruce, and perhaps a place where he had family or relations. It also suggests that Christie was wonderfully trusting of Bruce to supply him with such walking papers, allowing him to wander pretty well at will and to work for himself. With no apparent master on the scene, at liberty to take any job he could find and to collect his own wages, would Bruce not have had the air of a free man?[31] On the other hand, some twenty-years later, would not the servants of Simon McTavish and his wife, Marie-Marguerite Chaboillez, daughter of the slave-owning fur trader Charles Chaboillez, have appeared to be slaves? In June 1798, the imperious McTavish, head of the North West Company, just the sort of magnate we might picture as a hard-driving slave-master, hired Henry Taffe, a "free mulatto" from Quebec, to be his "House or Travelling Servant" for one year at a salary of £25, plus room, board and livery, "and in case of the said Henry Travelling with him to allow him a pair of boots and a Greatcoat." The following year, McTavish hired Samuel Luke, a "free negro," also from Quebec, as groom, coachman, and domestic servant for one year. Luke died within the next three years – perhaps travelling with McTavish, as there is no record of his death at Montreal or Quebec – and in March 1802, his widow, Sarah Johnson, placed their ten-year-old son, Samuel Luke Jr, as a servant to McTavish until he turned 21, an arrangement terminated prematurely by McTavish's death in July 1804.[32] McTavish seems to have made use of liveried blacks as status symbols, but none of these was a slave. Yet how was an observer to tell the difference in status between McTavish's black servants and the slave Bruce or the liveried slaves of John Campbell and Daniel Claus?

On the subject of status symbols, it would be well to shed the notion that black slaves were the exclusive preserve of a wealthy elite, flaunted as ornaments of success. If ostentation was a factor, it was singularly ineffective: many people, as we have seen, failed to notice that there were slaves about. Besides, one can scarcely picture the slave-owning clergymen and religious orders named earlier as feeling the need or inclination to indulge in needless expense or display. The idea that black slaves of this time were a luxury or a status symbol in Quebec does not hold water. While some masters surely were men and women of wealth and standing, others were artisans, farmers, shopkeepers, tavern-keepers, and the like. It was not a taste for showing off that made baker Joseph Berlinguet buy Rose in 1788 or 1789, or Indian trader John Stock take her off to the west, or farmer James Frazer cling to his slave, Robin, and Jane Cook hold Charlotte in slavery. Thomas John Sullivan bought Manuel Allen not for show but to work as a waiter in his tavern, and we can be pretty sure that in 1796, John Brooks, keeper of the seedy Black Horse tavern in the Quebec Suburb, did not pay £50 for Rose, about twenty-five, and £100 for Jacqho, thirty-six, to use them as window dressing.[33] The same goes for tailor John Mittleberger when he bought Nero for £60 in December 1780, shopkeeper Mary Jacobs when she paid £50 for Ruth Jane and Sylvie Jane in 1785, tanner Louis Gauthier when he acquired Rose, mentioned earlier, for £40 in March 1787, and hairdresser Daniel Carbry – he died "a poor man" in 1805 – when he bought Kitts, a fifteen-year-old "Negro boy," for $150 in August 1792.[34] Slaves were capital investments, property purchased as one would machinery or equipment, to be put to work in one's trade or occupation or to assist in the tasks of daily life. They might even serve as collateral: when George Westphall, formerly a lieutenant in the 2nd Battalion, 60th Regiment, was on the point of leaving Montreal for Halifax in November 1797, he left Ledy, a twenty-six-year-old "Mulato wench," with Richard Dillon, owner of the Montreal Hotel, as security for a loan of £20, and Lydia Saunders, a "Negro Woman," and her infant son with Thomas Powis of the Montreal Tea Gardens at Côte-St-Antoine (Westmount), as security for the payment of a debt of £27 4s. In both cases, Westphall was to get his slave property back if he paid off his debts within eighteen months.[35] Even in the case of slave-owning members of the élite such as Governor James Murray or Chief Justice William Smith, convenience also counted more than a desire to impress: they found the whites of the colony too independent to make trusty servants.[36]

Needless to say, a minuscule number of slaves, scattered and isolated from one another, could not produce a slave culture such as evolved in the American South, where slaves numbered about four million at the time of Abolition in 1865, or in the British sugar islands of the Caribbean, where the slave labour force on one plantation could number in the hundreds and the total had reached about 800,000 by the time of emancipation in 1834. No one has turned up any songs, music, dance, stories, speech patterns, folklore, religious practices, foods, recipes, dress, implements, etc., traceable to the slaves of Quebec. By the same token, a slave uprising was out of the question. Since the slave population never came close to equalling in size, let alone surpassing, the white population, as it did elsewhere, it was never perceived as a threat. No whites fell prey to guilt-induced nightmares of the slaves rising to exact revenge. No one dreamed of slave conspiracies, and none materialized. In 1799, when the Montreal slave-owners, stripped of the power to control their slaves, complained of the latter threatening a "general revolt," the legislature could not be persuaded to budge; there was not so much as a twitch from the public, the civil and military authorities, or the press. The "general revolt" had more the air of a contained labour dispute, to be settled between masters and slaves. Before this outbreak of insubordination, acts of protest by slaves were isolated affairs, limited generally to running away. We may fancy that every slave escape was an act of resistance to slavery, but it was not so.

Flight was a way out for anyone chafing in a position of subservience – soldier, seaman, servant, apprentice, slave. Most who took this route were expressing dissatisfaction with their lot, not proclaiming a desire to overturn the established order. The idea that slaves in Quebec might have engaged in violent acts of resistance such as arson, poisoning their masters, sabotaging of equipment, or just constant shirking or feigning illness, as sometimes occurred in slave societies, is wholly unsubstantiated.[37]

With its ingrained sense of entitlement facing no serious challenge until the late 1780s, Quebec society needed neither to concoct elaborate justifications of slavery, nor to crack the whip and turn slavery into a full-blown system of racial rules and laws, as those societies did where an ever-growing, aggrieved population of slaves and ex-slaves led to the imposition of ever-stricter, ever more intolerable controls. The right of property was sacred, slaves were property, and that was that. Smugly unconcerned on this score, free of any hate-breeding fear of blacks generally, the majority practised a kind of complacent, unreflecting racism that was generally untouched by the virulent, visceral, vocal strains that denied the humanity of all blacks and insisted on strict racial segregation, during or after slavery. Thus, from the depths of a winter holiday season in 1771, a Montreal correspondent, summing up the local news, could file this report to the *Quebec Gazette*:

> Dancing, Feasting, and Meriment, go swingingly round. – The greatest Harmony and the best Understanding now subsists between both Sexes – The Black and White mingling together in Nocturnal Assemblies form an undistinguished Band, where, throwing off the painful Restraint of Ceremony, our Youth freely unbend their Minds from the Labour of the Day, by indulging themselves in innocent and inoffensive Diversion. – A smart young Lieutenant t'other Day (according to the galant Mode) saluted his sable Partner with, "How do you feel E** this Morning, after your last night's Fatigue?" – So much for Montreal News.[38]

And, day after day for a year, in 1787–88, Loyalist Philip Peter Lansingh, the former sheriff of Charlotte County, New York, who had served in the American War of Independence as a lieutenant in the King's Royal Regiment of New York, ate his suppers at the home of Caesar Johonnot, sitting not in lofty isolation in a separate room but at the table with his black host and his family.[39]

Johonnot presents a good illustration of the fact that, although there may have been a presumption that blacks were slaves, there was no widespread conviction that they had to be so, that slavery was all that they were fit for, or that once they were freed, special laws were needed to ensure their subservience. The earliest record we have of him at Montreal finds him in court in 1786, prosecuting a white soldier for assault.[40] Three years later, he was hired by members of the business élite, including slave-owners James McGill and Robert Lester, a Quebec merchant, as the manager of their Montreal Distillery Company, a well-paid position that he held until the company folded in 1794.[41] In 1798, when surveyor William Fortune, an Irish-born Loyalist from South Carolina, needed someone to run his still at Pointe-Fortune on the

Ottawa River, he employed Johonnot at a salary of £50 a year, plus room and board. This was the same William Fortune who, in 1793, needing a house servant, had simply bought one, paying £30 to a Quebec tavern-keeper for "a certain Negroe Wench called Louise or Lisette about Twenty eight years of Age or thereabouts."[42]

As these cases show, servants and workers were needed, and society took it for granted that, if they were black, they could be owned outright or hired. Slavery in Quebec under the British had little to do with economics, and the colony never developed into a society dependent on slave labour. Slavery was convenient but not essential. It was supported not by racist theorizing but by an inbred belief in the primacy of all things European. The practice reflected social and cultural assumptions and values; it was no more an economic institution than buying a car as opposed to leasing one is an institution today. The institution was service: one could buy a servant or lease one. The choice was at the discretion of a master, and of no concern to the public. A closer look at the experiences of a few slaves will bear this out.

A FREE MAN SUBMITS TO SLAVERY

No one would go willingly into the nightmare world described at the head of this chapter, but on 24 March 1761, six months after the military surrender of New France to the British, Louis Antoine submitted to slavery. A man in his twenties, born a slave in St-Domingue but free for fourteen years past, he sold himself to merchant Dominique Gaudet of Lachine and Montreal on the following terms:

> Whereas the said Gaudet is willing to grant to him in marriage Catherine Baraca, his negro slave, about 18 years of age [she was fifteen], Louis Antoine has by these presents sold himself to the said Gaudet, the said Louis Antoine and Catherine Baraca to remain at the service and under the power, mastery and authority of the said Gaudet, who may as he chooses dispose of and sell them, as well as the children to be born of their marriage.
>
> By these presents, the said Gaudet, at his death, intends that the said Louis Antoine, Catherine Baraca and the children born of their marriage shall go free, his heirs to have no claim whatsoever upon them.[43]

The first part of this bargain was fulfilled one week later when Louis Antoine married Catherine Baraca in the Catholic church at Lachine.[44] It remained to be seen whether Gaudet would exercise his right to sell either one of them, or any children they might have, and whether they would all go free at his death, as he had pledged.

Assuming that Louis Antoine was a rational man of at least average intelligence, he would have had a fair idea of what awaited him. He knew slavery from his days as a slave at Cap Français (Cap Haïtien), and he had seen how it operated around Montreal, notably in the condition of Catherine Baraca and her parents, all slaves of Gaudet. He knew Gaudet, for whom he had probably worked before agreeing to become his slave.[45] The most striking feature of his contract, of course, is the mere fact that he struck such a bargain, entering into bondage of his own accord, weighing the risks and concluding that the prize was worth the sacrifice of his freedom. He knew that he was not signing his life away – or the lives of his wife and any children they might have – because physical violence played little part in slavery in Quebec. There were no slave patrols, bloodhounds, lynchings, and few, if any, whips and chains. The one case of wanton physical abuse by a Montreal master that has come to light in the forty-odd years that slavery yet had to run involved the savage whipping of a young white apprentice, not a black slave, in 1790; the public outrage in that case led to the quick prosecution of the master – he pleaded guilty and was fined £10, a hefty sum – suggesting that the community was not prepared to stomach this kind of extrajudicial savagery.[46] One cannot help but think that had such violence been the norm where slaves were concerned, it would have raised slavery's profile, provoked some outcry, and hastened slavery's end. No outcry came. As for chains, the only mention of these in relation to Montreal blacks under British rule comes well after slavery had ended, in the case of a prisoner who was shackled after attempting suicide while awaiting trial for murder.[47] Truly, Louis Antoine, in his twenties, had a reasonable expectation of outliving Gaudet, then in his sixties, and of surviving his enslavement.

Another striking aspect of the arrangement is what it tells us about slave-owners' regard for proprieties. We may think that Gaudet was an ogre for enslaving Louis Antoine; if we imagine that he saw in Louis Antoine's attachment to Catherine Baraca a chance to acquire a slave at no cost to himself, and for purposes of slave breeding, our revulsion is complete. This does not appear to have been the case; even had it been so, it should not blind us to two significant details – the contract itself and the wedding. Gaudet did not simply appropriate a black man and turn him into a slave against his will, but entered into a notarized contract for his services. This contract, or deed of sale, doubled as a sort of marriage contract; for all concerned, marriage meant not simply cohabitation or "jumping the broom," but a union sanctioned by a proper religious wedding, as we saw in the case of John Campbell's slaves Jeanne and François, or "Judith" and "John Gray." This was the rule for whites, and it extended to black slaves. Slaves could marry only with the consent of their owners. Not all owners imposed such hard conditions as Gaudet. The slaves Jacques César *dit* Jasmin and Marie Elisabeth Charles, for example, were freed by their respective owners when they married on 5 February 1763, although it had taken at least two years to persuade the dowager Baroness of Longueuil, the bride's owner, to agree to this, and she insisted that bride and groom remain at her (paid) service for three years following their wedding-emancipation.[48]

A slave marriage bound masters as well as the slave couple. Community standards played an important role, in that the general acknowledgment of the "sanctity" of marriage seems to have protected slave couples from being wantonly separated. There seem to have been no cases of regularly married slave spouses being sold away from each other. Remember that Peter McFarlane, in arrogating to himself the power of separating Catherine Coll from her husband in 1791, claimed as part of his justification that her marriage to Jacob Smith was invalid. There is a good illustration of this regard for matrimony as a "holy bond" not to be broken in a 1788 advertisement for the sale of a slave couple:

> To be SOLD together,
> A Handsome Negro Man and a beautiful Negro Woman married to one another; the man from twenty-three to twenty-four years of age, between five and an half and six English feet high; the woman from twenty two to twenty-three years of age; both of a good constitution. For further information, such as may be desirous of purchasing them must apply to Mr Pinguet, in the Lower-town of Quebec, Merchant.[49]

Few white North Americans would have been prepared to concede that a black man could be "handsome" and a black woman "beautiful." This is striking language; it is tainted here, however, because it is part of a sales pitch – how much of it was honest compliment, how much a vendor's hyperbole? However that may be, the advertiser's underscoring that the married couple would not be sold separately is just what we would expect to hear from a priest. Clergymen, of all people, could not in all conscience separate wedded couples while preaching the indissolubility of marriage. So, the anonymous advertiser, who was Reverend Jacques Guichaux, the parish priest of Ste-Famille on Île d'Orléans, offered Jeanne and Salé (i.e., John and Sally), whom he had bought from Montrealer Joseph Filteau nearly three years earlier, for sale as a unit. But what about their son, Michel Remy? Only six weeks old when Guichaux had bought the family in 1785, he was, now almost three, unmentioned in the advertisement. If the matrimonial bond was sacred, the slave family unit was not, and children were sometimes separated from their parents. But this was not the case with Jeanne and Salé's son – at least, not at this time.[50]

In all likelihood, then, Gaudet as a good Catholic had little choice but to respect the "indissoluble" marriage of Catherine Baraca to Louis Antoine once he had consented to it. This only compounds the paradox of his agreement with Louis Antoine. He claimed the right to sell any member of the family, yet promised that they would all go free at his death. To all appearances, his pledge was sincere – he went so far as to deny his heirs any claim to them. But how could he guarantee their eventual freedom if he sold any one of them? How could he respect their marriage and sell off wife or husband?

As already noted, Gaudet also owned Catherine Baraca's mother and father, Marie Anne and Pierre Baraca. He is said to have owned seventeen slaves, blacks or Panis, at one time or another, not to mention Louis Richard, a sixty-year-old white man who, in 1766, died at Gaudet's, "à qui il s'était donné" – to whom he had given himself. A white slave? Such cases of self-giving saw destitute white persons submit to a master's will until death, in return for room and board, basic care and a proper burial. It was a state akin to slavery, but white people *gave* themselves, where black Louis Antoine *sold* himself. And masters did not reserve the right to sell white people, as Gaudet did with Louis Antoine and his family.[51]

But then, Gaudet never did sell Louis Antoine, or his wife, or any of the three children who were born to them before he died. In fact, he probably never intended to. As far as we can tell from the contract of 1761, Louis Antoine entered into bondage solely to marry Catherine Baraca. He had to be reasonably sure that Gaudet would not defeat that purpose by selling him or his wife. And Gaudet clearly wanted to bind Louis Antoine to him, or he would not have set the terms that he did. From the language of the agreement, Gaudet even looked forward to Louis Antoine and his wife having children. Had he ever been tempted to renege on his promise and sell Louis Antoine, proving his title would have required him to produce the notarized agreement showing that Louis Antoine was not a slave for life (Louis Antoine, as a party to the agreement, would also have had his copy). Had he tried to sell any member of the family, in fact, a hint about the terms of the contract of 1761 would have given the buyers pause, raising the possibility of bothersome complications, perhaps even a court challenge similar to those mounted by the slaves Marie *dite* Manon and of André (see chapter 1). If any attempt had been made to keep them enslaved after Gaudet's death, it would have been difficult to circumvent this deed, even if the argument were made that a contract between two parties could not bind a third. But no such attempt was made. Gaudet lasted eight years and a day from the date of Louis Antoine's self-enslavement, dying on 25 March 1769 at the age of about 70. In that time, one of Louis Antoine's three children had died, as had his father-in-law. Two months after Gaudet's death, Louis Antoine and his wife had a fourth child, Marie Charlotte; her birth record noted that she was born of blacks "qui ont leur liberté" (who have their freedom). The contract was fulfilled to the letter, and perhaps even beyond, since it appears that Catherine Baraca's mother also went free, although no provision had been made for her in the deed of 1761.[52]

Louis Antoine's case reveals certain interesting aspects of slavery and of contemporary attitudes toward it. We discern in the slave an expectation of "fair" treatment, at least no worse than the treatment accorded domestic servants, and in the master a respect for community standards (a contract for services, formal wedding, sanctity of marriage, keeping one's word, etc.), even if those standards countenanced slavery. However harshly we may judge Gaudet for driving such a hard bargain for Catherine Baraca's hand, the experience was still a far cry from imported notions of slavery as a physical hell on earth. This is not to say that it was heaven: it was demeaning and dispiriting, and the hell of it was psychological. We can only wonder, for instance, how frequently Louis Antoine and his wife, made to feel inferior by their slave status, itself founded on a view of them as innately debased because they were black, found themselves praying under their breath for Gaudet's death, their family's passport to freedom, and how that made them feel.

Admittedly, cases of enslavement by consent were rare. Two others are known, one at Montreal and one near Quebec. The case of Marie Bulkley, as we have seen, was one of debt bondage: she sold herself as a slave for thirty years to pay off a debt. As we do not know her age – she may have been in her early teens – or circumstances, it is impossible to say how much of a choice she had, and whether she understood what she was doing. The other case also involved a form of limited-term enslavement, but was otherwise quite different from the situation of Louis Antoine and Marie Bulkley in that the contracting party, Élisabeth Mondina, was a white servant, and it was her yet unborn children, not herself, whom she gave up. In March 1782, unmarried and fearing that her pregnancy might cost her her job, she begged her employer, Executive Councillor Antoine Juchereau Duchesnay, seigneur of Beauport, to take the child at birth and keep him or her until the age of twenty-one, in return for which she pledged to serve Duchesnay for seven years at a pittance. There was no mention of who the father was, and it is possible that Élisabeth Mondina miscarried or that the child did not live long. Pregnant again the following year by Duchesnay's Haitian-born slave, François William – he was probably responsible for her first pregnancy – Élisabeth Mondina returned to the bargaining table:

> Marie Elisabeth Mondina, a woman of the age of thirty-four years, being for several years in the service of Mr Duchesnay, Esquire ... declared unto us that being pregnant by françois Wiliam, Negro belonging to Mr Duchesnay, and being about to marry him, she begs Mr Duchesnay to accept to keep her in his service together with her future husband. And the children who may be born of their marriage she gives to Mr Duchesnay until they reach the age of twenty-one years, after which they shall be free. For which she binds herself by these presents faithfully to serve Mr Duchesnay in all ways feasible, And that for wages she requires of Mr Duchesnay no more than her room and board and upkeep suitable to her station, for her and her children.
>
> And the said françois Wiliam intervening did declare that he consents that the children which the said Marie Elisabeth Mondina, his future wife, shall bear him belong to Mr Duchesnay until the age of twenty-one years for their room, board and upkeep suitable to their station, After which time of twenty-one years for each of the said children they shall be free to go where they please. Upon which Mr Duchesnay also intervening, did voluntarily declare by these presents that he consents to the marriage of the said françois Wiliam his Negro, with the said Marie Elisabeth Mondina, that he accepts voluntarily to house feed and maintain the said Marie Elisabeth Mondina according to her station, as well as their children who shall belong to the said Sieur Duchesnay, until the age of twenty-one years, And after which time they shall be free.

Here was an odd case where the children did not follow the status of their mother, a white woman, theoretically free. Élisabeth Mondina did not seek to worm her way out of her predicament by crying rape or using the black slave as a scapegoat. No less noteworthy is the fact that François William, though a slave, was not shut out of this sordid bargaining: he was asked to be a party to the arrangement and to consent to it.

On 5 August 1783, three days after entering into the compact, Élisabeth Mondina and François William were married. The first of their five children was born that September. All five were born into slavery, but with these qualifications: their servitude was not to last more than twenty-one years, and although they would belong to Duchesnay, he claimed no right to sell them.[53]

JUDAH'S SLAVES

For Jacob and Thomas, two slaves of Montreal merchant Samuel Judah, there was no question of consenting to slavery. Both men were among the many blacks taken prisoner in the American colonies during the American War of Independence. Thomas's experience offers a good illustration of the complications that could arise from a disputed title to a slave. Jacob's exhibits an exceptional instance of slave resistance. Both show the trust that slave masters placed in the law as they conceived it, and in both cases we get an idea of the qualms that whites felt – and those they did not feel – in treating blacks as property.

We catch periodic glimpses of Thomas over a period of a dozen years thanks to the drawn-out efforts made to untangle Judah's estate after his business failure in the mid-1780s. He might be the otherwise unidentified "nêgre du Sieur Judée Juif" who was a patient at the Hôtel-Dieu from 26 February to 1 March 1781,[54] but there is no telling for sure, since we do not know exactly when he came into Judah's possession, only that it was after August 1778. The nameless patient may have been Jacob, alias Isaac, who had been tossed from pillar to post during the war. He had apparently fought on the losing British side at the Battle of Saratoga in 1777, had been taken prisoner by the Americans, and was then captured in October 1780 at the home of American Colonel James Gordon in Ballston, New York, by Mohawk raiders led by Irish-born Lieutenant Patrick Langan of the King's Royal Regiment of New York. On behalf of the Mohawks, Langan had sold Jacob to Judah for £24 that November. At the same time, Judah paid Langan more than twice that price – £60 – for an unnamed "Negroe Wench" who had been captured with Jacob and was, in fact, his wife, although they were perhaps not formally married.[55]

Jacob, who claimed to be free by virtue of his loyal service under arms, did not suffer slavery gladly. On 7 April 1781, he attacked his master. Judah struck back – by filing a charge of assault against him. As the court record states:

> Samuel Judah Sworn Says that a Negro Man named Jacob was sold to him by Mr Lanzen [Langan] having Lived with him the deponant as his Servant Slave for about five Months; that he the said Negro Jacob did on Saturday last assault him the Deponent, and toke him by the Collar, and treated him the Defendant with great Insolence; that from his Behaviour and Insolence he has reason to think he will use him Ill and do him great Injury.

Court order the said Jacob Negro man to be committed to Prison for the above assault until he do find Security for his Good Behaviour towards the said Samuel Judah.[56]

Judah's decision to prosecute his slave rather than to discipline him himself may seem odd, as odd as the court's failure to impose any harsher penalty than ordering that the slave who had manhandled his master be detained until someone vouched for him. But who would post bail for a slave? Perhaps the magistrates assumed that Jacob would stew in jail until they released him, once they were satisfied that he had learned his lesson. Whatever their intentions, Judah's control over his slave property was impaired. His word was not law. Rather than impose his own rules, he had left it to the court to decide Jacob's fate, thereby depriving himself of his slave's services for an indefinite period. And if the court's ruling were to be taken at face value, a third party was to step between the master and his slave property to guarantee Jacob's future good conduct. This would give that person a responsibility that should have been Judah's alone, as Jacob's owner.

The treatment of Jacob on the part of both Judah and the court betrays a recognition that he was not simply property but a person, with rights and obligations. It was as if, in the eyes of the court, Jacob had been a common offender, which he was under the law: it made no distinction between whites and blacks. But why had Judah not punished Jacob himself instead of taking him to court? Where was the master's power to punish, or, as it is sometimes more dramatically termed in relation to slavery in the southern United States, the master's power of life and death over his slaves, an essential element in ensuring their submission?[57] We would expect that power to have applied in Quebec if we were to subscribe to the notion that, after the Conquest, slaves had lost whatever rights they may have had under French law to become, under British law, chattels with no rights at all.[58] The reality was quite different, and Judah's reliance on the courts in such a flagrant case points to a significant aspect of slavery in Montreal under British rule.

It may be that Judah was no physical match for his slave, and so could not discipline him on his own.[59] Since masters employed no overseers or slave-drivers to ensure their slaves' submission – the ownership of a slave or two could not justify the trouble and expense of hiring an overseer – where were they to turn? To the courts. In matters of strong discipline and punishment, rather than lay down the law, masters generally showed that they expected the courts, officers of the law, and penal institutions to play the role of overseer. In so doing, they acknowledged the power of the colony's legal apparatus over their slaves, counting on it to affirm the existing social order by keeping slaves in line. It is no wonder that they felt betrayed when, in the 1790s, the courts charted a course that ran steadily counter to their interests.

Consider the choices, fanciful and real, that presented themselves to the mind of merchant Pierre Guy when, in the fall of 1778, he grew exasperated at the misbehaviour of his slave, Fraser. Guy had bought him ten years earlier for £33 12s when

Fraser had been about ten years old. Lately, Fraser had taken to skipping out at night to go prowling for prostitutes, sneaking some of them back to Guy's. In 1776, during the American occupation of Montreal, Fraser, otherwise honest and upright, had purloined fifty livres' worth of goods from Guy's stores and given them to a "putain françoise" – a French whore, Guy confided to his friend, Quebec merchant François Baby. In a tone of rueful jest, he bemoaned his lack of power to turn Fraser into a castrato to cure him of his skirt-chasing. Selling Fraser seemed the only solution: some ship sailing from Quebec for the West Indies might be interested. Guy sought his friend's advice. In the meantime, he had had Fraser confined in jail. In the end, he sold Fraser the following March to fur trader Augustin Dubuque for 2,200 livres. In his letters to his friend, Guy did not muse on beating Fraser into submission, or putting him in irons – and the business of making a eunuch of him, if it sounds menacing, was no more than a grim private joke, born of frustration at his slave's antics. But Guy had obviously enlisted the support of the authorities, at least to the extent that he had had his slave jailed, probably on some charge of misconduct.[60]

Another good example of how the slave-owners proceeded is found in a letter to Guy's friend Baby from another of his correspondents. "I have a negro in prison at Quebec," Charles-Louis Tarieu de Lanaudière, writing from Chambly, informed Baby in September 1776. "I beg you to tell the provost to have him put in chains for fifteen days, hand and foot, then to remove them to teach him that as I know how to punish, so I know how to reward the well-behaved. No mercy. He is mine, I wish to make an example of him even if Mr [Thomas] Dunn allowed himself to be persuaded by him that he was free."[61] How revealing it is to find a master, wishing to make an example of his slave, instructing a third party to tell the sheriff how to go about the business rather than doing the deed himself.

The slave-owners' reliance on the machinery of the law is key to understanding not only slavery's demise, but also the rarity of whip-and-chain brutality on the part of the masters and the absence of vigilante action from the record of slavery in Quebec.[62] Physical brutality by masters or others was not a fixture of slavery; acts of violence by whites against blacks, or even blacks against blacks, were more common outside of slavery, perhaps simply because a master had an interest in protecting his slave property, whereas free blacks were on their own. The closest instance found of anything approaching vigilante action was the hounding of the black woman Marry Lewis, quite possibly the "négresse" Marie Louise, whose wedding Louis Antoine had attended in 1760.[63] The pursuit of Marry Lewis was described by a sergeant of artillery stationed at Montreal in a letter of January 1767 to Brigadier General Frederick Haldimand. It appears, from terms used in the letter and from the mere fact that it was addressed to Haldimand, that Marry Lewis may have been his former slave or servant:

> By request of your faithfull Servt. Marry Lewis, I make bold to send you these few lines to represent her grievances. She says that she went to the Gray Nuns,

for Three Months. They being so poor she was obliged to leave Them and go to service, on which St Luck La Corne applyd to one Justice Robertson in order to make her his Slave; she[,] knowing St. Luck had no order from you[,] would not; on which They used her very ill & strip'd her of her Cloaths, and keepd them for some Months, on which she was obliged to fly to the Country to get clear of St. Luck, yet he still sent in search of her, and hunted her from place to place & would not let her rest in any place untill St. Lucke was confined Three Months ago on Mr. Walker Mercht. Affair.

When she heard of St. Lucks confinement, came to Town and applyd for her Cloaths which she got and is at present at service in Town but on St. Luck's being acquitted she must fly for she declares she will sooner go to the savages than become his slave[.] she therefore Beggs of your Honr. either to send for her or be good enough to send her freedom sign'd by your own hand that she may live peaceably in any service she may chose. Your faithfull servt. Beggs you will write to Monsr. De Chambou [Deschambault] in Montreal with her freedom inclosed directed to her which will ease her of all her present fears.[64]

Haldimand had left Canada that year to take up his new post as commander in the British colonies of East and West Florida. He received the letter on 28 April, about a month after he had entered on his duties at Pensacola. His response, if any, is unknown. There was at least one redeeming note to this episode in that Marry Lewis had managed to enlist the sympathy of a soldier who took the trouble to put pen to paper and plead her case. It must also be noted that even the dogged St-Luc had sought the law's approval for his actions: he had "applyd to one Justice Robertson in order to make her his slave."[65] We do not know what possible grounds St-Luc may have had for his claim, and how Robertson ruled on his application.

Another curious instance of resort to the courts occurred in Montreal in May and June 1793 when, as we have seen, Colonel John Campbell, St-Luc's son-in-law, filed a charge of assault against "Violetta, a Negroe wench," who was then his slave or had been so until a few months earlier. According to the record of proceedings:

On a complaint against the Defendant for an assault and threatening. – Col. John Campbell the Prosecutor appeared this day in Court, and having heard his Affidavit read, taken before Mr Justice McCord, dated the twenty seventh day of May last, deposeth and saith, that he is still under the same apprehension from the threats and menaces of the said Defendant and from her malicious disposition, that she will do him some bodily hurt or to some of his family, and therefore prays Surety of the Peace. –

Violetta was bound over to keep the peace.[66] One would think that instead of publicly professing his fear of this woman and relying on the courts to restrain her, Campbell, the old soldier, would have simply shown her who was boss, so to speak. That he did not do so points to the same conclusion that we draw from Jacob's run-in with Samuel Judah: where disciplining slaves was concerned, masters counted on the apparatus of the law to crack the whip.

Like Violetta, Judah's slave, Jacob, was prosecuted and briefly imprisoned but not otherwise brutalized. And he definitely had sympathizers in high places. Major Robert Mathews of the 53rd Regiment, secretary to Haldimand, who was now governor and commander in chief, took an active interest in his case, either because he had known Jacob, or because men of his regiment recalled Jacob's service at Saratoga. Mathews asked Brigadier General Allan Maclean, commander of the forces at Montreal, to look into the matter. On 5 July 1781, Maclean reported on his efforts in a remarkable letter, expressing sympathy for Jacob, "the poor Negro man" whom he knew as Isaac. Maclean had taken up the matter with Judah, arguing that he should have ascertained, before buying Jacob, that the latter was really a slave. But Maclean had gone farther than the mere expression of his sentiments: he had posted Jacob's bail and urged him to flee to Quebec, where he would be out of harm's way. Jacob heeded Maclean's advice. It is not clear whether his wife accompanied him.[67]

As a result of Judah's bankruptcy in 1784, his assets were assigned to his creditors. The main creditor, to whom he owed the astronomical sum of about £40,000, was merchant Amos Hayton of London. As Hayton's attorneys, merchants Edward William Gray, the sheriff of the Montreal District, and William Lindsay of Quebec were appointed trustees of Judah's estate.[68] When Judah absconded to New York in 1786, Thomas fell into Gray's hands as part of the estate. Gray, who was then the owner of a black female slave named Sylvia,[69] communicated the news about Thomas to Hayton that summer:

> I forgot to mention to you that [Benjamin] Hart left S. Judah's Negro with me, but as the man asserts that Mr Love stole him, and that he is to be free at the age of twenty one, and by a Copy of a deed which Mr [David] David, who is empowered to claim him, shewed me, it appears that his former Master gave him to one of his Daughters on condition that he should serve her until he arrived at the Age of thirty one instead of twenty one, as he says, and then be free, there is reason to believe that Love did not come honestly by him, it would be in vain to attempt to dispose of him until that matter is cleared up, for which purpose Mr David has wrote to Philadelphia, and in the mean time I shall keep him in my house.[70]

At the end of 1786, Gray again wrote to Hayton that Thomas was still with him, "not having yet heard any thing further from the Claimant, and it being in vain to attempt to dispose of him, as no good title can be given, and few would purchase him under such circumstances."[71] After another three months, Thomas's situation was still no clearer, as far as Gray was concerned: "I cannot get any information respecting the Negro who is still with me and wish that business was ended, for tho' he is a clever fellow he is more expence to me than a hired Servant would be, and nobody would buy him under the circumstances I mentioned."[72]

By June 1787, Gray, who was getting to know "the Negro," and to feel for him, though he still could not bring himself to call him by a proper name, had formulated a plan:

> I inclose you copies of the papers concerning the Negro that you may come to some determination respecting him. Mr David says he has wrote to the Claimant several times since without receiving any answer, which appears to be very extraordinary, but if the man is entitled to his freedom at twenty one, as he says himself, and which is his present age, or at thirty one as mentioned in the writing, it would certainly be an act of great inhumanity and injustice to sell him for a slave – As he has behaved well since he has been with me and is willing to serve me, till he is thirty one years of Age, I will give you twenty Guineas for his time and then let him have his freedom, and take all risks upon myself, in order to make an end of the matter – if you accept of my offer you will of course signify the same in your answer, and on the contrary give such directions concerning him as you may think proper.[73]

Hayton is not having any of this, as we learn in a letter from Gray to Lindsay, his fellow trustee:

> Mr Hayton having requested me in a letter Dated the 19th July, to send the Negro man to him either by the *Integrity* or *Eweretta,* I purpose sending him by the first Vessel to Quebec, and shall direct him to call upon you on his arrival for your directions. Mr Hayton hopes that either of these Captains will give him his passage for his services during the Voyage, in what I imagine he will find himself mistaken, otherwise directs it to be paid and to have necessary Bedding &c. furnished, which you will please to see done – by next opportunity I will send you an extract of Mr Hayton's Letter concerning him.[74]

But Gray is once again stymied. On hearing of the plan to ship Thomas off to England, merchant David David steps in and, in the name of the mystery claimant, formally notifies Gray not to dispose of Thomas or else face a suit for damages. From David's protest we learn that Thomas was claimed by a Philadelphia widow named Chloe Forsyth, who maintained that she had bought Thomas on 7 August 1775, and that he had been "illegally kidnapped & taken away by a Captain Love belonging to the British Transports" on the withdrawal of the British forces from Philadelphia in June 1778.[75]

Miffed at this latest complication, and at Hayton, Gray takes up his pen again in August 1787 to notify Lindsay that Thomas will not be heading his way after all:

> Mr David the claimant of the Negro Man has protested against my sending him to England, which might put Mr Hayton to more expence than he would wish and has determined me to keep him 'till I hear further from him, in the mean time I send him a Copy of the Protest – he certainly was to blame to refuse my

offer in the manner he did, for if he did not think it sufficient why did he not say so, and not suddenly deprive me of him? I declare however that I would not have kept him for that very reason if I did not think it would injure him much by sending him away, and I do assure you I would not give a shilling more than I offered taking all risks upon myself as I proposed, for it is evident that he does not at all events belong to S. Judah's Estate and when the owner established his claim I should be either obliged to relinquish him or pay him such a compensation for the remainder of the time he has to serve as might be agreed on. – My Friend Hayton may perhaps imagine that I kept him to please myself but be assured that is not the case for I would rather have paid any price for a Servant than not have complied with his request in the manner it was made if I could have sent him away without subjecting him to greater damages and expence than the services of the Man would possibly compensate.[76]

Gray waited two months before advising Hayton of the latest snag:

Since you did not think proper to accept of my offer for the Negro Man[,] immediately on receipt of your Letter I wrote to Mr Lindsay to procure him passage but the day before he was to set off I was waited upon by Mr Beek with a Protest, of which I inclose you a Copy, which determined me not to send him without your further orders, as I did not think it advisable to subject you to the expence of an Action and the Damages that might be given against you[,] without your express consent.[77]

One year later, in October 1788, in writing to Hayton about what little progress had been made in the settlement of Judah's estate and what assets in his hands remained unsold, Gray observed that some resolution seemed in sight in Thomas's case: "The Negroe is also still with me[;] the Claim made to him will be determined next January term as the papers are at last come to D. David, the Claimants agent, when you shall be advised thereof."[78]

But January 1789 came and went, and nothing was done in court. After Gray's last letter on the subject, a full two years pass before Thomas is again mentioned in Gray's surviving correspondence. "I now inclose you the account current of the Estates of Samuel Judah," he writes Hayton on 19 October 1790. A lengthy passage fills us in on Thomas's life and a final decision that Gray has made about what to do with the "negro man" –

With respect to the negro man I must also add something least you should think I had an interest in detaining him so long as I have done, but if you recollect the reasons for my not sending him home as you desired, the impossibility of my disposing of him on account of the claim made by Mr David and the offer I made you, you will acquit me of any such intention, when at the same time, I assure you he has cost me more than a hired servant would have done, and ever since that period has rendered me very little service, besides he got married to a Soldiers [Troll?] by whom he has a child to whom his attention was mostly devoted – It now remains for me to give my reasons for sending him home, and first it was your desire, which has never been contradicted, secondly I know him to be capable of making as good a servant as ever existed, and as he was desirous of going himself I hope he will prove so to you[;] thirdly tho' David did not prosecute his claim, while it lay over here and the mans own pretensions to freedom as I before observed nobody would purchase him, and therefore I thought you had the best right to his Services, and lastly Mr Lindsay was of the same opinion, in consequence of all which I sent him to Quebec and Mr Lindsay is to get him a passage to England so I have done with him and the inclosures too –[79]

By the end of December, Gray had not heard whether Lindsay had finally shipped Thomas off to Hayton before ice had closed the port of Quebec for the winter. "I expected to have had the pleasure of receiving a letter from you before this time," he wrote reproachfully, "if it had only been to have informed me whether you had sent Thomas the Negro to Mr Hayton, and what expence attended that business, that I might have reimbursed you the amount."[80] At last, the "negro man" has a name. A letter must have come from Lindsay within the next day or two, probably informing Gray that Thomas was still in Quebec, because Gray wrote Lindsay on the subject one last time on 30 December. It was just a few lines: "Mrs Gray says she gave Thomas, the Negro the day he left Montreal or a day or two before[,] three or four old white Shirts, one of which she thinks was ruffled but cannot recollect any other particulars concerning them."[81] On this note about cast-off clothes, Thomas fades from view after spending more than four years in limbo because of his disputed ownership. There is no further word on whether he ever sailed for London.

SLAVERY WHITED OUT

This was the world of slavery in Montreal. At its core was an assumption, shared by English- and French-speakers, Catholics, Protestants, and Jews, of overall white superiority, a belief that whites had a natural right to treat blacks as property. Slavery need not be an involuntary servitude, or lifelong, and it did not require the depersonalization of blacks to the point where they became mere things. It was hereditary, in that the children born to a slave mother were slaves from birth. It was, above all, a convenience whose survival depended on its not being questioned. In different ways, the assumption of white supremacy underlay Dominique Gaudet's agreement with Louis Antoine, as it did Samuel Judah's purchase of Jacob, Edward William Gray's treatment of Thomas, and even Brigadier General Maclean's solicitude for Jacob, which was based, not on a repudiation of slavery, but on the belief that a white man had failed to exercise his power and duty to determine whether the black man that he

Marguerite de Lacorne St-Luc, daughter of Luc de Lacorne St-Luc, was only nine in 1784 when her father died, leaving her his "négresse." In 1808, she married Jacques Viger, who would later compile the first documentary record of slavery in Quebec.

had bought was slave or free. What right, other than the assumed right of white over black, did Gaudet have to propose the bargain that he did to Louis Antoine? What right did Judah have to buy Jacob, regardless of whether he was a free man? What right or title did Gray have, as trustee of Judah's estate or even in his capacity as sheriff, to hold on to Thomas and decide his fate, once he had determined, by mid-1787, that Thomas did not form part of Judah's estate, and particularly after the supposed rightful owner in Philadelphia failed to press her case? Yet for all the easy arrogance of these white men's assumptions, they could not summon the utter suspension of disbelief required to consider blacks mere chattels. Each in his own way, in words or deeds, recognized that the chattels had certain human and civil rights.[82] But when it came to disposing of this human property or settling disputes over ownership, slaves were treated as real property: the owner was expected to hold some recognizable title. Generally, this took the form of a deed of sale. Although manumissions were registered before a notary, no such formality was needed in the sale of a slave. A simple written record of the sale, signed by buyer and seller and a witness or two, would do. Even this was not always necessary, as witness Jacob and Thomas, seized by British forces as spoils of war and sold with little regard to their status. The only title then was that of white over black.[83]

Other than a dusty paper trail in the archives, slavery in Quebec left virtually no traces except in the memories of those who had taken an active part in it. The slight numbers of slaves, the absence of an Ontario-style gradual-abolition law or of the kind of overtly or implicitly segregationist enactments that followed slavery's fall in northern American states contributed to the collective amnesia. The statute books of Lower Canada, like the landscape, remained clear of all reminder that society had once subscribed to this practice. The calendar, too, is clear: there is no 1 August or any other firm date that one can point to or celebrate as marking the end of slavery in Quebec. It did not end with a ringing emancipation proclamation on some historic day; rather, like a style of dress, the fashion passed. Once it did, slaves were eager to put it behind them – it was no badge of pride – and slave-owners had no cause to speak of something which, to them, had seemed as mundane as powdered wigs and tricorn hats, and afterwards an embarrassing memory best forgotten. The subject did not come up.

This might explain why Jacques Viger, inveterate note-taker and collector that he was, in seeking to convince the public of the 1850s that Quebec had known slavery, cited old documents but no survivors. An adolescent when slavery ended, he himself may not have been conscious of it, or certain enough to rely on his childhood memories. But he might, for example, have heard his old uncle, Joseph Papineau (1752–1841), drop a word about Prince, the slave he had bought in 1792, or about those two petitions that he had presented to the Legislative Assembly on behalf of Montreal slave-owners, or about one or other of the slave transactions to which he had been privy as a notary. Viger might have discussed with his wife, Marguerite de Lacorne St-Luc (1775–1845), sometime in their thirty-seven years of married life, the fate of the slave woman that her father had left her at his death in 1784, when she was but nine years old. Perhaps she did not recollect the bequest, but she must have had some memory of acting as a sponsor at the baptism of the woman's first-born child four years later.[84] And what about the slaves that her older half-sister, Marie-Anne, Mrs John Campbell, had owned, or Thomas, the slave boy whom her mother had sold to Joseph Campeau in 1799? Are we to believe that none of Viger's acquaintances who had been eyewitnesses to slavery ever breathed a word about "the way things were" in his presence? If they had, he did not let on.

Treating slavery as an old story, over and done with, can make us forget that it was one chapter in the continuing story of race relations. The end of slavery was not the end of the story, any more than the rescue of crash victims ends with their being pulled from the wreck. When slavery crashed, the victims were left by the side of the road. The public silence on slavery among Viger's contemporaries stemmed not so much from embarrassment at the presence of its skeleton in their closet as from the fact that, generally speaking, their perception of blacks as alien and inferior had survived intact.

FIVE

Deer Out of a Cage

The end of slavery spelled a revolution in the lives of the slaves, but not in society at large. A matter of general unconcern while it lasted, it was as it faded an issue only to the few slave-owners who fought an ineffectual rearguard action to keep it going. No public funds went to slave-owners to compensate them for the loss of their human property, nor were freed slaves offered any public assistance. Absorbing the loss did not drive any slave-owners to rack and ruin. No segment of the economy declined from the loss of slave labour. Because black slaves were few, and because slavery did not end overnight but waned over several years, there was no flooding of the labour market with former slaves in search of work. The shift in their occupations – in many cases from domestic slavery to domestic service – was hardly perceptible.

David Walker, a powerful African-American writer of the 1820s, used a striking simile to contrast the handicapped state of freed blacks in his country with the world of opportunity open to whites. It was, he said, as if one were to place "one wild deer in an iron cage, where it will be secured, and hold another by the side of the same, then let it go, and expect the one in the cage to run as fast as the one at liberty."[1] The analogy applies to the blacks in Quebec, most of whom emerged from slavery – at its abolition or earlier – with their ambitions and abilities atrophied, their opportunities cramped by the restraints under which they had lived, and by their lack of resources. In some cases, freedom meant exchanging the tight cage of slavery for a roomier version, one that was more disorienting because it seemed so vast and open in comparison yet had its own invisible bars.

For some, the disorientation that accompanied freedom was geographical as well as psychological. This would have been the case for some slaves who, over the years, had found their way to freedom by running off. It would also have been the case for those who were sent away. Jack, for instance, a black boy of about sixteen years of age who had been marked down as "a Slave for life," was sold by the Mohawk trader Thomas Arakwente of Kahnawake to merchant James Holmes of St-Jean for £50 in May 1789. Three days later, Holmes resold Jack for 720 livres to François Boucher de Laperrière, of Boucherville, seigneur of Contrecoeur. In May 1794, de Laperrière and his wife, Marie Charles Pécaudy de Contrecoeur, freed "Jacques," then said to be about twenty-one, on condition that he move to "les postes les plus haut des païs d'en haut" (the farthest outposts of the Indian country), under pain of re-enslavement should he return.[2] The case of Harry, alias Michel Henry, was even more clearly one of freedom imposed as a punishment. In July 1776, Michel Eustache Gaspard Alain Chartier de Lotbinière, then a prisoner of war of the Americans, had bought the boy in Pennsylvania for £45. Harry came close to dying in 1787 but pulled through to serve de Lotbinière another twelve years. In November 1799, to punish him for some misconduct, de Lotbinière, seigneur of Vaudreuil, west of Montreal, and former speaker of the Legislative Assembly, set him free, at the same time banishing him from Vaudreuil with a warning that if he ever returned, "je le reprendrai Comme Mon Esclave & comme un Nègre que j'ai acheté" (I will seize him as my slave & as a Negro that I purchased).[3] Although exile from Vaudreuil was perhaps not as disorienting as Jack's banishment to the ends of the earth, it was still an expulsion of the slave from his familiar surroundings. This kind of high-handed behaviour on the part of masters might be likened to efforts made in the nineteenth century by American slave states to expel freed slaves lest their presence create unrest among those still in bondage.

Jack and Harry had somehow displeased their masters and had been freed for their pains. In effect, they were fired and ordered off the property, as though they had been employees rather than the property of their masters. To what extent might they or other slaves have counted on their misbehaviour provoking such a result? As we have seen, the headstrong Lisette, slave of the de Gaspé family, seems to have so exasperated her master that he thought to rid himself of her by setting her free, a move that, because of her lifelong attachment to the household, she resisted.

On at least two occasions, in which Montreal slaves were convicted of capital offences, the law imposed banishment, or what seems to have been a back-handed form of emancipation. Bruce, alias Brous, a slave of Lieutenant-Colonel Gabriel Christie, was sentenced to death in March 1773 for stealing £270 in cash from merchant Alexander Hay. However, on 6 May that year he was pardoned on the condition that within sixty days he leave the Province of Quebec, which then included all the territory that was later to be divided into Upper and Lower Canada, and more.[4] Two decades later, Tom, alias Thomas or Tom Grant, alternately identified as a "Negro boy" and a "mulatto lad" and allegedly a slave of merchant John Grant,[5] was jailed on 22 November 1794, accused of stealing twenty dollars from someone at Grant's house. If Tom had really been considered no more than a piece of property, his master might have settled this matter privately, inflicting whatever punishment he thought fit. He did not do so, and Tom's case went to court. The court appointed a lawyer to counsel him, but Tom put up no defence even though he faced the death penalty: in court in March 1795 he readily confessed to his crime and was accordingly sentenced to hang on 8 May. On March 16, however, he petitioned Governor Guy Carleton, Lord Dorchester, for a pardon. Dorchester acceded on 27 April on condition that, within thirty days, Tom "depart from and quit our said Province of Lower Canada, And be not at any time hereafter found at large within the Limits of the same or any part thereof without lawful cause."[6]

Who suffered most from this kind of banishment, slave or master? Whether the penalty imposed was hanging or banishment, the result for the master was the same: he or she was out one slave, and no law provided for compensation to be paid out of public funds, since no law recognized property in humans.[7] The slave's loss would have been much greater, of course, had he forfeited his life, but he did not; a downtrodden outcast on his home ground, was he any worse off as a masterless outcast abroad? All other things being equal, banishment would probably have been easier on Tom Grant in 1795 than on Bruce in 1773. Nothing in the terms of his pardon prevented Tom Grant from moving roughly eighty kilometres west to Upper Canada, where he would have been recognized as free under the gradual-abolition law of 1793, or the same distance south to Vermont, whose state constitution of 1777 prohibited slavery, or slightly farther afield, to Massachusetts (which then included the future state of Maine), where, in 1783, the courts had declared slavery incompatible with the equality-of-all provision in the state's constitution. But, in Bruce's day, before the American Revolution, slavery ruled in all the neighbouring colonies. It would have been difficult for a penniless black man to find a refuge where he might live free and work, without fear of re-enslavement.

It would be unreasonable to argue that Tom Grant had planned such an "escape" by deliberately setting out to commit a capital offence, risking his life in the hope that, once convicted, he would winkle a pardon out of the governor on terms that would leave him free to go where he pleased beyond the borders of the colony. But, given that more than one slave was freed for misbehaving, we must consider the possibility that the more crafty and determined among them, under the right circumstances and knowing their masters well, may have seen in misconduct – illegal or not – a back door to freedom. After all, an unruly slave posed a dilemma to a master; to keep him or her could be more trouble than it was worth, yet a mischievous character could render the slave unsaleable on the local market. To what extent some slaves might have intentionally rendered themselves at once unserviceable and unsaleable, goading their masters into washing their hands of them, is impossible to say.[8] The danger of tempting fate in this way, of course, was that instead of simply "firing" them, their frustrated masters might sell them up the river in fur-trade country, or down the river – to the West Indies, for instance – or that the courts might banish them to a foreign country or colony more inhospitable than Quebec.

SOMETHING TO TIDE THEM OVER

Of the slaves mentioned above, only Harry is known to have benefited from a severance package – a necessity in his case, considering that winter was coming on when he embarked on life as a free man. In condemning him to freedom, de Lotbinière obviously did not mean for him to die of cold. Besides twelve shillings to tide him over until he could provide for himself, he loaded Harry down with articles of clothing, including several suits, coats, cloaks, jackets, flannel underwear and mittens, eleven new shirts, and twelve vests (one of gold cloth).

The best long-term provision made by a master for a freed slave in the Montreal District was the gift bestowed, after some delay, by merchant François Dunoyer of Sorel on Jean-Baptiste Quéry. The French-born Dunoyer had owned Quéry's parents, Jean-Baptiste Quéry and Marianne Caploux, natives of Martinique, and the boy himself for many years. Marianne Caploux was a widow by February 1765, when Dunoyer freed her and her son in recognition of their long and loyal service, intending that "they should enjoy all the freedom, privileges, rights and liberty according to the usage and custom and in the manner in which the [natives of] European nations enjoy them in whatever place and under whatever government they find themselves." The unmarried Dunoyer also expressed the hope that they would remain with him as servants for the rest of his days. They did stay, and as Jean-Baptiste Quéry the younger was on the point of marrying in August 1772, Dunoyer gave him his home and farm on the banks of the Richelieu River (reserving the master bedroom for himself), with all its household furniture and housewares, its livestock, farm implements, tools and rolling stock, as well as other lots of land that he owned. Quéry signed his marriage contract with Madeleine Parenteau, a French Canadian from St-Michel-d'Yamaska, the following day, and married her the day after that. Then, in 1776, Dunoyer made out his will, leaving everything to Marianne Caploux that he had not already given to her son. She did not live to benefit from this largesse, as she died before Dunoyer, in 1788, at the reputed age of sixty-four. Just before his own death in 1792, Dunoyer made out a new will, leaving all to her son.[9]

No other former Montreal-area slaves found themselves so well secured from want as Jean-Baptiste Quéry. Still, like Harry, a few others did receive some small bounty from their masters. Rose (alias Marie Rose, Rose Raimbault), for instance, was left something of a trousseau by her mistress, Marie Louise Testard de Montigny. Seventy years old and in failing health in the fall of October 1791, Testard de Montigny, widow of Jean-Marie Raimbault, who had been a lieutenant in the French colonial troops, dictated her will, declaring Rose, "sa fille negre," free, and bequeathing to her a bed and bedclothes, a cow, and a pension of 30 livres (£1 5s) a year, consisting of the interest drawn on a capital of 600 livres. The widow Raimbault died in August 1799, when Rose was said to be in her thirties. In April 1805, Rose ceded her yearly pension in return for the capital of 600 livres.[10]

Although it marked a parting of the ways between master and slave, emancipation did not necessarily spell the severing of all ties between them. In the small world of Montreal, ex-slaves and former masters were bound to cross paths. Jane Cook, as we saw, had lost her slave Charlotte in 1798, but called on her in 1821 for help in proving her entitlement to an estate. Manuel Allen, after gaining his freedom in 1799, appears to have returned to work for his former master.[11] Catherine Guillet maintained cordial relations with the family of her former owner for decades. Born in St-Domingue to African parents,[12] Guillet is believed to have begun her life in Montreal in the 1790s as a slave of the painter François Malepart de Beaucourt and his wife, Benoite Gaëtan. Beaucourt, best known for the *Portrait d'une négresse,* which he painted in 1786 when he is thought to have been living in the French West Indies, died at Montreal in June 1794.[13] His widow, who was to outlive him by fifty years, is recorded over the next few years as the owner of several slaves. In early 1801, one of them, Catherine, "négresse de md beauCour a gée de 12 ans" (Mrs Beaucourt's twelve-year-old negress) was a patient at the Hôtel-Dieu; she was admitted again in January 1802, this time identified as Gaëtan's slave Marie, age eleven.[14] The estimated ages of Catherine/Marie jibe with the age of "about 18" given for Catherine Guillet in 1806 when, as a free woman working as a servant of John Trim, she married William Wright, the former slave of Loyalist merchant James Dunlop.[15] Indeed, at the birth of their first child, Marie Catherine Reith (*sic*) in 1807, Catherine Guillet was called Marie Catherine.[16] In 1810, the widowed Gaëtan married Gabriel Franchère Sr, and in May 1811 we find Franchère's daughter, Julie Victoire, acting as sponsor at the baptism of Catherine Guillet's daughter, Marie Charlotte Wright.[17] Widowed herself in 1825, Catherine Guillet married Jacob Abdella the following year.[18] On 26 June 1832, the two of them, under the names Jacob Abdallah and Catherine Diette, were arrested on what seems to have been a trumped-up charge of operating a bawdy house. They were tried and acquitted on 17 July under the names Jacob Abdallah and Catherine Curra.[19] The name "Curra" became "Cora" in the will that Benoite Gaëtan, recently widowed for a second time, dictated that same month. She left £6 to "Catherine Cora," whom she identified as the black woman married to the negro Jacob of the St-Joseph (or Récollets) Suburb. She also left all her clothes and furniture to her Franchère in-laws, with the suggestion that, should they find them unsuitable, they should give them away – "in which case, I urge them not to forget Catherine Cora."[20] Gaëtan named jeweller-clockmaker Jean-Baptiste Franchère as her executor. More than twenty years later, as the aged Catherine Guillet was about to leave Montreal, she gave a general power of attorney to this same Jean-Baptiste Franchère to manage her affairs.[21]

As solicitous as Benoite Gaëtan, François Dunoyer, or Marie Louise Testard de Montigny may have been about the welfare of their former slaves, it must be said that few slaves benefited from any lifetime, or even short-term, benevolence. Some went free with nothing more than the clothes on their backs. This would have been the case of those who walked out on their owners or were freed by the courts over the protests of their owners. Indeed, in the case of Marie *dite* Manon who, as we saw ear-

The Quebec-born, French-trained artist François Malepart de Beaucourt painted his *Portrait d'une négresse* in the mid-1780s when he and his wife are thought to have been living in the West Indies.

lier, was freed by order of General Thomas Gage in 1763, her frustrated owner refused to give her the clothes that she had left at his house, claiming that he was keeping them as compensation for items that she had stolen from him.[22] The slave Anne had her clothes but she was made to pay her way out of slavery, even if the sum was relatively modest. Merchant Pierre Roy had bought her for £20 16s 6d from a resident of Albany County, New York, in 1785, when she was about eleven years old. In August

1800, with slavery on its last legs, he agreed to free her (since baptized Marie Quine) in return for the "reimbursement" of 200 livres in five yearly instalments.[23]

The manumissions that exhibit the most puzzling mix of heart and heartlessness were those of Hilaire Lamour and his wife, Catherine, in 1787. Lamour was freed on 16 November as a reward for his twenty-five years of "true and faithful service" to Captain Daniel Robertson of the 84th Regiment of Foot (Royal Highland Emigrants), who had bought him at Martinique during the Seven Years War. The year 1787 seems to have been a slave-clearance year for Robertson. He had returned to Montreal after five years as commander at Michilimackinac. Shortly before leaving that post, he had freed his slave Jean Bonga, Bonga's wife, Jeanne or Jeannette, and their four children. Back in Montreal, whatever magnanimity Robertson may have shown in freeing Lamour was obviated by the fact that he held on to his wife. To obtain her release, Lamour had to buy her from Robertson, which he did on 3 December, only two weeks after his own emancipation. The price – £100 – was exorbitant, the highest recorded for a female slave sold at Montreal, and certainly more than a just-freed slave could pull out of a sock. Lamour must have borrowed heavily to amass that sum so quickly. But buying his wife did not make her free; she was now his slave. Going into debt to buy her put both of them in jeopardy. As we have seen, under British law creditors had the right until 1797 to seize black slaves in payment of the debts of their masters. Newly freed himself in 1787, Lamour probably had no other seizable asset than his wife. Should he default on his debts, Catherine could be seized and sold. Whether he recognized the danger or was alerted to it by someone else, Lamour formally emancipated his wife on 26 December, placing her beyond the reach of any creditor who might come after him.[24]

It may be that some slaves benefited from private assistance, pecuniary or otherwise, that went unmentioned in documentary records. The deed of manumission for John Trim, for example – a curious production that saw a woman identified as a widow from Upper Canada go before a notary at Quebec to free a slave at Montreal, without reference to any proof of her title to the slave – is quite pithy, offering no explanation of why Trim was freed and making no mention of a parting gift:

> Be it remembered that on this seventh day of October, in the year of our Lord one thousand seven hundred and Ninety three, before Us the undersigned Notaries Personally appeared Sarah Allen Widow of Edward Allen late of the Bay of Quinty in the province of Upper Canada Gentleman, which said Sarah Allen did and doth hereby free and Emancipate, Trim, a Negro Slave heretofore her property, at present resident at the House of Finlay Fisher of Montreal Schoolmaster – declaring the said Trim to be henceforth a free Negro, and renouncing all the Right, title or Claim which the said Sarah Allen ever had now hath or hereafter may have of in or to the said Negro or to his Service.[25]

The reference to Finlay Fisher might contain the barest clue that Trim, then perhaps in his late thirties, was receiving help in getting on his feet. Fisher, it will be remembered, was the man who, only the year before, had "aided, abetted and protected" the slave Jenny, claimed by Mary Jacobs (see chapter 2). It is possible that Trim learned to write from Fisher; he was soon to show that he could at least sign his name.

Whatever the conditions under which slaves were freed, freedom required considerable adjustment and exertion on their part. Where the pattern of their daily life had previously been dictated by their master, and their barest needs supplied, the survival of those who did not work as live-in servants now depended on their finding a roof to put over their heads, and work that would keep it there. When it came to housing, it is a sign of the change that occurred from the 1790s onward in the status of black slaves that, from *being* property, some went on to *acquire* real property in relatively short order. This was an important step at a time when the ownership of real estate was widely viewed as the measure of a person's stake in the country. Those who acquired or built a house possessed a fixed address. Not only could they shelter others less fortunate or less enterprising than themselves, but they were like beacons for black newcomers to town. They could be easily found, unlike tenants who might move from year to year, or sometimes every few months. Landed property also brought with it such attributes as the right to vote and to serve on juries. We shall see in later chapters to what extent these rights were extended to blacks. For the moment, we will content ourselves with identifying the black landholders.

LAND FOR BLACK LOYALISTS

"Nothing is so likely to make a man a good citizen as to make him a freeholder,"[26] an American politician observed in making the case for granting lands to freed slaves after the American Civil War. The first black landowners associated with Montreal at one time or another in their lives were not people who had been slaves in Canada but free blacks who received land grants as a reward for their fidelity to the Crown or for their services as members of Loyalist corps during the American War of Independence. The lands granted to these Loyalists were outside Montreal, most of them in what was soon to become Upper Canada.

Rubin Middleton, alternately identified as a "negroe" and a "mulattoe man," servant of a Montreal silversmith, narrowly escaped rotting in jail after he was convicted of rape in September 1781. Sentenced to nine months in jail and fined $100, he petitioned for a pardon, offering to serve in Sir John Johnson's corps, the King's Royal Regiment of New York. His petition was granted, his offer accepted, and he enlisted in the regiment, serving in the engineers' department. He survived the war and for his services was rewarded with a grant in Marysburgh, west of Kingston.[27]

Peter Becket, a native of Philadelphia, had served briefly in Butler's Rangers, based at Niagara, from 25 December 1777 to 31 May 1778, when he was discharged from that Loyalist corps as "unfit for service." He appears to have settled at Montreal by the beginning of 1783. After the war, he and his widowed mother, Mary Wright, received grants of land consisting of Lot 13 (200 acres) in the ninth concession of

Elizabethtown (Brockville), with a town lot attached; and half of Lot 7, i.e., 100 acres, in the seventh concession. They did not settle on their lands. In the fall of 1790, they sold their grants for thirty shillings to Montreal blacksmith Richard Wragg, the same New York Loyalist to whom, as we saw, Jacob Smith sold his land on the Ottawa River in 1794.[28]

John Powell (alias Jacques Paul, Jean Paul), said to be from Guadeloupe, received 100 acres in Lake Township (Lancaster, Ontario), District of Lunenburgh, for his "loyalty and services as a soldier" in Sir John Johnson's Royal Yorkers. Near the end of the American war, he and his African-born wife, Elizabeth, had spent some time in the Montreal area, at Terrebonne, when he was quartered there with others of the "régiment du brigadier Janson" (Johnson had recently been promoted brigadier general). Their only known child, a son named Louis, was born there in February 1783, and died the following July. After the war, Powell and his wife did apparently make a stab at working their Upper Canadian land, Lot 16 in the second concession of Lake Township. By the early 1790s, however, they had forsaken the hardships of country life for Montreal. The conveniences there included a hospital, where forty-year-old Elisabeth (sic), "négresse femme de jean powel nègre libre," spent three days in May 1792. Along with conveniences, however, urban life had its irritations. In the spring of 1795, the Powells accused Mary Fundy (alias Mary Campbell), a black woman who shared their home, of stealing a hat from him and a gown from her. In April 1796, Powell sold his Lancaster land to jeweller Thomas Powis, formerly of Quebec, who was soon to open the Montreal Tea Gardens at Côte St-Antoine (Westmount). Lot 16, which Powell claimed to have improved, he sold for 8d an acre, or £3 6s 6d in all. At the same time, he appointed Powis his agent for securing the deed to another 200 acres in the same township, Lot 17 in the 9th concession. Powell sold Powis those 200 acres too, but he was not to be paid until he held the deed in his hand and surrendered it to Powis. It appears that he never did secure this land grant.[29]

It is possible that some other black soldiers received land grants, or were entitled to the same but never took possession, like George Crane, who had served in the 84th Regiment. He married at Montreal in 1787 and a second time in 1794, when his occupation was given as a saddler. He died at Quebec in 1810, identified then as "a man of Colour, by trade a Saddler." But he and his first wife, claiming to be entitled to 250 acres, sold their claim for £2 in 1788, before they had even selected their land, so that they were never actually landowners.[30]

EX-SLAVES IN THE MARKET

Among Montrealers who are known to have been slaves, none was to show more dedication to the acquisition of real estate than John Trim. He alone among the former slaves treated land as an investment, something other than a property to occupy. But Trim was not the first known slave-turned-landowner. The first was Hilaire Lamour. In September 1793, six years after his emancipation, Lamour bought a 40'

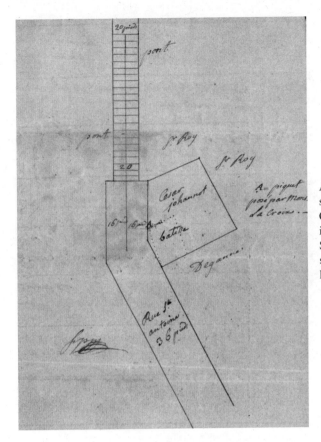

A surveyor's plan from 1797 shows the layout of distiller Caesar Johonnot's property in the west-side St-Antoine Suburb, by the bridge that, spanning the Petite Rivière, linked the suburb to the city.

by 130′ lot in the St-Laurent Suburb for 2,200 livres; he paid 1,400 livres down. By April 1794, he owed voyageur Antoine Badel *dit* Dufort 624 livres, the accumulated total of sums that Dufort had lent him from time to time (perhaps some of which had gone to pay the purchase price for Catherine in 1787). He promised to pay back the money by the following 1 September, but he was more than a year late. Final settlement of the debt on 30 October 1795 saw Lamour turn over to Dufort a strip of 10′ by 130′ of his lot. What Lamour and his wife did with their property – whether they built on it or not – is not known. They seem to have disposed of it by the summer of 1811, when Catherine died a pauper in the Hôpital-Général, the hospice run by the Grey Nuns.[31]

With Caesar Johonnot, we have a clearer idea of the use that he made of his property. He had been a slave at Boston until the early 1780s, where he had learned the distilling business from his master, Zachary Johonnot. In his will in 1783, the latter had left £50 to his former slave. Caesar Johonnot settled at Montreal within the next three years. His skills led to his being hired in 1789 as manager of the Montreal Distillery Company; besides his salary of five shillings a day, he was lodged rent-free in a company house. He held the position until the company's dissolution in 1794.[32] In April that year, he and his wife bought their own place, on the northwestern outskirts of the city. It consisted of a clapboarded log house and stable on a lot with forty-five

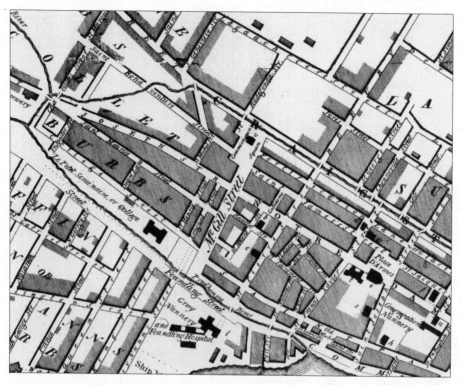

The bridge leading from the city to St-Antoine Suburb is visible to the northwest of McGill Street on this detail from an 1823 map. It stood to the east of the present-day intersection of St-Antoine and University (Craig and Ste-Geneviève) streets.

feet of frontage on the Chemin du Roi (St-Antoine Street) at the western extremity of the bridge that spanned the St-Martin River and linked the walled city to the St-Antoine Suburb. The price was 800 livres (just under £33 10s) plus an annuity of 35 livres a year to be paid from 1 August, and the annual seigneurial dues. Johonnot and his wife paid off the full purchase price by 2 January 1798.[33]

Johonnot invested heavily in his property. As of 31 December 1794, he owed 500 livres to a carpenter for carpentry and fencing work, a sum that he promised to pay by the following June. But it was 2 February 1797 before he managed to clear this debt, and it seems that he needed a loan to do so: two days before making his final payment, he had borrowed £25 from Dr Robert Jones, which he promised to pay back within two years, with interest at the going rate of six per cent. Eight months later, he secured a further loan of £40 from Jones, "for the purpose of Buying A Still and Building a Still home in the St Anthony Suberbs." Johonnot pledged to repay the loan, again at 6 per cent interest, on 30 January 1799.[34] In preparation for the building of this distillery, he had his property surveyed.[35] Another loan pertaining to this home distillery was recorded on 7 September 1797 when "Casar Johanot, an African, late overseer Distiller," borrowed £25 from notary Peter Lukin Sr, money lent "to enable him to make a new building adjoining to his present dwelling House." Johonnot was to repay the loan, without interest, on 7 September 1798; failing that, interest would accrue. Lukin acknowledged full payment of the debt on 6 October 1798.[36] Finally, on 11 January 1798, Johonnot acknowledged that he owed 515 livres to another carpenter "for as much remaining Due ... on the Building of a certain Wooden house for the use of a Distillery Upon the Land of the said Cesar Jonanote Next to his house." Johonnot promised to pay up on 17 July.[37]

He was hired on 23 January 1798 by Levy Solomon & Co. of Montreal and Cornwall for three years to work at Cornwall, where Solomon had a distillery, "or at any other port within the Provinces of Upper and Lower Canada." He was to be housed and fed, and paid ten dollars a month. A month later, on 26 February, in his absence from Montreal, his wife leased to a distiller from Quebec "that new part of the House she occupies in St Antoine Suburbs near this City formerly used by her husband as a distillery together with one small room in the House adjoining and all the ustensils for distilling." The lease ran from 16 February 1798 to 1 May 1799, at £20 a year.[38] Johonnot's employment with Levy Solomon & Co. ended before his three years were up, for on 9 October 1798 he contracted with William Fortune to work for two years as a distiller "in the distillery the property of the sd. William" at Pointe-Fortune on the Ottawa River. Besides room and board, Johonnot was to be paid £50 per year,

> and the said William Fortune for the good esteem which he hath doth by these Presents grant and bequeath unto the sd. Caesar, Half an Acre Superficial Measure of Land near and next his own Building in the Township of Hawkesbury in the Province of [the words Upper Canada are crossed out and the words] Lower Canada [are written in the margin], to have the sd. Caesar His Heirs and assigns to have and hold the sd. half an Acre of Land from henceforth for ever by virtue of these presents.

This was undoubtedly a perquisite designed to induce him to move to that remote settlement. The one condition placed on the gift was that if Johonnot or his heirs were to sell the land, Fortune was to have the first right to buy it.[39]

Johonnot's undoing came in 1799 when he defaulted on the repayment of the two loans from Dr Jones. In October, Jones sued for the recovery of those amounts, with interest, plus payment of a promissory note from Johonnot of 26 September that year in the amount of £3 16s, for a total of £77 3s 9d. The court ordered a seizure of Johonnot's assets to pay off his debt, plus court costs, for a total of £85 2s 10d or £85 16s 10d (court papers give different figures). His property in the St-Antoine Suburb was accordingly seized and auctioned off. Jones himself was the highest bidder, offering £58. But Johonnot's other creditors raised competing claims to the proceeds of the auction, and it was 21 August 1800 before these were settled and the ownership of the property could be formally transferred to Jones. Two months earlier, on 8 June, Johonnot had died at Sorel, leaving a pregnant wife and two young children.[40]

In the case of John Trim, only two and a half years elapsed between his emancipation and his first land purchase in April 1796. At the time, he was living with free blacks Henry Moore and his wife, Margaret Plauvier, in a rented house on St-Augustin Street, which ran along the inside of the western wall of the city. When the decrepit city walls were torn down in the first two decades of the nineteenth century, St-Augustin was broadened to become McGill Street, the east side being part of the city proper, the west side marking the limits of the western suburbs. Trim and the Moores seem to have pooled their resources so that at the expiration of Henry Moore's one-year lease of the house on St-Augustin Street, he and Trim bought their own place at Côte-Ste-Catherine (Outremont), on a long, narrow strip of land, 70′ wide by 12 lineal arpents deep (roughly 21 by 700 metres). Fruit trees graced the lot. This is just the kind of property we would associate with Trim, whose principal occupation was gardening, although he was occasionally referred to as a "curer of hams" and "dry salter," as well as a "trader," a term often used at the time to mean tavern keeper/grocer. The selling price was 600 livres, which Trim and Moore paid in cash on the spot. Besides the notaries, Trim was the only one of the parties to sign his name to the deed, the others making a cross.[41]

Two years later, for $350, Trim and Moore's wife bought the old wooden house on St-Augustin Street where they had lived before moving to Côte-Ste-Catherine. The property, on the east side of the future McGill Street, backed onto the former property of the Récollets priests.[42] Trim lived in that house for the rest of his life. A 220′ by 40′ lot next to his was offered for sale in 1810 with the boast that "from its size, scite and situation, [it] is well calculated for the building of extensive Stores, the

By 1793, the year of John Trim's manumission, when this view of the eastside Quebec Gate and Citadel Hill was taken, the old city walls were crumbling. St-Augustin Street, where Trim lived from 1798 until his death in 1833, ran along the inside of the western wall. The walls were torn down between 1801 and 1817, and St-Augustin, broadened, became McGill Street.

want of which is now very generally felt; or two Houses might be thereon built, with convenient yard-room to each." Yet a German immigrant who landed at Montreal in 1811, at the age of 15, was to claim many years later, with slight inexactitude, that, "At that time McGill street had only one building on it, and that was occupied by a colored man." In 1813, Trim's house was one of only five – two of them vacant – on McGill Street, with a sixth under construction. As for the property at Côte-Ste-Catherine, he may have kept it for his gardening business. In 1808, however, he first let it for the year, from 1 May, for 72 livres, and a few months later he and the widowed Margaret Moore sold the place for 720 livres.[43]

The McGill Street house was the last property that Trim bought with help from the Moores or anyone else. On his own, in May 1799, he bought a 100' by 138' vacant lot in St-Antoine Suburb ("au bout du fauxbourg St Antoine") for 170 livres, which he paid off in a year.[44] There were no real estate transactions for the next ten years, except for the disposal of the Côte-Ste-Catherine property in September 1808. Then, on 19 April 1809, Trim bought a sliver of land, 16' by 41½' in St-Antoine Suburb. He paid the purchase price of 102 livres on the spot. A little more than five years later, he bought a lot adjoining this one, 60' in front on Cemetery Street (de la Cathédrale) by 80' in depth, with a wooden house and stable on it, for £100.[45]

On 25 July 1818, Trim paid Charles William Grant, Baron de Longueuil, the new owner of the Récollets property, £110 cash for a 34' by 43' lot adjoining his McGill Street property. This was followed by another lull of almost ten years in his property-buying, during which time he lost his first wife, Charlotte, who died on 20 September 1823, and started a family with a young white woman, Fleurie Deniger. They had a daughter, Mary Ann, in 1825, a year before they married, and two other girls, Henriette and Charlotte, by the end of the decade.[46] In the last five years of his life, Trim made four more property purchases,[47] all in the St-Antoine Suburb:

- 10 July 1827 – a wooden house on a 40' by 160' lot on Janvier Street (de La Gauchetière between Mountain and Peel), price 1,500 livres
- 7 February 1828 – a 48' by 150' lot on St-Louis Street, backing onto his Janvier Street property, for £55 at a sheriff's sale
- 2 September 1829 – a 41' by 206' property, including a house, stables, shed, and well, on the "Main Street" (St-Antoine Street) of the suburb, price £275
- 19 September 1832 – a lot roughly 66' by 72' on Ste-Marguerite Street (Ste-Cécile), with a wooden house and several fruit trees on it, price at auction £96.

Unlike Johonnot, Becket, Lamour, and Powell, Trim still held his properties at his death. He left the usufruct of all his capital and property to his three daughters, but ownership was to pass to any "lawfully begotten" grandchildren. In a will that he made out in 1829, he indicated that he wanted his family to sell the McGill Street property after his death and move to one of his houses in the St-Antoine Suburb. But in his last will, drawn up in the fall of 1831, he dropped this stipulation. His first will had named three white executors – merchants Joseph Shuter and William Forsyth, and grocer Nicolaus Peter Mathias Kurczyn. He again named Forsyth and Kurczyn as executors in his last will of 1831, but Shuter was replaced by merchant Jacob DeWitt, a founder and leader of Montreal's American Presbyterian Society and the reform member of the Legislative Assembly for the county of Beauharnois.[48]

John Fleming was nowhere near as acquisitive as Trim, yet he, too, showed some ambition when, in 1804, only six months after he was freed by John Shuter, he simultaneously acquired not one lot, but two – Lot 52, measuring 90' by 45', on Gabriel Street (Ottawa), corner of Prince Street, and adjacent Lot 53, of the same dimensions but fronting on Prince.[49] It was the seigneurial system of land tenure that enabled a freed slave to become a landholder so soon after his emancipation. Fleming seems to have been the only black Montrealer to benefit from this system left over from the days of New France and originally intended to encourage settlement.[50] Seigneurs, who were granted lands by the crown, were virtually bound to concede lots to all comers who undertook to respect certain terms and conditions (settling on their land, developing it, etc.) besides paying nominal annual dues (*cens et rentes*). These *censitaires* in good standing could sell and bequeath their lands like any other landowners, the only difference being that on each such transfer the seigneur received a cut of the sale price (*lods et ventes*), and, of course, the new owner had to continue paying the annual dues. The Sulpician priests were the seigneurs of the island of Montreal, which was broken up into several fiefs and sub-fiefs. There was little unconceded land left on the island by the beginning of the nineteenth century, especially in the vicinity of the city. Trim, Lamour, Johonnot, and anyone else who bought lands already granted had to pay the purchase price as well as the annual seigneurial dues. But Fleming, in securing unconceded land in the Fief Nazareth, west of McGill Street, paid no purchase price. He needed no capital, no down payment, no mortgage, no collateral, no guarantor – all that he had to do was to subscribe to the conditions of his grant, i.e., to pay 72 livres (£3) a year as ground rent (*rente foncière*) for each of his two lots, plus a trifling sum of "six deniers Tournois de cens," to Mary Griffin and the nuns of the Hôtel-Dieu, who held the rights to the fief.[51] When a black man named Thomas Stockbird acquired a property opposite Fleming's in October 1810, it was from the then title-holder Paul Descary, not as a concession from Mary Griffin and the nuns.[52] A year after Fleming bought his two lots, he apparently came close to selling Lot 53 for £4, but that sale must have fallen through, because in 1816, Thomas McCord, who had acquired Mary Griffin's rights in the Fief Nazareth, sued Fleming for eleven years of arrears of the annual £3 payment on Lot 53. Fleming having no seizable goods worth £33, Lot 53 was seized by the sheriff and advertised for sale, the sale to take place on 10 December. But on 9 December, the court was advised that McCord and Fleming had settled their dispute. Indeed, on 28 November, Fleming had disposed of his two lots for £100.[53]

William Wright was even more fortunate than John Fleming in his acquisition of land and a house of his own, in that they came to him as a gift. A former slave of the wealthy businessman James Dunlop, a Scottish-born Loyalist from Virginia, Wright was a free man in 1806 when he married Catherine Guillet, then a live-in servant of

A modern-day artist used the specifications provided to the contractor in 1820 to produce this sketch of the house built for the former slave William Wright.

John and Charlotte Trim. Wright appears to have worked as Dunlop's servant until the latter's death in August 1815, and to have then lived at Trim's with his wife until 1820. While Dunlop left nothing to Wright in his will, he did order that his executors pay his debts, with the result that on 4 July 1820, five years after his master's death, Wright, then about sixty years old, received the not inconsiderable sum of £62 15s 9d "for as much due to him for wages from the estate of the late James Dunlop."[54] That same day, merchant Charles Frederick Hooffstetter, who handed Wright the wage settlement, and retired merchant Adam Ann Gordon gave him a house. In making the gift, they explained that, "feeling a friendship for William Wright, a negro, of this city, and commiserating his helpless state after spending or [sic] his life as a servant, and his present age threatening a want, they the said Adam Ann Gordon and Charles F. Hooffstetter of their free will have determined to ensure as much as in their power a competency against too great distress in his said Wm. Wright's old age."[55]

The two benefactors had hired a contractor to build the house at a cost of £100, on a lot they had purchased a few days earlier for £50. The house was to be thirty feet square and to contain two dwellings side by side, each with three rooms and a garret. Hooffstetter later paid an extra £15 10s to have the property fenced in, to run a fence down the middle of the yard, and to erect privies to serve two households. The house stood at the southwest corner of College (St-Paul) and Inspector Streets, in the Récollets Suburb. Wright and his wife, then childless – they had had five children, all of whom had died in infancy – were able to move in that September. They were responsible for paying £40 still owing on the price of the lot and the annual seigneurial dues. Under the terms of the gift, the house was to go to Wright's wife after his death; if she declined it, the property would be sold to provide her with an income.[56] A son, John, the only one of their children to survive to adulthood, was born there in 1823. William Wright died on 10 February 1825 at the reputed age of sixty-six. Catherine Guillet, about half his age, married widower Jacob Abdella in October 1826. They had three children, all of whom died before the age of two. Abdella left his wife in 1848, apparently moving to Canada West. She stayed on in the house until the mid-1850s (it was dilapidated by then, its roof leaking), when she went to live with her son, John Wright, at Quebec, where she died on 14 November 1862 at the reputed age of seventy-seven.[57]

Around the time that William Wright and Catherine Guillet were given their house in the Récollets Suburb, Othello Keeling, a labourer who was to be the widowed Guillet's tenant in 1825, bought a vacant lot on St-Louis Street in the same suburb for 2,000 livres. Keeling, who had been a slave or servant of fur-trade merchant John Gregory at his Fief Bellevue (Ste-Anne-de-Bellevue) at the turn of the century, was without the resources to develop his property, or even the wherewithal to pay it off. Thirteen years after buying it, he was obliged to return the vacant lot to the seller. He died at the reputed age of sixty, on 29 July 1834.[58]

SLAVERY DRIVES THE PRICE DOWN

Alexander Valentine[59] was another black Montrealer who, like John Trim, teamed up with friends or acquaintances to purchase a house. Of the Montreal real estate transactions involving blacks, this one most pointedly illustrates some of the difficulties in the caged deer's attempts to run as fast as the wild one.

Valentine was a domestic servant of Judge Arthur Davidson of the Court of King's Bench in February 1803 when he and carpenter Augustin Labadie bought a property on St-Charles-Borromée (Clark) Street, St-Laurent Suburb. The price was 3,000 livres, plus about 1,000 livres in encumbrances consisting of an annuity based on a capital of 600 livres, and about 400 livres in *lods et ventes* due to the Sulpicians for previous transfers of the property. The lot measured 39' 8" by 51', the house of squared logs (*pièces sur pièces*) 29' 8" by 25' 7". They paid the owner, cooper Étienne Roy, 500 livres down; another 500 was due him in September that year – they paid it on 10 October – and the remainder, with interest of six per cent a year, in four consecutive annual payments.[60]

In June 1804, Labadie and his wife sold their interest to the Valentines for 2,500 livres – 1,000 livres due to Roy to cover the encumbrances, plus 1,500 livres. Of the 1,500 livres portion, Valentine paid Labadie 787 livres 4 sols down, the remaining 713 livres 16 sols to be paid, without interest, on 1 May 1805. Valentine and his wife were to take possession on 1 November – earlier if they could come up with the balance owing to Labadie. Meanwhile, in July, the Labadies bought a house on nearby St-Urbain Street from peddlar John Threer, moving in on 1 September. The sale price was 1,500 livres – 800 livres payable on demand, and the balance, without interest, in May 1805 – plus an annuity of six per cent on a capital of 1,063 livres due to Angélique Blondeau, the widow of fur-trade merchant Gabriel Cotté, the previous owner. Labadie paid Threer the first instalment of 800 livres that August.[61]

On 9 October 1804, Valentine paid Roy the instalment then due on the price of his house, amounting to 620 livres, of which he had borrowed 422 livres from Davidson. Valentine undertook to pay back Davidson in four years, with interest. For his loan (and future sums he was to advance Valentine), Davidson held a mortgage on the property. Valentine made another yearly payment of 590 livres to Roy on 7 October 1805.[62] In the meantime, he and his wife – probably after consultation with Davidson or his son-in-law, lawyer David Ross – had become convinced that Labadie had overcharged them. They reneged on their agreement to pay him off by 1 May 1805. This made it impossible for Labadie to fulfill his obligation to pay off that same month the 700 livres that he owed on his house. In June, Labadie sued Valentine for the £29 14s 10d due to him, while Threer sued Labadie for the £29 s 4d owed him. Judge Davidson begged off sitting on this case pitting the Labadies against the Valentines, "one of the Defend[ts.] Being in my service."[63]

In their defence, lawyer Ross cast the Valentines as deer just out of a cage: they pleaded diminished responsibility on account of slavery.

> [H]aving been but lately liberated from the wretched and deplorable state of Slavery in which they had the misfortune to be born and being naturally of such weak capacities or understanding as to be altogether unable to count or reckon money and altogether ignorant of the value of Money and of the difference between one Sum and another[,] they the defendants were utterly incapable with safety to themselves of making and concluding with the Plaintiffs the Deed of Bargain and Sale of the fifteenth day of June last ... and cannot nor ought in law, justice, reason, conscience or equity to be bound thereby, and [...] they also say that being naturally of such weak capacities or understanding and utterly incapable with safety to themselves of contracting as aforesaid they the Defendants were greatly over-reached and imposed upon by the Plaintiffs in making and concluding with them the before mentioned bargain and Sale (which besides is of itself altogether inconsistent contradictory and absurd) ...[64]

The Labadies countered that the Valentines were far from being the clueless ex-slaves that they claimed to be. Both sides agreed to arbitration, which turned out to be an assessment of Valentine's financial acumen. Arbiters Louis Guy and Louis Chaboillez, both notaries, submitted their report on 16 October 1805, concluding that Valentine

> is absolutely ignorant of the monetary value of gold and silver species, that when he entered into the contract aforesaid, he was unable to discern whether the price of his acquisition was reasonable or exorbitant; wherefore from the information we have gathered and the maximum possible value of the land and house in question, we believe it just and fair to deduct from the sale price set by the Plaintiffs for the Defendants the sum of three hundred livres equivalent to twelve pounds ten shillings currency, which leaves a balance owing to the Plaintiffs of seventeen pounds four shillings and ten pence with interest from the first of May last.[65]

The court endorsed this finding, and in December Valentine and his wife paid Labadie £20 16s 10½d, the sum set by the arbiters, plus interest and costs. Most of the funds came from Davidson, whom the Valentines undertook to pay back in four years.[66]

With Labadie paid off, Valentine paid Roy another instalment on the price of the house on 17 October 1806, this time of 560 livres, of which 172 livres was his own money, and the rest (387 livres 10 sols) once more a loan from Davidson, repayable in three years or earlier, if possible. After Davidson's death, in May 1807, Valentine made the final payment to Roy of 500 livres, plus 36 livres in interest, on 16 March 1808, money borrowed from lawyer Ross. Valentine paid off his debt to Davidson's estate by 1 July 1814.[67]

The Labadies, for their part, had to sort out their problem with Threer. It was no doubt to accomplish this that, on 2 November 1805, Labadie borrowed 500 livres from Elizabeth Perras, the widow of merchant Simon Cavilhe, repayable with interest on 31 October 1806. But they still had not repaid her in December 1807, when they tried unsuccessfully to sell their house. Two months later, on 23 February 1808, declaring that they were about to leave the province, they gave notary Louis Guy a power of attorney, entrusting him with the responsibility of selling the house and paying off the widow Cavilhe.[68] The widow, growing impatient, sued the absent Labadies in February 1809, but Guy persuaded her to desist, pointing out that proceeding through the courts would only impose greater costs on the Labadies and make it more difficult for them to pay her. Guy must have promised to try to sell the house again, as Cavilhe's attorney, Joseph Quesnel, inquired that June whether he had made any progress in the matter. In late August, Quesnel informed Guy that Cavilhe now insisted on immediate payment of the debt, failing which she would return to court. In late October–early November, the public crier read out the offer of sale of the property at the door of Notre-Dame Church, and it seems that it was finally auctioned off.[69]

Notary Guy knew where the Labadies had gone, but we do not. Their departure is even more shrouded in mystery than their arrival. Of the Valentines, we know from their own claim in court in 1805 that they had been slaves until recently. They were quite possibly the illiterate black couple married at Montreal in 1800 under the names Alexander Smith and Catharine Fletcher. Near the end of her life, Valentine's wife, known as Catherine Mayson (also written Maisse, Mason, Masson, Maysan, Moysan), was identified as American-born, and it is likely that Valentine was also of American origin.[70] Labadie's wife was also American. Baptized Marie Angélique Price at St-Antoine by the slave-owning Reverend Louis Payet in 1798, she was said on that occasion to be the roughly twenty-five-year-old daughter of Richard Prêsse (Price), an Englishman, and Ann, a "femme metive" (mixed-race woman), farmers in Maryland. Her sponsors, Jacques Cartier and Marie Geneviève Cartier of St-Antoine, were respectively the future father and aunt of George-Étienne Cartier, one of the Fathers of Confederation; how the Cartiers came to act in that capacity, and how she, a native of Maryland, found herself living on the banks of the Richelieu River are questions that remain to be elucidated.[71] She and Labadie married at Montreal the following year. On that occasion, she was termed a "négresse"; her husband was not identified as black, only as the adult son of François Labadie and the late Marguerite Cuisy of the Parish of Montreal.[72] We have found no record of his birth, but assuming that

François Labadie, his father, was the man of that name who had been sponsor at the baptism in January 1793 of Marie Anne Houldin, the daughter of a former Montreal slave,[73] then Augustin must have been living in the Montreal area by the early 1790s, at the latest. We believe, hesitantly, that he was white. The only record found that suggests otherwise is a receipt from a representative of the widow Cotté in August 1807 that identified him as "Jean Bte Labadie negre."[74] This misidentification of Augustin Labadie is perplexing. It may be that he was black, or it may be that instead of delivering a payment in person, he had sent a black acquaintance – Jean Baptiste L'Africain, say (see below) – and the person making out the receipt had confused Labadie with this black emissary.[75]

While the Valentines had no children, seven were born to the Labadies in quick succession, and the first six just as quickly died. Their first four – Marie Angélique, Marie Victoire, Marie Julie (alias Marie Rose), and Marie Émilie – born between October 1800 and July 1803, all died before their first birthday; their fifth, Marie Louise, born in 1804, lived fourteen months; Louis Jacques Augustin lasted just seven weeks in 1806. The Labadies may have had better luck with their seventh child, Antoine Casimir, born on 22 December 1807; he appears to have been still living when they departed for points unknown in 1808.[76] Had both parents been black, we would have expected to find at least one black among the sponsors at the baptisms of the children, but all fourteen sponsors were white. These included Marie (also known as Polly) Fearson, wife of Montreal roads inspector (surveyor) Louis Charland, and godmother of Louis Jacques Augustin. The boy's godfather was nineteen-year-old Jacques Viger, the future Montreal mayor and historian of slavery, who was to succeed Charland as roads inspector after the latter's death in 1813. (The boy seems to have been named Louis for Charland, Jacques for Viger, and Augustin after his father.) Viger's aunt and uncle, Perrine Cherrier and Denis Viger, the latter a carpenter by trade and latterly a member of the Legislative Assembly for Montreal East, had been the godparents of the Labadie's second child, Marie Victoire. For black acquaintances of the Labadies, other than the Valentines, we must look elsewhere. Augustin Labadie was a witness at the wedding of Jean-Baptiste L'Africain and Charlotte Bonga in 1801, and godfather of their son, François-Xavier L'Africain, born in 1804.[77] Labadie and Charlotte Bonga also were the godparents of Marie Elizabeth Ferland, the daughter born in December 1803 to black labourer Jacques Ferland and his wife, Marie; with Bonga's mother, Jeanne (or Jeannette), Labadie was a sponsor in July 1803 at the baptism of Geneviève Fortennéter, daughter of black labourer Jean Fortennéter (alias Jean Fortune, John Fortunator); and with Mary Violet Jones, the future wife of shoemaker Narcisse Coudrin, he was a sponsor in November 1805 at the baptism of Pierre Augustin François, the son of Joseph François and Charlotte McGill.[78] A bill of November 1807 for professional services tendered by lawyer Joseph Bédard shows that Labadie sued Coudrin for damages in May that year, or at least took steps to launch such a suit.[79] While this list suggests that Labadie had friends or acquaintances among French-speaking blacks, Valentine similarly served as a witness at several baptisms, weddings and funerals, most of them involving English-speaking blacks.[80]

Unlike the Labadies, the childless Valentines remained in Montreal to the end of their days, he working as a carter after Judge Davidson's death. Valentine died on 18 November 1829 at the reputed age of 55 and was buried in the Protestant cemetery on Dorchester Street.[81] Catherine Mayson, his wife, put all the rooms in her own house up for rent and moved in to the house of a Mrs Grant. In 1831, she mortgaged the property on St-Charles-Borromée Street to Dr Daniel Arnoldi as security for payment of the £12 10s that she owed him "for medical attendance during several years past." From a lease of November 1833, by which she rented out two ground-floor rooms in her house to a white peddlar for $2 a month, it appears that she had returned to the house and lived upstairs, and that she also had other tenants living downstairs. In April 1834, she leased two rooms for slightly more than a year to a white carpenter, the terms of the lease requiring him to pay $3 a month and to act as caretaker of her building and yard. In May that year, she sold the house and lot to notary George Dorland Arnoldi, son of Dr Arnoldi, for an annuity of £20 a year, to be paid to her as long as she lived. She died nine years later, on 28 January 1843, at the reputed age of 84.[82]

The Mrs Grant with whom Catherine Mayson moved in after her husband's death was Mary Ann Drummond, a Jamaican who seems to have landed at Montreal shortly after 1800 and married labourer Jacob Grant in 1815 (their witnesses were John Trim and William Wright). In September 1829, two months before the death of Catherine Mayson's husband, Mary Ann Drummond had bought a two-storey house on St-Constant Street near Mignonne (de Bullion Street at de Maisonneuve Boulevard) in the St-Laurent Suburb. She was the only black woman of this time to buy a house on her own. Two weeks before she was to take possession, she paid the full price of £150 in cash. It was a wooden house on a 40′ by 124′ lot, bounded behind by the line separating the Fief Lagauchetière from the Fief Closse.[83]

Drummond and her husband had no children. He died in 1841; she survived by taking in washing and renting out rooms in her house, until it was destroyed on 8 July 1852 in a fire that, racing east, razed most of the buildings between present-day St-Laurent Blvd. and St-Denis Street, from de Maisonneuve Boulevard to Viger Avenue. In the Montreal city assessment rolls for 1853, her property at 19 St-Constant Street was listed twice, once as a vacant lot, property of Mary Ann Drummond, and also as a "Brick House unfinished, 10 Tenements," property of a contractor. Drummond's name never again turned up on the tax rolls or in city directories.[84]

Of one last black Montreal landowner of this time, Joseph François Demarin, we know nothing before February 1802, when, as Joseph François, "nègre libre," he bought a farm of 128¼ arpents at St-Eustache, in the seigneury of Mille-Îles, for 300 livres, paid in two instalments, the last on 24 May that same year. In his will, made out in March 1820, he left the farm and all that he owned to his "wife," Angélique Filiatreau (Angélique Filiatrault *dit* St-Louis). He and Filiatrault, by whom he had had two children, were not formally married until seven years later.[85]

BANDING TOGETHER

Leaving aside Demarin and the other sometime Montrealers whose lands lay away from the city (Becket, Middleton, Powell), we have ten blacks acquiring land at Montreal between 1793 and 1840. Most did not manage to hold on to their property. Although we know nothing of the use or disposal of the land bought by Thomas Stockbird in October 1810, we do know that, by 1840, the only black landowners left were John Trim's estate; Catherine Guillet, as the heir of her first husband, William Wright; and Mary Ann Drummond. Of the land transactions involving blacks, Trim's stand out for the number and size of his acquisitions; he was also the only one who owned a property within the limits of the old city. It is worth noting that, years before the age of the interprovincial and transcontinental railways, when much of the black population of Montreal would come to be concentrated on the west side, around the train stations, rail yards, and related facilities, Trim already favoured the west-side St-Antoine Suburb. He himself never lived there, but his daughters and their families would occupy some of his properties in the second half of the nineteenth century, forming an early black nucleus in that quarter.

The acquisition of property by blacks aroused no overt white opposition. In the cases outlined above, which constitute all the known real-estate acquisitions by blacks in Montreal up to the 1840s, whites did not refuse to sell to blacks or put up obstacles to such sales. Some whites even facilitated these transactions, as we saw, either by making outright gifts, as in Wright's case, or by offering loans, as in the cases of Johonnot and Valentine. Yet it is curious that the lands acquired by those first black property owners were, except for Trim's home on McGill Street, all located in the western and northern suburbs; none lay in the Quebec (or Ste-Marie) Suburb on the east side, where several black tenants leased flats and houses.

Whether property owners or tenants, blacks were scattered around the city. There was no area to which they were restricted, none from which they were barred. There was, however, a banding together of unrelated blacks in shared lodgings, which might hint at problems of discrimination in rental housing. As mentioned above, John Powell and his wife shared their place with Mary Fundy, who does not appear to have been a close friend: had she been so, it is unlikely that they would have charged her with theft as they did.[86] In 1819, three black men – Peter Dago, Titus Fortune, and Leonard Freeman – shared a house on St Nicolas Tolentine (St-Timothée) Street in the Quebec Suburb.[87] It is impossible to say whether this was by their own inclination, out of economic necessity, or because many landlords refused to rent to blacks, so that they were more or less obliged to share what lodgings they could find. In the winter of 1817–18, Dago and a Mrs Day, believed to be his mother, shared a place at Pointe-à-Callière, on the waterfront, with Ace Gabriel and William Meikins Nation. Gabriel left there and went to live with cook Richard Thompson, another black man, who operated a cake shop in the Quebec Suburb.[88] In March 1820, we find blacks Warren Glossen, George Binks, and Richard Jackson sharing a house in the Quebec Suburb.[89] In 1833, James Sampson and his wife, Elizabeth Ashley, shared a place with Robert Jackson, a black man from Quebec.[90] In coming together in this way, did blacks jump, or were they pushed? Probably both.

This cohabitation also occurred in houses owned by blacks. The Valentines and the Labadies shared the house on St-Charles-Borromée Street in 1803–04. In 1814, James Grant and his wife, Sally York, lived at John Fleming's house in the Ste-Anne Suburb.[91] In the spring of 1816, Jane Graham, a black woman from Upper Canada, was living with Jacques Fleming (John Fleming) and his wife.[92] As for the Valentines, Robert Williams lived with them, or rented a room in their house, in 1819; in 1825, it appears that newly married James Sampson and his wife, Elizabeth Ashley, were the Valentines' tenants.[93] Just after acquiring their house on St-Constant Street in 1829, as we saw, Mary Ann Drummond and her husband, Jacob Grant, briefly took in Valentine's widow, Catherine Mayson. In 1833, John Broome from Barbados and Jane Wilson from Bermuda, newly married, were tenants in Drummond's house (and all through the 1840s, after her husband's death, her tenant was cook John Francis, alias John François and Jean François St Elistan, a native of St-Domingue).[94] Blacks who were tenants of William Wright or, after his death, of his widow Catherine Guillet and her second husband, Jacob Abdella, included Mary Rusk, the widow of Joseph Pierson, Othello Keeling, and Peter Dago.[95]

Here again, John Trim offers an outstanding example. For the first few years of his residence on McGill Street, he shared the house with co-owners Henry Moore and his wife, Margaret Plauvier. We believe that Plauvier went on living there well after her husband's death in 1803, possibly until her own death at age 80 in 1827.[96] From about 1805 to 1820, Trim and his wife employed Catherine Guillet as a servant, and it is likely that Guillet's husband, William Wright, lived there for at least a few years before he and Guillet moved into their own house in September 1820. Labourer Abraham Low, believed to be of West Indian origin, moved from Quebec to Montreal around the end of 1814 and lived at Trim's for at least several months.[97] Robert Moore, previously employed and lodged at the City Tavern at St-Paul and St-Pierre Streets, lived at Trim's for about six months in 1815, probably from April or May until November, when he married Sente (Cynthia, Sintie) Williams. Four years after his wife's death in 1829, Moore would marry Trim's widow, Fleurie Deniger.[98] Jacob Abdella, a cook of Mediterranean origin – he was said at different times to be from Malta, Gibraltar, or Italy – boarded at Trim's for about four years, probably until the time of his wedding to American-born Mary Downing in January 1823. She died only five months later and, as we have seen, Abdella would go on to marry the widowed Guillet in 1826.[99]

THE FALLING OUT

In any probing of the roots of a Montreal black community, Trim is impossible to ignore. A former slave, married first to the doughty Charlotte, then to the French-Canadian Fleurie Deniger, who bore him three children, he was an incomparable embodiment of the link between the days of black slavery and the modern age, of "things as they were" and "things as they are." In Rome, he was determined to do as the Romans did. A canny, industrious black man in a white society, he knew how to use the tools of that society – money, the real estate market, the law, etc. – to his advantage, demonstrating that it was possible to surmount at least some of the handicaps that were a legacy of slavery. Of his material success, there is no doubt. As early as 1805, he had dealings with the lawyer and future chief justice James Reid, for which Reid paid him with a promissory note for £220. It is difficult to imagine what goods or services Trim could have provided that would have commanded such a high price; Reid's note said only that it was in payment "for value Received."[100] No other blacks of the period dealt in such large sums; Alexander Valentine, Augustin Labadie and his wife, John Fleming and others mentioned above struggled to come up with much lesser amounts. Trim's prosperity was no secret. When a dividing wall was built between his and neighbour Simon Clark's McGill Street properties in 1821, Clark's son instructed workmen to build it more than a foot inside Trim's property, pretexting that even if he deprived Trim of this narrow strip of land, "ça ne lui feroit pas grand tort il est assez riche" (he is rich enough that it will hardly hurt him).[101]

Material success may have brought Trim a measure of social acceptance from whites. His choice of executors, all whites, suggests that he mixed with them, at least in the course of business. A further hint that he was more in white eyes than just another "nègre" came in 1827 when, in the election of Assembly members for the County of Montreal, the polling clerk registered the aged Trim as a "Bourgeois," a term then used without pejorative connotation to identify men of some means and status.[102] This is the only known instance when the term, more or less equivalent to "gentleman," or to the old term "burgher," was applied to a black man of this time.

Trim's association with whites, culminating in his marriage to a young white woman in the mid-1820s, may have led him into conflicts with other blacks. Certainly, in his last years, he accused various blacks of misdeeds, including stalking, threatening and assaulting him, and stealing from him. There is an air of unreality to some of these charges, suggesting that they stemmed from emotional distress over the loss of Charlotte, his first wife, some dottiness in his old age, or the paranoia of a self-made man who, nearing his end, suspected those around him of coveting his wealth and possessions, and perhaps even his young wife. There may have been some foundation to his charges, but none was ever proven. At the time, all that was needed to have a person arraigned was a sworn complaint; the accused might then be released on posting security for good behaviour, or the case might go to trial on the strength of the accuser's complaint and the depositions of any witnesses he or she might bring forward. Criminal investigations, especially in relatively minor matters, were virtually unknown.[103]

In earlier years, Trim had had the odd run-in with various people. In October 1810, he complained of having been "grossly abused and insulted by ... Hazen Cross who ... threatened that he would kill him ... and his dog." Cross, a minor, was released on his promise to keep the peace for a year, his father and another man each posting a

£20 bond to guarantee his good behaviour.[104] In the fall of 1813, Trim complained of having been assaulted by a William Finch and threatened by Finch's son, James, when he went to fetch his grazing cow from a pasture belonging to Finch Sr. Trim swore that William Finch, "with a stick, gave Deponent a violent blow on the neck" and that James Finch had threatened that if he "came there again he should not go away a live." The Finches were each required to post £20 recognizances to keep the peace and be well behaved toward Trim for six months.[105] In the fall of 1818, Trim again complained of being abused, claiming that "this sixth day of November instant being in the New-Market place of this City, he was without the least provocation on his part assaulted and Struck by one Richard Thompson of the same place, labourer, who then and there abused and insulted this Deponent in the most shameful language." Thompson, who identified himself as a shopkeeper – he was probably the black cook and pastry shop owner of that name – was obliged to post a £10 bond, with two additional sureties of £5 each, to keep the peace for six months.[106] In 1820, it was a deranged man who disturbed the Trim household on a couple of occasions, walking into their home and creating a stir, or throwing stones at the house.[107] In 1823, Trim accused Jane Wilson, a "Servant Woman" – possibly his own servant – of assaulting and kicking him. We suspect that she was probably the Jane Wilson mentioned above as the wife of John Broome, tenants in the early 1830s of Mary Ann Drummond. Another intriguing aspect of this incident is that Trim filed his complaint on 2 September 1823, less than three weeks before the death of his wife, Charlotte. Unfortunately, the surviving records contain no further information on the servant Jane Wilson, the circumstances of the alleged assault or the disposition of the case.[108]

Trim met Fleurie Deniger in 1824, at the latest; their daughter, christened Mary Ann Shuter Trim, was born on 6 April 1825.[109] An interracial affair leading to the birth of a child might have been swept under the carpet, but the idea that Trim and Deniger might formalize their relationship and actually marry must have raised some eyebrows, and perhaps brought remonstrances from some of Trim's friends or acquaintances. He was black, she was white; he was a widower in his seventies, she was in her teens; he was well off, she was the penniless daughter of a deceased labourer. On 12 August 1825, Trim complained that at his house a Tally Reny Valentine "did ... threaten the said Deponent in a violent manner and provoke and challenge the said Deponent who from the behaviour and threats of the said Tally Reny Valentine, stands in bodily fear and danger of his life." As a result, Tally Reny Valentine was arrested on 15 August and detained until sometime in November.[110] It may be that this incident had nothing to do with Trim's marital plans, but as in the case of the 1823 run-in with Jane Wilson, we cannot help but note the timing of the incident in relation to the known facts of Trim's life. The name Tally Reny Valentine comes up in no other records: we suspect that the person might, in fact, be Alexander Valentine. By December 1825, Trim and Deniger had decided to marry, with the consent of her mother, Marianne Laventure *dit* Beaudin, and her stepfather, labourer Baptiste Poupart. A marriage contract was duly executed on 26 January 1826, and the couple were married on 2 April.[111]

Although some of the above cases leave room for speculation on the racial identities of the accused, no doubts exist for a string of accusations that Trim made in the last three years of his life. In the fall of 1830, he accused Robert Moore, his former lodger, of threatening to beat him, claiming that Moore also "followed him with evil intentions when he [Trim] has gone out at night." As a result, Moore had to post bonds to keep the peace on two occasions in the winter of 1830–31. Then, in September 1831, Trim sought to have Moore and Jacob Grant, the husband of Mary Ann Drummond, charged with grand larceny, suspecting that they had stolen clothing from his house and stashed the items around town, including at barber James Rollings' in St-Paul Street and at schoolmaster John Bruce's English and Classical Academy on McGill Street. A note on Trim's affidavit indicated that a search was made and "Nothing found."[112] Considering the distrust that Trim displayed toward his wife in his last will – "I desire that my wife Flavie Deniger shall have no controul whatsoever over the property or person of either one or another of my said Children," he stipulated[113] – and given that she would marry Moore five months after Trim's death, it is not unreasonable to suppose that Trim's charges may have sprung from a belief that Moore had already supplanted him in Deniger's affections.

With Jacob Abdella and his wife, Catherine Guillet, Trim went farther than voicing suspicions. On 25 June 1832, he and a Michael Coyle, believed to be white, formally accused them of running a bawdy house in their home. Besides Trim, the witnesses arrayed against them included another black man, Mauger Williams (also written Mager, or Major, Williams), and Abdella's tenants, the Metis Henry Thain and his wife Desolives Gauthier. Abdella and his wife were acquitted.[114] Finally, in November that year, two months before his death, Trim filed a strange complaint, ostensibly before his friend, Justice of the Peace Joseph Shuter. It almost seems that the complaint was registered to humour the old man. Trim alleged that a *Jacob* Julian and his wife *Catherine* Guerin (Jacob Abdella and Catherine Guillet again?) had frequently threatened to kill him, and that "Julian" had attacked and beaten him on or about the 15 October, "to the best of his recollection." The recognzance form of the accused stated that they and their sureties "personally came before me Joseph Shuter" – yet the form was signed not by Shuter but by another magistrate, and neither the accused nor the sureties signed it (or made their mark) as would have been required for it to be valid.[115]

Trim died on 26 January 1833. He was said to be seventy-eight years old. He was buried beside his first wife, Charlotte, in the Protestant burial ground on Dorchester Street (René Lévesque Boulevard).[116] Besides seeking to deny his widow any say in the upbringing of his children or the management of his estate, he left her nothing in his will. Under her marriage contract, however, Fleurie Deniger was entitled to an annuity of £24, plus a one-time payment of £10, both of which she would forfeit if she remarried, which she promptly did. On 22 June, she married waiter Robert Moore, widower and single father of thirteen-year-old Margaret Moore. A few days later, Deniger and her new husband successfully petitioned the courts to be named legal guardians of Deniger's three young daughters by Trim. Furthermore, in the summer of 1837, she and Moore entrusted to a notary the responsibility of managing the Trim estate.[117] So much for Trim's dying wish that she have no "controul" over her daughters and their inheritance. Moore and Deniger had a son, Robert, in November 1836, who lived only twenty-two months. In October 1838, a month after the boy's death, she accused Moore of beating her and threatening her with a sword; he was "in the habit of keeping a loaded musket under his bed, and being a person of disorderly and intemperate habits," she said, so much so that she feared for her life. She was not to fear much longer: Moore died the following February, at the reputed age of forty-eight.[118]

On 30 May 1838, Deniger was married a third time, to a sailor named Paul Coffin. Their daughter, Marie Catherine Eulalie Coffin, a stepsister to the Trim girls and to Margaret Moore, was born the following November; Jacob Abdella and Catherine Guillet were her godparents.[119] Familiarly known as Catherine or Emily Coffin, she lost her father some time within the next few years, because on 2 July 1842, Deniger married for a fourth time. Her new husband, carpenter James Carpenter, a widower, was a Prince Edward Island man, probably of East Indian descent.[120] In July 1843, he and Deniger successfully applied to the courts to be appointed legal guardians to her three Trim daughters, this even though the oldest, eighteen-year-old Mary Ann, had by then been married for two years. On the same day, they gave a lawyer a power of attorney to oversee the estate and to oblige the only active Trim executor, Kurczyn, to render an account of his stewardship.[121] Five months earlier, Deniger had had a daughter by Carpenter: Mary Elizabeth Carpenter (in French, Élisabeth Carpentier or Charpentier), like Emily Coffin, had Abdella and Guillet for godparents.[122]

Deniger's four marriages made for a complex blended family, with her three daughters by Trim entitled to the fruits of his estate, while their three stepsisters and successive stepfathers were not. We can only guess at the psychological effects that this and the successive male deaths and replacement fathers may have had on the children. Deniger herself, excluded from any claim to the estate, benefited nevertheless, as did her successive husbands and their children, insofar as they lived with her Trim daughters, in Trim properties, at least while the girls were minors. At her death in November 1860, however, Deniger was living not in one of the Trim houses but with her daughter Emily Coffin and son-in-law, black carpenter and contractor Mathew Bell, a native of South Carolina, in a rented dwelling on St-Antoine Street.[123]

To trace in detail the saga of Trim's descendants and their extended family, as well as the troubled state of his legacy, embroiled in legal disputes from the 1840s to the 1870s, would take us far beyond the scope of this work.[124] It is enough for our purposes to say that John Trim capitalized on his forty years of freedom and used his wits to accumulate a small fortune in landed property. The terms of his will, under which his children were to share in the use of his properties during their lifetimes while actual ownership was to pass to his lawful grandchildren, ensured as much as possible that his daughters, once grown, would have a roof over their heads and, whatever their individual merits, would not lack for suitors, while being protected from the risk that their husbands might squander their inheritance. It was a prudent plan. For a wild deer caged through the first thirty-odd years of his life, Trim had run at a remarkable clip once the cage door had sprung open for him in 1793, giving full play to his pent-up spirit of enterprise. His career of acquisition seems at times like an effort to erase the traces of his years of enforced deprivation, as if, in his mind, possession were nine points of the law of self-preservation: to have was to be. The tenth point was to have his name live on after him. He had at one time hoped for a son,[125] but the name of Trim passed with him. Becoming father to three girls in his last years, he did his best to give them a leg up in the world.

SIX

On Steamboats

The first institution established in Quebec to cater to blacks collapsed in less than a year, the victim of an occupational hazard.* On 2 March 1827, a Friday, the all-white American Presbyterian Sunday School Society of Montreal convened to hear members Ebenezer Muir and Dwight Plimpton Janes[1] state their case that "the condition of the 'blacks' in this city calls loudly upon the benevolent exertions of this Society." Earnest evangelical Protestants, they had in mind the religious and moral condition of blacks more than their socio-economic status, hence their proposed solution: a Sunday school. The society agreed, and No. 4 African School opened just two days later. Fourteen adults showed up for class that Sunday in the St-Paul Street premises provided by a society member. Within two weeks, attendance swelled to twenty-five. Then it dipped, down to sixteen in May, before plummeting to two or three through the summer, never to recover. At last, on 18 February 1828, No. 4 African School was folded into the main Sunday school housed at the church, on St-Jacques Street at the corner of McGill Street, a stone's throw from John Trim's home. In its annual report, the society attributed the shipwreck of No. 4 to one cause: "Upon the opening of the spring, the numbers decreased owing to their employment being principally on board Steam Boats."[2]

---

*I wish to thank Daniel Saint-Onge, an independent researcher specializing in the history of places of worship in Montreal, for drawing this episode to my attention.

AMERICAN PRESBYTERIAN CHURCH.

The American Presbyterian Church at St-Jacques and McGill streets. At the urging of grocer Dwight Plimpton Janes and tailor Ebenezer Muir, members of the church launched No. 4 African School, a Sunday school, in early 1827.

We may doubt that competition from the steamboats was the sole cause of No. 4 African School's demise, but it is undeniable that many black Montrealers worked on the steamers that ran on the St Lawrence River between Montreal and Quebec. They did so from the beginning of steam navigation in Canada, within a decade of the end of slavery, when the small, rickety sidewheelers required a crew of no more than a handful of men. As steamboats proliferated and grew in size and passenger capacity, all the while improving their appointments, staffing requirements increased, providing more employment and a greater diversity of jobs. Blacks served in various capacities, at first mostly as cooks, waiters, and "boots" (footwear cleaners).

The surviving records do not enable us to draw up an exhaustive list of the blacks who worked on these boats. A few crew lists and wage books of the early Molson steamers survive, but none, it seems, of the Montreal Steam Tow Boat Co., the other major line of Montreal-Quebec passenger boats launched in the 1820s by John Torrance in opposition to the St Lawrence Steamboat Co., as the Molson-run line was known from 1822. No relevant company records of the steamboat lines that arose to the west of Montreal in the 1820s have come down to us. These included the Upper Canada Line of stages and steamboats that operated on the St Lawrence route from Montreal to Kingston, launched by Horace Dickinson, a founder of the American Presbyterian Church in Montreal, one of the teachers at No. 4 African School in 1827, and a next-door neighbour of Trim's on McGill Street in the mid-1820s; and the Ottawa Steamboat Co., renamed the Ottawa and Rideau Forwarding Co. from 1835.

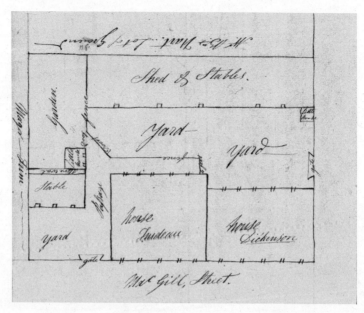

Horace Dickinson, owner of the Upper Canada Line of stages and steamboats and a teacher at No. 4 African School, lived next door to John Trim in 1824–26, as indicated by a notation on the left side of this rough sketch of the McGill Street property that Dickinson leased.

This 1838 watercolour of a waiter on the *British America* is the only known artwork that shows a black worker aboard the early Montreal–Quebec steamers.

The Molson records, however, and the odd newspaper reference, vital record, or hiring contract, provide sufficient evidence that early steam navigation was a major source of employment for black Montrealers.

The association of blacks with steamboats presaged their connection with the railways at the end of the century. The latter is relatively well known, but their role on the boats is forgotten. Certainly, the St Lawrence does not carry the same mythic load as the Mississippi, a stream freighted with memories of salvation and damnation, of blacks carried up to freedom, down to slavery; nor did it ever form, like the Mississippi and its tributaries, a black nexus, connecting black workers, slave and free, employed on steamboats and in the fur trade.[3] Slavery had ended before the first steamers appeared on the St Lawrence. No folklore has preserved the memory of early black steamboat workers on the St Lawrence, history and literature have ignored them, and only one artwork attests to their presence, a watercolour sketch of 1838 by a British military officer showing a waiter at work on the Torrance line's *British America*. By that time, steamers were well established, and many black men alternated between jobs on the boats, in domestic service, and as hotel waiters and porters. Washington Williams presents a good example. In late March 1841, he left his job as a groom to a well-to-do resident of the present-day Outremont district of Montreal "with the intention of engaging myself as a servant on board of the Steamboats which I expected would run sooner than they have." Since the steamboats had not yet started, he found work as a porter at Sword's Hotel. That same year, a traveller noted that the waiters on Lake Ontario steamers were "civil and attentive, and usually coloured men."[4] And we do know of at least one black woman who found employment on the boats: Margaret Sinclair, "an African," worked as cook aboard the Molson steamer *Quebec* in 1819. It is also possible that, as in the United States, some black women served as attendants in the "ladies' cabin" of these boats. Perhaps Margaret Sinclair had answered a help-wanted advertisement such as the one placed in newspapers by John Molson & Sons in 1817 seeking mates, stewards, cooks, and waiters for its steamers *Swiftsure* and *Malsham* – "Also Two Elderly Women to assist in Cooking and to wait upon Ladies, passengers."[5]

THE FIRST STEAMBOAT

At least three black men worked on John Molson's *Accommodation,* the first steamboat in British North America, launched at Montreal on 19 August 1809.[6] The earliest record of Robert Ashley's and Jean-Baptiste L'Africain's work on the steamer dates from 1 July that year, when each was paid £1 16s 8d for 11 days' work (3s 4d a day). The nature of the work they had performed is not specified, but since this pay day came more than one month before the boat's launch, it would have consisted of building work, perhaps on the cabin, which was completed that July.[7] Richard Rogers joined the crew the following year.

All three men may have been born in slavery, but L'Africain is the only one of whom we know this for sure. He shows up in Montreal records for the first time in 1796 when, as a fourteen-year-old slave of Benoite Gaëtan, widow of the painter François Malepart de Beaucourt, he was baptized at Notre-Dame Church. He probably came from the French West Indies. Whatever his land of origin, the slave boy of the 1790s was a free man by 1801.[8] Ashley may have come from England. He surfaces at the turn of the century as a free man, residing at Quebec and working as a steward on ships that sailed on the Quebec–London run; he was apparently associated with at least two such ships, the *Hope* and the *Adeona*.[9] Rogers was probably the twenty-eight-year-old "nègre libre" named Richard, a servant of Commissary General Isaac Winslow Clark, who turned up as a patient in the Hôtel-Dieu in February 1809. A later hospital record makes him a native of Upper Canada.[10] All three were married by the time the *Accommodation* was launched. L'Africain had married the former Michilimackinac slave Charlotte Bonga in Montreal in 1801. They had six children, not one of whom lived past the age of nine.[11] We do not know when and where Rogers married Asenath Myers. A daughter was born to them at Montreal in December 1809, and they had four more children over the next eleven years. Like L'Africain's children, they all died young, three of them within a year of their birth.[12] Ashley married at Quebec in 1802. He and his wife, Margaret Pearce, had better luck raising a family than L'Africain and Rogers did; three of their four children lived to adulthood. Their first was born at Quebec in 1804, the other three at Montreal in 1808, 1810, and 1815.[13]

With his seafaring experience, Ashley seems the kind of person that brewer John Molson, new to the shipping business, would have wanted for a crew member. Rogers had no experience on ships or boats that we know of, but he was the only one of the three who knew how to sign his name. Over the winter of 1809–10, before joining the crew of the *Accommodation,* he had operated a livery stable with a partner, indicating that, besides being literate, he possessed some entrepreneurial skills and business sense.[14] As a slave, L'Africain had known domestic service, but we do not know how he earned his living as a free man. Various records give his occupation as "labourer," a term so broad as to be practically meaningless. Perhaps he had worked for his friend, carpenter Augustin Labadie, which might explain his being hired to work on the building of the *Accommodation;* he does not seem to have been involved in the boat's operation. Beyond that, we cannot say what led Molson to hire them over other workers. To some extent, at least, he followed a practice that existed on seagoing ships, where many blacks found work as stewards and cooks. How common this practice was can be seen by dipping into travel accounts of the time. For example, in the journal of his trip to the West Coast fur-trade post of Fort Astoria, Gabriel Franchère, stepson of Benoite Gaëtan, noted that among the passengers and crew of the sailing ship *Tonquin* on which he sailed from New York on 6 September 1810, there were two blacks: "A mulatto steward" and "A coloured man as cook."[15] Thomas Storrow Brown, a Montreal merchant obliged to flee Lower Canada after commanding Patriote forces at St-Charles in the Rebellion of 1837, sailed away for Florida, noting of the crew of the ship that took him from New York City to Key West in September 1838 that the cook and steward were "both blacks." Brown, who was to return to Montreal six years later, gives us an inkling of the regard in which stewards were held by crew members and passengers: "The Steward and Waiter is the Captains great man in matters of comestibles, and like a prime minister or any other great man's great man, he is very obsequious [sic] to those from whom he expects favors, to wit, the Crew and those in the Steerage, who instinctively understand that there can be no chance for extra biscuit unless this important official is conciliated and propitiated."[16] Jeffrey Bolster, in his study of black seamen on American sailing ships, offered a more complex overall view: "Cooks and stewards, who were frequently black, inhabited an ambiguous social sphere belonging neither to the officers nor to the men. [...] Cooks' ability to bestow delicacies could inspire favoritism among forecastle hands, but stewards – the cabin servants – were often regarded as the captains' flunkies." These black workers were confined in a sense to a shipboard ghetto: "whites expected them to sail as cooks or stewards. These were service-oriented positions (even 'feminine' jobs in the minds of some whites) not defined by nautical skill and physical courage."[17]

In Ashley's case, it is easy enough to see how the idea of forsaking the perils of the North Atlantic for inland navigation might have appealed to a man in his position. It was wartime and Britain was locked in a fight to the finish with Napoleon. From June 1812, it would also be at war with the United States. Ashley was no swashbuckler; he was a ship steward, a married man getting on in years, with young children. Streaming between Montreal and Quebec would mean safer trips than the North Atlantic crossing – shorter ones, too, measured in days rather than weeks or months, less disruptive of family life, and easier on the constitution. It also promised its own excitement and status. As the first steamer on the St Lawrence, and only the third in service in the world, the *Accommodation* heralded a transportation revolution. As primitive as were its hull design and six-horsepower engine, it was as much a wonder to people of its day as the first car would be in the horse-and-buggy age nearly a century later. Working on such a boat would have conferred a cachet on the crew – blacks and whites – elevating them above the common run of riverboat hands.

But, as we have seen, Ashley was hired initially for other work than attending to cabin passengers or minding the food and drink. Here is the record of his wages for work on the boat that summer and fall:[18]

Pay day	Amount paid	Pay period	Rate per day
1 July	£1 16s 8d	11 days	3s 4d
8 July	£0 18s 4d	5½ days	[3s 4d]
15 July	£0 19s 2d	5¾ days	3s 4d
22 July	£0 17s –	4¼ days	[4s]
29 July	£1 – 3d	5¾ days	4s
2 August	£0 19s –	4¾ days	4s
12 August	£1 – –	5 days	4s
19 August	£0 16s –	4 days	[4s]

Pay day	Amount paid	Pay period	Rate per day
26 August	£0 16s –	4 days	[4s]
9 September	£1 18s –	9½ days	4s
5 October	£2 18s 3d	For work to 2 Oct.	–
7 October	£1 5s –	–	–
14 October	£1 7s –	6 days	4s 6d
21 October	£1 1s –	–	–
1 November	£1 4s –	6 days	[4s]
15 November	£0 10s –	2½ days	[4s]

The boat set off on her maiden run to Quebec on 1 November. As we can see from the record of his wages, totalling £19 5s 8d, the bulk of Ashley's work was done by then. He was not one of the regular six-man crew on that inaugural trip or on any other that she made that fall, it seems. The only record of wages paid to him after 1 November is for two and half days' work; a round trip between Montreal and Quebec took longer than that. Incidentally, the Molson records for 1808–10 show that he bought beer from Molson on only two occasions in those years – one-eighth of a hogshead (about 31 litres) of mild beer each time, at a cost of 5 shillings. It may be coincidence, but his first purchase, on 16 October 1809, came just after his pay had risen to 4s 6d a day from 4s, a 12.5 per cent increase; the second came on 11 November, after the *Accommodation* had completed her first round trip.[19]

L'Africain, for his part, seems to have stopped working in mid-July and then to have returned for part of a day in August. There are no records of any payments made to him between launch day in mid-August, when "John Africa" received 2s 6d, and the time when the boat went into operation, meaning that he was not engaged in any of the finishing work, the fitting of her engine and paddles, and her trials in September and October. But he seems to have done some work on her later in the year, perhaps in building the cookhouse on her deck or fitting her with a mast, because on 12 January 1810, in a final settling of the payroll for 1809, "John Lafrican" was paid £3 10s in "wages [for work] on board the Steam Boat."[20]

Ashley was back on board for the *Accommodation*'s one full season in 1810. L'Africain did not return, but Rogers now joined the crew. From mid-May to early June, trials were made of her refurbished engine and machinery, and she set off on her first trip of the season to Quebec on 5 June. On 18 June, Ashley was paid £3, and Rogers £3 10s. But what were their jobs? Not captain. Of all the blacks who worked on steamboats, not one made it to that position (knowledge of seamanship was not the issue, since many early steamboat masters had little or none). Not engineer or pilot. And, because William Boyce, who had filled the position of steward in 1809, was still there, presumably in the same capacity, that position was also taken. The only remaining possibilities were cook, fireman (stoker) or deckhand.

However, on 10 July, Molson paid Ashley £4 5s 9d "in full of wages this day inclusive & including 10/9 paid for Sundrys for the Steam Boat." The fact that Ashley was authorized to buy sundries (the odd article of food, drink or kitchenware, for

Steamboats, sailboats, rafts, and other watercraft were the main modes of transport in the early nineteenth century, when the highways were waterways.

which he would pay out of his pocket and be reimbursed) indicates that he had succeeded Boyce as steward. No one on the boat handled cash except the captain and the steward, the captain collecting fares, the steward collecting payment for drinks, snacks and the like. Indeed, on 1 August, the records identify Ashley as steward, and he continued in that job until the end of the season. By 3 August, he was being paid 5 shillings a day (that day he received £6 for 24 days' work). He earned a total of £31, a considerable improvement over the £19 5s 8d he had earned the previous year.[21]

Rogers' position on the boat is never specified. He may have worked as cook. Here is the record of his wages for the 1810 season:

Pay day	Amount paid	Pay period
18 June	£3 10s –	–
27 June	£2 5s –	On account
10 July	£3 5s –	–
3 August	£5 – –	On account
15 August	£4 – –	–
25 August	£2 10s –	–
8 September	£3 10s –	–
19 September	£2 15s –	–
2 October	£3 5s –	–
31 October	£6 15s –	–

He seems to have been paid 5 shillings a day, the same rate as Ashley, for a total of £33 10s.[22]

The *Accommodation* was scrapped in 1811. There are no records to show whether Ashley, L'Africain, or Rogers went on to work on the *Swiftsure,* Molson's second steamer, or on later boats over the next decade. Within that decade, all three men died. Their lives were short by today's standards. L'Africain was reputed to be about 35 when he died, perhaps from illness, on 20 November 1815.[23] Ashley's end may have been hastened by a beating he suffered on 15 November 1817, when he was "assaulted and kicked by one Alexander Todd," as he said. He died two months later, in his 40s – in poverty, it seems, because he was buried at the expense of the Anglican church.[24] Rogers seems to have spent most of the years from 1811 to 1818 working at, or out of, St-Jean on the Richelieu, northern terminal of the American steamers on Lake Champlain, the first of which had begun running in the same year that the *Accommodation* was launched on the St Lawrence. Steamboat service on the lake was interrupted during the War of 1812, resuming in 1815. Rogers' son, George, was born at St-Jean on 31 March 1814 and died there in March 1817.[25] Rogers was back at Montreal within a year or two, living on St-Maurice Street in the Récollets Suburb.[26] He was not working on steamboats at the time of his death. From 1 July 1820, he was hired for a month as a "servant" by innkeeper Ephraim Goodsell of LaPrairie, opposite Montreal. This was little more than a month after the inauguration of a steam ferry service between Montreal and LaPrairie, departure point of stage lines to St-Jean and the United States. On 8 July, however, Goodsell complained that Rogers had deserted him after only five days and that he was rumoured to be on the point of leaving the province. In fact, Rogers was about to take his final leave. He spent twenty days in the hospital that fall; discharged on 29 October, he died four days later, in his mid-thirties like L'Africain.[27]

A SHARED EXPERIENCE

Robert Ashley did not live to see it, but both of his daughters who grew to adulthood married men who worked on steamboats. James Sampson, for instance, possibly from Demerara (Guyana), who married Ashley's eldest daughter, Elizabeth (Betsy), in 1824, worked as cook aboard the *Quebec* from 7 to 21 September 1826.[28] Another black Montrealer, Robert Williams – Ashley had acted as witness at his wedding to Esther Thompson in 1816, and Williams was godfather of Ashley's youngest child, Margaret – took over the cook's job from Sampson from 22 September to 2 October, followed by yet another black Montrealer, Joseph Pierre (alias Joseph St-Pierre), from 3 October to 18 November. And, from 3 May to 2 June that year, Jacob Grant, the husband of Mary Ann Drummond, had worked as head waiter on board the *Quebec*.[29] Sampson may also have worked later on Ottawa River boats or on the building of the Rideau Canal, although when he was away at Bytown (Ottawa), the new settlement at the head of the canal, in the spring of 1828, he was said to be working as a barber. On another occasion, in September 1831, he was again reported to be in Upper Canada.[30]

John Patten (or Patton), who was to marry Ashley's second daughter, Ann, turns up at Montreal as a widower at the end of the 1820s. He and hairdresser William Goodrich, a native of Barbados, acted as the appraisers of the estate of Alexander Valentine in 1829.[31] Patten was recorded as a shoemaker in 1831 and 1834,[32] but either he changed occupations in the intervening years, or he alternated between steamboating in season and shoemaking in winter. In the summer and fall of 1832, 1833, and again in 1835, he served as mate on some of the Molson steamers. In the cholera summer of 1832, for instance, he was hired as mate on the *John Molson* on 24 August (after the epidemic had peaked), and was paid off on 5 December, earning a total of £9 16s 8d. He married Ann Ashley that October. His 1833 season, in which he earned £25 5s 10d, is more confusing, largely because his name was recorded as William as well as John: John Patten was hired on 25 June as mate of the *John Molson;* on 5 August, John Patton (*sic*) was paid £3 for his work as mate of the *John Molson* since 25 June. Then, on 27 August, John Patton was paid £3 12s 6d on account of his wages as mate of the *John Bull*. Patton seems to have transferred from one boat to another, although this payment is the only record of that. But, on 14 September, "William" Patton was paid £5 as mate of the *John Molson;* on 25 September, it was

The Montreal waterfront was a bustling place in the steamboat era. On 1 August 1834, the ships in port hoisted their colours in honour of the abolition of West Indian slavery, and black Montrealers met there for a celebratory dinner at Richard Owston's St George's Inn after an afternoon of speeches at the nearby Ste-Anne's Market.

John Patton who was paid £2 as mate of the *John Molson*. On another payday, 30 October, William Patton was recorded as receiving £3 as mate of the *John Molson*. At season's end, William Patton, mate of the *John Molson,* was paid £8 13s 4d balance in full on 21 November and discharged.[33]

There is no indication that any John or William Patten or Patton worked on the Molson boats in 1834. At the celebration by Montreal blacks of the coming into force of Britain's Slavery Abolition Act on 1 August that year, he was assigned the role of opening the meeting with a prayer. It seems odd, then, that he had not been among the black men present at Alexander Grant's house on 23 July 1833, when the bill had been discussed.[34] As in the case of the Sunday school students of 1827, his work may have called him away: from his 1833 steamboat engagements, we see that he was working aboard the *John Molson* from 25 June to 5 August that year.

In 1835, one source has John Patten beginning work as mate of the *Canada* on 26 April, while another says that John Patton was hired as mate on 27 April and was paid £2 on 30 May. This is just a minor variance in dates and names. Patten is said to have left the *Canada* in June, and, on 13 June, he began work as mate on the *John Bull*. Then, on 24 July, it is "Mrs Patton" who shows up to collect £8 – the "balance due her late husband, mate." Patten had died on the job, on 25 June; under the name William Patten, he was buried at Trois-Rivières, mid-way between Montreal and Quebec.[35]

In 1832, the year of her marriage to Patten, Ann Ashley had acted as witness at the wedding of John Broome (alias John Brown) and Jane Wilson. Broome worked as first waiter on the *Canada* for the full navigation season in 1833, from 15 May to 12 November, earning a total of £12 11s. In September, another black man, Cornelius Thompson, served as second waiter for eight days and was paid 10s 8d. Broome was back as first waiter on the *Canada* in 1834, from 21 April until his discharge on 17 October, making £10 10s 2d in all.[36] Unlike John Patten, Broome had managed to attend the abolitionist meeting at Alexander Grant's in the summer of 1833. Given their origins in Barbados and Bermuda respectively, and perhaps having family and friends still in the Islands, Broome and his wife would have felt a personal interest in this legislation. Yet when the law came into effect on 1 August 1834, it was a dark time in the Broome household. It was a summer of cholera. Jane Wilson had just given birth to their second child, Sarah, on 19 June. The 29 July was pay day, one of four that season, for Broome as first waiter on the *Canada;* he took home £2 15s. Two days later, his first child, Mary, died at the age of seventeen months. The next day was Liberation Day. They buried their daughter the day after that. John Broome himself died at the Montreal General Hospital on 19 May 1840 at the reputed age of 43, his wife outliving him by twenty-six years.[37]

Richard Thompson, "a man of Colour" from Niagara who was godfather of Robert Ashley's son, Thomas, is believed to be the Montreal man of that name who was hired as cook of the *Union* for the 1825 season at £3 per month, plus room and board on the boat. From 1823, this boat was the first steamer in regular service on the Ottawa River, plying between Grenville and Hull and, from 1826, Bytown. At Ashley's death in 1818, Thompson had been operating a pastry shop in the Quebec Suburb. Ten years later, he was cook aboard the Molson steamer *Waterloo* on the St Lawrence. He was in his eighties when he died on 19 August 1859.[38]

In connecting these people to the Ashley family, we see that steamboat work was not just an occupation but a shared experience that linked blacks of different origins, languages and faiths, contributing to the shaping of a small world. In American cities and other places with larger, more homogeneous black populations, a church or other institution might have served as the heart of a community. In Montreal, "the few sons of Africa within the city," as the *Gazette* referred to them in 1834[39] – some French-speaking, most English-speaking; some native-born, others relative newcomers from the West Indies, the United States, the British Isles, or farther afield; Anglicans, Baptists, Methodists, Presbyterians, Roman Catholics; not concentrated in one neighbourhood but spread out through the city – had neither the numbers nor the means to set up a separate church of their own. Unlike in Upper Canada, where black Baptist and Methodist churches of American inspiration had sprung up from the 1820s, no black church was established in Montreal or Lower Canada until the end of the century.[40] We might expect that some black Montrealers would have flocked to the American Presbyterian Church, considering the outreach efforts that it made in 1827 in setting up No. 4 African School. But in the 1820s and 1830s, Montreal's American Presbyterian congregation counted only one black member: Mrs Hester James, "coloured woman," was admitted on 15 January 1826 and left sometime in 1827.[41] The school may have rallied a good number of black pupils, for a few months, but the church itself did not. The word "American" in its name may have repelled blacks – it was not of a nature to reassure them, so long as slavery continued in the United States. If this was the case, it was ironic in that, among the white residents of Montreal, the church's early pastors and several of its members, because of their American experience of race, were among the most mindful of the plight of blacks.[42] In the absence of a common church, the "few sons of Africa" found a secular communion, notably in steamboats.

Who knows but that some steamboat connection did not underlie the hostilities between members of the Ashley clan and Jacob Abdella in the early 1830s? Abdella, who lived in Montreal from about 1820 to 1848, was recorded over the years as a labourer, peddlar, trader, dealer, confectioner, sailor, servant, cook, and pastry cook. The welter of occupational labels suggests a varied employment record, but it may hide a constant – that he was a versatile cook who happened to work, at different times, on his own account, in a private home, as an employee of a hotel, inn, or restaurant, and aboard the steamboats. In September–October 1834, for instance, he worked 26 days as a "sailor" on the Montreal–Quebec steamer *Favorite,* earning £1 14s 8d. Although there is no record of his employment in 1838, steamboat work may have accounted for his presence at Quebec in the fall of that year, where he was picked up while on a toot and locked up for three days, the records of the Quebec Jail identifying him as "dark" complexioned, 5 feet, 4 inches tall – and Irish![43] On 2 August 1830, Abdella accused Thomas Ashley and Peter Dago, who was then his tenant, of assaulting him. Dago and Ashley each had to post a £10 bond to keep the peace, the sureties for both of them being John Trim, who seems to have had his own bone to pick with Abdella around this time, and Abraham Low.[44] Again, on 30 September, Abdella accused Dago and, this time, Moses Ashley of assaulting him, in his house. Dago countered with an accusation of his own, saying that "he occupies a room in the House of one Jacob Abdallah [...] that last night he came to the House of the said Jacob Abdallah who with great violence prevented this deponent from entering his room, that at the same time the said Abdallah stabbed this deponent with a fork in the left side, which produced a very severe wound." Abdella had to post bail, promising to show up in court on 21 October. Dago also posted another £10 bond, with sureties Robert Williams and Robert Jackson, a Quebec-born black whose parents had been friends of the Ashleys.[45] The outcome of this unexplained spat is not known. In 1832, as we saw in a previous chapter, John Trim accused Abdella and his wife of operating a brothel. In March 1833, Thomas Ashley's brother-in-law, James Sampson, who shared a house with Robert Jackson, accused Abdella and his white tenant, Peter Peterson, of stealing a hog carcass from the yard of McGill Street innkeeper Thomas Brown English. Sampson said he had seen Jackson bring some of the meat into the house on several occasions. A search was made of Abdella's house but nothing was found.[46] Disputes of this kind flared up from time to time, pitting one group of blacks against another, but the absence of documentation makes it difficult to understand what provoked them and whether they represented a rift in the community or just some passing personal dispute. Despite their violent altercations in 1830, for example, Abdella and Dago were among the dozen men who gathered at Alexander Grant's for the abolition meeting in the summer of 1833.

Another figure we have met in Trim's entourage and who spent part of his working life on the steamers was Robert Moore. Testifying in May 1829 in a court case pitting Trim against a neighbour, Moore gave his occupation as "labourer." In fact, he was then employed as first waiter on the Molson steamer *Waterloo*. Hired on 21 April, he was to be discharged on 11 August. In 1834, he worked as first waiter on the *John Bull* from 28 May to 1 August, then as second waiter on the *Canada* from 12 August to 25 September, earning a total of £7 19s.[47]

Robert Williams, mentioned above as having succeeded James Sampson as cook aboard the *Quebec* in 1826, in fact held three successive jobs on that boat from 5 August to the close of navigation – cook's mate, cook, and boots, with a total of £3 18s 4d to show for his efforts. In 1831, he worked as a waiter on the *Lady of the Lake,* a steamer owned and operated since 1826 by James Greenfield, in opposition to the two main steamboat lines (by 1831, the Molsons and Torrances had become sleeping partners in Greenfield's boat). For the full seasons of 1833 and 1834, and the early part of 1835 (27 April–9 June), Williams worked as boots on the *Canada*.[48]

Joseph Pierre, Williams' successor as cook of the *Quebec* in 1826, was hired at 60 shillings a month on 3 October and had earned a total of £4 10s by the time he was discharged on 18 November. In 1834, he worked as cook aboard the *Voyageur* from

3 September.⁴⁹ He was, we believe, the Joseph Pierre who had been arrested at Quebec for assault in the summer of 1825, identified as 5′ 8″ tall, a fifty-year-old American-born man of a "dark" complexion. Jailed on 10 August, he was released on bail on 30 August. Ten years later, as a patient at the Hôtel-Dieu in Montreal, Joseph Pierre was identified as a forty-four-year-old "homme de Couleur" born in Bordeaux.⁵⁰

How small and hard the world of black Montrealers of this time could be is illustrated in incidents involving Pierre's wife, Sarah York. She is believed to be the Sarah York, "Black woman," 5′ 4″ tall, who was jailed at Quebec on 12 November 1817 on a charge of "having violently assaulted and beaten and seized by the throat W. Robinson." She was released by the Court of Quarter Sessions there on 19 January 1818.⁵¹ She and Pierre married at Montreal in 1822. In mid-September 1826, while her husband was away, perhaps on the boats, she complained that her landlord, farmer John Cross, had bodily expelled her from the house where she lived, nailing the door shut with all her clothing and furniture inside. In the fall of 1827, Pierre had to post a £10 bond to get her out of jail and guarantee her good behaviour for six months after she allegedly assaulted Catherine Guillet, Jacob Abdella's wife, and threatened to kill her. Two sureties were required; besides Pierre, John Broome also posted a £10 bond. Sarah York appears to have been possessed of a violent temper, but this incident at the end of October occurred when she must have been under emotional strain – her two children had died within months of each other, Joseph in February at the age of three, and 9½-month-old François-Xavier just that August.⁵² She and her husband had no other children, and Pierre died sometime between his hospital stay in 1835 and the summer of 1838. Perhaps his death contributed to another outburst on her part, on 12 August 1838, when Robert Moore complained that he had been assaulted by Sarah Pierre, "widow of One Joseph Pierre."⁵³ This is the only intimation we have of Joseph Pierre's death, for which we can find no official record, leading us to surmise that, unless he died and was buried somewhere else along the river like John Patten, he may have been the anonymous black man found drowned opposite Montreal three weeks earlier. As a newspaper reported: "On Sunday [22 July] the body of a colored man was observed floating near the Longueuil wharf of the Horse Boat, and was taken on shore. The hands were a good deal mutilated, and the body bore evident marks of having been a long time in the water. It is scarcely credible, yet t'is a fact, that notwithstanding the heat of the weather, and the publicity of the place, the body still lay exposed in the same spot at six o'clock on Monday evening."⁵⁴ In February 1840, Sarah York was arrested by a policeman who alleged that "at about ten of the clock P.M. [she] was visiting different taverns in this City and disturbing the public peace and tranquility by screaching and otherwise making a noise. That when requested to be peaceable ... she did assault and strike him and did further bite Deponent." For all the hard blows that life dealt her – and the blows that she dealt back – Sarah York outlived her husband by more than thirty years.⁵⁵

Of course, the blacks who worked on the riverboats did not all come from Montreal. Other river towns were represented on the crews, although to a lesser degree.

In April 1834, for instance, a Charles Williams died at Sorel, identified as "A coloured man employed as a Labourer on board one of the St Lawrence Steam Companys Steam Boats in this port."[56] John Shields, a "Man of Colour" from Quebec, who worked as a stevedore in the 1820s and early 1830s, was cook's mate aboard the *John Bull* from 22 May to 6 October 1837, then mess-room waiter on the *Canada* from 5 to 26 November. He may have succeeded Piers (Pierce) Dalton of Montreal in that last job: Dalton had been hired as the boat's mess-room waiter on 10 May, but there is no indication of when he was discharged.[57] Montrealer Mauger Williams was hired on the same day as Dalton as the *Canada*'s cook but was discharged eleven days later; he then worked as a sailor on the same boat from 18 June to 5 July. From 18 August to 16 October, he was boots aboard the *John Bull*. Williams had worked as cook aboard that boat in 1832, from 22 July to the end of the navigation season, earning a total of £9 2d. He had joined the boat that year five days after testifying for the prosecution against Jacob Abdella and his wife, in the bawdy-house case brought against them by John Trim.[58] With Mauger Williams on the *John Bull* for about three weeks in 1837 was Prince Phillips, who served as second waiter from 26 September to 8 December. The following year, Phillips found a job on dry land as a waiter at the Exchange Coffee House, the hotel at St-Paul and St-Pierre Streets whose courtyard was then the terminus of the Canada Steamboat and Mail Coach Co., successor to the Upper Canada Line. By 1840, he had set up in business as a cabinet-maker.[59]

"WHY ARE THERE NEGROES?"

The hiring of black workers by steamboat operators seems to have been a generally accepted practice. Did it cause tensions among the crews? In July 1831, Robert Williams of the *Lady of the Lake* accused the boat's fireman of assault, and in October 1836, Jacob Grant, then boots on the *Canada,* complained that the steward had assaulted him. The surviving documents, however, tell us too little about these incidents to allow us to judge whether they were racially motivated.[60] The testimony of Richard Rogers in a court case in September 1810 sheds a sidelight on the question. Appearing for the defence at the trial of John Forrest, a white sailor on the *Accommodation* who was charged with theft, Rogers said that Forrest had visited him at his home from 7 to 9 p.m. on the night of the theft. That two-hour visit would suggest that whites and blacks on the boats could fraternize.[61]

Some travellers left us revealing comments about racial attitudes up to mid-century. In his remarks to his daughter about the black cook aboard the ship that carried him from New York to Florida in 1838, for example, Thomas Storrow Brown, the once and future Montrealer, observed: "The Cook, a thick necked greasy nigger in tarry trousers, officiates in a kitchen six feet square. We devour his dainties with high relish, but should you on shore ever have a kitchen of similar dimensions and a similar functionary I should advise you whenever you give a dinner party to say nothing about it until the Cloth is removed."[62]

Closer to home, Charles Kadwell, a young English-born Montreal merchant on an excursion to Upper Canada in the summer of 1838, journalized in more patronizing language about a sunny couple who were among his three fellow passengers on the *Transit* as she steamed across Lake Ontario from Toronto to Niagara:

> While Seated at breakfast I could not help noticing the officiousness displayed by the coal black gentleman towards his lady fair, in fact they seemed as happy as matrimony could make them. He was completely *à la nigger:* rings on fingers & in ears, superfluous in breast pin & watch guard, & with respect to clothing appeared lately let loose from the hands of Master Snip. In fine, he was what I suppose he had the vanity to consider himself, *"a colored gentleman;"* these words having a highly important signification. His better half looked really very respectable, & from her "sweet accents" appeared not devoid of education; she was attired in a pelisse of rich silk, & her tout ensemble was such as to cause her to find favor in my eyes, & to wonder what propitious circumstances could have induced the happy pair to "lub" one another. They proceeded as far as the Falls where I lost them.[63]

In his flippant delineation of the "coal black gentleman," Kadwell sees black skin as the negation of propriety. The skin colour turns correct behaviour and attentiveness into "officiousness," and neat attire into a suit that is indecently new; ornamentation is outlandish and overdone, and if the creature seems at all like a gentleman, this is a pose – he is a "colored gentleman; these words having a highly important signification." The "lady fair," by contrast, is tastefully dressed, looks good, speaks white ... Between them, of course, there can be no real love, only its black-dialect caricature, "lub." On his return to Montreal on board the *Dolphin,* a small steamer that plied on the St Lawrence between Ogdensburg, New York, opposite Prescott, and Dickinson's Landing, west of Cornwall, for the Canada Steamboat and Mail Coach Co., Kadwell found all the berths in the men's cabin taken: "the black official informed me & another that (if we pleased!) he could provide room for us on the surface of the dining table!" The offer came not from a "purser" or "steward" or "cabin attendant," but from a person Kadwell saw fit to identify as a "black official." One senses that notions of black "officiousness" were still on his mind. Still, he and his weary fellow traveller gratefully accepted this offer of a tabletop bed.[64]

Venturing slightly beyond the period covered by this book, if only to show the persistence of a casually assumed white supremacy, we find even more striking ruminations jotted down by a young star of Quebec's political and intellectual firmament while on a business trip to New York City in early May 1850. Not yet thirty at the time, Pierre-Joseph-Olivier Chauveau, who would become the first premier of Quebec at Confederation, had already served six years in the parliament of the united Canadas (it sat at Montreal 1844–49) as member for the County of Quebec, and published a novel, *Charles Guérin,* still required reading today for students of Quebec literature. We catch him at his devotions in the French Catholic church on Canal Street in New York on 12 May. After noting the pleasing aspect of the congregants from France – "de beaux hommes et de belles femmes" – he turns his gaze on the blacks in attendance:

> But I must say, the negroes and negresses drew my whole attention, especially two old women, their heads wrapped in red scarves, whose muttered prayers were accompanied by awful gyrations, and whose flattened and hideous shapes were much more ape-like than womanly. I wondered how true it was, or not, that the negro is the missing link between man and monkey, as Yankees who are not abolitionists so starkly put it. In truth, these were not the first negroes and negresses that I had seen. All the steamboats and hotels from Montreal on were full of them, and at Irving House [hotel], hordes crowded the hallways through which I passed. But I cannot get used to the negro, always a zoological and social curiosity to my mind. Why are there negroes?[65]

The Fugitive Slave Act was wending its way through the US Congress at the time – it was signed into law on 18 September – eliciting wide sympathy for the plight of black Americans among men and women of feeling. Chauveau was clearly not one of them; his reflections were more in tune with the mid-century "scientific racism" that gave new wings to old theories of polygenesis, the idea that all humans could not have descended from a common ancestor, and that blacks were clearly a separate species, inferior to whites. His and Kadwell's private reflections speak for themselves, and for many kindred spirits whose attitudes, if not voiced publicly, found expression in the deeds of everyday life.

As Kadwell's observations tell us, blacks were occasionally to be found among the passengers on steamboats, not just among the crews. Several cases of racial discrimination against black passengers were recorded on the Great Lakes, as were accounts of assistance given by boat operators there to fugitive slaves from the United States seeking to cross into Canada. In Quebec, we know of no report of the mistreatment of black passengers before 1851. It is quite possible that such incidents did occur before this, but none was publicized, and black travellers themselves did not leave us much to go on. In the summer of 1832, for example, Paola Brown, a black resident of western Upper Canada, travelled down to Montreal and Quebec for the ostensible purpose of raising funds to build a church and school in the black refugee settlement of Colbornesburgh. On 5 September, he appears to have sailed from Montreal to Quebec as a deck passenger aboard the steamer *John Molson*. As silver-tongued and handy with a pen as he seems to have been, he left us no observations on that journey.[66] In 1851, however, Samuel Ringgold Ward, a black orator, journalist, and Congregationalist minister from New York, fleeing the land of the Fugitive Slave Act for Canada and travelling from Montreal to Toronto, complained of his brush with "negrophobia" on board the steamer *St Lawrence* on Lake St-Louis, just above Montreal. From the village of Beauharnois on 16 October, the eve of his thirty-fourth birthday,

A primitive painting from 1818 shows a turbaned black passenger seated on the port side of a small side-wheel paddleboat.

Ward, born a slave in Maryland, wrote in high dudgeon to Henry Bibb, himself a fugitive American slave and publisher of the *Voice of the Fugitive* newspaper in Sandwich (Windsor), Canada West:

> As an instance of Canadian Negro hate, I took passage to-day, at Lachine, for Kingston. I could get a cabin passage, on the steamer St Lawrence, which carries Her Majesty's Mail, upon no terms whatever! Mr. Kelly, the Purser, declared that there was no room for me. There were half-a-dozen state-room keys, uncalled for, in the office at the time! And the cabin saloon was much less crowded than was the deck. I concluded to sail but a short distance upon the infernal craft, but I could not have a cabin passage for over three hours! I therefore staid at this point, running the risk of finding a better chance in some other boat this evening. On Lake Champlain, the Francis Saultus [Saltus] gave me a cabin passage without hesitancy. So the America, Fashion, and Buckeye State, on Lake Erie, and the Arctic on Lake Michigan. The same is true on the Hudson River. All of these are Yankee vessels, plying in Yankee waters, and run by Yankee captains. But the St Lawrence, under the patronage of the British Government, and sailing upon British waters, with a British subject for a captain, compels a black man to take a deck passage – or none … The boast of Englishmen, of their freedom from social negrophobia, is about as empty as the Yankee boast of democracy.[67]

Bibb published Ward's eye-opening letter in his newspaper. With Ward's indignation on record, it is strange to find him whitewashing the unhappy incident in the autobiography that he published four years later, in which he summed up his Montreal–Toronto trip of 1851 as "a most delightful passage of two days."[68]

How many others like purser Kelly saw blacks as fit to serve on steamboats perhaps, but unfit to be served? Well might we wonder about the views of the Browns, Kadwells, Chauveaus, Kellys, and their ilk, the values upon which they acted and which they passed on. Some powerful white chemistry must have been at work in 1860 for Brown, the one-time Patriote, sixteen years after his return from Florida, to marry a slave-owner of St Augustine as Americans North and South hurtled toward their murderous divorce.[69] If only Selina Simmons, the young black girl from Florida who served the Browns, and others like her had consigned their thoughts to paper![70]

Without a black draft of history, it is too easy to white out the black past. What was once a sin of omission begins to look, as it persists, like wilful blindness and denial. Reading accounts of the *Accommodation*'s career, for instance, we would never know that black hands had worked her. A half century ago, the author of a master's thesis ventured to suggest in respect of her crew that "it might be interesting to speculate on the racial origin of one named John Lafrican."[71] It is high time we moved beyond speculation – about L'Africain, Robert Ashley, Richard Rogers, and about blacks generally.

SEVEN

JACKS OF ALL TRADES

The enormity of slavery and the shadow that it cast can make it difficult to look back on the blacks of the early nineteenth century as other than icons of constant sorrow. Seeing them exclusively in that poor light does them as great an historical injustice as erasing them from our collective memory. They become flat projections of present-day sympathies rather than the humans that they were – part of the action, so to speak, obeying the same impulses that drove everyone else. Like whites in search of work, they would go where the jobs were, nearby or off in fur-trade country. In the early 1820s, some surely would have gravitated to the site of the Lachine Canal, whether to work on its construction or to provide some service to the workers there; in the economic slowdown that resulted in a loss of jobs at Montreal in the second half of the 1820s, some might have sniffed out the opportunities presented by large public works such as the building of the Rideau Canal. In times of war, they might have enlisted in the army or the militia.

Steamboat hands, like any seasonal workers, had to find ways to keep body and soul together in the off-season, which could run to half the year (November to May). As we saw with Washington Williams, some black men alternated between steamboat work, domestic service, and employment at hotels or restaurants; mate John Patten worked as a shoemaker, cook James Sampson was once said to be a barber, and steamboat and hotel waiter Prince Phillips metamorphosed into a cabinet-maker. Steward Robert Ashley was once identified as a baker.[1] To make a living, people frequently changed jobs, or sometimes held two simultaneously, turning their varied skills to account.

This versatility, as well as the sometimes bewildering variations in the way names were recorded, can make it difficult to pin down the occupation of free blacks at any given time. The task is further complicated by the fact that, after slavery, the labelling of blacks as such becomes more the exception than the rule, at least in the public records. It is a fact that in scouring old documents, much as one might wince at unwarranted racial designations – who today would think of labelling a newborn a "negro" at his baptism, or a couple as "both blacks" at their wedding? – there is something historically invaluable in these jottings. They tell us unambiguously that blacks were present – where and when, and what they were up to – besides shedding light on the attitudes of those whites who recorded their presence.

Just as slaves were frequently termed "servants," free blacks were often "servants" or "labourers." These were facile, catch-all designations. In a kind of one-size-fits all categorization, all black males were identified as "labourers" at one time or another. The slave Tom Grant was so identified when he worked as a servant of Colonel John Campbell in 1794.[2] So was John Baine, the sexton of the Anglican Church in 1803–04, and so was Thomas Cockburn when he worked as a raftsman in 1809.[3] Caesar Johonnot, manager of the Montreal Distillery Company from 1789 to 1794, did not escape being tagged with the all-purpose designator, nor did Alexander Grant, the leading black figure in Montreal in the 1830s, who operated his own high-end hairdressing salon, as well as a clothes-cleaning business.[4] The term was applied to the gamut of manual workers – skilled, semi-skilled and unskilled, slaves, the self-employed as well as hired hands. As for the term "servant," it was sometimes just a synonym for "employee," as it had once been a euphemism for slave. Even in the case of domestic servants, conditions varied from liveried attendance on a grandee such as Simon McTavish to drudgery in the service of an artisan, and from an engagement of several years to one of a few days. We cannot rely on the terms "labourer" and "servant" to enlighten us about their occupations, nor can we argue, solely on the basis of these labels, that blacks were confined to the meanest jobs, since the labels tell us nothing about the work they did.

Even the more specific designations can be misleading. John Trim and John Pruyn were both "gardeners," for example, a term that suggests a relatively humble status. But Trim went beyond gardening, into the grocery or provisioning business and accumulating real estate. Although he continued to be identified as a gardener until his death, the odd document after 1815 refers to him as a "trader"; in a few instances, he is a "curer of meat" or something similar.[5] Pruyn, the husband of Rosalie Bonga, a "trader" on Vitré Street (Viger Avenue) in 1819–20, was a "gardener" by the mid-1820s. In the years 1824–27, he grew fruits and vegetables in the northeastern St-Louis Suburb on land that he leased in a share-cropping arrangement, his rent amounting to half of his crop. Unlike Trim, he never owned land or employed domestic servants.[6] Joseph Pierson was identified variously as a labourer, cook, and "pâtissier." During the War of 1812, he occupied a property east of the city, at St Mary's Current, that contained, among other facilities, an oven and a small dairy – suggesting that, rather than toiling as a hired cook, he had probably already launched his own business, the "eating house" that he was operating on Notre-Dame Street at his death in 1815. It may not have been the most prosperous establishment, but it was his own, and he answered to no master.[7]

To argue that blacks were confined to the lowest levels of the labour pool is to oversimplify. Slavery had left its mark on blacks and whites. If, after slavery, many blacks worked as house servants, barbers, cleaners, waiters, cooks, farmhands, gardeners, grooms, hairdressers, seamstresses, laundresses, etc., this was to be expected. They took the domestic skills that they had picked up in slavery, or that their slave parents had passed on to them, and put them to remunerative use, filling the service jobs that they knew and that white society was used to seeing them perform. Some may have been content with that, but many wanted more out of life. The more enterprising, ambitious, or fortunate developed humdrum jobs into a business of their own. We can only imagine the purposefulness and effort that it took for a former slave like John Trim to prosper as he did. In the case of Caesar Johonnot, who had picked up his knowledge of distilling as a slave in Boston, building his own distillery may not have been the wisest move, since the expense ruined him; his skills were in demand and would have assured him continued employment and a decent living. Either way, like John Trim or Joseph Pierson and several others, he was not stuck in a dead-end job at the lowest pay, and had it not been for his untimely death in 1800, he might have passed on his knowledge to his sons.

Others seeking a better life were not so skilful or fortunate as Trim et al. and succumbed to the lure of liquor, illicit activity, and petty crime. Richard Jackson, a young man from Albany, New York, went that route. Two glimpses of his life, a decade apart, convey the sadness of his situation. As a youth of seventeen or so, he worked as a servant for businessman Charles Porteous in 1819. Porteous stood up for him in the spring of 1820 when he was charged with theft (and acquitted), testifying that in the four or five months that Jackson had worked for him, he had "found him an honest attentive and faithful servant, & wd have engaged him again could he have found him."[8] Was a life of domestic service the best that Jackson could look forward to? Flash forward to his home in 1831. He and his wife, both drunk, are fighting. A man steps in on Mrs Jackson's side and, in the ensuing knockdown, chews off part of Jackson's lower lip. It is a squalid picture of a man at rock bottom, who, scarred for life, would not rise. A few months later, he and William Murphy (another black man in the same boat) along with several whites were jailed – Jackson for two months, Murphy for three – for operating a bawdy house.[9]

The variety of jobs that blacks held, and the entrepreneurial skills and strong work ethic that some of them displayed, make it impossible to state categorically that they were restricted to the worst jobs. On the other hand, they were denied what might be considered the best. Slavery had generally deprived them of schooling, training, and opportunities, and imprinted on white minds a view of blacks as fit to serve, unfit to lead. As a result, blacks were for the most part shut out of those jobs and positions that, in the view of society at large, carried authority, commanded respect or reflected in some way their potential or intellectual attainments. A modern-day "human resources" manager would shudder at the waste.

PUBLIC SERVICE, THE PROFESSIONS, AND THE ARTS

There were no blacks in government or public administration in Lower Canada. One man of apparently mixed-race background served in what we would today consider a white-collar, public service position. The problem lies in ascertaining the racial identity of this man, Halifax-born William Wright, who, from a clerk in the Adjutant General's Department at Quebec in the 1820s and 1830s, rose to the rank of chief clerk, then served in the latter post at Montreal from 1839 until three years before his death in 1869. He was also a prominent Mason, master for some years of St George's Lodge, No. 643 (English Registry), at Montreal.[10] Was he partly black? If so, his attainments were out of the ordinary. Even more extraordinary would be those of his Quebec-born sons, William and Henry Blake Wright, who would be respectively the first accredited "coloured" medical doctor and notary in British North America. An examination of the sons' careers, which unfolded in the second half of the nineteenth century, falls outside our purview: William, who graduated in medicine from McGill University in 1848 at the age of twenty, taught at the university for thirty years, co-founded and edited *The Medical Chronicle or Montreal Monthly Journal of Medicine & Surgery* in the 1850s, and was also ordained an Anglican priest in 1874; his younger brother, Henry, practised as a notary from 1861 to 1903. It is Dr William Wright who gives us the first indication that the family was other than white: in the census form that he filled out in 1861 as owner of the house that they occupied, he listed his father, five siblings, and a servant (but not his English-born mother, Mary Blake) in the column headed "Coloured Persons Mulatto or Indian"; opposite each of their names, he wrote: "Creole." This term, found in no other Montreal census returns that year, can cover a variety of racial or ethnic blendings. The Wrights never publicly identified themselves as "coloured," and there is no evidence of any close association between them and black Montrealers, but decades later, Dr Wright, by then a widower of seventy-three, and his sixty-nine-year-old sister, Henrietta, who shared his home on Ste-Famille Street, were counted as "black" in the census of 1901.[11] Was this the truth as volunteered by the Wrights, or the rash jotting of a census taker? One might think that if there was an occasion when someone might have played the "race card," it was in 1882–83 when medical students at McGill rebelled against Dr Wright's antiquated teaching and forced his retirement. Yet race is nowhere mentioned as an element in the dispute.[12] Given these circumstances, perhaps we should resist counting William Wright *père* as "black." The mystery remains.

The only "public servants" in Montreal whom we know to have been black, other than the occasional hangman (see chapter 9), were of a far different class than the Wrights. In November 1785, Henri Moore, believed to be John Trim's friend Henry Moore, was one of four men hired for a month by Montreal's chimney inspector to sweep every chimney in the city proper. Those doing the rooftop work were to be paid $10, those on the ground $9.[13] In November 1818, Peter Dago, Warren Glossen, John Hyers, and Prince Thomson (alias Thomas Thompson) were hired by Emmanuel d'Aubreville, captain of the night watch, as the city's lamplighters on a six-month

Quebec-born Dr William Wright (1827–1908), shown here as a young man, identified his whole family, except his mother, as "coloured" in the census of 1861. In 1901, a census-taker identified him as "black." His father, also called William, served as chief clerk in the Adjutant General's Department at Monreal.

Below
Dr Wright as a man of mature years.

A large Celtic cross marks the grave of Dr William Wright and his wife, Margaret Mason Harbeson, in Mount Royal Cemetery. The truncated column on the right marks that of his parents, William Wright (1804–1869), a native of Halifax, and Mary Blake.

contract. A law enacted earlier that year had entrusted to the magistrates who administered the cities of Montreal and Quebec the responsibility for lighting city streets, a service previously provided by public-spirited merchants and others. Even before those private street lamps went up, it seems that some blacks may have eked out a living by going out at night with a lantern and lighting the way home for the well-heeled. In describing a nocturnal walk home from a friend's in November 1791, Dr Henry Loedel said that he and his wife were accompanied by "a Negro who carried a Lanthern before them." This lampman also acted as a sort of bodyguard, tackling a white lout who threatened Loedel.[14] The watch and public street lighting were instituted on 1 May 1818. For the first six months, the watch consisted of D'Aubreville, his deputy, and a band of 20 rough-and-ready characters who were hired at three shillings a night. They worked out of the former Récollets convent, located behind John Trim's house. In the fall, when the white watchmen refused to carry on with lamplighting duties any longer, D'Aubreville, with the approval of the magistrates who administered the city, recruited the four black men. Their job consisted in lighting and maintaining all the oil street lamps in the city and suburbs, for two shillings a lamp per month.[15] Dago had worked as a lamplighter when the street lighting was still in private hands. He had arrived in Lower Canada from his native New York state as a teenager in 1810, only to be arrested on crossing the border for a theft committed on the road, at Plattsburgh. A street-wise survivor who, unlike his friend Richard Jackson, managed to keep his head above water, Dago engaged in a mixture of licit and illicit jobs, eventually settling into the business of dyer and scourer, which he carried on until his death in 1868.[16] Glossen did not live so long: he was hanged for burglary in October 1823 at the reputed age of thirty-five.[17] In the 1830s, blacks Thomas Cockburn, Jacob Simpson, Richard Jackson and William Murphy, dissolute characters by then, given to drink and the running of bawdy houses, engaged in what we would consider a public work, but as private entrepreneurs: they cleaned privies, surely one of the most unpleasant, if necessary, labouring jobs.[18] So much for blacks in public service.

The liberal professions were white preserves – there were no black teachers, notaries, lawyers, judges, doctors, or pastors. Nor were there any black architects, artists, writers, or musicians in the city and vicinity who earned a living from their art, although some black men did serve as drummers and buglers in the army or the militia, and others who played an instrument – usually the fiddle – were engaged to play at private frolics. We can only wonder where a twenty-five-year-old Quebec slave like Lowcanes had learned to play "the Violin very well," as his master claimed in 1775.[19] We hardly picture masters hiring a music teacher for their slaves, or most free blacks having the wherewithal to buy an instrument or to pay for lessons. And as anyone knows who has ever plucked a string, it takes a good deal of practice to produce a pleasing sound from such an instrument – who had the time to spare? At Quebec, in 1781, Bob, "a Nigro man," dropped by the home of an acquaintance to wish her a happy New Year, and "played upon the Fiddle near the Window."[20] A mulatto named Morris Emery apparently fiddled away at parties around St-Armand, on the Vermont border around 1800.[21] American-born Stephen Rogers, who spent time at Montreal in the first decade of the century and then farmed on the seigneury of D'Ailleboust, northeast of Montreal, played the fiddle at a holiday season party in the winter of 1815–16, as we know from his complaint that he was assaulted on "the third of January [1816] last past, being in a house at Cote St. Pierre in the parish of Berthier ... where he had been Called to play the Fiddle."[22] Thomas Perks, a mulatto from Nova Scotia living at the fort at Coteau-du-Lac in 1821, played the fiddle at a dance on 13 August when he was mortally injured in a bar fight.[23] Abraham Low, usually termed a labourer, trader, or peddlar, was identified as a musician in 1834. Seven years later, we hear of him noodling on a flute outdoors in St-Dominique Street, apparently for his own amusement.[24]

Perhaps the closest that Montreal came to seeing a professional black artist at work was in the summer of 1824, when William Alexander Brown proposed an evening of

> AFRICAN THEATRE.
> At the request of several Gentlemen Mr Turnbull has been induced to allow the occupation of the New Market Theatre by Mr BROWN the African, for one night only; in consequence of which Mr Brown respectfully informs the Public, that on Monday Evening the 16th August, will be presented, select Scenes from the most admired Plays. Doors will open at Seven, and Performances to Commence at 8 O'Clock. Boxes 2s 6d, – Pit 1s 3d. Box Tickets to [be] had at the Box Office, during the day on Monday, Pit Tickets at the Door.[25]

Three years earlier, in New York City, Brown, a former ship steward from St Vincent, had founded the African Theatre, the first black theatre company in the Ameri-

A high-stepping tambourine player beats out the rhythm at a dance in this scene published in 1809. From fifers, drummers, and buglers in the army and militia to fiddlers at parties, quite a few black men were musicians.

> RUN AWAY from the Subscriber (on the Eighteenth Instant) a Negro man named *Lowcanes*, aged twenty-five Years, thin faced, and remarkable long hair tied behind, about five feet ten inches high, speaks good French, no English, plays the Violin very well. He had on when he went off a light coloured short coat with a red cape to it, waistcoat and breeches: Whoever secures the said Negro man so that his Master may have him again shall have sixteen Dollars reward, and charges from
> 22d *November*, 1775.   WILLIAM GILL.

Lowcanes, a slave, "plays the violin very well," says this notice of his escape in 1775.

cas. Rival theatre managers and others who could not stomach the idea of seeing blacks intrude on what they considered a white cultural preserve did their best to drive him out of business, disrupting performances and trashing the venues. By the end of 1823, the company was finished in New York. Brown's subsequent life is a mystery. He is thought to have taken some members of the troupe on tour, or to have set up a new company at Albany. He made at least one hop across the border to Montreal. Whether this was a solo effort, or whether other black actors travelled with him, we cannot tell.[26]

Other than Brown, most if not all of those "gentlemen" who persuaded theatre manager John Duplessis Turnbull[27] to open his doors to this rare spectacle would have been white. There were not enough black Montrealers to make such a performance pay, and fewer still who could have spared the price of admission. In an age of widespread illiteracy, we might also assume that many of them lacked the language skills to savour "select Scenes from the most admired Plays," but we would be wrong on two counts. For one thing, black New Yorkers of all stripes had flocked to the theatre, which presented everything from Shakespeare – straight or adapted – to pantomime, and there is no reason to believe that black Montrealers would have responded any differently. And, on the score of literacy, it should be noted that just two and a half years after Brown's visit, a survey of the first-day class at No. 4 African School found that seven of the fourteen adults present could read "tolerably" or better – not bad for working-class Montrealers of the time, black or white, English-speaking or French.[28]

Did the African Theatre ever take the stage that 16 August? Brown was up against stiff competition. The paying public seeking entertainment probably would have chosen to attend the circus, tried and true, rather than a performance that would perhaps have struck them as a mere novelty. That evening, West & Blanchard's crowd-pleasing circus, which featured theatrical as well as equestrian acts, drew "a very full House of the first respectability" for the last performance of *Timour the Tartar*, complete with live horses. Besides, Turnbull's own commitment to promoting the African Theatre was probably not what it might have been, as he was seeking to interest the circus in performing a melodrama of his own composition.[29] Be that as it may, no review or report of the African Theatre performance appeared in the newspapers. Nothing more was heard of "Mr Brown the African" and his theatrical venture in Montreal.

TRADESMEN AND ARTISANS

Black tradesmen, especially cooks, shoemakers, and barber-hairdressers, were a less rarefied species than black actors. As we have seen, some of them – including a woman, Margaret Sinclair – worked as cooks aboard the steamboats. Reference has also been made to cook Joseph Pierson and his restaurant, and to Richard Thompson, who operated a pastry shop and worked on the steamers. Cooking is a very portable skill, and so when a person such as Jacob Abdella is identified as a cook, without further specification, it is impossible to tell whether he was working on land or on the boats, on his own account or as someone's hired help. It is likely that many blacks identified as cooks and waiters plied their trade on the water. In many cases, however, their places of employment were unspecified. Pierre Alex, for example, born in St-Domingue, was identified in 1815 as a thirty-five-year-old black cook, without further precision.[30] Another native of St-Domingue, James Noël, active in the early 1820s, was tagged at different times as a "nègre domestique" and a "nègre cuisinier."[31] Yet another Haitian native, Jean François, who arrived in Montreal by way of Bytown (Ottawa) in the summer of 1835, was occasionally identified as a cook.[32] David Bristow, of unknown origin, who turned up at the end of the 1830s, would also work as a cook in the ensuing decade.[33] English-born David Woolford, who first shows up in the records in 1840 when he married Caroline O'Reilly, a Canadian-born "coloured woman" (perhaps from Upper Canada), worked as a baker.[34]

Shoemakers included Ebert Weldin, supposedly a mulatto, who plied his trade from the mid-1790s until at least the early 1820s;[35] Narcisse Coudrin, possibly from New Orleans, active between 1805 and 1811, who seems to have left town after the death of his wife, Mary Violet Jones, in the latter year;[36] and, around 1820, James Croni, born at Ste-Anne-du-Sud (Ste-Anne-de-la-Pocatière) below Quebec, whose mother, Catherine Barbe, a native of French Guiana and former slave of Laughlin Smith, seigneur of Ste-Anne-du-Sud, died at Montreal in 1825.[37] John Patten, active at Montreal from the end of the 1820s until his death in 1835, seems to have alternated between shoemaking and working on the steamboats, as we saw in the last chapter. In the summer of 1834, Catharine Crowell, a twice-widowed woman "of colour," placed her fifteen-year-old son, William Brusler Fortune, as an apprentice to a shoemaker until he turned twenty-one.[38] Thomas H. Smith, one of the 12 "Coloured brethren" who met at Alexander Grant's in July 1833 to discuss the British anti-slavery bill then in the works, was possibly the shoemaker identified two years earlier as Thomas Smyth.[39]

Barber-hairdressers seem to make a later appearance. No doubt some had picked up this skill as slaves – as had Jean Louis, from St-Domingue, advertised for sale in 1793 as a "bon perruquier" as well as a "bon Cuisinier."[40] But there seems to be no mention of free blacks earning their living at this trade in the first two decades of the nineteenth century; one suspects that some "labourers" of that time may, in fact, have been barbers and hairdressers. The first such person of whom there is a record is William Goodrich, born in Barbados to a white businessman and "a Negro slave named Francis [sic]"; he surfaced at Quebec in 1820 before moving to Montreal. He married the widow Chloe Pierce there in 1826, and died four years later.[41] James Rollings set up his home and shop on St-Paul Street in 1826, and promptly got into a spat with his neighbour, a jeweller, after he put up a barber pole. Rollings's shop was across the street from where Alexander Grant would set up as a hairdresser and scourer in 1830. Rollings was enumerated there as a "perruquier" in the census of 1831.[42] There is no trace of him after 1834. Grant, who moved his shop to McGill Street, then to Notre-Dame Street, remained in business as a "fashionable hair cutter, perfumer and peruke maker," until his death in August 1838. He employed at least one

"At dinner we were much amused by the antics of one of the Black waiters who flourished the dishes over our heads in a most alarming manner." Katherine Jane Ellice, a member of Governor-General Lord Durham's entourage, recorded the scene in words and watercolours while on a quick tour from Montreal to the United States in 1838.

other black hairdresser, George Nixon, who lived with him and his wife in 1836. Cecilia (Celia) Farley, Grant's widow, carried on the business for another seven or eight months after his death, disposing of the hairdressing equipment and shop fixtures in April 1839.[43] In 1835, Grant served as a witness at the wedding of James Grantham, an English-born black, who appears to have worked briefly as a barber in the mid-1830s before embarking on a career as a wholesale and retail tobacconist.[44] In the 1840s, Grantham would have a few business dealings with James Smith, a hairdresser of West Indian origin who would operate a tony shop at various locations on Notre-Dame Street for more than thirty years from 1840. For the first few years, Smith occupied Grant's old shop; it is quite possible that it was he who bought Grant's hairdressing equipment and supplies at auction in 1839.[45] Solomon Molliston, believed to have come from New York City in the early 1830s, practised as a barber and hairdresser from at least 1834 to his death in 1840. In February 1834, he was among the witnesses at the wedding of hairdresser Joseph Shaw, who had been one of the twelve men to attend the anti-slavery meeting at Grant's the previous summer.[46] Robert Gordon, a "mulatto," seems to have set up shop in 1837, operating as a barber-hairdresser-wigmaker on St-Paul Street before moving to a location opposite Ste-Anne's Market (Place d'Youville) around 1842. The market building, where black Montrealers had celebrated the coming into force of the British emancipation act in 1834, housed the Canadian parliament from 1844 to 1849. A barber located across the street from such a hirsute assemblage could count on a brisk trade. But after a Tory mob burned down the parliament building in 1849, Montreal lost its status as capital – and away went the bewhiskered politicians and functionaries. Gordon died a "pauper," unmarried, in May 1854, at the age of about fifty.[47]

Now and then we catch a glimpse of other skilled and semi-skilled free workers, such as saddler George Crane, mentioned in a previous chapter as active at the turn of the century at Montreal, then at Quebec. Much earlier, another who had moved between the two cities was Jean François Dominique *dit* Mentor, a Montreal slave-turned-silversmith, who plied his craft at Montreal and Quebec and died at Montreal in 1773.[48] Morris Thompson was a metal worker of a different stamp: a foundryman, he was hired by merchant Peter McGill in 1824 to work as a "journeyman moulder" at the Marmora Iron Works in Upper Canada.[49] Later still, precious metal became the stock-in-trade of John Wright, the only child of ex-slaves William Wright and Catherine Guillet to live to adulthood. Apprenticed to a gilder in 1839, at age sixteen, he worked in Montreal for about a decade after learning his trade, and then moved to Quebec in the 1850s.[50] Tailors, like shoemakers, were in more general demand than gilders, yet no black tailor seems to have set up shop before Cubit Giles, whose presence at Montreal was not recorded until the early 1840s.[51]

FARMERS AND FARMHANDS

A few black farmers were recorded on the island of Montreal in the early years of the century, three of them closely linked. Robert Boston, John Dolphin, and Henry Thomson are believed to have farmed leased land, or to have been hired to farm the lands of others, as there is no record of their buying land themselves. Records of births, marriages, and deaths show how closely they were connected. For example, Boston, reputedly thirty-four, and Dolphin, twenty-eight, were married on the same day at the same church in 1806.[52] Boston's wife, Mary Ann Hunter, was said to be a twenty-year-old "négresse" from Philadelphia; Dolphin's was identified as thirty-year-old Elizabeth Jarvis. Boston's wife died on 13 July 1809.[53] Three years later, as a "Negroe" farmer at St-Michel (now the St-Michel district of Montreal), he married again, with Dolphin as his witness. This second Mrs Boston, identified as nineteen-year-old Betsy Thomson, died on 19 January 1813, less than five months after their wedding.[54] Then, Boston's nine-year-old son by his first wife, Robert Hunter Boston, died on 5 June, two days before John Thomson, the ten-year-old son of "negroes" Henry and Phillis Thomson, who farmed nearby at Petite Côte (Rosemont Blvd.). Boston was a witness at John Thomson's burial, as he was again at the burial of the Thomsons' thirteen-year-old son, Henry, on 13 September.[55]

Elizabeth Jarvis, Dolphin's wife, died in July 1812, a month after the beginning of the War of 1812; at her death, she was identified as Lydia Dolphin, "a Negress" of about twenty-six, and her husband, John Dalphen (*sic*), was said to be of St-Michel.[56]

Just as Dolphin and Robert Boston had married together in 1806, Dolphin and Henry Thomson enlisted together in Lieutenant-Colonel Charles Michel de Salaberry's Corps of Canadian Voltigeurs on 16 February 1813. Dolphin's enlistment form identified him as the thirty-one-year-old son of John Dolphin, 5′ 7″ tall, complexion "noire nègre" (negro black), hair "de laine" (woolly), eyes "noir." Thomson, described in the same terms as Dolphin, was down as the son of Thomas Thompson, height 5′ 4″, age thirty-five, the maximum age for Voltigeurs recruits.[57] He may have understated his age: at his death on 2 January 1819 he was said to be fifty-six, which would have made him about fifty in 1813. Certainly, if he did serve with the Voltigeurs, it was not for long. He was present at the funerals of his two sons the following summer, and, in April 1814, he was hired for a year as a "servant and laborer" to work a farm at St-Michel for Montreal merchant David Stansfeld.[58] As for Dolphin, he may have transferred from the militia to the army: a John Dolphin served in the 8th (King's) Regiment, which was stationed at Montreal in 1815 after serving in Upper Canada during the war. When Henry and Phillis Thomson had a daughter in the fall of 1815 they named her Lydia, probably after Dolphin's late wife. At the end of 1816, Dolphin and William Appleby, a carpenter, leased a farm just outside the city for six years from 1 May 1817, but they had a violent falling-out in February 1818 when Appleby and his wife went at Dolphin with axe and tongs, putting him in the hospital for fifteen days. No trace of Dolphin has been found after his discharge from the hospital.[59]

The former slave John Fleming, under the name Jacques Flemming, was identified as a "nègre cultivateur" (negro farmer) in 1813 at the birth of his son, Jacques. He was separated from Julia Johnson, his legal wife, and his current "wife" was called Magdeleine Carmel. When he sold his land in November 1816 she was called Magdeleine Thompson. On other occasions she was Madelaine Fleming or, as in 1820, when she was accused of operating a waterfront bordello and gambling den, "a Colerd woman by the name of Flemming."[60]

Others designated in Montreal records as farmers seem to have lived in the city off and on, or to have visited, but to have done their farming elsewhere. Such was the case of Joseph François Demarin, who, as mentioned in a previous chapter, farmed at St-Eustache from 1802 until his death in 1829. Fiddler Stephen Rogers, mentioned above, and his wife Ann Garner (or Gardner), both American-born blacks, settled on the seigneury of D'Ailleboust, in the area of Ste-Elisabeth and Ste-Mélanie, northeast of Montreal. At the christening of their daughter, Elvira, in Montreal in 1807, Rogers was identified as a farmer of D'Ailleboust, and he seems to have continued farming in that area for the next few decades.[61]

Farmer Cato Giles shows up briefly in Montreal records in 1819. The church burial record of his teenage daughter, Catharine, in August identified him as a "sometime farmer in St Andrews."[62] He had actually farmed, not at St Andrew's (St-André-d'Argenteuil) up the Ottawa River, but at St-Armand or Philipsburg, on the Vermont border. Giles, who may have begun his life in Canada as a slave,[63] was free by 1797, as we know from the account books of Philipsburg merchant and innkeeper Phillip Ruiter, the agent of the seigneury of St-Armand. These records show charges for various items (cloth, wheat, salt, tea, rum, tobacco, corn, flour, peas) which Giles bought from Ruiter between 1797 and 1812, as well as for services, e.g., rental of a house, "to winter your Cows 5 mths," "to pasturing Your heifer," etc. Giles paid his debts partly in cash, partly in labour – his own or that of his wife, Hannah – by "shoping & drawing wood," "spliting rails," "cleaning hemp," "hoeing & planting," "Cutting Weeds," "By Your wife Spining 58½ Run of Yarn at 7½d per run." Their daughter, Hannah Giles, "spinster," married Montreal "labourer" George Williams on 6 December 1819, the two of them termed "people of colour."[64]

In 1820, we get a fleeting glimpse of the travails of the Curtis family, who appear to have come from Vermont. Isaac Curtis may have been a farmer, or a steamboat hand, or both. The first sign of the family's presence comes on 7 March with the baptism of Louis Samuel Curtis, "né dans les Etats de Vermont" (born in the states of Vermont) to "farmer" Isaac Curtis and his wife, Sarah Brown. At their daughter Charlotte's baptism on 17 May, Isaac Curtis's occupation was given as "matelot" (sailor). Five days after her baptism, Charlotte, who was said to be fourteen, entered the Hôtel-Dieu. She left the hospital on 2 June, but returned again 10 June, this time for eighteen days. Her mother, meanwhile, identified as an American-born "Negrêse" – the only one in the family who could sign her name – was admitted on 17 June and died there on 1 July. At her burial, her husband was again identified as a sailor. Charlotte herself returned to the hospital on 9 July and died there on 26 July.[65]

Labourer Thomas Fidler was hired as a "servant" for one year by furrier George Clark in July 1809 to work on a farm at St-Michel for $10 (£2 10s) a month plus board. By mutual consent, the agreement was cancelled on 26 December. Fidler, who had worked to 23 December, was paid in all £10 14s 5d. A few days later, he and Richard Rogers, "both persons of color," formed a partnership to operate a livery stable until the following 1 May.[66] Rogers, as we saw, then went to work aboard the steamer *Accommodation*. It is not entirely clear whether Fidler farmed the land at St-Michel for Clark, or whether he was merely a farmhand. There is no doubt about the status of English-born Isaac Newton, who was hired by explorer and fur-trade merchant Sir Alexander Mackenzie for one year from 1 November 1804 to work on the latter's farm on Mount Royal. Newton was to be paid $9 a month, "with lodging only and the use of a patch of ground for the purpose of planting potatoes and corn." At the same time, Mackenzie leased the farm for one and half years to Scottish gardener Alexander Reid, in return for half the produce of the farm, garden, and orchard. Reid was to keep the place in good order, "for which purposes he will be allowed the labor of the black man Isaac during the above term free of any expense."[67]

IN THE FUR TRADE

Without the fur trade, there would have been no Canada as we know it. From the moment of Montreal's foundation in 1642, this trade in animal skins was not only the city's economic mainstay, but also fuelled the exploration of the continent, shaped westward expansion and economic development for both the French and British colonial empires in North America, and lay at the root of the frequent conflicts between settlers and aboriginal populations and between the colonies of the different European powers. In the late eighteenth century, it was also a hive of slave-owners and one of the principal channels through which black slaves reached the city, or left it, as can be seen from the numerous references in this book to blacks owned or trafficked by fur traders. Although the fur trade's economic importance for Montreal declined from the end of the eighteenth century, around the time that slavery came to an end, and all but disappeared with the merger of the North West and Hudson's Bay companies in 1821, it remained a major employer well beyond that time, and even American concerns recruited voyageur crews from Montreal and the surrounding area. Some of the voyageurs were black.[68] And as we have seen, leading figures of the trade such as Simon McTavish, James McGill, and Sir Alexander Mackenzie also employed free blacks in their homes or on their farms.

There was another, more indirect, way in which the fur trade may have affected the lives of blacks. "Traveling in the exotic and adventurous 'Indian country' opened voyageurs to new cultural beliefs and practices," fur-trade historian Caroline Podruchny has written.[69] She makes no mention of blacks in her book, but one cannot help but wonder whether this mind-expanding role of the fur trade did not help to make voyageurs less standoffish than other colonists in dealing with blacks. Certainly we find interesting instances of interaction between voyageurs and Montreal blacks, from the financial assistance provided to Hilaire Lamour by voyageur Antoine Badel *dit* Dufort, to the sale by voyageur Jean-Baptiste Mallet of his property at Côte-Ste-Catherine to John Trim and Henry Moore in 1796, to voyageur Joseph Colombeau's standing as godfather to Caesar Johonnot's daughter, Catherine, in 1797, and the marriage in the first decade of the nineteenth century of Johonnot's widow, Margaret Campbell, to sometime voyageur François Houle.

Among the black Montrealers who worked in the fur trade were John Darlington, a "Negre Libre" hired in April 1777 by trader Ezekiel Solomon to travel to the fur-trading post of Petit Nord (in Northern Ontario), where he was to winter, then return with canoes of goods or furs. On his return to Montreal, he was to be paid 600 francs.[70] Peter Canon from Virginia, sometimes termed a "mulâtre," more often a "nègre," probably also worked at the trade in the mid-1780s: at the burial of one of his children in 1785, he and his wife were said to be residents of the "Pays d'En-Haut" (the upper country), at that time usually signifying fur-trade land.[71] Constant, a slave, obtained the consent of his master, Pierre Fortier, in 1794 to hire on with fur trader Jean-Baptiste Tabeau. As a "milieu" (middleman in a canoe), he was to paddle to Michilimackinac, then still in British hands, and winter there for three years, for a total of 1,300 livres, minus 600 livres that were to go to Fortier in three annual instalments. Fortier promised to free his slave at the end of the three years, providing he received his payments and that Constant behaved.[72] In the fall of 1803, William Dowling was hired as a "Bout Batteaux" (literally, endman, i.e., frontman or steersman in a canoe) for 1,200 livres to paddle up to Michilimackinac, now an American post, and spend two years working there for Montreal trader Toussaint Pothier. The

Michilimackinac Company hired Dowling in January 1808 as a steersman, to travel to Michilimackinac or nearby St Joseph Island, spend the summer as a domestic, then return as a steersman, for a total of 300 livres.[73] Dowling's positions indicate that, on the water at least, he had more experience and responsibility than Constant; where the latter's job as middleman was paddling or bailing, Dowling's was to either direct the canoe's course by commanding its crew from the front, or to steer it from the stern. A Thomas Macloude who spent three weeks at the Hôtel-Dieu in the summer of 1806, was registered as a "nègre" voyageur, about thirty-six years old.[74] Like Peter Canon, but thirty years later, Thomas Parker (alias Thomas Parker Irving or Irvine) is thought to have worked in the fur trade, judging from a reference to him and his wife, Patty Williams, in 1818 as living in the "pays d'en haut."[75]

The best-known blacks with a Montreal connection who engaged in the fur trade were the Bonga brothers, Étienne and especially Pierre (known respectively as Stephen and Peter in English), former slaves of Captain Daniel Robertson at Michilimackinac. On the point of returning to Montreal in 1787 after five years as military commander of that post, Robertson had freed Jean Bonga and his wife Jeanne, as well as their two sons and two daughters. The Bongas kept a tavern at Michilimackinac. Shortly after the death of Jean Bonga in January 1795, his widow had moved to Montreal with her daughters, Charlotte, who would soon marry Jean-Baptiste L'Africain, and Rosalie, who would become the wife of John Pruyn.[76] Étienne may have accompanied them too, but Pierre remained in fur-trade country. Through 1800–06, Pierre, married to a Chippewa woman, was with Alexander Henry the Younger of the North West Company on his trading ventures in the areas of the Red and Pembina Rivers in present-day Manitoba, Minnesota, and North Dakota. In his journal, Henry noted the birth of Pierre's daughter, Blanche, on 12 March 1802 at his fort on the Pembina River: "Pierre's wife was delivered of a daughter, the first new fruit in this Fort, and a very black."[77]

Of Étienne, we know only that he died unmarried and childless at Montreal on 2 November 1804; he was identified as a twenty-eight-year old voyageur, the "servant" of Sir Alexander Mackenzie's cousin, Roderick Mackenzie, a partner in the North West Company. Roderick Mackenzie, after years in the field, had lately settled at Terrebonne. Within days of Étienne's death, his brother-in-law Jean-Baptiste L'Africain went to court to have a curator named to protect the interests of the absent Pierre in the estate. An inventory of Étienne's belongings, the first known itemized statement of a black Montrealer's assets, showed that he owned little – a total of 408 livres 10 sols' worth, mostly in clothing – but that he was owed 3,150 livres, 3,000 of that by McTavish, Frobisher & Co., then the leading firm in the North West Company partnership. At Kaministiquia (Thunder Bay, Ontario) on 21 July 1806, Pierre Bonga, just back from the Red River country, "Nègre, Voyageur, et Engagé de la Compagnie du Nord Ouest," authorized a fellow voyageur to collect the 1,263 livres, 7 sols coming to him from his brother's estate.[78]

Pierre Bonga, who had four children – Jean-Baptiste, Blanche, Étienne, and George – "by a Woman of the Indian Country," sent them to Montreal to be baptized, schooled and trained in the service of North West Company partners. The baptism record of his seven-year-old son Étienne (Stephen) in 1810 identified Peter Bongo (*sic*) vaguely as "in the service" of the North West Company. In Montreal in 1813, the boy's court-appointed guardian, North West partner Archibald Norman McLeod, bound him until age twenty-one as a servant to Angus Shaw, another partner in the fur-trade concern. Blanche Bonga, nine, and George, about seven, were baptized in 1811, their father's occupation given as a North West "labourer." But Pierre Bonga was said to be an interpreter for the company in 1812, when his thirteen-year-old son Jean-Baptiste was indentured to McLeod. During the virtual war that raged between the Montreal-based North West Company and the London-based Hudson's Bay Company from 1811 to 1821, Pierre Bonga was among the North Westers at Fort William (the former Kaministiquia) when that post was captured by Lord Selkirk on 12–13 August 1816. Pierre Bonga died in what is now Minnesota, in 1831. Early the following year, his widowed sisters in Montreal, Charlotte and Rosalie, accepted £11 in return for renouncing all rights to his estate in favour of his sons, George and Étienne. The deed recording this says that Pierre Bonga had died intestate; no one seems to have been aware of the will that he had made out at Montreal in 1815, in which he had left everything to his children.[79]

Glasgow Crawford (alias Glasco, Crawford Glasgow), husband of Phillis Araquandie (Arakwente), a Mohawk from Kahnawake, was another black man from the Montreal area engaged in the fur trade in the final days of the showdown between the North West and Hudson's Bay companies. He worked for the Hudson's Bay concern as a middleman and cook from 1818 to 1821, serving in the Athabasca Department, centred on the lake of that name in what is now northwestern Saskatchewan and northeastern Alberta. George Simpson, the future Montreal governor of the company, ran that department in 1820–21. On 24 November 1820, he noted in his journal that Simon McGillivray Jr, the Metis who commanded the North West's Fort Chippewyan, "complained that Glasgow our Cook was in the habit of chastising his children and had this afternoon thrown down and kicked his little girl; it appears however that there is no ground for the charge; the man happens to be a Negro and the children have taken umbrage at his complexion, it being a shade darker than their own."[80] The following March, a little pilfering and his linguistic skills appear to have doomed Crawford to spend one more year than he had bargained for in the company's service. As Simpson noted on 3 March:

> Examined our Trader Mr [Jacques] Chastellain & Glasgow the Cook very particularly relative to a petty theft of Tea & Flour; they pleaded Guilty which gives me a firm hold of both; if the services of the former are required for another year, he must either remain on my terms or submit to a heavy fine; the latter will be a most useful Man to Mr Brown in the Mountain, as he speaks English, French & Iroquois fluently, he did intend going to Canada this season having a considerable Balance in the Compys. hands but he must now prepare for another campaign.[81]

In old age, George Bonga of Minnesota, son of voyageur Pierre Bonga and his Indian wife, regretted that as a schoolboy in Montreal, "as there was no one, to take any particular interest about me, I did not get as good an education, as I might have had."

But the merger of the London and Montreal-based fur trade rivals that year resulted in sharp cutbacks in the voyageur labour force, and Crawford returned to Montreal after all. "Glasco & wife" were recorded in the mid-1830s as residents of Kahnawake. The only other black living there was Joseph Thompson, a native of Schenectady, New York, who, around 1848, would settle at Huntingdon, on the Châteauguay River near the New York border, with his French-Canadian wife.[82] In a list of Kahnawake residents drawn up in 1836, Indian Department superintendent James Hughes wrote opposite their names that Glasco and the as yet unmarried Thompson had been "turned out of the village several times [as not entitled to occupy Indian lands] but have always returned."[83]

There was another sort of voyageur in the early nineteenth century, the "voyageur des cages," or "cageux," a raftsman, one of those who sailed the large timber cribs down the rapids-strewn Ottawa and St Lawrence Rivers to Quebec. Like the fur trade, the timber trade kept many men on the move, away from home for extended periods. This export trade gained great impetus during the Napoleonic Wars, when Britain's navy could no longer rely on its traditional supplies of timber from the countries of

Baptized at Montreal in 1810 when he was about seven years old, Étienne (Stephen) Bonga, brother of George, was indentured there in 1813 to North West Company partner Angus Shaw. He was to remain with Shaw until he turned twenty-one.

the Baltic Sea. North America offered a seemingly boundless supply of this resource. It came not only from Lower and Upper Canada and New Brunswick, but also from the Vermont and New York shores of Lake Champlain, down the Richelieu River to the St Lawrence and thence to Quebec, the one outlet for the trade before the mid-1820s when canals connected the remote northern portions of those states with the Hudson River and the port of New York. There is an early hint of this connection in a notice placed in the *Quebec Gazette* in 1771 by William Gilliland, a pioneer settler on the New York side of Lake Champlain, concerning his black slave, Ireland, and a sixteen-year-old white servant who had fled together. Of his white servant, Gilliland said that he was "remarkable for the Number of Masters he has served, having lived with almost every Stave-Cutter on the Lake."[84]

From the suit that he filed against timber dealer Charles Bennet in 1793, we suspect that Caesar Hunkings was employed in the trade, and seeking to recover lost wages, but the surviving court records do not enlighten us on this score or on the outcome of the case.[85] In 1804, however, Castor Jay, a black man born near Albany, New York, was hired as a "voyageur des cages" by Simon and John McNabb for 48 livres a month to work at assembling timber cribs at the head of the Bay of Quinte in Upper Canada, and to help run them down to Quebec.[86] Thomas Cockburn was hired in March 1809 for the same kind of work, up the Ottawa River, by the timber firm of Cameron & McMillan, at 54 livres a month. Cockburn, who was said to have come from Ireland, was married that November, at the end of the rafting season, to the widow Mary McArty.[87] Two months later, Cameron & McMillan hired Henry Garrett as a "labourer" in the same line, but for 90 livres a month.[88] Rafting work, or some other river trade, may have accounted for Garrett's presence in 1827 at Quebec, where he was arrested for assaulting a constable who tried to break up a brawl.[89] At her death at Montreal in 1816, Silvia Lee was identified as "a black woman, wife of William Lee of Fort Wellington [Prescott] Upper Canada a raftsman." Cockburn, Garrett and Jay were relatively young men, but William Lee was a veteran, a Loyalist who had served in the American War of Independence as a volunteer with Captain Henry Bird in the 8th Regiment, then stationed at Detroit.[90]

BLACK MEN IN ARMS

The military, like the fur trade, accounted for the presence of a good number of black slaves, and also recruited free blacks. In the days of empire, Britain's soldiers ranged farther afield than the fur traders. Some officers posted to Quebec landed there with a slave or two picked up while on service in the West Indies or elsewhere. Other slaves arrived in the province as prizes captured in military raids during the American War of Independence. At the same time, blacks such as Peter Becket, Rubin Middleton, and John Powell served with Loyalist corps, and later, during the War of 1812, as we have seen, farmers John Dolphin and Henry Thomson enlisted in the militia. Other blacks tasted of the military life in these years of endless hostilities.

Only ten years after the formal end of the war with its American colonies and their allies France and Spain, Britain was again at war with France, a conflict that soon engulfed all of Europe and which, but for a brief truce in 1802–03, was to rage on from 1793 until Napoleon's final defeat in June 1815. Posing a more immediate threat to British North America was the war with the United States, which broke out in June 1812 and kept Canadians and Americans on pins and needles for almost three years, almost coinciding with the last three years of the Napoleonic wars. Soldiers were understandably in demand for the protection of the colonies, and every foreigner was eyed as a possible spy or enemy agent. Entering Lower Canada in July 1793 after working as a "labourer" at Grande Isle, Vermont, George Lewis (or Louis), registered with the authorities as required by law – except that he waited a full year before doing so. In July 1794, just out of the hospital, he stated before a Justice of the Peace that in his twelve months in Canada he had, among other things, "enlisted ... in the 1st Battalion of the 60 Regiment from which I was discharged. I now live as a hired Servant with Thomas McCord of Montreal Esquire and intend to remain in this province."[91]

In general, those blacks who served in the army arrived at Montreal with their units, while those in the militia were residents who enlisted there. Some army regiments did recruit locally, however, and some black Montrealers were induced – by the levy money, if nothing else – to sign up. The New Brunswick Regiment of Fencible Infantry, for example, created in 1803 and elevated to the line in 1810 as the 104th Regiment of Foot, actively recruited at Montreal and Quebec from the fall of 1803, offering a bounty of five guineas to every approved recruit, and promising each a grant of not less than 200 acres of land in New Brunswick at the reduction of the corps.[92] How alluring such blandishments must have been to a Henry McEvoy, only recently freed from slavery. As we saw earlier, as a slave boy convinced that Britain had abolished slavery and set him free, he had hired himself out in January 1802 as a servant. His deed of indenture to William Byrne and his son, Philip, had said nothing about wages: the Byrnes simply agreed to lodge, feed, and clothe him, etc. They also reserved the right to assign his services to anyone they pleased. On 21 May 1804, they ceded their rights under the deed to Sir John Johnson. Shortly afterward, Henry McEvoy enlisted in the New Brunswick Regiment. He served until 24 September, when he and nine other recruits were transferred to the York Rangers, a black corps created in 1803 for garrison duty. It was disbanded in 1805, most of its able-bodied men going on to serve in other regiments, including the Royal African Corps.[93]

"There were ... Negroes in the [New Brunswick] Regiment but their number was distinctly limited to the pioneers, one to each company, and perhaps some of the drummers," a historian of the 104th wrote. All the pioneers were "negroes," the same author tells us, and these road builders and construction workers were the only members of the regiment allowed to sport full beards.[94] As for black drummers, an officer who had taken part in the overland trip from Fredericton to Quebec by six of the regiment's ten companies in the winter of 1813 wrote of that gruelling experience a half-century later, recalling a moment of levity provided by one Harry Grant of New Brunswick: "Some of the men would run the tobagans down the hills sitting on them, and would frequently capsize. Our big black drummer [Grant] straddled the big drum, which was lashed to a tobagan, to try the experiment, but it got off the track, shooting him off at high velocity, and the sable African came up some distance from where he disappeared, a white man exciting roars of laughter."[95]

Richard Houldin, like Henry McEvoy, was an early recruit to the regiment. He had married the "négresse" Marianne Ambroise at Montreal in 1786, and they had had four children in the next eight years.[96] Houldin enlisted on 19 October 1804. We know nothing else of him, other than that in November 1814, near the end of the War of 1812, he transferred to the 10th Royal Veterans Battalion, and that he died sometime before his wife did in 1819.[97] Houldin's wife was, we believe, the anonymous female slave whom Legislative Councillor Luc de Lacorne St-Luc, at his death in 1784, had bequeathed to his nine-year-old daughter, Marguerite, "avec Liberté de La Rendre Libre à Sa volonté" (with power to free her if and when she so desires). In view of her marriage to Houldin less than two years later, it appears that Marianne Ambroise was freed by her young mistress, the future wife of Jacques Viger. There are strong

A Pioneer of the 104th (New Brunswick) Regiment. The former slave Henry McEvoy enlisted in this newly formed regiment at Montreal in 1804, when it was called His Majesty's New Brunswick Regiment of Fencible Infantry.

hints of Marianne Ambroise's connection to the St-Luc family in that, in 1788, Marguerite de Lacorne St-Luc, then only thirteen, was the sponsor at the baptism of the Houldins' first-born child, Richard, and that Ambroise herself was identified at her death in 1819 as "Marie Anne négresse connue sous le nom de Saint Luc" (Marie Anne, negress known by the name of Saint Luc).[98] The Houldins had three other children besides Richard, one of whom, Marie Louise, born in 1791, lived only five months.[99] The other two, Marie Anne and Marie Euphrosine, born respectively in 1793 and 1794, lived until the mid-nineteenth century. Marie Anne was married young to another private in the New Brunswick Regiment, the Scotsman Andrew Holiday. Although no record of their marriage has been found at Montreal, they had a "legitimate" child in June 1806, when Marie Anne was only thirteen.[100] Sometime after her husband's discharge in May 1817, when the regiment, then stationed at Montreal, was disbanded, they moved to Berthier, where he worked as a tailor. In 1830, he petitioned the government for land in Chertsey Township, north of Montreal, as a reward for his military services. He was dead by the summer of 1848, but his widow was still living in early 1851.[101]

A black drummer of the 7th Regiment of Foot (Royal Fusiliers) in 1787. The regiment was stationed in Quebec at the start of the American War of Independence and again in the early 1790s.

Charles Falkner (alias Falkendow, Faulkner, Forkindor, or Forkindon) was yet another black Montrealer who joined the New Brunswick Fencibles. He enlisted on 28 April 1804 and served successively as a private and drummer until June 1812, when he transferred to the Canadian Regiment of Fencible Infantry. He was serving as a musician in the latter regiment at Quebec in August 1812 when his son, James, was born there; the boy died at Sorel the following December. As a reward for his services during the war, Charles Falkner was among the black veterans who were granted land in Oro Township in Upper Canada.[102]

Henry Clarke, who served as a private, then as a bugler, in the 104th from 16 November 1809 to 24 May 1817, was probably the black man of that name who died at Montreal two and a half years later. He was buried anonymously – "a man unknown, an African," who had died at the Hôtel-Dieu on 30 November 1819, according to the church record. He was not so unknown at the hospital, where the records identified him as Henry Clarke, a "neigre" born at Baltimore, allegedly forty-two years old.[103]

Peter Zamphier was discharged on 19 May 1819 after serving nineteen and a half years as a drummer in the 49th (Hertfordshire) Regiment. He received a pension of

9 pence a day, and a grant of 100 acres behind Perth in Upper Canada. He spent about three months on his land before some "old wounds" reopened, and he had to leave for Montreal to get medical attention, as he later claimed. In Montreal, on 27 August 1819, he married seventeen-year-old Charlotte Meunier (alias Charlotte Thain). At their wedding, he was identified as a labourer of Sorel. Both he and his bride were termed "people of Colour." In the summer of 1824, as Peter Zomphire, he was employed as a cook at Berthier, across the St Lawrence from Sorel, when he voted in the elections on 29 July. That fall, he addressed a petition to the government explaining that after he had left his land near Perth in 1819, it had been given to someone else, so that he wished for a new grant, hoping, "in consequence of his Wounds being healed that he will be able to cultivate it and earn a Subsistance for himself and family." He was granted about 100 acres in Abercrombie Township in the Laurentians, but four years later he still had not fulfilled the conditions of this grant (he probably had not yet settled on it). Both of his children were baptized at Sorel, in 1827 and 1828, and as a resident of that parish in 1830 he pleaded with the government for an extension of the time allowed to fulfill his settlement duties in Abercrombie.[104]

John Baptiste Gaspard was identified as a "nègre" and a soldier in the 89th Regiment in August 1813, at the baptism of his daughter, Mary Sarah. Gaspard was then absent from the city, but his wife, Ann Carbett, was present.[105] William Feeler, "a black man," husband of Tibby Prejumier, "a woman of colour," served in the War of 1812 as a private in the Corps of Provincial Royal Artillery Drivers, according to the August 1814 baptism record of his daughter, Mary.[106]

John Williams also served in the War of 1812, in the same Voltigeurs corps in which John Dolphin and Henry Thomson enlisted. He and his wife, Dorcas Moses, were identified as a black couple from Boston when their daughter, Maria, reputedly fourteen years old, was admitted to hospital at Montreal in April 1806. Maria Williams was still at Montreal in early 1811 when she was among several women arrested on charges of lewdness. Five years later, she was living at Quebec, where she was identified as "an adult negro woman, daughter of the late John Williams, private Soldier in His Majesty's late Regiment of Canadian Voltigeurs, and of Dorcas, his Wife." It appears that Williams may have been among the earliest Voltigeurs recruits, signing up in April, almost two months before the declaration of war.[107]

For the wartime militia service of other blacks, there is more solid evidence than these incidental mentions in vital records. Castor Jay, the former raftsman, enrolled in the Voltigeurs before Sergeant-Major Louis Cramer on 10 December 1812, his enlistment papers identifying him as "a person of color," thirty-one years old, 5' 4", son of James Jay.[108] Later that same month, Thomas Cockburn, another former raftsman, also enlisted in the Voltigeurs. His papers identified him as a twenty-eight-year-old "négro," son of Charles Cockburn, 5' 4½", with a black complexion, woolly hair, and black eyes. He was on duty at Gananoque, Upper Canada, in August 1813. He served to the end of the war. Surviving pay lists show him through the fall of 1814 and until 24 March 1815 as a private in Captain Emmanuel D'Aubreville's company, based at

St-Philippe-de-Laprairie, opposite Montreal.[109] The Jacob Simpson who served as a private in Captain Charles Taché's company of Voltigeurs in 1814–15 is believed to be the black Montrealer of that name who was Cockburn's crony (and possibly his brother-in-law).[110]

Abraham Low was living at Quebec when he enlisted in Colonel Joseph Bouchette's Quebec Volunteers under the name "Abram Volunteer" on 10 December 1812, receiving £2 5s "outfit money." The muster roll of 25 November–24 December that year lists him under "Drummers, Bugles, or Fifers." He served in Captain Robert Christie's company, and was paid 7¾d a day (£1 for a month of 31 days), slightly more than privates, who received 6d a day (15s 6d a month of 31 days). On 16 February 1813, Christie's company was attached to the 4th Battalion Select Embodied Militia of Lower Canada, headquartered at St-Thomas-de-Montmagny, below Quebec. Abram or Abraham Volunteer continued in the service until 4 November 1814, when he was marked down as having deserted. He moved to Montreal where, as he later stated, he lived at John Trim's. Thirty years later, under a program to award land to the 1812 veterans, Low filed an application claiming that he was "regularly discharged at Quebec, that his discharge has been lost in his own possession." On 17 September 1845, he received £20 in scrip from the Commissioner of Crown Lands, "in Commutation of my claim for One Hundred acres of Land." But Low, perhaps in need of cash, had jumped the gun: a week earlier, he had sold his anticipated reward for £9 17s 6d.[111]

Gabriel Johonnot, the son of distiller Caesar Johonnot, served in Captain J.E. Faribault's company of the 1st Battalion, Select Embodied Militia, during the war. Gabriel Jannot (*sic*) was listed as a drummer or bugler in the muster roll of 25 May–24 June 1814, and subsequently as a private, until January 1815. The roll for 25 December 1814–24 January 1815 carried the remark opposite his name: "Sick at Beauport." That may have been a strategic illness – he had just married at Quebec that December. From January to the disbanding of the corps at the end of March 1815, he was back to bugling, in Captain George Finlay's company. Perhaps it was some revelry on the corps's disbandment that led to his being charged with assault on 25 March; Gabriel Janot, "negre de Quebec," had to post a £20 bond to keep the peace for six months.[112] He returned to Montreal after the war. Another young black Montrealer who served in Faribault's company with Johonnot in 1814 was Hero Richardson, identified as a "negro native of Green Island residing in this city." The Green Island here referred to is believed to be a village near Troy, New York. He was reportedly seventeen when he enlisted in the Voltigeurs on 30 May 1814 for the duration of the war "et même Six mois après la guerre s'il en est requis" (and even for six months after the war if needed). Richardson served as a private in Faribault's company until 28 March 1815.[113]

The Treaty of Ghent, signed in Belgium on Christmas Eve 1814, officially ended the conflict, but it took several weeks before news of the peace reached North America. A general demobilization followed at the end of March 1815. Like everyone else,

Lieutenant William Clark of the Voltigeurs was in the dark about the treaty on 16 January 1815 when he recruited Robert Williams of Montreal for as long as the war lasted. Williams, who was paid a bounty or "outfit money" of £4 7s 6d upon enlisting, was identified as a "naigre," the twenty-five-year-old son of Adams Williams, 5′ 5″, with black skin, black hair and black eyes.[114] Similarly, Thomas Williams enlisted in Captain John F. Mackay's company of Voltigeurs at Quebec on 3 February 1815. He is believed to be the same Thomas Williams who later lived in Montreal and who was hired there in 1819 as a travelling servant by former fur trader John Ogilvy, the commissioner named by Britain under Articles 6 and 7 of the Treaty of Ghent to establish the boundary with the United States on the upper St Lawrence and Great Lakes. For £3 10s a month, Williams was to attend Ogilvy as a domestic servant or cook, "or in such other employment as he may be required & attend his master in all his travels" from 1 May to the end of the navigation season.[115]

If some men were late to join the war effort, others had been early, as we saw in the case of John Williams. American-born Jacques Williamson, a carpenter, enlisted in the Voltigeurs on 5 May 1812 before Captain Louis Juchereau Duchesnay, and was paid a bounty of £4. His enlistment deed identified him as a resident of the Quebec Suburb, the thirty-four-year-old son of John Williamson (at his wedding fifteen years earlier, almost to the day, he had been said to be 20). He was described as 5′ 7″, of a "mulâtre" complexion, with black eyes and hair "en laine."[116] He achieved something unmatched by any other coloured man in the service: by the fall of 1814, he was promoted to sergeant. The surviving muster rolls show him as serving in that capacity in Captain William Johnson's company from about October 1814 to March 1815, when the corps was discharged.[117]

George Crozier, a friend of cook Joseph Pierson,[118] was another early bird. He enlisted in the Voltigeurs on 21 May 1812, before Captain Jean-Baptiste René Hertel de Rouville. His enlistment form did not say outright that he was a "negro," but described him as being of a black complexion, with black hair and black eyes. He was identified as a twenty-two-year-old resident of Montreal, 5′ 5″, the son of George Crozer. He was serving as a private in de Rouville's company in the spring of 1814, but by the fall he was the company bugler, and was then bugler in Captain J. D'Estimauville's company from December through to 24 March 1815.[119] Another bugler, William Thomas, who volunteered for the 1st Battalion of Select Embodied Militia at Quebec in early 1813 and served in different companies until the corps was disbanded at the end of March 1815, is believed to have been the black man of that name who later lived in Montreal.[120]

We have no idea whether any of those black 1812ers who were born in the United States felt uneasy about taking up arms against their country of origin. More broadly, we do not know whether any black Montrealers of American birth, particularly those arrived since the turn of the century, were as disturbed as their white counterparts at the outbreak of hostilities, and whether they considered themselves directly concerned by Governor-General Sir George Prevost's proclamations of 9 July and 19 September 1812 requiring Americans to swear allegiance to the Crown or leave the country. Did they, in short, think of themselves as Americans? We suspect that they did not, at least, not so much as to feel conflicted. In the eyes of American blacks at this time and for years to come, Canada represented a haven. Those who moved to Canada did so in the belief that they had something to gain by quitting the republic to live under the crown. If not free of prejudice, Canada was at least free of laws regulating what blacks could be and do.

It is another question as to whether the authorities saw them as enemy aliens of doubtful loyalty, aliens whose loyalty was assured, or a class apart – aliens by race but not by national origin – who were not required to swear an oath of allegiance. Did the authorities, in fact, see them at all?

One white American who could not bring himself to renounce his citizenship when war came was Massachusetts-born Arthur Tappan, who had operated a dry-goods business with fellow American Henry Devereux Sewall in Montreal since 1809. They closed up shop and returned to the United States on the outbreak of the war. Tappan, who moved to New York City, would go on to become a wealthy, well-known philanthropist and a pillar of American abolitionism. There is a hint that at least one black family, that of John Pruyn and Rosalie Bonga, may have crossed into the United States in the years of sabre rattling that preceded the war. At the baptism of their daughter Marie Elizabeth Pruyn in November 1815, the parents were identified as Jean Praime and Rosalie Bongar, "demeurant dans les etats unis. tous deux nègres, la mere seule est catholique. n'étant dans landroit qu'en passant" (living in the United States, both negroes, only the mother is Catholic, they are just passing through).[121] This was partly true: both parents were black, Rosalie Bonga was Roman Catholic, and, from the fact that two of their children were baptized Catholics and three Presbyterians, we assume that Pruyn, with his New York Dutch name, was Presbyterian or of some similar Protestant denomination. That they were just passing through is more than doubtful: they had married at Montreal in 1806, their son William was born there in 1807, and they lived there continuously from 1815 until their deaths.[122] The birth records of their children, however, suggest that, if not in transit in 1815, they were returning after an absence of several years. William, their first child, was baptized two days after his birth in April 1807; Jane was said to be four months old when she was baptized in September 1815; and Eliza was a little more than one month old at her baptism in May 1819.[123] But Marie Elizabeth was said to be three years old at her baptism in November 1815, and John Jr seven at his baptism in November 1816.[124] From their ages, John Jr and Marie Elizabeth would have been born respectively in 1809 and 1812. Why would their parents have waited years to register their births, when their other children, born at Montreal, were baptized within a few months of their births?[125] It does appear that they were absent from the city when John and Marie Elizabeth were born. Perhaps they had been living in the United States, as Marie Elizabeth's baptism record stated.

WOMEN'S WORK

Where women are concerned, the problem of determining occupation is compounded by that "delicacy" in many public records that left members of the "fair sex," black or white, untainted by any label other than their civil status, i.e., "wife," "widow," or, in the case of single females, "spinster." This discretion probably accounts for the fact that a prison log of the 1830s containing detailed descriptions of all the male inmates of the Montreal jail offers no such data about any of the female occupants.[126] Where men were routinely identified by occupation, even if it was only as "labourer" or "servant," women rarely were. We must depend on incidental mentions here and there.

Louise, a free black woman married to a slave, was dealing in tobacco in 1761, as we know from the suit she filed against a white customer for payment.[127] In 1810, Mary Rusk, the estranged wife of Joseph Pierson, identified herself as the domestic servant of a man named Coats or Coates when she charged her husband with assault.[128] Margaret Sinclair, as we saw, was working as a steamboat cook when she died in 1819. We would never know that Catherine Guillet worked as a household servant for John Trim and his wife from roughly 1805 to 1820 were it not for her deposition in 1828 in a court case pitting Trim against a neighbour. Nor would we know that she held any kind of paying job after she left Trim's service, were it not for the prosecution of a thief in 1821, when Guillet testified that she worked as a washerwoman.[129] When Mary Ann Drummond bought her house in 1829, no mention was made of her occupation; she was identified simply as the wife of "laborer" Jacob Grant.[130] But the fact that she paid the full price of £150 in cash then and there causes us to wonder how she came by all that ready money. City directories, which did not make their regular appearance at Montreal until 1842, identified the occupation of the by then widowed Drummond as "washing." It was probably as a washerwoman that she had managed to penny-pinch the funds to buy the house. Marie Elizabeth Pruyn, who married widower Abraham Low in the early 1830s, was also a washerwoman, as we know from an incident in October 1846 when, as Isabella Lowe, she was accused of stealing "about four or five cotton shifts of the value of two shillings each and various other articles" from the man for whom she worked.[131]

Legitimate employment opportunities for women were few and generally restricted to domestic work or something akin to it – household servant, laundress, cook, "femme de journées" (charwoman), seamstress, etc. Catherine Lamour, for instance, appears to have worked as a seamstress in 1795 and to have employed a white assistant. In November that year, she accused Marie Lapierre, wife of Pierre Henry, of stealing a calico woman's jacket, two calico petticoats, several men's shirts, and two silver thimbles. She identified Lapierre as a woman who, for about a month, had been "accoutumée de travailler a la Couture pour cette deposante, et de garder la Maison pendant son absence" (doing sewing work for the deponent and minding the house when she had to go out).[132] Maryland native Marie Angélique Price was identified as a twenty-year-old "négresse libre, femme de journées" when she married carpenter

Augustin Labadie in 1799.[133] So was Massachusetts native Mary Violet Jones a "femme de journées" when she married shoemaker Narcisse Coudrin in 1807.[134] Catherine Salter, the widow of onetime lamplighter John Hyers, then wife of Edward Baird (or Beard), was hired at the end of August 1831 by schoolmaster John Lyle "to wash in [his] dwelling house ... during four successive days."[135]

In two instances, girls of unspecified origin and parentage crop up in the first two decades of the nineteenth century to be indentured as domestic servants. Eve was said to be already a servant of merchant Baruch Berold Levy in February 1809 when, at the age of about sixteen, she allegedly expressed a desire to be legally bound to him as a servant until she turned twenty-one. Levy applied to the courts to name a "tutor ad hoc" for this minor, that is, a guardian who would act in that capacity for the sole purpose of indenturing her to him. We would like to think that the court inquired into Eve's background – where had she come from? Where were her parents or relations? – before appointing jailer Gwyn Owen Radford as her tutor on 22 February, but the records contain not a word on that score. Radford promptly placed her as a servant with Levy for five years.[136] One year later, Eve skipped and became the subject of the last notice ever published offering a reward for a runaway black servant, its language almost a throwback to the time of slavery.[137]

Caroline took longer to place, it seems, but much less than a year to sour on her servant's role. She was said to be about fourteen in March 1818, a "négresse" whom provision merchant Cornelius Chatfield claimed to have taken into his home. As Levy had done with Eve, Chatfield applied to the court for a guardian to be named, to place her as a servant. How and why he had taken her in is never explained, nor do the records contain any information about her background. On 24 March, the court appointed cabinet-maker Samuel Frost as her guardian. On the following 14 December, Frost bound Caroline to Chatfield until she turned twenty-one. She ran off that same night, as Chatfield complained to the authorities the next day, alleging that "Caroline, a black girl, this deponents indented Servant did yesterday evening desert and abandon his Service, and is now Secreted in a house in the St-Joseph Suburbs of this City. Wherefore he prays that a Warrant may issue to apprehend the said Caroline his said Servant So that she may be dealt with according to Law."[138]

As intriguing as the cases of Eve and Caroline are, with many other women, we simply do not know whether they did any remunerated work, although we may assume that they did so to supplement their meager household income. From destitution, alcoholism, or the lack of better job opportunities, some women turned to prostitution.[139] This could lead to frequent jail terms for "disorderliness" and petty theft, and, in several cases, to an early grave. Such was the fate of Emilia, born in slavery to John Gray and Judith (John Fleming and Julia Johnson) in 1797, jailed twenty-six times at Quebec between 1815 and 1829 under the name Amelia Fleming, who died at Montreal in 1831 at age thirty-three.[140] Maria Williams, the Boston-born daughter of John Williams and Dorcas Moses, who left Montreal for Quebec at about the same time as Emilia Fleming, died of tuberculosis in the jail there on 16 February 1817.[141] Martha Curtis Hyers, born at Montreal to John Hyers and Catherine

Salter, jailed for the first time at thirteen for theft and helping to run a bawdy house, married at fifteen to Richard Jackson and widowed at nineteen, died of venereal disease in the Montreal jail on 25 November 1841 at age twenty-one.[142] Montreal-born Nancy Feeler, daughter of William Feeler and Tibby Prejumier, after serving nine jail terms between July 1832 and September 1834, moved to Quebec, where she was sentenced to jail on twenty-one occasions beginning in April 1835 and died behind bars of an "inflammation of the lungs" on 5 November 1838 at age twenty-eight.[143] If Quebec exerted a pull on some of these destitute Montreal women, it was probably owing to its being a bustling seaport, with money to be made from sex-starved sailors.[144]

A WORD ABOUT WAGES

There seems to be no hard evidence of racial discrimination in hiring, or at least no documented cases of blacks being refused a job because of their skin colour. The lack of documentation does not mean that discrimination did not occur, but only that there is no record of it. Employers hired whomever they wished; anyone who felt unjustly turned away had no recourse. All that we can say is that black job-seekers probably found some doors shut against them, or learned from others what doors not to knock at. As a rule, however, if they managed to get a foot in the door, they do not appear to have been victims of wage discrimination. The wage records for the Molson steamers, for example, suggest no short-changing of black employees. As concerns military service, pay scales for the different ranks were set by regulation, and so a private, black or white, received a private's pay. The problem was that few blacks were destined to rise above that lowest rank, although the strange workings of prejudice meant that black musicians were in fashion and, as we saw in the case of Abraham Low, those who served as buglers, fifers, or drummers, like their white counterparts, were paid slightly more than privates. In the fur trade, too, blacks appear to have been paid the going rates.

That being said, some employment contracts do hint at discrepancies, although we cannot say with certainty that these were rooted in racial discrimination. The four black lamplighters hired as part of the night watch in the fall of 1818, for example, were hired as a crew at a monthly wage of two shillings per lamp, while the watchmen proper, all white, were hired individually for three shillings a night. We can only speculate as to what led the captain of the watch to select four black men for a job previously performed by the white watchmen. It must be noted, too, that it was much easier to monitor the productivity of the lamplighters, whose job was more mechanical, than of the watchmen, whose job was to maintain the public peace and security. With the former, one had simply to check whether the lamps were lit and well maintained, with enough oil and wick each evening to last until dawn. From the number of street lamps they tended, the lamplighters may each have earned as much as a watchman, but this is not clear.[145]

When Morris Thompson was hired for six months as a journeyman moulder for the Marmora Iron Works in 1824, it was at the rate of four shillings a day, "& thus to continue during all the said term unless Mr Charles Hay of the said works after the first month find the said Maurice Thompson equal to other men whose wages are five shillings a day to allow him the same Sum for the remainder of the said term." The employer also was to pay Thompson's passage from Montreal to the works in Upper Canada. On the same day that he hired Thompson, a single man, Peter McGill hired another moulder for Marmora, Michel Thifaut, a married man, for six shillings a day, part of that to be sent monthly to his wife back in Montreal. Besides his passage to Upper Canada, Thifaut was to get room and board. Was the omission of room and board from Morris's contract an oversight? Was Thifaut paid more because he was white, or married, or was it that he had more to offer than Thompson in the way of skills and experience? Note that his wages were not only higher than Thompson's but also than those of the "other men whose wages are five shillings a day."[146]

By the terms of his indenture to gilder John Smith in 1839, John Wright, said to be seventeen (he was sixteen), was to get "sufficient meat, drink & lodging fitting for an apprentice," and to be paid £5 the first year, his wages increasing by £1 a year, to £8 in his fourth and final year. Only three and a half years later, Smith hired a fifteen-year-old white apprentice for five years, at £10 to start, his wages to rise by £2 a year to £18 in his final year. What accounted for this unequal treatment?[147]

The recruitment of a fur-trade crew of fourteen men, one of them black, in the spring of 1821 should, we suppose, provide a clear indication of whether the lone black employee, a former slave, was the victim of wage discrimination. The hiring was done at Quebec, not at Montreal, but this case is cited here simply to demonstrate that, although materials are available for a comparative study of black and white wages and working conditions, drawing firm conclusions on the subject of racial bias is not a straightforward matter. The men were hired over a period of two weeks by *bourgeois* James Mackenzie for the North West Company, most of them for a period of seventeen months (May 1821–October 1822).[148] The table on the following page summarizes the terms of their respective contracts. The men are listed in the chronological order of their hiring. The third on the list is the man previously identified as Nero Bartholomy, once a slave of tailor Ralph Gray of Quebec and Beauport, and, at this time, a widower and cook.

Some contracts are in French, others in English. Presumably, the English terms "meat & drink" were equivalent to the French "logé et nourri" (literally, housed and fed), so that all – the seamen on their ship, and the landsmen on shore – were provided with room and board. The wages are given at times in pounds and shillings, at others in dollars, sometimes per month, sometimes per year. In the simplified table on page 215, the French terms have been translated and the wages converted into dollars (£1 or 20s = $4). The monthly wage is given as well as the total to be paid to each man, leaving out the "other benefits." The men are listed in descending order of their total known wages.

Hirings by James Mackenzie for the North West Company, April–May 1821

Date	Name	Position	Term	Wage	Other benefits
23 April	Léon Roi	Chasseur/pêcheur/voyageur	1/5/21–1/10/22	20s/mo	R&B, fish & game, eq.
24 April	Augustin Billodeau	Marinier	1/5/21–nav season	£2.10/mo	R&B
	Nero Barthelomy	Marmiton Cook	1/5/21–1/10/22	£15	R&B, fish & game, eq.
	Thos Nugent	Charpentier & chaloupier	1/5/21–1/10/22	£15/yr	R&B, fish & game, eq.
	Pierre Lapointe	Blacksmith	24/4/21–24/04/22	£15/yr	Meat & drink, eq.
27 April	Louis Fauché	Marmiton or Cook	1/5/21–1/10/22	£12/yr	R&B, fish & game, eq.
	Ignace Gravelle	Chasseur/pêcheur/voyageur	1/5/21–1/10/22	£12.10/yr	R&B, fish & game, eq.
	Joseph La Rochelle	Charpentier & menuisier	1/5/21–1/10/22	£15/yr	R&B, fish & game, eq.
	Charles Bara	Marinier	1/5/21–nav season	£2.10/mo	R&B
30 April	François Martin	Marmiton & Cook	$5/mo	1/5/21–nav season	R&B
	Richard Harris	Seaman	1/5/21–trip duration	$10/mo	Meat & drink
	John Fortune	Seaman	11/5/21–for summer	$10/mo	Meat & drink
7 May	Olivier Boucher	Fisherman & engagé	7/5/21–for 17 mos	£1/mo	Meat & drink, eq.
	James Brown	Seaman	3/5/21–nav season	$10/mo	Meat & drink

R&B = "logé et nourri," i.e., room and board; fish & game = a share in the fish and meat caught; eq. = standard equipment (footwear, blanket, etc.); nav season = the navigation season

James Mackenzie's hirings (wages in dollars)

Name	Position	Wage	Total
Léon Roi	Hunter/fisher/voyageur	$8.00/mo for 17 mos	$136.00
Thos Nugent	Carpenter–boat builder	$5.00/mo for 17 mos	$85.00
Pierre Lapointe	Blacksmith (or cooper)	$5.00/mo for 17 mos	$85.00
Joseph La Rochelle	Carpenter-joiner	$5.00/mo for 17 mos	$85.00
Ignace Gravelle	Hunter/fisher/voyageur	$4.16/mo for 17 mos	$70.80
Louis Fauché	Cook	$4.00/mo for 17 mos	$68.00
Olivier Boucher	Fisher & hired man	$4.00/mo for 17 mos	$68.00
Nero Barthelomy	Cook	$3.06/mo for 17 mos	$52.00
Augustin Billodeau	Seaman	$10.00/mo for nav season	–
Charles Bara	Seaman	$10.00/mo for nav season	–
James Brown	Seaman	$10.00/mo for nav season	–
Richard Harris	Seaman	$10.00/mo for trip duration	–
John Fortune	Seaman	$10.00/mo for the summer	–
François Martin	Cook	$5.00/mo for nav season	–

Some preliminary observations: The expedition was bound not for the West by canoe but for the North by ship. Several of the hiring contracts give the destination as the "North Posts" and "la Baie" (the Bay), without further particulars. This was at the time when the North West Company merged with the Hudson's Bay Company, and so the northern destination could conceivably have been Hudson's Bay, though it was more probably somewhere out on the Gulf of St Lawrence or toward Labrador, or perhaps even up the Saguenay River.[149] The ages of the men are not recorded, but Nero Bartholomy would have been in his sixties, a rather advanced age to be heading off on an outback adventure.[150] Would his age and fitness have been a factor in setting his wages? Finding no later records of him at Quebec, we cannot help but wonder whether he ever made it back. Literacy does not appear to have counted in the determination of wages. Of the fourteen men, none was hired for clerical work, although blacksmith Pierre Lapointe and seaman Richard Harris were each required to "render a faithful account of all that will be put in his possession." Harris, carpenter–boat builder Thomas Nugent, and seaman John Fortune were the only ones who signed their names to their contracts; Bartholomy and the other recruits signed theirs with an X. We note also that there was some carelessness in the drafting of the contracts. Lapointe, for example, was hired as a blacksmith, but the part of his contract setting out his wages and benefits gives his job as "cooper"; and while the contract refers to his being hired for a term of one year and five months from 24 April 1821, it also states that his term is to end on 24 April 1822, or in twelve months (hence the discrepancy between the two tables with regard to the duration of his term).

In the list of total wages in the second table, we see a glaring contrast between the sums paid to the two men hired as hunter-fisherman-voyageur, Léon Roi and Ignace Gravelle, the one receiving $136, the other $70.80 for the same term. The first table

Voyageurs prepare to portage around rapids. Missing from such depictions is any hint of black participation in the fur trade.

shows that they both were to enjoy the same "other benefits." Both were white men, and so racial discrimination cannot account for the striking difference in their pay. Perhaps it was a question of experience. Just as striking, if we refer to the list of monthly wages in the second table, is the fact that Nero Bartholomy, hired as cook, was paid less per month than the other cooks; he was, in fact, the lowest paid of the fourteen. If we refer to the first table, we see that he was the only one whose contract did not spell out how much he was to be paid per month or per year: he was to serve for seventeen months and be paid £13. Is it possible that in the drafting of his contract, the words "per year" were inadvertently omitted, and that he was to be paid at the *annual* rate of £13, making his monthly wage $4.33 instead of $3.06, and his total wages for the seventeen months £18 8s 4d, or about $73.60 rather than $52? One suspects that there was no error, that his monthly wage really was the lowest of the fourteen, and that his total wages were the lowest among those of the eight men hired for the full seventeen months. Even the five seamen hired for mostly shorter terms at $10 a month would conceivably have earned more than he did; if they worked from 1 May to the end of October, and even into November, they earned a total of at least $60. Only François Martin who, from the fact that he was hired for the navigation season, appears to have been a ship's cook, would have earned less than Nero Bartholomy in total wages, but in the space of six months he would have pocketed $30 while Nero Bartholomy would have earned $26. Nero Batholomy may not have been the last hired, first fired – he was, in fact, one of the first hired – but he was the one who was paid the least. If his age and physical fitness were not a factor in setting his wages, then what?

The above observations are not the fruit of an exhaustive comparison of the wages paid to black and white workers in different fields. There is certainly room for a closer examination of the subject, for which the records cited here might serve as a starting point.

EIGHT

Political Colours

Justice William Badgley gave it as his opinion in 1859 that, since the institution of British rule a century before, blacks had "enjoyed the same Civil rights as other ... subjects of the Crown in the Colony, without any disqualification whatever by reason of their complexion."[1] The fact that black slavery endured for about forty years after the Conquest jars with this assertion. To be sure, blacks did not labour under legal disabilities of the sort that barred Roman Catholics from election to the British House of Commons before the passage of the Roman Catholic Relief Act of 1829. Nor were they held back by Christian oaths of office such as those that hobbled the Jews of Lower Canada and kept them from sitting in the Legislative Assembly until the early 1830s. On paper, there were no rights enjoyed by whites that were denied to blacks. But unwritten rules saw to their disqualification as surely as written ones.

In the field of politics, these unwritten rules virtually barred blacks from public office. Paradoxically, unwritten rules meant that blacks held the right to vote. We have glimpsed Peter Zamphier voting at Berthier in 1824 and John Trim voting in 1827, but whether blacks exercised the right to vote from the moment that an elective Legislative Assembly was set up under the Constitutional Act of 1791 is difficult to say, as detailed records of the earliest elections are lacking. We do know, however, that blacks in Lower Canada were voting, untrammelled, by the second decade of the nineteenth century.

VOTING IN THE COUNTRY

Two black voters left their mark on the election in the County of Bedford in the summer of 1820.* Rural Bedford, on the Vermont border, was not urban Montreal, but a look at this election and its consequences can serve as a useful introduction to the electoral mores of a time when, in town as in country, voting took place in public, polls could go on for weeks, treating (providing free drinks and food) was common, and the death of the monarch entailed the dissolution of parliaments and a new general election. In Bedford, as in other counties, the right to vote rested on ownership of property that yielded a revenue of 40 shillings sterling a year or more. In Montreal, as in other cities and boroughs, the property had to yield £5 a year; tenants there also had the right to vote as long as they had been living in the electoral district for one year and paid annual rent of at least £10.[2] Women who met the property qualifications held the right to vote, mainly because the Constitutional Act of 1791 did not specify that voters had to be male. Nor did it specify that they had to be white: hence the enfranchisement of blacks. As one historian has written, "Everyone meeting the qualifications – women, Indians, and Negroes – could vote."[3]

In the case of women, however, not everyone agreed that the law allowed them to vote, and social conventions, notably the view that politics was a field too muddy for the "fair sex," rendered their right precarious. When a woman tried to vote in the East Ward of Montreal in 1827, for example, the poll clerk noted opposite her name: "Voter a woman. Candidates agreed not to take female votes."[4] Black voters fared better. At least they never faced this sort of gentlemen's agreement to shut them out of the polling, and the right to vote was not taken away from them, as it was from Quebec women from 1834 to 1836, and then definitively from 1849 (and not restored until 1918 for federal elections, and 1940 for provincial elections).[5]

The Bedford election of June–July 1820 can be quickly summarized. Joseph Franchère had been elected in April, but the arrival of news from England that George III had died in January meant that the incumbent had to submit to re-election. Tory John Jones Jr vied with him for the right to represent the county. A first poll was held 27–30 June in St-Mathias for the inhabitants of the northern part of the county, and then a second poll opened in the border village of St-Armand on 3 July. It did not close until 20 July. Jones won, but Franchère's supporters, citing abuses, petitioned the Assembly to nullify the election and call a new one. In hearings at Quebec from 26 January to 13 February 1821 the Assembly uncovered many irregularities, but it was not until 31 December, a year and a half after the election, that Jones was unseated. A by-election was called for February 1822.[6] That was when Justus Billings bought a farm.

---

*I thank Francis Black, historical illustrator and researcher, for first calling my attention to this election.

In town and country, affrays at the polls like the one depicted here were a common occurrence in the days of open voting.

Billings' name, in various forms (Justin Billings, "Justis Bennings, a Negro," Justus Bennings), had come up at the inquiry into the 1820 election. A propertyless tenant farmer, and therefore unqualified to vote, he was one of several such who had left the poll after refusing to swear the voter's oath, only to return "refreshed" – Billings was said to have been "not so much intoxicated as the others" – on a later day, to take the oath and vote for Jones. One witness produced a list of more than 200 unqualified people who had voted.[7] It appears that the other black voter, a woman, was "bought" with a pair of shoes, but the testimony that cabinet-maker Allan Hungerford gave about her is, in some respects, confusing and self-incriminating:[8]

> Q. Did Mr Lemay [Franchère's agent] or his friends, and which of them, promise to give a certain sum to a negro wench to induce her to vote?
> A. There was a negro wench who said eight persons had offered her a quarter dollar each, if she would vote for Mr Franchère, but that she would not do so, the persons who had offered her the money she represented as being the friends of Mr Jones.
> Q. Who did this negro wench vote for?
> A. She voted for Mr Jones.
> Q. Do you know if the said negro wench is a free woman, and was she married at the time?
> A. I do not know, I believe she is a widow and that she is free.
> Q. Did this negro wench appear at the Poll in the dress of a man or of a woman?

A. As a woman.
....

Q. Have you any knowledge that the negro wench you have mentioned, had received a pair of red morocco shoes to induce her to vote for Mr Jones?
A. I know that she afterwards, received a pair of black morocco shoes.
Q. Do you know who gave the said shoes, and if they were given to her for having voted?
A. I do – I gave the shoes myself.
Q. On whose behalf did you give them?
A. On my own behalf.

No other witness mentioned the "negro wench," a term that was a throwback to the days of slavery and that was rarely, if ever, used in public speech in Montreal by 1820. The question of whether she was a "free woman" is also jarringly anachronistic: was there anyone at the seat of power in 1820 who seriously believed that slaves still walked the land ... and did nothing about it? Her tentative identification as a widow suggests that she was probably Hannah Caesar, the widow of the black fiddler recorded at Philipsburg, next to St-Armand, at the turn of the century under the name "Morris the blackman," and in 1816, as a mulatto, "the late Morris Emery of Caldwell's manor a Musician."[9]

Justus Billings and Hannah Caesar, if it was she, helped to elect John Jones, and their walk-on parts in the cheating that the inquiry exposed contributed to his unseating. Billings or those who pulled his strings seem to have learned their lesson from this episode, i.e., discretion is the better part of vote rigging. Accordingly, in February 1822, just before the by-election to fill Jones' seat, Billings became fully enfranchised through a hocus-pocus land transaction effected before notary Léon Lalanne, who had been one of Jones' agents in the 1820 contest. Billings paid $50 for eighty acres in the seigneury of St-Armand, on the understanding that within a year the seller, James Ayer, would reimburse the $50 and get his land back. If anyone was counting on this sort of tactic to tip the vote against Franchère, the gambit did not pay off. Franchère won back his seat in March, and Ayer came close to losing his land. "Owing to pecuniary inability," he was unable to come up with the $50 to buy it back within the appointed time. In February 1823, Billings, "from good will towards the said James," gave him a year's extension. A year stretched into two. In the end, it was the summer of 1825 before Ayer was able to redeem his eighty acres.[10]

One telling aspect of this episode is that no one expressed surprise at blacks voting, or objected to the votes of Justus Billings and Hannah Caesar on racial grounds. This is one indication that the participation of blacks in the Bedford election of 1820 was no innovation and that blacks had voted there before. It is possible that a refusal or disinclination to accept that blacks could be qualified to vote predisposed some people to challenge Justus Billings and Hannah Caesar. From the evidence presented at the inquiry, however, it seems that race was not an issue in their case, any more than in the case of hundreds of whites who had also voted irregularly.

VOTING IN TOWN

The fact that blacks exercised their right to vote before 1820 is confirmed by the record of the election that year in the two-seat East Ward of Montreal, for which polling took place between 8 and 20 March (the records for the West Ward, the only other electoral district in the city, have not survived). Three candidates vied for the two seats: brewer and steamboat owner John Molson, an incumbent; and newcomers Thomas Busby, a merchant, and Hugues Heney, a lawyer. Molson and Busby were establishment men, or Tories, while Heney ran with the "popular" party, or Parti canadien. At least ten blacks turned out to vote: Thomas Cockburn, Peter Dago, William Filler (Feeler), Warren Glossen, Jacob Grant, Murray Hall, John Hyres (Hyers), Isaac Newton, Jacob Simpson, and Richard Thompson. Eight of them did so without difficulty or obstruction, other than the requirement that Murray Hall swear to his eligibility.[11] Two would-be voters – Jacob Simpson, identified as a labourer and tenant of the west side St-Joseph Suburb, and "domestique" Jacob Grant, a tenant of the north-side St-Laurent Suburb – were deemed not qualified. The voting register does not specify the reasons for which they were turned down, but in Simpson's case the explanation is obvious: he lived in the West Ward, not in the East. As for Grant, the reason for his exclusion is unknown, but it is unlikely that race was a factor, considering that eight other black men did cast their votes. That the votes of the eight black electors were not protested by any candidates and elicited no comment in the public prints – indeed, the fact that the poll book itself makes no reference to their race – indicates quite clearly, along with the Bedford election, that the participation of blacks in elections was no novelty, but an accepted fact in town and country.[12]

Like all voters, the eight who concern us were identified in the poll book by name, occupation, property qualification, and place of residence. To this perfunctory identification might be added such information as can be gleaned from other sources about their ages, origins, and marital status to see whether there was a pattern to their voting. The table on the following page ranks these voters in descending order by age, although the best surviving information on that score is sparse and conflicting. For four of the voters, at least one contemporary source professes to identify their origins, but the origins of the other four are a mystery. We are on somewhat firmer ground when it comes to their marital status.

These profiles reveal nothing startling. All were male, none was a property owner, all were "labourers" except for Richard Thompson (who kept a shop), and all but Thomas Cockburn were recorded as residents of the Quebec Suburb. Cockburn was said to be a resident of the city proper, but this is questionable; court records, which show that he, Dago, and Glossen all ran afoul of the law at this time, make him a resident of the Quebec Suburb.[13] We also know that Dago, Glossen, and Hyers, the three youngest of the eight, had worked together as lamplighters in 1818–19. But nothing in these profiles helps us to understand how the black electors voted. Hall and Newton, perhaps the two oldest, plumped for Busby, while Feeler and Glossen plumped for Molson. Thompson, among the oldest, cast his two votes, one each for Molson and

Black voters in the 1820 election, East Ward Montreal

Name	Age (approx)	Occupation	Residence	Property qualification	Marital status	Origin
Murray Hall	60	Labourer	Quebec Suburb	Tenant	Married	–
Isaac Newton	50	Labourer	Quebec Suburb	Tenant	Married	England
Richard Thompson	50	Shopkeeper	Quebec Suburb	Tenant	Single	Niagara
William Feeler	40	Labourer	Quebec Suburb	Tenant	Married	–
Thomas Cockburn	35	Labourer	"en ville"	Tenant	Married	Ireland
Warren Glossen	30	Labourer	Quebec suburb	Tenant	Single	US (Vt)
John Hyers	25	Labourer	Quebec suburb	Tenant	Married	–
Peter Dago	25	Labourer	Quebec suburb	Tenant	Single	US (NY)

Busby. Dago and Hyers, the two youngest, both voted for Molson and Heney. Cockburn picked Busby and Heney. Together they gave five votes to Molson, four to Busby, and three to Heney.[14] The final tally was Heney 906, Busby 646, Molson 541. The fact that last-place finisher Molson won the most black votes may have had something to do with his stature as a major employer (and/or a judicious application of free beer?). Heney held his seat until 1832, but Busby never got to take his. As happened at Bedford and elsewhere, the death of the King signalled a new election; fur-trade merchant Thomas Thain captured Busby's seat in July (the poll book of that election has not come to light). It may be significant that none of the eight black East Ward voters of March 1820 – all of them English-speaking – pinned all their hopes on Heney, in the way that some plumped for Molson or Busby. The younger voters were at least willing to give Heney one of their two votes, while the older ones voted more conservatively. But this is the kind of voting pattern we might expect to find among English-speakers as a whole. The one conclusion that we can draw is that there was nothing like a concerted "black vote."

THE AMERICAN WAY, THE BRITISH WAY

If race was an issue in politics, it was a white-on-white one, pitting the French-Canadian majority, backers of Louis-Joseph Papineau's Parti canadien (which, despite its name, rallied some English-speakers) against *les Anglais,* a term that referred not to the English proper, but to a mostly English-speaking minority that was opposed to the majority's aspirations as expressed by Papineau's party. The majority had the numbers but not the power to which it would have been entitled had the system been democratic; through control of the Legislative Council and the executive, the minority had the power without the numerical strength. The ruling oligarchy and supporters of the established order stood ever more staunchly for the British connection, while the majority discovered a kinship with the oppressed whites of the world – Americans of the revolutionary era, the Irish under the British yoke, Italians struggling against Austrian rule, Greeks fighting for independence from Turkey, Poles rising against the Russian tsar ... . When Dr Robert Nelson, the rebel son of an Irish Loyalist, led an armed incursion into the colony from Vermont in February 1838 to fan the guttering flame of rebellion, he seized the occasion to read a declaration of Lower-Canadian independence, proclaiming, among other things, an end to civil disabilities affecting *les sauvages,* i.e., Canadian Indians. Across the lines, the staging of the first national "Negro Convention" at Philadelphia in September 1830 and the launching of William Lloyd Garrison's abolitionist weekly *The Liberator* at Boston on New Year's Day 1831 signalled an intensification of the American struggle against slavery, a trend confirmed by the founding of the American Anti-Slavery Society at Philadelphia in 1833. The forces of progress in Quebec were not inspired. Slavery was dead, and race, in its American sense of white versus black, did not enter the picture (although Wolfred Nelson, the patriote hero of the battle of St-Denis in 1837, did later become a member of the Paris-based Institut d'Afrique, which fought against the slave trade and promoted development in Africa).[15]

Which side were black Montrealers to take in the endless, all-consuming white-on-white debate that degenerated through the 1830s into paralysis of the legislature by 1836, armed conflict in 1837–38 and suspension of representative government from 1837 to 1841? The accepted view is that blacks in Canada hewed to the status quo and refused to accept the ever more insistent contention of advanced "reformers" in both Lower and Upper Canada that British colonial rule had grown intolerably oppressive. William Lyon Mackenzie, the Upper Canadian grievance-monger *extraordinaire,* summed up this view in writing about blacks in his province:

> Nearly all of them are opposed to every species of reform in the civil institutions of the colony – they are so extravagantly loyal to the Executive that to the utmost of their power they uphold all the abuses of government and support those who profit by them ... I regret that an unfounded fear of a union with the United States on the part of the colored population should have induced them to oppose reform and free institutions in this colony, whenever they have had the power to do so. The apology I make for them in this matter is that they have not been educated as freemen.[16]

The fact is that it would have been difficult for race-conscious blacks in Upper or Lower Canada to get excited about the abuses of which whites complained. Partiality in the distribution of public offices and government patronage? No black had ever tasted this manna. No blacks could wholeheartedly join in the cry for "No taxation without representation" when no conceivable representation at that time spared them a thought. Whether the Legislative Council was appointed or elected, a burning question for the Parti patriote, as the Parti canadien came to be called from the late 1820s, was all the same to those for whom there was no possibility of ever being appointed

A sabre-wielding Colonel Allan McNabb, at left, is accompanied by his black servant in this caricature of an episode in the Rebellions of 1837–1838. Of black Canadians it was said: "They would die by the weapons of war to support the country that gives liberty and equality to all subjects alike."

or elected. As for the "unfounded fear" of union with the United States, reformers themselves inspired that with the waxing admiration they expressed through the 1830s for American democratic institutions, and with their warnings of an American-style revolution in the making, if only to tweak Tory noses.[17]

If, for some whites, Papineau foremost among them,[18] American republican democracy was the solution to the abuses of a monarchical system, the opposite was true for blacks. Democracy, as exemplified by the United States, had not put an end to slavery; it seemed powerless or unwilling to do so, and those American states that had freed themselves from the taint of slavery had hastened to enact segregation to various extents. "Tyrannical" Britain, on the other hand, legislated slavery to death without bloodshed, in 1833. Even before it had done so, David Walker, the black American anti-slavery pamphleteer, had written:

> The English are the best friends the coloured people have upon earth. Though they have oppressed us a little and have colonies now in the West Indies which oppress us *sorely*. – Yet notwithstanding they (the English) have done one hundred times more for the melioration of our condition, than all the other nations

of the earth put together. The blacks cannot but respect the English as a nation, notwithstanding they have treated us a little cruel.

... We have here and there, in other nations, good friends. But as a nation, the English are our friends.[19]

After 1833, some thoughtful blacks, reflecting on the accidents of history, may even have blessed providence for separating Britain from its American colonies fifty years earlier. Britain's loss of the thirteen colonies in 1783 meant that when it moved to abolish slavery far and wide, it faced the stout opposition only of West Indian planters, whom it compensated to the tune of £20,000,000. Would it have contemplated abolition if it had had to contend against the American South as well and faced the prospect of a ruinous compensation scheme?[20] Regardless of systems of government, Canadian blacks had a down-to-earth reason to be leery of any rapprochement with the United States: hands across the border could lead to the end of the Canadas as a haven for fugitive American slaves. This argument would be raised at mid-century when disgruntled Montreal Tories briefly turned away from Britain and campaigned for the annexation of Canada to the United States. The passage of the American Fugitive Slave Law in 1850 would be one argument cited to help kill that annexationist enthusiasm.[21]

Under the circumstances, attacks on Britain and praise for American democracy were not likely to find favour with blacks in the Canadas.[22] In Montreal, blacks generally did not see a place for themselves in the Patriote ranks, and the Patriotes, focused on their struggle to establish the principle of majority rule, had no time for the concerns of a marginal minority. Nevertheless, Mackenzie's suggestion that blacks closed their eyes to "all the abuses of government" and blindly supported the status quo is not entirely borne out by the facts. Blacks had their fight, and whites had theirs, as two black Torontonians, Peter Gallego and E.L. de St. Remy, made clear in the prospectus for a political journal that they proposed to publish in 1839. Their approach reflects the basic political stance of blacks in both Lower and Upper Canada more cogently and accurately than does Mackenzie's analysis:

> As regards our colored fellow subjects, it is needless to say that their *character, rights, and welfare,* in every application of the word, here and everywhere else, *will be always our main object*.
>
> Knowing that public opinion in England is more enlightened than in any other country, or even than her own colonies, we will on that account, as well as from a grateful sense of her great measure of national justice towards us, and from many other cogent reasons, (the interest of this colony, in general, being by no means the least,) support and defend by all honorable means, with all our force and might, the connection of the Canadas with the mother country. We will by our words and writings, as well as swords, fight the battles of that just and free Monarchy, whenever called on, and no consideration, however specious or plausible, shall ever make us pause or hesitate.

With regard to *local* reforms, which do not compromise the safety of the connection, we will not pledge ourselves to any man or party. We remain free to take whichever side appears, to us, the most just and beneficial to the province, without considering the parties or persons who propose them. Let not the public, however, forget that we, who have had the *experience of uncontrolled popular government,* and who know what real grievances are, will not be easily duped into the belief that we are under oppression, whilst we feel no such thing.[23]

STORM CLOUDS AND DIRTY TRICKS

Shopkeeper Richard Thompson again cast his vote in the East Ward of Montreal in August 1824. This time, he voted for James Leslie and James Stuart. Stuart, a stout supporter of the Parti canadien until 1822, when he had switched sides, lagged in the polling and ultimately withdrew with 225 votes to his name. Leslie, a liberal-minded Scottish-born merchant making his start in politics, topped the poll with 559 votes; incumbent Heney polled 364.[24] Oddly, considering the participation of blacks in the East Ward election of March 1820, Thompson appears to be the only black who voted in this contest, and it seems that no blacks at all voted in the West Ward election at the end of July. The polling there lasted only three days, and the general turnout was low compared with that in the East Ward; only 140 votes were cast for Papineau, 137 for the other winning candidate, Pierre de Rocheblave, and 111 for the loser, stationer James Brown, the former publisher of the *Montreal Gazette.*[25]

In the West Ward in 1827, blacks voted Tory to a man. Here the lines were clearly drawn. Party leader Papineau and Dr Robert Nelson for the Parti canadien squared off against merchant Peter McGill, a director and future president of the Bank of Montreal, and Clerk of the Peace John Delisle. Four black men voted in that contest: Jacob Abdella, identified as a labourer and owner of his house on College Street; hairdresser James Rollings, a tenant in St-Paul Street; John Trim, owner of his home on McGill Street; and carter Alexander Valentine, set down as a "yeoman" and owner of his home on St-Charles-Borromée Street. All four voted for McGill and Delisle, who went down to defeat, polling respectively 415 and 395 votes to Papineau's and Nelson's 593 and 592.[26] Three of the four black voters were property owners,[27] whereas all those who had voted in the East Ward in 1820 had been tenants. The three homeowners – Abdella, Trim, and Valentine – also voted that same month in the election for the two members to represent the County of Montreal. To do this, they had to travel to the village of St-Laurent, several kilometres northwest of the city, where the poll was held. Trim, about seventy years old, who was registered as a *bourgeois,* cast a plumper for lawyer James Charles Grant. Valentine, in his fifties, did the same. Jacob Abdeloe (*sic*), who would have been in his thirties, was the only one among them to cast his two votes. One went to Grant, the other to Joseph Perrault, who carried the day with fellow incumbent Joseph Valois, a Pointe-Claire farmer, when Grant, trailing, withdrew from the contest.[28]

Two contests held in the spring of 1832 show that blacks were not as utterly conservative as Mackenzie made them out to be. In the first, a by-election held 3–6 April to fill the East Ward seat vacated by Hugues Heney, Jacob Grant, not qualified to vote in 1820 but now owner (through his wife, Mary Ann Drummond) of a house in St-Constant Street, voted for the moderate Patriote standard-bearer, Clément-Charles Sabrevois de Bleury. His opponent, Olivier Berthelet, carried the day by 354 votes to 297. We will never know how black labourer William Murphy, a tenant in St-Laurent Suburb for the previous seven months, might have voted. He was turned back for failing to meet the one-year residence requirement.[29] The by-election held 25 April–22 May to fill one of two seats in the West Ward was much more noisy and violent. John Trim, registered this time as a gardener, voted for Tory Stanley Bagg, as did James Rollings. But Jacob Abdella, who had voted Tory in 1827, backed the Irish-born Daniel Tracey, editor of the *Vindicator* newspaper, the English voice of the Patriotes. So did scourer Alexander Grant, in his early thirties like Abdella, and voting in his first election. Three French-Canadian men were killed on 21 May when troops called to maintain order at the poll in Place d'Armes opened fire on a crowd, stoking the popular sense of grievance. When the poll closed the next day, Tracey squeaked in with 691 votes, four more than Bagg. Within a month, cholera blew in with the immigrant ships, death ruled, and a pall settled over all. Tracey died of cholera in July.[30]

As we can see, the number of blacks who exercised their right to vote in these years was never great, which might be seen as a reflection of the relatively small size of the city's black population and the little weight that it carried in public affairs. The fact that only twelve "coloured brethren" showed up at Alexander Grant's in 1833 for a discussion of the British emancipation bill points to the same truth: the numbers were not there. It was not until the overheated general election of 1834 that anyone took notice of black voters and thought it worthwhile to solicit their support.

Backers of the British party, desperate for votes, hit on this idea. It sprang from a dirty trick. Patriotes and Tories were at daggers drawn by the time the poll in the West Ward opened on 28 October. Since February, the Patriotes had been campaigning up and down the land, agitating the 92 Resolutions, the Legislative Assembly's strongly worded, provocative summation of grievances, denounced by the Tories as treasonous. Moderates on both sides shuddered at the rising tone of the rhetoric that presaged a violent showdown. The bulk of the province was behind the Patriotes, but in the heavily English-speaking West Ward, the Tories thought they stood a chance. Five days before the opening of the poll, the *Montreal Gazette* reported on the meeting of 21 October at which the Patriotes had nominated their champions, Papineau and Robert Nelson, to run against Tories William Walker and gardener John Donnellan, the founding president of the St Patrick's Society. No one from the newspaper was present at this meeting, but "if we are to credit public report, and rely upon printed placards which have been circulated throughout the city" (by Donnellan supporters), Nelson, himself of Anglo-Irish roots, had derided a suggestion that only an Irishman could represent Irish constituents. He was reported to have said:

> Are we to be told, by a paltry handful of presumptuous and conceited Irishmen, that they have a right to send an Irishman to the House of Assembly, as well might our German fellow-citizens insist upon our nominating one of them, or I will go further and say that if we are to yield to the pretensions of the Irish, the *Niggers,* who are numerous likewise, would have an equal right to send one of their body to the House.[31]

The *Gazette* claimed to have cleaned up Nelson's language because, "if report speaks true," he had referred to the Germans as "sausage-makers." Yet the bowdlerizing editor had let the word *"Niggers"* go, in italics. The report of Nelson's speech was heartily denied by the Patriote press. A good proportion of Irish Catholics backed the Patriotes – it was reported elsewhere that Irish, American-born, and French-Canadian voters had attended the nomination meeting.[32] If Nelson really had been dismissive, it was no doubt about attempts to paint Donnellan as the great Irish hope. However distorted the report of Nelson's comments, it served as a pretext for an unprecedented appeal by the newspaper to three groups of voters – the Irish, the Germans, and the blacks. Speaking to the latter without addressing them directly, the *Gazette* observed:

> As to the coloured portion of our community, they are not so numerous nor so wealthy as the others we have mentioned, but they have never forfeited their right to a decent and proper regard for their feelings, by any set of misconduct. Here they are freemen, and fully entitled to the exercise of their privileges as BRITISH subjects in whatever way it may suit their inclination. The colour of the body can have no effect on the qualities of the mind, and the sons of Africa will ever receive in this Province, the respect that is their due, so long as they support the laws and the constitution which confers upon them all the blessings of BRITISH liberty. While they are persecuted almost to death by the *free* and independent citizens of AMERICA, and debarred of their privileges, here they are really equal, and no doubt at the coming elections, such of them as have votes or influence, will show their disapproval of a party by whom they are contemned and despised, by voting against Dr Nelson.[33]

Not quite three months after the coming into force of Britain's emancipation law, the writer of that paragraph knew the value, in appealing to black voters, of playing the British card and raising the bogey of America. "It is supposed all Canada [Upper and Lower] contains about seven thousand colored inhabitants," a black Philadelphian who had moved to Toronto, wrote that September. "The king of Great Britain has not more faithful and loyal subjects in any part of his dominion – that I can safely say. They would die by the weapons of war to support the country that gives liberty and equality to all subjects alike."[34] And, as Alexander Grant had remarked in his keynote address at the celebration of West Indian emancipation on 1 August, Britain

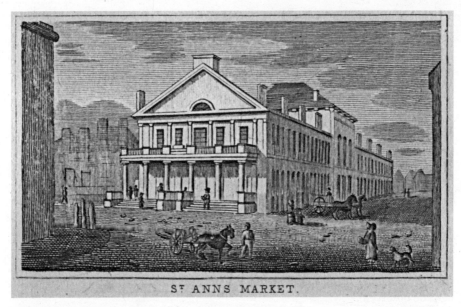

In the Ste-Anne Market building on 1 August 1834, black Montrealers met to hear Alexander Grant deliver his speech saluting West Indian emancipation. The building was later refurbished and housed the Canadian parliament from 1844 to 1849.

had set an example that the United States would do well to heed if it hoped to avert a catastrophe:

> Will she [America] have the effrontery – will she be so ridiculously absurd as to call herself the "land of liberty," while she holds in slavery 2,000,000 of her fellow-creatures; But will these continue to kiss the lash? Will they continue to be insensible to that liberty which their brethren in almost every other part of the world enjoy? I answer no! They will duly estimate the blessing; they will burst asunder their chains, and awful will be the lesson to those who will have the folly to oppose them. – But I hope the dreadful catastrophe will be prevented by a timely following of the noble example of England, and prove that she is in reality, and not merely in name, "the land of the brave and the home of the free."[35]

AN INFLUENTIAL VOICE

The *Gazette* writer probably had Grant in mind when he appealed to black Montrealers with "votes or influence" in the fall of 1834, implicitly acknowledging that some of them could read, that they were politically aware and active, that they might exert an influence on fellow blacks which no white could match, and that, through their votes at least, blacks had a modicum of political power that was worth harnessing in a pinch. If the press, for once, found blacks worthy of notice as other than objects of censure, pity, or ridicule, it was to some extent because Grant had brought blacks to the notice of the press. Since his arrival on the scene in 1830, he had shown that he recognized the value of newspapers in making blackness visible, beginning with a simple advertisement for his scouring business. He may have learned some lessons in public relations – and made useful contacts – in 1832 from his acquaintance with Paola Brown, a black American refugee who visited Montreal and Quebec in that grim year, enlisting the support of the press as he solicited funds for the black settlement of Colbornesburgh, near Guelph, Upper Canada.[36] In the summer of 1833, as we have seen, Grant convened a meeting at his home to express the support of black Montrealers for the British emancipation bill then wending its way through Parliament, taking care to communicate the result of their deliberations to the newspapers. While the *Gazette* published their communiqué without comment, the *Vindicator* drew attention to it with a telling paragraph:[37]

> [W]e comply with the request of our fellow-citizens of colour, and give publication to the Resolutions which they passed at a meeting held on the subject. The proceedings will be read with interest, and we congratulate the persons who signed them, on the public spirit they showed, and the sympathy they evinced in favor of the numerous and unhappy class of our fellow-creatures in whose behalf they came forward.

This marked the first time that anyone in Montreal had openly credited blacks with public spirit. The following June, Grant addressed an open letter to "The Colored Brethren Residents of Montreal," complaining of the denial of certain rights and privileges to blacks, which the laws "strictly entitle us to, such as serving on Juries &c." The letter was published in the *Montreal Herald* of 15 May 1834; unfortunately, no copy of that issue of the newspaper seems to have survived, so that the only inkling we have of the contents of the letter comes from a brief quotation and a sympathetic editorial comment in the *Vindicator*:

> Being advocates for the extension of Civil Rights to all persons without difference of color or creed we cannot but regret that Mr Grant's Brethren should have to complain of the partiality of public officers. As far as the Jury Law provides there is no distinction. If the colored men are excluded it can be attributed only to those who are intrusted with the execution of the Law and of which officers the House of Assembly complain.[38]

So much for blacks closing their eyes to the abuses of officialdom. Even if there is reason to believe that Grant phrased his complaints more diplomatically than the *Vindicator* did – in its partisan way, it targeted the "partiality of public officers"; his target was the partiality of the public at large – he nevertheless drew attention to an "abuse" that touched blacks directly. This grievance happened to suit the Patriote agenda, complementing the party's longstanding complaints about the way juries were constituted, with some classes of whites favoured over others. Grant next intruded on the public consciousness in August with the speech he gave at the celebration of West Indian emancipation. This loyal effusion, an unabashed tribute to British rule, suited the Tory agenda, and was published in the *Gazette,* but not in the *Vindicator.*

When it came time to vote that fall, Grant, hairdresser, tenant, St-Paul Street, shied away from the Patriote side, whose candidate he had supported in 1832. On 30 October, he voted for the Tory ticket. John Patten, shoemaker, tenant of St-Henry Street – the man who had opened the 1 August celebrations with a prayer – voted the same way. The next day, a Friday, a *"grand riot"* caused the returning officer to close the poll after half an hour, and to adjourn voting to the following Monday.[39] Walker and Donnellan charged that the mayhem had begun with an attack on their supporters by a gang of notorious toughs. Meanwhile, Thomas Brown English's General Brock Tavern, on McGill Street, served as the headquarters of the Tory gangs throughout the election.[40]

With both sides tense, suspicious, and seeking every possible advantage, many voters were challenged at the poll by the candidates against whom they voted. On 5 November, Walker challenged Jacob Abdella, "dealer," who voted for Papineau and Nelson. Abdella's successful justification of his right to vote was that "[h]e intends voting by virtue of a property in St-Joseph Suburb of which his wife had possession before his marriage with her, that he heard his wife say at their wedding that she held the property by virtue of the will of her first husband, that he has a copy of that will in his possession, that he has been married for more than nine years and that he has always collected the income and revenues which the property yielded." Five days later, it was "labourer" John Broome's turn to be grilled by Papineau when he turned out to vote for Walker and Donnellan. Before his vote was accepted, Broome, tenant of a house on St-Charles-Borromée Street, explained that "[b]efore the first of October 1833 the said John Broome lived in a house belonging to Jacob Grant and since the first of October 1833, he resides in a house belonging to one Albreck, paying four and a half dollars per month. He was born in Barbados."[41]

No other blacks voted in the West Ward. In the East Ward, where polling was somewhat calmer, Jacob Grant, labourer, proprietor of a house in St-Constant Street, cast one vote for Tory Sydney Bellingham; Bellingham's two opponents, James Leslie and Joseph Roy, won handily. That poll, at the house of Mayor Jacques Viger, opened on 31 October and closed on 11 November.[42] Meanwhile, voting and challenges and rampages by stone-throwing, club-wielding gangs went on in the West Ward until, on Monday, 17 November, the returning officer, at wits' end, called a halt and proclaimed Papineau and Nelson the victors. The count stood at 588 for Papineau, 587 for Nelson, 554 for Walker, and 547 for Donnellan.

The end of the election did not bring an immediate return of calm as threats of mob violence continued for several days. An attack on the house of McGill Street innkeeper Patrick Brennan by four or five men in the early hours of 25 November may have been one of the late sputterings of election mayhem. Thomas English of the

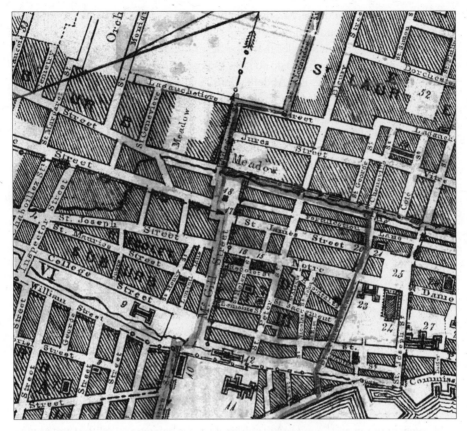

Ste-Anne Market (no. 12 on the map) was a stroll away from Jacob Abdella's house at the southwest corner of College and Inspector streets, from the Trim home on the east side of McGill facing St-Maurice Street, and from Alexander Grant's on St-Paul Street near St-Pierre (St Peter on the map). Other landmarks included the Hôpital-Général (11), the new Notre-Dame Church (24) facing Place d'Armes (25), the Hôtel-Dieu (27) on St-Paul at St-Joseph (now St-Sulpice) Street, and the Anglican Christ Church (26) on the north side of Notre Dame Street east of Place d'Armes.

nearby General Brock Tavern identified Robert Jackson, a "Coloured man," as one of those who had pelted the house with sticks and stones. Jackson was accused of riot and released on a £20 bond pending his appearance at the next sitting of the Court of Quarter Sessions in January. Alexander Grant acted as one of his sureties. When the court convened, the grand jury declined to indict Jackson.[43]

Of the five black Montrealers known to have cast their votes in the East and West Wards in this showdown election, only Jacob Abdella stuck by Papineau's party. We cannot, of course, extrapolate from this that one-fifth of Montreal's black population favoured the "popular" side in politics over the champions of the British connection, any more than we should interpret the mostly stand-pat votes cast by blacks over the years as unqualified support for misrule. Considering their exclusion from political office and patronage, it is a wonder that they bestirred themselves to vote at all. That some of them took the trouble to do so rather suggests a conscientiousness in the performance of a public duty. For Abdella, Trim, and Valentine to vote in town, then journey to the outlying village of St-Laurent to vote in the county election in 1827, seems like service above and beyond the call of duty. Besides serving in the defence of the country, as soldiers or militiamen, voting was pretty well the only public duty that blacks were allowed to perform. In voting, they were less concerned with taking sides on the issues that agitated the white majority than with maintaining a system which, however imperfect, had left them free since the turn of the century without subsequently hobbling them with laws to keep them "in their place." How else to explain the political conduct of a man like Alexander Grant, the only black voter who, besides voting this way or that, left us a few words about his views? It was his choice to leave New York, where slavery had officially ended in 1827, for Montreal. He must have had his reasons to not only expatriate himself but to encourage others to do the same. As he would later state, "Being, what is termed, a man of colour, and extremely anxious that all my friends should enjoy the same degree of liberty and happiness which I possess, I have always been active in promoting the permanent settlement of them in the Canadas."[44] In the Canadas, we find him voting for an anti-establishment candidate, then singing the praises of Britain, deploring the silent rule that deprived blacks of their right to sit on juries, yet voting, when the crunch came, for the old guard that sustained the very people who applied that unwritten, exclusionary rule. By the fall of 1834, Grant had established his credentials as an articulate spokesman for the black population. Politically divided as Lower Canada was, both sides in Montreal paid some attention and found in his public utterances elements that dovetailed with their views. Had there been no unwritten rules, he might have been considered worthy of some public appointment. Had the political class, and voters generally, been open to a black candidacy, we have to think that he would have been the first to be considered, by one side or the other. From improbable, that notion became impossible: after 1834, there would be no other elections in his lifetime.

THE BLACKS CONCERNED

The black turnouts at successive elections and at the meeting that Grant called in the summer of 1833 to discuss the British abolition bill, while seeming to underline the small size of the black population, may give us an indication of which black Montrealers, besides Alexander Grant, showed an active concern for public affairs. Of the ten men who turned out to vote in the East Ward in 1820, four or five – William Feeler, Warren Glossen, John Hyers, Isaac Newton, and probably Murray Hall – died within that decade; we have no other record of their participation, and it is therefore impossible to gauge the level of their interest. Similarly, John Broome and John Patten, relative newcomers to town who voted in 1834, died before any other electoral contest took place. But Broome was present at Grant's for the abolition meeting and, if Patten was not, as we saw in a previous chapter, it may simply have been that his work on the steamboats called him away; he did play a role in the celebration of West Indian emancipation on 1 August 1834. We have already mentioned the exertions of Jacob Abdella, John Trim, and Alexander Valentine in voting in both the town and county elections in 1827, but since Valentine died in 1829, he too is to some extent an unknown quantity. From what we know of Trim's life, and of his participation in the elections of 1827 and 1832, there seems little doubt of his sustained interest in *la chose publique*; from his resolute support of losing Tory candidates, we might even say that politics was one area in his life where he was signally unsuccessful. He died six months before the 1833 meeting at Grant's. As far as we can judge, Jacob Abdella and Jacob Grant displayed considerable public spirit, and perhaps in a more open-minded way than Trim. Both turned out to vote in election after election – even if Grant was disqualified in 1820, he made the effort – which implies a concern for domestic affairs, and both were present for the meeting at Grant's which, dealing with the proposed abolition of slavery in the British empire, concerned world affairs. In the increasingly polarized political climate of the 1830s, Abdella was the only black voter that we know of who stuck by the Patriote candidates; Jacob Grant, like Alexander Grant, voted for a Patriote in 1832, but then supported the Tories in 1834.

Admittedly, the turnout of blacks at a few elections and at one meeting on a public issue offers a very imperfect measure of their level of awareness and active involvement in public affairs. By that measure alone, Peter Dago's record seems unremarkable: he votes in 1820, and thirteen years later, turns up at Alexander Grant's for the abolition meeting. In these years, his brushes with the law – over everything from unpaid dog taxes and selling liquor without a licence to keeping bawdy houses, theft, and receiving stolen goods – and his reputation for shady dealings tend to overshadow other aspects of his life.[45] From a distance of nearly 200 years, we may see him as something of a wastrel. It is difficult, if not impossible, to know what went on behind the scenes, but if we look for a moment beyond the period covered by this study, we find that beyond those two early manifestations of interest in public affairs he is said to have played an active role at a meeting of the Consultation Committee of Coloured People of Montreal in April 1846.[46] This, together with various instances when he extended a helping hand to others,[47] may suggest that he kept a closer eye on matters of particular concern to blacks and played a more active role in the affairs of the embryonic community than our long-distance impressions would allow. While the ex-slave John Trim aimed for a kind of middle-class respectability, and Alexander Grant confidently asserted his own, Dago never sought to prove or improve himself. He set his sights on surviving, by hook or by crook, and succeeded, lasting until 1868.[48]

NINE

THE COLOUR OF JUSTICE

Even though the political institutions of the day took virtually no notice of them, blacks exercised their right to vote. When it came to judicial institutions, whose proceedings had a much more immediate impact on their lives, unwritten rules kept blacks from serving on juries – at a time when juries sat on all but the most minor criminal trials. Thus property owners John Fleming, "a Negro Servant," of the Ste-Anne Suburb, carter Alexander Valentine of St-Charles-Borromée Street in the St-Laurent Suburb, John Trim of McGill Street, "labourer" Thomas Cockburn, tenant of a house on St Nicholas Tolentine Street in the Quebec Suburb, and Jacob Simpson, "labourer," tenant of St-Joseph Street (Notre-Dame west of McGill) in the Récollets Suburb, made it onto the lists of persons qualified to serve as jurors in the second decade of the century, but were never called.[1] Similarly, "labourer" Jacob Grant, as owner of a house on St-Constant Street, got no farther than having his name entered on a list of potential jurors in 1833.[2] Other black Montrealers fit the bill, but none appear to have been called for jury duty before the 1850s. Sheriffs bore direct responsibility for this exclusion by virtue of the fact that they decided which persons on the lists should be summoned to form the panels from which jurors were selected at trial. Some may have considered blacks incompetent, others may have given no thought to the matter: the idea of blacks sitting on juries was simply unheard of. Whatever their own views and prejudices, sheriffs may also have excluded blacks in the belief that whites would object to sharing a jury bench with them, or refuse to have a black man assess their guilt or innocence.[3]

Society at large had no problem with all-white, all-male juries. If the process of jury selection was criticized, debate focused on the proportion of English-speaking versus French-speaking jurors, city dwellers versus country folk, merchants versus farmers and tradesmen, etc. No one made a public issue of black exclusion until Alexander Grant did so in 1834. This says something about white attitudes, to be sure, but also about a reluctance or inability of black Montrealers before Grant's day to voice their collective grievances. It would be a mistake to see in the absence of blacks from juries a sign that they themselves refused to serve. In the many cases, civil as well as criminal, in which they were involved as accusers, defendants, petitioners, plaintiffs and witnesses, there is not the slightest hint that they repudiated the white man's law or boycotted the judicial system. In discussing racial bias in Quebec's lower criminal courts of this period, Donald Fyson cites the negative views of the colonial justice system held by aboriginal peoples who, with rare exceptions, clung to their traditional ways, and hints at a black resistance to the system when he states, for example, that "not all Blacks ... rejected the legitimacy of European criminal justice."[4] There is no evidence that any blacks rejected the legitimacy of the courts. The fact is, the approaches to the dominant society by aboriginals and blacks were, on the whole, diametrically opposed. Indians wanted out; blacks wanted in. While aboriginals clung collectively to their deeply rooted identities as separate peoples or nations, the blacks, cut off from their roots, desired nothing more than to be seen as full-fledged British subjects, to blend in and to avail themselves of the opportunities, services and institutions, rights and privileges that integration seemed to promise.[5]

The administration of justice, however, remained resolutely white – with one exception. It was not only from juries that blacks were absent. In the entire machinery of justice and the state, outside of soldiering, no position, paid or unpaid, was open to them but that of public executioner – in French, *bourreau* or, more ceremoniously, *exécuteur de la haute justice* or *maître des hautes oeuvres*, as in the English "lord high executioner." There is considerable irony in the formal titles, when applied to blacks, as few of them could aspire to be acknowledged as *maître* (master or lord) in any field, and the word *haute* (high) signified no other elevation than a literal one: the scaffold or raised platform on which the executioner performed his grim task. The high-sounding title, in fact, branded its holder and his family as low and disreputable, resulting in their being ostracized by "decent" people and therefore condemned to associate with none but the "indecent." As only outcasts could be persuaded to undertake such a loathsome job, it was generally offered to accused felons or convicts who were spared prosecution or pardoned in return for performing this public service. Whites often filled the position, as we would expect where the general population and the criminal element were so overwhelmingly white, but the bloody work of meting out pain and death was widely considered a natural fit for blacks well into the nineteenth century.[6] Not trusted to try one of their peers or to serve a summons, make an arrest or a seizure, walk a beat or push a pencil in the service of the law, they could nonetheless be licensed to kill, flog, or brand for the good of all. Bailiff, constable, watchman, jailer, juror, clerk, crier – however humble, any position in the edifice of justice that would have called on them to display a modicum of intellect, judgment, tact or discretion, to exert authority or command respect, was off limits. These were the unwritten rules, one sign that, even after slavery had died, the racial perceptions at its heart lived on.

THE BLACK HANGMEN

Perhaps because information on the subject is rather scattered and elusive, no one has yet undertaken a comprehensive study of the subject of colonial executioners under both French and British rule.[7] The dishonourable character of the position did not change from one regime to the next. While New France made do with one hangman at a time, based at Quebec, the British soon made efforts to retain one per judicial district. If the panoply of gruesome punishments at the executioner's disposal was less extensive under the British, an increasing population provided an ever-renewable supply of candidates for the physical penalties that remained. Burning at the stake was out, as was *la question* (torture to extract a confession), but there was still death by hanging and, more frequently, flogging, the pillory, and branding or burning in the hand.

The colony's first black hangman was a slave from Martinique who landed at Quebec in 1733. In the face of complaints from the authorities in New France that they could find no fitting candidate for the job, the French minister of marine, Jean Frédéric Phélypeaux, Comte de Maurepas, responsible for colonial affairs, had advised them in 1728 to consider having "a negro from the Islands" bought for them at the Crown's expense. Gilles Le Noir (or Lenoir), a Frenchman sent out to fill the position, turned out to be an incompetent sot. From 1729, there was repeated mention in correspondence between the colonial and home authorities that "a negro would be more suitable than anyone else."[8] What made a black man the ideal choice? Not knowledge of the executioner's art: hangmen generally learned their trade on the job. We might suppose that a slave could be counted on to do what he was told, but a soldier unquestioningly followed orders, too, so it was not simply the habit of obedience that made a black slave more suitable. Neither was servile status the criterion, because no one raised the possibility of hiring a Panis. The man most suited to be held up as a pariah was the pariah by birth: a black man.

On instructions from Maurepas, Intendant Hocquart took steps in 1731 to have a slave bought in Martinique to be the colony's *bourreau*. It was another two years before a suitable candidate, in the person of Malgein, baptized Mathieu Léveillé, could be found, bought, and shipped to Quebec via Louisbourg. To him would have fallen the job of extracting, under torture, a confession of arson from the slave Marie Josèphe Angélique in 1734, and then hanging her and throwing her corpse into the flames, in accordance with the sentence of the court. It was a dirty, lonely job, but someone had to do it. To provide some companionship for their hangman, the authorities later imported a black female slave, Denise, who was intended to be his wife. But Mathieu Léveillé, already ailing before Denise's arrival, never regained his health and died unmarried in September 1743. Hocquart assured the home authorities that he would try to sell the jilted Denise to recover the 1,500 livres that she had cost.[9]

Mathieu Léveillé was thought to have been done in by the climate, and this dissuaded the French authorities from ever looking again for a slave from the tropics to be hangman in Canada.[10] Before his last illness, however, another French colony in North America had found a hangman among the slaves of Martinique. The slave François had been sentenced to death there for murder in July 1741 when word came from France that Louisbourg, the fortress on Île Royale (Cape Breton), was in search of an executioner. The Conseil Supérieur of Martinique offered to commute François's death sentence if he agreed to take on the paid position. He agreed, his life was spared, and he was set free to go earn his living – and the general opprobrium – in the northern colony.[11]

Under British rule, importing a slave seemed the answer for the newly appointed provost marshal (sheriff) of Montreal in 1767. In October, anxious at the prospect of having to organize his first execution since his formal appointment two years earlier, Edward William Gray, not yet twenty-five years old, dashed off a plea to Major Philip Skene, a British half-pay officer and founder of Skenesborough (Whitehall) at the foot of Lake Champlain in the sister colony of New York:

> The Robber Lapoint received Sentence of Death this Day and is to be executed on the 28th Inst. and as there is Little hope of his being pardoned I must beg you will be so kind as to send me the Negroe Man you promised me for an Executioner by return of the Courier without fail as I am in the greatest distress for want of a Person to do that business & the consequence of its not being done would not only entirely ruin me but the two Gentlemen who are my Security's – When you send him you will please tutor him for the purpose, but keep the matter a secret from every other person, particularly the Couriers, who I have told he is a Negroe I have bought of you, otherwise, so refined are the French People's notions of honour, that I do not think I could prevail even upon them to suffer him to come along with them. The Fellow therefore must likewise keep his business to himself, and when I have done with him I will either return him to you or keep him entirely and account with you for his value. Your doing me this favour will lay me under the Greatest obligation which I shall ever gratefully remember.[12]

Gray's intended mail-order hangman was probably the Skene slave who, during the War of Independence, after escaping from American forces, landed at St-Jean in early October 1778 and promptly appealed to Governor Haldimand for his freedom (see Appendix III). In his petition, Rathass Coffee, as his name was written, claimed that during the Seven Years War (1756–63), he had jumped ship to the British side, probably from a Spanish vessel at the British attack on Havana in June 1762, and been promised his freedom by Skene, a participant in that attack. If Coffee was Gray's intended hangman in 1767, it appears that, in the end, he was spared the duty of an all-expenses paid trip to Montreal to kill a man, as a suitable executioner was found at Quebec in the person of John May, believed to have been white.[13]

But other blacks did do hangman's duty, including, in one peculiar instance of frontier justice, a female. In 1777, the former slave Ann Wiley and a French-Canadian man were charged with robbing and setting fire to a storehouse at Detroit, then part of the judicial district of Montreal. In view of the capital nature of their offence, they should have been sent to Montreal for trial, but Justice of the Peace Philippe Dejean, a former Montreal merchant, summoned a jury at Detroit and tried them on the spot. Convicted on the sole count of robbery, they were both sentenced to hang, but Dejean could get no one to do the deed. Colonel Henry Hamilton, lieutenant-governor of Detroit (and later of Quebec), solved the problem by offering to pardon Ann Wiley if she would execute her accomplice, which she did. The execution of a woman was a relatively rare occurrence, execution *by* a woman the rarest. Racial prejudice in this instance did not operate so baldly as to dictate that the black should die and the white be spared, but we may wonder whether Hamilton and Dejean would have made the offer to Ann Wiley had she been white. We cannot help but suspect that, suppressing what would have been a natural aversion to impose this duty on a female, they cast Ann Wiley as the executioner because she came wrapped in a black skin.[14] If so, black skin saved her life, which would be racism with an awful twist.

In the notes to his *Les Anciens Canadiens,* an aged Philippe Aubert de Gaspé offered a hazy recollection of stories he had heard after his arrival at Quebec as a nine-year-old schoolboy in 1795 about the late black executioner named Bob, universally loved and fondly remembered:

> This Ethiopian should have inspired the horror that all feel towards those who follow his trade; but, no, Bob was welcomed into people's homes like anyone else, bore the character of a perfectly honest man, ran errands, and everyone loved him. As much as I can recollect, there was something very affecting in Bob's story: Fate had made him executioner much against his will. He shed tears whenever he had to perform his cruel duty. I do not know why it is that my memory, so faithful when it comes to recalling everything that I saw and heard from my earliest childhood, fails me when I plumb it for an explanation of this sympathy with which Bob was favoured.[15]

De Gaspé wrote when he was in his seventies, and the passage of time may have given a patina of romance to his memories; certainly no other instance has been recorded of a white populace taking to heart its public executioner, and a black one at that. In the twentieth century, Quebec provincial archivist Pierre-Georges Roy was convinced that "Bob" was Alexander Webb, whom he identified as a black man convicted of burglary at Quebec in 1784 and pardoned at the foot of the gallows. Roy reasoned that the authorities were looking for a hangman and that Webb must have been spared the noose on his agreeing to take on the role. This seems to disregard the obvious – there already had to be a serving hangman if Webb came within an inch of being hanged. As a matter of fact, Alexander Webb was convicted in May 1785, not 1784; he was sentenced to hang that 15 June, respited at the last moment, and officially pardoned on 23 June on condition that he leave the province within three months.[16] Evidently, "Bob" was not Alexander Webb. Who, then? Historian Marcel Trudel, notwithstanding de Gaspé's claim that "Bob" had ceased to be hangman by the mid-1790s, believed that he was George Burns, a black man who served as hangman at Quebec in the first years of the nineteenth century.[17]

The records of the day can be utterly confusing when it comes to assigning names to blacks, but in the case of "Bob" it is the stabs in the dark of later writers that have sown confusion. No more George than he was Alexander, "Bob" was most probably ... Bob, as de Gaspé said. Indeed, "Bob a Nigro man," and a rather companionable one at that, was jailed at Quebec on 13 January 1781, on "Suspition of Felony" concerning some stolen rum. He was still in jail at the end of April.[18] We do not know the outcome of this case, but in seeking the identity of Bob, the black hangman, we would do better to consider this suspected black felon than anyone bearing some other name. Bob was very probably the hangman mentioned in a report of proceedings in the Court of King's Bench at Quebec in November 1789: "Robert Lane the Hangman, charged with Felony, was discharged by proclamation."[19] Surviving court records contain no confirmation that Robert Lane was black, but only an indictment charging him with a burglary committed the previous 7 August. The grand jury found "No bill," that is, there was insufficient evidence to support the indictment. Robert Lane was still the executioner at Quebec at the time of his death in February 1796, at the reputed age of about forty-eight. This was shortly after young de Gaspé arrived in town, and the passing of Bob would explain why stories about him circulated at the time.[20]

Unless Bob was employed at Montreal as well as at Quebec, it seems that another black hangman was active in the province in the 1780s. More than fifty years after the fact, Montreal-born Paschal Cerré, then a resident of Missouri, recalled that when he had lived at Montreal between 1781 and 1787 he had seen "several blacks there. One was executioner."[21]

There was certainly another black executioner at Quebec in the first years of the nineteenth century. This was the man that Trudel mistook for Bob. George Burns moved to Quebec around the turn of the century from Montreal, where his daughter, Marie Joseph, was born in June 1798.[22] He may have taken up the job at Quebec later that year, after the death in September of the then hangman, Thomas Wall. At the birth of his daughter, Marguerite, at Quebec in 1804, Burns was identified as a "labourer."[23] A parish census in 1805 enumerated him as the hangman, and we have de Gaspé as a witness that he was serving as executioner for the district in 1806. De

Gaspé, an articling law student that year, saw Burns at work and left a vivid picture in his *Mémoires,* though he did not name him:

> One Friday in 1806, a criminal was placed in the pillory for some odious crime. The offended populace began its attack on him, which turned frenzied when soldiers from the barracks joined in. The rampaging mob first ransacked the carts of the *habitants* in the market place, taking forcible possession of every article they found there – eggs, vegetables, calves' heads, feet, flesh and offal – over the cries of the women who sought to protect their goods. After pelting the criminal, they went after the executioner, whom they pursued under the wagons where he sought refuge. Try as he might to dart under the carts, under the very hooves of the horses, the poor negro, lithe as a snake, could not escape the blows of both the public and the *habitants* whose goods were being pillaged.
>
> The mob then turned its fury on the constables who were attempting to restore order. Assailed on all sides, some of them sought refuge in the cathedral, or in the seminary, while others ran off down the côte de Léry, where they were pursued beyond Hope Gate.
>
> The mayhem was at its height when Colonel [Isaac] Brock arrived on the scene ...[24]

Burns clearly did not benefit from the affection that Quebecers were said to have showered on Bob. He died in office on 2 October that year at the age of about fifty.[25]

Another onetime Montrealer, Abraham Edwards – a "malato," according to one description; "Negro, very thick lips," said another – convicted of theft and jailed for two years at Quebec in December 1815, appealed for a pardon at the beginning of 1817, volunteering to serve out the time remaining in his sentence as hangman at Trois-Rivières. Edwards' offer was transmitted to Governor-General Sir John Coape Sherbrooke by the sheriff of Trois-Rivières. Some hurried consultations took place, the governor inquiring of the chief justice "whether there is any objection to Abraham Edwards now a prisoner in the Quebec Gaol ... being pardoned for the purpose of becoming public Executioner at Three Rivers." No objection being raised, notice of the pardon and instructions to deliver Edwards to Trois-Rivières were sent in mid-March to de Gaspé, now the sheriff of Quebec. The official pardon was issued on 21 March on condition that Edwards "engage himself to Do and perform all and every the Duties of Public Executioner of and for the District of Three Rivers for and during the rest and residue of the said Term of two Years yet unexpired, and that he do within seven days next after the date of these Presents depart from the said District of Quebec for the Town of Three Rivers." Edwards' choice of Trois-Rivières seems odd, but his heart probably had its reasons. Barely two months after his arrival there, "Abraham Edwards, labourer, Batchelor a Man of colour who is of Age, and has no Tutors Curators or Parents in the Country, and who declares himself unable to sign his name," married Adeline Rivers, a woman in much the same circumstances.[26]

BENJAMIN FIELD

We do not know when or under what circumstances Benjamin Field became the executioner at Montreal, only that he was hired by 1819. He was possibly the child Ben Field, the younger of two New Jersey slaves of that name who, left masterless by the Revolution, sailed for Nova Scotia in 1783 on the British evacuation of New York.[27] He may have embarked on his career as early as the first decade of the century, before the death of his wife in 1810. A reference to him, in French, in December 1808 called him Benjamin Jx or Ix, which could be construed as the equivalent of Benjamin X in English, an attempt to preserve his anonymity. With a wink to its readers, a newspaper alluded to the hangman, without naming him, in 1816 as "un peu basané," somewhat swarthy.[28]

The first explicit reference we have found to Field as hangman comes in a list of inmates of the house of correction in 1819: Benjamin Field, "Hangman," and Joseph Field, "Hangman's Son," are recorded as having been committed by magistrate Thomas McCord on 22 May 1819 "until further orders." A year later, in a complaint filed on 10 May 1820, a resident of the Papineau Road accused Benjamin Field, "boureau du District de Montréal," of operating a brothel on that street. Clearly, Field's official occupation was an open secret by then.[29] He was jailed that day, "being charged on oath with having Kept and maintained a house of ill fame and with having allowed persons of both sexes to assemble there drinking and misbehaving themselves to the great annoyance of the public peace and tranquility of the neighbourhood." Arrested as found-ins and charged as "public vagabonds and Bawds" were his son Joseph, his daughter Mary, his son-in-law Anthony Billow (alias Beleau, Bellew, Bellow, Bellows, etc.), and Jane Graham, wife of Henry Garret, a black woman arrested several times as a prostitute. Joseph Field remained incarcerated until July 1822, and Benjamin until September 1824 – more than four years, when the offence usually brought a jail term of at most a few months.[30]

From jail, Field moved to a house on St-Charles-Borromée Street, owned by Sheriff Frederick William Ermatinger,[31] probably because of problems finding a landlord who was willing to have the hangman as a tenant. The arrangement soon ended as, on the strength of depositions by residents of the area and of a constable who raided his home, Field, "a man of Colour, who acts as Hangman for the District," returned to jail on 14 April 1825, accused of keeping a bawdy house. Five found-ins, including Mary Field and Jane Graham, "all persons of ill fame vagabonds & prostitutes," were also incarcerated. Field was not discharged until 2 June 1827.[32]

On both of these occasions, he was not sentenced by the courts, as it appears from the jail and court records that he never underwent a trial but was simply lodged in the jail on the warrant of committal issued at the time of his arrest. Home, however bleak, was not some cramped cell: "A whole ward is occupied for the detention of the Common hangman, which in some measure prevents the classification of prisoners," the grand jury of the Court of Quarter Sessions complained in July 1823 in

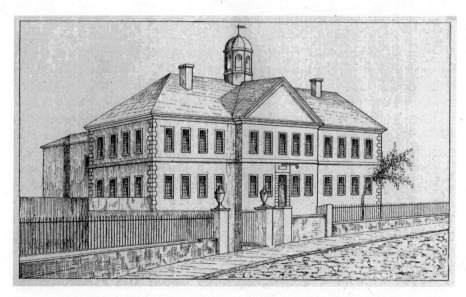

This was the Montreal Jail from 1803 to 1836. A ward in the jail was hangman Benjamin Field's home for much of the 1820s.

calling attention to problems at the jail. In other words, Field's jailhouse home took up space that could have been used to separate minor offenders and debtors from hard-core criminals.[33] If the hangman took up so much room – possibly the reason he had had to find other lodgings in the fall of 1824 – it was undoubtedly because members of his family lodged with him. Sharing Field's quarters at one time – and his duties as hangman – was his son-in-law, Beleau, as he was called in a newspaper report in May 1822:

> ATTEMPTED SUICIDE. – Monday last [22 May], the man named Beleau, son-in-law to the hangman, who resides in the prison of this city, attempted to slit his throat with a razor. He was found unconscious in a pool of his own blood. A surgeon was called who after examining the wound declared it to be not a mortal one. There is, it is said, a deep gash on the left side of the neck but the trachea artery is untouched. The reason for this desperate attempt is unknown.[34]

Only six days earlier, Billow had finished serving a one-year jail term for grand larceny. He died before September 1825, when Mary Field was identified as the widow of Anthony Bellows – "he was hangman" – or widow of Anthony Bellew, "the late Executioner."[35] As for Field, in June 1826 he was briefly treated in hospital, where he was identified as Benjimin Feelds, 58, "Negre Natif de l'Amirique." What became of him after his release from jail one year later is a mystery. One suspects that he did not live much longer.

Throughout the period 1808–27, when Field is known to have lived in Montreal, the salary of the public executioner was set at £27 sterling a year.[36] On top of that, the executioner received room and board, and perhaps also extra payment for every punishment that he inflicted. As Sheriff Gray had had occasion to explain in 1784:

> In my agreement with the Executioner I am to pay him Five Guineas for every Execution, and two Guineas for every other Punishment, over and above his Wages, which comes to something more than what I charge [the government] including the Allowance for Provisions, for I pay him regularly every Week a Guinea, besides many smaller Sums that I am obliged to give him from time to time ... I could not get him to take less, nor do I think it by any Means an extraordinary charge for such Business.[37]

Again in 1786, in referring to the payments to the hangman, Gray stated that "it has been a custom every [sic] since I have been in Office, to allow him 40/ [shillings] for every such punishment, be there more or less, and on that account I could never get any yet to inflict them for less."[38] The combined wage of a guinea a week plus premiums in the 1780s amounted to considerably more than £27 sterling per year, and it seems inconceivable that a hangman's emoluments would have been cut back so drastically twenty, thirty, and forty years on.

THE QUALITY OF JUSTICE

If the readiness to assign such a repugnant job – and no other – to blacks speaks of a low regard for them, we would expect to find that attitude reflected in the operation of the legal system as a whole. We would think, for example, that the flimsiest evidence would suffice to convict them, that their sentences would be pitiless, and that, as accusers, they would be given short shrift by white judges and all-white juries in cases where the defendants were white. A scouring of the court records of the period shows no such discriminatory practices; nothing close to a "racial profiling" or persecution of blacks or preferential treatment of whites is detectable in the way the criminal justice system worked. In effect, this is to say that the presence of blacks on juries would have made no significant difference, for better or worse, in the verdicts of the courts. Yet they were arbitrarily excluded. There was no legal basis for their exclusion, if they were of age and met the property qualification, which, in the period under consideration, never amounted to more than a tenancy of £15 a year. They had a right to serve. Denying them the opportunity to do so was a good way to promote civic irresponsibility, just as locking them out of political office and public appointments, in the long run, could only foster apathy and cynicism toward public affairs. In their absence, the potential existed for racial bias in the verdicts of criminal court juries in cases where blacks appeared as defendants or accusers. The legacy of this system is a lasting conviction that racial bias was not just a possibility but the reality.

That the law itself could be harsh, no one can deny. Hanging offences were many, defence lawyers had no right to address juries, and criminal appeals were unknown. In capital cases, however, juries often managed to reduce the offence so that the convict would be spared; if the death sentence was pronounced, it was frequently commuted to banishment through a conditional pardon. From the early 1820s, in crimes where the mandatory sentence was death but judges did not mean it to be enforced, the death sentence was "recorded" but not "pronounced," signalling to the parties and to the authorities that the sentence should be commuted.[39]

Although hangings were not so common as the law allowed, the other physical punishments – whipping, branding, and the pillory – were applied with relative frequency, and for what today would be considered petty infractions. For a theft or burglary, it seems – the surviving records do not specify the offence – "George a Nagre" and two whites, one of them a woman, were each sentenced in May 1765 to receive 50 "stripes" on their naked backs. What did one have to do to merit such a thrashing? Not much, as witness "George a Negroe," in trouble again two months later, on his own this time. At his arraignment on 22 July, he pleaded guilty to stealing "Two pieces of Silk Ribband Value Eleven pence Stirling" from merchant John Grant. His sentence called for him to be carted – "Stript Naked to the Waist and tyed at a Cart Tail at the Goal and there to Receive 10 Stripes & at Mr Deschambaux Corner 10 Stripes & at the first Street this Side the Generals 10 Stripes and at Mr Landrieux Corner 10 Stripes and proceed to the Court Corner and there receive ten Stripes & on the Parade 10 Stripes."[40]

Being hauled half-dressed through the streets on a cart and suffering sixty cracks of the whip for filching two ribbons seems wildly excessive to us today, but the punishment was inflicted on more than one offender in the eighteenth century (by the nineteenth century, thirty-nine lashes was the maximum inflicted outside the military). Blacks were not singled out as the targets of prosecutorial zealotry, even when slavery ruled. Thus, "the Negro Cesar" accused of assaulting and beating a white man named Antoine Chatelain in April 1781 was discharged within a month, after the ailing Chatelain failed to show up in court to press his case. Mongo, a slave of Jean-Baptiste Hervieux, indicted on a charge of assaulting Jean-Baptiste Solquin, a white man, in November 1783, was granted a postponement at his request to the next sitting of the Court of Quarter Sessions and released in the meantime on posting a recognizance of £25. When the case next came up the following April, it was again put off, to July. In July, Solquin failed to show up, so the case was again put off. Finally, on 12 October 1784, with Solquin absent yet again, Mongo was discharged.[41]

What is known of the experience of Isaac Newton is interesting if only because he appeared before various courts over a period of forty years, from the heyday of slavery in the 1780s to well beyond its passing, and his misadventures placed his fate in the hands of players at every rung of the system. His first known run-in with the law occurred at Quebec in 1786, when he was accused of receiving stolen goods. He was tried at the May Term of the Court of King's Bench, and acquitted.[42] After working for a time as a domestic servant for the Quebec harbour master,[43] then moving upriver to Montreal, he was arrested and jailed there in November 1794 for stealing 20 shillings' worth of cloth from merchant Elias Smith. Tried and convicted by a jury of the Court of King's Bench in March 1795, he was sentenced to six months in jail, at the end of which time he was to return to court to be branded in the hand. On 31 August, a contrite Newton petitioned Governor-General Lord Dorchester, pleading that he

> did not know the consequence of the Crime, at the time he committed it, but is now deeply impressed with the most heart felt Contrition and remorse, and truly sorry He is He ever transgressed the laws of his Country [...] Your Petitioner therefore humbly implores your Excellency (that in consideration of his youth inexperience and General good Character before He committed this his first Crime, and also his orderly behaviour while under Confinement, as will fully appear by the annexed Certificate) to be graciously pleased to remit a most dreadful part of the Sentence (to be burned in the Hand) ...

Attached to the petition was a certificate from jailer Jacob Kuhn attesting to Newton's good conduct as a prisoner. Newton had left his petition rather late, since he was to be branded at the September term of the court, which was about to open. If Dorchester was to do anything for him, it would have to be done quickly. So it was. On 2 September, which must have been as soon as the petition reached him at Quebec, Dorchester ordered that a pardon be drafted. Since this could not possibly be done in time to prevent the execution of the sentence, he ordered that Chief Justice James Monk be advised of the coming pardon and that he take steps to ensure that the branding was suspended.[44]

More than twenty years elapse before we again find Newton in trouble, this time in February 1816, accused of stealing a pork shoulder from a tavern-keeper at the market. The tavern-keeper had not seen Newton take his cut of meat, but on finding it missing, he had been informed that a "Négre" had run off with it. The tavern-keeper and a butcher from the market had gone off in search of the thief and had caught up with Newton a few streets away, who was found to be carrying the stolen pork under his coat. The butcher swore that Newton was the man who had filched it. While not ironclad, the evidence was incriminating, even damning, if racial bias were to colour the jury's deliberations. Newton was nevertheless acquitted in the Court of Quarter Sessions on 22 April.[45]

Finally, in March 1824, Newton and three other people were jailed on charges of keeping a disorderly house, disturbing the peace, and "being persons of ill fame." After spending more than three months in jail awaiting trial, they were discharged on 19 July, the grand jury of the Court of Quarter Sessions having chosen to ignore the indictment.[46]

If Newton's experiences highlight some of the harsh features of justice – the possibility of branding, and long pre-trial detention between court terms, which certainly made it difficult for a poor person to hold a job and earn an income – this was a reality for all, white and black. There was nothing unusual in the handling of his cases that would indicate he was the victim of racial bias. On the contrary, two acquittals, one pardon, a jailer's testimonial as to his good conduct, and the dismissal of the bawdy-house charges argue that he benefited from what fairness and small mercies the all-white, all-male system had to offer.

For the most part, Montreal court records, especially after 1800, contained no reference to the race of the accused unless it was in some incidental way in the course of testimony. In this respect, the records of the trial of James Grant were unusual. In November 1814, he was accused of a capital offence: stealing a cow. He had allegedly taken the animal from a farm in the east-side Quebec Suburb, driven it across town to John Fleming's house – where Grant and his wife lived – in the Ste-Anne Suburb, slaughtered it, and salted the meat in a barrel. The cover of the deposition by the cow's owner identified the case as "The King agnst. James Grant B.M." At first glance, if we did not know who James Grant was, we might take "B.M." to be a job title, degree or professional designation; however, the puzzling letters were simply an abbreviation for "Black Man." The entries in the register of the Court of King's Bench at Grant's trial the following March were less coy, identifying the case as "Dominus Rex v. James Grant a Negro." At his arraignment on 3 March 1815, the court appointed lawyer James C. Grant to represent James Grant B.M. Witnesses at the trial on 6 March included blacks John Fleming, Henry Garret, and Garret's wife, Jane Graham. James Grant B.M., who is believed to have moved to Lower Canada from New York State around 1804, claimed that he had bought the cow from some American acquaintances. Fleming testified that this was the explanation that he had overheard Grant give to his wife, Sally York. The exculpatory evidence seems rather weak, but Grant B.M. was acquitted.[47]

CAPITAL CASES

If we look at capital cases in the Montreal courts between 1760 and 1840, we find seven death sentences recorded against blacks in that eighty-year period; two, at most, were carried out. Warren Glossen was executed in 1823, and possibly Thomas Bruce in 1778.[48] As we saw in an earlier chapter, two slaves sentenced to death for theft in a dwelling house – Bruce in 1773, and Tom Grant in 1795 – were pardoned on condition that they leave the province.[49] It seems that Bruce, however, remained on the spot or returned, and that he was the Thomas Bruce sentenced to death in 1778. Accused of stealing "a great quantity of Liquors, Soap, Sugar and other effects" from a merchant in St-Paul Street on the night of 4–5 September 1777, he had fled to Quebec, where he had been captured the following winter, and returned to Montreal to be tried. He was convicted of felony and burglary in March 1778 and sentenced to hang on 10 April, but there seems to be no record of his execution or death.[50] Reuben Chambers, a "mulatto" sentenced to death in 1824 for murdering a white man in an altercation at a logging bee near St Andrew's (St-André-d'Argenteuil) the previous year, was repeatedly reprieved every six months in the face of doubts about his sanity until, in 1827, his death sentence was commuted to transportation. The fifth person sentenced to death, Elizabeth Williams, a twenty-three-year-old single woman from St-Benoît (Mirabel), daughter of a black labourer and a French-Canadian woman, was convicted in the Court of Queen's Bench in August 1840 of the murder of her baby, born in secret on 10 March, whom she had kept until 11 April, when she left him in the woods to die. Sentenced to hang on 9 October, she was saved from execution by the intercession of "the Notables and other inhabitants of the County of Two Mountains," including the Anglican rector and Roman Catholic parish priest of St Andrew's, military and militia commanders, and two justices of the peace, who appealed to Governor-General Lord Sydenham on her behalf:

> That among the unfortunate Individuals in the Gaol of Montreal, condemned to suffer death at the last Court of Criminal pleas, is Elizabeth Williams of the Seigniory of Argenteuil, in this County, convicted of the murder of her child, aged five weeks, under circumstances demonstrating her imbecility of mind, more clearly, than a wilful intention of depriving her infant of life.
>
> That Your Petitioners, under the circumstances of the weakness of mind of the said Elizabeth Williams, esteem it their duty to recommend her as an object of commiseration.
>
> Wherefore Your Petitioners respectfully Implore the extension of the Royal Clemency to the said Elizabeth Williams and commutation of the punishment of death into such other as Your Excellency may deem fit to decree.

Sydenham commuted her sentence to three years in the house of correction.[51]

As whites were all too ready to belittle the mental capacities of blacks, whether to exploit or ostracize them, or to claim a protectorate over them as poor souls in need of guidance, we cannot but be skeptical of the "imbecility" of Elizabeth Williams and the "insanity" of Reuben Chambers, even if these claims by their defenders may have served their purpose at the time. Elizabeth Williams may have been a simpleton, but she may just as well have been suffering from postpartum depression, aggravated by her distress as a single mother (the father never came forward during her ordeal) and hiding a child whose existence she did not dare reveal. In her torment and confusion, she would have had to take but one short step to go from denying his existence to denying him existence.[52] In Chambers' case, there was evidence that his derangement was of recent appearance, and perhaps only a passing aberration. As he sat in the Montreal jail awaiting his trial, a committee of the Legislative Council looking into the state of facilities for the care of the insane queried Sheriff Ermatinger about the institutions under his charge. Ermatinger responded in January 1824 that he had seven prisoners of various degrees of insanity in the jail, among them Chambers, whom he characterized as "Insane and dangerous and frequently outrageous."[53] Yet a witness who had known Chambers for about a year testified at his trial on 5 March that "he always appeared to have his senses." Another who had known him for two years "never knew him to be insane, always heard he was a quarrelsome man when he was where liquor could be found." Daniel de Hertel, a prominent resident of Argenteuil, testified that Chambers, "at different times in his service during last summer," had behaved a little oddly at times, but never violently, although a boy had left De Hertel's service after complaining of being abused by Chambers. Yet another witness spoke of Chambers as a man "much altered" since he had last seen him; Chambers was "a man of great strength and [who] used to knock people about a good deal," he testified. Dr William Dunbar Selby, the medical attendant at the jail, said that he had not seen Chambers when he first arrived, "but was told he had behaved very violently to some of the persons in gaol & he at one time attempted to hang himself." On that occasion, Selby had helped to cut him down. Chambers was "locked up in a room by himself and he has since that time been fastened by one leg to the wall."[54] Whatever "insanity" afflicted him in 1823–24, Chambers later had the presence of mind to seek a pardon. Governor-General Lord Dalhousie pardoned him in 1827 on condition that he "be transported to the Island of Bermuda ... for and during the term of his natural life ... subject and liable to all such and the same laws, rules and regulations as are or shall be in force at the said Island of Bermuda with respect to convicts transported from Great Britain."[55]

Unlike the above one-time offenders, Warren Glossen played with fire for five years. On 9 May 1818, he and another black man, Wyman (or Weyman) Virginia, were indicted for grand larceny in the theft over several months of £100 worth of leather from the store of merchant George Forsyth, £140 worth of leather belonging to Forsyth stored in the warehouse of James McDouall & Co., and the theft of £20 worth of butter and cheese from McDouall & Co. A third black man, William Meikins (or Meakins) Nation, was originally implicated in the theft of the leather, but he does not seem to have been prosecuted. Glossen and Virginia both pleaded not guilty at their arraignment on a charge of grand larceny on 9 May, but at the trial three days later of the case of *R v. Weyman Virginia and Warren Glossen*, Virginia alone was tried, no explanation being recorded as to why there were no proceedings against Glossen. Virginia was found guilty and sentenced to two years' hard labour in the house of correction.[56] The following November, Glossen was among the four black men who were hired by Emmanuel d'Aubreville, the captain of the night watch, as the city lamplighters for six months. Two months into the contract, Glossen was up on charges that he and watchman John Bowman (or Baumann) had stolen a sheep from D'Aubreville, of all people. At the time, he and Bowman shared a house in the Récollets Suburb. William C. Virginia from Fairfax, Vermont, brother of Wyman Virginia, provided Glossen with an alibi, claiming that since his arrival in Montreal on 18 January, he had lived with Glossen, and that on the night of 20 January, when the sheep was stolen, Glossen was home from 7 o'clock on. François Houle, the husband of Caesar Johonnot's widow, told a different story:

> That on Wednesday last the twentieth day of January instant during the night, John Bowman and Warren brought to the house where the said John Bowman and the said William live, a sheep, a piece of which the said Warren brought to

deponent's wife – That he, the deponent, saw the said John Bowman and Warren bring the sheep as aforesaid and saw them butcher it – But that he did not learn where they had obtained it. And further says the deponent that the said William was present when the said Bowman and Warren cut up the said sheep.

Houle's evidence notwithstanding, the Grand Jury of the Court of King's Bench found no bill, and Glossen was discharged.[57]

That summer, "Warren Gaussen alias Glasford Warren" was arrested and convicted in Sessions Court for keeping a disorderly house. On 19 July, he was ordered jailed until 30 July, on which day he was to be pilloried for one hour and then released.[58] Less than a month after his exposure in the pillory (a punishment likely administered by Benjamin Field), Glossen faced a charge of assault, but that case was apparently settled out of court.[59] He had another close call in March 1820 when he and two other black men were accused of theft. The stolen goods – chickens and half a cord of wood – were found in the house that Glossen shared with co-accused George Binks and Richard Jackson in the Quebec Suburb. The grand jury found no bill against Glossen, and Jackson was acquitted at trial, but Binks, found guilty of petty larceny, was sentenced on 20 May to three months' hard labour in the house of correction and to receive thirty-nine lashes in the market place on 2 June.[60]

Glossen finally came a cropper in 1823. In January, he and his crony, Bowman, were part of a gang that stole about £15 worth of merchandise from a dry goods shop on McGill Street. A few nights later, they broke into the Lachine offices of forwarders Whiting & Crane, from which they stole goods, money, and the company's books. Tried on 1 September for the first burglary, they were all acquitted of that charge but found guilty of petty larceny. On 5 September, they were tried for the burglary at Whiting & Crane; Glossen, Peter Johnson, and Jean-Baptiste Albert were found guilty as charged, while Bowman and Joseph Yager (or Jaeger) were convicted of grand larceny. Glossen, Albert, and Johnson were sentenced to hang, but Johnson had his sentence commuted to five years on the treadmill at Quebec. For the petty larceny at the dry goods store, Bowman and Yager were each sentenced to six months' hard labour and to receive thirty-nine lashes on the bare back at the market place; for grand larceny, they got twelve months in jail, consecutive to their six months in the house of correction. "The Lord have mercy on my Soul," a dazed Glossen repeated over and over as, supported by friends and attended by the Reverend John Bethune, rector of Christ Church, he mounted the gallows on the morning of 24 October to be hanged by Benjamin Field.[61]

A SPANISH-SPEAKING IMMIGRANT FACES THE NOOSE

In addition to James Grant B.M. and the six black convicts above, at least three others risked the death penalty: Manuel Firmin, a "mulâtre espagnol" from South America, who faced various charges in the 1820s and 1830s as he moved from Quebec to Montreal to Trois-Rivières to Sorel;[62] William Collins, charged with murder in 1826;

and Alexander Johomnot, accused of stealing above the value of forty shillings in a dwelling house that same year. Firmin was perhaps the most intriguing of the three, given the ingenuity he displayed, the scrapes he got into, his seeming ability as an immigrant to get his bearings (at least for a while) – and because, as in the case of Isaac Newton, his brushes with the criminal justice system at every level over time revealed that, if the law was harsh, the quality of mercy was not so strained that it was denied to blacks.

In his first few years in Lower Canada, he seems to have been just another young man launched, perhaps by misadventure, on a career as a thief. A coloured, Spanish-speaking immigrant moving from place to place as he sought to adjust, he is first glimpsed at Quebec at the end of May 1818, when he was arrested for the theft of a pair of shoes worth five shillings. On being convicted, he was sentenced on 23 June to receive 39 lashes and to spend six months in the house of correction. From Quebec, he moved to the neighbouring Huron village of Lorette, where Grand Chief Nicolas Vincent complained in January 1820 that Firmin had caused a great deal of trouble in the roughly one and a half months that he had lived there. He was said to have no visible means of support, no fixed address, and to live an idle, disorderly life, and he was reputed to be a dangerous man and a disturber of the peace. Firmin left the village before he could be arrested on a charge of being idle and disorderly.[63] By that fall, he had moved on to Montreal, where he was arrested for stealing a coat worth £5 from a tailor's shop and a gold ring worth £2 10s from the store of jeweller James Adams Dwight on 4 November. He was indicted on 9 November on two counts of stealing privately from a shop, but it appears that the Crown did not proceed with the charge of stealing the ring. Firmin was tried that same day on the one count and convicted of grand larceny. On 15 November, he was sentenced to 12 months in the house of correction.[64]

There, he fell in with hardened criminals – James Kelly, Halifax-born Tobias Burke, Portuguese-born Vathis De Selby, and English-born John Whiteman. They cowed other inmates, threatened to break out or burn down the jail, and generally caused a ruckus. All but Firmin did break out, and were caught. On 3 March 1821, they set fire to straw in a room at the house of correction, but the fire was put out before it did much damage. The five of them were charged with arson and pleaded not guilty at their arraignment on 5 May in the Court of Oyer and Terminer. Since they were all detained on previous convictions, there was no rush to try them. At the end of the court term on 14 May, they were ordered transferred to the jail, once they had finished serving their time in the house of correction, "for further proceedings to be had against them." At their trial on 7 November, Kelly was found guilty of arson, Burke and Whiteman of being accessories, and all three were sentenced to hang, but Firmin and De Selby, the two aliens in the group, were acquitted.[65] For Firmin, acquittal came as his twelve-month sentence for grand larceny was about to expire, a happy coincidence. The following 8 May, he was charged with grand larceny, but this time the grand jury found "No Bill." A little more than a week later, prosecutors tried their hand again with a charge of petty larceny, but again the grand jury found "No Bill."[66]

At this point, Firmin's life seems to have undergone a striking change. Within months of his last brush with the law, he forsook Montreal for Trois-Rivières. He seems to have found his footing there. During his residence of about eight years, he married a woman named Marie McLeod, and in 1826 he acquired a town lot from Joseph Boucher de Niverville, seigneur of the Fief Niverville. One condition of his grant was that he build a house on the lot within two years.[67] This interlude of domesticity ended in the summer of 1830, when he was convicted of obtaining a watch under false pretences and sentenced to three months in the house of correction at Trois-Rivières. After serving about a month, he escaped and fled to the United States. From St-Jean, his wife, left without support, petitioned Governor-General Lord Aylmer in February 1831 to pardon her husband and allow him to return. She gave a detailed account of the circumstances that had led to his wrongful conviction, as she alleged. Without being pardoned, Firmin returned in July or August 1832 and was re-arrested. He pleaded guilty to the charge of escaping custody and was sentenced on 13 September to one month in the house of correction followed by one month in jail. On 17 September, he addressed an appeal to the governor for a pardon. Nine area notables, including the sometime slave-owning Reverend John Doty, recommended him to the clemency of the governor. In forwarding his petition to Quebec on 5 October, Justice Edward Bowen himself wrote in a covering note:

> I enclose you a Petition from an unfortunate poor devil, a mulatto, confined in the House of Correction at Three Rivers, praying for a Pardon. He is strongly recommended by the Bar and I know the Judges would have no objection. He found the door of the house of correction open two years since and naturally walked off. About three months ago he was arrested for having done so & is now remanded under his former Sentence & to be imprisoned for the latter offence during one month.

Pardoned ten days later,[68] Firmin moved to Sorel. It was as a Sorel resident, on business at Quebec in the spring of 1833, that he played a role in what smacks of a con game. Toward the end of April, farmer Louis Deguire *dit* Desrosiers of St-Michel-d'Yamaska went down to Quebec to sell fish at the market in Lower Town. Off went Firmin to Quebec, to sell fish too. And another Sorel resident, Joseph Asselin, also turned up there. According to Desrosiers, Asselin invited him into a tavern for a drink, saying he wanted him to take a letter back home. It turned out that Asselin had no money to pay for their drinks, so Desrosiers took out his purse and paid. The next thing he knew, his purse, containing about $23, was gone, as was Asselin. Desrosiers ran out after Asselin, and bumped into "Emanuelle Firmain homme de Couleur." Desrosiers told Firmin that he had just been robbed by Asselin, and Firmin told Desrosiers that he would go after Asselin. Desrosiers tried to keep up, but fell behind. Finally, he caught up to Firmin, who held up the stolen purse, crying out, "It's your purse! Asselin had it!" And according to Desrosiers, Firmin gave him back his purse at Sorel, but with only about $9 in it.

Firmin also gave his version of events. He stated that after Desrosiers had told him that he had been robbed by a man who had worked as a butcher at Sorel and sold lamb there in June 1832, he told Desrosiers that he knew that man as Joseph Asselin. At Desrosiers's request, Firmin went looking for Asselin, found him, seized him by the collar and demanded to know whether he had robbed Louis Deguire *dit* Desrosiers. Asselin said he did not know anyone of that name, but he took a purse from his pocket that contained a little more than $9. Asselin gave purse and money to a Mr Jones, who gave it to Firmin, all before the eyes of an assistant clerk of the market at Quebec. And Firmin gave purse and money to Desrosiers. Firmin had to post a bond guaranteeing that he would give evidence at Asselin's trial in Montreal, but there seems to be no record of such a trial.[69]

The New Years' Day theft of a trunk full of cash from the home of a neighbour in 1834 proved Firmin's undoing. The evidence showed that Firmin, who seems to have been working as a dealer in pork as well as fish, had invited the victim and several other neighbours to his house for a party and slipped out during the evening to steal the cash. Arraigned on one count of burglary on 4 March, he was tried and convicted the next day, the Crown filing a *nolle prosequi* on a second charge. He was sentenced to hang on 23 May. The court records note that "Judgment of death in this cause was not pronounced by the Court but was ordered to be recorded and is now recorded," a formula which, as we have seen, indicated that the court did not consider that the death penalty should be enforced.[70] Firmin accordingly appealed to the governor for a pardon. On 26 June, his death sentence was commuted to transportation to Bermuda or any other place that the authorities chose. He was ordered held in the Montreal jail until arrangements could be made for his departure. The papers were prepared – but something went wrong and Firmin did not go. He remained in the Montreal jail, from where, in November, he petitioned to be released. On 20 December, he was granted a new pardon, this one ordering that within ten days he transport himself out of Lower Canada "in such manner and to such a place as our Governor Lieutenant-Governor or person administering the Government shall direct." Firmin and his wife went to the United States. Then, on 17 December 1836, his wife appealed to the governor, Lord Gosford, to allow him to return, pleading that she was gravely ill and without resources at Trois-Rivières, where she was visiting her parents. Firmin had been working as a cook at the Columbia Hotel in Albany, New York, she said, a job he had just been obliged to give up because of swelling in his legs.[71] The request appears to have been denied, as there seems to be no further trace of Firmin in Lower Canada.

AN EVEN-HANDED APPROACH

In all his run-ins with the law, Firmin was never accused of a crime of violence, unless it be the charge of arson levelled against him at Montreal for the fire at the house of correction, of which he was acquitted. His were mostly small-time property crimes, but they carried big-time penalties, from flogging to hanging. William Collins also faced the death penalty, but for the crime of murder. He was part of a group that had tried to crash a wedding party on the night of 15 August 1826. Thomas Halbert, who turned them away, was kicked and struck with a rock during a melee, suffering injuries from which he died two days later. Several prosecution witnesses, portraying Halbert as the innocent victim, testified that the "colored man," Collins, had struck the fatal blow. The defence sought to present the affair as a dust-up in which Collins and his friends were leaving the scene after being turned away, when they were attacked by a band of stick-wielding Irishmen who had come rushing out of the house where the party was going on. Peter Dago led off a string of six witnesses who impugned the credibility and character of the main prosecution witness, a white woman who had served time in prison for running a bawdy house. Collins and co-accused James Lang, a white man, were convicted of manslaughter and sentenced on 9 September to be burned in the hand in open court and to spend six months in jail. They pleaded for mercy, and as a result were spared the burning in the hand.[72] In the end, the penalty they suffered for a homicide was lighter than that inflicted on Firmin for the theft of a pair of shoes. As for Alexander Johonnot, the posthumous son of distiller Caesar Johonnot, he too faced the death penalty for property crime. He had embarked on a career of petty crime by the age of sixteen, perhaps under the tutelage of his reprobate stepfather, François Houle. By the fall of 1826, when he was staring at the noose for stealing $25, he had at least five convictions under his belt, which had earned him five terms behind bars and two public whippings (in 1819 and 1822, likely at the hands of Benjamin Field). At his trial in February 1827, he was convicted and, at the age of twenty-six, banished from Lower Canada.[73]

From these and other cases cited elsewhere in this book, we can see that most of the criminal prosecutions of blacks in the Montreal area in this period were for theft, assault, and morals charges. They were rarely accused of the more violent crimes – armed robbery, homicide, and rape. One of the few accused of armed robbery was Warren Glossen's acquaintance, William Meikins Nation. He was charged along with four white men, including Tobias Burke, one of Manuel Firmin's jailhouse acquaintances, in a violent home invasion in the St-Laurent Suburb in the spring of 1818. The grand jury of the Court of King's Bench returned a True Bill on the indictment for all the accused except Nation.[74] Other than Reuben Chambers, Elizabeth Williams, and William Collins, the only person charged with anything approaching murder before 1840 was servant William Thompson of Berthier. He was accused in 1815 of attempting to break into his former master's house with the intent to kill him, a charge supported by no other evidence than the word of that master, as we will see. The only case of rape in eighty years was that of Rubin Middleton, mentioned in an earlier chapter. Middleton, an American-born "mulatto," was convicted in 1781 of raping a ten-year-old white girl. Surely, if racial passions had ruled, this was one case where the authorities and the public, already on edge from six years of war with the Americans, would have called for blood. Middleton was sentenced to a jail term of nine months and fined £25, then pardoned on his offering to serve, not as hangman, but as a soldier – hardly excessive punishment in the circumstances.[75]

The same apparent even-handedness shown in the treatment of accused blacks is found in the prosecution of cases where blacks were the victims, accusers, or simply witnesses. William Feeler's experience in 1820 is instructive on this score. Called to

A pair of sketches of Montreal in 1824 taken from Citadel Hill. The hill marked the eastern end of Notre Dame Street, where Joseph Pierson had his restaurant when he was fatally stabbed by a soldier in 1815. The street is seen on the left, below the cannon, in the view toward the west. The other view looks southwest toward the river.

testify against a white man accused of assaulting another white, Feeler complained that the accused had threatened to beat him up if he testified; as a result, the accused was made to post a peace bond. Standard procedure, we think, and so it was: no rules kept blacks from testifying against whites, blacks had recourse to the law when they saw fit, and their complaints were heeded and not simply brushed aside.[76]

In the period under consideration, we know of two blacks who died violent deaths. Joseph Pierson, the eating-house owner, was fatally stabbed with a bayonet in 1815; and Thomas Perks, a mulatto from Nova Scotia living at the fort of Coteau-du-Lac, died in 1821 as the result of a fight at a dance, where he had played the fiddle. In neither case did the authorities secure a conviction, but this does not appear to have been the result of laxity on their part.

In Perks' case, a local lout was promptly arrested and prosecuted for murder. Evidence suggested that Perks, angered by horseplay that had ended with the tipping of the bench on which he was sitting, had offered to fight any man present. Joseph Leclerc (or Leclair) stepped up. The tavern keeper told them to take their fight outside. Leclerc fought dirty: "Perks ... was in the act of taking off his coat when Leclerc knocked him down with a body-blow; repeated his blows upon his rising, and, getting him down, either knelt or attempted to kneel on his breast – Next day, the deceased, after vomiting a great deal of blood, died, having previously declared that some one had knelt upon his breast and broken his heart." Low blows in a bar fight between two willing participants did not add up to murder, the jury found, acquitting Leclerc at his trial in October.[77]

The facts were more troubling in Pierson's case because the evidence pointed to soldiers as the killers. Four men of the 8th (King's) Regiment, customers at his cook shop on 8 March 1815, had refused to pay their bill. Pierson chased after them to collect when one of the soldiers struck him on the head while another stabbed him in the stomach. Pierson died in the early hours of 10 March. A young Dr Robert Nelson testified at the inquest that the stab in the stomach had been fatal. Pierson himself had identified a William Thompson as one of the four soldiers implicated, though he was not the one who had struck him. Thompson denied that he had been present, and found a fellow soldier to vouch for him. From items left at the scene, the circumstantial evidence presented by other soldiers, and his own suspicious conduct, the evidence pointed to Private James Douglas, but he too denied involvement. The inquest jury ruled it murder by a soldier unknown. Douglas was arrested for the murder and spent the summer in jail awaiting his trial. At the next term of the Court of King's Bench in September, however, the grand jury deemed the evidence insufficient and declined to return a bill of indictment. Douglas was freed.[78]

It is possible that blacks were involved in Pierson's death. Two soldiers of the 8th Regiment mentioned in depositions were John Dolphin and William Thompson. Neither was identified by race, but we have seen that a black farmer called John Dolphin had enlisted in the militia in the War of 1812. Evidence in Pierson's case showed that Private John Dolphin of the 8th Regiment was one of four soldiers who had been absent from roll call at the time when Pierson was stabbed. Dolphin was not a common name – were there really two men of that name in Montreal at the same time, or had militiaman Dolphin joined the 8th Regiment sometime during the war? As for William Thompson, Pierson himself had implicated a soldier of that name.[79] This might be the black William Thompson (or Thomson) who surfaced in the Montreal area around this time. Thompson worked briefly as a domestic servant for Thomas Webster, an English immigrant who had set up as a merchant at Berthier in 1815. It is possible that after the general demobilization that took place in March, soldier Thompson, for lack of anything better, found employment in domestic service. Webster's servant was certainly no veteran at domestic work: when Webster sacked him on 23 September, after repeated warnings "on account of his continual habit of drinking," an angry Thompson told Webster that he was "the first master he had served and that he ... would never serve another." Four nights later, Webster charged, Thompson tried to break into his house to kill him. Thompson was arrested on 28 September and held in the Montreal jail until 30 October, when, as the records of the Court of Quarter Sessions state, "The Defendant being in Custody was brought up and no person appeared during the setting of this Sessions to prosecute him. The Court on motion of Mr Viger order that the said William Thompson be discharged and he is discharged accordingly." This was an error. Thompson was being held for trial in the high court, not in Sessions Court. Unaware of his discharge, a grand jury of the Court of Oyer and Terminer proceeded to indict him the following March for attempting to break into Webster's home with intent to commit murder. Too late – the bird had been freed. The prosecution was abandoned.[80]

If we suspect that blacks may have had a hand in killing Pierson or of abetting his murderer, it is because the pugnacious Pierson had a knack for antagonizing one and all, including his black acquaintances, even those closest to him. Hanna Caesar, a black woman, had accused him and his lover, Julia Johnson, of assaulting her in 1804, and in 1805 Pierson had been fined for assaulting black farmer Stephen Rogers.[81] In 1807, he had had to post a £10 bond after being accused in another assault case, the outcome of which is unknown.[82] Finally, in June 1810, only eight months after they married, his wife, Mary Rusk, charged him with assault, painting him in a brutal light:

> Mary Rusk, Wife of Joseph Pearson, of Montreal, being duly Sworn upon the Holy evangelists deposeth and saith that Yesterday the fifteenth June instant at about the hour of two o'clock in the afternoon this deponent being at Work in the House of Mr Coats where she lives in the Capacity of Servant, She was without any Provocation on her part Violently assaulted and Struck with a Stick and fist by Joseph Pearson, her husband, deposeth further, that yesterday about seven in the evening this deponent being in Notre Dame Street on her way to Doctor [Benjamin] Green's She was overtook by her said husband, who insulted her very much, and pulled this deponent's bonnet about saying that if she would not speak to him he would knock her deponents brains out. That this deponent did not go in to Doctor Green's as She intended, and went round about

and got as far as Mr Justice [Thomas] McCord's, Where she went in his house, that her said husband went into the sd. House by force and there violently assaulted and Struck this deponent and tried to drag deponent out of the said house, that from the threats and menaces made to her deponent by her sd. Husband she has every reason to believe and doth verily believe that her life is in danger. Wherefore She prays Justice in the premisses.

Mary Rusk's deposition left out one important detail that must have been evident to the official who took her statement: she was pregnant, about to give birth to their son, Valentine. Pierson was arrested and released on his own £10 recognizance to keep the peace.[83] He was, as the evidence indicates, not an easy man. We can easily conceive that if an aggrieved Pierson squared off in 1815 with a band of unruly soldiers fresh from the field of battle, they would come to blows. This is not to exculpate his killers, only to suggest that those war-bitten soldiers, black or white, rarely on the best of terms with civilians, had met him as they would an enemy. They would have felt no remorse in dispatching him, just as others who had known him would have felt little sympathy. Mary Rusk was not at his bedside when he died, nor for that matter was his lover, Julia Johnson, by whom he had had a daughter in 1812.[84] In the end, there was not so much as a hint that Pierson had ever had a wife, a lover, a child, or a friend in the world.

Six years later, Mary Rusk testified in a case which shows that the authorities acted as diligently in relatively minor offences as they did in the prosecution of the capital cases outlined above. This one, although the charge was grand larceny, involved nothing more than the opportunistic theft of some laundry. Rusk, who, after Pierson's death, had married black labourer Peter Abraham, now went by the name of Mary Abraham (or Abram).[85] In the summer of 1821, she was living with Catherine Guillet and William Wright on College Street. One day in early July, Guillet, after doing some washing for businessman Andrew Porteous,[86] spread the items out to dry in her yard. A young man named Henry Johnson, happening by, jumped the fence, scooped up three tablecloths and a shift, and ran off. Rusk and a neighbour raised the alarm. The neighbour and another man working nearby, both whites, chased the thief, caught him, and recovered the stolen articles. Convicted of a reduced charge of petty larceny, Johnson was sentenced in November to twelve months at hard labour and to receive the standard thirty-nine lashes – more work for Benjamin Field.[87]

In one case in 1840 in which race appears to have been a factor, Abraham Low, himself a man who exhibited a violent streak, perhaps exacerbated by alcohol, accused a white trader of assaulting him. According to Low, on the evening of 21 July he went "to the house of one Luke Stewart Trader and politely asked change for two dollars when the said Stewart without cause or provocation grossly abused Deponent and did incite another person then in the said house to strike him, this person being unknown to Deponent. That the said Stewart did also ... violently assault beat and strike Deponent." Stewart was required to post a £40 bond to keep the peace, with two additional £20 sureties.[88]

THE BETSY FREEMAN AFFAIR

It would be too fastidious to summarize every court case involving blacks only to hammer home the point already made – that the criminal justice system of the day, resolutely white, did not betray racial bias in its handling of cases involving blacks, whether they were the accused or the accusers. But three cases that arose in the summer of 1836, all involving Alexander Grant, present a few new elements while reinforcing these points in a dramatic way. All three proceedings stemmed from a visit to Montreal by former resident Ann Gelston. She had been the first person baptized in the newly founded American Presbyterian Church of Montreal, on 13 April 1823, before the church even had its own minister or building. She had moved to New York around the end of that year. She had subsequently married a man named Ebenezer Marvin and, in the mid-1830s, they lived at Charlotte, North Carolina.[89] In June 1836, to escape the oppressive southern heat – she was in "an advanced state of pregnancy" – Gelston journeyed north to Montreal to stay with her sister and brother-in-law, Phoebe Worth Gelston and jeweller James Adams Dwight, on College Street. Attending her on the trip was Betsy Freeman (alias Betsy Marvin), a black girl aged between fourteen and sixteen. Word of the girl's presence in town reached Grant, who recorded that

> understanding that a few days since, a young Female, of the name of "Betsy Marvin," arrived in this city with a Lady of that name, who stated herself to be her Mistress, but who upon enquiry, appeared to be the Wife of a Slave-holder in North Carolina; this excited my suspicion, and acting upon the advice of several persons, who though not of the coloured race, are warm friends of humanity, I immediately called upon the girl, who stated to me that she was a Slave; that she was 14 years of age, that she had witnessed her Grandfather led handcuffed to be sold, and that her master, when she left North Carolina, had proceeded to "Mobile" with 30 more human beings for sale.
>
> After hearing the young girl's statement, I enquired if she wished to remain with her Mistress? She said no; that her Mistress had ill-treated her; that she was now in a free country, and did not wish to be longer a Slave. I replied, by the benevolent Laws of England which are in operation here, you are really free, and may at this moment go where you please; she said she would be glad to do so, but she had no friend to protect her, and to get her a situation. I told her that I would protect her, that I had a house, and that my Wife would be her friend; she then collected her wearing apparel and followed me to my house.[90]

That was on Sunday, 12 June. On Monday, the 13th, Ann Gelston swore out a complaint before a justice of the peace that Betsy Freeman, "a Servant duly Engaged to the deponent," had deserted her service, "in direct violation of the said Engagement." Dr Daniel Arnoldi, the magistrate who received her complaint, was also her physician

Black Montrealers flocked to the courthouse on 14–15 June 1836, anxious to hear how the court would decide the fate of Betsy Freeman.

and the prison doctor.[91] Acting on the complaint, High Constable Benjamin Delisle went to Grant's house in St-Paul Street and demanded that he surrender Betsy Freeman, which Grant readily did, "conceiving he [Delisle] acted under legal authority."

> Proceeding with Mr Delisle, I stated that we had better go to the Police Office as the nearest and best station for a Magistrate; he said no, that Dr Arnoldi would be the best Magistrate, as he had issued the writ for the girl's apprehension; on our arrival at the Doctor's study I attempted an explanation of the poor girl's case; the Doctor instantly interrupted me, though I addressed him by the title of "your Honor," and treated him with all possible respect. He appeared so well acquainted with the supposed merits of the case, that he desired me to hold my tongue, and turning to the girl said, "you infernal Devil, why did you leave your Mistress?" she replied that her Mistress had ill-treated her, that she was in a free country, and wished to be free. Doctor Arnoldi said "hold your tongue, you Devil, if you do not go back to your Mistress, I will put you in a solitary dungeon and confine you there six months." The girl thus frightened, said she would rather return to her Mistress than go to Prison; she did return, and I understand her Mistress confined her in a Garret 24 hours. Upon my endeavouring to plead for the girl, the honorable Magistrate took me by the collar and degraded himself by kicking me.[92]

Grant sought advice from hardware merchant Cyrus Brewster, undoubtedly one of those who "though not of the coloured race, are warm friends of humanity," who urged him to enlist the help of lawyer Charles Ovide Perrault and to apply for a writ of habeas corpus, which would oblige Gelston to produce Betsy Freeman in court and let the court determine Betsy's status. Since it proved impossible to secure the writ that evening, and there were fears that Betsy would be spirited across the border before the courts could act, Grant enlisted the help of a handful of black men to keep watch on the Dwight house overnight. Disturbances around the house through the night led to Grant and two other men, George Nixon and Moses Powell Wormley, being charged the next day with riot. On that Tuesday, 14 June, Grant secured the writ of habeas corpus.[93] He also laid a charge of assault and battery against Arnoldi for having kicked him. The doctor-cum-magistrate was arrested and released on a £10 recognizance to appear at his trial.[94]

The criminal cases against Grant and Arnoldi would be heard later, but the writ of habeas corpus ordered Ann Gelston to produce Betsy Freeman before the Court of King's Bench that very day. High Constable Delisle picked up Betsy Freeman and took her before the court, attended by "a great number of other colored persons." But Gelston begged off, Doctor Arnoldi certifying that she was bedridden and could not leave the house. To the disappointment of the many blacks present, who "evinced the greatest zeal and the warmest sympathy for one they supposed to be a slave," the court put off the hearing until the next day and ordered that, in the meantime, Betsy be taken back to the Dwight house.[95]

On Wednesday, 15 June, lawyer Charles Dewey Day, appearing for the absent Ann Gelston, presented her side of the case as consigned in an affidavit that she had signed before magistrate Arnoldi. Gelston swore that Betsy Freeman, about sixteen years old, was born free and never a slave, that she was her husband's "servant or apprentice," bound out at the age of about fourteen, with her mother's consent, under the North Carolina law "for indenturing free black children." The indenture was on record in a North Carolina court, she said, and she believed that her husband was "bound in a penalty of one thousand dollars ... (and at least five hundred dollars) to restore the said Elizabeth to the said Court which is the Guardian of all free colored children." Gelston denied ever mistreating the girl and claimed "that the said Elizabeth is desirous of remaining in the service of the said Ann Gelston and of avoiding all communication with the said Grant and the people of her own colour by whom he is supported and encouraged in his attempt to seduce the said Elizabeth from the care & service of the said Ann Gelston."[96]

Grant's lawyer, Perrault, suggested that Gelston was playing semantic games, using the term "apprentice" to mask Betsy Freeman's slave status. The fact that Gelston did not have a copy of Betsy's alleged indenture meant that her claim was unsubstantiated, he argued. Besides, even if Betsy were Gelston's "apprentice," she may have been the slave of whoever had bound her over to Gelston. But Grant and his lawyer had no proof that Betsy was a slave. To settle the question, the court put Betsy herself in the witness box. To the judge's questions, she replied that she was fifteen or sixteen, that she was under no restraint, that she came from Carolina and wished to return there with her mistress. The justices, with a nod to Grant's humane motives in the affair, told her that she was free to do as she pleased, whereupon Betsy rejoined her mistress. "This fact is strong evidence of the Lady's kindness to her servant," one newspaper remarked, perhaps presuming too much.[97]

Betsy Freeman was called to testify for the prosecution on 19 July when Arnoldi was tried in the Court of Quarter Sessions for assaulting Grant. Grant, Wormley, and High Constable Delisle also gave evidence. Arnoldi called no witnesses. The jury pronounced him guilty, and on the motion of Perrault, counsel for the prosecution, the court imposed a fine of ten shillings. The Patriote newspaper *The Vindicator* rushed to print the news in one sentence, and to editorialize pointedly in a second: "Daniel Arnoldi, Esq. one of the Justices of the Peace for this District, was found guilty to-day, by a petit Jury, in the Court of Quarter Sessions, of assault and battery on Alexander Grant, a colored man. We should think that it is full time to purify our Commission of the Peace."[98]

The trial of Grant, Wormley, and hairdresser George Nixon, who worked for Grant and lived with him, came on before Chief Justice James Reid and Justice George Pyke of the Court of King's Bench on 7 September. By then, Ann Gelston and Betsy Freeman had left Montreal. Members of the Dwight household testified about the harrowing night they had spent when five or six black men had noisily besieged their house, at one point breaking a window and firing a shot into the ceiling. According to the defence, "the coloured men, and Grant in particular, had sought only to keep things peaceful and orderly, but trouble broke out nevertheless, the fault of an unknown sailor, armed with a sabre and firearm, who was the author of the disturbance and riot."[99] The jury of ten French-Canadians and two English speakers retired briefly to deliberate and returned a verdict of acquittal for all three accused (see Appendix IV).

We cheer the outcome of the Betsy Freeman affair today. Granted, Betsy Freeman returned to her mistress after trying to flee, and her status remained unclear. But it seems unlikely that she was Ann Gelston's slave. Everyone associated with Gelston denied the allegation. As a former resident of Montreal (and possibly of areas along the border), Gelston herself would have known that she was tempting fate by bringing a slave into British territory, or falsely claiming under oath that Betsy was free. And had Grant remained convinced, after the habeas corpus hearing, that Betsy was truly a slave, he would, we think, have persisted in his efforts to secure her freedom. He and his associates seem rather to have accepted that they had been mistaken. Perhaps Ann Gelston did run into more heat than she deserved. Granted, too, the Dwight household had been subjected to a terrifying ordeal, for which whoever was responsible, whether a drunken white sailor or some hot-headed black protestor, was never called to account. But, as in 1833, when Grant had called the "Colored Brethren" together for the first time and succeeded in disseminating their views on the British abolition bill, and in 1834, when he had drawn public attention to the barring of blacks from juries, the summer of 1836 marked some small revolutions and affirmative steps.

For the first time, a "colored man" had arraigned a ranking member of society – a doctor and magistrate, no less – on a criminal charge and secured his conviction before four of his colleagues and an all-white jury. And three black "labourers," as the indictment so vaguely termed them, on trial before another all-white court, to which the white victims looked for retribution, cleared themselves of charges that they were violent troublemakers. Through it all, there was a general recognition that Grant had acted from disinterested motives. His star rose as no black star ever had over Montreal. "Mr Grant is, although differing with us in politics, an intelligent, industrious, and humane man of color," the *Vindicator* had remarked in July.[100] In this rare, public acknowledgment of black intelligence, industry, and humanity, we may see an antidote to the perverted language used in old slave-sale advertisements, as in the very last one, for Charlotte, the "excellent Negro Wench," almost forty years before – "She has no fault, and is very honest, sober and industrious" – where the praise was meant to seal her condemnation to slavery.

A POLITICAL COLOURING

If there was a fly in Grant's anointment, it was politics. For some, the legal contests were a cover for political skirmishing. The *Vindicator*'s brief encomium hinted at this in noting that Grant's political views were at odds with those of the newspaper, edited by Papineau lieutenant Edmund Bailey O'Callaghan.[101] They were equally at odds with those of his lawyer, Perrault, the young Patriote member of the Legislative Assembly for Vaudreuil, where he had been elected in 1834, and a writer for the Patriote newspaper *La Minerve*. Indeed, Perrault probably wrote, or dictated, *La Minerve*'s coverage of Grant's three court cases, in which he himself was a front-line participant. He would die at the age of twenty-eight, fighting British regulars at St-Denis in the Rebellion of 1837.[102] His older brother, Louis, printer of the *Vindicator*, would spend the rebellions holed up in Vermont, as would Patriote hero Ludger Duvernay, editor of *La Minerve,* who also happened to be the foreman of the grand jury that indicted Arnoldi. Vermont-born lawyer Charles Dewey Day may have been induced by old business ties between his father and the Gelstons to represent Ann Gelston at the habeas corpus hearing in June, but he was also a prominent and outspoken Tory, eager to dispel notions that American expatriates in Lower Canada were all Patriote sympathizers.[103] As we can see, Daniel Arnoldi, who was at once Gelston's doctor and the magistrate who ordered the arrest of her maid, was not the only one who played a dual role in the affair. His conviction for assault was a victory for Grant and the blacks of Montreal, but it was also a coup for the Patriotes, who obviously relished the thought of bagging a magistrate considered a puppet of the oligarchy, thus giving the Tories a black eye.[104] As the *Vindicator* said in reporting on the charge against Arnoldi, "A long time has the community demanded some improvement in the Magistracy of this city."[105] And, as the author of a sketch of lawyer Perrault's life said, "He waged a relentless war on the judges, magistrates and public servants who, through their venality and dispiriting influence, dishonoured the positions which they occupied."[106] On one level, the issue was a black one; on another, it was white.

Daniel Arnoldi is remembered as the founding president of the College of Physicians and Surgeons of Lower Canada, forerunner of the Quebec body of that name;[107] Charles Dewey Day, in the stones of Chancellor Day Hall at McGill University, with which he was long associated; Ludger Duvernay as the founder of the patriotic St-Jean-Baptiste Society, whose headquarters bear his name; Edmund Bailey O'Callaghan for his voluminous and valuable historical publications as the New York State archivist; and Charles Ovide Perrault as a tragic young hero of an unfinished revolution. As for Betsy Freeman, she was soon forgotten. So was Grant, after his death from a skull fracture a few hours after he was thrown from his horse on the night of 20 August 1838 as he rode home from the races. "Mr Grant was a man of colour, but respectable and upright," *L'Ami du peuple,* an establishment newspaper, observed in what was at once a eulogy of the man and a libel of his race.[108]

TEN

Shoulder to Shoulder, Arm in Arm

Blacks and whites could be partners in crime, as we saw in the case of Warren Glossen and his band of burglars. The criminal underworld was thus a place where the wall of prejudice was sometimes breached, and where ability, reliability and determination to get the job done were qualifications that trumped considerations of skin colour. In licit enterprises, too, blacks and whites worked together – on steamboats, on timber rafts, in the fur trade, in hotels and restaurants, in domestic service, etc. – but mostly at arm's length, with blacks routinely excluded from positions of power and trust. In two areas, however – apprenticeship and intermarriage – racial barriers were lowered or at times fell away completely. It is difficult to gauge the extent of the racial mixing that occurred here, since the racial identity of the parties is not always clear. Gauging society's reaction to interracial unions and "miscegenation" is also problematic: for the parties concerned, the simple fact of entering into such a union spoke volumes, but society's views on the subject were rather muffled.

Apprenticeships were the trade schools of the day. The relationship between master and apprentice was often closer than that between a master and hired domestic servant. In the latter case the master sometimes knew little more than the servant's name, and their respective roles were essentially to command and to obey. The role of the apprentice, on the other hand, was to learn, and the master's to impart knowledge and skills. The responsibilities of each were spelled out in a contract. The apprentice paid tuition not in cash but in service, by assisting the master in his or her trade or occupation or, in the case of some female apprentices, by helping the mistress to keep house. In

Blacks and whites stand shoulder to shoulder to keep foxhunters from riding across a farm in this "real scene in Montreal" by British sporting artist Henry Alken (1785–1851).

return, master or mistress generally supplied the apprentice's basic needs for shelter, food, clothing, laundry, etc. For our purposes, the key difference between apprenticeship and schooling in Montreal up to 1840 was that, although there were no black schoolteachers, the teacher of an apprentice could be black.

Occupational training was not the sole educational function of apprenticeships. In several cases, it is a telling sign of the hopes that illiterate parents entertained for their children that, in placing them with a master, they required that they be taught reading and writing. Some contracts even stipulated that the apprentice was to be spared from his regular duties to attend school. Besides offering this benefit of schooling, apprenticeships often operated as a social coping mechanism for parents who were unable to care for their offspring. The placement of children, especially the very young, often resulted from the death or prolonged absence of one or both parents, or some other major change in the family's circumstances. Apprenticeships, in such cases, served as something close to foster care.

BLACK TEACHERS, WHITE PUPILS

In September 1805, shoemaker Narcisse Coudrin began a one-year apprenticeship with master shoemaker Benjamin Hagar, acknowledging himself as "not being Compleat Master of the said Arts." After only six months, master and apprentice agreed to cut short their arrangement. Coudrin must have possessed the skills he needed to make and repair footwear because, the following year, as a master shoemaker himself, it was his turn to take on apprentices: two white boys. Fifteen-year-old Antoine

Gravelle of the St-Laurent Suburb was apprenticed to him for four years on 2 April 1807, and Germain Auchu, thirteen years old, joined him, also for a four-year-term, the following 21 December. The older boy was indentured by his father for the purpose of learning the trade, but Auchu was placed by his godmother under circumstances that showed he needed not only a skill for the future but a home for the present. She had raised the boy since the age of two, she said; his father and sole support had since died, his only remaining relatives were at Quebec, and she could no longer bear the expense of caring for him. To "save him from distress" and to enable him to earn a living, she had got him to try his hand at shoemaking, which he seemed to enjoy; and so, with the boy's consent, she placed him with Coudrin.[1] It is noteworthy to find whites, so soon after the end of slavery, ready to place their trust in a black artisan. We might be tempted to think that Auchu's godmother was driven by desperation, and that she might not have turned to a black man given a choice. But this is a worst-case supposition: there is no hint in the boy's indenture of any preoccupation with Coudrin being black. In the case of the other apprentice, Antoine Gravelle, nothing suggests that his placement was anything but routine. The fact that Coudrin took these two boys under his wing tells us that his skills were recognized, that he did enough business to justify the hiring of two helpers, and that, while we have no idea of his income, he earned enough that he could afford to house, clothe and feed them.

In the 1830s, Alexander Grant had a succession of white apprentices, beginning, as far as can be determined, in October 1833 when he took on James Taylor for three years as an apprentice barber-hairdresser. No deed of apprenticeship has come to light for Alexander McPherson, but in June 1835 a court found him guilty of deserting Grant's service and ordered him to return within twenty-four hours. McPherson failed to comply, and Grant sought to have him arrested. The incident shows how seriously masters, black or white, took the enforcement of apprenticeship contracts. Grant may have tried a different working arrangement in the wake of this incident: while he seems to have taken on another white apprentice in 1836, he also hired George Nixon, a black man, who worked and lived with him. This is one of only three known instances before 1840 in which a black employer had a black employee, the others being John Trim's employment of Catherine Guillet as a servant in the first two decades of the century, and Richard Thompson's employment of Ace Gabriel at his pastry shop in 1818. In the summer of 1837, Grant hired fourteen-year-old William Pennell as an apprentice; the boy was supposed to remain with him until he reached the age of majority, but the indenture was cancelled by mutual consent that November. Grant's next apprentice appears to have been a boy named Whalon or Whalen, who was probably Irish. On 12 February 1838, the boy's mother, Mary Whalon, accused Grant and his wife of assaulting her when she "entered the shop of One Alexander Grant situated in Notre Dame Street of this City, for the purpose of seeing her child." Up to this point, all of Grant's apprentices appear to have been English-speaking, like Grant and his wife. But to draw a French-speaking clientele or to accommodate those among his customers who spoke French, it made sense to hire an apprentice who spoke the language. Mary Whalon's stormy visit seems to have decided Grant. The very next day, he advertised for a new apprentice, a bilingual boy of fourteen or fifteen with good recommendations. "A Canadian boy would be preferred," he indicated, meaning French-Canadian.[2]

Robert Gordon and James Smith, two other black barber-hairdressers who set up shop in the second half of the 1830s, also took on white apprentices, beginning in the following decade. Gordon hired a sixteen-year-old French Canadian, Pierre Tison, for four years from 4 February 1842, and Smith hired his first apprentice, fifteen-year-old Moïse Gosselin, for two years beginning on 1 May that same year. No other apprentices indentured to Gordon are known, but Smith continued to have white apprentices – as many as three at a time – for the next three decades, the last one hired for five years in the spring of 1873.[3]

English-born James Grantham, a schemer of some sophistication despite his illiteracy,[4] seems to have begun his career in Montreal as a barber (perhaps working for Grant) and may have lived with the Grants before his marriage in December 1835. He had set up home in the Quebec Suburb in the spring of 1836[5] and was established as a tobacconist before the end of the decade. In May 1839, he hired French Canadian Alexandre Chaland as a journeyman tobacconist for five months. He also had another French Canadian, Joseph Champagne, working for him then, either as an apprentice or as an employee: that July, he accused Champagne of deserting his service.[6] Grantham would employ a succession of white workers or apprentices until his death in 1861. In April 1841, he took on sixteen-year-old Joseph Silvan; in May, he took on another apprentice, Charles Renaud, about nineteen, who remained with him only until 1 May 1842. At about the same time, he hired tobacconist Pierre Lonay for one year to "make segars at four & six pence per thousand and plugs (twelve to a pound) at four & six pence per hundred pounds." In the spring of 1843, he hired journeyman George Knower for four months to make cigars at 5 pence per hundred for the first two months and 6 pence per hundred for the last two. On June 1845, he hired twenty-one-year-old John Lappin as an apprentice tobacconist for two years, but Lappin quit two months later, complaining that Grantham had neglected to teach him the business.[7]

Whether it was that he thought himself hard done by, that his illiteracy left him with a chip on his shoulder, or that he was chronically disputatious by nature, Grantham seemed to get into spats, prosecutions, or lawsuits with practically everyone he dealt with, including his landlords, his tenants, and even his wife. In some cases, he seems to have been provoked or to have been the victim of injustice. In May 1838, for example, he complained twice that he had been beaten by grocer Thomas Panton. Both complaints seem to relate to the same incident on 9 May, when he had gone to the store of Panton & Foster "to ask for some articles belonging to him."[8] The following November, he laid a charge of assault against Alexander Grant's widow, Celia Farley. His complaint has not been found, but she had to post a £20 security for her promise to appear in court in January 1839, to keep the peace, and to be of good behaviour toward Grantham.[9] It is difficult to conceive of the recently widowed Celia Farley springing at Grantham, if she did so, without provocation. In the summer of 1839, he accused a layabout of stealing 2¾ pounds of snuff from him.

A police constable spotted the man in the market trying to sell the snuff and arrested him on suspicion. He was indicted that October, but the grand jury found no bill.[10] In Grantham's estimation, race was at the root of an incident that occurred in 1840. He filed a complaint that summer alleging that a Thomas Cawthorn, often drunk, was "in the habit of swearing and screaming at Deponent and impedes and incommodes peaceable inhabitants and particularly the persons in Deponents employ. That the pretext of the said Hawthorn [sic] for interfering habitually with deponent is that Deponent is a man of color." Flavien Paquette, who worked as Grantham's clerk and lived in his house in the Quebec Suburb, reported that, on the evening of 23 July, Cawthorn had shown up at the door of Grantham's store and, learning that Grantham was absent, asked Paquette to filch a cigar for him – Grantham would never know. The episode ended with Cawthorn being obliged to post a £20 bond to keep the peace.[11]

Testimony in a civil court case in 1843 offers a glimpse into Grantham's household and business. He was identified as a wholesale and retail tobacconist, and a married man, although his wife was not living with him. He had two children with him, said to be eight and five years old, presumably his daughters Julie and Mary Rebecca.[12] The only woman living in the house was Elizabeth Anderson, a twenty-six-year-old widow who, besides being Grantham's live-in housekeeper, tended his shop. She had a seven-year-old child with her. She had been with Grantham since about 1839. "There is on the first flat Five rooms, namely the shop room the Kitchen the Parlour, the dining room and the bedroom [...] There are three other apartments in the upper part of Mr Grantham's House." He employed seven people – four men and three women, all whites, it seems. Besides Anderson, the women were Rosa and Margaret Welsh, who worked at the house but did not lodge there. Of the four male employees, two were clerks; the other two, though their duties were not specified in the testimony, must have been tobacconists.[13]

Prince Phillips, a Grantham acquaintance, was another black Montrealer who had at least one white apprentice. Phillips, who had worked as a steamboat waiter in the fall of 1837 and then found a job as a waiter at the Exchange Coffee House, was accused of theft by the owner of that hostelry in the fall of 1838. Grantham acted as one of his sureties when he was released on £50 bail.[14] The charge was dropped a few months later. Phillips then set up as a joiner and cabinet-maker. In the summer of 1840, he filed a complaint against his white apprentice, John Jeremiah Collins, for disobedience and for disturbing the peace by "swearing, screaming and calling out murder" while drunk.[15]

WHITE TEACHERS, BLACK PUPILS

Of course, it was more common to find white masters with black apprentices than the reverse. In the decade before the British Conquest, Jean François Dominique *dit* Mentor, a freed slave, had trained as a silversmith. Mentor's owner, merchant Dominique Nafrechoux, was a resident of Longue-Pointe in 1745 when, feeling his age, he filed with a notary a sealed note, dated 30 September 1744, providing for Mentor's eventual freedom:

> I Nafrechoux certify having granted his freedom to Jean François Dominique Mentor my Negro from the moment of my death as a reward for the good services he has done me and for the devotion and faithfulness that he always has shown in my service. It is my intention and that he take all that is of use to him, leaving him master of himself to go where he pleases while going on living as an honest man and taking care to pray God for me.[16]

Nafrechoux died in 1748, and on 22 April 1749, Mentor, now free, apprenticed himself for six years to silversmith Ignace Delezenne, a maker of church vessels, tableware, and the trade silver used by fur traders. Delezenne, who kept a shop on the Place d'Armes, was to provide all his basic needs as well as to pay him 150 livres at the expiry of the apprenticeship. Delezenne moved to Quebec in mid-1752, and Mentor followed. If his apprenticeship ran to term, it would have ended in 1755. At Quebec, on 15 May 1756, Delezenne hired Mentor as a journeyman silversmith for two years at 200 livres a year; Mentor could stay on for a third year at 300 livres, if he wished. There is a suggestion in this contract that their earlier working arrangement had Mentor acting as a general dog's body as well as learning the trade; the new contract specified that Mentor would work only at the operation of the shop. Perhaps it was to take care of the other chores that, on 4 May 1757, Delezenne bought a black slave named Pierre, about eighteen years old, for 1,192 livres. Both Mentor and Delezenne practised their trade under the French and under the British. Mentor was identified as a silversmith, about fifty years old, at his death at Montreal on 8 May 1773.[17]

William Becket, believed to be the son of black Loyalist Peter Becket and his wife Mary Richardson, was nine and half years old when he was placed with merchant Levy Solomon as a domestic servant in March 1793. The boy was to remain with Solomon until he turned 21. Solomon undertook to send him to school for four years – between the ages of 12 and 16 – to learn the three Rs.[18] Presumably William's mother had died, since the following year Becket married Marie Denoyer, with whom he had cohabited for some time. In March 1794, four months before their wedding, they had had a son, Joseph, who lived only two days.[19] Their relations appear to have been rocky after that unhappy episode. In mid-June, Denoyer, then employed as a servant by Samuel Kipp, a Loyalist who had served as a captain in Delancey's Rangers during the American War of Independence, accused Becket of abusing her. She declared that "as a result of the poor conduct of her husband and the disorderly state of his house, she was obliged to leave him, though she was ill at the time, to try to earn an honest living elsewhere – that for the last three months her husband has continually threatened to kill her."[20] Some reconciliation must have taken place, however, because they married on 11 July.

Apprenticeships of blacks became quite common after 1800. If nothing else, this suggests that, where work was concerned, the wall of prejudice was not so high or impenetrable that whites refused to pass on their skills to blacks. So Tobias Johnson, an illiterate "Negro man" born in Schenectady, New York, placed his ten-year-old son, Jean-Baptiste Johnson, as an apprentice farmer with Walter Chase of Chatham on the Ottawa River in May 1801. Chase was to have the boy taught to read and write, to provide him with "meat, drink, lodging, washing and wearing apparel fitting for such an apprentice, treat him with humanity as he would his own Son," and, at the end of his period of servitude, to give him two new suits of clothing – "one for Sunday wear and one for everyday wear" – and a two-year-old colt. In March 1805, John Door, "a Negro boy of this City," his age unspecified, bound himself as an apprentice and servant to Bartholomew Corrigan for two years "to learn how to trade in the Country." He was to get boarding and washing, plus thirty-one dollars a year, payable in monthly instalments.[21]

In the case of five-year-old Mary Ann and three-year-old James (alias Jacko), two children of Elizabeth Franklin, we may form some idea from their mother's circumstances of the reason they were apprenticed at such tender ages. When she placed both as apprentices on 28 May 1804, she was living in the St-Laurent Suburb and identified as Elizabeth, "commonly called Betsy, a Negro Wench, born as she declared in Connecticut, & brought up by one Jacob Henry there." Only a month earlier she had given birth to a boy, Joseph, whose father, identified as Carter, "neigre, journalier," was the man previously mentioned under the name Castor Jay. Jay was also the father of Elizabeth's son James, but not, it appears, of Mary Ann. On 24 April, at the very time that Joseph was born, Castor Jay was hired to work as a raftsman running timber cribs down from the Bay of Quinte in Upper Canada to Quebec. His departure would have left Elizabeth, with her three young children, in the lurch. This, we believe, would account for her placing the two older children as apprenticed servants a month later. Mary Ann was indentured to tailor Edward Dalton, of the Quebec Suburb, and was to remain in Dalton's service until she turned twenty-one. James was placed as a servant to tailor Nicolas Boissy, also of the Quebec Suburb, until he too turned twenty-one. Joseph, the newborn, died on 29 June. We hear no more of James, but Mary Ann's indenture seems to have been terminated early: in September 1806, when she was about to turn seven, she, now identified as the daughter of Elizabeth Franklin and Edward Green (who does not appear to have lived in Montreal), was indentured by her mother as a domestic servant to merchant Moses Carnahan and his wife, of the Bay of Quinte. Under the terms of her apprenticeship, Mary Ann was to remain with the Carnahans until 25 October 1817, her eighteenth birthday; she was to be "instructed in sewing reading and writing," and at the end of her eleven years of service, she was to get "a new suit of wearing apparel complete and also a bed and beding."[22]

Gabriel Johonnot, the son of distiller Caesar Johonnot, was fourteen when he was apprenticed by his mother to butcher and former tavern-keeper James Seabrook in 1807 for a term of seven years. He was to be paid £6 a year, in monthly instalments of ten shillings, with a severance payment of an extra £6 at the end of his term. He never received his £6 bonus, however, because the apprenticeship was cut short, and in June 1809 his mother placed him as a servant with merchant Moses Northrop. This arrangement also fell through. By March 1811, Gabriel Johonnot was living at the Hôtel-Dieu and working there as an *infirmier*, a nurse or orderly.[23]

Isaac Newton Wily, named after his godfather, Isaac Newton, whose brushes with the legal system are detailed in the previous chapter, was only four years old when he was apprenticed to a furrier. Born on 17 December 1804 to "labourer" William Wily,[24] a native of Philadelphia, and Peggy Christie (alias Margaret July), he was placed by his father as a servant to George Clark in the summer of 1809. At the time, his mother seems to have been absent, and his father gravely ill. William Wily had been a patient in hospital for a month in April–May and had then been re-admitted for another month in June. Hospital records show that he returned again on 25 July. The deed of apprenticeship for his son was drawn up at the hospital on 3 August. William Wily died there a little more than three weeks later. Under the terms of Isaac's indenture, he was to remain with Clark until he turned twenty-one. At the end of his sixteen-odd years of service, Clark was to give him two new suits of clothes and $40. In June 1815, Clark, about to return to England, transferred the boy, then ten years old, to merchant tailor James Burr Prime, who took over Clark's obligations under the apprenticeship deed of 1809.[25]

Charles Parker was apparently almost six years old in the summer of 1813 when he, too, was apprenticed by his father, Thomas Parker (alias Thomas Parker Irving), "a person of Color," until he reached the age of majority. He was indentured to tavern-keeper Joshua Whitney of Quebec as a house servant. Among other things, Whitney was to give the boy "schooling to fit him for an ordinary education" (*sic*).[26] Here again, as with Isaac Wily, death had a hand. The boy's twenty-six-year-old mother, Penelope Lennox, had died on 28 June, probably from complications of childbirth: her daughter, Susannah, born on 19 June, outlived her by just one day.[27] Thomas Parker was to take a new wife the following January, in the person of Patty Williams (John Trim was a witness), but it seems that he may have worked at some occupation that kept him away from Montreal, making it impossible for him to take care of his children. Indeed, the absence of birth records in Montreal for any of his four children but Susannah suggests that the family may have moved from the hinterland to Montreal around the time of her birth. Two years after Charles's indenture, a tutor, or guardian, had to be appointed by the court for the purpose of placing his younger brother, Alvin, then said to be about five, as a domestic servant with hatter Jabez Dean DeWitt. The court record did not identify Alvin's parents, except to say that his father was out of the province and his mother dead. When William, the eldest child of the family, died at the Hôpital-Général of the Grey Nuns in 1818 at the age of thirteen and a half, his parents, again unnamed, were said to be "résidans dans les pays d'en haut" (living in the upper country).[28]

Death was once more a player when William Brusler Fortune, the fifteen-year-old son of Titus Fortune and Catharine Crowell, was apprenticed to shoemaker Richard Adams in 1834. His father had died when William was not yet one year old.

His mother had apparently remarried, but her second husband, Jonathan Moss, was also dead by 1834. That summer saw the return of the cholera that had wreaked such havoc two years earlier. Besides the fact that her son was of age to learn a trade – he must have had some schooling since he knew how to write – Catherine Crowell may have thought it advisable to waste no time in providing for his future as best she could. In July, she applied to the court to be formally appointed his guardian, and on the 16th of that month she had him squared away until the age of twenty-one. She died two weeks later.[29]

One might have doubts about the identification of apprentice shoemaker Ebert Weldin as a "mulatto," since the only evidence that has come to light that he or anyone in his family was coloured is a published notice of his flight from his master, Loyalist John Tieple, at Sault-au-Récollet in 1792.[30] But "mulatto" was Tieple's word. He knew Ebert Weldin, saw him in the flesh, and must have had some reason to label him so – which we, knowing Weldin only from old papers, are in no position to refute. (Might he have been part Indian?) If we accept that Ebert Weldin was a "mulatto," we find that the apprenticeship deeds for him and his siblings, all made when slavery still flourished, form a series showing that their father, "yeoman" James Weldin, gave some serious thought to their future.

On 2 February 1789, Mary Weldin, said to be ten years old, was apprenticed to innkeeper and former Indian interpreter Simon Clark and his wife, Eve, for seven and a half years. She was to be taught housewifery and reading, and to be kept properly fed and clothed. At the end of her term, she was to be given two new suits of clothing, "one for Sundays and the other for working days with suitable linen," as well as "a Good Milk Cow and a Bible." She ended up staying with Clark for eleven years or so; she knew John Trim, who moved into the property next door to Clark's on St-Augustin Street in 1798.[31] Ebert, the elder of the Weldin siblings, was the next to find a place, three months later. He was apprenticed to Tieple on 1 May, at the age of sixteen, to learn the trade of shoemaker. Tieple, who had served as a sergeant in the King's Royal Regiment of New York in the American War of Independence, was a "master cordiner" (shoemaker) as well as an innkeeper and tanner. Ebert Weldin was to serve as his apprentice until he turned twenty-one. At the end of his apprenticeship, Tieple was to give him a complete set of shoemaker's tools as well as one full set of clothes – "Coat, waistcoat and breeches, hat, shoes, stockings with suitable linen."[32] Elizabeth Weldin, said to have been born in August 1780, would have been just shy of nine years old when she was apprenticed on 21 July 1789 to shoemaker William Clark and his wife, Elizabeth, until she turned eighteen. Like her sister Mary, she was to be taught housewifery, reading, and writing. But her father did not insist on as much of a "trousseau" for her as for her older sister: the Clarks were to send her out into the world at the end of her apprenticeship with one new suit of clothes and a Bible.[33]

Within the space of just over six months, then, three of the four children in the family, ranging in age from almost nine to sixteen years, were provided for. This burst of placements hints at some change in the family fortunes. It is probable that the children's mother, identified in the deeds of indenture only as Anna, had died recently and that this had spurred the widowed James Weldin to find places for his children. It is also possible that his intended remarriage had something to do with Ebert Weldin's escapade in 1792. On Sunday, 7 October, Ebert and a French-Canadian man who worked for Tieple as a tanner and currier ran off. Tieple offered a $20 reward for their return.[34] Less than a year later, his father, identified as a master cooper of Ste-Rose on Île Jésus (Laval), married Marie Anne Amringer of St-Eustache. She was eighteen years old, younger than her stepson.[35]

In the meantime, Elie, the last of the children of James Weldin's first marriage, had been taken care of. On 13 March 1792, at the age of sixteen, he was placed as a servant to Captain John Jones of Augusta, Upper Canada, until 10 June 1797, which was probably his twenty-first birthday. Jones was the brother of the occasional slave-trader Daniel Jones of Brockville, and of Dr Solomon Jones of Augusta, who as a member of the Upper Canada House of Assembly in 1798 would vote in favour of reopening the colony's borders to slave imports.[36] Elie Weldin was to receive the usual necessities during his apprenticeship, and quite a package on his graduation:

> a Working suit of Cloathes & a Sunday suit; – Likewise a Cow and a pair of Stears of about two years old. Promises the said Capn. Jones to Endeavour to Draw from Government a Land for the said Elie Welding, his Servant when his time will be Expired, and if he Cannot succeed to Draw said Land from Government, he promises by these presents to Give him his said Servant one hundred acres of his own Lands at the River Reydow [Rideau].[37]

Through these apprenticeships, James Weldin evidently hoped to see his children well launched on their adult life, the boys with a trade and the basic tools or facilities that they would need, the girls trained in housewifery, with not only domestic skills but also the ability to read and write, something their brothers lacked.

It was a very different kind of skill that John Wright, the only surviving child of Catherine Guillet and William Wright, was to learn. One may wonder whose idea it was to apprentice this son of former slaves to a gilder. Odds are that it was his choice: there was an elegance to his signature which, besides indicating that he had been to school and practised handwriting, hints at an artistic bent. Perhaps his mother had something to do with it if, as it appears, she had spent her youth as a slave of the artist François Malepart de Beaucourt. John Wright had just turned sixteen at the end of 1839 when his mother and stepfather, Jacob Abdella, applied to the court to be appointed his legal guardians. The application, misstating his age as seventeen (someone scratched out the word *seize* and substituted *dix sept*), was granted on 10 December; the next day, he was placed with gilder John Smith until he turned twenty-one. Because he was said to be a year older than he really was, that meant an engagement of four years rather than five. He was to get "sufficient meat, drink & lodging fitting for an apprentice," and to be paid £5 the first year, his wages increasing by £1 each year, up to £8 in his fourth and final year.[38] There is no information on his years of apprenticeship; that he made the grade can be deduced from the fact that he did later set up as a gilder. The first indication of this comes in the fall of 1848, after his mother, abandoned by Abdella, had been reduced to selling some of her furniture. Cook David Bristow bought it, no doubt as an accommodation. A month later, John Wright, identified as Jean Baptiste Wright, gilder, bought the furniture back from Bristow for the price that he had paid – £3 9s 7½d. The Montreal city directory for 1854 listed John Wright, gilder, at College and Inspector streets, the family home that had been given to his father in 1820.[39] He then moved to Quebec, where he took out a full-page advertisement in the city directory for 1855–56:[40]

JOHN WRIGHT,
CARVER & GILDER,
MANUFACTURER OF
PICTURE AND MIRROR FRAMES,
WINDOW CORNICES &c, &c,
CHURCH, STEAMBOAT & GENERAL
DECORATOR,
LOOKING GLASSES RE-SILVERED,
FRAMES REPAIRED & RE-GILT,
MAPS, MOUNTED & VARNISHED,
and all sorts of job work executed with despatch, in a superior style
of workmanship and at the lowest possible remunerating prices.

No. 7,
St John Street, without

No example of Wright's work is known. The census of January 1861 found him and his mother living in the St-Jean Ward of Quebec. It identified him as a gilder, born in Montreal, coloured, living in a single-storey board house. He had been baptized a Presbyterian, but the census identified him as a Roman Catholic. His age was said to be twenty-nine – he was, in fact, thirty-seven.[41] His mother died in November 1862. Three years later, when he was almost forty-two, he married a white woman and acquired an instant family – two boys, four-year-old Hilarion Lazare Réal Trudel and Charles Hector Michel Trudel, age two and half, sons of his wife, Anna Perrin, from her first marriage. Wright and Perrin had a daughter of their own in April 1866 called Marie Catherine Anna Wright. Her baptismal record spelled the name Writh, and identified the father as William Writh, gilder.[42]

SOME MARRIAGES

The American abolitionist Samuel Ringgold Ward, speaking of white attitudes toward blacks in Ontario after the passage of the American Fugitive Slave Law of 1850, noted what had struck him as an anomaly during his own residence there in 1851–53. He had never detected the slightest trace of "Negro-hate," he said, in anyone "recognized ... as a gentleman. Either that class do not participate in the feeling, or their good sense and good taste and good breeding forbid its appearance."[43] Those who did harbour feelings of "Negro-hate" were mainly the lower-class Canadians – yet they intermarried with blacks:

> while you get so much evidence of the aversion betwixt these classes, you see it to be no strange thing, but a very common thing, for a black labourer to have a white wife, of a like class. In other circumstances, one would not wonder at it; but considering the bitter feeling of the whites, it is, to say the least of it, an anomaly, that blacks should propose on the one hand, and that whites should accept on the other. However, the history of poor human nature and its actions is full of these anomalies. It is certainly without pain that I add, these matches, so far as I know, are happy ones. How far this anomaly may tend in future to correct the prejudice, I cannot tell.[44]

To complete the parallel, we might add that while the lower classes from which the "Negro-haters" allegedly sprang also produced their opposite, members of the upper classes, ostensibly free of racial prejudice, never deigned to marry blacks.

With some qualification, this view of intermarriage in Canada West is also a fair representation of the situation at Montreal in the period that concerns us. We have seen that some who would pass for gentlemen, men like Charles Kadwell and Pierre J.O. Chauveau, were not above the private expression of racial prejudices, although perhaps "good taste" did serve to mask their sentiments from public view. It is a fact that most marriages between whites and blacks up to 1840 involved working-class men and women. It is also a fact that most of these, like John Wright's marriage in 1865, were unions of black males and white females. These matches, as far as we know, were not all happy ones; they were like all marriages – some happy, some not, some a little of both. For example, John Trim's second marriage, to Fleurie Deniger, would have to be classed among the unhappy ones, although it seems that this had little to do with racial considerations and a great deal to do with the disparity in age between husband and wife, and with the fact that, in Trim's estimation, no woman could ever measure up to Charlotte, his first wife and soulmate.

We can only speculate as to how these unions came about: whether the parties knowingly defied convention, or whether they simply did not see race as a barrier. In the same way that the history of slavery is as much a study of white attitudes as of black exploitation, these mixed marriages – "that blacks should propose on the one hand, and that whites should accept" – were a two-sided coin. We might assume that the reason black men married white women is that there was a shortage of eligible black females, and they had no choice. But white women had a choice; there was no shortage of white males, yet they accepted the hand of a black man. If it were to be suggested, on the other hand, that black males chose to marry white women because, in the context of the times, this was a step up, particularly for a former slave, would it not have been a step down for a white woman – and why would she have taken that step? And if, as occasionally happened, a white man proposed and a black woman accepted, it is difficult to see how either party would be motivated to enter into such a union by a desire to rise in the world or to "make a statement" about race. It does seem that mutual attraction, practical needs, or both trumped racial considerations. Picture, for example, the plight of Caesar Johonnot's widow, Margaret Campbell, in the summer of 1800: she had lost both her husband and her home, had two young children, and was expecting a third. In her situation, a helping hand in the shape of a breadwinner, black or white, was a matter of life and death, we might say. Even in less dramatic circumstances, marriage was often a matter of practical necessity; for single parents, it was practically essential. The general impression today that intermarriage between blacks and whites was taboo is a notion that may say as much about our own prejudices – about race and class, or about the backwardness that it pleases us to see in those who inhabit the lantern-lit past – and needs to be reassessed.

Whether anyone in Quebec – churches, public officials, families – frowned on such unions, they went on. No law proscribed them. There is no evidence of obstructions placed in their way, that anyone was animated by "Negro-hate" to the point of threatening the couples with violence,[45] or that they were otherwise ostracized for it by their families or by whites or blacks in general. It may be, however, that a white woman who was the widow of a black man, particularly if she had children of mixed race, was marked for life as an unsuitable wife for a white man. Suspicions in this regard are aroused by the case of Fleurie Deniger who, after the death of her first husband, Trim, was married three times, each time to a coloured man. But her exceptional story cannot be taken as representative.

How many such marriages took place? They were frequent enough that, in researching the lives of black Montrealers at this time, one cannot take for granted that the spouse of a black man or woman was also black. In his brief experience in Ontario in the mid-nineteenth century, Ward found interracial unions to be "a very common thing." In his study of slavery, Marcel Trudel counted forty-five unions between whites and slaves or former slaves in the hundred years from 1713 to 1812 across French Canada; thirty-four involved an Indian spouse, eleven a black one.[46] The latter included the marriage of the slave François William and Élisabeth Mondina at Beauport in 1783, discussed in an earlier chapter, and that of the former de Lotbinière slave Louis Joseph *dit* Pompé in 1809 to Catherine Robidoux of Oka, glimpsed earlier. There are scattered references in the preceding pages to several exogamous unions between blacks and Indians as well as between blacks and whites. Leaving aside the relations of blacks and Amerindians, a field of study in its own right, here is a recapitulation of those black-and-white marriages in chronological order, along with others not yet mentioned, of persons who lived at Montreal at some time or married there. There seem to have been twenty-one in all, involving twenty black spouses (one of them, Joseph François Demarin, appears to have married twice). These twenty were sixteen males and four females. In several cases, although it seems reasonably clear that the parties were joined in a formal union, no record can be found. In the case of Jacob Smith and Catherine Coll, it is fortunate that the minister who performed the ceremony at his home testified to that effect in court, as no other record of their wedding exists. In other such cases, determining the approximate year of the wedding depends on fragmentary evidence such as the birth date of a first known child or some other such indication. (In the following list, parentheses containing the mention of a single year signify that the child was born and died in the same year.)

ca 1782 Peter Canon, a black man from Virginia, married Marie Louise Loignon. He died on 16 October 1797, said to be fifty years old. She died on 24 April 1823, said to be about sixty. Children: François (alias Pierre, Pitre; 1783), Jean Joseph (alias Pierre; 1784), anonymous (1785), François (1787), Marie Amable (b. 1788), Marie Louise (b. 1791) and Claude (b. 1797). The first four children died within a year; the date of death of the last three is unknown.

ca 1785 Charles Gaspar, alias Jean Gaspard, "nègre Protestant," married Marguerite Tessier. Children: Jean (b. 1786) and Marguerite Amable (b. 1792).

ca 1790 Joseph François Demarin, black farmer, married Angélique Lavallée *dit* Jolibois. No children, apparently. Demarin married again in 1827.

1791 American-born mulatto Catherine Coll married Jacob Smith on 17 October. She died on 11 September 1817, said to be fifty-one. Her husband's date of death is unknown (he was perhaps the Jacob Smith who died "in the Protestant poorhouse" of Montreal on 31 March 1826 at age seventy-three). Children: Catherine (1798), Christopher (1799), John Frederick (1800), and Henry Charles (1801).

1793 Henry Taffe (or Taaffe), "free mulatto," hired as a servant for one year by Simon McTavish in 1798, married Rose Moreau at Quebec on 7 March. Children: Marie-Thérèse (1794–1797), Marguerite (1796), and Henriette (b. 1799).

1794 Black cooper Jean Barthélemy of Quebec married Ursule Démet (Demette, Desmettes) of Montreal on 30 June. They lived at Quebec. They had no children of their own, but on 12 September 1796 they virtually adopted a seven-month-old mixed-race girl, whose mother, a black woman identified as Baid, lived aboard the ship *Le Favori* and placed her daughter with the Barthélemys until the girl reached age twenty-one, because she did not have the means to care for her. Barthélemy and his wife had the girl baptized on 18 September, under the name Ursule. (In 1799, Barthélemy was a witness at the wedding at Quebec of his friend, the former black slave Joseph Beaumenil, to the white servant woman Marie Thérèse Laisné.) Barthélemy was still living in September 1836, but Démet appears to have died before then.

1794 Widower Peter Becket, Loyalist son of blacks William Becket and Mary Wright of Philadelphia, married Marie Denoyer on 11 July. (Becket's first wife was a Mary Richardson. They were married on 26 January 1783 and had a son, William, born that same year. It is not clear whether Mary Richardson was black or white.) Children: Joseph (1794). Peter Becket died on 25 July 1809, said to be fifty-eight.

ca 1795 George Burns, the future hangman at Quebec, married Josephe Dubreuil, daughter of François Dubreuil and Brigitte Henry of Chambly. In 1798, Burns and his wife were residents of Montreal, where their daughter, Marie Joseph, was born in June. Their daughter Marguerite was born at Quebec in 1804. Burns died on 10 October 1806, said to be about fifty. Children: Marie Joseph (b. 1798), Marguerite (b. 1804).

1797 Jacques Williamson, carpenter, American-born mulatto, son of John Williamson and Mary Mangelay (alias Marie Mosolé), married Marie Louise Bleau, daughter of François Bleau and Marie-Françoise Jasmin of Ste-Anne-de-Mascouche, on 8 May. He was said to be twenty years old, she twenty-four. She died on 6 August 1845 at age seventy three, he on 23 July 1850, said to be seventy-two. Children: Jacques Louis (b. 1797), Marie Louise (b. 1799), Marie Emélie (1801–1870), Jacques (died 1803), Jacques-Noël (1803–1809), Emélie (b. 1806).

1799 Marie Angélique Price, a coloured woman from Maryland said to be twenty-six years old, married Augustin Labadie, carpenter, on 25 November. Children: Marie Angélique (1800–1801), Marie Victoire (1801), Marie Julie, alias Marie Rose (1802), Marie Émilie (1803), Marie Louise (1804–1805), Louis Jacques Augustin (1806) and Antoine Casimir (b. 1807). They left Montreal for parts unknown in early 1808.

1802 Caesar Hunkings, black labourer, married the widow Marie Marguerite Colleret *dit* Bourguignon on 27 June. Hunkings died on 28 September 1807, said to be about sixty years old. His widow died in March 1838 at age seventy-nine. Children: Marie Françoise (1804).

ca 1805 Thomas Snider (alias Scheneider), "nègre," formerly of Terrebonne, married Marie Picard. Children: Charles (died 1807).

ca 1806 Marie Anne Houldin, daughter of Richard Houldin, private in the New Brunswick Regiment of Fencible Infantry (later the 104th Regiment), and former black slave Marie Anne Ambroise, married Andrew Holiday of Roxbury, Scotland, also a private in the New Brunswick Regiment. Marie Anne Houldin, still living in 1851, was only thirteen when their daughter Marie Louise was born in 1806. They may have had other children later, somewhere else than at Montreal.

1818 William Thompson, "nègre," son of the late Pierre (Peter?) Thompson and Marie Goudé, possibly a soldier in the 8th Regiment in the War of 1812, then a servant and cook at Berthier, married Desanges Blais of Yamachiche on 31 August. Thompson died in an accident on 19 June 1828, at the reputed age of 32. Children: Marguerite Eulalie (1819–1909), Éléonore (1820–1900), and François (1824–1825). Marguerite Eulalie Thompson was married at Berthier on 14 September 1847 to white farmer Félix Clément.

1820 Marie Euphrosine Houldin, daughter of the late Richard Houldin and Marie Anne Ambroise, married carter Martin Parent, a widower, on 31 January. Euphrosine died before October 1850. Her husband died on 23 July 1834. Children: Joseph (b. 1821), Emilie (b. 1822), Marguerite (b. 1825), Brigitte

(b. 1826), Jean Baptiste (b. 1829), Marie Euphrosine (1830–1838) and Louis Moyse, alias Martin (1834).

1826 John Trim, slave freed in 1793, childless widower, married Fleurie Deniger, a minor, daughter of the late Toussaint Deniger, labourer, and Marianne Laventure *dit* Beaudin, on 2 April. Trim died on 26 January 1833, said to be seventy-eight. His wife, who went on to marry three more times, died on 23 November 1860, her age given as sixty-two (she was a minor at her wedding in 1826, so she would have been in her early to mid-fifties at her death). Children: Mary Ann Shuter (1825–1866), Henriette (b. 1827), and Charlotte (b. 1829).

1827 Joseph François Demarin, black farmer, widower, married Angélique Filiatrault *dit* St Louis at St-Eustache after they had cohabited for many years. Demarin died on 22 September 1829, his age given as about 78. Children: Joseph and Angélique Demarin. At their wedding, the parents legitimized their two children. Joseph is believed to be the "illegitimate" boy christened Joseph (no family name) at St-François-de-Sales Church on Île Jésus (Laval) on 12 March 1802. Angélique's birthdate is unknown, but she was said to be of the age of majority on 24 October 1836 when, as Angélique Desmarais, she married Louis Dufour of Ste-Scholastique at St-Eustache. Her daughter, Sophie Dufour, married at Ste-Agathe on 22 August 1864 to Isaac Constantineau, was among the pioneer settlers of St-Faustin in the Laurentians.

1833 Robert Moore, widower, black servant, and steamboat waiter, married Fleurie Deniger, widow of John Trim, on 22 June 1833. Moore died on 6 February 1839. Deniger went on to marry a third time. Children: Robert (1836–1838).

1834 Solomon Molliston (or Molleston), a black barber and hairdresser believed to have come from New York, married Irish widow Bridget (Biddy) Conway on 2 December. Molliston died 23 January 1840. Children: Solomon (1834–1839); Solomon (1839–1840).

1835 James Grantham, from England, briefly a barber, then a tobacconist, married Mary Ann Ferris on 14 December. This was not a happy union. Grantham accused his wife of being a violent drunk and had her locked up four times in 1839–1840, for periods of six days to six weeks. In May 1840, she accused him of abuse, and he was bound to keep the peace. Nothing more has been found about Ferris after the birth of her son, James Jr, in 1841. Grantham later remarried. He died on 16 June 1861. Children of his marriage to Ferris: Julie (b. 1836), Rebecca (b. ca 1839), and James (b. 1841, appears to have died in infancy). Rebecca married James Harrison at the Wesleyan Methodist Church in Toronto on 31 December 1866.

1839 Paul Coffin, labourer and sailor, married twice-widowed Fleurie Deniger on 30 May. He died sometime before the summer of 1842, when his widow married a fourth time. Children: Marie Catherine Eulalie (b. 1839), known as Catherine or Emily Coffin.

Marguerite Eulalie Thompson, born at Berthier (Berthierville) in 1819, is the earliest Quebec-born coloured person of whom a photograph survives. The daughter of black cook William Thompson and his white wife, Desanges Blais, she married white farmer Félix Clément in 1847; they farmed at St-Gabriel-de-Brandon. After her husband's death in 1870, Eulalie and her children shuttled back and forth between St-Gabriel and the mill town of Woonsocket, Rhode Island, finally settling in Woonsocket, where she died on 27 April 1909. This undated photograph in the possession of her descendants shows her with her youngest child, Maxime (1864–1924).

To this list could be added some of the figures already mentioned as active in the early decades of the nineteenth century but who married (or remarried) after 1840. These would include:

1842 Joseph Thompson, son of Thomas and Anne Thompson of Schenectady, New York, married Marie Olive Ouellet, daughter of Germain Ouellet and Magdeleine Dumont of St-Pascal-de-Kamouraska, at Caughnawaga (Kahnawake) on 23 May. Born in the last decade or so of the eighteenth century, he seems to have moved to Canada in his youth and split his time between Montreal and the Mohawk reservation of Kahnawake before settling in Huntingdon around 1848. Thompson died on 3 July 1880, his age given as 100, but perhaps closer to 85. Children: Mary (b. ca 1850, died in childhood).

1842 Thrice-widowed Fleurie Deniger married James Carpenter, a coloured widower from Prince Edward Island, on 2 July. Deniger died on 23 November 1860. Carpenter went on to marry a Scottish widow, Mary Fleming, and died in 1875, at the reputed age of 84. Children: Mary Elizabeth (b. 1843).

1843 James Smith, hairdresser, married English-born Louisa Martin on 3 April. From 1840, he occupied the Notre-Dame Street shop that Alexander Grant had occupied in 1837–38. Children: Martha (ca 1849–1871), Charlotte (d. 1851), Benjamin (1851), Abby (1855–1863), Alfred (1858–1860) and Verbena (1862).

ca 1846 James Grantham, tobacconist, married Irish-born Eliza Gilchrist. They were later said to have eight children, although one appears to have been a daughter born to him and his first wife, Mary Ferris; in the absence of birth records for most of the others, one suspects that some were Gilchrist's children by a previous marriage.

1849 Charlotte Trim, youngest daughter of John Trim and Fleurie Deniger, married Irish-born carter Thomas Tinsley on 10 February. Tinsley's parents had died at Montreal in the cholera epidemic of 1832. Children: Flora (b. 1845?), Thomas Charles (b. 1849), Edmond Richard (b. 1852), Elizabeth (b. 1855), Amable (b. 1858), Marguerite (b. 1860), and William Henry (b. 1871).

1851 Peter Dago, dyer and scourer, born in New York state, son of Titus (alias Francis) Dago and Sara Knolstine (alias Nadine Day), married Scholastique Diller, of German and French-Canadian descent, daughter of Baptiste Diller and Marie St-Louis, on 18 September. Diller died on 22 April 1857. Dago remarried in 1865. Children: Mary Scholastique Philomène (1843–1872), Francisco (b. 1849), and Peter (1854–1858). The two older children, born out of wedlock, were legitimized at their parents' wedding.

1865 Peter Dago, widower, married Irishwoman Helen Coffey, the twenty-five-year-old daughter of Thomas Coffey and Helen Parke, on 7 August. Dago died on 16 August 1868 (buried under the name Peter Vago), his age said to be seventy-six. Children: Ellen Theresa Coffey (b. 1860), Peter (b. 1863), and Marie Jeanne (b. 1866) Dago.

1865 John Wright, gilder, son of former Montreal slaves Catherine Guillet and William Wright, married widow Anna Perrin at Quebec on 2 October. Children: Hilarion Lazare Réal Trudel (b. 1861) and Charles Hector Michel Trudel (b. 1863), sons of Perrin's first marriage; Marie Catherine Anna Wright (b. 1866).

If we were to count informal unions, we would have to add to the list such names as those of Reuben Thomas and Thérèse Masson, identified in 1793 as "Rubin Thomas otherwise called Jupiter a black Man, and one therese Maçon who lives with the said Jupiter as his wife." But there is no way of knowing when they began living together or how long their life together lasted. Thérèse Masson is believed to have died on 31 December 1832, but she and Thomas may have separated as early as 1793–94, when she exposed him as a receiver of stolen goods and accused him of beating her.[47]

PERSISTENT ENIGMAS

Persistent doubts about the racial identity of some figures render a study of interracial unions necessarily speculative. In earlier chapters, we encountered Jacob Smith and Augustin Labadie, who in the absence of any racial identification might be *presumed* white. Both men married women who were at least partly black. The racial identity of Halifax-born William Wright Sr (1804–1869), identified by his son, a medical doctor and priest, as "Creole," and whose wife was white, remains a mystery. There are also cases where it is not clear whether a wife was black or white. For example, at first glance it might seem that the woman identified at her wedding to Thomas Cockburn (alias Adam Cockburn) in 1809 as the widow Mary McArty was white.[48] But the records of the Hôtel-Dieu show that a forty-eight-year-old black man identified as Pitre Macarti – a French rendering of Peter McCarthy – was a patient there in May 1802, evidence of the presence of at least one McCarthy who was black.[49] It is possible that this Peter McCarthy was the father, or perhaps even the first husband, of Mary McArty. At her death in 1870, Mary McArty was buried under the name Marie Saint Martin.[50] This suggests a family connection with Jeanie (alias Jane, Geneviève) Martin, the wife of Jacob Simpson, a couple who were close to the Cockburns. When the Simpsons' son, Charles, was born in October 1821, his parents were identified as labourer John Simpson and Janet Summertan; her family name, as recorded, was probably an anglicized version of Saint-Martin (the sponsors were blacks John Pruyn and Catherine Salter, the wife of John Hyers). At the boy's death six months later, the parents were called Jacob Simpson and Jeanie Martin, "people of colour."[51] It is possible that Mary McArty/Saint Martin and Jeanie Martin/Summertan were, in fact, sisters.

One of the more puzzling cases is that of Caesar Johonnot's wife, usually called Margaret Campbell during his lifetime. Presumably she was black. The fact that Johonnot signed as a witness at the burial of a black woman named Mary Campbell, who was "living at His Excellency General [Gabriel] Christie" when she died in February 1797 at the reported age of fifty-one, might hint at some connection between his wife and this older woman with the same family name.[52] Yet while he is clearly identified as black in numerous surviving documents, his wife never was, and even her name is a matter of some doubt. If she was black and her name was Campbell, her ties to other black Campbells may have sprung not from a family connection but from the bonds of slavery, i.e., they had been slaves of someone named Campbell. Also, if she was black, her subsequent marriage to the ne'er-do-well François Houle was one of the rarer cases of a union of a white male and a black female, and the children born of this union were of mixed race. If, as seems less probable, she was white, then her marriage to Johonnot and, briefly, to black labourer François Masson were interracial unions, and it is the children of Johonnot and Masson who were of mixed race, while their younger Houle stepbrothers and stepsisters were white. One way or another, one of her relationships was exogamous.

She was, to all appearances, a resourceful woman. In Johonnot's absence from home in 1798, she took charge of leasing out the distillery on their property. She later found situations for her oldest son, Gabriel. Later still, while Houle was a poor provider, she did her part to keep the family afloat by working as a seamstress: James McGill's widow, who employed her as "ma couturière," left her £10 in her will.[53] As to her racial identity and marital status, it does not help that we have been unable to find any record of her marriages, nor of her birth and death. She seems to have wed Johonnot sometime before August 1787. They had five children: Ruth, who died in January 1789; Gabriel, born circa 1792; Jean-Baptiste, who lived only five months (1795–1796); Catherine, 1797–1852, and Alexander, born in December 1800, six months after his father's death. Theirs was a mixed marriage at least in the religious sense – she Roman Catholic, he Protestant – as we understand from the fact that when their daughter, Catherine, was baptized, Johonnot was made to promise that he would raise her in the Catholic faith. Their son Alexander was also baptized a Catholic, identified as the son of the late Cesar Jean Nout and Marguerite Camille.[54]

Margaret Campbell appears to have then married a black labourer named François Masson: when their son, also called François Masson, was born in July 1803, he was said to be the child of the "lawful marriage" of François Messon and Marguerite Déjanot. François Masson Sr, said to be fifty-five years old, died three months after the birth of his son. The boy himself lived less than six months; at his death in January 1804, his parents were identified as François Masson and Marguerite Campbell.[55] Within the next two years, Margaret Campbell married Houle. When she placed her son Gabriel as an apprentice to butcher James Seabrook in 1807, the deed identified her as Margaret Campbell; two years later, another deed of indenture for Gabriel, this one to merchant Moses Northrop, identified her as Margaret Johnno, wife of Francis Wool (i.e., François Houle) and widow of Cesar Johnno.[56]

The name by which she had been generally known undergoes an odd francization at this time. In the 1790s, it had been given in French on various occasions as Camel, Camille, or some facsimile of Campbell, but in 1806 she was called Marguerite Loisel when she and Houle buried their nineteen-day-old daughter, Marie Marguerite. Some variation of this name clings to her for more than a decade – at the birth of their daughter Sophie in 1807; at the death of their four-year-old daughter Adélaïde in 1813; in July 1817, when she accuses Houle of beating her and threatening to kill her and her child; and again the following year, when she accuses Emmanuel D'Aubreville, captain of the night watch, of assault, a case that she did not pursue.[57] In these years, if she is identified by any name other than Loisel, Loiselle, or Houle, her married name, it is not Campbell. When in the fall of 1810 her son Gabriel was admitted to hospital for three weeks as the result of a severe beating at the hands of his stepfather, he was registered at the Hôtel-Dieu as Gabriel Major, "nègre agé de 18 ans fils de John Major dit Jeannot et de Marguerite Trudel." Again hospitalized in March 1811, he was once more called Gabriel Major, but his parents were identified as Siser Jennon and Marguerite Trudelle.[58] How the name Campbell evolved into Loiselle and Trudel (and Johonnot into Major) is a mystery; the fact that it did leads us to wonder whether Campbell really was her name to begin with, or an English version of a French name.[59]

Life in the Houle household was clearly unpleasant, and the head of the household soon reaped what he had sown, his grown stepchildren fighting back with their fists or in the courts. He accused his stepson, Gabriel Johonnot, of assault in September 1815, and the young man was bound over to keep the peace. In November 1818, it was Catherine Janot's (*sic*) turn to accuse Houle of assault and battery.[60]

Houle worked off and on for various fur companies. He was jailed from 6 September 1823 to sometime in January 1824, charged with a theft aboard the steamer *Laprairie*. He was jailed again on 23 October 1825 until the following April, this time accused of concealing himself on someone's property with "felonious intent." He was back in jail from 12 June 1826 until 9 September, on suspicion of vagrancy and of being involved in "some gangs of robbers." On 31 March 1827, he was charged with being a vagrant with no visible means of support, and remained in jail until 17 May.[61]

This seedy life must have taken a toll on Margaret Campbell and made her long for her days with Johonnot. But, of all the members of her family, perhaps Alexander, her youngest child by Johonnot, was the one most damaged by this domestic hell. He seems to have followed his stepfather into a life of crime. On 23 September 1817, Houle had to post a £15 bond to guarantee the court appearance of Alexander (named Alexis Jonneau) on 21 October. In January 1818, as Alexander Jonneau (and Janneau), "alias Alexander Hoole," he was arrested and charged with petty larceny – on Christmas Eve, he had stolen a horse collar with bells on it – convicted and sentenced to three months in the house of correction. In November 1819, he was indicted for stealing tablecloths and towels from an auctioneer's shop the previous May. Acquitted of a charge of stealing privately from a shop, he was found guilty of petty larceny, for which he was sentenced to receive 39 lashes in the public marketplace, followed by three months in jail. In January 1821, he was convicted of petty larceny and sentenced to three months' hard labour in the house of correction. Up on another charge of petty theft that April, he was convicted on 27 April and sentenced three days later to six months of hard labour in the house of correction. In 1822, he again faced a charge of petty larceny for stealing a saw; tried and convicted on 11 May, he was sentenced on 20 May to six months' hard labour in the house of correction, plus 39 lashes in the marketplace. In February 1825, under the name Alexander John, he was jailed, along with Robert Ellis and a Joseph St-Martin, on suspicion of theft, though it does not appear that he was prosecuted.[62]

Acquaintance with the likes of Robert Ellis spelled serious trouble. An African-American, Ellis stands along with Warren Glossen as a good illustration that blacks and whites rubbed shoulders in the Montreal underworld of the day. Alexander Johonnot was not the only child of Margaret Campbell's who became entangled with him. In 1823–24, Ellis faced a charge of shoplifting jewellry from a shop in St-Paul Street on 12 March 1823. On the night of the theft, he had given two rings stolen from the shop to Alexander's stepsister, Sophie Houle. Sophie Houle and Catherine Johonnot – court documents identified her as Catherine John, wife of Anthony Hinksman, although they were not yet formally married – were among the witnesses called by the prosecution; Peter Dago was a witness for the defence. Ellis was acquitted at his trial on 9 March 1824.[63] He was implicated in other offences at Montreal. As we saw, he and Alexander Johonnot and another man were jailed on suspicion of theft in February 1825, but they seem to have been released within a few weeks. Ellis was back in jail on 11 July that year, charged in a midnight robbery at the rectory of St-Martin Parish (Laval) on the night of 21 September 1824. Ellis remained incarcerated until November, when he was released, was committed to jail once more on 1 March 1826 on the same robbery charge, and was finally discharged on 9 September 1826 on an order from the Court of King's Bench.[64]

Just twenty days later, a replay of the St-Martin robbery, with fatal consequences, took place 300 kilometres away, at Pointe-Lévy, across the St Lawrence from Quebec.[65] At about 1 a.m., a band of men robbed the Reverend Michel Masse, the parish priest. Ellis, who wore a wig but "could not effectually disguise himself," held a loaded pistol to Masse's breast to get him to hand over the key to a chest from which they stole £1,800 in gold and silver coins. Pierre Beaudry, the mastermind, insisted that Ellis remain with him guarding the priest while others went searching for the iron chest: "Beaudrie said that he wished Ellis to stay with him as he had more confidence in him than any other person," Patrick McEwen (alias Patrick Daly), one of the gang, later testified. All the members of the gang except Beaudry were soon captured. Ellis and McEwen had managed to make it as far upriver as Trois-Rivières. The jailer there wrote to his counterpart at Quebec:

> I have been busily employed in attending to the orders of the Magistrates, relative to a Black fellow who has been taken on suspicion of having been a party concerned in the robbery lately committed at Point Levi – I also received two others for the same offence, upon one of whom, a sum of money amounting to £155, was found, the greater part consisting of Gold – Black Bob, (as he is called) had also a large amount but I cannot say how much.[66]

Four of the prisoners, including "Black Bob" Ellis were tried before Judge Edward Bowen of the Court of King's Bench at the end of March. William Ross was tried separately, at his request, before Judge James Kerr. McEwen, a key witness for the prosecution, had been in jail at Montreal with Ellis in September. "When in jail at Montreal I got acquainted with a man of colour of the name of Robert Ellis; he was confined in a cell opposite to mine, and I spoke to him several times; I saw him in Quebec about ten days after." Ellis, Ross, and Benjamin Johnson (who was captured at Longueuil), were sentenced on 31 March to be hanged in front of the jail on 21 April. Brothers Michel and Jean-Baptiste Monarque were sentenced the same day to be hanged near the church at Pointe-Lévy on the 24th. Ellis, Ross, and Johnson were accordingly executed at 10 a.m. on 21 April.[67] Three days later, the Monarque brothers were taken across the river to Pointe-Lévy. In the shadow of the gallows, the sheriff announced that Michel, the younger one, had been reprieved. Jean-Baptiste was hanged alone.

Alexander Johonnot was lucky to escape a similar fate. The crunch came for him at Montreal at about the same time as it did for Ellis at Quebec. Jailed from 7 October 1826, he was tried in the Court of King's Bench on 26 February 1827 for stealing $25 from a patron in a canteen. He called no witnesses. Convicted of stealing above the value of 40 shillings in a dwelling house, a capital offence, he was spared the noose but banished from the province for seven years.[68]

Alexander's banishment may have been the signal for a wholesale exodus of Margaret Campbell's family – all but her daughter Catherine and her son-in-law, Anthony Hinksman. From 1 February 1828, Hinksman leased a house and lot on Canal Street in St-Joseph Suburb, for 15 months. The next year, as Anthony Hinxman, he was charged with a "felony," but this may have been a mistake – he was discharged the day after his arrest. The 1831 census identified him as Anthony Kinckman, labourer, a tenant in College Street, the street where Jacob Abdella lived. There were four people in the family: two males aged between 30 and 60, one married, one not; two females aged between fourteen and forty-five, one married, one not; three Church of England, one Roman Catholic. In May 1831, Hinksman and John Patten acted as sureties for whites Guillaume and Agathe (Florentin) Laverdure when they were charged with keeping a bawdy house. They each posted £5 bonds as sureties for Guillaume Laverdure, and £10 each as bail for Agathe Laverdure. (Robert Williams and Edward Baird, the second husband of Catherine Salter, each provided sureties for another accused in the same affair.) In 1832, with the city in the grip of a devastating cholera epidemic, Catherine Johnson – read Johonnot – married Anthony Hinksman on 22 July, with John Patten and Ann Ashley in attendance. One year later, Anthony Ingston – read Hinksman – was among the blacks who turned up at Alexander Grant's to adopt resolutions in support of the British abolition bill. That is the last we hear of members of the Johonnot family at Montreal.[69]

FREAKS OF NATURE, FIGMENTS OF THE IMAGINATION

If there were any villains responsible for the decline in Margaret Campbell's fortunes, they were the Fates that robbed her of Caesar Johonnot and gave her François Houle. Race had little to do with it, although any of her contemporaries who were aware of the family's travails, with a dash of "Negro-hate" thrown in, might have been tempted to see in them a confirmation of the dissolute improvidence of blacks or of the evils of "amalgamation," the term then used, especially across the border, for the union of blacks and whites. "Miscegenation" came later, a word coined by two New York journalists in an effort to discredit incumbent President Abraham Lincoln and his antislavery Republicans in the 1864 election. They produced an anonymous pamphlet under that title, advocating interracial union as the salvation of the United States, whose pale, pinched, Anglo-Saxon population was doomed to wither away without an accession of tonic black blood. In a pitch that was sure to fire Irish voters, they suggested that the Irish, being "a more brutal race and lower in civilization than the negro," had all to gain from interracial mating. The idea was to rouse anti-Republican feeling and entrap Lincoln and others into endorsing this nonsense disguised as earnest idealism, and then expose them for the folly of their views. "Ably argued," a Montreal newspaper commented after receiving a copy, "but we do not think he [the anonymous author] will find many readers in this part of the world."[70]

If Montrealers of the 1860s would not take to the promotion of "miscegenation," what about those of Margaret Campbell's day? How did they view mixed marriages? From the fact that black-and-white unions did occur among the "lower classes," we know that such unions found a measure of acceptance there. That their "betters" did not indulge at all suggests that they wholly disapproved of the idea, and that the same "good taste" that Samuel Ringgold Ward saw as stifling the public expression of racism in the upper classes caused them to view interracial mixing as, at the very least, in "bad taste." Witness the remarks of the Reverend James Taylor Dickinson, son of Horace Dickinson, the founder of the Upper Canada Line of stages and steamboats and teacher at No. 4 African School. James Dickinson had left Montreal to study at Yale College, where he graduated in 1826, thereafter settling in Connecticut. As an ardent abolitionist and pastor of the Second Congregational Church in Norwich, he preached a strong anti-slavery sermon on American Independence Day, 1834. He had this to say in rebutting the charge that abolitionists favoured "amalgamation": "This is altogether false – ... With the subject of intermarriages we have nothing to do. We do not desire to see such things take place, nor on the other hand do we think it wise or proper to make laws against them. If, in here and there an instance, the two races shall intermarry, we shall consider them as persons of *bad taste,* and there we shall leave the matter."[71] This was the gentlemanly form of racism: interracial unions were unquestionably something to be discouraged, not by recourse to loud or violent opposition or to prohibitive laws, but by a frown of disdain and the tut-tutting of men and women of taste.

Closer to home, a piece of journalistic sensationalism in the summer of 1821, and a rejoinder to it, show that some Montrealers were inclined to swallow and propagate – others not – the hoary notion that "mulattos," the fruit of interracial unions, were freaks or begetters of freaks. Indeed, the initial report in the *Montreal Herald* ran under the heading *"Lusus Naturae,"* a freak of nature:

> *Lusus Naturae.* – Last week a mulatto woman of Laprairie was delivered of an animal, that, on account of its singularity, deserves to be noticed. Its head was of a natural shape, but from the forehead sprouted two horns, about 2½ inches apart, one of them curling up and the other down. It had sockets but no eyes, and the mouth and nose were split, in a manner nearly resembling those of a sheep. The trunk was human; in the thighs and legs, however, there were no bones, the left one terminating in a bear's paw, and the right in a sheep's foot. The animal was female; its tone strange, as if composed of that of several animals. It was christened, and died in half an hour after its birth. The father was a mulatto. We have omitted to mention that on each hand (which, together with the arms, resembled the fore paws of a land tortoise,) it had five fingers and a thumb.[72]

The bilingual *Montreal Gazette* published a translation of this lurid fable for the edification of its French-language readers.[73] One of them was moved to set the record straight in a letter to the French-language *Spectateur canadien:*

> *Lusus Naturae.* – On 9 July, a stranger who identified himself as Joseph Ennuel, mulatto, a native of New Orleans, presented a deformed female child for baptism who was given the name Marguerite. The child was cold and at death's door, her breath coming slowly and with difficulty. She had previously uttered two cries, like those of any other children. Her features seemed placed higher on her face than they normally are: the mouth, the nose, the eyes were but half-formed, and of forehead there was none. The cap of her skull was not closed, exposing agglutinations of blood and two strips of flesh which the women present likened to the lobes of a heart. They furthermore stated that the bones of the thighs and legs were not deformed; the hands, besides the thumbs, had five fingers; the skin was of the common tone. The water for the baptism had to be poured on her cheek. I do not know why, in the last Gazette, this child is called an animal; and all her attributes which are likened to those of a bear, a sheep, a land tortoise, as well as the references to curved horns and the cries of several animals, are not *lusus naturae*, but *lusus imaginationis*.[74]

The girl (christened Magdelaine, not Marguerite) died the day she was born – the *Herald* got that right.[75] Substitute the word "lady" for "mulatto woman" in the original report, and make the father a "gentleman" instead of a "mulatto," and this cruel class- and race-based fabrication never would have seen print.

Some people, the editors of the *Herald* and the *Gazette* among them, it seems, believed it to be within the realm of possibility that mulattoes could give birth to "an animal," not simply a child with a profound congenital malformation. To those inclined to believe that blacks were a species separate from whites and that mixing the two would yield a subhuman hybrid, this story might have seemed plausible, a hideous confirmation of the penalty for violating the laws of nature.

The press of the 1820s could publish such a vicious misrepresentation of Magdelaine Ennuel safe in the knowledge that many readers would find it credible and that few, other than those who had actually seen her, were in a position to contest the account *viva voce,* and that fewer still would trouble to write a refutation. Reputable medical men and ethnologists, believers in the supremacy of whites, would add their "scientific" support to old theories of blacks and whites as separate species whose mixing resulted in the degradation of the superior breed. Who could argue against science?[76] Not the small coloured population of Montreal. It did not have the means to express its disbelief or indignation, and if collectively affronted, was in no position to mount an effective protest. There was then no Alexander Grant to rally the troops and set down their complaints in prose that could command attention, as there would be in the mid-1830s.

ELEVEN

One Thousand Characters in Search of an Author or Two

Various elements of Montreal's population affirmed their collective identities and bonds in the mid-1830s by founding national societies. In 1834–35, the English, French, Germans, Irish, and Scots did so, as did the *nation canadienne* with the launching of the Société St-Jean-Baptiste. These were white clubs: no blacks identified with any of these groups or joined them. Each was a combination cultural association, social club, political forum, and mutual-aid society, the importance of these roles varying from group to group according to their interests, social status, and present needs. Blacks, as a group, were in no position to launch their own society. Their individual origins were too diverse to enable a sense of membership in one nation, with a common culture, language, or religion. It would be 1863 before Montreal blacks set on foot their first association – and, even then, the St Augustine Society was strictly a benevolent organization, with a religious tinge but no national or patriotic colouring beyond the hint in its name.[1] In naming their societies after a Christian saint, the English picked George, the Irish Patrick, the Scots Andrew, and the *Canadiens* John the Baptist; black Montrealers would choose Augustine of Hippo, the fifth-century father of the Christian church, author of the famous *Confessions,* and an African. But this was thirty years in the future, in a different setting with different actors.

Oddly enough, if the blacks of the 1830s did not consider themselves a nation, others had seen them in that light for decades. Of the several terms that whites in Quebec used to identify blacks in the eighteenth and early nineteenth century, none is more suggestive than *nègre de nation* and its variants

– meaning, literally, "Negro by nationality" or "of the Negro nation." There was no English equivalent. "African" came close. It was ambiguous in that it was sometimes used to denote a black person, at other times a native of Africa; either way, it anchored that person by birth or ancestry to one continent. But where was the homeland of the *nation nègre*? Everywhere and nowhere. The nation was African, in a sense, but it was also severed from Africa. There was no white nation. Whites were *Allemand de nation, Français de nation, Irlandais de nation,* etc., never *de nation blanche.* No nation encompassed all whites. Blacks, however, whether born down the road, or elsewhere in the Americas, in Europe or in Africa, were liable to be classed as *de nation nègre.* The plain *nègre* and *négresse* were, of course, the most commonly used terms (English-speakers just as frequently used "negro," "negress," "black man," or "black woman"). But references to the *nation nègre* were not uncommon.

François Dominique *dit* Mentor, for example, was tagged a *nègre de nation* in his first year as a free man when he apprenticed himself to a Montreal silversmith on 22 April 1749.[2] At Lachine, fifty-year-old Charles, "negre de nation," died on 14 May 1767.[3] The following 10 July, Pierre, "Neigre de nation," died at Montreal at age twenty.[4] Marie Charlotte, daughter of Louis Antoine and his wife Catherine Baraca, both "Nègres de nation," was born at Montreal on 24 May 1769 and died only five months later, stamped a "naigresse de nacion."[5] When Élisabeth, the seven-year-old slave of Montreal notary Pierre Panet, was baptized on 18 September 1770, she was recorded as a "Negresse de nation," but someone struck out the words "de nation," leaving her a "Negresse" pure and simple (the deletion itself is intriguing).[6] At her death at Quebec on New Year's Day 1778 at the reputed age of fifty-two, Susanne, a slave of the merchant Louis Parent, was a "négresse de nation."[7] Jacques Michel, "nègre de nation," died a slave of Michel Eustache Gaspard Alain Chartier de Lotbinière, seigneur of Vaudreuil, on 23 July 1779 at the age of about twenty-two.[8] Dianne, "negresse de nation," about thirty, was presented as a gift to the sisters of the Hôtel-Dieu in Montreal on 20 April 1784.[9] The twelve-year-old slave of Reverend Louis Payet called Pompé, "de nation nègre," was baptized under the name Jean-Baptiste at St-Antoine on 13 September 1789.[10] Marie Joseph Elizabeth, "de nation nègre," was about twenty-one when she was baptized at Berthier on 20 February 1793.[11] When distillery manager Caesar Johonnot bought a house at Montreal on 14 April 1794, the deed of sale termed him "naigre de nation."[12] Farmer Stephen Rogers and Ann Garner, the American-born parents of Basiliste Rogers, were "nègres de nation" when she was baptized at age three at Sainte-Élisabeth in the seigneury of D'Ailleboust on 24 February 1815.[13] Angélique Anne, "négresse de nation," was a forty-eight-year-old servant of Jacques Cartier, father of the future Sir George-Étienne Cartier, when she died at St-Antoine on 28 September 1823.[14] Most of the time, the designation was used in the recording of vital statistics, a task handled by the churches, but in the examples above we see that it was also applied to Mentor when he signed up to learn a trade and to Caesar Johonnot when he bought a house. It could, in other words, come up at any time, even when national or ethnic origin and race were irrelevant to the business at hand.

This "Negro nation" was a product of the plundering of Africa's human resources and the obliteration of African ethnic origins and identities in the melting pot of slavery. It was at once a myth and a truth in embryo, a figment of the white imagination that, in time, would become more or less fact. As North American whites persisted in lumping together all persons with dark skin or negroid features as undifferentiated "blacks," regardless of their place of birth or their ancestral origins, and to exclude them from full participation in society, so blacks would come to forge something approaching a nation of their own, rooted in a shared history and experience of rejection and mistreatment. It would be a nation within nations, identifying with the state or country in which its members found themselves; it would also be a nation apart from any state, transcending political boundaries, its passport a black skin. In *The Souls of Black Folk* (1903), W.E.B. Dubois famously wrote of the "double consciousness" or "twoness" of American blacks in the apartheid system that prevailed in his country. On the basis of the old French expression, we might as well speak of a dual nationality.[15]

Black Montrealers of the 1830s were far from any "national" affirmation, although some of them took a few small steps in this decade, under the leadership of Alexander Grant, to express a collective existence and identity, or at least to act in concert and speak with one voice on issues that particularly concerned them, such as the British Abolition Bill of 1833, or the plight of Betsy Freeman in 1836. But while white groups of the day sought to assert their cultural distinctness from one another, the thrust of the black effort was the reverse. Marginalized on the basis of skin colour and few in number, they sought acceptance, regardless of their origins, as members of society's mainstream. Freshly rid of slavery, their goal was integration; they wished to prove that if the dominant society would only let them in the door, it would see that no essential difference separated them from whites. They envisaged doing in Rome as the Romans did. Thus, rather than move to set up a black church, they adhered to the existing white ones. They did not seek to set up their own school; as well intentioned as it might have been, the American Presbyterian Church's short-lived No. 4 African School of 1827 may have elicited an ambivalent response from some of its intended beneficiaries – gratitude for the service, but an uneasiness at its segregated nature. Erecting separate facilities for blacks, particularly when the initiative came from whites, served only to institutionalize and entrench a colour line.[16] As for the judicial system, black Montrealers of this time never stood off and refused to recognize white justice, civil or criminal. If anything, their attitude, tempered by their experience that the fair word of the written law did not always trump the unwritten laws that governed people's minds, remained closer to that of the fugitive American slave in Upper Canada who said: "When I reached English territory, I had a comfort in the law."[17] From the first days of British rule, they accepted it, abiding by its decisions, appearing as witnesses, and using it themselves as plaintiffs and accusers when they saw fit. Before Grant's appearance on the scene, no effort had been made to articulate the point that blacks did not want to be seen as distinct but as equal. The repeated spurning of their advances would later lead them to give up the effort and conclude that they had no choice but to forge the "Negro nation." A black joke of the 1850s stands as a commentary on the laughable thinness of the rapprochement and equality that rewarded their efforts at integration:

> "How much do you charge, massa magistrate, to marry me and Miss Dinah?"
> "Well, Clem, I'll marry you for two dollars."
> "Two dollars! What you charge to marry white folks, massa?"
> "We generally charge five dollars, Clem."
> "Well, you marry us like white folks, and I'll give you five dollars, too."
> "Why, Clem, that's a curious notion, but as you desire it I'll marry you like white folks for five dollars."
> The ceremony being over, and Clem and Dinah being one, the magistrate asked for his fee.
> "Oh, no, massa! You no come up to de 'greement."
> "How so, Clem, what is lacking?"
> "Why, you no kiss de bride."
> "Get out of my office, you black rascal."[18]

We might look on the history of blacks at Montreal from 1760 to 1840 as a piece of absurdist theatre in which, over time, one thousand people with little in common beyond a history of subjection were thrown onto a stage and expected to perform. Some central figures stand out, entering and exiting in succession, as if on cue: Caesar Johonnot from the mid-1780s to 1800; then Charlotte and John Trim, who take us to the 1830s; followed by Alexander Grant, the first to realize that this play needed speaking parts. He no sooner delivers a few lines than he dies. His absence leaves the cast speechless again, or mumbling indistinctly – with Peter Dago, the ubiquitous silent witness of more than fifty years, weaving his way among the players.

At 150 or 200 years' remove, some actions, even small, peripheral ones by bit players in the drama, are worth a thousand words. Three such scenes, commentaries on the main event, come readily to mind. Each is haunting in its own way.

The first occurs in the thick of the American War of Independence. Raiders from Canada swoop down on Cherry Valley, New York, on 11 November 1778. The wife of the Reverend Samuel Dunlap, the Presbyterian minister of the place, is among those killed; Dunlap, his daughter and "two negroes of his" are taken captive to Canada. A week later, both sides agree to exchange an equal number of prisoners. For this purpose, Dunlap, his daughter and his two slaves are counted as two. In this prisoner swap, two blacks count for no more than Dunlap's dead wife. The "negroes" are nonentities returned without requiring any "royalists" in exchange. Only in the arithmetic of race, we think, could someone be no one, and two plus two equal two.[19]

Almost twenty years later, American actor John Durang, who had spent the winter of 1797–98 at Montreal performing with Rickett's Circus from Philadelphia, was travelling to Quebec, the tour's next stop, when he and a few other members of the troupe stopped one spring evening at a humble farmhouse at Rivière-du-Loup (Louiseville). There, as Durang recorded in a memoir of his life:

> After we had smoked a segar and took a drink, a black lady entered the house in great stile. She was dress'd in a blue riding habit, black hat and feathers, a whip in her hand, gold watch, gold chain and locket around the neck, lacet boots, a red satin under west, her figure tall, slender, and well shaped. She had a polite address; she talk'd very familier and ask us where we come from and our business. ... She made her exit with a swiming courtsey; who she was I know not.[20]

The fleeting glimpse of this woman, appearing out of nowhere, obviously not a member of the farming household, so remarkable in her dress, the breeziness of her polite but familiar manner, without a hint of servility or reticence, presents such a contrast to the black reality conveyed by other records that it is tempting to see her as a figment of Durang's imagination. But it is scarcely conceivable that a white American would have gone to the trouble of inventing a "black lady" only to cast her in such an inconclusive scene. If Durang was not fabulating, then she must have been a slave: the blue and red of her outfit are reminiscent of the colours worn by Colonel John Campbell's liveried slaves. But her riding habit and whip cannot have been common accoutrements for slaves, particularly female ones, and no slave livery ran to a gold watch, watch chain and a locket. Besides, in Durang's eyes she was not a "negro wench," in the parlance of the day, but a very uncommon "black lady." Some rich man's mistress? Surely no black family in Quebec had the means to pay for such finery in the days when Charlotte and Judith had just bade their goodbyes to slavery. Durang's "lady" does not fit neatly into the jigsaw puzzle of the drab world inhabited by black Quebecers of the day. The only place where she can conceivably fit is some corner near two other women we have met: E**, the "sable partner" of a "smart young Lieutenant" in the wartime winter frolics of 1776–77 at Montreal, and M.A.J., the polished "woman of colour" at Quebec in the summer of 1803, ready to set off for "any part of Europe" as a ladies' maid.[21]

Something about Durang's "lady" suggests there is hope for the past. But flash forward to September 1844, six years after Alexander Grant had left the stage. Jane Wilson, the widow of John Broome, was obliged to put an end to the one-woman protest that she had conducted through the summer. A white woman on her street complained that "Mme Broom, femme de couleur," had stood outside her house day after day for several months, shouting insults and threats. What could have provoked this marathon of vituperation? The records that survive do not explain what made her shout so persistently, or what it was that she shouted, but Jane Wilson was made to swear to keep the peace on pain of a penalty of £20.[22] Out of earshot, her loud and artless cries become for us a silent picture, a work of art, Jane Wilson's *Shout,* like Edvard Munch's *The Scream.* Mme Broom, *femme de couleur*, had a quarrel with the world; at some level, it had to do with race. Curtain.

ONE ROAD NOT TAKEN

For blacks who had had their fill of condescension, mistreatment, slights or just cold Canadian winters, it would seem that Montreal businessman and City Councillor John William Dunscomb, newly elected to the first parliament of the united Canadas in March 1841, offered a ticket out. A native of Bermuda like Jane Wilson, but white and well connected, Dunscomb maintained personal and business ties to his native island and to the islands of the Caribbean from which he imported rum, sugar, molasses, cigars, and other products for his wholesale grocery business.[23] Perhaps those contacts, and maybe a good word from Jeremiah Leaycraft, his former partner who had only recently moved to Kingston in Jamaica,[24] had helped him to secure his appointment that spring as Jamaican immigration agent in Canada, under Jamaica's Immigration Act of 1840. Dunscomb advertised his nomination in June:

> The undersigned hereby give notice that they have been duly appointed AGENTS for CANADA, under the Immigration Act of the Island of Jamaica, and that they are prepared to grant FREE PASSAGES to JAMAICA, in accordance with the liberal provisions of the Act, to such members of the COLOURED POPULATION, (*of good character*) as may feel disposed to avail themselves of the advantages offered.
>
> Applications for further information may be made at the Office of the Agency in Montreal.
>
> J.W. DUNSCOMB & CO.
St. Sacrament Street[25]

We find no hint that any of the one hundred or so black residents of Montreal at the time took advantage of this program, devised by the Jamaican authorities under Governor Sir Charles Metcalfe (who was to serve as governor-general of Canada from 1843 through 1845). One reason is that they were not the intended targets of the plan, although Dunscomb did advertise it in Montreal publications.

The plan focused on the recruitment of agricultural workers to fill a shortage of plantation labour created in the wake of emancipation and the end of the apprentice system in 1838 – not a line of work that was likely to appeal to urban blacks settled in Montreal. In Canada, the likely recruits were thought to be refugees from American slavery in Upper Canada. But there, too, removal to Jamaica did not excite great interest. As a Jamaican immigration official later wrote: "At the commencement of Mr Dunscomb's Agency the number of people of color in Upper Canada was estimated at 12,000, increased annually by fugitive slaves from the United States, but though unsettled in their circumstances and anxiously desirous of seeking a permanent home in the West Indies not more than 169 could be induced to visit Jamaica of whom more than one half returned dissatisfied."[26]

In 1841, Dunscomb, to whom Jamaica's agent-general of immigrants had sent £500 "for the purpose of furthering the removal of the coloured people from Upper

Governor-General Sir Charles Metcalfe, formerly governor of Jamaica, opens parliament in the former Ste-Anne Market building in 1845.

Canada," had shipped twenty-five people to Jamaica. Jamaican authorities entertained high hopes for the coming year, as the agent-general of immigration advised Governor Metcalfe at the end of September:

> Your Excellency will be glad to learn that there is a prospect of a considerable influx of labourers from Upper Canada, consisting of coloured people, who have settled in that province, but disliking the climate, are desirous of removing to one more congenial. I have reason to believe they would prove an useful class of labourers, and be likely to assist in improving our cultivation of some of the minor productions, more particularly that of cotton and tobacco ... it is more than probable, that the approach of winter will expedite the movement of those who have determined on settling here.[27]

But the enterprise seems to have fallen flat in 1842. In mid-October, only a few days after the press of his commercial affairs had led him to resign his seat in the Canadian parliament,[28] Dunscomb advertised for "Persons of color, – of good character" to take free passage to Jamaica aboard a "first class ship" that was to sail from Quebec around 25 October. The deadline for applications was 22 October.[29] It appears that no emigrants sailed for Jamaica that year. The following year, however, 110 were sent out

The parliament building was destroyed in a fire set by an angry Tory mob on 25 April 1849.

under Dunscomb's auspices. "During 1844, and 1845 considerable efforts were made by this Gentleman and through the instrumentality of Mr Stephen Virginia, an intelligent colored farmer from Upper Canada, to prosecute this branch of emigration upon a more extended scale than formerly."[30] Virginia, who had been living in Jamaica for more than a year, raised the hopes of the authorities there: he intended to return to Canada to gather his family and others whom he knew to be eager to move to the island. They gave him the funds necessary for their travel costs and asked him to report on the prospects for further emigration. Another Upper Canadian, Peter Gallego, a young black man who had studied at Upper Canada College and the University of Toronto, also took part in the effort. Between 1841 and 1844, he made several trips to Jamaica, at first as the agent of a black convention held at Ancaster, Canada West, then as an agent of the Jamaican government; in 1844 he published a pamphlet to encourage black emigration to Jamaica. A grand total of thirty-four black emigrants sailed off that year.[31] In view of the poor results and prospects, the Jamaican authorities notified Dunscomb in January 1845 that they had no choice but to cancel the program and terminate his employment as their agent as of 31 March.[32]

Jamaica was not the only Caribbean colony that faced a labour shortage after slavery's end and that looked to British North America, among other places, for immigrants. Trinidad did the same. The lieutenant-governor of Nova Scotia issued a proclamation concerning Trinidad's scheme, inviting would-be emigrants to submit their names to the provincial secretary. The British consul at New York was appointed agent for Trinidad, and he offered $5 to cover the costs of travel to New York for any blacks in Canada or in the Maritime colonies who were interested.[33] In Canada West, surgeon Thomas Rolph, who hatched various plans to draw British immigrants to Canada, also sought to promote the emigration of blacks to Trinidad between 1841 and 1843, latterly as an agent of the Trinidadian government.[34] Canadian authorities were leery and dismissive of his efforts. As Sir George Arthur, lieutenant-governor of Upper Canada, wrote to Governor General Lord Sydenham:

> Doctor Rolph's course is not very intelligible to me; for, whilst he is so strenuous an advocate for peopling the Province, it would seem that he is equally busy in promoting Emigration from it ... If Her Majesty's Government desire to promote the removal of the Black Population, something may, perhaps, be done in it on a small scale; – it should be remembered, however, that they are firm Defenders of our Soil; – but, where the Doctor proposes to find from three to five hundred People of Color, who *wish* to proceed to Trinidad, I am at a loss to conjecture![35]

Sydenham, for his part, considered Rolph's plan "amusing" – and unacceptable: "I am quite opposed to losing any of these men from the Canadas, and should countenance no such scheme."[36] The same points that Arthur and Sydenham raised against Rolph's Trinidad scheme held for Dunscomb's efforts on behalf of Jamaica: both tended to depopulate Canada of some of its most loyal subjects, at a time when the Rebellions were still fresh in everyone's mind and the prospect of war with the United States, sooner or later, was always a concern. "With some exceptions they are ... a well conducted and orderly set of People," Sydenham wrote of the blacks in Canada to Colonial Secretary Lord John Russell. "Their condition and prospects in Upper Canada are at least as good as any which Trinidad would afford, and their loyalty to the queen and gratitude for the favor shewn to their race under British laws renders them valuable subjects in these Colonies."[37]

LIFE AND DEATH GO ON

Natural attrition, not emigration schemes, accounted for whatever population losses occurred among the blacks of Montreal. John Broome, Jane Wilson's husband, died in 1840, as we saw, as did Solomon Molliston, the barber, and his son of the same name.[38] In 1841, Thomas Cockburn, identified as Adam Cockburn, "a Colored Man, of intemperate habits, and destitute," died of "misery and intemperance," hours after he was found lying drunk and frozen on a street in Griffintown; Jacob Grant, Mary Ann Drummond's husband, and Martha Hyers, the widowed twenty-one-year-old prostitute, also died that year.[39] Longtime resident Brigitte Lafortune, a fifty-five-year-old native of the West Indies, and John Low, the seven-year-old son of Abraham Low and Elizabeth Pruyn, passed away in 1842, as did another of their sons, Richard, only four months after he was born.[40] The year 1843 saw the deaths of Catherine Mayson, the aged widow of Alexander Valentine, at the Hôpital-Général, and of newly married Washington Williams, twenty-three, the young man whom we saw in 1841 leave domestic service too early in the spring to land his hoped-for steamboat job, and settle instead for a job at Patrick Swords' Hotel.[41] Low lost another son shortly after birth in 1844, and in the spring of 1845 his eldest, nineteen-year-old Jacob, went paddling off to the fur-trade country on a three-year contract with the Hudson's Bay Company. Low himself would die in his son's absence, in 1846.[42] The black population suffered only two deaths that we know of in 1845 – Quebec-born Robert Jackson, forty-four, who made a deathbed conversion to Catholicism, and American-born William Murphy, who lived his last years in an alcoholic haze and died in jail, where he had begun serving a two-month term for disorderliness.[43] Murphy had been one of the booze-and-bawdy-house crowd with Thomas Cockburn, Jacob Simpson, and Martha Hyers' husband, Richard Jackson, who had all predeceased him. An inquest ruled that he had "died by the visitation of God," finding that –

> William Murphy a colored man was committed on the 18th August instant to the common jail of this District on a charge of vagrancy. When committed, deceased exhibited a degree of mental aberration, and was also in a feeble and debilitated state, from which he did not recover, but gradually declined until the twenty fourth day of August instant on which day deceased died. During his illness, deceased received every care and attention, not only from the Physician of the jail but also from the Officers and inmates of that institution.[44]

The physician of the jail, Daniel Arnoldi, we have already met. The coroner's report included a note from him:

> The other Day I had began a Report upon the Case of Wm Murphy deeming it a Case of Mental Aberration – but being unwilling to pronounce decidedly upon it from first Sight: – I thought proper to delay that Measure till further observation would Sanction that Opinion as he exhibited not only an alarming degree of fatuity, but considerable bodily prostration, which I could not readily account for. – I therefore prescribed restoratives and generous Diet. – but no change for the better took place and he gradually sank from sheer debility.

This slow attrition in the small black population was offset by an accession of new blood through an even slower natural increase – against at least fourteen deaths there were seven births between 1840 and 1845, among them those of the two Low boys mentioned above who died in infancy – and a trickle of immigration, which would increase after 1850.[45] New faces that appear around this time include cook

David Bristow, who married Alexander Grant's widow, Celia Farley, in 1840; Virginian Thomas Brooks, who married sixteen-year-old Mary Ann Trim in 1841; joiner James Carpenter, a widower from Prince Edward Island who jumped ship at Quebec in 1840 and married Mary Ann Trim's widowed mother at Montreal in 1842; Charles Meads, who would prosper as an "oil boiler" and put up apartment houses on Versailles Street, hoping the rents would assure the financial future of his three children before he succumbed to a fatal illness in May 1863, only three months after his wife, Quebec-born Nancy Feron (alias Nancy Faren, Ann Farrell, Nancy Farrell, Ann Feron, and Nancy Meade), had dozed off while smoking a pipe and burned to death; Samuel Queen, the boardinghouse-keeper who, in 1843, married Caroline Curtin, the daughter of Barbados-born stevedore John Curtin of Quebec; and Isaac Taylor of Baltimore, who would marry Harriet (Henriette) Trim in 1846.[46] Another newcomer was Antonio, the young slave who had been cabin boy aboard the *Amistad,* the Cuban slave-transporting ship at the heart of a famous legal case in the United States in 1839–41. After the US Supreme Court ruling in the case on 9 March 1841, Antonio was to be shipped back to slavery in Cuba, but abolitionists short-circuited that plan by packing him off to Montreal. Dwight Janes probably had a hand in this. As a resident of Connecticut in 1839, the co-founder of Montreal's short-lived No. 4 African School had been the one to alert prominent abolitionists to the cargo of kidnapped Africans aboard the ship. Shortly after testifying in the case in the US District Court in New Haven on 7 January 1840, he had moved back to Montreal.[47] Another who may have played a part was the Reverend G.W. Perkins, the second pastor (1830–39) of Montreal's American Presbyterian Church, who had moved to Meriden, Connecticut in 1839, where he was active in the anti-slavery cause.[48]

THE NUMBERS AGAIN

As mentioned in passing earlier, about one hundred blacks lived at Montreal in the early 1840s. It is impossible at this stage to give a more definite figure, just as it is impossible to be more specific for the period 1760–1840 than to say there were roughly 1,000 (at last count 1,011, including 66 – 39 males, 23 females, and 4 slaves of unspecified gender – whose names are unknown). The census conducted in 1842 does not really firm up the count. Like previous censuses, it named the heads of households only. Thus, we find 47 unnamed blacks – 33 females and 14 males – listed in white households or establishments, most of them as servants or employees. We could take a stab at identifying the odd one – Catherine Mayson was undoubtedly the black female enumerated as a resident of the Hôpital-Général, and Washington Williams was probably one of two black males listed at Swords' Hotel[49] – but identifying most with certainty is not possible.

Even "black" households pose problems. Peter Dago, for instance, was enumerated as the head of a household on Vitré Street, St-Laurent Ward, but the census gave no indication that he or any of the eight other occupants were black. Six of them were

Vermont native Dwight P. Janes (1801–1878), a founding member of the American Presbyterian Church in Montreal, played a key role in the celebrated Amistad slave case in the United States in 1839.

said to be American born, and two of German origin – probably Scholastique Diller, with whom Dago would have a child the following year and whom he would marry in 1851, and her sister Caroline, who would marry John Taylor, a black Marylander, in 1850.[50] The census counted the "Widow Brooms" (Jane Wilson) as the head of a household on St-Charles-Borromée Street consisting of three black females, one of whom, between five and fourteen years old, would have been her eight-year-old daughter Sarah. The other two were married women (widows were counted as married), one between fourteen and forty-five, the other older than forty-five, one of them born in Bermuda, and one of "African origin"; one had been in Canada nineteen years, the other twenty-seven. Two were members of the Church of England – this would be Jane Wilson and her daughter – and one was a British Wesleyan Methodist. Jane Wilson was born in Bermuda, and it seems that she was the woman between fourteen and forty-five years of age, the one who had lived in Canada for about nineteen years. Who, then, was the second adult, the one of African origin, over forty-five, about twenty-seven years a resident of Canada, a Methodist, counted as married but probably widowed like Jane Wilson? Considering the possibilities, and proceeding by elimination, we might hazard that she was Sarah York, sometimes called Celeste, the widow of Joseph Pierre, a sometime steamboat worker like John Broome (Broome, recall, had acted as a surety for her in 1827 when she was accused of assaulting Catherine Guillet). At her death in 1871, Sarah York's age would be given as ninety, though she was probably in her seventies.[51]

The difficulties we face in counting and identifying free black Montrealers are not unlike those we faced in enumerating slaves. Those left unnamed in one source, such as the census of 1842, might be identified by name elsewhere, but we cannot be sure that they are the same. Those who could not write their names had them recorded by others in sometimes unrecognizable forms. As we saw in the last chapter, Mary McArty, who married Thomas Cockburn in 1809, was Marie Saint Martin at her death, and Jeanie Martin was elsewhere Janet Summertan. This name game would go on throughout the century.[52]

And, just as the course of slavery ran differently in Quebec than in Ontario and elsewhere, so did its aftermath. For reasons having to do with geography, transportation, language, religion, and a host of other factors, more American blacks reached landlocked English, Protestant, Upper Canada and settled there than in French and Catholic Lower Canada, which was open to the sea and reputedly colder.[53] While blacks were estimated to number in the thousands in Upper Canada, they numbered in the hundreds in Lower Canada. Many of the blacks in Upper Canada were American refugees, awaiting the fall of slavery to enable their return home.[54] The presence of large numbers of American blacks there undoubtedly contributed to the founding at Toronto in 1837 of the Upper Canada Anti-Slavery Society, the first such organization in Canada. No such group had arisen earlier to oppose slavery at home or in the British Empire. Now that Britain had cleansed itself of that stain, some Anglo-Canadians felt free to cast stones at American slavery.[55] In Lower Canada, access to the sea favoured a different mix, blacks coming by land from the United States, but also by ship from the West Indies, from across the Atlantic, occasionally from South America, and from the eastern seaboard of the United States. The patterns of settlement were different, too. Lower Canada had nothing like the settlements of black American refugees that sprouted in the upper province from the late 1820s. These settlements drew the support and attention of anti-slavery groups in the United States, and of missionary efforts there and in Britain; they were useful props in abolitionist propaganda against American slavery, and the publicity they received attracted more blacks to Upper Canada. As a result, British and American references to the experience of blacks in Canada tended to focus on southwestern Upper Canada, to the exclusion of blacks elsewhere, notably at Montreal, the largest city and leading centre of population, commerce, finance, and industry in either of the Canadas. The smaller number of blacks in Lower Canada had nothing to do with the one province being more hostile and the other more welcoming. If anything, overt acts of hostility were more prevalent in Upper Canada, where the larger size of the black population and its concentration in settlements made it an easier target for segregationists. The sprinkling of blacks in Lower Canada did not provide the same pretext for open manifestations of racism, nor did it offer touring abolitionists the same quick study.

One consequence of this is that historical accounts of blacks in Canada, relying on the wealth of published material about refugees in Upper Canada – and about concentrations of blacks in the maritime colony of Nova Scotia, which had its own distinctive patterns of black immigration and settlement – ignore Quebec through most of the nineteenth century, from the end of slavery to the age of the Canadian Pacific Railway beginning in the mid-1880s. As for Quebec's place in the history of blacks in Canada, and Montreal's in particular, the historiography is woefully deficient – an irony, in view of the fact that the source material, although largely unpublished, is comparatively abundant, as the present study demonstrates.

Ironic, too, that in Quebec, of all places, there has been a strange willingness – and a needless one – to credit the British parliament for delivering the *coup de grâce* to slavery in 1833. This is particularly notable, considering that in the prevailing historical view Britain could do no right in regard to Quebec in the 1830s. By this view every measure emanating from London was misguided or noxious, every appointment inept, and these missteps culminated in the Russell Resolutions of 1837, the mission of Lord Durham in 1838 and his ever-contentious report, and the subsequent attempt to crush French Quebec through the legislative union of Lower and Upper Canada in 1841. Yet the honour of ending slavery in Quebec is ceded to the otherwise "perfidious Albion" without question, as if such an overall positive measure were something extraneous, a milestone in the history of blacks in Quebec, but not in the history of Quebec. Here is the nub of a persistent problem: the segregation of histories. To include a chapter on blacks in a survey of Quebec's or Canada's past only serves to highlight the distinction. "Black history" is not woven into the fabric, as it should be; it is a separate piece of cloth, requiring a separate treatment. It is a qualified history, just as a "gentleman of colour" was not quite a gentleman, and Mme Broom was not quite a woman but a "femme de couleur."

"Black history" is a field that presents at least a double paradox. For one thing, it serves to combat racism while at the same time perpetuating it. It seeks to record a past previously ignored, in an effort to correct old misrepresentations and to account for the present state of our societies; at the same time, it sustains the racial distinctions that we deplore. If we condemn racial discrimination, we must want to be done with it. A second paradox flows from this: the ultimate, unspoken goal of "Black history" is to write itself out of existence. It is a history so rooted in racism that it could not exist without it. Eradicate racism, and black history becomes history, period. How long it will take for this to occur is impossible to tell, but it surely will – and ages from now people will look back on us as benighted souls who were still sorting humans according to skin colour, just as we shudder at that barbarian gene in past generations that made black slavery so widely acceptable.

We are not there yet; hence this book. Like it or not, we have this legacy to deal with.

APPENDIX I
NEWSPAPER NOTICES

A. SLAVE SALES AND FUGITIVES

Quebec's early newspapers printed ninety-four notices concerning the sales of black slaves and the flights of black prisoners, ship deserters, servants, and slaves. The first such notice appeared in 1765, the last in 1810. They concern about eighty-five different people, although the anonymity of the slaves offered for sale makes it difficult to be certain of the exact number. They are verbal snapshots of black men, women, and children. Many contain interesting details about their subjects' physical appearance, scars or injuries, linguistic and other abilities, habits, dress, and so on. We learn, for instance, that about one-fifth are scarred by smallpox, and about one-third speak, or can get along in, two languages or more. This one plays the violin, that one wears a wig, this man "shaves his Head and takes Scotch Snuff," that woman "makes butter to perfection;" here is a slave who speaks "good English and French, a little Dutch and Earse;" here is another who stutters.

In all, about forty slaves were offered for sale in forty-three notices, the last published in 1798.[1] Some were put up for sale more than once; some were sold singly; some with one or two others. Some forty-five blacks took part in fifty escapes that were the subject of a notice. The breakdown by locality of the advertised sales and escapes is shown in the table.

Advertised sales of black slaves and escapes of black fugitives, 1760–1840

Place	Sales	Escapes	Total
Montreal	11	17	28
Quebec	31	30	61
Elsewhere	1	4	5
Total	43	51	94

There are fifty-one published notices for fifty escapes; this is because Joe, the slave of Quebec printer William Brown, was the subject of two notices when he broke out of jail in 1786, one by the sheriff (no. 54), and one by Brown (no. 55), each offering a reward for his capture. The one slave (no. 72) who was "elsewhere" than at Montreal or Quebec when advertised for sale was a female living at Trois-Rivières. Of the escapes that occurred "elsewhere," one took place at Willsboro, New York, on Lake Champlain in 1771 (no. 16); one at the military post of Carleton Island, at the foot of Lake Ontario, in 1780 (no. 34); one at Berthier (Berthierville), northeast of Montreal, in 1791 (no. 77); and one at New Richmond in the Gaspé in 1794 (no. 87).

On four vital points – names, ages, origins, and status – the notices are deficient:

Names. As a rule, the slaves offered for sale went unnamed, while fugitives were named. Only one slave offered for sale, Caesar (no. 65), was identified by name, whereas only two runaways (nos 2 and 18) were unnamed. Slave-masters seem to be identified in sixty-three of the notices; in some cases, however, the persons named were not the actual owners but agents acting for them. On this score, it must be noted that if a notice referred readers to the printer of a newspaper, this did not generally mean that the printer was the owner of the slave advertised. Other than William Brown, printer of the *Quebec Gazette*, who published several notices concerning his own slave, the printers were usually acting as intermediaries.

In the case of fugitives, it was in the interest of the advertiser to provide as full a picture as possible, to facilitate recognition and capture; hence the identification by name. Morally, too, there was an element of reproof in fugitive notices: the runaways were considered to have acted reprehensibly, whether they had broken out of jail, deserted a ship, or escaped a master. The reverse was true of slaves offered for sale: here, the idea was to speak well of them to entice buyers, and owners succinctly touted the skills and industriousness of their human merchandise. The two notices published within four months about Bett (nos 57 and 58), one as a fugitive and the other as a slave for sale, may serve to illustrate this contrast. When she ran away in March 1787, her owners, merchant partners James Johnston and John Purss of Quebec, advertised her delinquency, naming her and adding that she was "eighteen years old, middle stature, speaks the English, French and German languages well ... was big with child, and within a few days of her time." We are given to understand that her age, pregnancy, and flight all pointed to her irresponsibility. In the context of her escape, the mention of her language skills also sounded a warning that the three languages she spoke were like so many disguises that she might don to facilitate her escape; her fluency was an asset only to herself. Bett was retaken, and when Johnston & Purss advertised her for sale that July, they avoided reminding prospective buyers that she was the pregnant runaway they might have read about only four months earlier. They also avoided giving any hint that she was the Bett who, in May, having lost her baby, had been briefly held on suspicion of murdering the child.[2] They gave neither her name nor their own; parties interested in buying a "stout, healthy, active negro woman" were referred to the printer of the newspaper for information. The sales pitch mentioned her age, which in this context constituted a plus – she was young, "active" – and the fact that she had had the smallpox was also a positive trait since this meant that she was now immune. Other selling points were that she "can cook, wash and iron, work at plain needle-work, and is very handy in the care of children; may suit an English, French, or German family, as she speaks those three Languages." Her knowledge of languages is here promoted, like her other skills, as an asset to her owners.

Ages. Was Bett really eighteen? Where ages are given, they are generally such rough estimates as to be no more than indications of childhood and adulthood. The slave Ishmaël, for example, was said to be thirty-five at his first advertised escape attempt in 1779 (no. 29), and still about thirty-five at his third in 1788 (no. 64), although he had been bumped up to "about 36" on his second attempt in 1784 (no. 45).

Origins. A more or less explicit indication of origin is provided for only thirteen of the advertised runaways and slaves. Of these, only eight (nos 4, 16, 21, 29, 32, 33, 76, and 79) are stated to have been natives of a particular place, and one other (no. 24), from the fact that he was said to speak English with a "Guinea accent," is presumed to have been born in west Africa. The other four (nos 43, 47, 56, and 88) are said to have come from New York, Detroit, or Upper Canada, but this is no guarantee that they were born there. From the fact that some spoke Dutch or German, we might infer that they came respectively from New York and Pennsylvania, just as those who spoke English and French had probably lived for some time somewhere between Quebec and the Mississippi. They were not necessarily born in those places, however.

Status. It is not always clear, in the case of fugitives, whether the subject of the notice was a slave. In Pompey, "a Sailor Negro Slave," we have a deserting seaman who is also unequivocally a slave (no. 15), and Joe, "a negro man slave," is both a prison escapee and a fugitive slave (no. 55). The language of other notices was not always so explicit. While most of the notices up to 1798 concern slaves, the word "slave" itself appears in only six of them (nos. 4, 15, 29, 35, 55, and 61).

Although the notices are about blacks, they are also about whites, revealing a pervasive sense of entitlement to the use and disposal of blacks. We see this, for example, in an owner offering his "negro wench" for sale for no other reason than that he has "no use for her at present" – oh, and at the same time, "Likewise will be disposed of a handsome Bay MARE" (no. 43); or when tailor Ralph Gray offers to sell either one of his two "negro women ... as they disagree together" (no. 38).

A statistical analysis of the ninety-four notices would be of limited value in drawing hard conclusions about the slaves in general. For one thing, they represent only a portion of the sales and escapes. Another is that the picture they present might be lopsided, blacks at Quebec being perhaps overrepresented by virtue of the fact that Quebec was home to the colony's only newspaper for much of the time that slavery lasted. However, it is possible to establish the following facts. More males than females were the subject of notices: fifty-three of the former versus thirty-two of the latter. In the fifty cases where the rewards offered for fugitive black slaves, servants, deserting seamen, or jailbreakers were specified, the average was about $9 (roughly $9.50 for males and $7.50 for females). Of the fifty escapes advertised, most took place in the milder months (when the rivers were navigable): thirty-seven between April and October, six in November, one each in December and January, three in February, and two in March. We should not read too much into the relatively high number of escapes in November: two of those were jailbreaks, meaning that the timing was less a matter of choice than of circumstance, and one was a repeat attempt by a Quebec slave who had first tried to escape the previous summer. As for the three escapes in February, one, in 1786, was the jailbreak by William Brown's slave Joe, who had made at least five previous attempts to get away since 1774; another, in 1784, was the second attempt of the Montreal slave Ishmaël, who had previously escaped in the summer of 1779 and was to do so again in the summer of 1788.

In scouring old newspapers in search of blacks or slaves, we must guard against the temptation to overreach and to read them into the copy when they simply are not there. One such misreading more than a century ago led historian Robin Winks to state that, in Quebec, "the last known private advertisements for slaves appeared ... in 1821." In support of this, Winks cited a statement made by Hubert Neilson in his 1906 paper, "Slavery in Old Canada." In a footnote, Neilson had written: "Mr. G.M. Fairchild informs me that he has seen advertisements concerning slaves in the columns of the Quebec Mercury as late as 1820 or 1821." The fact is, no slave advertisements appeared in the *Mercury* in 1820 or 1821, or in any other year for that matter. The only possible explanation for the error by Neilson's informant is that he mistook for slave advertisements the notices about three absconding white apprentices that the *Mercury* published in 1820–21, each illustrated with the image of a running figure, like the logos that newspapers of the eighteenth century had used in notices about slaves. This would be an inconsequential error were it not for the fact that it has helped perpetuate the myth that slavery in Quebec persisted beyond the first years of the nineteenth century.[3]

Here are a few cases, of lesser consequence, where modern-day authors have mistakenly read blacks into newspaper notices. In her comparative study of black female slaves in Canada and Jamaica, Maureen G. Elgersman wrote: "Newspaper advertisements best help to understand the material level at which Black women in Canada lived. In 1778, Dufy Desaulniers, a resident of Montreal, offered a reward for the return of her escaped female slave who was 'dressed in striped calico of the ordinary cut.'" This led Elgersman to speculate about the significance of the slave's poor clothing – which can tell us nothing about black women in Canada for the simple reason that, as the advertisement stated, this slave of Marie Thomas Fleury de la Gorgendière, the widow of merchant Thomas Ignace Trottier *dit* Dufy Desaulniers, was a Panis:

> SIX PIASTRES A GAGNER.
> IL s'est enfui, le 14 du courant, une Panise appartenant à Madame Veuve DUFY DESAUNIER, âgée d'environ trente-cinq ans, habillée d'une indienne rayée, d'une taille ordinaire, d'une corpulence passable. Quiconque la ramenera, aura une récompense de SIX PIASTRES, & sera remboursé des frais qui seront prouvés avoir été faits pour la retrouver.

Oddly enough, on the basis of this same notice, Marcel Trudel also counted this Indian woman as a black slave.[4]

In her 2006 study of the slave Marie Josèphe Angélique, Afua Cooper fell into a similar error in discussing the importance of slave advertisements. "These advertisements give us insight into the enslaved people, their condition, and their responses to slavery. A couple of examples will suffice," she wrote, citing as her first example a notice from 1769 concerning a man called Joseph Negrié. A careful reading of this notice, and a comparison of the English and French versions that ran in the same newspaper, should have made it clear that Negrié was not a black man and not a slave:

> JOSEPH NEGRIÉ, a young Man, about 22 Years of Age, of a brown Complexion, slim made, 5 Feet 3 Inches high, his Face as if he had lately had the Small-Pox; small Legs, speaks French and English tolerably well, though French by Birth; run-away in the Night between the 7th and 8th Instant, from Peter du Calvet, Esq; of Montreal, with whom he was engaged for a Number of Years. The Public are desired not to employ the said Joseph Negrié; and all Captains of Vessels, who may take him on Board, are forwarn'd from carrying him out of the Province, as they will be pursued to the utmost Rigour of the Law. Whoever shall discover said Negrié, are desired to inform his Master, Peter du Calvet, Esq; at Montreal, or Mr Thomas Lee, Merchant in Quebec, and they shall be rewarded.

The name and graphic might suggest that Joseph Negrié was a fugitive slave, but he was, in fact, a white indentured servant.

Cooper is not the first to transform this French-born white servant of merchant Pierre Ducalvet into a black slave. Hubert Neilson had done so a century before, followed by Trudel, then by Daniel Gay, who listed him among the slaves whose names might hint at their origins – Negrié (or Négrié) sounding like "négrier," a French word for slave-trader or slave ship.[5]

We cannot assume that every slave in Quebec was black or that every black was a slave, nor that everyone identified at the time as "swarthy," "tawny," or of "brown" or "dark" or even "black" complexion was a black person. Gay, for instance, theorized on the basis of a notice of 1765 about a British army deserter named James Case, a man of "brown Complexion," that the presence of English blacks in New France went back a long way. But there was nothing in the notice to suggest that Case was black. He was said to be "five Feet five Inches and an Half high, brown Complexion, long thin Visage grey Eyes, dark brown hair, born in Lancashire Old England, and Parish of Wiggan, by trade a Weaver." The presence in Quebec of a Lancashire weaver serving in the 28th Regiment of Foot in 1765 suggests nothing about New France, which was no more, or about the presence of blacks in North America.[6] Case had a brown complexion, as did Joseph Negrié and any number of other apprentices, servants, and deserters (see accused murderer Louis Braban *dit* Lamie in notice 84, and Catherine Elizabeth Renoe in n15); all this meant was that they were not fair-skinned and fair-haired, not that they were blacks. And when we find an angry man, falsely named by a woman as the father of her child, denouncing her as untrustworthy, "a Convict, three Times sold in America," we are reminded that there was a time when white lawbreakers in some colonies were sentenced to be sold into servitude.[7]

The preceding notices were reasonably clear. Here is one from 1766 that is not: "To Be Sold, An indented Servant Woman, who has Three Years and Eight Months to serve. For further Particulars enquire of the Printers." We suspect that this woman was a white indentured servant, and that it was her indenture, not herself, that was for sale. For this reason, this notice is not included in the advertisements concerning blacks, but certainty eludes us in her case.[8]

The newspapers that published the notices presented here were as follows.

Quebec Gazette. This was the colony's first newspaper, printed by William Brown and Thomas Gilmore at Quebec. The first issue appeared on 21 June 1764. In 1774, Brown became sole owner. Publication of the bilingual weekly was suspended from 1 December 1775 to 14 March 1776, during the American invasion of Quebec. The issue of 19 March 1789 was the last published by Brown, who died on 22 March that year. His nephew, eighteen-year-old Samuel Neilson, succeeded him, but he died on 10 January 1793 at the age of twenty-two. Samuel's younger brother, sixteen-year-old John Neilson, then took over the reins and continued in that position well into the next century.[9]

Montreal Gazette. French printer Fleury Mesplet moved to Montreal from Philadelphia on the coat-tails of the American invasion force of 1775–76 and was left stranded by the American retreat. The French-language paper that he launched on 3 June 1778, under the name of *Gazette du commerce et littéraire,* was soon renamed the *Gazette littéraire du district de Montréal.* Publication ceased in June 1779. On 25

August 1785, Mesplet came out with a new newspaper, the bilingual *Montreal Gazette*. After his death on 24 January 1794, his widow continued publishing the paper until 13 February. Silent for more than a year, the *Montreal Gazette* was reborn on 3 August 1795, under the ownership of Montreal postmaster Edward Edwards.

Quebec Herald. William Moore launched his weekly *Quebec Herald and Universal Miscellany* on 24 November 1788, and then renamed it the *Quebec Herald, Miscellany & Advertiser* when he began to print it twice a week. Regular publication ceased in 1792, and publication stopped altogether in 1793.

Quebec Mercury. The first issue of this stoutly English Quebec newspaper, under the editorship of Thomas Cary, appeared on 5 January 1805, after the end of slavery in Quebec. It did not publish slave advertisements. It is included here only because in June 1806 it happened to publish the offer of a rather steep reward – five guineas apiece – for the capture of three deserters, including one black seaman, from a ship moored near Quebec.

Canadian Courant & Montreal Advertiser. Like the *Mercury,* this Montreal newspaper, launched in 1807 by American expatriate Nahum Mower, never published notices concerning slaves. However, in 1810, the *Courant* was one of the two Montreal newspapers that published the last notice of a reward offered for an absconding black indentured servant.

Other newspapers were launched from the 1790s onward, but none published notices of black slaves or fugitives.

Breaking down the number of advertisements published by each newspaper, we find that the *Quebec Gazette,* with its longer and steadier publication record, carried seventy-three, the *Montreal Gazette* eighteen, the *Quebec Herald* seven, and the *Mercury* and *Courant* one each. This makes for a total of one hundred, but since some of these were the same advertisement carried in more than one newspaper, we can say that the actual number of distinct advertisements was ninety-four. Counted as one is any advertisement that appeared at the same time in both English and French, or in two different newspapers, or that ran in several successive issues of the same newspaper. But if the same notice appeared at intervals of a month or more – indicating, say, renewed attempts to sell a slave – it is counted as a new one each time it is revived.

In the *Quebec Gazette,* the first notice of a black slave for sale was published on 18 June 1767, and the last on 9 October 1793. The *Montreal Gazette* printed its first slave-sale advertisement on 23 August 1786 and its last on 22 January 1798. (The first newspaper advertisement for the sale of a slave at Montreal was published in the *Quebec Gazette* of 13 April 1769.) The first notice for the sale of a slave in the *Quebec Herald* was published on 25 May 1789, the last on 14 April 1791.[10]

The notices are presented in chronological order and numbered sequentially. Where they concern a person who is, or is believed to be, the subject of more than one notice, the notice number is followed in square brackets by the numbers of the other notices for that person. Thus, the first notice for William Brown's slave, Joe, is no. 21 [22, 28, 30, 54, 55], the next 22 [21, 28, 30, 54, 55], and so on. In the case of the escape of the slave Ben in 1788, a first cursory notice and a second more detailed one that followed more than a month later are treated as two versions of the one advertisement and presented together, the one numbered 62 and the other 62b. Similarly, the two notices, with slightly different wording, published a week apart in April 1789 for the sale of a twenty-eight-year-old male slave are treated as one and numbered 67 and 67b. The source newspaper for the advertisements is given in square brackets at the end of each notice. The text of the notices is preceded by a tag line giving the place of the sale or escape; the month in which the sale was to take place or when the escape occurred; whether the notice concerns a sale or an escape; whether the subject was male or female (and the subject's estimated age); and, finally, whether the notice was accompanied by a logo, or visual cue, showing a running or standing figure.

As much as we may associate these logos with slave advertisements, in Lower Canada they are not sure indicators of slave status. They also figured in notices concerning white fugitives well into the 19th century, as we saw in the case of the notices for runaway apprentices published in the *Quebec Mercury* of 1820–21. Furthermore, where slaves were concerned, we might assume that the image of a running figure would indicate an escape, and that of a standing figure a sale, but the use of such logos was far from consistent from newspaper to newspaper. The *Montreal Gazette*, for example, did not use them until after it had published its last notice concerning slaves. The first time that a logo appeared in that newspaper, on 23 December 1799, it accompanied a notice about a runaway white apprentice.

– 1765 –

1 *Quebec – June – Escape/Male – Running logo*
RUN-AWAY from the Subscriber on Tuesday Morning last [25 June], a Negro Man, named *Drummond,* near six Feet high, walks heavily: Had on when he went away a dark coloured Cloth Coat and Leather breeches. Whoever takes up, and secures the said Negro, so that his Master may have him again, shall have FOUR DOLLARS Reward, and all reasonable Charges, paid by

JOHN MCCORD

Speaks very bad English, and next to no French.[11]

[*Quebec Gazette,* 27 June 1765]

– 1766 –

2 *Quebec – August – Escape/Female (24) – Running logo*
RUN-AWAY, *on Saturday the 22d of August, 1766, from* I. WERDEN, *in Quebec,*
A NEGRO GIRL, of about 24 Years of Age, pitted with the Small-pox, speaks good English: Had on a black Gown and red Callimanco Petticoat; and suppos'd to have Cash, both Gold and Silver, with her. Whoever apprehends said Negro Girl, and brings her back to said Werden, or to Mrs *Mary Wiggans*, at Montreal, shall have ONE PISTOLE Reward, and all necessary Charges, paid by

I. WERDEN.[12]

[*Quebec Gazette,* 1 September 1766]

SLAVE SALES AND FUGITIVES   315

3 [20] *Montreal – September – Escape/Male – Running logo*
RUN-AWAY, the 25th Instant, from Mr *Grant,* Merchant at Montreal, a Negro Man, named Brouce, the Property of Lieutenant-Colonel *Christie*: He is a Stout well made Fellow, about 5 Feet 5 Inches high, speaks English and French, and stammers a little in his Speech, Whoever secures the said Negro, and delivers him to the said Mr *Grant,* or to *David Elves,* Esq, shall be paid a Reward of TWO DOLLARS, and all reasonable Charges.[13]

Montreal, 25th *September* 1766.
[*Quebec Gazette,* 6 October 1766]

– 1767 –

4 *Montreal – May – Escape/Male (23) – Running logo*
RUN-AWAY, from *James Crofton,* Vintner in Montreal, the Third of May, 1767, a Mulatto Negro Slave, named Andrew,[14] born in Maryland, Twenty-three Years of Age, middle sized, very active and sprightly, has a remarkable large Mouth, thick Lips, his Fingers crooked, speaks good English and French, a little Dutch and Earse; is supposed to have with him forged Certificates of his Freedom, and Passes. Whoever takes up and secures the said Negro, so that his Master may have him again, shall have EIGHT DOLLARS Reward, besides all reasonable Charges, paid by Mr Henry Boone, Merchant, at Quebec, or James Crofton, at Montreal.

N.B. He is remarkable for being clean dress'd and wearing a Handkerchief tied round his Head; is very well known to all the Gentlemen at Quebec, that has been in Montreal, and who have used my House, and was Three Months with Mr Joseph Howard, of Montreal Merchant, last Summer in Quebec.[15]

[*Quebec Gazette,* 14 May 1767]

5 *Quebec – June – Private sale/Male (15) – Standing logo*
TO BE SOLD
A Healthy NEGRO BOY, about 15 Years of Age, well qualified to wait on a Gentleman as a body Servant. For further Particulars enquire of the Printers.[16]

[*Quebec Gazette,* 18 June 1767]

– 1768 –

6 *Quebec – July – Escape/Male – No logo*
RUN away on the 11th Instant, a Mulatto Man named WILL, the Property of Eleazar Levy,[17] he is much known in Canada, he speaks French, English and Spanish. All Masters of Ships, or others are hereby cautioned against conveying or assisting him to get off. Any Person that will return him to the House of his Master, or give intelligence that will be the Means of his being taken, shall receive FOUR DOLLARS Reward, and all Charges, paid by

SARAH LEVY.
[*Quebec Gazette,* 15 July 1768]

7 *Quebec – October – Escape/Male (40) – Running logo*
RUN-AWAY, on Thursday Night, the 18th Instant, from Mr Grant, at St Roch, a Negro Man, named Dick, about 40 Years of Age, 5 Feet 10 Inches: Had on a blue short Coat and green Waistcoat; wears a Cap with an old Hat; shaves his Head and takes Scotch Snuff. He carried with him a brown Frock and Scarlet Waistcoat with Gold Basket Buttons, and some Bed-Cloaths. Any Person who apprehends the said Negroe, shall receive FIVE POUNDS reward, upon returning him to the Owner.
Quebec, 19th *October*, 1768.

Il s'est échappé, dimanche le soir, de chez Mr Grant, à St Roch, un Nègre nommé DICK, agé d'environ 40 ans, de la taille de 5 pieds dix pouces: Il portoit un court habit rouge et une veste verte; il porte un bonnet avec un vieux chapeau, il a les cheveux rasés, prend du tabac d'Ecosse: Il a emporté avec lui un surtout brun, et une veste écarlate, avec des boutons de fil d'or, et quelques fournitures de lit. Toute personne qui arrétera le dit Nègre, aura CINQUE LIVRES de récompense, en le remettant au propriétaire.[18]
Québec, le 19 *Octobre,* 1768.

[*Quebec Gazette,* 27 October 1768]

8 *Quebec – November – Private sale/female (11) – No logo*
TO BE SOLD, a very healthy handy Negro Girl, about Eleven Years of Age, speaks both French and English. Enquire of the Printers hereof.

[*Quebec Gazette,* 17 November 1768]

– 1769 –

9 [11] *Quebec – February – Private sale/Female (25), Male (9 mos), Male (23) – No logo*
AS MILES PRENTIES, Tavern-keeper in the Lower-Town of Quebec, intends leaving the Province, he requests all Persons who have any Demands upon him, to give in their Accounts, and he also requests all Persons who are indebted to him, to make speedy Payment, so as he may be the better able to pay off his just Debts: –

Mr Prenties has to sell a Negro Woman, aged 25 Years, with a Mulatto Male Child, 9 Months old; she was formerly the Property of General Murray; she can be well recommended for a good House-servant, handles Milk well, and makes Butter to Perfection: Likewise a Negro Man, aged 23 Years, a very good House-servant, understands waiting upon a Gentleman, and looks well in Livery.[19]

[*Quebec Gazette,* 23 February 1769]

10 *Montreal – April – Private sale/Male (15) – No logo*
WHEREAS John Ferguson,[20] intends leaving this Province June next, all those who have any demands on him, are desired to bring their Accounts to be settled, and all those indebted to him are desired to make immediate Payment, otherwise their Accounts will be put into the Hands of an Attorney without further Notice. To be sold at the same Time, a healthy Negro boy, about 15 Years of Age, who has had the Small-

Pox, and is a compleat Cook; also a Horse, Chaise, Calash, and all his Household Furniture. –
    Montreal, 3 April, 1769.   [*Quebec Gazette*, 13 April 1769]

11 [9] *Quebec – June – Public sale/Female (25), Male (9 mos), Male (23) – No logo*
TO BE SOLD, at Public Vendue, on Friday the 16th Instant, a Negro Woman, aged 25 Years, with a Mulatto Male Child, 9 Months old. She can be well recommended for a good House Servant. – Likewise a Negro Man, aged 23 Years, a very good House Servant, and understands a good deal of Cookery.
                                          [*Quebec Gazette,* 15 June 1769]

12 [14] *Quebec – August – Private sale/Male (22–23) – No logo*
TO BE SOLD, for no Fault, the Owner having no Employ for him, a likely Negro Fellow, about 22 or 23 years of Age, understands Cooking, waiting at Table, and Household-work, &c. &c. He speaks both English and French. For further Particulars enquire of the Printers.[21]
                                     [*Quebec Gazette,* 17 August 1769]

13 *Quebec – September – Escape/Female (27) – No logo*
RAN-AWAY, on the 11th of September last, a Negro Woman, named Susannah, about 27 Years of Age, and about 5 Feet 10 Inches high, smooth fac'd, speaks English, and a little French. Whoever apprehends and secures the said Negro Woman, so that her Master may have her again, shall receive a Reward of TEN DOLLARS, by applying to Messrs *Dobie & Frobisher,* Merchants at Montreal, or to the Printers hereof.[22]
    N.B. Whoever harbours or conceals said Negro Woman, will be prosecuted to the utmost Rigour of the Law.
    Quebec, 18th October, 1769.
                                       [*Quebec Gazette,* 19 October 1769]

                        – *1770* –
14 [12] *Quebec – May – Private sale/Male (23–24) – Standing logo*
                      TO BE SOLD,
For no Fault, the Owner having no Employ for him,
A likely NEGRO FELLOW, about 23 or 24 years of Age; understands Cooking, waiting at Table, and Household Work, &c. &c. He speaks both English and French. For further particulars enquire of the Printers.
                                         [*Quebec Gazette*, 3 May 1770]

                        – *1771* –
15 *Quebec – August – Escape/Male – Running logo*
RUN-AWAY from the Subscribers, in the Night of the 12th Inst. a Sailor Negro Slave named POMPEY, about 5 Feet 5 Inches high, and is Robust; he was lately bought of Mr *Perras*,[23] Merchant in this Town; had on when he went away a brown Jacket and breeches. Whoever brings him to the Subscribers shall have EIGHT DOLLARS

Reward, and reasonable Charges paid. Any Person harbouring him will be prosecuted according to the utmost Rigour of the Law, by

JOHNSTON & PURSS[24]

[*Quebec Gazette,* 15 August 1771]

16 *Willsborough, New York – August – Escape/Male (28) – No logo*

SIX DOLLARS REWARD,

TO any Person or persons who shall discover and secure the following Persons, who absconded on Sunday Night the 18th Instant, from their Master the Subscriber, residing in Willsborough, Lake Champlain.

FRANCIS FREELAND, a bound Servant, suppos'd to be about 16, tho' small of his Age, remarkable for the Number of Masters he has served, having lived with almost every Stave-Cutter on the Lake, and Mr Charles Hay, of Quebec.; speaks English and French fluently: Took with him two Pair of Tow Cloth Trowsers, two Shirts of the same, almost new, and one old red Coat.

IRELAND, a Negro Man, aged about 28 Years, a straight well-made likely Fellow, about 5 Feet 6 or 7 Inches high, speaks English tolerably plain, but no other Language, except that of his native Country, *Guinea;* as he has liv'd with me, without any Appearance of Discontent, for upwards of 13 Years, it is supposed he has been seduced by the little Fellow that is gone off with him, and who is well known to many in Canada for his Villany. – For the above Reward, or Half of it for either, apply to Moses Hazen, Esq, at St John's, Mr John McCord, Merchant in Quebec, Mr Thomas McCord, Merchant in Montreal, or to

WILLIAM GILLILAND[25]

Willsborough, 20th *August,* 1771.

[*Quebec Gazette,* 19 September 1771]

– *1774* –

17 *Quebec – September – Private sale/Male (18) – No logo*

TO BE SOLD,

A Likely NEGRO LAD about 18 Years old.

Enquire of the Printers.

[*Quebec Gazette,* 8 September 1774]

– *1775* –

18 *Montreal – August – Escape/Male (22) – Running logo*

RUN AWAY from Mr *Orillat's* Farm on the Island of Montreal, the 20th Ult. A Negro about five Feet five or six Inches high, well-made, about twenty-two Years of Age, a mild Countenance, long Visage, with a small Scar on the left Side of his Neck joining the Jaw-bone, occasioned by a Gland not yet cur'd: he had on when he went away a short grey Coat of English Drugget. Whoever brings him back to Mr John Orillat shall have a reasonable Reward.[26]

[*Quebec Gazette,* 7 September 1775]

19 *Quebec – November – Escape/Male (25) – No logo*
RUN AWAY from the Subscriber (on the Eighteenth Instant) a Negro man named *Lowcanes,* aged twenty-five Years, thin faced, and remarkable long hair tied behind, about five feet ten inches high, speaks good French, no English, plays the Violin very well. He had on when he went off a light coloured short coat with a red cape to it, waistcoat and breeches: Whoever secures the said Negro man so that his Master may have him again shall have sixteen Dollars reward, and charges from
    22d *November,* 1775.   WILLIAM GILL.[27]
[*Quebec Gazette,* 30 November 1775]

– *1777* –

20 [3] *Montreal – September – Escape/Male (35) – No logo*
                                           Montreal, *September* 15, 1777
WHEREAS in the Night between the 4th and 5th instant, the cellar of John Jones, in Saint Paul Street, near the barrack, was broke open, and a great quantity of Liquors, Soap, Sugar and other effects were stolen and taken therefrom; And whereas there is the strongest reason to suspect that the said burglary and robbery was committed by a Negro man called *Bruce,* tall, well made, with a high Nose and very black complexion, about thirty-five years of age, who has since absconded: Notice is hereby given to all Captains of Militia and other peace Officers to use their utmost endeavours to apprehend the said *Bruce* and to send him in safe custody to the Goal of Montreal; and all persons are hereby strictly forbid to harbour or conceal the said Bruce on pain of being prosecuted with the utmost of the severity of the Law. A reward of FOUR POUNDS and all reasonable charges will be paid to the person who shall apprehend him and secure him as aforesaid, by
                                           EDWD. WM. GRAY, Sheriff.
[*Quebec Gazette,* 18 September 1777]

21 [22, 28, 30, 54, 55] *Quebec – November – Escape/Male (20) – Standing logo*
RANAWAY from the Printing-office in Quebec, on Saturday evening the twenty-second instant, a Negro Lad named JOE,[28] born in Africa, about twenty years of age, about five feet and an half high, full round fac'd, a little marked with the small-pox, speaks English and French tolerably; he had on when he went away an old green fur-cap, an old sky-blue broad-cloth coat, an old grey ratteen jacket, leather breeches, brown leggings and Canadian macassins. All persons are hereby forewarned from harbouring or aiding him to escape, as they may depend on being prosecuted to the utmost rigour of the Law, and whoever will give information where he is harboured, or bring him back, shall have FOUR DOLLARS Reward from
                                                    THE PRINTER.
[*Quebec Gazette,* 27 November 1777]

– *1778* –

22 [21,28,30,54,55] *Quebec – January – Escape/Male (20) – Standing logo*
RANAWAY from the Printing-Office in Quebec, on Sunday night the twenty-fifth instant, a Negro Lad named JOE, born in Africa, about twenty years of age, about five feet and an half high, full round fac'd, a little marked with the small-pox, speaks English and French tolerably; he had on when he went away a new green fur-cap, a blue suit of cloaths, a pair of grey worsted stockings and Canadian macassins. All persons are hereby forewarned from harbouring or aiding him to escape, as they may depend on being prosecuted to the utmost rigour of the Law, and whoever will give information where he is harboured, or bring him back, shall have EIGHT DOLLARS Reward from

THE PRINTER.
[*Quebec Gazette,* 29 January 1778]

23 *Quebec – February – Private sale/Female (28) – No logo*
TO BE SOLD
A Likely mulatto wench, 28 years old, healthy and strong; has had the small-pox and meazles; understands cooking, also to keep a house in order; can work at her needle, and is remarkably careful of young children.

Any family wanting a servant, may be informed of further particulars by applying to Mr Samuel Morin[29] in the Upper-town.

The price will be fixed at a word. – 11th February, 1778.

[*Quebec Gazette,* 12 February 1778]

24 *Montreal – May – Escape/Male – Standing logo*
RAN AWAY on Saturday night the 10th Instant, a Negro man named JACK, about five feet eight inches high, had on when he went away a red coat, faced with green, buff waistcoat and breeches, and an old blanket coat, speaks no other tongue but English, and that upon the Guinea accent, his foretop turned back, very black, with a large beard, was lately purchased of Captain Covells, of colonel Peters Volunteers. Whoever will secure the said Negro, that his Master may get him again, shall have a Reward of EIGHT DOLLARS and all reasonable charges paid by Finlay & Gregory, merchants near the Market-place, Montreal.[30]

Montreal, May 13, 1778.

[*Quebec Gazette*, 21 May 1778]

25 *Quebec – July – Escape/Male (18) – Standing logo*
RUN away on Friday night the 10th instant, from Mr Prentice's, a Mulatto fellow call'd Jacob, about eighteen years of age, had on when he went away a light brown fustian short Coat, white cloth Waistcoat and Breeches, and a round Hat, about five feet five inches high, well made and very active, speaks little or no French. Whoever secures and brings said Mulatto to Mr Miles Prentice in Quebec, or to Mr Thomas Richardson, at the Coffee-House Montreal, shall receive FOUR DOLLARS Reward and reasonable charges.

All Captains and Masters of vessels are desired not to take on board said Mulatto.
– Quebec, July 22, 1778.[31]

[*Quebec Gazette,* 23 July 1778]

26 [27] *Quebec – August – Escape/Female – No logo*
RAN AWAY from my service, on Tuesday night the 18th instant, A Mulatto Negress named BELL. I do hereby promise a reward of FOUR DOLLARS to any person who will apprehend said Negress and bring her to me, or lodge her in his Majesty's gaol in Quebec. She wore when she went away a striped woollen jacket and petticoat, and had no shoes or stockings on. I do caution all persons from harbouring said Negress, as I am determined to punish any person in whose custody she may be found to the utmost rigour of the law.

Quebec, August 19, 1778. GEO. HIPPS.

[*Quebec Gazette,* 20 August 1778]

27 [26] *Quebec – October – Escape/Female – Standing logo*
RUN away from Mr George Hipps on Thursday last [29 Oct.], a Mulatto wench named BELL, this is to give notice, that any person or persons whatsoever who harbours the said Girl may depend that he will go to the utmost rigour of the Law. When she went away she had upon her a Callico gown and Petticoat, a dress'd Cap, and a black silk Handkerchief.[32]

Quebec, *November* 3, 1778.

[*Quebec Gazette,* 5 November 1778]

28 [21, 22, 30, 54, 55] *Quebec – December – Escape/Male (21) – Standing logo*
RAN AWAY from the Printing-Office in Quebec, on Tuesday last [22 Dec.] about five o'clock in the evening, a Negro Lad named *JOE,* born in Africa, about twenty-one years of age, about five feet and a half high, full round fac'd, a little marked with the small-pox, speaks English and French tolerably: he had on when he went away an old green fur cap, a dark ratteen Coat and double-breasted jacket of the same, with yellow gilt buttons to each, a pair of black Manchester velvet breeches, grey worsted stockings and a pair of Indian Macassins. All persons are hereby forewarned from harbouring or aiding him to escape, as they may depend on being prosecuted to the utmost rigour of the Law, and whoever will give information where he is harboured, or bring him back, shall have FOUR DOLLARS Reward from

THE PRINTER.

[*Quebec Gazette,* 24 December 1778]

– *1779* –

29 [45, 64] *Montreal – July – Escape/Male (35) – Standing logo*
TEN DOLLARS REWARD.
RUN-AWAY from the Subscriber, a Negro Slave named Ishmaël, about 35 years old, 5 feet 8 inches high, pretty much marked with the Small-pox, wears his own Hair which is black, long and curly; has black Eyes, broad Shoulders, and tone of voice pe-

culiar to New-England, where he was born; reads English tolerably well, and can speak a little French: He had on an old Hat bedawbed with white Paint, an Ozcabrig Frock and Trowsers, a check Shirt, a short white flannel Jacket, and a pair of Mochinsons.

If any person apprehends said NEGRO, and gives notice thereof to the Subscriber living at the Batoe-gate, he or she shall receive *TEN DOLLARS* Reward, besides all reasonable Charges; but, whoever carries him off, entertains, or employs him after this public notice, will be prosecuted according to Law.
Montreal, July 16, 1779.   JOHN TURNER.[33]
[*Quebec Gazette,* 29 July 1779]

30 [21, 22, 28, 54, 55]   *Quebec – September – Escape/Male (22) – Standing logo*
RUN-AWAY

FROM the Printing-Office in *Quebec,* on Thursday last [16 Sept.] about seven o'Clock in the evening, a Negro Lad named JOE, born in Africa, near twenty-two years of age, about five feet and a half high, full round fac'd, a little marked with the Small pox, speaks English and French tolerably: he had on when he went away a dark Ratteen Coat tore about the arms, and a double breasted Jacket of the same, with yellow gilt buttons to each; greasy leather breeches, old thread Stockings, and a pair of Canadian Macassins. All persons are hereby forewarned from harbouring or aiding him to escape, and Masters of Vessels from carrying him off, as they may depend on being prosecuted to the utmost rigour of the Law; and whoever will give information where he is harboured, or bring him back, shall have FOUR DOLLARS Reward from
THE PRINTER.
Quebec, September 23, 1779.

[*Quebec Gazette*, 23 September 1779]

31 [36, 37, 39, 41, 44]   *Quebec – September – Private sale/Male (21) – No logo*
TO BE SOLD

A Robust, Likely, Healthy Negro Fellow, about twenty-one years of age, speaks English and French well, and has had the Small-pox. – For further particulars enquire of the Printer.

[*Quebec Gazette,* 30 September 1779]

32   *Quebec – September – Escape/Male – Standing logo*
RUNAWAY from the ship Susannah, Captain Ballantyne, on Monday evening last [27 Sept.], a black Boy named JNo. THOMPSON, height about 5 feet 3 or 4 inches, born in Spanish-Town, Jamaica, had on when he went away a brown Waistcoat with a flannel wrapper and black knit Breeches, without any Stockings. Whoever brings the same Boy to Mr Simon Fraser's, or on board the same Ship, shall receive ONE GUINEA Reward.

[*Quebec Gazette,* 30 September 1779]

33 *Quebec – October – Escape/Male (18), Female (26) – Standing logo*
RAN-AWAY
From the Subscriber, on Sunday morning the 24th ult. About four o'Clock, a Negro Lad named *NEMO,* born in Albany, near eighteen years of age, about five feet high, full round fac'd, a little mark'd with the Small pox, speaks English and French tolerably; he had on when he went away a double breasted Jacket of strip'd flannel, old worsted Stockings, and a pair of English Shoes. Also a Negro Wench named *CASH,* twenty-six years old, about 5 feet 8 inches high, speaks English and French very fluently; she carried with her a considerable quantity of Linen and other valuable Effects not her own; and as she has also taken with her a large bundle of wearing apparel belonging to herself, consisting of a black sattin Cloak, Caps, Bonnets, Ruffles, Ribbons, six or seven Petticoats, a pair of old Stays, and many other articles of value which cannot be ascertained, it is likely she may change her dress. All persons are hereby forewarned from harbouring or aiding them to escape; and Masters of vessels from carrying them off, as they may depend on being prosecuted to the utmost rigour of the Law; and whoever will give information where they are harboured, or bring them back to the Subscriber at Quebec, or to Mr George Ross, Merchant at Sorel, shall have TEN DOLLARS Reward for each, and all reasonable charges.
HUGH RITCHIE.[34]
N.B. The Lad was seen at Sorel on Friday morning the 29th ult. And there is reason to believe they are both lurking thereabout.

Quebec, November 2, 1779.
[*Quebec Gazette,* 4 November 1779]

– 1780 –

34 *Carleton Island – July – Escape/Male (25) – No logo*
RANAWAY from Carleton-Island the 18th July last, a Negro Lad named FORTUNE, about 25 Years of Age, 5 feet 5 inches high, has lost the toes off his right Foot, speaks English and a little French, had on when he ran away a red Jacket, coarse Shirt, and canvas Trowsers. Whoever secures said Negro so that his Master may recover him again, shall receive EIGHT DOLLARS Reward and all reasonable Expences paid by the Printer or Mr McMurray of Montreal; and any one that harbours or conceals, &c. said Negro will be prosecuted as the Law directs.[35]
[*Quebec Gazette,* 10 August 1780]

– 1781 –

35 *Montreal – June – Escape/Male (24) – Standing logo*
RUN away from the subscriber, the 27th of June last, a Negro man named NERO, 24 years of age, about 5 feet nine inches high; took with him a short blue Coat lined with red serge; a short grey Coat; one ditto of green blanket; a double-breasted green Jacket, one ditto of Ticken with Trowsers of the same, a Fustian Waistcoat and breeches. – Whoever apprehends the said negro and secures him, so that his Master may have him, shall receive FIFTY SHILLINGS Reward and all reasonable charges

paid, by applying to Mr William Laing in Quebec, if the Negro should be taken near it, but if near Montreal apply to the owner.

JOHN MITTLEBERGER.[36]

N.B. All persons are hereby forbid to harbour or employ the above described slave, or they may depend on being prosecuted with the utmost rigour of the Law, all Captains of Vessels and others, are forewarned not to carry him off at their peril, strick search will be made, and Warrants issued for that purpose.
Montreal, 24th August, 1781.

[Quebec Gazette, 4 October 1781]

36 [31, 37, 39, 41, 44] Quebec – October – Private sale/Male (22) – No logo
ANY person bound for the West Indies, desirous of purchasing a likely, robust, active, healthy Negro man (who has had the Small pox) about twenty two years of age, speaks English and French both remarkably well, may apply to the Printer hereof.

[Quebec Gazette, 18 October 1781]

37 [31, 36, 39, 41, 44] Quebec – December – Private sale/Male (21) – No logo
TO BE SOLD,
A Likely, Robust, Active, Healthy NEGRO LAD, about twenty one years of age; he speaks English and French both remarkably well, and has had the Small-pox.
    For further particulars apply to the Printer.

[Quebec Gazette, 6 December 1781]

38   Quebec – December – Private sale/Female (30 or 18) – No logo
MR R. GRAY, at New-Garden near Quebec, having two likely, healthy NEGRO WOMEN, both brought up to house-work, the one aged about thirty and the other about eighteen years, is desirous of disposing of one of them as they disagree together. They have both had the Small-pox and can be well recommended.[37]

[Quebec Gazette, 20 December 1781]

– 1782 –

39 [31, 36, 37, 41, 44] Quebec – May – Private sale/Male (21) – No logo
TO BE SOLD,
A Likely, Robust, Active, Healthy NEGRO LAD, about twenty one years of age; he speaks English and French both remarkably well, and has had the Small-pox.
    For further particulars apply to the Printer.

[Quebec Gazette, 2 May 1782]

40 Quebec – October – Public sale/Male – No logo
To be Sold by Auction, by Sketchley & Freeman, at their Public Sale Room, Notre Dame Street, Quebec, this present Thursday the 3d Instant, and the following days:
A large quantity of Dry Goods and Liquors, consisting of Woolen Cloths, Irish Linens and Sheetings, Checks and striped Cottons, printed Callicoes, Chintz, Gauzes, Pocket Handkerchiefs, Hosiery, boys Hats, a large quantity of French Paper, Gold and Sil-

ver Watches, Raisins, Soap, Glass, Tumblers, Goblets, Ladies white and colour'd Gloves, Patna Chintz, &c. &c.

Also a few Puncheons of exceeding fine Rum, a small quantity of choice Claret, Madeira and Port Wines.

The sale to begin at 10 o'Clock in the morning.
And on Saturday [5 Oct.] punctually at 11 o'clock in the morning, will be sold by Auction, by Sketchley & Freeman, at their Public Sale Room, aforesaid,
A Smart, Young and Healthy NEGRO Man, well qualified to make a good servant.

[*Quebec Gazette*, 3 October 1782]

– 1783 –

41 [31, 36, 37, 39, 44] *Quebec – January – Private sale/Male (21) – No logo*
TO BE SOLD,
A Likely, Robust, Active, Healthy NEGRO LAD, about twenty one years of age; he speaks English and French both remarkably well, and has had the Small-pox.
For further particulars apply to the Printer.

[*Quebec Gazette*, 23 January 1783]

42 *Quebec – July – Escape/Male (20) – Standing logo*
RAN AWAY,
FROM the Subscriber, on Thursday the 31st Ult. a Negro Lad named CHARLES, about 20 years of age, four feet four or five inches high, with a white mark on the right side of his forehead; speaks English and a little French and German; had on when he went away, a short grey jacket, and large linen trowsers. Whoever will give information of him and put him again in my hands, shall have THREE GUINEAS Reward.
Quebec, August 7, 1783.   PRE. GUEROUT.[38]

[*Quebec Gazette*, 14 August 1783]

43 *Quebec – November – Private sale/Female (18) – No logo*
TO BE SOLD
A NEGRO WENCH about 18 years of age, who came lately from New-York with the Loyalists. – She has had the Small Pox – The Wench has a good character and is exposed to sale only from the owner having no use for her at present.
Likewise will be disposed of a handsome Bay MARE.
For particulars enquire of the Printer.

[*Quebec Gazette*, 6 November 1783]

– 1784 –

44 [31, 36, 37, 39, 41] *Quebec – January – Private sale/Male (25) – No logo*
TO BE SOLD,
A Healthy NEGRO LAD, who has had the Small-Pox, and is about 25 Years of Age.
For more ample information apply to the Printer.

[*Quebec Gazette*, 15 January 1784]

45 [29,64] *Montreal – February – Escape/Male (36) – No logo*
FOURTEEN DOLLARS Reward.
RUN-AWAY, on Sunday Night last [28 Feb.], from the Subscriber, a Negro-Man, named ISHMAEL, about 36 Years of Age, and nearly 5 Feet 6 Inches high; of a remarkably down-cast Countenance, and a black and copper coloured mixt Complexion; his Hair is short, strong black and curly; and his Face much pitted with the small Pox. He wants some of his Upper-fore Teeth, as likewise the first Joint of the fourth Finger of his left Hand; and besides, on the middle of his Right-Leg, he has a fresh Eschar from a Horse Kick lately received and cured; had on when he went off, a round Hat cocked up behind and blue silk Band; a red plush Waistcoat; a pair of blue Bath coating Leggings and Breeches in one; and a Pair of Shoes and Metal Buckles.

He came from Claverac near Albany in 1776, with his former Master, C. Spencer; can speak and read English tolerably well, and understands a little Dutch and French; he passes himself, 'tis said, as a Free Negro, the more easily to effect unnoticed his intended Escape out of the Province. Whoever will apprehend the said Negro-Man, and deliver him to the Subscriber, Merchant, Montreal, shall receive the above Reward, and all reasonable Charges from

JOHN TURNER.
Montreal, March 1, 1784.

[*Quebec Gazette,* 11 March 1784]

46 *Quebec – March – Private sale/Female – No logo*
A VENDRE
UNE NEGRESSE qui est présentement en ville. L'on pourra s'adresser à Madame Perrault pour le prix.[39]

[*Quebec Gazette,* 4 March 1784]

47 *Quebec – May – Private (or public) sale/Female (15–16) – No logo*
TO BE SOLD by Private Sale,
A Likely healthy NEGRO Wench, between 15 and 16 years of age, brought up in the province of New-York, understands all sorts of house work, and has had the Smallpox. Any person desirous of purchasing such a Wench, may see her at the house of Mr John Brooks in the Upper-Town, where the conditions of sale may be made known; and if she should not be sold before the 30th instant, she will on that day be exposed to publick sale.

Quebec, May 10, 1784.

[*Quebec Gazette,* 13 May 1784]

48 *Quebec – August – Escape/Male (28), Male (?) – Standing logo*
RAN AWAY
FROM the Subscriber on Thursday the 12th August last, a Negro man named Tight;[40] about twenty-eight years of age, about 5 feet 8 inches high, speaks English and a little German; he went away in company with a Negro man belonging to Capt. Laforce

named Snow,[41] tall and slender, who speaks English and French. They were seen crossing the River St Lawrence from the South side to L'Assomption about the first instant, and are supposed to have gone towards the Lake behind Montreal. Whoever will apprehend the first mentioned Negro named Tight, and secure him so tightly that his master may have him again, shall have *Forty Shillings* reward, and all reasonable charges, paid by Mr Christy Cramer, Merchant in Montreal, or the Subscriber in Quebec.

Quebec, 7th September, 1784.   JOHN SAUL.

[*Quebec Gazette,* 9 September 1784]

49 *Quebec – September – Private sale/Female (23) – No logo*
TO BE SOLD,
A GOOD healthy Negro girl, 23 years of age, speaks good French and English, and has had the small-pox. For further particulars apply to *Michael Cornud*,[42] Merchant, Quebec.

[*Quebec Gazette,* 2 September 1784]

50 *Quebec – October – Private sale/Female (limited term) – No logo*
TO BE SOLD,
BETWEEN Seven and Eight Years unexpired of the time of service of a black Girl, on Indenture, aged between Twenty and thirty; the purchaser will receive satisfactory accounts respecting her honesty, sobriety and good temper. Enquire of the Printer.[43]

To be sold also, an English fashion Chaise, iron axle-tree, and brass boxes, almost new and perfectly sound and unshaken.

[*Quebec Gazette,* 21 October 1784]

– *1785* –

51 *Quebec – May – Private sale/Female (26), child (?), and Male (13) – No logo*
A Gentleman going to England has for sale, a Negro-wench, with her child, about 26 years of age, who understands thoroughly every kind of house-work, particularly washing and cookery: And a stout Negro-boy, 13 years old: Also a good horse, cariole and harness. – For particulars enquire at Mr William Roxburgh's, Upper-Town.[44]

Quebec, 10th May, 1785.

[*Quebec Gazette,* 12 May 1785]

52 *Quebec – May – Escape/Male (38) – Standing logo*
RANAWAY *the 28th or 29th of last Month,*
A NEGRO MAN named CUFF, about 38 years of age, 5 feet 8 inches high; had on when he went away, a white shirt, a drab coloured waistcoat, the sleeves of old stockings, a blue great coat, round hat, with a band and buckle, a pair of green leggins, and black buckles in his shoes; he has some scars on his temples, and a scar on one of his hands. Whoever will apprehend him and bring him to the Subscriber, shall have

SIX DOLLARS reward, and all reasonable charges paid. Captains of vessels and others are requested not to harbour or carry off said Negro.

Quebec, 6th June, 1785. ELIZABETH McNIELL.[45]

[*Quebec Gazette,* 9 June 1785]

53 *Quebec – September – Escape/Male (30) – No logo*
RUN AWAY on Thursday morning last [15 Sept.] from the Subscriber, A Mullatto man Named Tom Brooks, Aged Thirty years, about five feet eight Inches high, strong made, had on a Mixed Brown Coat and Weastcoat, Green trowsers, a white Beaver hat with broad Gold-lace; speaks English and French perfectly; was in Company with one Richard Sutton by trade a Carpenter, who had on a Blue Jacket, a pair of white trowsers and new hat. Whoever Secures the said Mullatto or Sutton, so that the Subscriber may be informed of it, shall have a Reward of Five Pounds.

Quebec Sept. 22d. 1785. ROBT. M. GUTHRIE.[46]

[*Montreal Gazette,* 29 September 1785]

– *1786* –

54 [21, 22, 28, 30, 55] *Quebec – February – Escape/Male – No logo*
BROKE out of his Majesty's Goal the 18th February, 1786, between the hours of six and eleven o'clock in the morning, JOHN PETERS a Criminal, about five feet eight inches high, had on him a brown coat, westcoat and breeches, a pair of Indian shoes and a round hat, has a fair complexion, thin visage and fair hair, round shoulders, and about thirty years of age. – ALSO, JOE, a Negro man, the property of Mr William Brown, printer, had on him a blue great coat, a red outside Jacket, a white under Jacket, and black breeches, and a round hat, of a sulky look, thick lips, and about five feet eight inches high. Whoever will apprehend the said Prisoners, so as they may be returned to his Majesty's Goal, shall receive a Reward of FIVE POUNDS Currency for each, by applying to Jas. Shepherd, Esq. Sheriff, or to John Hill, gaol-keeper. And all persons whatsoever that harbour or shelter the said prisoners, shall be prosecuted to the utmost rigor of the Law.

[*Quebec Gazette,* 23 February 1786]

55 [21, 22, 28, 30, 54] *Quebec – February – Escape/Male (26) – Standing logo*
Printing-Office, *Quebec, 1st May,* 1786.
BROKE out of His Majesty's Gaol in Quebec, on Saturday morning the 18th of February last, a NEGRO MAN SLAVE named JOE, born in Africa, twenty-six years of age, about five feet seven inches high, a little pitted with the small-pox, has several scars on his legs, speaks English and French fluently, and is by trade a Pressman; he had on him when he broke out a blue great coat, a red out-side jacket, a white under jacket, and round hat. He was seen some time ago in the parish of l'Ange Gardien below the falls of Montmorency. All persons are hereby forewarned from harbouring or aiding him to escape, as they may depend on being prosecuted to the utmost rigor of the Law; and whoever will give information where he is harboured, so that he may

SLAVE SALES AND FUGITIVES   329

be had again, shall receive THREE GUINEAS Reward from the Printer of this Gazette.[47]

[*Quebec Gazette*, 4 May 1786]

56 Montreal – August – Private sale/Male (24) – No logo
To be Sold by Private Sale.
A Mulatto, of about 24 Years old, just arrived from Detroit; has had the small Pox, speaks good English and French; those who chuses to purchase him, may inquire at the Subscriber.

Montreal, 23 August 1786.   Jos. ROY

[*Montreal Gazette*, 24 August 1786]

– *1787* –

57 [58] Quebec – March – Escape/Female (18) – No logo
RAN-AWAY from the subscribers, between the hours of seven and eight o'clock yesterday evening [7 March], a NEGRO WENCH, named BETT, about eighteen years old, middle stature, speaks the English, French and German languages well; had on when she went away, a blue Kersey Jacket and Pettycoat, a dark cotton Cap with yellow strings, and an Indian Shawl round her neck, was big with child, and within a few days of her time.

Whoever will apprehend said Negress, and secure her return, shall be paid A REWARD of TWENTY DOLLARS, and all reasonable expenses.

Any person who may harbour or conceal the said Negress, will be prosecuted to the rigour of the law, by

JOHNSTON & PURSS.

[*Quebec Gazette*, 8 March 1787]

58 [57] Quebec – July – Private sale/Female (18) – No logo
FOR SALE,
A STOUT, healthy, active NEGRO WOMAN, about eighteen years old, has had the small pox, she has been used to a family, can cook, wash and iron, work at plain needle-work, and is very handy in the care of children; may suit an English, French, or German family, as she speaks those three Languages.

For further information enquire of the Printer.

[*Quebec Gazette*, 5 July 1787]

59 Quebec – October/November – Escape/Male – No logo
THE WIDOW PERRAULT gives notice to the Public, that her NEGRO Servant, known under the name of Alexis, made his escape from her house a few days ago; she therefore forewarns all persons who may harbour him or give him strong liquor, or make him work, that they will be prosecuted to the utmost rigour of the law.[48]

[*Quebec Gazette*, 8 November 1787]

– *1788* –

60 *Quebec – March – Private sale/Female (22–23), Male (23–24) – No logo*
To be SOLD together,
A handsome Negro Man and a beautiful negro Woman married to one another; the man from twenty-three to twenty-four years of age, between five and a half and six English feet high; the woman from twenty-two to twenty-three years of age; both of a good constitution. For further information, such as may be desirous of purchasing them must apply to Mr Pinguet, in the Lower-town of Quebec, Merchant.[49]

[*Quebec Gazette,* 27 March 1788]

61 *Quebec – April – Escape/Male (26–27) – Standing logo*
RUN away on Sunday last the 13th inst. from the Subscribers, a NEGRO MAN named Caleb, aged about twenty-six or twenty-seven years, five feet eight inches high, had on when he went off a dark blew great coat, drab coat and vest, dark blue breeches, white stockings and a round hat: All persons are required not to harbour or employ the said Negro Slave, or they will be prosecuted according to law. Any person who will bring and deliver him up at Quebec, shall have all reasonable expences paid, and be rewarded by
Quebec, 16th April, 1788.   MATHEW & JOHN MACNIDERS.[50]

[*Quebec Gazette,* 17 April 1788]

62 *Montreal – April – Escape/Male (13) – Standing logo*
RUN away on the 24th instant, a Negro Boy named BEN,[51] about thirteen years of age, five feet four or five inches high, black hair, and very streight; had on when he went off a blue round jacket and trowsers, and a round hat. Whoever will apprehend the said boy and return him to his master at Mr *Levy Solomons'*, shall be well rewarded and all expences paid. All persons are forewarned to harbour or employ said negro, under pain of being prosecuted as the law directs.
Montreal, 28th April, 1788   M. MICHAELS

[*Quebec Gazette,* 8 May 1788]

62b
RUN away on the 24th April last, a Mulatto Boy named BEN, about thirteen years of age, five feet four or five inches high, streight black hair, not tied, well limbed; had on when he went off a blue round jacket and trowsers, and a round hat; speaks good English and some broken French. Whoever will apprehend the said boy and return him to his master at Mr *Levy Solomon's,* shall receive FIVE POUNDS Reward, and all necessary expences paid. All persons whatsoever within this province, as well as masters of vessels, are forewarned to harbour or employ said Mulattoe, under pain of being prosecuted as the law directs.
Montreal, 5th June, 1788   M. MICHAELS

[*Quebec Gazette,* 19 June 1788]

63 *Quebec – June – Escape/Male (18) – Standing logo*
RUN AWAY from the Schooner Lucy, a Mulatto fellow named PASCAL PURO, the property of John Sargent;[52] he is about eighteen years of age, a stout strong lad, about five feet six or seven inches high, talks good English, writes and reads, has a scar under one of his ears, calls himself a fee-man,[53] is supposed to be concealed in some house in this town.

Any person harbouring or taking away said fellow, will be dealt with agreeable to law. FOUR DOLLARS Reward will be given any person giving information, so that he may be secured, by applying to
Quebec, June 3d 1788. CONSTANT FREEMAN.
[*Quebec Gazette,* 5 June 1788, supplement]

64 [29, 45] *Montreal – June – Escape/Male (35) – Standing logo*
RUN away from the Subscriber on Saturday morning [5 June], a Negro man named ISHMAEL, aged about thirty-five years, five feet eight inches high, black short curled hair, marked with the small pox, wants some teeth, and a joint to his left hand little finger; speaks English, a little French and Dutch; had on when he ran away a round hat, a sailor's blue jacket, a white waistcoat, blue trousers and no shoes, &c. It is supposed he will call himself a free negro.

Whoever apprehends said Negro, and brings him to his master, shall receive the promised Reward, and all reasonable Charges.
Montreal, 7th June, 1788. JOHN TURNER, Senior.
[*Quebec Gazette,* 26 June 1788]

65 *Quebec – August – Public sale/Male – No logo*
BY PUBLIC AUCTION,
Will be sold on Saturday next the 23d inst. at Ferguson's tavern in the Lower town:

ABOUT twenty-five pipes and hogsheads of Old Madeira Wine, from fifteen to twenty pipes and hogsheads Port ditto, both of which are of the first quality and truly genuine, and are absolutely to be sold without reserve. Samples may be seen previous to the sale, by applying to the Brokers.

Sale to begin at 7 o'clock in the evening, by
Quebec, 19 August 1788. MELVIN & BURNS.
N.B. At same time and place will be sold, a likely healthy NEGRO Man named Caesar.[54]

[*Quebec Gazette,* 21 August 1788]

– 1789 –
66 *Montreal – January – Private sale/Female (15) – No logo*
A VENDRE
PAR le Soussigné, Une jeune Négresse d'environ 15 ans, parlant Anglois & François, & au fait du train d'un ménage.

J.F. PERRAULT[55]
[*Montreal Gazette,* 29 January 1789]

67 *Montreal – April – Private sale/Male (28) – No logo*
To Be SOLD,
A Stout, healthy NEGRO MAN, about 28 years of age. Is an excellent Cook. Enquire of the Printer.
Montreal, 1st April, 1789.

[*Montreal Gazette*, 2 April 1789]

67b
To Be SOLD,
A Stout, healthy NEGRO MAN, about 28 years of age. Is an excellent Cook, and very fit for working on a Farm. Enquire of the Printer.
Montreal, 1st April, 1789.

[*Montreal Gazette*, 9 April 1789]

68 [71] *Quebec – May – Private sale/Female (26) – No logo*

Quebec, May 25th, 1789.
FOR SALE,
A Stout, Healthy
MULATTO GIRL,
26 years of age, or thereabout.
Enquire of the Printer.

[*Quebec Herald*, 18–25 May 1789]

69 *Quebec – Spring – Escape/Female – Standing logo*

Quebec, Dec. 14, 1789.
RUN AWAY
From the Subscriber, last spring, a Negro wench named *Ruth,* it is suspected she is about St John's.

If any person will apprehend the said Negro wench and deliver her to Mr Fitch, at St John's, Mr Dillon at Montreal, or the Subscriber in Quebec, all reasonable expences will be paid, by

JOHN SAUL.[56]
[*Quebec Herald*, 14 December 1789]

70 *Quebec – August – Escape/ Male (35) – Running logo*
IL S'ENFUIT DE QUÉBEC LUNDI DERNIER MATIN, un NEGRE nommé JOE[57] ou CUFF, âgé d'environ 35 ans, environ 5 pieds 10 pouces de haut. Il avoit quand il partit un capot rouge, une paire de grandes culotes de Cotton rayé. Il a aussi l'oeil droit couvert de blanc, parle François et Anglois. Les Capitaines et Officiers de Milice sont priés de l'arrêter et en donner avis à l'IMPRIMEUR, ou à Mr BELLECOUR chez le Sieur *Jo. Delisle,* au Cul-de-Sac à Québec, et ils seront raisonnablement récompensés; et toutes personnes qui le cacheront ou lui donneront asile seront poursuivies selon la rigueur de la loi à cet égard. – Quebec, 3 Septembre, 1789.

[*Quebec Gazette,* 3 September 1789]

71 [68] *Quebec – September – Private sale/Female – No logo*
Quebec, Sept. 14, 1789.

TO BE SOLD
(*With a Warranted title,*)
A Stout Healthy
MULLATO WOMAN,
At a moderate price, – Apply
To the Printer.

[*Quebec Herald*, 7–14 September 1789]

72 *Trois-Rivières – September – Private Sale/Female – No logo*
TO BE SOLD
A Young, Able and healthy Negro Woman.

For further particulars enquire at the Printing Office, Mountain street Quebec.
Three-Rivers, 22d. September, 1789

[*Quebec Gazette*, 1 October 1789]

– *1790* –

73 *Quebec – April – Private sale/Female – Standing logo*
TO BE SOLD

A Young Healthy NEGRO WOMAN capable of most kind of business is a good cook and house-maid, understands milking cows and making butter, and of undoubted sobriety and honesty – *For particulars apply to the printer.*

[*Quebec Herald* and *Quebec Gazette*, 22 April 1790]

74 *Montreal – October – Escape/Male (27) – Running logo*
RUN AWAY

From the Subscriber, a Negro Man, named Richard, about five foot seven inches high, twenty seven years of age, and has a cast in one eye; had on when he went away, a dark brown jacket and long trousers, whoever will apprehend and return him to the Subscriber, shall receive TWO GUINEAS Reward, and all reasonable expences paid.

Montreal, 20th Oct. 1790. ROSSETER HOYLE.

[*Quebec Gazette,* 28 October 1790/*Quebec Herald,* 4 November 1790]

– *1791* –

75 [76] *Quebec – March – Private sale/Male (18–19) – Standing logo*
Quebec, March 17, 1791.

TO BE SOLD,
A YOUNG,
NEGRO LAD,

About 18 or 19 years of age, strong and very healthy, has had the small pox and measles, brought up to the farming business, and understands it well.

He speaks the *English, French* and *German* Languages well.

Any person who had a mind to purchase the same, for further particulars apply to the *Printer.*

[*Quebec Herald,* 17 March 1791)

76 [75] *Quebec – April – Public sale/Male (18–19) – No logo*

Quebec, 14th April, 1791.

ADVERTISEMENT.
To be SOLD *by* AUCTION, *on*
Tuesday *the 26th instant, at the house of*
Mr John Goudie, *No. 43,*
Champlain Street, Lower-town,
A Compleat sett of hand organs, half a dozen mahogany chairs, one elegant four post mahogany bedstead, several other bedsteads, beds and bedding, tables, a clock, looking glasses, a quantity of porter in hogsheads, also a quantity of kitchen furniture.

LIKEWISE
TO BE SOLD,
A young NEGRO LAD about 18 or 19 years of age, strong and very healthy, has had the small pox and measles, born in Philadelphia, brought up to House work, can shave and dress hair, he speaks English and French.

Any person who has a mind to purchase before the day of SALE, for particulars apply to the Proprietor.

[*Quebec Herald,* 14 April 1791]

77 *Berthier – July – Escape/Female (30) – Running logo*

RUN AWAY
From the Subscriber in the Night of the 13th Instant:
A NEGRO WENCH, named Cloe, about thirty years old, pretty stout made, but not tall; speaks English and French, the latter not fluently. As she has taken all her own cloaths and some which did not belong to her, it is uncertain what dress she may wear. She is supposed to have gone off in a canoe with a man of low stature and dark complexion, who speaks English, Dutch, and French. She got out of a garret window by the help of a ladder. – Whoever will apprehend and return the said wench to the Subscriber at Berthier, or give notice to him, or to the Printer hereof, where she may be found, shall be liberally rewarded, and all reasonable expences paid.

Berthier, 21st July, 1791   J. JOSEPH[58]

[*Quebec Gazette*, 28 July 1791]

78 *Montreal – November – Public sale/Female (25) – No logo*

J. A. GRAY.
Has for sale at his Stores in Saint Joseph's street,
Next the Grand Parade,
Double and single Glocester Cheese
London Porter, in Hampers of 3 dozen each.

ALSO TO BE SOLD,
A healthy Negro Woman aged about twenty five, a tolerable good Cook, understands Washing and the business appertaining to a female Servant. – She will be disposed of on very moderate terms.[59]

Montreal, 2d November 1791
[*Montreal Gazette*, 3 November 1791]

– 1792 –

79 *Quebec – February – Escape/Male (30) – Running logo*
IL S'EST ENFUI UN NEGRE NOMME JACK APPARTENANT à William Grant, Ecuyer, de Quebec. Il portoit une bougrine de drap bleu épais doublé de flanelle blanche, et un Gilet de même couleur; des Grandes Culottes ou braies de grosse étofe brune. Il a environ 30 ans, né en Afrique, d'environ 5 pieds 8 pouces de haut, robuste, parle Anglois et François. Quiconque arrêtera le susdit Nègre et l'amenera à son Maître ou à David Alexandre Grant Ecuyer l'Isle Ste. Helene près de Montréal, ou à Mr Hardie à St Jean recevra une guinée de recompense, et sera remboursé de tous fraix raisonables. Quiconque l'azilera ou le cachera sera poursuivi suivant la loi. On pense qu'il tâchera de séchaper dans les Etats Unis, ayant été vu Vendredi le 2 du courant aux Grondines cheminant vers Montréal, ou St Jean.

[*Quebec Gazette*, 15 March 1792]

80 *Montreal – October – Escape/Male (19) – No logo*
TWENTY DOLLARS REWARD.
RAN away from the Subscriber on Sunday the 7th instant, a Mulatto apprentice about nineteen years of age, and about 5 feet 9 inches high a Shoe-maker by trade, had on when he went away a brown Surtout coat, a Jean Coat and Leggins, a pair of boots and new coarse Hat.

Also a Canadian man about twenty-six years of age, much marked with the small-pox, speaks broken English, had with him a brown Surtout coat, a brown coat and striped vest, he is a Tanner and Currier by trade. Whosoever apprehends the above mentioned men, and delivers them at Montreal, or to the Subscriber at Sault au Recollet shall receive the above reward and all reasonable charges, paid by

JOHN TIEPLE.

N.B. The apprentice's name is Eber Welden,[60] and the Canadian Pierre Agie.

[*Montreal Gazette*, 11 October 1792]

81 *Montreal – November – Escape/Male – No logo*
Montreal, 20th November 1792.
BROKE Goal and escaped on Sunday the 18th instant about eight o'Clock in the evening, William Spencer, a Negro, charged with petty larceny; he is about five feet and six inches high, well made, and wore a short blue Jacket, and red waistcoat, black breeches, a round hat and generally a wig.

JACOB KUHN, Goaler.

All Officers of Militia in the country, as well as all other His Majesty's subjects are hereby required to use their utmost diligence in apprehending the said criminal and to lodge him in any of the goals of this Province, the respective keepers whereof are hereby required to receive the said William Spencer into their custody and him safely keep until he shall be discharged by due course of law; and as a further encouragement a reward of four dollars and all reasonable charges shall be paid on the criminal being committed to any of the said Goals, by

EDW. WM. GRAY, *Sheriff.*
[*Montreal Gazette,* 22 November 1792]

– *1793* –
82 *Montreal – February – Private sale/Male (22) – No logo*
A VENDRE

UN Mulâtre âgé de 22 ans, bon Perruquier pour homme & pour femme, & bon Cuisinier; il faut s'adresser à Mr Jean Routier, Riviere du Chene, ou a Mr Jean-Marie Hupé, Fauxbourg St Antoine.[61]

Montréal, *20 fevrier 1793.*
[*Montreal Gazette,* 21 February 1793]

83 *Montreal – March – Private sale/Female (25) – No logo*
TO BE SOLD.

A Very stout Negro wench of about 25 years of age, she can Wash, iron, Cook, and do any kind of House work. For further particulars apply to Mr McMurray.[62]

[*Montreal Gazette,* 21 March 1793]

84 *Montreal – May – Escape/Male (20) – No logo*

Montreal, *12th May 1793.*

BROKE Goal and escaped, this morning, *Louis Braban dit Lamie,* a Canadian, charged with murder, about five feet ten inches high, brown complexion, and dark brown hair; had on a blue Capot and Trousers, canadian shoes, a check silk handkerchief and a round hat, and is stout and well made. Also *John Hitlenger,* a soldier in the second battalion of the Sixtieth Regiment, a German, charged with robbery; he is about five feet four inches high and twenty eight years of age, fair complexion and light brown hair; had on a short blanket coat, a green waistcoat and white breeches with shoes. Also *Jacob Simpson,*[63] a Negro, indicted for petty larceny; he is about five feet two inches high and about twenty years of age, had on a green jacket and old brown trousers.

JACOB KUHN, Goaler.

All Captains and Officers of Militia, in the several country parishes, as well as all other His Majesty's subjects, are hereby required to use their utmost diligence to apprehend the said Criminals, and to lodge them in any of the goals of this Province, the respective keepers whereof are likewise required to receive them into their custody and them safely keep until they shall be discharged by due course of law; and as a further encouragement a reward of eight Dollars, with all reasonable expences, will be paid for each of the said Criminals, on their being committed to any of the said Goals, by

EDW. WM. GRAY, *Sheriff.*
[*Montreal Gazette* and *Quebec Gazette*, 16 May 1793]

85 Montreal – May – Private sale/Male (16) – No logo
TO BE SOLD
A Mulatto Boy sixteen years old, capable of Cooking and doing all kind of House Work, any person wishing to purchase, enquire of the Printer.

[*Montreal Gazette*, 16 May 1793]

86 Quebec – October – Private sale/Male (23) – No logo
TO BE SOLD,
A Likely, healthy, Stout MULATTO Young Man, aged Twenty-three Years, has been used to House-work, speaks both French and English, and is fit for any kind of hard Labour. – Inquire of the Printer. – *Quebec, 9th October,* 1793.

[*Quebec Gazette,* 17 October 1793]

– *1794* –
87 Gaspé – April – Escape/Male (38-40) – Running logo
RUN away from the Subscriber, at New Richmond in the district of Gaspié on Saturday the 29th of April, A NEGRO MAN named *Isaac,* who calls himself *Charles* some times: He is about five feet eight or ten inches high, speaks good English and some broken French and Micmac, aged about thirty-eight or forty years, has lost some of his fore-teeth, and has the ends of both his great toes frozen off. Whoever will take up said Negro and confine him in any of the jails or prisons in the province of Lower Canada, and notify the Subscriber by the earliest opportunity, shall receive a Reward of TWENTY DOLLARS, as the said Negro has been guilty of theft and many other misdemeanors.

AZARIAH PRITCHARD, senr.[64]
[*Quebec Gazette,* 22 May 1794, supplement]

– *1795* –
88 Montreal – December – Private sale/Female (12–13) – No logo
FOR SALE
A Young healthy Negro Wench between 12 and 13 years of age, lately from Upper Canada, where she was brought up. – Enquire of Gibb & Prior.[65]
Montreal 24 December 1795.

[*Montreal Gazette,* 28 December 1795]

– *1796* –
89 Montreal – November – Escape/Male (18) – No logo
BROKE out of and escaped from the Common Gaol of the said District, in the night

between the 14 and 15th inst. the following prisoners, to wit. Noah Drew and Moses Little Bailey, convicted of uttering and passing false and counterfeit money, Recompence Tiffany, charged with suspicion of circulating false money and Thomas Etherington, a mulatto charged with stealing in a dwelling house. – The said Noah Drew is about 27 years of age, about 5 feet 7 inches high, fair complexion and black hair, had on a blue coat, black waistcoat olive colored breeches and white hat, Moses Little Bailey is about 20 years of age, about 5 feet 2 inches high, pale complexion and light colored hair, had on a grey nankeen coat, waistcoat and trowsers, and a black hat. Recompence Tiffany is about 30 years of age, 5 feet 7 inches high, fair complexion and light brown hair, had on a short brown cloth coat, a stript corduroy waistcoat, and light blue cloth trowsers. Thomas Etherington is about 18 years of age, about 5 feet 4 inches high, very slender and an ill looking countenance, had on a brown bath coating jacket and trowsers, an old black hat, and walks somewhat lame.

JACOB KUHN Gaoler.

All Captains of militia, in the several Parishs, as well as all Constables and other Peace officers in and for the District aforesaid, are required to use their utmost diligence to apprehend the above named criminals and them to commit to any of his Majesty's Gaols in this Province, the respective keepers whereof are hereby required to receive them into their custody, and them safely to keep, until they shall be discharged by due course of Law; and as a further encouragement a reward of 40 shillings will be paid for each of the criminals on their being committed as aforesaid with all reasonable expences by

Montreal 20th Nov. 1796. EDWD. WM: GRAY Sheriff.[66]

[Montreal Gazette, 21 November 1796]

– *1797* –

90 Montreal – July – Private sale/Female (17) (limited term) – No logo
FOR SALE.
Ten years Service of a Negro Girl aged about seventeen years – Enquire of the Printers.

[Montreal Gazette, 31 July 1797]

– *1798* –

91 Montreal – January – Private sale/Female (30) – No logo
FOR SALE.[67]
An excellent Negro Wench aged about 30 years, can do all kind of work belonging to a house particularly washing and ironing. She has no fault, and is very honest, sober and industrious. Enquire at the Printing Office.

Montreal 18 January 1798.

[Montreal Gazette, 22 January 1798]

92 Montreal – August – Escape/Male (?), Female (?), Female (4) – No logo
NINE DOLLARS REWARD. [68]
RAN away from the Subscriber, on the 12th instant, a Negro Man named Robin or Bob he is about five feet six inches high, had on when he went away, a coarse shirt

and trowsers, a light coloured cloth waistcoat, felt hat, and old shoes, also a Negro Woman named Lydia or Lil, partly of the mulatto colour, about five feet high had on a blue and white striped short gown, a blue drugget petticoat and black silk bonnet, she is thick and well set, they may possibly change their cloathes; they took with them a mulatto child, named Jane about four years old. Any person taking up and securing said Negroes and Child, so that the owner gets them again, shall have the above reward and all reasonable charges paid by,

JAMES FRAZER.

N.S. All masters of vessels and all others are hereby forbid to harbour, employ, carry off, or conceal, said negroes, as they will be prosecuted in the highest manner, the said James Frazer hath the Protection of Government for said negroes.

Current of St Marys near Montreal, August 12th 1798.

[*Montreal Gazette,* 20 August 1798]

– *1806* –

93 Quebec – June – Escape/Male (27) – No logo

DESERTED.

BETWIXT last night and this morning, from the ship *Ellison,* Capt. Alexander Suter, lying off Sillery, *John Watson,* about 47 years of age, with short black hair, about 5 feet 6 or 7 inches high, stoutish made, fresh coloured, had on a blue jacket & trowsers, and a red flannel shirt; Also *William Henry,* a negro, 27 years old, about 5 feet 7 or 8 inches high, slender made, had on a red flannel shirt, blue jacket & trowsers; Also *William Shaw,* an apprentice, 19 years of age, about 5 feet 6 or 7 inches high, with light hair, pale complexion, and a little marked with the small pox. They carried off the ships skiff. Any person bringing all or either of the said deserters, to any magistrate, so that he or they may be secured, shall, on such security, receive a reward of *FIVE GUINEAS* for each of them, and ONE GUINEA for the skiff by applying to the subscribing captain, on board.

Quebec, June 16th, 1806. ALEXANDER SUTER.

[*Quebec Mercury,* 16 June 1806]

94 Montreal – March – Escape/Female – No logo

Cinq Piastres de Récompense.[69]

ENFUIE de chez le soussigné Samedi au soir le 24 du courant, une Negresse engagée au service du soussigné, nommée EVE. Elle est d'environ 5 pieds de hauteur, bien-faite, et marquée au front de la petite vérole. Quiconque en donnera information ou l'amenera a Mr Polley, recevra la récompense susdite, et quiconque retirera ou logera la dite Eve sera poursuivi suivant la loi.

BORUCK B. LEVY.
[*Montreal Gazette*, 9 April 1810]

94b

RUN AWAY

FROM the Subscriber, on the night of the 24th inst. an indented Black Girl, by the name of EVE; she had a mark on her forehead occasioned by the Small-Pox. Whoever will apprehend and deliver her into the care of Mr Wm. Polley, will receive Five Dollars Reward, and all necessary charges paid. All persons are hereby forbid harboring or trusting her upon the penalty of the law.

Montreal March 26th 1810 BORUCK B. LEVY

[*Canadian Courant*, 23 April 1810]

B. MISCELLANEOUS NOTICES REFERRING TO BLACKS

1 *Quebec, 1765*
WHEREAS several scandalous Aspersions have been thrown out against the Character of Williams Conyngham, of the City of Quebec Esq; late Coroner for that District, relative to his conduct in that Office, on an Inquest taken before him on the body of a Negroe Man, found lying dead on the beach at Wolfe's Cove, on the 9th Day of April Instant; and that the said Williams Conyngham had exceeded his Power of a Coroner therein, and several other injurious Reflections and Expressions, tending greatly to the prejudice of his Character.

We the Subscribers, Members of the Jury on said Inquest, being desirous to do that which in Justice ought to be done, do hereby publickly declare, That, according to the best of our Knowledge and belief, the said Williams Conyngham has, in no Respect Whatsoever, acted otherwise than became the Duty of his Office, he having, during the whole Time, taken the utmost Pains to discover the true Cause of the said Negroe Man's Death, and for that Purpose did, with much candour and Patience, go thro' very long and complicated Examinations, which we, agreeable to our Oaths, did desire him from Time to Time to take; and we also declare, that the said Williams Conyngham, during the Course of said Inquest, behaved himself as became an honest Man, and able in his Profession. Witness our Hands, at Quebec, this 20th Day of April 1765.

John Dancer, Foreman, *John Watmough, John Baird, Samuel Morin, John Dalglish, George Gregory, Edward Chinn, Jacob Rowe, John Aitkin, William Holland, William Bondfield.*[70]

[*Quebec Gazette*, 25 April 1765]

2 *Montreal, 1799*
Whereas, it has been reported that I suspected the servant of Mr John M'Intire, at the Coteau du Lac, Innkeeper, to have taken a considerable sum of money from me at his house, in the month of February last, and as such a report might injure the repute of his servants and hurt his custom, I do therefore in justice to him and his family, hereby publicly declare, that I am fully convinced, that it was not any person belonging to his house or family, who took the money from me. Given under my Hand at Cornwall, this 11th day of July 1799.

MICHAEL V. KOUGHNER[71]

[*Montreal Gazette*, 26 August and 9 September 1799]

MISCELLANEOUS NOTICES 341

3 *Montreal, 1799*
BY Virtue of a Writ of Execution issued out of His Majesty's Court of King's Bench, holding Civil Pleas, in and for the said District, at the suit of Robert Jones, Esquire, against the Lands and Tenements of Caesar Johannot, to be directed, I have seized and taken in execution, as belonging to the said Caesar Johannot, an Emplacement or Lot of Ground, situate in the Saint Antoine Suburbs of Montreal; consisting of forty-five feet in front to the line of one Marcheterre, junior, bounded on the North-east by the Representative of the Widow Sarasin, and on the South-West by a lot of ground belonging to Joseph Degan, with two wooden houses thereon built; and also a small point of land bounded by the rivulet and a small house adjoining thereto, with a stable thereon built: Now do I hereby give notice, that the said premises will be sold and adjudged to the highest bidder, at my Office, in the City of Montreal, on Tuesday the twenty-fifth day of March next, at eleven of the clock in the forenoon; at which time and place the Conditions of Sale will be made known.[72]
EDW. WM. GRAY, SHERIFF.
All and every person or persons having Claims on the above described premises, by mortgage or other right or incumbrance, are hereby advertised to give notice thereof to the said Sheriff, at his Office aforesaid, according to law. – *Montreal, 14th November, 1799.*
[*Quebec Gazette,* 21 November 1799]

4 *Montreal, 1800*
BY Virtue of a writ of execution issued out of His Majesty's Court of King's Bench, holding civil pleas in and for the said District, at the suit of the Honorable Pierre Louis Panet, against the lands and tenements of Nathaniel Hazard Tredwell, to me directed, I have seized and taken in execution, as belonging to the said Nathaniel Hazard Tredwell, a certain parcel of land, distinguished by the name and appellation of the *Petit Rocher,* on the Grand River, in the Seigniory of Argenteuil, in the District of Montreal aforesaid, composed of lots number twenty, twenty one and twenty two, making together fifteen acres and half a perch in front, on the Grand River, running in depth as follows; twelve acres and half a perch above runs in depth to the river *du nord,* diminishing by the inclination of eight degrees, from one line to the other, and the other three acres below extent to half the distance between the two rivers; the whole bounded in front by the said Grand River, in depth part to the river du nord, and part of the land of Hyacinthe, a negro,[73] on one side above to Joseph Berthe, and below half to land belonging to Madgelaine Blais, and half to the said Hyacinthe, with a wooden house and a stable thereon erected as the said premises are and extend: now I do hereby give notice that the said premises will be sold and adjudged to the highest bidder at the Church door of the parish of the Lake of the Two Mountains, in the District aforesaid, on Monday the fourth day of August next, at ten of the clock in the forenoon; at which time and place the conditions of sale will be made known.
EDW. WM. GRAY, Sheriff.
All and every person or persons having claims on the above described premises, by mortgage, or other right or incumbrance, are hereby advertised to give notice

thereof to the said Sheriff, at his Office in the City of Montreal, according to law. – *Montreal, 27th March 1800.*

[*Quebec Gazette*, 3 April 1800]

5 *Montreal, 1803*

NOTICE.

AUGUSTIN LABADIE and ALEXANDER VOLUMTEN[74] of the City of Montreal, have purchased of Etienne Roland and Magdeleine Provost his wife, by deed of the 3rd instant before the undersigned notary, an emplacement with a house thereon erected, situate in the St Lawrence Suburbs, containing thirty three feet in front by fifty one feet in depth; bounded in front by St Charles Street, in the rear by the seller, on one side by Michel Belan, and on the other side by Charles Heupe.

All persons having claims on the emplacement and house above described by mortgage or other right or incumbrance, are hereby required to give notice to the subscriber at his office in the City of Montreal, St Gabriel street No. 4, before the first of May next, otherwise the purchasers will avail themselves of this advertisement.

J.M. MONDELET, N.P.

Montreal, February 5, 1803.

[*Montreal Gazette*, 7 February 1803]

6 *Quebec, 1809*

REWARD. – Whereas a small BOAT belonging to the Brig *Harriet Garland* of Liverpool, was about a week ago taken away by a black man and two other seamen of the above vessel, and left at Wolfe's Cove, where it remained for a few days, and as they have not since returned it is supposed they have disposed of it, any person or persons who can give such information as may lead to the recovery of said boat, shall receive FIVE GUINEAS Reward, by applying to

PATTERSON & CO.

Quebec, 22d June, 1809

Custom-house buildings.[75]

[*Quebec Gazette*, 22 June 1809]

7 *Montreal, 1810*

FOR SALE,

A LOT OF GROUND situate in St Augustin-Street, of about two hundred and twenty feet in front, by about forty feet in depth, bounded in the rear by the Jesuits' Garden, on one side by Philip Ross and on the other by John Trim. This lot, from its size, scite and situation, is well calculated for the building of extensive Stores, the want of which is now very generally felt; or two Houses might be thereon built, with convenient yard-room to each.[76]

For particulars apply to

MDE. PERRAULT.

May 5.

[*Montreal Gazette*, 7 May 1810]

MISCELLANEOUS NOTICES

8 *Montreal, 1812*

Advertisement.

NOTICE is hereby given that WILLIAM LAMOUR,[77] an elderly negro man, has been discharged from my service. All persons are warned not to deliver any articles to him on my account, as I will not be responsible.

This man is well known, having formerly lived some time at the Hospital of l'Hotel Dieu.

March 14,   MARY DONNELLAN.

[*Montreal Herald,* 14 March 1812]

9 *Montreal, 1812*

BY virtue of a WRIT OF EXECUTION issued out of His Majesty's Court of King's Bench, holding civil pleas in and for the district of Montreal aforesaid, at the suit of Thomas McCord, of the City of Montreal, in the said District, Esquire, against the lands and tenements of John Fleming of the same place, yeoman, to me directed; I have seized and taken in execution as belonging to the said JOHN FLEMING, a lot of land or emplacement situated in the Fief Nazareth, in the said City of Montreal, containing forty-five feet in front, by ninety feet in depth, bounded in the front by Prince Street, on the northwest side by Alexander McCullock, on the southeast side by lot No. 52, in the possession of the said John Fleming, and in the rear by lots Nos. 45 and 46, the said described lot being known and distinguished by No. 53, and containing four thousand and fifty feet or thereabouts in superficies. Now I do hereby give notice, that the said lot of land or emplacement will be sold and adjudged to the highest bidder, at my Office, in the City of Montreal aforesaid, on TUESDAY, the TENTH day of DECEMBER next, at ELEVEN o'clock in the forenoon, at which time and place the conditions of sale will be made known.

FREDk. W. EMATINGER, Sheriff

All and every person or persons having claims on the above described lot of land or emplacement, by mortgage, or other right or incumbrance, are hereby advertised to give notice thereof to the said Sheriff, at his Office, aforesaid, according to Law; and further that no opposition *afin d'annuller* or *afin de distraire,* the whole or any part of the said lot of land or emplacement, or *afin de charge* or *servitude* on the same, will be received by the said Sheriff during the fifteen days previous to the sale thereof.

Sheriff's Office, 1st August, 1816.

[*Quebec Gazette,* 8 August 1816]

C. THREE EARLIEST ADVERTISEMENTS BY BLACKS

1 *Quebec, 1803*
WANTED a place to attend one or more Ladies to any part of Europe, a woman of colour lately arrived, that can bring an unspotted character from the lady she attended, a line directed to M.A.J. will be attended to if left at the Printing-Office.
    Quebec, 11th July, 1803.[78]

[*Quebec Gazette*, 14 July 1803]

2 *Montreal, 1824*
AFRICAN THEATRE.[79]
At the request of several Gentlemen Mr Turnbull has been induced to allow the occupation of the New Market Theatre by Mr BROWN the African, for one night only; in consequence of which Mr Brown respectfully informs the Public, that on
Monday Evening the 16th August,
Will be presented, select Scenes from the most admired Plays.
Doors will open at Seven, and Performances to Commence at 8 O'Clock. Boxes 2s 6d, – Pit 1s 3d. Box Tickets to [be] had at the Box Office, during the day on Monday, Pit Tickets at the Door.

[*Spectateur canadien*, 14 August 1824]

3 *Montreal, 1830*
ECONOMY AND ELEGANCE.
OLD garments cleansed and made to look AS WELL AS NEW, by ALEXANDER GRANT, *from New-York,* at No. 80 St Paul Street nearly opposite to Mr Rollings, Barber.
    Orders will be received at Mr Rollings' *Barber,* St Paul Street.[80]
    22d May, 1830.

[*Canadian Courant*, 21 July 1830]

Appendix II

Slavery in the Judges' eyes

The "freedom suits" of four Missouri slaves, adult children of the former Montreal slave Rose, in the Circuit Court of St Louis in the mid-nineteenth century led the court to query three Montreal judges on the question of the former legal status of slavery in Canada. Justices James Reid and Samuel Gale were examined before a rogatory commission in 1846 in the case of *Pierre v. Gabriel S. Chouteau,* and Justice William Badgley testified in the case of *Mary Charlotte v. Gabriel Chouteau* in 1859.

TESTIMONY OF JAMES REID

[James Reid (ca 1769–1848), retired Chief Justice of the Montreal Court of King's Bench, was examined on the part of the plaintiff Pierre before commissioner John Samuel McCord, judge of the Montreal District Circuit Court, on 9 April 1846. Frederick Griffin, was counsel for the plaintiff; Robert Shore Milnes Bouchette, was counsel for the defendant.[1]]

QUESTION 1: *What is your name and profession, and where do you reside?*
ANSWER: My name is James Reid, late Chief Justice of the Court of King's Bench at Montreal, where I now reside.
QUESTION 2: *Do you know the parties in this cause, and are you interested in this suit?*
ANSWER: I do not know the parties, nor either of them, nor am I interested in the event of this suit.

QUESTION 3: *How long have you resided in Canada, and are you well acquainted with the laws and usages of Canada?*
ANSWER: I have resided fifty-eight years in Canada, during which time I have had occasion to become acquainted with the laws and usages of that country.

QUESTION 4: *What judicial situation did you hold in Canada, and how long did you hold the same?*
ANSWER: I have held the situation of one of the Puisné Justices of the before mentioned Court of King's Bench for the District of Montreal, for seventeen years, and subsequently, the situation of Chief Justice of the same Court, for nearly fifteen years.

QUESTION 5: *When did Canada pass from the dominion of the French government to that of the British government?*
ANSWER: Canada came under the dominion of the British Government by capitulation to the British arms in September 1760, and the Country was afterwards ceded to Great Britain by treaty of Peace in 1763.

QUESTION 6: *Was slavery of Negroes, or other persons, recognized and allowed by law in Canada, while the country was under the dominion of the French Government?*
ANSWER: Slavery would appear to have been practised in Canada to a certain extent while under the dominion of the French Government, although I can find no law by which it was there introduced or recognized previous to the year 1709, when, by an Ordinance of Mr Raudot, the *Intendant* of the Colony, permission was given to the colonists to purchase negroes and *Panis,* from the Indians, on the principle that they would prove useful in the cultivation of the soil. – This Ordinance would seem to have been made in order to confirm a practice which had previously existed, but for which there was no law, by authorizing slavery in the particular cases referred to: – the *Intendant* relies also upon the principle he invokes that all Colonies should be placed upon the same footing in regard to slavery, as those in the West Indies. Slavery formed no part of the public law of France, but required the Legislative authority of the Crown for its establishment, and accordingly we find, that by this authority, it was introduced into the West India Islands by the *Code Noir* in 1685. – It has been doubted, whether Mr Raudot or any governor of a particular Colony, could establish therein, such a general principle of public law, as Slavery, without the special authority of the Crown; and it may be inferred, from the expressions used, that Mr Raudot was under this impression by his stating that he made the above Ordinance *"sous le bon plaisir de sa Majesté"* – which *"bon plaisir"* I see no where noticed or confirmed. It is certain, however, that from the time of this Ordinance, and even before, Slavery of Negroes and *Panis,* as therein stated, had been practised, and was still continued in the Colony in 1736, as by an Ordinance of Mr Hocquart, the then *Intendant,* of the first of September of that year, a form for the emancipation of slaves is established and directed to be observed. So far the existence, if not the legality, of Slavery would appear.

QUESTION 7: *Did any of the articles of capitulation granted to the Canadians upon* their surrender of Canada to the British arms in September 1760 bear reference to slaves then in Canada?

ANSWER: The forty-seventh article referred to them particularly.

QUESTION 8: *Did that article extend to such of the children of the Negroes and Panis therein mentioned as were born in Canada after the capitulation?*

ANSWER: I think not. Children born under the British dominion, where slavery is not known or established, cannot be considered as slaves, whatever their parents may have been.

QUESTION 9: *Did any and what change in the civil and criminal laws of Canada take place on the capitulation of the Country to the British arms in September 1760?*

ANSWER: In regard of the French and Canadians, the laws and customs of the Country, as formerly administered and recognized, were temporarily continued. In regard of Merchants and traders, and others, I believe, the laws of England prevailed.

QUESTION 10: *What was the legal effect of the King's Proclamation of the Seventh of October 1763, on Slavery in Canada?*

ANSWER: I consider the legal effect of that proclamation was, to carry with it the abolition of Slavery of every Kind in the Colony; – the exception contained in the forty-seventh article of the capitulation of September 1760, referred only to such *Negroes* and *Panis,* as were then in existence, but could not be extended to their issue subsequently born.

QUESTION 11: *Was slavery ever afterwards (except in regard to the* Negroes *and* Panis *mentioned in the 47th article of the capitulation) recognized by law, or as being legal in Canada?*

ANSWER: As far as I know and believe, Slavery after that period (except in the cases referred to) was never recognized, nor considered as being legal in Canada.

QUESTION 12: *Was the King's Proclamation of the seventh of October 1763 ever repealed?*

ANSWER: It was virtually repealed by the Act of the British parliament 14 George III, chapter 83 [the Quebec Act], by which a new system of jurisprudence was introduced. The administration of the criminal law of England in criminal matters, having been thereby established, and came into operation in May 1775.

QUESTION 13: *Was the Question of the Legality or non legality of Slavery in Canada ever tested in any of the Courts of justice in Canada, – and, if yea, what was the result of the test?*

ANSWER: I am informed that a case was determined in the Court of King's Bench at Montreal, and that by the Judgment of that Court of the eighteenth of February 1800, one *Robin* alias *Robert,* who had been arrested as a slave for leaving his Master, was brought before the Court on a writ of *Habeas corpus,* and discharged, on the ground, that no slavery existed in Canada.

(The witness was then, by Mr Bouchette, the Defendant's Counsel, cross-examined, and answered as follows. –)

CROSS-QUESTION 1: *Were not the Intendants under the French Government in Canada invested with certain legislative as well as judicial powers?*

ANSWER: I believe they were.

CROSS-QUESTION 2: *What were the terms and language of Mr Intendant Raudot's commission, in so far as it invests him with legislative powers?*

ANSWER: I cannot say, not having been able to see or know the nature of his Commission.

CROSS-QUESTION 3: *Do not the words* "sous le bon plaisir de sa Majesté" *used in Mr Raudot's Ordinance of 1709, to which you advert, signify* sauf le bon plaisir, *and would not the Ordinance in question be in full power until* le bon plaisir *of His Majesty to the contrary would have been expressed?*

ANSWER: The words *"sous le bon plaisir de sa Majesté"* used by Mr Raudot, in his Ordinance of 1709, are not words of course, or of general use in any of the Ordinances of the *Intendants* in Canada, and are not to be found in any of the Ordinances of Mr Raudot, during his administration as *Intendant*, as far as I can discover, except in the particular Ordinance in question. As the King of France had the power of control over the Colonial legislature, it is reasonable to suppose, that when reference was made by it to that controul, or *"bon plaisir,"* the expression of such *bon plaisir* became necessary to give validity to the Act or Ordinance thus submitted, especially on matters of importance arising in the Colony. – The establishment of Slavery was an act of high authority in any Legislature, and more especially in such a subordinate Legislature as that vested in an Intendant in Canada, and my opinion is, that Mr Raudot had no more power to establish Slavery in the Colony, than he had to establish torture or death for any new offence occurring there without the consent and authority of the King.

CROSS-QUESTION 4: *Did not Mr Hocquart the Intendant's Ordinance of the 1st of September 1736 assume the legal existence of Slavery in Canada under the French Government?*

ANSWER: The language of that Ordinance implies that he did.

CROSS-QUESTION 5: *Is not the precise language of the 47th Article of the Capitulation, referred to in your examination in Chief, as follows?*

"Art. XLVII – les nègres et panis des deux sexes resteront en leur qualité d'Esclaves en la possession des Français et Canadiens à qui ils appartiennent; il leur sera libre de les garder à leur service ou de les vendre; et ils pourront aussi continuer à les faire élever dans la religion romaine."–

"Accordé, excepté ceux qui auront été faits prisonniers." –

ANSWER: Yes.

CROSS-QUESTION 6: *Do the articles of capitulation in question contain any proviso or limitation as to slaves, beyond the restriction as to prisoners, – and did the conquerors stipulate any thing as to the freedom of the offspring of Slaves?*

ANSWER: The articles of capitulation contain no proviso or limitation as to slaves, except as to prisoners, nor do the conquerors appear to have stipulated any thing as to the offspring of Slaves.

CROSS-QUESTION 7: *In your examination in Chief you state that the legal effect of the King's Proclamation of the 7th of October 1763 was to carry with it the abolition of Slavery of every kind – would you please state whether it had that effect* in

Florida, the Grenadines, Dominica, St. Vincent, *and* Tobago, *which are therein mentioned, as well as the Government of Quebec?*

ANSWER: In my answer to the tenth interrogatory in Chief, I stated that the effect of the Proclamation of 1763 was the abolition of slavery of every kind *in the Colony*, having a reference to the Colony of Quebec, as the only one in question. I cannot say what effect this Proclamation may have had in the Floridas and other places mentioned in this Interrogatory, not being acquainted with the then existing laws in those places, – but I do not think that this Proclamation could have had the effect to abolish Slavery there, if it was there legally established and recognized.

CROSS-QUESTION 8: *Assuming that the Proclamation abolished Slavery in the Government of Quebec, was not the Proclamation revoked by the 14th George III, ch. 83, Sec. 4, and all and every the Ordinance and Ordinances made under it annulled and made void?*

ANSWER: The British Statute 14th George III, ch. 83, s. 4, annulled and made void all the provisions of the Proclamation of 7th October 1763, as to their subsequent operation, in order to make way for a more efficient system of Government, but this did not affect the rights of Colonists who had become, and continued to be, British subjects under that Proclamation, whereby they became entitled to the full enjoyment of their personal freedom, as much as to the air they breathed.

CROSS-QUESTION 9: *Are you aware of the existence of any Act of the Parliament of Great Britain subsequently to the King's Proclamation adverted to, and posterior in date even to the Quebec Act (14 Geo. III, cap. 83) recognizing slavery in the Province of Quebec, and regulating the importation of slaves therein?*

ANSWER: The British Statute 30 George III, chapter 27, which I presume is now alluded to, was made for encouraging a particular description of persons, citizens and subjects of the United States, and the territories and countries thereunto belonging, to settle with their property and effects in His Majesty's territories in America, into which they were required to emigrate in British vessels, owned by British subjects, and having first obtained a license from the Governor, or Lieutenant Governor, of the Colony or Province &ca for that purpose. I do not consider this Statute as introducing Slavery, or permitting its existence in any part of this Colony, but in a very limited manner to a particular description of persons only, and under particular circumstances. The great object of the Statute was to secure to immigrants the same right over the property they brought with them as they held by the laws of the Country from which they came, This was necessary in regard of Negroes, as the British Parliament, aware that no slavery existed in any of His Majesty's territories in North America, thought it advisable to hold out an inducement to persons coming from Countries where Slavery was authorized, by securing to them the services of those slaves they brought with them, so that it is through this limited channel only that this slavery, for the few years it existed, can be traced to any part of the Colony. The Statute referred to, while it constitutes a particular exception, recognizes the general rule that no slavery existed in His Majesty's North American Colonies.

CROSS-QUESTION 10: *Is not the Province of Quebec mentioned in the 30th George*

III, chap. 27, that portion of the British dominions in America now known as Canada, with some modifications of boundary?
ANSWER: It is.
CROSS-QUESTION 11: *Was the Province of Quebec divided by Royal Proclamation in 1791 into two Provinces, called Upper Canada, and Lower Canada?*
ANSWER: It was.
CROSS-QUESTION 12: *Are you aware of the passing of any law by the Provincial Parliament of Upper Canada after its erection into a separate Province, recognizing the institution of slavery, and providing for its gradual abolition?*
ANSWER: There is an act of the Provincial Parliament of Upper Canada of 33rd George III, chapter 7, made for the purpose of preventing the further introduction of Slaves into that Province. This Act appears to have reference solely to the slaves brought into that Province, in which immigrants were encouraged to settle, under the British Statute 30 George III, cap. 27, and provides for the abolition of a slavery which had so partially existed.
CROSS-QUESTION 13: *Are you aware of any similar act passed by the Legislature of Lower Canada, and if such an act existed would you not have a knowledge of the fact?*
ANSWER: I have no knowledge of any similar act of the Legislature in Lower Canada. Had such an act existed, it is probable I should have known it. There would not seem to have been any need of such an act in Lower Canada, as slavery was never known to exist there under any period of the British Government. The immigrants who brought slaves with them under the British Statute 30 George III, ch. 27, appear to have gone to Upper Canada, where the means of settlement were principally provided.
CROSS-QUESTION 14: *Were not the laws and Institutions of the Province of Quebec common to Upper and Lower Canada, up to the separate erection of those Provinces in 1791?*
ANSWER: They were.
CROSS-QUESTION 15: *Have you any knowledge that any person or persons has or have held and possessed one or more slave or slaves in Canada? – If yea please to state by whom such slave or slaves were possessed and at what time.*
ANSWER: I have no such knowledge. –

TESTIMONY OF SAMUEL GALE

[Samuel Gale (1783–1865), judge of the Court of King's (Queen's) Bench, Montreal, was examined on the part of the plaintiff Pierre before commissioner John Samuel McCord, on 27 April 1846. Frederick Griffin was counsel for the plaintiff; Robert Shore Milnes Bouchette was counsel for the defendant.[2]]

QUESTION 1: *What is your name, and your profession, and where do you reside?*
ANSWER: My name is Samuel Gale, – I am one of the Justices of the Court of Queen's

Bench for the District of Montreal in the Province of Canada, – and I reside in the City of Montreal.

QUESTION 2: *Do you know the parties, and are you interested in the event of this suit?*

ANSWER: No.

QUESTION 3: *How long have you resided in Canada, and are you well acquainted with the laws and usages of that Country?*

ANSWER: I have resided in Canada for upwards of fifty years, and am acquainted with the laws and usages of that Country.

QUESTION 4: *How long have you been a Judge of the Court of Queen's Bench for the District of Montreal, – and how long did you practise the law before you were raised to the Bench?*

ANSWER: I was appointed one of the Justices, or Judges, of the Court of King's Bench in the year 1834, and have held my appointment from that time as Judge to the present day, originally as Judge of the *King's* Bench, and subsequently as Judge of the *Queen's* Bench, that is to say – of the same Court under different appellations; – I had practised the law twenty-six years before I was called to the Bench.

QUESTION 5: *When did Canada pass from under the dominion of the French Government, to that of the British Government?*

ANSWER: The Conquest of Canada was effected by the British Government from the French Government in the years 1759 and 1760, and the definitive cession of the Country from the latter Government to the former was established by the treaty of peace concluded between those powers in February 1763.

QUESTION 6: *Was slavery of negroes, or of other persons, recognized and allowed by law in Canada, while the country was under the dominion of the French Government?*

ANSWER: I believe that a modified system of slavery respecting negroes, and some others, was *de facto* exercised in Canada in various instances while the Country remained under the French dominion, but I cannot undertake to say, that such *de facto* exercise of slavery was justifiable under sufficient legitimate enactment, and a correct interpretation of the laws as they then stood; – my opinion is the contrary.

QUESTION 7: *Did any and what change take place in the laws of Canada when the Country came under the dominion of the British Government, – and what was the effect of such change – firstly, – in regard to Negroes and Panis then in existence and secondly – in regard to Negroes and Panis subsequently born in the Country?*

ANSWER: Several changes took place in the law of Canada when the country came under the dominion of the British Government. Among others, the rights of the subjects or inhabitants became more extensive, and the British public or national law and rights superceded the French. The legal effect of these changes would, in my opinion, have been *per se* (unless barred by direct stipulations to the contrary,) to extinguish slavery, and put an end to any pretended right of man in his fellow creatures as forming part of his goods, chattels, or property, and would have extended (stipulations expressly to the contrary excepted,) as well to abolish slavery, and to give freedom to the *Negroes* and *Panis* then in existence, as to the same effect in regard to *Negroes* and *Panis* subsequently born in the Country. The law of England bestows on all its subjects, of every color, equal rights to personal freedom, and legal protection.

QUESTION 8: *Did the 47th Article of the capitulation of Canada to the British arms, in September 1760, extend to such of the Children of the* Negroes *and* Panis *therein mentioned as were born in Canada after the capitulation?*

ANSWER: The 47th article of the capitulation in September 1760 did not extend to such of the children of the *Negroes* and *Panis* therein mentioned as were born in Canada after the capitulation. And my opinion further is – that the same 47th article could not have legitimately been enforced after the treaty of peace of February 1763, even as to those *Negroes* and *Panis* previously held in slavery, and who continued in Canada, for a capitulation is only a temporary act or agreement by commanders, or subordinate powers, subject to be afterwards modified, changed, or set aside by the mutual agreement under a treaty of peace of the sovereign powers on both sides. The treaty of peace did not sanction such a violation of the British public law as would have been established by a continuation of Slavery in Canada, and the powers of no military commander, as such, could extend to establish permanently, a law at variance with the public law of the Sovereign, or Sovereignty, under which he served.

QUESTION 9: *Was Slavery (except of the Negroes and Panis mentioned in the said 47th article,) recognized by the law of Canada, at any time subsequent to the capitulation of September 1760?*

ANSWER: Slavery was never recognized by the law of Canada at any time subsequent to the capitulation of September 1760.

QUESTION 10: *Was the King's Proclamation of the 7th of October 1763 ever revoked or repealed, – and if it was, by what law, and from what date was it so repealed?*

ANSWER: Some of the provisions of the Proclamation of the 7th of October 1763 – such as those relating to the civil Government of Canada, (then *"the Province of Quebec,"*) and the powers of the governor and other civil officers thereof, were revoked and made void from the first day of May 1775, by the Statute of the British Parliament, 14th George the third, chapter 83, passed in the preceding year, and commonly called "the Quebec Act."

QUESTION 11: *Did the revocation or repeal of that proclamation effect the revival of any laws respecting slavery in existence before the capitulation?*

ANSWER: No revocation, annullment, or change of the Proclamation of 1763 ever had the effect of reviving any laws respecting slavery in existence before the capitulation of 1760, or of reviving or establishing slavery in Canada.

QUESTION 12: *Was the legality of the slavery of* Negroes, Panis, *or other persons, ever tested in the Courts of Justice in Lower Canada, – and if it was – what was the result of the test?*

ANSWER: The question of the existence or legality of slavery *in Lower Canada* of *Negroes* or *Panis* has been brought before the Courts of Justice there, and all slavery has been adjudged illegal in Lower Canada. There was a case decided in the Court of King's Bench, at Montreal, on the eighteenth of February in the year one thousand eight hundred, on the Petition of a Negro called Robin, *alias* Robert, who was held as a slave by one James Fraser: the Judgment of the Court set him free. There have been cases of a like description, before and since, as I believe, and the illegality of slavery in Lower Canada is a matter too clear, and too well established to admit of doubt, altho' the laws in that particular, are the same as they have been ever since the cession of the Province by the Treaty of Peace of 1763.

QUESTION 13: *Are any or either of the Judges who decided the case to which you refer now alive?*

ANSWER: I believe the Judges who decided the case of the Negro Robin *alias* Robert, before mentioned, were the Chief Justice Monk, and the Judges Ogden and Panet: – I have a personal knowledge of the death of one of them, namely, Judge Panet, who died in Montreal, and the other two died in England, as I have understood and believe, a number of years ago.

(The witness then answered to the cross-questions of Mr Bouchette, the Defendant's Counsel as follows.)

CROSS-QUESTION 1: *Was not the modified form of slavery which in your examination-in-Chief you say existed* de facto *in Canada under the French Government continued for some years – and how many years, to the best of your knowledge, after the conquest, and therefore under the British Government?*

ANSWER: I cannot say that the modified system of slavery which existed *de facto* under the French Government, mentioned in my examination in Chief, continued *de facto* in Canada after the treaty of Peace, altho' it is probable that several of those who before were held in slavery continued to be so held if they made no application to the proper authorities to be discharged, or declared free. The agency of the Courts of Justice of course would not be exercised between individual and individual, unless demanded; and it is therefore most likely that there were instances of persons called slaves, who continued to remain as such with the persons who were called their masters, long after the conquest of Canada, and while it continued one Province. Such voluntary acquiescence in servitude might be owing to various motives, – such as affection or ignorance of their rights – or fear. But no legal inference could be drawn from the exercise of such assumed ownership on the one hand, while no objection was raised on the other. In the thirtyfirst year of the reign of George the third (A.D. 1790,) a Statute of the Parliament of Great Britain was passed for the division of what had, until then, been the Province of Quebec, otherwise called the Province of Canada, into two separate Provinces, of which one was called Upper Canada, and the other Lower Canada. And two years afterwards (this division of the Province of Canada having in that interval been effected,) the Legislature of the Province called Upper Canada passed a Statute (33 George III, chap. 7,) confirming the service during life, of such negroes, and others, as had been previously bought or brought into Upper Canada under a license from the Governor, but expressly declaring at the same time that no negro, or other person, who should afterwards come or be brought into Upper Canada, and no child thereafter born of a negro or other person should be subject to such service, but should be free after the age of twenty-five years.

CROSS-QUESTION 2: *Did not the Intendants under the French Government in Canada possess certain Legislative as well as judicial & administrative powers?*

ANSWER: The Intendants under the French Government in Canada possessed, in virtue of their commissions, Legislative powers to a certain extent, as well as judicial and administrative powers.

CROSS-QUESTION 3: *Were not the Ordinances by them made under and by virtue of their Commissions, declared as valid and binding as if* "émanés de nos Cours Souveraines, nonobstant toutes prises à partie, édits, ordonnances, et autres choses à ce contraire," *and are not the French terms quoted, the language of the Intendants' commission?*

ANSWER: The Ordinances of the Intendants, when made in virtue of their commission, and within its legal limits, were valid and binding according to the French terms quoted in this cross-interrogatory, and the terms so quoted form a part of the terms or language used in the Commission of the Intendants, which, however, are not to be taken alone, but in connexion with the rest of the context, or other portions of the Commission. The powers of the Intendants were limited to the extent of the commission under which they were appointed, and their commissions required them to act in conformity to the Royal Edicts and Ordinances for France, and according to the custom of Paris, and could not, in my opinion, be interpreted by legitimate and legal construction to authorize the Intendants to pass laws inconsistent with the public law and public rights of subjects, as they existed in France, and in the custom of Paris, where slavery would not have been in accordance with the laws. To authorize the Intendants, or others, to give a legitimate sanction to the establishment of slavery in Canada, would have been inconsistent with the public rights of the subjects or dwellers in the custom of Paris, and must have required, in my opinion, express and positive authority to that effect. Such express authority was not conferred by their commissions. The Intendants and others having Legislative authority in Canada, were appointed, it must be considered, according to their commission, to uphold and preserve the public rights of all subjects and indwellers in conformity with the custom of Paris, and not to abolish these rights as regarded innocent persons of particular classes or races, or of peculiar colour.

TO CROSS-QUESTION 4: *Were any and what formalities required by any and what Ordinance in Canada under the French dominion for the manumission or emancipation of Slaves?*

ANSWER: An Edict or ordinance of Mr Hocquart, one of the Intendants of Canada in 1736, required masters who gave freedom or emancipation to their slaves, to do so by written document passed before public Notaries, and declared all other forms of emancipation null and of no effect. An Edict or ordinance of a previous Intendant, Mr Raudot, had been antecedently passed, which declared, among other things, that it would be useful to the Colony to hold Negroes, and Indians of a distinct nation called Panis, as slaves, and therefore that the negroes and Panis who had been, or might be bought, should be held by the purchasers as their slaves. This is an ordinance under which slavery existed *de facto* in Canada, while under the French Government, the establishment whereof, as I have already stated, exceeded, as I conceive, the limits of the legal authority conferred upon the Intendants, and would, consequently, not have been regarded as binding under a correct and legitimate interpretation of the law.

CROSS-QUESTION 5: *Is there any thing in the language of the treaty of Peace of 1763 modifying, changing or setting aside any particular article of the capitulation of September 1760?*

ANSWER: The language of the treaty of peace is such as to cede the Province, in full sovereignty, to the King and Crown of Great Britain, without any conditions as respected those inhabitants who chose to remain in it, except that they were to have the free exercise of the Roman Catholic religion, in so far as the laws of Great Britain might permit. Any article of the capitulation therefore which was not in accordance with the perfect sovereignty and right of Legislation of the Crown and Legislature of Great Britain, or was inconsistent with the public law thereof, must have been modified by the treaty of Peace, which rendered all the French inhabitants, who thought fit to continue in Canada, British subjects, entitled to the freedom and privileges, and subject to the duties of such, and having a right to retain and hold real estates and chattels in all things which the English public law allowed to be a legitimate object of property, but subject to the operation of such public law, and to the legislation of Parliament. By the proclamation also of His Britannic Majesty, issued a few months after the treaty of peace in 1763, it was declared that all persons inhabiting in, or resorting to Canada, might confide in the Royal protection for the enjoyment of the benefit of the laws of England.

CROSS-QUESTION 6: *Did not the British statute of the 14th George III, chapter 83, commonly called "The Quebec Act," continue in full force all the laws and customs of Canada, and declare expressly "that in all matters of controversy relative to property and civil rights, resort shall be had to the laws of Canada"?*

ANSWER: No, – that statute did not confirm in full force all the laws and customs of Canada. It however declared "that, in all matters of controversy relative to property and civil rights," resort should be had to the laws of Canada, but the term "property" used in that statute does not mean *man,* or a *fellow creature;* and the blacks or *Panis,* under the English public law, are just as much entitled to *civil rights* as their white neighbours.

CROSS-QUESTION 7: *Are you aware of the existence of any, and what act of the Parliament of Great Britain, subsequently to the Quebec Act, regulating the importation of slaves into the Province of Quebec? – And, if there is such as act, or ever was one, when was it repealed?*

ANSWER: I am aware of an act passed by the Parliament of Great Britain in the thirtieth year of the reign of George the third (chapter 27,) authorizing settlers from the United States, under a license from the Governor, to import into the Province of Quebec, and other places, negroes and household furniture, with some other things, to a certain amount, free of duty. But this act which declares that negroes may be so imported did not declare that they should be slaves in the Province of Quebec, otherwise called the Province of Canada, after they were so imported; – it did not therefore alter the illegal nature of Slavery under the pre-existing law of Canada. And, if slaves were so imported while the Province of Quebec, or Canada, existed as a single Province, under the dominion of England, they would legally, as I believe, no more have continued slaves there, than they would continue slaves in England, supposing that a statute should declare that negroes, with a certain quantity of baggage, might be imported into England free of duty. It is true, that after the Province of Canada was divided into two Provinces, one of the divisions thereof, namely, the Province of Upper Canada, passed an act (the 33rd George III, chapter 7,) which confirmed, as I have stated in a former answer, the service during life of such negroes and others as had before been bought or brought under license to Upper Canada, but expressly declared that none who should afterwards come or be brought or born in Upper Canada should be subject to such service. The provisions of this act of Upper Canada (33 Geo. III, c. 7,) were indispensable, as I conceive, to render legal the servitude for life of the negroes, or others, bought or brought under license into Upper Canada, but did not extend to the other division of the former Province of Quebec or Canada, called the Province of Lower Canada.

CROSS-QUESTION 8: *In your examination in chief you state that slavery was never recognized by the law of Canada subsequent to the capitulation of September 1760, – Is the provincial act of the 33rd George III, chap. 7, passed in Upper Canada in 1793, a part of the law of Canada, or is it not?*

ANSWER: When I spoke in my examination in chief of the law of Canada, I spoke of the law of the Province of Canada or Quebec, not of the law of what was a different Province called Upper Canada, altho' formed out of a portion of what had been the territory of Canada. I should not call a statute of the State of Maine since its separation from Massachusetts, a law of Massachusetts, altho' it be a law of what once formed part of the territory of Massachusetts. The provincial act, 33 George III, chap. 7, passed in the Province of Upper Canada, after its division from the Province of Canada, was never a part of the law of the Province of Canada or Quebec. The last named Province had then ceased to exist, – nor was any law of similar import or effect to the last mentioned Upper Canadian statute ever passed in what constituted the other and larger division of the Province of Canada, namely, the Province of Lower Canada. The similarity or partial identity of the names of the provinces does however occasion some danger of apparent ambiguity or confusion, unless prevented by much care and precision. The two Provinces of Lower and Upper Canada have again been re-united, under the name of the Province of Canada, by the Statute of the Imperial Parliament, 3 & 4 Victoria, chapter 35, and once more form one government.

CROSS-QUESTION 9: *Was not the Province of Upper Canada a part of the original Province of Quebec, which comprised also Lower Canada, and does not the Upper Canada act, 33 George III, chap. 7, legislate for a state of things or institutions that must have been co-extensive with the Province of Quebec, and therefore existing in Lower, as well as Upper, Canada?*

ANSWER: The Province of Upper Canada, as appears by my preceding answers, was a part of the former Province of Quebec, whose territory comprised also Lower Canada. And the Provincial act 33 George III, chap. 7, in this cross-interrogatory referred to, legislated for a state of things or institutions not indeed co-extensive with the former Province of Quebec, (for Upper Canada had already abrogated the French laws, and substituted the English laws as the rule of decision,) but for a state of things or institutions under which, as I believe, the Negroes and Panis were entitled to the same rights as they were in the rest of the former Province of Quebec, namely, Lower Canada. And by this Provincial act of Upper Canada certain Negroes and others previously bought and imported under license were deprived of rights during their own lives, as I have before stated, whereas no such act was ever passed by Lower Canada.

CROSS-QUESTION 10: *Have you any personal knowledge – and what knowledge, of the particulars of the case of* Robin alias Robert, *or of any other case which you believe exists of the like description, and of the grounds of the Judgment?*

ANSWER: I have no personal knowledge of the particulars of the case of Robin *alias* Robert, other than having seen the record of the proceedings and Judgment. I knew two or three individuals when a child who were held, as I understood from themselves and others, as slaves, but who were induced to apply to the Courts of justice to be declared free, and, as I also understood, were so declared. One of these, as nearly as I recollect, was called Phillis, and lived at Sorel in this District; and there was also another, whose name I cannot call to mind. These things are however, as I believe, fifty years bygone or more, – and I do not now recollect having myself seen any more recent instances of persons residing in Lower Canada who were held as slaves.

CROSS-QUESTION 16: – *Have you any recollection of the* de facto *existence of Slavery in any part of Canada, – or have you not heard of slaves being owned and held long after the conquest by inhabitants of the province?*

ANSWER: I have no recollection on the subject beyond what is contained in the last and preceding answers. I have heard of slaves being owned and held in the Province of Canada after the Conquest, but I never heard of any one retained in slavery in Lower Canada subsequent to the division of Canada into two Provinces by the act of the Parliament of Great Britain of 1790, if they applied to the Courts to be discharged.

TESTIMONY OF WILLIAM BADGLEY

[William Badgley (1801–1888), judge of the Superior Court of Canada East, was examined on the part of the plaintiff Mary Charlotte before Commissioner Charles A. Terroux, notary public and justice of the peace, on 5 February 1859. Frederick Griffin was counsel for the plaintiff; John J.C. Abbott was counsel for the defendant.[3]]

QUESTION 1: *What is your name, age and profession, where do you reside, and how long have you resided in Canada?*
ANSWER: William Badgley, aged fifty-seven Years, a lawyer by profession, now a Judge of the Superior Court for Lower Canada, – at present, and since my birth, with occasional intervals, a resident of the city of Montreal.
QUESTION 2: *What judicial or other public situations, or Offices, have you held in Canada, during what periods did you hold the same respectively, and were you ever a member of Parliament of the present Province of Canada, or of the Parliament of either of the Sections thereof formerly known, respectively, as Lower Canada, and Upper Canada?*
ANSWER: From 1840 to 1847, in the judicial Office of Commissioner of Bankrupts at Montreal, and also Circuit Judge during the three latter Years of that period; from 1847 to 1855, a member of the Parliament of Canada, and in that interval, from 1847 to 1848, Attorney General for Lower Canada; since 1855, a Judge of the Superior Court for Lower Canada.
QUESTION 3: *Are you well acquainted with the laws which were in force in Canada, or La Nouvelle France, while it was a Colony of France?*
ANSWER: Professional and Official pursuits and duties required my becoming acquainted with the laws of French Colonial Canada.
QUESTION 4: *Was the slavery of Negroes, or other persons, recognized or allowed, either by the public law of France, or by any other law of local application in Canada or La Nouvelle France, while it was under the dominion of the French government?*
ANSWER: Slavery was not tolerated in France, either by the public or the municipal law; on the contrary, it was repugnant to all the known, recognized maxims, usages and jurisprudence, which constituted the State, and characterized a Kingdom in which uniformity of fundamental law prevailed. Slavery and Serfdom, of every description, were finally, and absolutely, abolished in France, by the Edict of Louis the Tenth, *le Huttin,* in 1315; and the last slave sale in that country was that of a Jew, in 1296, for three hundred livres. (*Guyot's Répertoire de Jurisprudence, v° Esclavage*). The French legists unite in considering the question of freedom as an elementary principle of French jurisprudence. "Nous ne connoissons point d'esclaves en France, tous les hommes y sont libres." "En France, par un long usage qui a force de loi, les esclaves deviennent libres dès qu'ils ont le bonheur d'y entrer." "On ne connoit point d'esclave en France, et quiconque a mis le pied dans ce Royaume est gratifié de la liberté." (*Ib., Causes Célèbres, p. 30*). "Ainsi la liberté a régné dans ce Royaume avec tout son éclat, et de telle manière que dès qu'un esclave y a mis le pied, il y acquiert la liberté; tous les auteurs attestent que c'est une maxime du droit français." (*Ibid.* p. 11). "De nos maximes, de nos usages, de Notre jurisprudence il suit, nécessairement, qu'il ne peut y avoir d'esclave dans ce Royaume." (*Ib.* [blank space])

These citations from the writings and collections of French jurisprudence, by Denizart, Guyot, and others, to which many more of a similar character might be added, express the unanimous opinion of French jurists, and the declaration of French jurisprudence, upon the subject of freedom in France. Although slavery was thus denounced, throughout the Kingdom, by its fundamental laws, it was found expedient and necessary to encourage and recognize *la traite des Nègres* in particular portions of its territorial dominions abroad, from the special circumstances of the climate and productions of those localities; and hence, by exceptional legislation for the French West-indian colonies, by the royal Edict of March 1685, commonly known as the *Code Noir*, which bears the following title: "Le Code Noir, ou l'Edit du Roi servant à règlement pour le gouvernement et l'administration de la justice et de police des Isles Françaises de l'Amérique, et pour la discipline et le commerce des Nègres et esclaves dans le dit Pays;" and its objects are stated in the preamble to be "y maintenir la discipline de l'Eglise Catholique &ca. et y régler ce qui concerne l'état et la qualité de nos esclaves dans nos dites isles;" and subsequently in Louisiana, in the successive Royal grants to [Antoine] Crozat in 1712 and the *Compagnie d'Occident* in 1717, and by the Royal Edict of 1724, which also was a *Code Noir*, specially enacted for Louisiana. By this special exceptional legislation, the title to slaves, and the legality of slavery itself, was recognized in those particular places in the French dominions. These Edicts were enactments of positive law, specially promulgated for those particular colonies alone, and necessarily became part of their municipal law.

Denizart, after stating the general principle of freedom, proceeds: "Le bien de l'état a exigé d'autres maximes dans les colonies Françaises de l'Amérique méridionale, et de l'Afrique. Nos rois ont permis d'acheter et de posséder des esclaves Nègres dans ces pays." The author then refers to the Edict of 1685, as having been registered in the island of St° Domingo, and proceeds: "Cet Edit sert de règlement pour la police des isles de l'Amérique française ... Il y a un autre édit du mois de Mars 1724, qui sert de règlement pour l'administration de la Justice, police, discipline, et le commerce des esclaves nègres dans les colonies de la Louisiane; on le nomme aussi le *Code Noir*, et ses dispositions ne diffèrent qu'en bien peu de choses de celles de l'Edit du mois de Mars 1685, *pour les isles.*" (*3 Coll. de Jur: v° Nègres*). "En effet, depuis que les isles de l'Amérique font partie de la domination de Nôtre Souverain, la nécessité de soutenir, d'entretenir les habitations, a introduit la traite des Nègres; leur vente, leur achapt, sont autorisés par les loix publiques, que je rapporte suivant l'Edit de 1685." ... "Si en France on ne connois point d'esclaves, si la seule arrivée dans ce Royaume procure la liberté, ce privilège cesse à l'égard des esclaves nègres françois. Quelle en est la raison? C'est qu'en France, c'est que par une loi de la France, même les esclaves Nègres de nos colonies sont constitués dans un esclavage nécessaire, et autorisé." (case of the Negro, *Boucaux* in the *Causes célèbres* de M. Gayot de Pitaval, vol: XV.)

The same report explains the origin of that particular colonial slave legislation, and which may also be found in other law authors. "Il s'est présenté plusieurs compagnies pour former un établissement dans les isles de l'Amérique, Saint Domingue et autres, et y faire un commerce considérable. Le Roi, pour faciliter cet établissement, concède à ces compagnies toutes les terres incultes de ces isles, autorise la traite des nègres, qui s'échangent contre des marchandises, et comme ces Nègres sont destinés au défrichement et à la culture des terres, ensemble de toutes les denrées qui y croissent, l'utilité du commerce qui ne se fait dans les colonies que par le moyen de toutes ces opérations, a déterminé le Souverain à donner son Edit en 1685, par lequel, en reglant l'administration de la police sur ces nègres, il regle en même tems leur état et leur condition; il déroge à cette maxime du droit français; il veut que ces nègres restent esclaves, à fin de pouvoir mieux les contenir dans l'exercise de leurs travaux qui contribuent à rendre le commerce florissant dans le royaume, et à y entretenir l'abondance." Again, – "L'Edit de 1685 a réellement constitué l'esclavage dans les colonies; les Nègres que l'on y amene de la côte de Guinée sont esclaves &^{ca}. Le Souverain l'a aussi statué par une loi qui est demeurée en vigueur depuis ce tems-là, et de son exécution dépendent la culture des terres de ce pays, la prospérité de Nôtre commerce, la conservation de cette partie des États de Nôtre Monarque: mais, en même tems que c'est une loi nécessaire pour nos colonies, tout son effet y réside sans l'étendue au delà de ces nouvelles acquisitions: ... ainsi, nul avantage à tirer de cet édit hors de nos colonies." (*Ibid.*)

The intercourse between the mother country and those slave colonies, and the application and enforcement of the principle of French freedom in favor of Negro slave servants brought from the West-indian colonies into France by their Masters, occasioned the enactment of further special, exceptional, but at the same time positive, laws, respecting that particular class, namely, the royal edict of October 1716, and its modification by its interpretative Royal declaration of fifteenth December 1738, which preserved the slave status of the colonial Negro whilst in France, and protected the rights of the master; but only upon the observance of positive conditions, a failure of any one of which, under the Edict of 1716, gave the slave his liberty, and under that of 1738 not only subjected him to royal confiscation, *pour être renvoyé aux colonies,* but imposed upon the Master a penalty of one thousand livres for each such slave.

Exceptional as these royal Edicts were to the public law of freedom acknowledged in France, even they were not generally admitted by the provincial parliaments of France, and were registered only in those of Dijon, Rennes and Grenoble. They were neither registered by, nor offered for registration to, the parliament of Paris, and Denizart, *loco citato,* remarks, "parce qu'on les a considérés comme contraire au droit commun du royaume, suivant lequel tout homme est libre dès qu'il habite dans les pays soumis à nos rois." "Depuis l'Édit de 1315, la France est non seulement rentrée dans son premier droit de franchise, elle a encore conservée celui de ne souffrir dans ses États aucuns esclaves." (The *Procureur du Roi,* in Boucaux's case.)

The case of Francisco, the Pondicherry Negro, purchased there in early life by his master, and brought as his servant to France, where he obtained his liberty in 1759, by the concurrent decisions of the two highest tribunals of the Country (Denizart, *loco citato*), and the case of Boucaux, the St^o. Domingo Negro slave, also brought to France as his servant by his Master, and who likewise obtained his freedom there by similar decisions, are celebrated in the annals of French litigation; the latter case, as already stated, is reported at length in M. Gayot de Pitaval's *Causes célèbres,* volume XV. These decisions were in affirmance of the principle of freedom in the Kingdom of France, and of the exceptional character of those edictal enactments, as applicable only to a particular class of persons, and to particular colonial localities, namely, Negro slaves belonging originally to the African and West-Indian colonies alone.

From the foregoing, to which much additional authority might be added, it is evident, 1st that the public law of the parent state did not recognize slavery in France or its territorial dominions, but declared it illegal, and it was, therefore, antagonistic to the local law of her slave colonies in that respect; 2^{ndly}, that the same fundamental rights of the French people extended through all the dominions of France, *tous les états du Royaume,* where her laws prevailed, without special exceptions of particular places; and 3^{rdly} that the exceptional status of slavery was confined to those slave colonies, *colonies françoises de l'Amérique méridionale et de l'Afrique,* and to the Colony of Louisiana, above mentioned; and even for these required no less authority for its establishment and recognition than the positive, express legislative declaration of the Royal Will.

Proceeding from France to Canada, the Colonial Archives shew the establishment, by letters patent in 1663, of a Sovereign or Superior Council for the colony, *Conseil Souverain ou Supérieur de Québec,* to whom were intrusted full administrative and judicial powers in the last resort, *pour y juger souverainement et en dernier ressort,* subject only to the King's pleasure, and according to the "loix et ordonnances de Notre Royaume, et y procéder autant qu'il se pourra en la forme et manière qui se pratique et se garde dans le ressort de Notre Cour de Parlement de Paris." In the year 1674, Canada became a Crown Colony, open to all the King's subjects, the proprietary *Compagnie des Indes Occidentales* to whom the King had granted the Country in 1664 having been broken up, and having abandoned their charter in the former year. The effect resulting from the establishment of the Superior Council, and the introduction of the laws and ordinances of the Kingdom, and of the laws and usages of the *Prévôté de Paris,* was to make these the laws of the Colony, and at the same time to bring with them, for the benefit of the colonists, those fundamental laws of France which regulated the public rights of persons resident in, or being within the precincts of, the *Prévôté de Paris* in Canada. From that time all persons coming in or brought into the Province, becoming subject to the penalty of those laws, were entitled to demand and to receive, the protection afforded by them, in the same manner as in a home province of old France, and especially in that of the *Prévôté de Paris.*

From the establishment of the Superior Council in 1663, no subsequently enacted or promulgated royal legislation could have legal effect, or become operative, in Canada, without its special adoption and registration by the Superior Council, nor unless it was otherwise found to be applicable to the state of the Colony. The only public royal acts of France which received colonial registration since 1663, and in which any reference is had to slaves, *esclaves,* were the following, which I have selected in their order of date, namely:

1st the neutrality treaty of November 1686, between England and France, with particular reference to their respective American Colonies; by the tenth article of which the Indian allies of either state and their slaves, were not to be removed or disturbed;

2nd the Royal grant of Louisiana to Crozat in 1712, which, by the 14th clause, authorized the grantee alone to trade to Guinea for negroes, for the local purposes of the Colony and the cultivation of his grant; and for their sale, for local purposes only, by him to the Colonists alone, who at the time numbered but twenty-eight families, composed, according to Charlevoix of "des marchands, des cabaretiers, et des ouvriers, qui ne se fixoient en aucun endroit;"

3rd The Royal grant of 1717, after Crozat's death, of Louisiana to the *Compagnie d'Occident,* with similar privileges of trading for Negroes;

4th the Royal declaration of 1721, for terminating the legal conflicts arising from the double appointments of tutors to minors in France, and also in the Colony; which, being an enactment of general colonial requirement, applied as well to the free as in the slave Colonies. The general reason for this enactment is stated to be, the conflicts in the tutorial appointments; but, in addition to that general reason, the King took advantage of it to regulate a local evil which was growing in the slave colonies, namely, the enfranchisement of Negroes by their owners whilst the latter were minors. The preamble mentions the evil with reference to the negroes themselves, who, it is stated, "comme nous avons été informés, employés à la culture des terres, étant regardés dans nos colonies comme des effets mobiliers, suivant les lois qui y sont établies les mineurs abusent souvent du droit que l'émancipation leur donne de disposer de leurs nègres, et en ruinant par là les habitations qui leur sont propres, font encore un préjudice considérable à nos colonies, dont la principale utilité dépend du travail des nègres qui font valoir les terres, &ca." The emancipation of the minor, referred to above, was a power granted to him, judicially, to trade, and to manage his Estate, as if he was of the full age of French majority – twenty-five years. The fourth article of this public act, therefore, specially prohibits even the emancipated minor, until his twenty-fifth year, from disposing of his Negroes, "qui servent à exploiter leurs habitations," the terms of this provision shewing this to be a special provision applicable only to the French slave islands;

5th the Edict of October 1727, whereby the foreign trade of the colonies is regulated, and in which special provisions are necessarily enacted with regard to Negroes landing, or being on board of Vessels touching at, or trading with, the colonies;

and lastly, the arrêt of July 1745, which, assimilating fugitive slaves from foreign or enemies' colonies to wrecks on the coasts of the Kingdom, appropriated them, or their proceeds, to the Royal benefit. No other French public act, referring to slavery, has been registered in the Colony; these will be found in the first volume of the *Edits, Ordonnances Royaux, Déclarations et arrêts du Conseil d'Etat du Roi concernant le Canada,* published by authority, in 8vo form, in 1854, and none of them introduced slavery into, or recognized it in, French Canada.

Neither the edict of 1685, or *code noir* of the French West-Indian islands, nor the other exceptional enactment above referred to, respecting negro slaves in France, nor even the edict of 1724, the Louisiana *Code Noir,* were registered, or offered for registration, in the Superior Council of Quebec, and they were, therefore, inoperative in Canada. [blank space] The Royal grants of 1712 and 1717 of Louisiana, necessarily were so registered, because Louisiana was thereby separated from Canada, of which until 1712, it formed a portion. "Hors le cas prévu par la loi, hors le pays mentionné, qui est le seul objet de la loi, cet esclavage cesse, et la liberté reprend tous ses droits."

The consequence of the want of this Provincial Parliamentary or Colonial registration is well explained in the following remarks of the King's advocate, *Procureur du Roi,* addressed to the judicial assessors of the Court before which the trial of the St. Domingo negro slave, Boucaux, was proceeding, and are in full conformity with French law in that respect. After remarking upon the specially exceptional character of the edicts of 1685 and 1716, he proceeds: "ces deux édits n'ont ni l'un ni l'autre été enrégistrés au parlement de Paris, et n'ont point été envoyé au Greffe de ce siège: peut-être que ce défaut de formalité attirera vôtre attention, et que vous vous reglerez sur ce principe, que la loi ne peut avoir d'execution ni d'effet que par sa publicité; en ce cas, il n'en faudroit point davantage pour rendre inutiles tous les raisonnemens, et pour détruire toutes les inductions que la partie de M. Tribard (c'est-à-dire la partie du Maître) tire de ces Edits; par la même raison, il n'en faudroit point davantage pour remettre celle de M. Mallet (viz. celle du Nègre) dans le même état que les esclaves étrangers, à qui l'on ne conteste point le privilêge de la liberté dans toute l'étendue du Royaume." (*Causes Célèbres* XV, 54). It must hence be manifest, that no public law of France introduced, or established, or recognized slavery in Canada, as a Colonial status. To use a common form of expression, the common law of France neither established nor protected slavery in Canada: that conclusion is established by the fact, that upon the Grant of Louisiana to Crozat in 1712, and its formation into a separate colony, dissevered by the Royal letters patent from the Province of Canada, of which, till that separation, it had formed a part, the King deemed it necessary exceptionally and specially to provide, on the subject of slavery, in favour of the grantee, Crozat, by giving him special permissions to purchase slaves in Guinea and sell them in Louisiana, and afterwards, in 1717, extended the same privilege to his successors, the *Compagnie d'occident;* and finally in 1727 [*sic*: read 1724], by his Royal Edict of that year, made a *Code Noir* specially for that colony, whilst no such legislation was ever contemplated for, or extended to Canada. I refer particularly to the first Royal grant of Canada, of April 1627, to the *Compagnie des cents associés,* the Letters patent establishing that Company, its articles of association, and the various Royal and public documents connected with that Company, including that of its dissolution, the Second Royal grant of Canada, in May 1664, to the *Compagnie des Indes occidentales,* the constitution and erection of this latter company, with the special article of the Grant in their favour of *les Isles de l'Amérique appellées les Antilles,* all of which are of record in the first volume of the before cited Edits, Ordonnances Royaux &ca., and in which neither slaves nor slavery are mentioned or can be implied. I have seen in the possession of a Collector of old colonial records, a note or extract from representations said to have been made from Canada to the Home Government, upon the subject of the introduction of Negroes as contained in the official letters of the Governor de Denonville, and the Intendant de Champigny, of the tenth of August, thirty first of October, and sixth of November 1688, to the Secretary of State in Paris; there are no means of verifying their correctness in this country, but as connected with this subject and bearing evidence of interest in the Matter, I cite the extract, which is as follows[:]

"Monsr. de Lagny écrit[:] Les gens de travail et les domestiques sont d'une rareté extrême, et d'une cherté si extraordinaire, qu'il ruinent tous ceux qui font quelque entreprise. On croit que le meilleur moyen serait d'avoir des esclaves nègres. Le Procureur Général du Conseil, qui est à Paris, assure, que si sa Majesté agrée cette proposition, quelqu'un des principaux habitants en ferait acheter aux isles à l'arrivé des Vaisseaux de Guinée et il est lui même dans cette résolution."

The Secretary's answer in the following year, 1689, was simply, that the King made no particular objection to the project, but suggested at the same time, "il est bon de leur faire remarquer, qu'il est à craindre que ces nègres qui viennent d'un climat si différent ne perissent en Canada, et le projet seroit inutile." This Negro project remained without effect, and was never put into execution, nor do I find from examination of the provincial records, that any further representation was made upon the matter.

A kind of servitude, however, had grown up in the Colony from other causes. The prisoners taken in war by their Indian captors, whose lives had been spared, were, by force of Indian customs, reduced to servitude, and called slaves, *servi,* less *à serviendo quam servando;* a servitude, at all events, the result of captivity in war, by which the Indian Masters secured to themselves the material advantage of their prisoners' service. The Indian tributaries of France soon became induced to preserve their captives from other, but more venal, motives. The service-market of Canada, at that period, as shewn in the representations above extracted, and as we learn from Charlevoix, was in great need of supply, and hence the wants of the Colonists raised the cupidity of the Indians, whose predatory excursions, far and near, enabled them to supply the former and secure the latter.

The Western tribes of *Pawnees* appear to have been the great source from which their prisoners proceeded, so much so indeed, that all the Indian servants of the Colony became included under that general appellation (*Panis*). These Captives were not placed or sold in Canada alone, but were disposed of in the slave holding Carolinas, and in the other British provinces, where no slavery was established. (See the preamble to Raudot's Ordinance of 1709).

In 1671, Negro slaves were first introduced into Carolina; and already, at that time, the number in Virginia amounted to two thousand (see Holmes's American Annals.); so that negroes might be brought as captives into Canada as well [as] Pawnees (*Panis*), and both became subjects of sale and barter – whether legal or otherwise was not considered – they were subjected to the law of *le plus fort;* and the colonists, almost exclusively the residents of the towns, benefited by this enforced servitude, and converted them into domestic servants. Even white persons from the British colonies, taken by the Indians, were subjected to the same treatment and consequence; and it suffices to refer to the inhabitants of Deerfield, who were taken by the French Indians and sold in Canada, from which they were only redeemed on payment of ransom money. That a strong opinion prevailed against its validity, and that arbitrary measures were needed to secure a continuance of such useful service, and to prevent the seduction therefrom of the purchased *Panis* and negroes, will be found in the terms of the preamble of the ordinance of the Intendant Raudot, of the thirteenth of April 1709, intituled "Ordonnance au sujet des nègres, et des sauvages appellés Panis." (Edits et Ordo &ca. Vol II, 271).

It must be observed, that this Ordinance was the *Acte* of the Intendant alone, and stands unsupported by the sanction of either the Sovereign Superior Council in the Colony, in whose archives it was not registered, or of the Crown in France. Its preamble plainly indicates the reason of its origin and promulgation, namely, the opposition made to the traffic in, and the sale and purchase of, Indian and negro captives, – the interference with the claims of their purchasers for their compulsory servitude, – and the application in Canada in their favour of the principles of personal freedom, extended by the public law of France to all persons coming within its territorial dominions, where slavery was not exceptionally established *par la loi de l'État,* or by the positive enactment of the Royal will: hence the purchased servitude could not be enforced, and the purchased *Panis* and Negroes, almost in every instance, quitted the service of their purchasers, "ce qui fait, qu'ils quittent quasi toujours leurs maîtres."

The legal references, above recorded, of the public law of France, of its operation and effect throughout the French dominions, and of the fact of the local establishment of slavery in her above-mentioned French slave colonies alone & only by means of the exceptional laws above-mentioned, strongly qualify the concluding portion of the preamble of the Ordinance, in which the Intendant, objecting to the attempts at interference with the forced servitude, because the purchased negroes and *Panis* were told that they could not be retained in servitude, and were entitled to freedom, "sous prétexte qu'en France il n'y a point d'esclaves," boldly asserts: "ce qui ne se trouve pas toujours vrai, par rapport aux Colonies qui en dépendent, puisque dans les Isles de ce continent tous les Negres que les habitans achètent sont toujours regardés comme tels," – the Intendant's deduction therefrom is a curious *non sequitur* – "et comme toutes les colonies doivent être regardées sur le même pied, et que les peuples de la nation Panis sont aussi nécessaires aux habitans de ce pays pour la culture des terres et autres ouvrages qu'on pourroit entreprendre, comme les Nègres le sont aux Isles, et que même ces sortes d'engagements sont très utiles à cette Colonie, étant nécessaire d'en assurer la propriété à ceux qui en ont achetés et qui en acheteront à l'avenir: Nous, sous le bon plaisir de Sa Majesté, Ordonnons, que tous les Panis et Nègres qui ont été achetés et qui seront dans la suite appartiendront en pleine propriété à ceux qui les ont achetés, comme étant leurs esclaves." It will be observed, that the Intendant himself refers to the slavery of the *Isles de l'Amérique* as being local in its nature, and furnishes in his *Ordonnance* one, and among many, of the various arbitrary and legally unjustifiable acts for which his official career in Canada was long noted among the Colonists, and of which traces are met with in the traditionary remarks and statements handed down to this time.

The enforcing authority of this Ordinance will not a little depend upon the delegated power of its framer to make a public law. The Royal commission invested him with the legal functions of administering the law in all matters, civil and criminal, "conformément à nos édits et ordonnances, et à la Coûtume de Notre bonne ville, prévôté et vicomté de Paris," in force in the Colony; and further, "de faire avec le Conseil Superieur tous les règlemens que vous estimerez nécessaires pour *la police générale* du dit pays, ensemble pour les foires et marchés, ventes, achats, et débits de toutes denrées et marchandises;" and, in case of necessary despatch, "nous vous donnons pouvoir et faculté par ces même presentes, de les faire seul, &ca." Such delegation of Royal power might have justified the enactment of a *Police reglement,* preventing interference with service and prohibiting "qui que ce soit de les débaucher (les Panis et Nègres) sous peine de cinquante livres d'amende," but could not thereby override the public law of the state, which was repugnant to slavery, and annul the maxims, usages and jurisprudence of the Kingdom, or of the Prévôté de Paris, by which freedom was maintained in French territory; nor introduce into Canada by implication, *uno afflatu,* all the exceptional legislation specially made for other particular Colonies; nor validate the slavery of the purchased Indian from his having been a mere prisoner of war, or of a Negro from the colour of his complexion. Moreover, the Intendant himself is constrained to declare the doubtful character of his Ordinance, in as much as he promulgated it subject to the King's confirmation – "Nous, sous le bon plaisir de sa Majesté, Ordonnons &[ca]." – the limitation itself is of a very peculiar character, and I have been able to discover the like restriction in only two other Intendants' Ordinances, from among about one hundred and fifty in number that I have examined from a very early period down to the time of the Conquest of the Province, and both of those Ordinances had reference to what might be called Royal *interests,* – one, by the same Raudot, in 1710, for the appointment of a Judicial officer at Montreal; and the other, in 1744, by another Intendant for regulating the Current value in the Colony of certain moneys of account and coins. No other Intendant's Ordinance professed to reach to a matter of state policy, or of public laws, and therefore, no other was restricted in the terms as above. The Confirmation of Raudot's Ordinance of 1709, *sous le bon plaisir de sa Majesté,* was never given; and of this, the appended copy of the ordinance, with the certificate attached, is proof. The signature thereto "Geo Pownall" is that of the late Sir George Pownall, Secretary and Registrar of the Province whose signature I recognize from having frequently seen such appended to public official documents in his official capacity; he was knighted, I think in 1790, and died in 1834.[4] Raudot was appointed in 1701, relieved from his Intendancy by his successor's appointment in March 1710, and returned to France, where he probably satisfied himself of the propriety of not requiring the Royal sanction to his Ordinance. A copy of Raudot's commission as Intendant, duly authenticated by the Certificate and signature of the said Sir George Pownall, secretary and Registrar of the Province, is also hereto appended.

I have been unable to discover a single judicial enforcement of the slave principle recorded during the existence of the French dominion over Canada: it is probable that the penalty was so financially effective in preventing interference with a compulsory service that even the patriotic opponents of the arbitrary ordinance hesitated before embarking in a litigation which, in the Colony itself, would be opposed by the self-interest of the wealthy, and, probably of the Intendant himself, and his subordinate judicial dependants; and which, at all events, could not be carried on without considerable expense, before it could receive final adjudication by the Appellate jurisdiction of the Parliament of Paris.

Although the absolute nullity of the Ordinance, with reference to the establishment of slavery in Canada, cannot be doubted, from what has been above stated, that nullity manifestly follows from the following additional reasons.

Upon the trial of Boucaux, already referred to, it was unhesitatingly admitted by the Counsel for both parties, as well as by the *Procureur du Roi,* that the slave status could attach only to the Negro of the West-Indian and African Colonies, because he was a slave there *par la loi de l'État,* and that such a status did not extend, even by implication, to any other person, or to servitude for any other cause, except that arising out of the necessarily peculiar cultivation of the West-Indian Estates.

As stated above, the same fact of the localizing of the slavery is also expressed in the preamble of the ordinance by Raudot himself. The argument urged by the Counsel for the Master, in Boucaux's case, rested solely and entirely upon the local application and effect of the exceptional Edicts of 1685 and 1716, and candidly exempted from their operation all but the Negro slaves of those island colonies [–] "on ne connoît point, il est vrai, d'esclaves en France, et quiconque a mis le pied dans ce Royaume, est gratifié de la liberté. Mais quelle est l'application, et quelle est la distinction du principe? Le principe est vrai dans le cas où tout autre esclave qu'un esclave Nègre arrivera dans ce Royaume. Par exemple, qu'un étranger, qu'un négociant François, arrive dans ce Royaume avec des sauvages qu'il prétendra être ses esclaves; qu'un Espagnol, qu'un Anglois, vienne en ce Royaume avec des esclaves Nègres dépendans des colonies de sa nation; voilà le cas dans lequel, par la loi, par le privilège de la franchise de ce Royaume, la chaîne de l'esclavage se brisera, et la liberté sera acquise à de pareils esclaves." The King's advocate adopts this opinion without hesitation, and thereupon claims for Boucaux that liberty which was conceded to all foreign slaves coming into the territories of the Kingdom, and then concludes: "de nos maximes, de nos usages, de notre jurisprudence, il suit nécessairement, qu'il ne peut y avoir d'esclaves dans ce Royaume." (*Causes Célèbres,* Vol. XV).

I have desired to state at length, and in the language of the French jurisprudence itself, the grounds upon which I have rested my opinion of the nullity of Raudot's Ordinance, which can derive no presumptive support from the mere fact of the complexion of the Canadian Negro being the same as that of the West-Indian Negro, a presumption which, however extravagant and unfounded in itself, when applied to the negro, cannot, in any manner, apply to the *Panis* Indian captive; nor simply from the Intendant's assurance that the labour of the *panis* or negro would be beneficial to Canada.

I have refrained from testing the Validity of Raudot's Ordinance by modern notions and feelings, but have confined myself to the established jurisprudence of

France, which was law in Canada, and to its recorded Judgments, co-eval and co-incident with the Ordinance itself; hence my professional conviction, that neither slavery itself, nor the slavery of any purchased *Panis* or negro, would have been sustained in the appellate tribunals of France, notwithstanding the purchase of the subject, or the existence of an abusive practice arbitrarily attempted to be legalized by the Ordinance of the Intendant Raudot.

It only remains to say a word upon the *Ordonnance* of the Intendant Hocquart of the first of september 1736, which, in form, is not obnoxious to the nullities attachable to that of Mr Raudot. It is of a more *Police* character, intended as a preventitive to litigation, and a preservative of the subject of proof of a particular fact, & simply provides for the legal ascertainment of a fixed mode of enfranchisement, by a written proof of the fact, requiring the *Acte* to be established by writing, authentically executed before Notaries Public, functionaries to whose *actes* full faith and evidence were given by Law, and verbal testimony avoided thereby. I need not add, that any other effect that might be ascribed to this second Ordinance would be obnoxious to the same nullities as were applied to the former.

The necessary deductions from the authorities and facts stated, which have been carefully considered and supported by the references, in general literally transcribed, are, – that the public law of France did not allow or recognize the Slavery of Negroes or other persons, either in France or in French Canada; – that the only law of local application in Canada was a nullity; – and that though a forced servitude *de facto* existed in the Colony, it was an abusive servitude, *servitude d'abus,* not sustained by any law having authoritative legal sanction for its support; unlike Louisiana in this respect, where the Royal permission was given to traffic in slaves, and where the King not only sanctioned slavery by *la loi de l'État,* but enacted the Edict of 1724 to regulate its police, justice and administration in the Colony; Canada possessed none of these, no authentic documents can be found in her archives or records which regulate the mode, or period or effect of servitude, the extent of the Master's power, the period of the enforced subjection or any of its incidents or consequences, either affecting the purchased person himself, or his offspring, or any Act of Police, justice or administration connected with slavery. The reason is manifest, because the servitude, such as it existed, was simply by the abuse of power, in those who held the *Panis* and Negroes, and from the fear of the penalty imposed upon "ceux qui les débauchent." Yet slavery was not a legal status established par *la loi de l'Etat,* or by Royal sanction, and could have had no legal force upon the person of the so called slave (*esclave*). The difference between slavery legally established, and enforced service of longer or shorter duration, must be manifest, as respects Canada, as not to require further observation.

QUESTION 5: *Did the capitulation of the Canadians to the British arms, in September 1760, effect any, and what, change in the legal status or condition of Negroes, or other persons, then held by the Canadians as slaves?*

ANSWER: As I do not recognize the legal existence of a slave status in Canada previous to the capitulation of 1760, because that status could have been established by

Royal enactment only, and which was in fact never made for Canada, the only effect of the particular stipulation in the Capitulation regarding *Panis* and Negroes was, to leave them with the same natural rights that they previously possessed. Even admitting the existence of an abusive servitude *de facto,* as regarded that class of inhabitants, the 47th Article of the Capitulation only stipulated, that the Panis and negroes should remain in the same quality of slaves, *resteront dans la même qualité d'esclaves,* in the possession of those who held them, as they were before that stipulation; whilst, by other articles, all the inhabitants remaining in the Colony became subjects of the King of England, and were no longer to be governed by the laws and usages established for the Colony, thus the entire body of the People, of every class, so remaining and conquered by the arms of the Crown of England, became subjects of that Crown, by Act and operation of law. In the well known case of Campbell and Hall, Lord Mansfield says: "in the acquisition by conquest, it is limited by the constitution to the King's authority to grant or refuse a capitulation; if he refuse and put all the inhabitants to the sword, all the lands belong to him; if he receive the inhabitants under his protection and grant them their property, he has the power to fix the conditions: the conquest virtually naturalizes the inhabitants by the Act and operation of law, and they become subjects of the Crown of England." It was also well urged in that case, that "it is not, as formerly, when the conqueror gained captives and slaves and absolute rights by the law of nations, but now the conqueror obtains dominion and subjects." Hence the effect of the capitulation was to operate a change from the abusive slavery by which that class of persons had been constrained *en qualité d'esclaves,* to the possession by them of personal and public rights as British subjects.

The capitulation of Montreal in september 1760 differs in this particular from that of Quebec in september 1759: both were careful for the full and entire protection of the inhabitants in all their property & effects, houses and Goods, and even protected those of the Military and religious Orders, and enabling all to dispose of their property, if they determined upon returning to France; whilst in the former only was contained the stipulation respecting *Panis* & Negroes, the latter not mentioning these at all. The necessity for any mention of this particular class of persons could only have arisen from the unsatisfactory relation subsisting between the purchasers and the purchased *Panis* & Negroes; had these been considered as legal property, no special reference to them would have been made, but the fact is the traffic was chiefly local from the intercourse subsisting between the French Indians and the residents of Montreal, where the Indian trade was carried on at certain regular periods.

QUESTION 6: *Did the capitulation effect any, and what, change in the legal status or condition of the* Children *of such Negro, or other slaves, born after the capitulation?*
ANSWER: Every capitulation in itself is nothing but a merely temporary consequence of superior military power and cannot be extended to affect a subsequent condition of things; nor could it extend to the children of those Negroes and *Panis* born after the capitulation, who, being born subjects of the King of England, could not be af-

fected by any laws and usages previously established for the colony, which, even if not set aside by the capitulation, would have ceased to exist in this particular, as being repugnant to the public law of the conquering state.

QUESTION 7: *Did the Treaty of Paris of the tenth of february 1763, and the King's Proclamation of the seventh of October in the same Year, or either of them, effect any, and what, change in the legal status or condition – 1st of the negroes, or other persons, held by the Canadians as slaves at the time of the capitulation, – and 2^{ndly} of the children born in Canada of such Negroes or other persons, either after the capitulation, or after the treaty of Peace?*

ANSWER: They did so, not only by themselves but also in connexion with other public documents applicable to the Colony. By the capitulation of 1760, the French inhabitants remaining in Canada not only became subjects of the King of England, but were deprived of their former municipal laws, the Custom of Paris, and the laws and usages established for the country, under which they had been previously governed.

The following letter from the Marquis de Vaudreuil, Governor of Canada, to M. de Belestre, Governor of Detroit, dated the day after the capitulation, otherwise interesting in itself, is peculiarly so, as it indicated his appreciation of the effects of the capitulation. The Marquis observes: "Le Général Anglais a déclaré que les Canadians [sic] devenaient sujets de S.M. Britannique, et par cette raison le peuple n'a point été conservé dans la coûtume de Paris."

"À Montréal, le 9 Septr. 1760.

"Je vous apprends, monsieur, que j'ai été dans la nécessité de capituler à l'armée du Général Amherst. Cette ville est, vous savez, sans défense, nos troupes étoient considérablement diminuées, nos moyens et ressources totalement épuisés.

"Nous étions entourés par trois armées qui réunies formoient au moins 30,000 hommes. Le Général Amherst était au 6 de ce mois à la vue des murs de cette ville, le Général Murray à portée d'un de nos fauxbourgs, et l'armée du lac Champlain étoit à Laprairie et à Longueuil. Dans ces circonstances, ne pouvant rien espérer des efforts ni même du sacrifice des troupes, j'ai pris sagement le parti de capituler avec le Général Amherst, à des conditions très avantageuses pour les colons, et particulièrement pour les habitans du Détroit. En effet, ils conservent le libre exercice de leur religion, et sont maintenus en la possession de leurs biens meubles, immeubles, et leur pelletries; ils ont aussi le commerce libre comme les propres sujets du Roi de la Grande Bretagne.

"Les mêmes conditions sont accordées aux militaires et ils peuvent commettre des procureurs pour user en leur absence de leurs droits; eux et tous les citoyens en général peuvent vendre aux Anglois et aux François leurs biens, et en faire passer le produit en France, ou l'emporter avec lui, s'ils jugent à propos de s'y retirer à la paix.

"Ils conservent leurs Nègres et Panis, mais ils sont obligés de rendre ceux pris des Anglois.

"Le Général anglois a déclaré que les Canadiens devenoient sujets de S. M. Britannique, et par cette raison le peuple n'a point été conservé dans la coûtume de Paris.

"À l'égard des troupes, il a été imposé la condition de ne point servir pendant la présente guerre, et de mettre bas les armes; elles doivent être envoyées en France. Vous ferez donc, Monsieur, rassembler les Officiers et soldats qui sont dans votre poste, vous les ferez mettre bas les armes, et vous vous rendrez avec eux à tel port que l'on jugera à propos pour de là passer en France.

"Les Citoyens et habitans de Détroit seront conséquemment sous le commandement de l'Officier que le général Amherst aura destiné pour ce lieu.

"Voux ferez passer copie de ma lettre aux Miamis et Scactanons, supposé qu'il eut quelques soldats, a fin qu'eux et les habitans s'y conforment.

"Je compte avoir le plaisir de vous voir en France, avec tous nos Messieurs, Madame de Belestre jouit d'une parfaite santé.

"J'ai l'honneur d'être, très sincèrement,
    "Monsieur, votre très humble,
        & très obeissant Serviteur.
           (signé) Vaudreuil."

The French Governor himself thus admits the cessation of the former laws and usages of the Colony; the difference in the capitulation of Montreal and that of Grenada, a conquest also mentioned in the Treaty of Peace, and in the Proclamation of 1763, is manifest. By the former, the French Canadian colonists were deprived of their governing laws and usages, by the latter capitulation, these were preserved to them. 5th Article of the Grenada capitulation: "They shall preserve their civil government, their laws, customs and ordinances; justice shall be administered by the same officers who are now in employment, &ca. *Answer:* They become British subjects, but shall continue to be governed by their present laws until His Majesty's pleasure is known." See case of Campbell & Hall, where Lord Mansfield, in his judgment, says: "3^{rdly} Articles of capitulation upon which the conquest is surrendered, and treaties of Peace by which it is ceded, are sacred and inviolable, according to their true intent."

The treaty of Peace of 1763 only secured the liberty of the free exercise of the Roman Catholic religion for the inhabitants of Canada, whilst the proclamation erected the conquered province into a provincial government, the Government of Quebec, – gave power to the Governor to summon general Assemblies, and with them and the Colonial council to make laws for the Colony, as near as might be agreeable to the laws of England, but assuring in the mean time to all inhabitants, and to all persons resorting to the Colony, the enjoyment of the benefit of the laws of England, pledging the Royal declaration to give power, under the great Seal of England, to the Governor of the Province, to erect Courts of judicature and public justice, for hearing and determining all causes, criminal and civil, according to law and equity, and as near as might be agreeable to the laws of England.

The Royal Commission of November 1763 to the first Governor, General Murray, did grant these powers; and among others, the power at once to constitute such Courts of Justice for hearing and determining such causes according to law and equity, &ca; and the commission of September 1766 (nearly three years later), by which the first chief Justice of the Province, William Hey, Esquire, was appointed, made it incumbent upon that high functionary to administer justice in the Province, "according to the laws and customs of that part of our Kingdom of Great Britain called England." Extracts from the former, and a copy of the latter, both duly authenticated, are hereto appended. By the above mentioned public documents, plainly expressing the King's will, the introduction into the Colony was of course made of the laws of England, public and municipal; the former regulating the status of individuals, making all persons naturalized subjects, and giving to them the personal and civil rights of British subjects, and the latter, or common law, so far as applicable to the state of the Colony.

It is a well known principle of English law, that "upon the conquest of a Country the law remains unchanged until the will of the Conqueror is expressed:" that must be taken as between subject and subject only, not as between the Sovereign and subject; and it is also established, that the power to alter the laws of a conquered country is a power vested in the Crown, without any limitation as to the advice under which it may be exercised, whether by proclamation or charter (*3 Knapp's Privy Council Reports, 1835, Johnson vs. Reira.*)

There can be no reasonable doubt, that the proclamation and commissions, above referred to, plainly express the will of the King for the substitution in the colony of the law of England for the laws and usages which prevailed in the French time. That the law of England did so prevail, unmistakeably at least within the apprehension of the Chief law-Officer of the Crown in Canada, appears from the draught of the Report prepared by Mr (afterwards Baron) Maseres, Attorney General for the Province, for submission by the Governor General and Council of the Province to the King in 1769; in which, observing upon the effect of the capitulation, it is remarked: "by which (namely, the 42nd article, and General Amherst's answer thereto,) it should seem, that these Your Majesty's new subjects in this Province were put up on the same footing as Your Majesty's other subjects in other parts of Your Majesty's British dominions with respect to the laws by which they were to be governed, and the power of legislation that was to be exercised over them for the time to come; and that the continuance or abolition of their former laws and customs was to depend entirely upon the future counsels which Your Majesty, in your royal wisdom, should find it expedient to pursue." (*Maseres' Collection of Commissions &ca, London 1772, 4to*). As mere matter of fact, the English law was the prevailing and recognized law of the colony, and, on that very account, became obnoxious to the strong representations against its continuance made by the French colonists to the Government at home for its removal, and the restoration of the old French system.

It is manifest, from these citations and references, that the law of England became the measure of Justice, and of the personal and public rights of every class of the inhabitants of the Province: that the negroes and *Panis,* with the other resident colonists, by their submission to those laws, became liable to all their penalties, and consequently, had a right to all their privileges and protection.

If in fact the status of slavery ever had legal existence in the Colony, it became absolutely abolished by contact with the laws of England. A similar question of the status of individuals in the Colony, as to the enjoyment of civil rights, arose in a case in 1835, in which it was held, in effect, by the vice Chancellor of England, giving the Judgment of the Privy Council in appeal from the Colony, that the status of the party must be decided by the public law, the law of England; and *that* being settled, the municipal law then applied itself to the rights or property in contest. The Vice Chancellor in the course of his Judgment observed: "the Cession of the country to England of course varied the law of the country in respect of the Sovereign: when the King of England became King of Canada, the natives of Canada became his subjects. Canada became part of his dominions, subject to be governed by its local laws. By the change of Sovereignty, it happened, that the law of England, and not the law of France or French Canada, would, of necessity, determine the question. (*3 Knapp's P.C. Rep. Donagani vs Donegani.*)

The status of slavery, must, therefore, be settled by the law of England; but that law does not, in principle, recognize the existence of Slavery, except as the creature of municipal laws; holding, that slavery is not a natural, but a municipal relation, an institution confined to certain places, and that a mere change from a place of contrary custom is sufficient by that law to secure freedom. These principles were established, after great argument, in the case of the Virginia Negro Somerset against his master Stewart, in which the Court of King's Bench, Lord Mansfield presiding, distinctly and expressly recognized the principle, that the status of slavery was a municipal relation; an institution, therefore, confined to certain places, and necessarily dropped in a Country where such municipal relation did not subsist. (*Lofft's Rep: & 20 State Trials.*)

Coleridge, in a note to 1 Bl: Com [William Blackstone's *Commentaries on the Laws of England*]: p. 127, remarks upon the case, "the principle of decision is, that slavery is not a state recognized by the law of nature generally, or by the law of England locally; and, wherein it legally exists, it does so only by the force of some local law. Whenever, therefore, a slave comes from a place where it is recognized, into a place under the English law, he ceases to be a slave, because the local law loses its force, and the English law itself neither suffers the relation, nor will, by the *comitas inter communitates,* enforce any local law contrary to the law of nature." As long therefore, as the law of England acknowledges the law of nature to be its great principle and rule, so long must it reject a claim to a right of property in a man, or in his labour and industry, founded on his being born of a captive, or on his being seized violently by a third person, and sold to the Claimant. To use Lord Mansfield's very forcible language, "the state of Slavery is of such a nature, that it is incapable of being introduced on any reasons, moral or political, but only by positive law, which preserves its force long after the reasons, occasion, and time itself, from whence it was created, are erased from memory. It is so odious, that nothing can be suffered to support it but positive law."

This English legal system was further sustained by the terms of the before-mentioned commission to the Chief Justice of the King's Bench, and of the Commissions of other Officials in Canada, and continued in full operation until the Year 1774, when the British Statute 14 George III, chapter 83, was passed, which recalled the French laws with reference to property and civil rights. Under this statute no interference was allowed with what had already been acquired or judicially determined under the operation of the English law. Under this system of English law, public and private slavery had no legal existence from the cession of the Country, as regarded the *Panis* and negroes referred to above, much less their children, born after the capitulation and the treaty of Peace, who were free-born. Burge says, "Children born in England of parents who had been in the Colonies, were not only at the time of birth absolutely free, but continued so. There could be no ground for considering that the children would become slaves even if they had returned to the Colonies. Such was the admitted law of Jamaica, and it is believed of every other West-Indian colony." (*I Burge's Commentaries on Colonial & Foreign laws, p. 757.*) This is a conclusion of the law of the Country of the birth; not because the birth occurred in this or that locality, but because it occurred under the protection of the particular system of the law of the Country of the birth being itself repugnant to slavery. [blank space] In the case of Lunsford vs. Coquillon, 2 Martin's Louisiana Reports, page 408, before the Supreme Court of that State, it was assumed, that if the status of slavery were dissolved, according to the law of the domicile of the owner, and of the slave who lives with him, it would be considered as having legally ceased to exist in every other place. So the incipient right to freedom of the issue of a female slave, registered according to the laws of Pennsylvania, would prevail in Kentucky, notwithstanding her removal to the latter state. Her freedom was not impaired by forcibly removing her into Kentucky to defeat her attempt to assert her freedom, nor by her subsequent removal, *voluntary* or forced, into the state of Louisiana (*I Burge, loco citato*). Children born therefore after the capitulation, and after the treaty, are unquestionably free-born; and with reference to them, it is difficult to discover a legal principle which would sanction the position, that a person in possession of the status of freedom could, by his own act, subject himself to that of slavery. (*I Burge, p. 750. See also the case of Serjt. Rawle's Reports, p. 305 & seq.*)

QUESTION 8: *Was the King's proclamation of the seventh of October 1763, ever recognized by the British Parliament as being legal, and was it ever revoked or repealed?*

ANSWER: It was so recognized by the British Act for Canada, of 14 George III, Chapter 83 (Known as *the Quebec Act*), intituled, "An act for making more effectual provision for the Government of the Province of Quebec, &ca," which came into operation in May 1755 [*sic*: read 1775]. By this Act, the Criminal law of England was continued in the Province, the "laws of Canada" were to be resorted to "in all matters of controversy relative to property and civil rights," and in all causes thereafter, to be instituted in any of the Courts of Justice, with respect to such property and rights, were to be determined agreeable to "the laws and customs of Canada;" but the Act did not affect the personal rights of Colonists, acquired under the proclamation and treaty.

QUESTION 9: *Were any municipal or other assessments or taxes raised or levied in Canada, for the expenses and purposes of Government, at the time of the Capitulation; – by what law or laws were they raised or levied, – and were Slaves mentioned in any such law or laws as property?*

ANSWER: The Royal Edict of February 1748, which imposed assessments or taxes upon a great variety of articles, does not make mention of slaves. By the *Code Noir* of 1685, the West-Indian slaves were expressly declared to be moveable property, *meubles;* and, so also by the Louisiana *Code Noir* of 1724; but these laws, in that respect, were municipal, and not applicable to Canada. No law of Canada, at any time, has brought the purchased Negroes and *Panis* within any such declaration, or converted them into goods and Chattels.

QUESTION 10: *Since Canada came under the dominion of the British Crown or Government, have Negroes been permitted, in the Courts of Justice in that Country, to testify as witnesses in Civil and criminal cases, and have they been, and are they, Eligible to serve as Jurors, or to vote at Elections? in fact, have they, by reason of their Colour, laboured, or do they labour, under any legal disabilities what ever that white men, in the same Country, did not, and do not, labour under?*

ANSWER: Since the establishment of the British dominion in Canada, negroes have enjoyed the same Civil rights as other natural born, or naturalized, subjects of the Crown in the Colony, without any disqualification whatever by reason of their complexion.

QUESTION 11: *Was the subject of slavery ever brought under the consideration of the Governor and Council of Canada, or Province of Quebec, before its division into Lower and Upper Canada, – or under the consideration of either branch of the Parliament of either Lower or Upper Canada after that division, – and if so, how was it brought under consideration, and what was the result?*

ANSWER: No application was made, or attempted, to the Governor and Council (the then Provincial Legislature) from 1764 to 1791; a negative proof of its *non*-existence, during that time. It was brought under the Notice of the Parliament of Lower Canada in the several Years 1793, 1799, 1800, and 1801; but the prevailing impression in Lower Canada was so powerful against the belief in the possible existence of slavery, that no legislation was allowed or had upon the subject. The bills introduced before the House of Assembly were dropped, and no action whatever was taken before the Legislative Council. Since 1801, no attempt whatever at legislation upon the matter has been made.[5] I subjoin extracts from the proceedings of the Lower Canada Parliament, as officially reported in the Journals of the House of Assembly for the Years above mentioned, which I have compared with the entries in those books, acknowledged in this country to be authoritative. The Original Manuscript Journals were destroyed at the burning of the Parliament buildings in Montreal in 1849. These parliamentary proceedings only arose from the dread of the United States' slaves, brought into the Province after the Declaration of Independence, being continued as slaves, and differing from the servitude in the French time. In the second session of the first Parliament of Upper Canada, held in 1793, a provincial act, 33 George III, Chapter 7, was passed, "to prevent the further introduction of slaves, and to limit the term of contracts for servitude within this Province," which originated in the passing of the British statute of 1790, 30 George III, Chapter 27, "for encouraging new settlers in His Majesty's Colonies and plantations in America." The British statute was unequivocally a mere emigration act, declaring, in effect, the expediency of giving encouragement to persons that were disposed, from among the resident inhabitants of the United States generally, to come and settle in the scantily populated Bahamas, Bermudas, the Province of Quebec, and Nova Scotia, &ca. The enticement offered for their encouragement to come within those British territories with their families, *Negroes,* furniture, implements of husbandry and cloathing, was a freedom from duty upon a particular valued amount of these imported effects for each white person of the family, and for each Negro brought in. Having thus encouraged their entrance into the Province, the Statute at the same time discouraged their departure from it, by withholding legal sanction from all sales or bargains which those settlers might make of their Negroes, furniture or cloathing within twelve months after their arrival. The Statute necessarily referred to Negroes, by reason of the existence of Negro slavery in some, and of the residence of free negroes in others of the United States, to which the general object and purport of the Statute addressed itself. Virginia, the Carolinas, and other States, maintained the institution of slavery, whilst Pennsylvania and the New England states had abolished it altogether, after strenuous endeavours for the purpose from the early part of the Eighteenth century. It was finally abolished in Pennsylvania in 1780, and Connecticut and Massachusetts soon followed the example. From the commencement of the War of Independence to its close, by the peace of 1783, the slave and Negro population, respectively, of the United States had been considerably reduced. The slave states lost by deportation to the West Indies alone, it is said, upwards of ten thousand slaves; whilst the Negro population of the New England states, without reference to Pennsylvania and New York, had also suffered a reduction from 5,249 in 1776 in Massachusetts, to 4,377 in 1784, and from 6,464 in 1774 in Connecticut, to 4,373 in 1782. Many of both classes had doubtless found their way into the British territories, including Canada; and hence, the belief in 1790, that many loyalists still resident in those different States might be enticed by the allurement of the Statute to come into the British territories. This Statute was manifestly a law for the occasion, including objects and things, as well as persons, white and black, within its professed aim and intention, namely, the withdrawal of population and capital from the United States for the benefit of British interests. No professional reputation, however elevated, would justify to itself an attempt to fasten the Slave institution upon Canada by implication alone; and any such attempt, made from the words of the Statute, would be a gross and unwarrantable perversion of every legal rule in the construction of Statutes. The British Act must rest upon its own terms *pro re nata*; and whilst in themselves they expressed and created a special exemption, they at the same time recognized the existence of the general principle of freedom in those British territories into which the United States' subjects, or citizens, were encouraged to come with their families, Negroes, furniture, implements of husbandry and clothing, by the offer of an exemption from fiscal duty upon a limited value of those effects, which they were expected to bring with them.

I have already stated the fact, that the Upper Canada Act originated in the intended application of the British Statute, which will be manifest from the Provincial modification imposed by it upon the power of license granted to the Lieutenant Governor by the British Act, and without which the benefit of the latter could not be obtained at all. It is notorious, as matter of historical fact, that in 1783-4 there were upwards of ten thousand persons resident in the Upper part of the then Province of Quebec, namely, now Upper Canada, and that they were, with few exceptions, loyalist emigrants, who had left the United States to continue under British allegiance. Of this number, a large proportion were from the New England States; and the result was manifested at the earliest opportunity afforded to them, after the establishment of Upper Canada as a separate Province under the act of 1791, the 31 George III, Chapter 31, which, for the first time, gave effect to the Royal promise contained in the proclamation of the formation Parliamentary Assemblies in the Province: up to that time the local Government had been conducted by a Governor and Council, the latter of whom were, with scarcely an exception, composed of public officers resident at or near the seat of Government. At the first sessions of the Parliament of that Province, Upper Canada, the French laws and customs were abolished, as "being manifestly and avowedly intended for the accommodation of His Majesty's (French) Canadian subjects," and not for "British subjects born and educated in countries where the English laws were established," and the laws of England were therefore substituted by Act passed on the fifteenth of October 1792, 32 George III Chapter 1.

In July 1793, in the second session of the same Parliament, the Act 33 George III, Chapter 7, above referred to, was passed, and the reason stated in the preamble was, because it was "unjust that a people who enjoy freedom by law should encourage the introduction of slaves," and because it was "highly expedient to abolish slavery in this Province, so far as the same may gradually be done without violating private property." This provincial act absolutely deprived the Lieutenant Governor of the power of granting the necessary "license for the importation of any negro or other person to be subjected to the condition of a slave, or to a bounden involuntary service for life," and relieved such Negro or other person from such slavery or involuntary life-service. It then proceeded to reduce voluntary contracts of service to a period of Nine years, and while it sustained existing contracts with reference to Negroes who had come or been brought into the Province, in virtue of Public authority, or of any act of the Parliament of Great Britain, it gave relief to the children born of slaves, who were thereafter to remain in the service of their Master only until their twenty-fifth year; manifestly a compensation to the master for his care and support of them from their birth, whilst their children were to be free-born subjects. This Provincial Act was, to a certain extent, a modification of the Connecticut Act of 1784, for a similar purpose; and I apprehend, cannot be viewed as sustaining the

Slavery of any but those slaves who had been brought into the Province under the pledge of the public faith, or by contract.

QUESTION 12: *Was the question of the legality of the slavery of negroes, or other persons, ever tested in any of the Courts of Justice in the Province of Quebec, – or, after its division, in any of those in Lower Canada? and if yea, what was the result of the test?*

ANSWER: The question has been tested, but not frequently, in the Civil courts of the Province of Quebec, that is, in the Courts of King's Bench and Common Pleas, as well before as subsequent to its division into the two governments of Lower and Upper Canada; and, from an examination of the cases brought before those Courts, the result was unfavourable to the existence of slavery, or to its recognition. I subjoin the following cases, which I have taken from the authentic registers of the Courts of Justice in Montreal, in which such litigation took place; and which seem to apply to Negroes from the United States

Hoyle vs Fisher & wife: – Action to recover possession of, and to hold "two negro wenches," Sylvia-Jane, and Ruth-Jane, sold by the Defendant, by Notarial Act of fourth December 1785, which assigned them to one Jacobs during their natural lives. The Defendant made default to appear, and the cause went undefended; the Court in consequence, by Judgment of the Eighteenth March 1788, adopting the Plaintiff's demand, condemned the Defendants to deliver up the wenches or pay £50 currency.

Poiré vs LaGord: – Action to recover back the price paid by the Plaintiff for John Brown, a negro, sold as a slave by the Defendant. The record states, that Brown was not a slave, and the Judgment of the third of July 1788, in conformity with the records, was in favour of the plaintiff.

Mittleberger vs Langan: – An action, similar to the one last-mentioned, for the price paid for a Negro, named *Nero*. The record shews that the Negro had been made a prisoner of war by the Mohawk Indians, at Ballston in the State of New York, from the property of his master Colonel Gordon, and brought into Montreal, where the Plaintiff [*sic*: read Defendant] as the agent of the Mohawks, sold him, that he was confined in the *Provôt's* prison at Montreal, as a prisoner of War, and received military rations as such, and that on his being discharged from the prison, by Brigadier McLean, the Commanding Officer, he returned to his former Master, Colonel Gordon, at Ballston, where he had been seen by the witness. On this Evidence the Plaintiff obtained Judgment in his favour on the twentieth of January, 1789.

Turner & wife vs Sullivan: – Action for balance of price for *Manuel,* sold as a slave. Manuel had been sold as a slave for his natural life, and had afterwards, on the same day, entered into articles of servitude with Sullivan, the Defendant, to serve him for five years, and then be free. The plea was, that Manuel was not a slave, and that the

Plaintiffs had deceitfully represented him as being a slave, and thereby obtained from the defendant certain payments amounting to £18, on account of the price; and of which payments the Defendant by an incidental demand claimed the repayment, with damages &ca. Manuel himself intervened in the cause, and claimed his freedom under the law of the land. In February 1799, the Court dismissed the Action, for want of any title in the plaintiffs to transfer any property in Manuel, and, on the incidental demand, condemned the Plaintiffs to repay the £18 to the defendant.

Smith vs McFarlane: – Action in trespass for taking away Catherine Coll, the Plaintiff's wife, and for retaining her cloathes. Plea not proved, and verdict for the Plaintiff for £50 currency. Appeal to the Court of King's Bench, who Ordered, Nineteenth July 1793, a *venire de novo,* on technical objections to the regularity and sufficiency of the pleadings, and from defect of proof, on both sides, at the trial. Upon the return of the record to the Court below, the Common Pleas Judgment was rendered on the twenty eighth day of February 1794, after much argument, chiefly upon technical grounds of informality in the pleadings fyled, and upon the mode of proceeding to proof on the two questions of marriage and slavery, whether it should be before the Court according to the procedure of the French Court, or before a Jury according to English practice. By the Judgment the Defendant was Ordered to replead, and to establish an issue: the Court expressing its opinion upon the two points of proof above-mentioned in the following terms, copied from the authentic register of the Court of that day: – "Ces deux points sont deux questions purement de droit, dans la manière que les parties offrent de les établir, ce ne pouvant être des questions de fait, *car les loix de cette province n'admettent point de mariage légitime, ni d'esclavage de fait, sans titre authentique et loix expresses.*"

The King, on the application of Robin, a black man, for a writ of habeas corpus: – The Negro, Robin, had been purchased in the City of New York in 1783, whilst still in British possession, and became his master's servant, with whom he removed to Nova Scotia, and afterwards to Newfoundland [*sic*: read P.E.I.], and finally came with him to Montreal. After his arrival in Montreal, he was committed to the common gaol of the District, by warrant of three Justices of the Peace, for absenting himself from his owner's house without leave. On *habeas Corpus* granted, and after arguments *in Banco* before Chief Justice Monk and Judges Ogden and Panet, the negro was discharged, by Judgment rendered on the Eighteenth of February, 1800.

Copies of the several before-mentioned Judgments, duly authenticated, are hereto annexed.

The Registers of the Courts have been carefully examined by me since 1761 until after 1802, and no other cases connected with slavery have been found. The above, except those of Manuel and Robin, chiefly turn upon the rights of the parties under the contracts of sale between themselves, as purchasers and vendors, in relation to the consideration money, and apart from the individual rights of the negro or subject sold, to hold himself no slave. Such contracts for sale may be valid as between the parties, and the law would readily hold them upon their Contracts but the person of the slave was not the object of litigation. It is only in those of Manuel and Robin, where the negroes themselves were personally in Court, and in both of these they were relieved from the effect of servitude. It is not to be wondered at that judicial opinion was not sooner expressed. Judicial action cannot be expected to arise *ex mero motu* of the Judges themselves, and Courts must be moved before their opinion can be required.

It is singular, however, that no case can be found of record in the archives of the Courts, under the British or French rule, in which involuntary servitude has been judicially sustained, or in which application for freedom has been judicially denied; and it is still more singular, that none of the cases above mentioned applied to the purchased Negroes or *Panis,* the so-called *Esclaves* of the French rule, or to their descendants, and offspring, of whom some may still have existed *en qualité d'Esclaves,* as before the capitulation, but not by constraint of law, or of the judgments of Courts of Justice. The contracts of servitude above referred to, with others to which I have had access, executed in Montreal from 1780 to 1790 or 1792, always stipulate the sale either of a life service, for "the terms of his natural life" or for a longer or shorter period of service, but in no case does it interfere with the acquisitions of the purchased persons, or stipulate regulations over his wife and children: the ingredients of slavery, in no case that I have examined, are added to or form part of the contract, which is limited in all of them to mere service, more or less prolonged. So also in the French time it did not assume any other shape than mere enforced service, *pour sa vie durante,* or for a certain number of years of service, and most assuredly never did descend from the parent to the children.

Appendix III
Spoils of War

While Quebec and the American colonies briefly fluttered together under the British flag, before the opening shots of the American Revolution were fired at Lexington on 19 April 1775, Jacob Thomas of Dutchess County, New York, occasionally travelled to Montreal with slaves to sell.[1] In September 1770, he sold Jeannette, a black woman in her thirties, on approval to Jean Orillat, a Montrealer who from the last days of New France had prospered at the fur trade and related business. Six months later, Orillat paid Thomas 700 livres, plus a grey mare and a colt, for her. On that occasion, Thomas also sold Orillat a whole "famille esclave nègre" for £100 – father, mother and three children, ages one to four years.[2] Then, on 2 March 1772, Thomas and John Fulton sold Cesar, "a negroe man servant," to fur trader James Morrison for £60, promising that if Morrison "shall find any fault to the Said Negroe from this date to the month of June next [,] on our or either of our returns to this place [,] we will oblige ourselves to take him the said Negroe and Return the Money again."[3] On 15 April, Thomas sold Cato, a "Negro man Slave," to merchant Thomas Barron. Cato proved to be defective merchandise: apparently, he was epileptic. In June 1774, Barron, crying fraud, sued for £150, claiming that Thomas had known at the time of the sale that Cato did "Labour and Languish under the distemper & pain of fitts convulsive falling sickness & many other Disorders," and was unable to work.[4] A month before Barron went to court, Thomas sold another slave at Montreal – Marie, in her teens or early twenties – to lawyer Pierre Panet on 2 May, James Morrison witnessing the transaction.[5]

War intervened, putting paid to Barron's suit over Cato, it seems, and interrupting this cross-border trade for eight years.[6] Blacks continued to cross the lines, a few under their own steam, but most as captives – either slaves of Loyalists, or taken in arms or seized here and there by British forces and their Indian allies, to be sold as slaves or held as prisoners, virtually at the whim of their captors. In 1779, Lieutenant-Colonel Daniel Claus, the Indian Department's deputy agent for the Six Nations Confederacy, reported hearing that "the five Nations [Iroquois] brought many Negro prisoners to Niagara which Majr. [Walter] Butler never delivered up [as prisoners], but kept [as slaves], & satisfied the Indns. for them."[7] A private of the King's Royal Regiment of New York (KRRNY) complained in early 1792 that "Black people that has been of great Service to his Majesty's Scouts has this late Summer came in Voluntarily with me in hopes of gaining there freedom, but for their Loyalty they now are render'd Slaves in Montreall."[8] This despite the promises of British commanders in the American colonies that slaves of rebel masters would be freed if they crossed to Britain's side.[9]

From the beginning of the war, blacks trickled into Quebec, usually one or two at a time. George Long, "a Negro," captured at the Battle of Hubbardton in Vermont on 7 July 1777, and Newport, also "a Negro," from Newbury, Massachusetts, taken the previous day at Skenesboro (Whitehall), New York, were sent to jail at Quebec.[10] Also held at Quebec, Joseph King called on Governor Haldimand in October 1778 to set him free in recognition of his loyalty:

> Your Petitioner has Been twice taken by the Yankeys And Sold by them Each time At Publick Vandue. he has Made his Escape And brought two white Men with him through the woods. he was Servant to Cpt. McCoy last winter In Montreal And Came here [Quebec] last Spring. Your Petitioner has gon through Many Perils And Danger of his life In Making his Escape from the Yankeys. he hoaps that your Excellency through the Abundance of your benevolence Will Grant him his liberty for Which your Poor Petitioner As In duty bound Will for Ever Pray.[11]

A slave identified as Rathass Coffee entered Canada at St-Jean, the port of entry from New York and Vermont, in early October 1778. He claimed to have jumped ship to the British side at Havana during the Seven Years' War and to have spent the ensuing years with Captain Philip Skene of Skenesboro, who had promised him fifty acres and a cow, but never delivered and kept him as his slave. Captured by Americans at Ticonderoga, he said in a petition to Haldimand:

> I made My Escape with two white Men to St. Johns And has Gon through Many perils And Dangers by Both Land And Water. My Master Was taken Prisoner Also And Made his Escape. Your Petitioner begs through Your Great Clemency And Goodness that you'l be pleas'd to Look Into the State of his Case And Grant his Liberty ...

Loyalist leader Sir John Johnson (1741–1830) was a large landowner and a slave-owner. One of his houses, at Williamstown, Ont., is now a national historic site.

Your Petitioner thinks its Avery hard Case that he Can Neither Get his Agreement Nor his Liberty.[12]

In the summer of 1779, a Mohawk chief known as Captain John had captured a black man, slave of a Major Hopkins, an American officer who had been killed in action on 14 Mile Island in Lake George, New York. The man was sent a prisoner to Chambly, and Captain John wanted compensation for his loss. Haldimand promised that December to pay him "an allowance for the Negroe."[13] Jack and Charles, slaves of Andrew Wemple, a captain of New York's Tryon (Fulton) County militia who deserted to the British in May 1780, arrived from the Mohawk Valley with their master on 25 May. Wemple also brought with him Peter Martin, "Col. Butlers Negro," who would join his master, Lieutenant-Colonel John Butler, commander of Butler's Rangers, at Niagara. In 1793, Peter Martin would play a part in sparking the government of Upper Canada to legislate limits to slavery.[14]

The trickle swelled at the end of May 1780, when Lieutenant-Colonel Sir John Johnson, commander of the KRRNY, led a force of his "Royal Greens" and Indians on a raid into the Mohawk Valley of New York. This was his home territory, the area that his late father, Sir William Johnson, had ruled, where John Johnson had grown up and which he, as a loyal subject of the king, had had to flee after the outbreak of the American Revolution. The raiding party came away with several prisoners, and, as Johnson mentioned in an account he sent to Haldimand on 3 June: "One hundred and forty three Loyalists and a Number of Women and Children[,] with About thirty blacks[,] Male and female[,] came off with us – Seventeen of the latter belong to Colonels Claus[,] Johnson and myself[.] some are Claimed by White Men and Indians who are endeavouring to dispose of them[.] I should therefore be glad to have your Excellencys directions concerning them."[15] Haldimand congratulated Johnson on the success of his mission and expressed dismay that anyone on the British side would claim possession of slaves belonging to loyal subjects: "I am surprised that any White people can Claim the Negroes who belong to You, Colonel Claus, or any other Person in the King's Service, and I am persuaded that Lt. Col. Campbell will take Such Steps with the Indians, as will Convince them that they Can have no Pretensions to ye Negroes who are the property of the King's faithfull Subjects – I hope the Mohawks Entertain better Sentiments than to importune You with any Such Claim."[16]

Johnson spoke only of slaves of loyal subjects in replying to Haldimand on 12 June, putting in a good word for John Campbell, the superintendent of the Indian Department: "Some Negroes the property of good Subjects have been disposed of by the Indians, but I hope they will be recovered with Little expence to the Owners. Colonel Campbell did everything in his power to prevent their disposing of them, and released some from them."[17] What of captured slaves who had belonged to American rebels? On 24 July, Haldimand's secretary asked Johnson to send Campbell "all the Information in your Power relative to the negroes brought in by Scouting Parties, as he has directions to transmit to His Excellency a list of them, specifying from whom they were taken, and by whom they have been purchased, as the General will be Under the necessity of reclaiming them as Prisoners of War."[18] Campbell's report of 10 August listed six men and two women:

Return of Negroes taken by Sir John Johnson's Party in May 1780 and Sold by Indians to inhabitants of Montreal and others[19]

Negros		By whom purchased	Whom they did belong to
Men	Women		
1		Mr Gamelin[20]	Mr Conine Loyalist
1		Mr Jordan	Mr Conine Loyalist
1		Doctor Delisle	Mr Smith a Rebell
	1	Mr Grant at Lachine	Mr Fonda a Rebell
1		Capt. Sherwood	Mr Wemp a Rebell
1		John Demoauck	Mr Fonda a Rebell
1	1	Saml. Anderson	Mr Fonda d[itt]o.

If this report constituted a true sketch of the sales of blacks captured on Johnson's raid, only two of the eight blacks sold were the property of a "faithful subject," Mr Conine (Conyn) of Butler's Rangers, stationed at Niagara. The names of Johnson's and Claus's slaves were not mentioned, but they, along with all but the first on Campbell's list, were enumerated in the "Return of Negroes & Negroe Wench's brought into the Province by Parties under the Command and Direction of Lieut. Colo. Sir John Johnson Bart," filed one year later, after more blacks had been captured, notably in October 1780 in a raid on Ballston, New York, led by Captain John Munro of the 1st Battalion, KRRNY, assisted by Mohawks under the command of Lieutenant Patrick Langan. That table (see p. 387) shows only one slave belonging to Loyalist John

Conyn. In addition, the purchaser identified in the second-last entry above as John Demoauck, i.e., Mohawk captain John Deseronto, would show up in the later list as the captor, not the purchaser, of a Fonda slave named William, sold to a Mr McDonell.

The seizure and sale of black captives continued to raise questions and provoke disputes. Some disagreement clearly lay behind the affidavit sworn by Randal Hewit before Montreal commissioner of the peace John Porteous on 9 March 1781 concerning a black woman taken in the Ballston raid:

> This day came before me Randel Huet [sic], and maketh Oath on the Holy Evangelists of Almighty God, that in the month of October last, he belonged to the Indian Department, on an Expedition to Balls Town Commanded by Capt. John Monroe, That in the House of Tyranes Collins a Rebel Captn. Now a Prisoner in this City, he the said Huet took into his possession a Negroe Wench who was endeavouring to escape out of a Window in said Collins's House in Balls Town aforesaid, and conveyed her out of the House and gave her to Matthew Snetzsinger, who also belonged to the Indian Department, and that afterwards said Snetzsinger by his consent sold said Negroe Wench unto John Howell, also belonging to the Indian Departmt. on said Expedition and further sayeth not.[21]

If that statement sounded defensive, the letter that Brigadier General Allan Maclean, commander of the British forces in the Montreal District, wrote to Haldimand's secretary, Major Robert Mathews of the 53rd Regiment, on 5 July 1781 about another Ballston captive was altogether different. It concerned Jacob, alias Isaac, who had been captured with his master, American Colonel James Gordon. Although he claimed to be a free man, and seemed to have witnesses to the fact, Jacob was sold, along with his wife, on behalf of their Mohawk captors by Lieutenant Langan to Montreal merchant Samuel Judah for a total of £84. Jacob had been jailed in April 1781 on a charge of assaulting Judah, when Maclean intervened on his behalf at the request of Haldimand's secretary:

> My dear Mathews,
> On the receipt of your Letter I Sett out Executing your request, in procuring poor Isaac his help mate. this I did with pleasure, as your wishes were those of Humanity & Charity.
>   Your friend Isaac I have the honour of being acquainted with, and have more than once heard his whole adventures, and I did Endeavour to relieve his distress. He and his wife were brought in here Last November with about 16 more of the Same Colour, and they were all Sold. Isaac then declared he was a Free Man for the reasons you mention, and I do Confess I was of the Same Opinion. in the spring Isaac obtained a hearing before the Justice's & the poor Creature sent me Word that there was a Corporal & men belonging to the Light infantry of the 53 Regt. that knew him Carrying Arms with Genl. Burgoyne's Army, When his Poor Massa was Killed and Isaac himself taken prisoner. I

found out the men of the 53d. and they made Oath to what [the] poor Negro man advanced in his defence. the Justices declined passing Sentence, but admitted Isaac to bail. When no other person Would bail the poor Creature, and that he was remanded to prison, I bailed him, and advised him to Sett out for Quebec, where he would be at the head of the fountain of money, where the Sons of Israel could not or darest not Seize upon him by Violence. Isaac also said that Even had he not taken up Arms for the King, as he had come in of his own accord, no man in Canada had a right to Claim him as his Property, as Sir Henry Clinton had by proclamation declared all Slaves belonging to Even Rebells free that came to take protection under the Kings Standard. So your poor Negro man does not want kindnesses. before the receipt of Your Letter I sent for Mr Judah, about the fair Consort & help mate of Isaac, Judah told [me] he had purchased the man & Woman from Sir John Johnson, that a bill of Sale was made out to him and Signed by Lieut. Langdale [Langan] of Sir Johns, that he paid 80 Guineas for Isaac & his wife that the money was paid to Langdale as Agent to Sir John that a Number of Other Negroes were sold at the Same time by the Same persons to Other People, that he would Send to his Correspondent at Quebec immediatly to Seize upon Isaac as his Property. that it was no business of his to Enquire whether Lieut. Langdale, had, or had not a right to Sell the man and Wench; he had paid for them.

    I told him I believed he was mistaken, that it was most certainly his affair to know whether or not Isaac was the Property of the Seller, before he bought him. he then told me Isaac had robed him and taken goods out of his Shop, and he would have him taken up for a robery that he had Letters from Mr. [Nathaniel] Day, the Commissary Genl. and from Mr [Conrad] Gugy[22] acquainting him that Isaac had Sold Some of the goods upon the Road to Quebec And that he neither Would or Could afford to be 80 Guineas out of Pocket upon Isaac and his wife. So that unless the Humain, and good Natured Capt. [William] Twiss will interpose Poor Isaac, tho in fact a Free Man, will get again into the Fangs of this hard hearted Isralite[.] for my Part finding that Sir John was the Principale in this business, I avoided Saying any more on the Subject, only to Explain the Whole Affair to you[.] I have only to Add that I Shall Ever be happy to be able to Execute any request of Yours perfectly Convinced, that Your great goodness of heart, and your benevolence are the Motives of Your Conduct. I am with truth & Sincerity My dear Mathews, Yours &c

                                                                 Allan Maclean[23]

    Only eleven days later, Haldimand wrote to Johnson, Campbell, and Claus, ordering them to file detailed reports on the blacks brought into Canada by the forces under their command.[24] He stated as his reasons for wanting the information:

> Several Complaints having been made upon the Subject of selling Negroes brought into this Province by Scouting Parties, who alledge a right to Freedom,

and others belonging to Loyalists who are obliged to relinquish their Properties, or reclaim them by paying the Money for which they were sold, I must desire that you will upon the most minute enquiry give into brigadier General Maclean a Return of all Negroes who have been brought into this Province by parties in any respect under your direction specifying their names, their former Masters, whether Loyalists or Rebels, by whom brought in, by whom and to whom sold, for what price, and where they are at present, that the grievances now complained of may be redressed and such arrangements made as will prevent them in future.

Campbell filed this slim return on 30 July:

Return of Negroes brought in to the Province from the Colonies by Scouting Party belonging to the Indian Department[25]

Names:	Roger[26]
Number:	1
Former master:	Major A. Vanschock
Former place of residence:	Saratoga
By Whome taken:	Lt. Johnson
To Whome sold:	———
For what price:	———
In whose possession at present:	Lt. Johnson
Where taken:	At Fort St Ann's in Arms Octr. 1780.

N.B. There were other Negroes taken in to the Province by Indians who have been reported to the Commander in Chief last year and are now returned by Lieut. Col. Sir John Johnson

Johnson's report, undated but filed at the same time as Campbell's, is reproduced here with slight changes to the format and headings. The names are given in the same order as in the original, but they have been numbered for easier reference.[27]

Return of Negroes & Negroe Wench's brought into the Province by Parties under the Command and Direction of Lieut. Colo. Sir John Johnson Bart.[28]

1. Name:	Tom
Former master:	Conyne
Loyalist or Rebel property:	Loyalist
Brought in by:	Canada Indians
Sold to:	Jacob Jordan Esq.
Price:	£12.10
Whereabouts:	Montreal with Mr Jordan

2. Name: CHARLES
Former master: Smyth
Loyalist or Rebel property: Rebel
Sold to: Revd. Mr Delisle
Price: £20
Whereabouts: Montreal with Mr Delisle

3. Name: NERO
Former master: Col. Gordon
Loyalist or Rebel property: Rebel
Brought in by: Mohawk Indians
Sold to: John Mittleberger
Price: £60
Whereabouts: Montreal in the Provost Goal
Remarks: *Taken at Balls Town making his escape out of a Window in Col. Gordons House. Runed away some time ago from his late Master.*

4. Name: JACOB
Former master: Col. Gordon
Loyalist or Rebel property: Rebel
Brought in by: Mohawk Rangers
Sold to: Samuel Judah
Price: £24
Whereabouts: Quebec
Remarks: *Taken at the same place [as no. 3] endeavouring to make his escape – also runed away from his late Master.*

5. Name: A NEGROE WENCH[29]
Former master: Col. Gordon
Loyalist or Rebel property: Rebel
Brought in by: Mohawk Rangers
Sold to: Samuel Judah
Price: £60
Whereabouts: Montreal with Mr Judah
Remarks: *Sold by Sir John Johnson in lieu of a Negroe Wench & Child of his Property which Col. Gordon exchanged for this Wench.*

6. Name: BETTY[30]
Former master: Capt. Collins
Loyalist or Rebel property: Rebel
Brought in by: Mohawk Indns.
Sold to: John Gregory
Price: £45
Whereabouts: Montreal with Mr Gregory

7. Name: TOM
Former master: Col. Fisher
Loyalist or Rebel property: Rebel
Brought in by: Mohawk Indns.
Sold to: Capt. [Andrew] Thomson
Price: £25
Whereabouts: Montreal with Mr Langan
Remarks: *Sold by Capt. Thomson of Col. Butlers Rangers, to Sir John Johnson who gave him to Mr Langan.*

8. Name: JACK
Former master: Barny Wemple
Loyalist or Rebel property: Rebel
Brought in by: Royal Rt. N.Y.
Whereabouts: Montreal with Capt. Anderson[31]
Remarks: *Since Dead*

9. Name: DIANA
Former master: Adam Fonda
Loyalist or Rebel property: Rebel
Brought in by: Royal Rt. N.Y.
Whereabouts: Montreal with Capt. Anderson

10. Name: WILLIAM
Former master: Major Fonda
Loyalist or Rebel property: Rebel
Brought in by: Mohawk Indns.
Sold to: Mr McDonell
Price: £30
Whereabouts: Quebec
Remarks: *Taken at his Masters house by Capt. John the Mohawk, with a Waggon & Horses which he got ready to convey his Mistress to Schenectady.*

11. Name: COMBWOOD[32]
Former master: J. Wemple
Loyalist or Rebel property: Rebel
Brought in by: Mohawk Indns.
Sold to: Capt. Sherwood
Price: £12.10
Whereabouts: St Johns with Capt. Sherwood

12. Name: CATHARINE
Former master: Dow Fonda
Loyalist or Rebel property: Rebel

Brought in by:	Canada Indns.
Sold to:	John Grant
Price:	£12.10
Whereabouts:	St Genevieve with Capt. A. McDonell
Remarks: *Sold by John Grant to Capt. Alexander McDonell.*

13. Name:	SIMON
Whereabouts:	Niagara with A. Wemple
Remarks: *A Free Negroe, who formerly lived with Capt. Fisher.*

14. Name:	BOATSWAIN
Former master:	Lewis Clement
Loyalist or Rebel property:	Loyalist
Brought in by:	Canada Indns.
Whereabouts:	Niagara with his former Master

15. Name:	JANE
Former master:	Lewis Clement
Loyalist or Rebel property:	Loyalist
Brought in by:	Canada Indns.
Whereabouts:	Niagara with her former Master

16. Name:	DICK
Former master:	Col. Butler
Loyalist or Rebel property:	Loyalist
Brought in by:	Mohawk Rangers
Whereabouts:	Niagara with his former Master

17. Name:	JACK
Former master:	Wm. Bowen
Loyalist or Rebel property:	Loyalist
Brought in by:	Royl. Rt. N.Y.
Sold to:	Capt. J. McDonell
Price:	£70
Whereabouts:	Niagara with Capt. McDonell
Remarks: *Sold by Wm. Bowen his former Master, to Capt. John McDonell of Col. Butlers Rangers.*

18. Name:	PEGGY
Former master:	Mr Young
Loyalist or Rebel property:	Loyalist
Brought in by:	Royl. Rt. N.Y.
Whereabouts:	Niagara with her former Master

19. Name: MINK[33]
Former master: Capt. Herkamer
Loyalist or Rebel property: Loyalist
Whereabouts: Coteau du Lac with his former Master

20. Name: TANSE
Former master: Adam Fonda
Loyalist or Rebel property: Rebel
Whereabouts: Coteau du Lac
Remarks: *Came in with Sir John Johnson, and are now employed in Capt. Herkamers Com^y. of Batteau Men.*

21. Name: CATO
Former master: Pruyme
Loyalist or Rebel property: Rebel
Whereabouts: Coteau du Lac
Remarks: *Came in with Sir John Johnson, and are now employed in Capt. Herkamers Com^y. of Batteau Men.*

22. Name: JACK
Former master: Major Fonda
Loyalist or Rebel property: Rebel
Whereabouts: Coteau du Lac
Remarks: *Came in with Sir John Johnson, and are now employed in Capt. Herkamers Com^y. of Batteau Men.*

23. Name: JACK
Former master: Major Fonda
Loyalist or Rebel property: Rebel
Whereabouts: Coteau du Lac
Remarks: *Came in with Sir John Johnson, and are now employed in Capt. Herkamers Com^y. of Batteau Men.*

24. Name: WILLIAM
Former master: Sir J. Johnson
Loyalist or Rebel property: Loyalist
Brought in by: R.R.N.Y.
Whereabouts: with his Master

25. Name: FRANK
Former master: Sir J. Johnson
Loyalist or Rebel property: Loyalist
Brought in by: R.R.N.Y.
Whereabouts: with his Master

26. Name: FARY
Former master: Sir J. Johnson
Loyalist or Rebel property: Loyalist
Brought in by: R.R.N.Y.
Whereabouts: with his Master

27. Name: JACK
Former master: Sir J. Johnson
Loyalist or Rebel property: Loyalist
Brought in by: R.R.N.Y.
Whereabouts: with his Master

28. Name: ABRAHAM
Former master: Sir J. Johnson
Loyalist or Rebel property: Loyalist
Brought in by: R.R.N.Y.
Whereabouts: with his Master

29. Name: TOM
Former master: Sir J. Johnson
Loyalist or Rebel property: Loyalist
Brought in by: R.R.N.Y.
Whereabouts: with his Master

30. Name: SAM
Former master: Sir J. Johnson
Loyalist or Rebel property: Loyalist
Brought in by: R.R.N.Y.
Whereabouts: with his Master
Remarks: *Since Dead. All those marked for Sir John Johnson Joyned him in the Mohawk River.*

31. Name: JACOB A BOY
Former master: Sir J. Johnson
Loyalist or Rebel property: Loyalist
Brought in by: R.R.N.Y.
Whereabouts: with his Master

32. Name: TANAE A BOY[34]
Former master: Sir J. Johnson
Loyalist or Rebel property: Loyalist
Brought in by: R.R.N.Y.
Whereabouts: with his Master

33. Name: **PHILLIS**
Former master: Sir J. Johnson
Loyalist or Rebel property: Loyalist
Brought in by: R.R.N.Y.
Whereabouts: with her Master

34. Name: **BETTY**
Former master: Sir J. Johnson
Loyalist or Rebel property: Loyalist
Brought in by: R.R.N.Y.
Whereabouts: with her Master

35. Name: **JUDE**
Former master: Sir J. Johnson
Loyalist or Rebel property: Loyalist
Brought in by: R.R.N.Y.
Whereabouts: with her Master

36. Name: **JANE**
Former master: Sir J. Johnson
Loyalist or Rebel property: Loyalist
Brought in by: R.R.N.Y.
Whereabouts: with her Master

37. Name: **HAGAR**
Former master: Sir J. Johnson
Loyalist or Rebel property: Loyalist
Brought in by: R.R.N.Y.
Whereabouts: with her Master

38. Name: **NICHOLAS**
Former master: Col. Claus
Loyalist or Rebel property: Loyalist
Brought in by: Mohawk Rangers
Whereabouts: with his Master

39. Name: **TOM**
Former master: Col. Claus
Loyalist or Rebel property: Loyalist
Brought in by: Mohawk Rangers
Whereabouts: with his Master

40. Name: PETER
Former master: Col. Claus
Loyalist or Rebel property: Loyalist
Brought in by: Mohawk Rangers
Whereabouts: with his Master

41. Name: MARIA
Former master: Col. Claus
Loyalist or Rebel property: Loyalist
Brought in by: Mohawk Rangers
Whereabouts: with her Master

42. Name: A NEGROE MAN NAME UNKNOWN
Brought in by: by a Soldr. of ye 8th Regt.
Remarks: *Sold by a Soldier of the 8th Regt. To Lieut. Herkamer of the Corps of Rangers, who sold him to Ensign [Walter] Sutherland of the R.R.N.Y.*

43. Name: CHARLES GRANDISON
Former master: Col. Warner
Loyalist or Rebel property: Rebel
Brought in by: Mohawk Indns.
Remarks: *Sent a Prisoner to Fort Chambly – The Indians still claim the allowance promised them by ye Commandr. in Chief.*

N.B. Several others carried to Niagara by Indians & white men.

Of the blacks on Johnson's list, only Simon (no. 13) was identified as free. Charles Grandison (no. 43) was not identified as free, but as the property of a rebel; yet, he was not sold as other slaves of Americans were, but was detained as a prisoner of war at Chambly. Two of the persons named, Jack (no. 8) and Sam (no. 30), had died by the time this list was prepared, and eight others were no longer in the Montreal District: six (nos 13–18) were at Niagara, and two (nos 4 and 10) at Quebec.

One of those at Quebec was Jacob (no. 4), who had fled from his master, Samuel Judah. The only other fugitive was Nero (no. 3), another man captured, like Jacob, at Colonel Gordon's in Ballston and sold by Langan, acting for the Mohawk captors.[35] Bought for £60 by tailor John Mittleberger on 5 December 1780, Nero had run away from him on 27 June 1781. Mittleberger learned on 12 July that Nero was then in military custody, held as a prisoner of war – not as a runaway slave – by Brigadier General Maclean, the same commander who assisted Jacob in eluding Judah. This explains why the list placed Nero at "Montreal in the Provost Goal," the military detention facility. Runaway slaves and servants were normally held in the common jail. As soon as he learned of Nero's detention, Mittleberger tried to gain possession of him, securing a certificate of ownership from Langan. But Maclean would not give

SPOILS OF WAR 395

him up, and sometime within the next month or so Nero either escaped or was discharged from custody and vanished. Mittleberger published a notice of Nero's flight and offered a reward of fifty shillings for his return, all to no avail.[36] He never saw his slave again. Seven years later, he sued Langan for the return of the £60 that he had paid for Nero, plus £25 4s in damages. Langan argued that he was not responsible for "the oppressive act of Brigadier General McLean," who had retired to England after the war, and besides, if Mittleberger considered him liable, he should not have waited so long to sue him. The delay in launching the suit seems attributable to the fact that Mittleberger had only recently learned that Nero was back with Gordon, as his slave, in Ballston.[37] At the trial on 10 January 1789, a witness testified that he had spoken to Gordon and Nero at Ballston the previous fall, and that "Gordon told this depont., that said negro was his property and that he came back to his service upon being discharged from the Provot of Montreal by Brigadier Maclean his commanding officer, and that the said negro himself told this depont., that he had drawn provisions at Montreal as a prisoner."[38] Judges John Fraser and Jean-Baptiste René Hertel de Rouville awarded Mittleberger £60, with interest from 4 July 1788, when he had filed his suit, plus court costs.[39]

MISSING FROM THE LIST

In a deposition that he gave in the Nero case, John Munro, the captain of the KRRNY who had commanded the expedition against Ballston, and now a resident of Upper Canada, stated:

> That the troops and indians under his command did capture a number of negroes, which negroes were claimed by the respective white men and indians who captured them, and were brought to Montreal and sold as was customary in such cases, all excepting a negro named Dublin who being known to be a freeman was liberated and enlisted in His Majesty's service. This deponent further adds that he never considered these captured negroes as ordinary prisoners of war and consequently did not report to the Commander-in-Chief or any other Commanding Officer ...[40]

How many "negroes" taken prisoner went unreported like this? We saw above how Daniel Claus claimed in 1779 that blacks captured by Iroquois raiders and taken to Niagara had not been declared as prisoners but kept as slaves by an officer. At least four black prisoners were captured by Munro's troops at Ballston. It appears that, at the time, he considered them booty rather than regular prisoners of war, but that the following year, Haldimand's call for an account of black prisoners had led him to report them to Johnson, his commanding officer. So the four – Nero, Jacob, an unnamed "Negro Wench" and Betty (nos. 3, 4, 5 and 6) – appear on Johnson's list. But from Munro's deposition, eight years after the fact, it seems that he had never seen fit to re-

IL s'eft enfui de chez le fouffigné le 27 Juin dernier, un Négre nommé NERO, âgé de 24 ans, environ cinq pieds neuf pouces de haut; il a pris avec lui un habit court bleu, doublé de ferge rouge, un habit court gris, un ditto de couverte verte, une bougrine verte croifée, un ditto et une paire de grandes culottes de coutil, une paire de culottes et une vefte de futaine.—Quiconque prendra le dit Négre et l'amenera à fon maitre, ou le mettra en lieu de fûreté, recevra une récompenfe de CINQUANTE SHELLINGS et tous les frais raifonnables, en s'adreffant à Mr. Wm. LAING à Québec en cas qu'il eft pris aux environs, mais s'il eft pris plus de Montréal il faut s'adreffer au propriétaire. JEAN MITTLEBERGER.

N. B. L'on défend par ces préfentes à toute perfonne de retirer ou employer l'efclave ci-deffus défigné, fans quoi ils peuvent être perfuadés d'être pourfuivis fuivant toute la rigueur des loix; l'on prévient tous les Capitaines de vaiffeau et autres de ne pas l'amener à leur péril, en ce qu'il en fera fait une ftricte recherche les ordres étant déjà fuffis à cet effet.———— Montréal, le 24 Août, 1781.

RUN away from the fubfcriber, the 27th of June laft, a Negro man named NERO, 24 years of age, about 5 feet nine inches high; took with him a fhort blue Coat lined with red ferge; a fhort grey Coat; one ditto of green blanket; a double-breafted green Jacket, one ditto of Ticken with Trowfers of the fame, a Fuftian Waiftcoat and breeches.— Whoever apprehends the faid Negro and fecures him, fo that his Mafter may have him, fhall receive FIFTY SHILLINGS Reward and all reafonable charges paid, by applying to Mr. WILLIAM LAING in Quebec, if the Negro fhould be taken near it, but if near Montreal apply to the owner. JOHN MITTLEBERGER.

N. B. All perfons are hereby forbid to harbour or employ the above-defcribed flave, or they may depend on being profecuted with the utmoft rigour of the Law, all Captains of Veffels and others, are forewarned not to carry him off at their peril, ftrict fearch will be made and Warrants are iffued for that purpofe.

Montreal, 24th Auguft, 1781.

Captured at Ballston, New York, in October 1780, Nero was sold for £60 to Montreal tailor John Mittleberger. He fled in June 1781, was held briefly as a prisoner of war, and then returned to Ballston and his American master.

port the capture of Dublin, perhaps because "being known to be a freeman," Dublin was not treated as a piece of property and sold, but was "liberated and enlisted." We may wonder how much Dublin's liberation depended on his readiness to enlist, or how much choice he had in the matter.[41] In any case, blacks, slave or free, were clearly not on the same footing as whites in Munro's books.

Two other blacks who surfaced in the Montreal area at this time did not make it onto any list of prisoners. At least one of them should have. It is not known when and where Samuel Peak was captured, and whether he had been a slave, but Guillaume Chevalier de Lorimier, the Indian Department agent at Caughnawaga, ransomed him from his Mohawk captors in June 1780. In gratitude for his deliverance, Peak bound himself to de Lorimier for five years as a domestic servant.[42] It is possible that Rubin (alias Robert or Reuben) Middleton entered the province not as a prisoner but under his own steam, but he too underwent a form of captivity – and a liberation à la Dublin. He was employed as a "Mulatto Man Servant" by Montreal silversmith James Poupard when he was tried and convicted on 11 September 1781 for raping a ten-year-old girl in Poupard's service. Middleton was sentenced to nine months in jail and fined £25. He was not to be released from jail until he had paid the fine. His prospects of raising such a sum while in detention were nil.[43] Preferring a stint in the king's service to an eternity in the king's jail, he appealed to Haldimand that November:

> That your Petitioner by Sentence of the Court of Kings-Bench held in this City in the month of September last past, was Sentenced to be Committed to Goal for the Space of Nine Months and then to Pay a Fine of One Hundred Dollars to the Crown. That he is in no ways able to pay the said fine, nor has he any future prospect so to do;
> That he came into the Province with a view to render all the services in his Power to His Majesty's Government and is still desirous to do so in the Capacity of a Soldier in the Corps Commanded by the Honble Sir John Johnson or otherwise.
> May it therefore please your Excellency to grant your Petitioners Pardon & release on his Entering into His Majesty's Service forthwith and he will as in duty bound Ever Pray.[44]

Haldimand took him at his word. In mid-December, Mathews, his secretary, wrote to Sheriff Edward William Gray:

> His Excellency the Governor having thought fit to Remit the fine and imprisonment to which the Negroe was Sentenced on Condition of his inlisting as a Soldier in the Kings Service, as proposed by himself, I am directed to Signify to You His Excellencys Pleasure that you do release him from Confinement and administer to Him the Oath of Allegiance as is Customary to all Other Recruits – He is to be delivered over to Sir John Johnsons Second battalion having him-

self Made Choice of that Corps, but he is to be inlisted for Life as in the Standing Army – His Pardon will be sent to You in Time to be pleaded at the Next Meeting of the Court of King's Bench.[45]

In ordering Captain Robert Leake to receive Middleton as a soldier, Mathews offered this recommendation: "As the Negroe is a good Artificer [skilled craftsman], I am further to Acquaint You it is His Excellency's Pleasure that he join the Engineer Department when applied for by Capt. Twiss." Writing the same day to Capt. William Twiss, commander of the Royal Engineers, Mathews mentioned that Haldimand had been informed that Middleton "is a good Carpenter." A week later, Leake advised Mathews that Sheriff Gray had delivered "the Mulattoe Man, Middleton," to him and that Middleton, "engaged as a Soldier in the 2d. Battn., is now in Quarters waiting for the orders of Capt. Twiss, and I have every reason to imagine from the enquiries I have made into his character, he will be usefull as an Artificer, and free from future censure." After the war, Middleton was rewarded for his services with a land grant in Cataraqui Township No. 5 (Marysburgh), west of Kingston.[46]

HERKIMER'S BATTEAU COMPANY

Fourteen people listed in Johnson's table of 1781 were his own slaves, and four belonged to his brother-in-law, Claus.[47] One of Johnson's listed slaves, Sam (no. 30), had died since his arrival at Montreal. Although it is easy to conceive of Claus employing four slaves as servants in his household, Johnson clearly had more than he could use, especially considering that he owned other slaves besides those on this list. Some were put to work in Herkimer's Batteau Company, based at the fort of Coteau-du-Lac at the foot of Lake St Francis, west of Montreal.

This company was formed in the summer of 1780 with two practical objectives. It was to forward goods and supplies up the St Lawrence to the military post of Carleton Island at the foot of Lake Ontario. At the same time, it was meant to occupy idle Loyalist refugees who were drawing rations from government but contributing nothing to the war effort, although they were willing and able to serve in some other capacity than as fighting men. The company was to be made up of three officers, ten foremen, and forty workmen. Captain Johan Joost Herkimer of the Indian Department, another Mohawk Valley Loyalist, was placed in command.[48]

From the first, several blacks were among the workmen assigned to Herkimer. Struggling with start-up problems concerning pay and supplies for his company, he wrote to Haldimand's secretary on 30 August 1780: "I have twenty three private Men in my Employ at present. – I am at great Loss for want of Instructions ... The People under my Care are in great Want of Cloathing, particularly several Negroes are quite Naked ... Col. Butler Writes me that he will send thirty Men, including Negroes, which he has to spare ..."[49] It appears that Butler and others considered the company to be a dumping ground for unneeded slaves, young and old: their owners would be relieved of the expense of caring for them and could expect to draw their wages.

Major John Ross, who commanded the fort at Coteau-du-Lac, complained that most men of Herkimer's company were unfit for the job. Lieutenant Jacob Maurer, Inspector of Batteaux, was sent to check on this and "to throw them into order, that they May become useful." He was instructed to see to it that:

> When they are not Employed Batteauing, they are to be in the Engineers Service, & to Receive pay as other Loyalists, which is 1/ Currency & a Gill of Rum per Day, exclusive of their Standing Subsistance – When Batteauing they must be paid by the Trip exclusive, in the like manner, of their Subsistence, but considering it in Your Calculation, So as to Pay them as Much, or Nearly as Much in the Whole as you give Canadians, by Which, it is Supposed those, who work well, May earn 2/ or 2/6 per Day – His Excellency does not think proper to Pay them by the Day, for the idle would reap as Much Benefit as the Industrious ... It Seems that Mr Herkimer is Collecting Women & Children rather than Men – You will please to inform him that this is not the Intention.[50]

Maurer's inspection confirmed Ross's view. In early October, he reported that he had found whites employed who were not refugees and not entitled to provisions from government, and old men with their wives and children drawing rations – "we already Victual 72 Souls & I am very Sure Captn. Harkamann [sic] Couldn't Mann 2 Batteaux" with them. A quick cleanup was needed, and Maurer was given the job. Herkimer was sternly rebuked: "Your Company being intended for Service, and not as Invalids or a nursery for Women & Children who can be as well taken care of, and at much less expense to Government" at the refugee settlements downriver than at Coteau-du-Lac.[51] By the end of October, Maurer reported that he had discharged six white men, five of whom were not Loyalists; two other white men unfit for the boat service he kept on, one to work on the small boat canal built at Coteau to bypass the rapids there, and the other, a carpenter, to make oars, paddles and setting poles for the boatmen. Of the black men in the company, he wrote:

> The 2 old Negroes who are Coopers I have Provided with Tools & ordered to Prepare wood to make 200 4 gallon keggs for the use of the Batteaux Men; and as Numbers of Barrells are Wanted for the Service in the Course of the year, whenever they have finish'd the keggs they may be employed in making Barrells. There remain 4 more old Negroes belonging to Sr John, whom I orderd to remain until his return to know what he intends to do.[52]

Despite Maurer's efforts, mismanagement would plague the company throughout the war, and Herkimer came close to being dismissed.

From the list compiled by Major John Nairne, Inspector of Loyalists, of people entitled to receive rations as Loyalists that November,[53] we find that at least fourteen of the thirty-five such persons in "Harkiman's" company at Coteau-du-Lac were blacks. While thirteen of the whites had family members with them, or at least one child, all fourteen blacks were on their own. They were:

1. Thomas Brookes
2. Ketoe Brine
3. John Conine
4. Tans Fondoe
5. Jack Fondoe Senr.
6. Jack Fondoe Junr.
7. Mink Harkiman
8. William Johnson
9. Frank Johnson
10. Quack Johnson
11. Ferry Johnson
12. Jupiter Johnson
13. Johnson Wench, female child above six years old.
14. Caesar Pratt

A comparison of this list of November 1780 with Johnson's of July 1781 will show that Herkimer's slave, Mink Harkiman (no. 7), is Mink (no. 19) on Johnson's list, and that the men here identified as Ketoe Brine (Cato Pruyn), Tans Fondoe (Fonda), and the two Jack Fondoes, senior and junior, (nos 2, 4, 5, 6) correspond to Cato, Tanse, Jack, and Jack (nos 21, 20, 22, 23), all slaves who had formerly belonged to Americans but were not sold into slavery in Montreal. These five were still members of Herkimer's company in the summer of 1781. None of Johnson's slaves – all those here given the name Johnson – were identified as members of the batteau corps in the 1781 list. William, Frank, and Ferry Johnson (nos. 8, 9, 11) correspond to William, Frank, and Farry (nos. 24, 25, 26) on Johnson's list; Quack Johnson (no. 10) might be the Johnson slave identified as Jack (no. 27) on that list. There is no telling which of the several females slaves belonging to Johnson might be the "Johnson wench" listed here (no. 13).

Of the other boatmen, Thomas Brookes (no. 1), John Conine (no. 3), and Caesar Pratt (no. 14) were slaves of Loyalists serving at Niagara in Butler's Rangers. John Conine, for instance, belonged to Lieutenant John Conyn, who, in requesting the return of his slave at the end of the war, complained of having been denied his slave's wages. "You undoubtedly have a right to his pay," Lieutenant-Colonel Butler harrumphed, promising to write Herkimer, his protégé, about it.[54] But this question of who should get the wages, at least for work done in the Engineers' Service, had been determined at the end of 1781 by Captain Twiss of the Royal Engineers, upon his visit to Coteau-du-Lac:

> Amongst the Batteaux Men, I found several Slaves, and others who were treated as such, tho' they appear to have a just claim to their Freedom; these Men have been frequently employed in the Engineers' Department and the Money due to them for work, has been paid to their Masters, but as Ensn. Tinling reported to me, that this practice made them work with a very ill will,

I directed, that in future each Individual should receive his own Money, according to the Pay List made out from the Cheque Book.[55]

Haldimand himself had heartily agreed with Twiss's decision: "You did perfectly right," he wrote, "to direct that the Amount of the Extra Work done by them in your Department should in future be paid to themselves. I shall require a particular return of them to be given in specifying the Circumstances of their Engagement."[56]

Like Conyn, Captain Andrew Bradt, the master of Caesar Pratt (no. 14), also wanted his slave back at war's end, and Butler, his commanding officer, again intervened, writing to Herkimer and to Haldimand's secretary. Maurer, as Herkimer's supervisor, also wrote to Haldimand's office for directions on how to handle such requests. The instructions he received were that "all such Negroes be given up on the Requisitions of their Owners, provided they produce Sufficient Proofs of their Property, and give full acknowledgments or Receipts for them, which must be taken in the most ample manner, to prevent future Claims, and to have the necessary recourse to Those Persons who receive them, should different Applications be made for the same Negros."[57]

Thomas Brookes (no. 1) was the subject of just such competing claims. As early as March 1781, Private Niclos Schylor (Nicholas Schuyler) of Butler's Rangers addressed a piteous petition to Haldimand for the return of "one of my negors" who had been taken as a prisoner to Niagara and who was then in the possession of "Doctor Gothery of the Rangers."[58] The slave was unnamed, but Dr Robert Maghlin Guthrie of Butler's Rangers, who settled at Quebec after the war, then at L'Assomption, near Montreal, had a slave named Tom (or Thomas) Brooks, who ran away from him in 1785. Guthrie offered a reward of £5 for information about him, describing him as a "Mullatto ... Aged Thirty years, about five feet eight Inches high, strong made, ... speaks English and French perfectly."[59]

POSTWAR ARRANGEMENTS

With the end of war came the questions of settling old cross-border accounts and, naturally, of settling the Loyalists. Sir John Johnson sought Haldimand's permission for an exchange of slaves with American Major Jelles Fonda:

> Having had an Application from Major Fonda, of Tryon County, to return him his Negros, brought in by me in 1780, in Consequence of Lieutenant Colonel Butlers Acquainting him that I would Willingly do so, provided I could Obtain Your Excellency's Approbation, As I imagine he would be glad to return me some of mine in lieu of them, that are in his Neighbourhood, I should be glad to have your Excellency's pleasure on that head.[60]

Haldimand's secretary replied, essentially repeating the instructions that had been given to Maurer about securing proof of ownership and proper receipts for any blacks returned to their masters.[61] Presumably the Fonda slaves Johnson had in mind included the two Jack "Fondoes" who had served in Herkimer's company (nos 5 and 6 on that list, nos 22 and 23 on Johnson's). In some cases, Americans came looking for their slaves. In March 1784, for instance, Yohannes Decker journeyed to Montreal from New York state, in search of Pompey, a boy he had purchased in 1774, who had been "Captivated by the Indians at the Settlement of Kississing" in 1779 and reportedly sold to Lieutenant George McGinn of the Indian Department for $11. McGinn had sold him to a Mr Beaubin (Baubin, Beaubain) of L'Assomption, where Decker met up with him, but Beaubain would not hand him over. Decker returned home, hoping that the government would order the return of his slave.[62] Diana (no. 9 on Johnson's list) was the subject of horse-trading between Montreal merchant Alexander Campbell and her former American master, Adam Fonda. Campbell explained the negotiation in a letter to Haldimand's secretary:

> Having sent to Albany to Endeavour to recover Some of my depts, find a Certain Adam Fonda of Caughnawago, of Tryon's County, who gives a reason for his not paying his Dept, that a Certain Negro Wench named Dine, born in his Own family, & his Actual property, was taken away from his House by Capt. Saml. Anderson of Sr John Johnson's first Battalion and Detained by him as his property. Now the Same Adam Fonda being willing to pay this dept has Sent a power of Attorney to take his wench, and sell her, to pay his dept. As no Magistrate has a right to give an Order for taking this wench, or does not Choose to do any thing without his Excellency's Directions, beg the favour of you to signify this Affair to the Govr. that he may order it, as to him Seems Best.[63]

At far-off Michilimackinac, post commander Captain Daniel Robertson of the 84th Regiment wondered what to do with three blacks left behind by his predecessor, Lieutenant-Governor Patrick Sinclair. Sinclair had captured the three – "an Old Man & Woman and a Young Woman" – in the course of an unsuccessful attack on Spanish St Louis in 1780, and had told Robertson to return them to their masters at the peace. But Robertson was loath to do so, as he considered their masters "a sett of Spanish Rascalls," and that he or Sinclair had a better right to the slaves. It is possible that two of the three were Jean Bonga and his wife, Jeannette, who were Robertson's slaves there until he freed them in 1787 along with their four young children before leaving Michilimackinac to return to Montreal.[64]

All through the war, blacks had come in, mostly by land, a few by ship, some as prisoners, as runaway American slaves availing themselves of British promises of freedom, as slaves of Loyalists, and as freemen. In late 1782, when the fighting was pretty well over, two prisoners – Roger, the one black captive declared by Lieutenant Colonel John Campbell in 1780 as having been brought into Canada by the Indian Department, and Plato, an old man captured around 1779 and belonging to an American named Stringe – asked for permission to remain in Canada. Plato, however, appears to have changed his mind, writing to Haldimand in the summer of 1783: "I hope you will excuse these few lines from a poor slave who could wish to go again to his own Master & Mistress, As the Gentleman I live with at present Mr St Luc says he is very willing to let me go with the first party who sets off from here, if your Excellency has no objection."[65] By the end of 1782, only one black, named Abraham, captured in the Mohawk Valley in 1781, was still held prisoner at Montreal.[66]

From Lachine in the spring of 1784, Stephen DeLancey, Inspector of Loyalists, wrote to Haldimand's secretary: "There is several Black men in this neighborhood who Joind the British army & came off with the Loyalists, I will be glad to have his Excellency's Instructions about them. They have applied to me to know if they will have land and other priviledges that the loyalists have."[67] Mathews told DeLancey to forward all information about prospective black settlers to Sir John Johnson, to whom Haldimand had already written on the subject. Johnson was of the opinion that "the Negroes Mr DeLancey Alludes to must be the property of Loyalists, many of Whom, as Well as those stiling themselves freemen, have served in some or other of the Corps, and Consequently I should suppose, entitled to the same proportion of land as the other Men are."[68]

Like Rubin Middleton, Cato Pruyn (no. 21 on Johnson's list, no. 2 on the list of batteaumen), often called Cato Prime, sometimes Cato Prince, was one of those who had served, and who shared in these land grants. He received 200 acres – Lot 10 in the second concession of Lake (Lancaster) Township – in what was to become Upper Canada. Several other blacks, including Tanse (no. 20 on Johnson's list, no. 4 on the list of batteaumen) were also granted lands in Lancaster.[69] Both Cato Pruyn and Tanse had been slaves of American masters, yet they were not enslaved in Canada or returned to them after the war, in contrast with the former slaves of Major Jelles Fonda, whom Sir John Johnson, as we saw, intended to exchange for some of his own slaves left behind in New York.

BACK TO BUSINESS

With peace restored, it did not take long for the pre-war slave traffic in which Jacob Thomas had engaged to resume. The ink was barely dry on the Treaty of Paris, signed on 3 September 1783, when Daniel Jones, who had kept a tavern at Montreal during the war, was at Albany buying a slave couple, Tite (alias Tight) and Ruth, that November. In Albany again the following February, Jones bought Phoebe, a woman of about seventeen. Jones, one of the founders of Brockville, Ontario, took his three slaves to Quebec where, on 24 May, he sold Phoebe for £30 to innkeeper Pierce Ryan, and the next day, sold Tight and Ruth to baker John Saul for £88. Jones married at Montreal three weeks later. At the turn of the century, Phoebe, by then widowed and a free woman, would move to Montreal. In 1788, Jones would sell an eight-year-old slave girl, Elizabeth, to his brother, Dr Solomon Jones of Augusta, Upper Canada, and in 1794 he would sell fifteen-year-old Sylvie, bought in New York, probably around Albany, to Nicolas Berthelet of Longue-Pointe.[70]

Early 1785 appears to have been a busy time for the slave traffic between upper

New York State and Montreal. James Morrison, one of Jacob Thomas's old customers, took Sarah, a "Negro wench," on consignment from Hugh McAdam of Saratoga, who packed her off to Montreal on 20 February with the following note:

> She has no fault to my knolage. She Will not Drink and so fare as I have seen she is honest. many upertunitys She has had to have Shown her Dishonesty had she been so in Clined. I am sorry to give You the trouble, She Cost me Sixty five pounds Should not like to Sell her under. Should you not be Able to get Cash you may sell her for furrs of any Kind you think will Suit our market and send them Down By the Return Sladges.[71]

Morrison sold Sarah and wrote back to McAdam somewhat boastfully on 10 March:

> I have disposed of your Negroe Wench Sarah agreeable to your letter of the 20[me] Feby. there was several Wenches brought here at the same time[;] their Masters was obliged to sell them at vendue[.] one sold for 25 Guineas another at 21 but I sold yours at private sale for Eighteen half Joes and has given a bill of sale of her on the strength of your letter otherwise she would not have sold for more than the others. I have sent the money with Mr Coll McGregor to be delivered to you on his way to Albany and put his receipt on the bill of sale a Copy of which I did not think necessary to send you.[72]

Morrison claimed perhaps more business acumen than he deserved in outselling all the other purveyors of "Wenches." He did not let on to McAdam who the buyer was, and did not send him a copy of the bill of sale, which might have given the game away. The buyer was his brother-in-law, Charles Le Pallieur (Lepailleur), a merchant like him, and also clerk of the Court of Common Pleas. Morrison had sold Sarah to him on 9 March for £36, or "Eighteen half Joes" (Johannes) as he put it in his letter. Four years later, when Sarah was said to be about twenty-four, Le Pallieur would sell her back to Morrison for exactly the same price, and Morrison would flip her the same day for £50 to Joseph Anderson.[73]

Two days before McAdam shipped Sarah to Montreal, Peter Hubbard of Loonenburgh, Albany County (Athens, Greene County), bought Bell, a "Negro wench," about thirty-eight, for £50 New York currency from Roger Magrath of Coeymans, in the same county. A copy of the bill of sale in the records of J.G. Beek, a Dutch-born notary, auctioneer, and surveyor of customs at the port of Montreal,[74] bears the note: "Sold to Charles Beaubain." No other detail is offered of who brought her into Canada, or when exactly she was sold to Beaubain, although it appears to have been in the spring of 1785.[75] This copy of a bill of sale for black slaves from New York State is no. 2 of four found together in Beek's record book. Together, the four bills account for nine slaves. All the transactions in New York took place between 15 and 19 February 1785. In three of the sales, covering four slaves, the buyer was Peter Hubbard, identified in one bill as Captain Peter Hubbard.[76] Besides Bell, the other slaves bought by Hubbard, all females, were:

- *Flora:* a "Negro wench," said to be twenty-five years old, bought on 15 February for £60 New York currency from Ezra Reed, of Claverack district, Albany County. The copy of the bill of sale (no. 3) bears the note: "Sold to Beaubien Desrivières."
- *Sibilla and Pegg:* Sibilla, a twenty-year-old "Negro wench," and her two-year-old daughter, Pegg, were bought for a total of £80 New York currency on 15 February from William Roe of Loonenburgh. The copy of the bill of sale (no. 4) bears the note: "Sold to Alexr. Fisher." It seems that, in Montreal, Pegg went by the name Marguerite. She was said to be 11 in the fall of 1791 when she was admitted to the Hôtel-Dieu as "marguerite négresse appartenent a mr ficher."[77]

The one bill of sale (no. 1 in this set) that did not involve Hubbard was for five slaves bought on 19 February by David McKinstry and Henry Hull of Hillsdale in Albany County from Cornelius Hogeboom of Kinderhook. The "true copy" of the bill of sale in Beek's records mentions no sale price, a rather serious omission. The copy identifies the slaves as "A Negro wentch," about thirty-two; "two wenches," about eleven and five; and "two small Negro Boys," about nine and two. A marginal note says: "One Boy Nine Years old sold to Mr John Grant. One d[itt]o of Two Years to [Pierre Amable] Debonne Esq."[78] The eleven-year-old girl was Anne, the slave whom McKinstry sold on 8 March to merchant Pierre Roy, who subsequently had her baptized under the name Marie Quine, and whom he finally freed in August 1800.[79]

Also bound for Montreal in the spring of 1785, William Ward of Newfane, Vermont, paid Elijah Cady of Kinderhook £250 New York currency for four black slaves on 1 April. On 4 April, he sold Joseph, about twenty, previously a slave in Providence, Rhode Island, and Litchfield, Connecticut, for £50 Quebec currency (£80 New York) to Joseph Hébert, militia captain of LaPrairie. He sold the other three – Toby, twenty-four, his nineteen-year-old wife Sarah, and a six-month-old boy, presumably their son – for $425 (£170 New York currency) "in open market" on 26 April to a William Campbell, who resold them for $300 on 6 May – "in open market" again – to Dr Charles Blake, a former army surgeon. Sarah was still with Blake at her death in 1799.[80] Campbell sold at a considerable loss, and the speculation was not a profitable one for Ward, either – he simply broke even.

As we see from Ward's venture, New Yorkers were not the only Americans engaged in this postwar traffic. On 1 February 1786, another man with strong Vermont connections, Levi Allen, brother of the famed Ethan Allen, leader of the Green Mountain Boys, sold two slaves, Mimi and Prince, both said to be in their mid-thirties, to Montreal merchant John McNamara, for £70.[81] The deed of sale was passed before notary Beek. It was before Beek, in his capacity as notary, that Morrison, acting for Hugh McAdam, sold Sarah to Charles Le Pallieur on 9 March 1785, and before Beek again that he bought her back and resold her to Joseph Anderson on 6 June 1789. As notary or auctioneer, or both, Beek handled the sales of Bell, Flora, Sibilla and her daughter, Pegg, and the five unnamed slaves that McKinstry and Hull had bought in New York on 19 February 1785. On 6 April, Beek also auctioned off the "Négresse" Rose, a woman said to be in her twenties, to Montrealer Pierre Mézière on behalf of Martin McEvoy. This, at least, was what Mézière declared five years later when he sold Rose and her five-year-old son, Henri, and in 1794 when he sold Rose's daughter, Marie Anne (alias Jeanne), who was then ten or eleven years old.[82] We do not know where Rose came from. McEvoy was possibly the Martin McEvoy who served as a captain of the Royal Catholic Volunteers, a short-lived Loyalist corps raised in British-occupied Philadelphia in 1777, until he was discharged following a general court martial at Flushing, New York, in September 1778 that found him guilty of stealing a horse and a cow, and kicking a fellow officer.[83]

McEvoy, who appears to have lived for a time at St-Jean, had a hand in several transactions in 1786 that involved New Hampshire slave-traders. In November, he acted as a witness at what appears to have been the sale of Dick (alias Dick Gun), a six-year-old mulatto, by Joseph Barney of Richmond, New Hampshire, to Benjamin Hammond of Saratoga, New York, or to someone who soon afterward sold Dick to Hammond. This transaction is rather murky, since the name of the buyer does not appear on the document, which consists of a simple endorsement by Barney of the contract by which he had purchased Dick on the previous 19 October for £20 from William Gillchress (sic) of Shrewsbury, Vermont. The witnesses to that earlier transaction signed their names Elisha Fullam and Lucy Yeomans. The back of it bears the cryptic endorsement: "Novembr ye 15 1786/Receivd the Contents of the Within Bill/By Me – Joseph Barney/29 Nover. 1786 –/Witness present: Martin McEvoy/John Carven." The document is attached to a deed of sale, passed before notary Beek on 11 January 1787, for Dick by Benjamin Hammond to Paul Larchevêque dit La Promenade of Lachine for £30. Almost seven years later, Dick was christened Paul in the Catholic church at Lachine.[84]

Joseph Barney, mentioned above, was the same man who, on 15 November 1786, sold Catherine Coll to Andrew Mabon of St-Jean, who subsequently sold her to tailor Peter McFarlane of Montreal (see chapter 2). On that same 15 November, McEvoy bought Prince, a black man in his late forties, from a resident of Walpole, New Hampshire, whose name was given as Elisha Fullman – probably the same man who had signed his name Elisha Fullam as a witness to the sale of Dick Gun to Barney on 19 October. Furthermore, McEvoy sold Prince on 12 December to a man identified as Elisha Yeoman, who may well have been connected to Lucy Yeomans, the other witness to the sale of Dick to Barney.[85]

It is clear from the patterns of sale and resale that men such as Daniel Jones, Peter Hubbard, Joseph Barney, Martin McEvoy, David McKinstry, Henry Hull, and William Ward bought slaves as trade goods, not to be their servants. In most of the cases cited, they were buying American slaves to supply the postwar Canadian market. They were American residents who thought that there was money to be made in feeding the Quebec demand for "servants," or who, resolved to move to Canada or, in Jones's case, to stay in Canada after the war, bought a few American slaves, counting on finding buyers for them in Canada. Besides Jones and McEvoy, those who moved to Canada are thought to have included William Ward, who was to die in Montreal in 1788.[86] Hugh McAdam of Saratoga, who shipped his slave across the border to be sold in

1785, is believed to be the innkeeper Hugh McAdams who died at Montreal in 1824 at the ripe age of eighty.

The cross-border traffic in groups of slaves seems to have run its course by the end of 1786. No evidence has come to light of later dealings of this sort,[87] although as the activities of Daniel Jones show, traders still occasionally bought individual slaves in New York State for resale in Quebec.

Appendix IV

The King v. Alexander Grant, George Nixon & Moses Powell Wormley

This trial for riot stemmed from the efforts of black Montrealers in June 1836 to rescue Betsy Freeman, the "servant" of a visitor from North Carolina. Alexander Grant, as we saw in chapter 9, had reason to believe that Betsy was a slave. Fearing that she might be whisked away before the courts could look into the matter, Grant posted men to watch the house where she was staying. A commotion through the night of 13 June led to Grant, Nixon, and Wormley being arrested the next morning. Their trial took place in the Court of King's Bench on 7 September before Chief Justice James Reid and Justice George Pyke.

THE INDICTMENT[1]

At His Majesty's Court of Kings Bench for the District of Montreal begun and holden at the Court House in the City of Montreal for the cognizance of all crimes and criminal offences on Saturday the twenty seventh day of August in the seventh Year of the reign of our Sovereign Lord William the Fourth by the grace of God of the United Kingdom of Great Britain and Ireland King, Defender of the Faith, before the Honourable James Reid, Esquire, Chief Justice of His Majesty's said Court of Kings Bench and the Honourable George Pyke, Jean Roch Rolland, and Samuel Gale Esquires Justices of the same Court:

The Jurors for our Lord the King upon their Oath present that Alexander Grant, Late of the parish of Montreal in the County of Montreal in the District of Montreal, Labourer, George Nixon, Late of the same Parish, Labourer, and Moses Powell Wormley, Late of the same Parish, Labourer, on the thirteenth day of June in the sixth year of the Reign of our Sovereign Lord William the Fourth, by the grace of God of the United Kingdom of Great Britain and Ireland, King, Defender of the Faith, with force and arms at the Parish aforesaid in the county aforesaid in the District aforesaid, did unlawfully, riotously, routously, tumultuously, violently and outrageously make a great noise disturbance and affray near to and about the dwelling house of James Adams Dwight there situate unlawfully, riotously, routously, tumultuously, violently and outrageously stay and continue near to and about the dwelling house of the said James Adams Dwight Making such their noise disturbance and affray for a long space of time, to wit, for the space of five hours, and during that time there did unlawfully, riotously, routously, tumultuously, violently and outrageously shoot off a certain gun loaded with gunpowder and leaden shot at and against the said dwelling house and through a certain window parcel thereof and thereby then and there not only greatly terrified and alarmed the said James Adams Dwight and his family and disturbed and disquieted them in the peaceable and quiet possession use and occupation of the said dwelling house but also then and there broke to pieces shattered and damaged the glass, to wit, three panes of glass of Great value then and there affixed and belonging to the said windows and then and there with loud and horrid oaths and imprecations unlawfully, riotously, routously, tumultuously, violently and outrageously menaced and threatened the said James Adams Dwight to shoot him through the body and other wrongs to the said James Adams Dwight then and there unlawfully, riotously, routously, tumultuously, violently and outrageously did to the great damage of the said James Adams Dwight and against the peace of our said Lord the King his crown and dignity.

THE TRIAL

The Defendants being ready for their trial the following jurors were called and Sworn to try the issue joined on this Indictment viz.:

Leandre Leguerrier	Jean Bte Belanger
Patrick Brennan	Etienne Isabelle
Gregory Dunning	André Gauthier
Jean Bte Vaillancour	Jeremie Laporte fils de Charles
Charles Fournier dit Prefontaine	Louis Bellefleur
Pierre Denaud dit Detaillis	Jean Bte Pigeon

The Attorney General [C.R. Ogden] opened the case and called James Adams Dwight, John Gass, Phoebe M Dwight, Sarah Ann Dwight, Mary ORourke, Elizabeth Edwards Dwight and Benjamin Delisle who were Sworn and Examined as witnesses on behalf of the Crown.

The Attorney for the defence called Silas Brewster,[2] Alexander M Delisle, William

Brewster, John Craig, William Pollock, Peter Lawson, James Grantham, Edward Twaddle and Edward Thompson, who were likewise Sworn and Examined as witnesses on behalf of the defendants.[3]

For the Crown[4]

JAMES ADAMS DWIGHT, lives in Montreal, – he is a watch maker, lives in College Street – his house has 2 stories – he is married & has 6 children – W^s. had a sister, Mad^e. Martin [Marvin] in the States who came here on a visit to W'^{s}. family in June last – she had a couloured Child w^h. her – the child was absent on Sunday evening and Mrs Martin was advised to have the Child [word missing], who was [one word illegible] aged about 16 years – the girl was restored to the house on the Monday. – About 9 oClk in the evening he observed a number of persons sitting near his house, W^s. made no enquiry of them – W^s. a little after 10 oClk went to bed after shut^g. up his house. – After he had been in bed a short time, he was woke up by a great noise at the door – he opened his window, and saw a number of 5 or 6 persons of colour who demanded the Young girl – W^s reasoned w^h. them, that he could not give her up nor allow them to come into his house – these persons w^d not listen to him, he shut his window and put on his dress – they then knocked at the door with sticks & stones – & w^d. occasionally stop their noise at times & asked W^s. if the girl was a slave – the Wits seized that occasion to say, she was not – W^s. remained in this state, when a stone or piece of lime was thrown in though the front window into the room – the Son of W^s. was w^h. him who spoke to these persons – This kind of menacing & noise continued until about 2 o'Clock in the morn^g. – when they endeavoured to get in behind the house, and the Yard not being well closed, he was told, by his daughter that these persons are on the gallery behind the house – the Ws. became alarmed – there was a glass door in the back part of the house – & W^s. went to defend it – There was a light in this part of the house – they threatened the persons in the house & after some time they broke the glass in the back window – W^s. then told them they were house breakers – they said they were not – They then introduced a gun thro' the window about 18 or 20 inches and also the point of a sword – they also introduced the hand and opened the door by lifting the latch, – W^s. then told them not to proceed, or if they did it would be at their peril – the Gun was fired, & the shot struck the ceiling & knocked down a part of the ceiling of the room –

His soon [sic] took a Nail & fastened the door again when these persons retired a little into the Yard but came back again occasionally to the house & renewed their attacks – it was then beginning to get a little lighter –

Does not think there were more than three or 4 of them behind the house –

D^t. Alex Grant was there among these persons George Dickson was there also, and also the Defd^t. Moses Powell Wormley was there also – thinks he saw Wormley on the gallery –

All the persons he saw there that evening were coloured persons, to the number of 5 or 6 – and there were 3 or 4 panes of glass were broken in his window & door – This struck terror into the W^s. and his family, & he could not then tell what might be the consequence –

X^d.

W^s. had fallen asleep before he heard the noise it might then be about ½ past ten o'Clock – when he saw D^t. *Grant* there – also *Nixon* – when noise began – Grant stood at a little distance, but changed his situation – that when they were knocking at the door he saw the D^t. *Nixon* there – Did not know which of them spoke or threw stones – Thinks that Grant fired the Gun, but cannot say positively – saw no drunk man, no white people there – he counted 6 persons there, but they might be changing as they were moving about –

Knows D^t. Grant – is told he is a turbulent man, and he is of that opinion from the conversation he has had with him. –

JOHN GASS – K^s. the residence of last W^s. – he was there the eveng. of the riot in June last – he saw, *Grant* who stood three or 4 Yards from the others – did not see the other Defend^s. – they were all talking together – it was then between 9 & 10 Clk – W^s spoke to Grant that evening he asked if W^s. was Mr Brewster he s^d. no – told Grant where Brewster was to be found – W^s. was aware of the circumstances of the girl of colour, & he [Grant] told W^s. he was there on that account, that they did not mean to do any thing that night, but were to wait till next day. W^s. did not stop above 2 minutes, & when he went away he left Grant there – Grant s^d. the people had no occasion to be alarmed, as they meant not to do any thing.

X^d.

Grant was very quiet when he saw him – and not like a man disposed to cause disturbance – Grant was then 20 Yd^s. from Dwights house –

PHOEBE M. DWIGHT, wife of first W^s. – was at home in the eveng of 1 [sic] June – M^{rs}. Marvin was there that night – when her husband came home, he went soon after to bed, and w. shortly after woke up by a violent noise at the door – he got up opened the window & asked the people why they made that noise – She saw a gun fired into the house that night and several panes of glass – saw the Defd^s. *Warmley,* and *Dixon* there that evening – this riot continued almost the whole night observed that a part of the plaster was carried off by the Shot –

X^d.

It was the 13 June, saw *Grant* sometimes near and sometimes at a distance from the house saw him between 10 & 11 & near 12 and acts of violence were committed while he was there – she went to the window frequently & looked through – Thinks she saw *Wormley* every time she looked out – Has seen *Wormley* in town some time before this night – It was a common star light night – There were Candles in the house – thinks she could distinguish the Defd^s. sufficiently well – and from the room where there was a night light she could tell the persons she saw – *Nixon* was there, & was very troublesome and remained till day light in the morn^g. when Mr Delisle came to arrest him –

That Grant wore a dark green coat – she saw him also after light in the Morn^g. – when she first saw him it was about nine oClk –

SARAH ANNE DWIGHT – daughter of first W^s. was at home on the evg of 13 June – remembers to have heard the noise about one oClk at night – she heard a gun discharged – she heard persons on the Gallery did not see them – About 2 or 3 o'Clock in the morng. she saw D^t. *Grant* – also *Nixon,* who was [singing?] when she saw him – saw also *Walmley* – saw none others she could recognize –

X^d.

Is positive as to *Grant* & *Dixon* to have seen them, she may mistake as to *Wamley* – does not recollect to have seen Walmley before then – she took particular trouble every time she looked out, and next morn^g when she saw them in the light – she is sure they were the same she saw next morn^g – Grant wore a dark green coat – cannot say as to the dress of Walmley, but Nixon was dressed in white Jacket & pantaloons – did not see them in actual violence – There were six or seven persons altogether –

They were too much alarmed by the stones that were thrown to go near the window – there was a single night light in the room q^h. gave but a dim light –

MARY OROURKE – was living at Dwights in June, rem. that on night of 13 a riot at house – it began about 11 or 12 oClk & cont^d. till 3 oClk in the morn^g – She heard a gun fired into the house – towards morn^g. she saw several persons, Grant – The even^g before she saw Warmley about 9 o'Clock –

X^d.

It was in the morn^g only when she saw these persons – cannot say how Walmely was dressed the even^g before when she saw him – he was walking about –

ELIZABETH EDWARDS DWIGHT – daughter of first W^s. In the night of 13 June last she was woke up by a noise in the night between eleven & 12 – heard a loud knocking at the door – the noise increased, & seemed to be the noise of several persons, q^h. contin^d. till 3 o'Clock in the morn^g. heard a gun fired, & picked up some of the shot That about 3 o'Clk in the morn^g. she saw Defd^t. Grant – does not know the others – She saw four persons there in all – the whole family was much disturbed.

X^d.

Grant had a green coat on – cannot say what kind of Coat it was – The noise that awoke her was a knock^g. at the door – it was between eleven & 12, & thinks the noise began then –

BENJ^n. DELISLE High Constable, was called upon the 14th June last to the assistance of Mr Dwight it was between 4 & 5 oClk [a.m.] – went to D.'s house, and saw the

Deft. Grant, and Nixon, but not Walmley – there were other persons of colour there – saw the place where the shot had been fired & the mark of the Shot in the ceiling – X^d.

It might be between 5 & 6 when he went to Dwights – That the night before Grant went for W^s. and went w^h. him to house of one Forbes, it was to obtain a Habeas Corpus – in order to stop the girl, as he heard that the daughter of Mr Dwight was going to the States – From thence he & Grant [went] to M^r [Justice Samuel] Gale's office, where they remained ¾ hour that Mr Brewster accompanied them – That he understood that as the Court was then sitting they must apply to the Court – but on stating by Grant the danger that the girl might be taken away that night or next morn^g early – Grant appeared much interested for the fate of the girl from generous motives – From Mr Gale's they returned to M^r [lawyer Charles Ovide] Perrault's office, it might then be about 10 oClk at night W^s spoke to Grant next morn^g knocked at Dwight's house where W^s. was, the W^s. told him he had better not come in, as the girl was not going away – saw Nixon w^h. a little cane in his hand.

Defence
Mr Hart & Mr Perrault were heard for Defdts.

SILAS BREWSTER, In the month of June last, Grant called upon him stating there was a coloured girl at Mr Dwights, who had left that house & gone to Grant's house – & had remained there till next morn^g – on the Monday morn^g the 13 June he told W^s. that the girl had been arrested by an order from Dr Arnoldi – W^s. advised Grant to sue out a Writ of Hab. Corpus – advised him to call on Mr Perrault – and the follow^g part of that day was employed in getting the Writ – this was towards the evening – That same even^g. Grant and Mr Perrault & W^s. went to Mr Gale's to get the Writ – at first Mr Gale sd he would grant the writ, but when they returned between 9 & 10 Mr Gale s^d. he would not grant the writ in Term time – so that the matter stood over next morn^g – That W^s. parted with Grant at his own door about 10 oClk – & told Grant it would be better to keep watch near the house that night, that the girl might not be carried away in the mean time –

Has generally heard the character of Grant favorably spoken of –

ALEX. MORRIS DELISLE,[5] Clerk of Crown – Prepared Writ of Hab. Cor. thinks it was ½ past nine o'Clk when he left Mr Gale's – who remitted the parties till next day – always considered Grant as a quiet honest man –

W^M BREWSTER, lives near Mr Dwights – In the evening of 13 June last W^s went home about 10 o'Clk – when he got home saw several persons in the Street some whites as well as blacks – enquired what was the matter of Grant, there was great excitement about the young girl – Grant told him they would keep a guard there to prevent the girl being carried away in the night, but that there would be no violence exercised to take the girl – as he trusted the Girl [*sic:* read court] w^d liberate her – there were persons there of the neighbourhood, who appeared interested – W^s. left Grant there – In the night he heard knocks & noise at Mr Dwight's house – the general opinion was that the girl was to be carried off in the night, he got up, saw a number of persons there – the blacks seemed much excited, some of them w^d. go up to the door & make a noise & come away again – There seemed to be no concert among them – Got up & spoke from his window to the persons there – he Saw a white man with a Sword in his hands, asked them why they made that noise – asked if Grant was there – they said he was not – asked if Grant Knew or had directed such noise – they said No – The man who had the sword struck ag^t. the house of W^s. w^h it and seemed in liquor – There was a number of white persons among them, they sang Rule Britannia[6] – Has always heard Grant well spoken of, and who took always great interest for those who were slaves –

When he saw the persons mount the steps of the gallery, he tho^t. it was other persons – he heard the report of a gun, got up & went out, but could not tell one person from another, & thinks it was impossible to do so –

X^d.

When he got up, and spoke at the window to these persons, he asked if Mr Grant was there, they told him he was not – he cannot say he was not –

JOHN CRAIG, hairdresser – lives opposite Grants[7] – shut up his shop at 9 oClk, went to Mr Grants, Nixon, the Defd^t. shut up Grant's shop, & went w^h him to College street there he heard Grant speak to the people of colour there that it would be better to wait till to morrow & take the course of law – W^s. staid some time – went away & came back again, as Grant had asked him to watch there – That he did not then see Nixon – was told he had gone home – went to Grants house where Nixon lived, and saw him in bed, and left him there – it was then about 11 o'Clock – W^s. returned to Dwights place where he remained some time, saw Grant there – W^s. was w^h him, sometimes near the house and some times at a distance from it – Saw a Young man who was a Sailor a White man – he had a sword w^h q^h he knocked at the door – he saw this sailor who also fired a gun – When this happened, Grant was at some distance with another coloured man – did not see him make any disturbance at all – W^s. returned w^h Grant & went home, this was half-an hour after the gun was fired – some of the persons then returned w^h Mr Grant – Did not see Nixon till next morng he had a white dress on & grey trowsers –

X^d.

Cannot say that Nixon might not have got out of bed and gone to Dwights after –

~~CECILIA GRANT~~[8]

WLLM FULLER[9] K^s D^t. was at Dwights till about 10 oClk on the evn^g of 13 June last – saw Mr Brewster there & 5 or 6 coloured men, & some boys – heard Grant enjoin the persons there to be quiet & keep watch, & next morn^g. they would have recourse to law.

PETER LAWSON lives near Dwights – saw Grant & some other persons one evening – had conversation w^h Grant & others whom he did not know – Grant s^d. he was there to see the girl was not carried away that night. – Grant was in the house of W^s. about 10 o'Clk and may have remained there about hf. an hour, he heard Grant tell the people to remain quiet, & to rescue the girl, if she was carried off – W^s. heard no noise that night after he went to bed – Never heard any thing ag^t. the character of Grant until this affair. –

JAMES GRANTHAM, was at Dwights about ½ an hour about 8 oClk – Grant was there, but went away to town about law matters – W^s. went away soon after Grant –

WM TWADDLE,[10] saw Grant that even^g at Dwight's – it was after dark a little, spoke to him – he s^d. he wanted to prevent the girl from being carried away that even^g – Considers Grant a quiet, industrious Man –

EDWD. THOMPSON. In the beg^g. of June Wormley came to his service in begin^g. of June last, & is still w^h. him – he is a quiet man –

THE VERDICT[11]

The Evidence being closed the Honble. Mr Chief Justice Reid charged the jury who retired to deliberate on their verdict under the Charge of Alexander Fornet, a Constable Sworn to keep them, and having returned into Court are called over, all appear and say, by Leandre Leguerrier their foreman, that they are agreed on their verdict and that they find the defendants Severally not guilty in manner and form as laid in the Indictment and so they say all.

Abbreviations

APC	United Church of Canada Records, American Presbyterian Church of Montreal, BANQ, P603, S2, SS14
BANQ	Bibliothèque et Archives nationales du Québec, Montreal
BANQ-Q	Bibliothèque et Archives nationales du Québec, Quebec
BRH	*Bulletin des recherches historiques*
CD	Montreal city directories (generally called Lovell's)
CO	Colonial Office records, National Archives (United Kingdom)
CCP	Court of Common Pleas, BANQ, TL16 (files S2, registers S3 and S4)
CQS	Court of General Quarter Sessions of the Peace, BANQ, TL 32, S1 (files SS1, registers SS11)
CQS-Q	Court of General Quarter Sessions of the Peace, Quebec, BANQ-Q, TL31, S1
CWS	Court of Weekly Sessions of the Peace, BANQ, TL36, S1; and TL32, S38, for cases of January 1832–February 1834, November 1837–July 1839, and tavern licences.
DCB	*Dictionary of Canadian Biography.* Toronto and Quebec: University of Toronto and Université Laval, 15 vols., 1966–2005.
HP	Haldimand Papers, LAC, MG21, Add. Mss. 21661–21892
HDM	Hôtel-Dieu de Montréal
HDQ	Hôtel-Dieu de Québec (microfilm at BANQ)
JALC	*Journals of the House of Assembly of Lower Canada*
JAUC	*Journals of the House of Assembly of Upper Canada*
JCLQ	*Journals of the Legislative Council of Quebec*

JCUC   *Journals of the Legislative Council of Upper Canada*
JHN   *Journal of Negro History*
KB   Court of King's Bench, criminal side, BANQ, TL19, S1 (files SS1, register SS11, indictments SS38, administrative documents SS777). This includes the records of courts of Oyer & Terminer and General Gaol Delivery, an extension of the Court of King's Bench that sat, when required, outside the regular terms of that court.
KBCV   Court of King's Bench, civil side, BANQ, TL19, S4
KB-Q   Court of King's Bench, Quebec, criminal side, BANQ-Q, TL18, S1, SS1
KRRNY   King's Royal Regiment of New York
LAC   Library and Archives Canada
MA   Molson Archives, LAC, MG28 III 57
MUA   McGill University Archives
MURB   McGill University, Department of Rare Books and Manuscripts
NEHGR   New England Historical and Genealogical Register
POBR   Mount Royal Cemetery, Protestant Old Burial Records
PRDH   Projet de recherche en démographie historique, Université de Montréal (available at www.genealogie.umontreal.ca/en/)
PROB   Prerogative Court of Canterbury and related Probate Jurisdictions: Will Registers, National Archives of the United Kingdom
QB   Court of Queen's Bench, criminal side, TL19, S1
RAPQ   *Rapport de l'Archiviste de la province de Québec*
RPM   Registre de la prison – Montréal, BANQ, E17, S1, SS1
RPQ   Registre de la prison – Québec, BANQ-Q, E17, accessed online at various times in 2006–2008 at www.banq.qc.ca/portal/dt/accueil.jsp)
SLCC   Circuit Court Case Files, Office of the Circuit Clerk, St Louis, Missouri State Archives, Office of the Secretary of State, accessed online at various times in 2006–2008 at http://stlcourtrecords.wustl.edu
TC   Trusteeships and curatorships, BANQ, CC601 S1, Cour supérieure, dossiers des tutelles et curatelles
UMBC   Université de Montréal, division des Archives, P0058, Collection Louis-François-Georges Baby
WO   War Office records, National Archives of the United Kingdom

NOTES

Most of the sources cited were consulted in manuscript or on microfilm. Some are now available online, and more will be in the years to come, making them more readily accessible.

Most archival documents from the Bibliothèque et Archives nationales du Québec (BANQ) were consulted at the Montreal branch. This includes microfilm copies of notarial deeds and of all the vital statistics records of Quebec churches, whose manuscript originals may be kept at other branches. For this reason, the repository is identified simply as BANQ. In the case of manuscript records found only at the Quebec branch, the repository is identified as BANQ-Q.

The old manuscript admission records of the Hôtel-Dieu de Montréal (HDM) are held by the Soeurs Hospitalières de Saint-Joseph at their convent adjacent to the hospital. The admission and death records for the Hôtel-Dieu de Québec are on microfilm at the BANQ. References to them are given as BANQ, HDQ.

The early *Journals of the House of Assembly of Upper Canada (JAUC)* are found in the *Sixth Report of the Bureau of Archives for the province of Ontario, 1909;* likewise, the early *Journals of the Legislative Council of Upper Canada (JCUC)* are in the *Seventh Report of the Bureau of Archives for the province of Ontario, 1910.*

The name of the Scotch Presbyterian Church in St Gabriel Street, whose records are frequently cited, is shortened to St Gabriel Presbyterian Church.

The place of publication of the newspapers cited is Montreal unless otherwise indicated.

INTRODUCTION

1 CQS, *Alex. Grant v. Alex. McPherson*, Grant affidavit, 25 June 1835. CWS, register, 23 June 1835, *Alexander Grant v. Alexander McPherson*. Pilarczyk, "'Too Well Used by His Master': Judicial Enforcement of Servants' Rights in Montreal, 1830–1845," and "The Law of Servants and the Servants of the Law: Enforcing Masters' Rights in Montreal, 1830–1845." The prosecution by Alexander Grant is mentioned in the latter at page 799. In another case cited on page 812, *John Russell v. John Lewis*, Lewis is believed to have been a black seaman (CWS, register, 23 June 1841).
2 See *Census of the Canadas 1860–61*, 1:4–43, "No. I – Lower Canada Personal Census, by Origin, 1861"; 1:161–365, "No. 5 – Lower Canada Personal Census, by Ages, 1861." Except in quotations, the French forms of the ward names (as of the suburb names) are used, even though they were routinely translated at the time as St Ann, St James, St Lawrence, St Mary, etc.
3 The problem of judging those who practised slavery is the subject of an eloquent personal statement in Boulle, *Race et esclavage dans la France de l'Ancien Régime*, 11.
4 Gay, *Les Noirs du Québec*, 84. Trudel, *Dictionnaire des esclaves et de leurs propriétaires au Canada Français* (hereafter *Dictionnaire*), 91, 115, 120, 351, 359. See Appendix I n4.
5 See Appendix I/A, notices 26 and 92.
6 Caesar Hunkin (*sic*) sued a timber dealer for a debt of £11 2s 3d in 1793. His name was recorded as Cesar Hernking in 1801 at the burial of Nancy Buckley, the slave of tailor Benaiah Gibb Sr. A year later, he was Cesar Hunkins at his wedding to a white woman identified, in English, as Mary Margaret Lapron (Marie Marguerite Colleret *dit* Bourguignon, widow of François Leprohon). At the birth of their daughter Marie Françoise in April 1804, Hunkings was identified as César, and, at her death one month later, as César Angune. He died on 28 September 1807, at age sixty or so. No evidence has been found of his having been a slave in Canada, but he may have been a descendant of slaves owned by a Col. Hunkings of Portsmouth, NH, in the early eighteenth century, one of whom was called Caesar Hunkings. In 1774, a Mark Hunking of Barrington, NH, advertised the flight of a slave named Caesar in the *Boston Gazette* (BANQ, register of Christ Church, 14 April 1801; register of Notre-Dame Church, 14 March 1798, 13 April, and 14 May 1804, 30 September 1807, 10 October 1814, 7 March 1838; register of St Gabriel Presbyterian Church, 27 June 1802. CCP, *Caesar Hunkin v. Charles Bennet*, 13 November 1793. CQS, docket for April 1796, and register, 28 April 1796. POBR 1:223. *Boston Gazette*, 25 July 1774. Gooding, "Records of the South Church of Portsmouth, NH," 427. Trudel, *Dictionnaire*, 95–6, 119).
7 At her death at Montreal in June 1813, the "negress" Mary Young was said to be 106, which was probably a great exaggeration (BANQ, register of St Gabriel Presbyterian Church, 23 June 1813).
8 Only two references have been found to certificate-carrying blacks in Quebec. One is in a 1767 notice concerning the fugitive slave Andrew who "is supposed to have with him forged Certificates of his Freedom, and Passes" (see Appendix I/A, notice 4). The second concerns Joseph Louis Robertson (alias Louis Joseph Robisson, Louis Robinson), identified at his wedding at Berthier in 1797 as the thirty-one-year-old New York-born son of a mulatto and an Englishwoman, and the holder of a certificate attesting to his freedom issued at Sorel 15 September

NOTES TO PAGES 9–17

1796 by Loyalist Captain Edward Jessup, the founder of Prescott, Ont. (BANQ, register of Ste-Geneviève Church, Berthier, 24 March and 29 May 1797).
9 Her first name was written variously as Flavie, Fleure, Fleurie, Flora, Flore, Florence, Marie, Marie Flavie or Mary, and her family name as Dagenais, Dajennais, Deligny, Dénigé, de Nisier, de Nisiez, Denniger, Desnaigé, Desnegé, etc.
10 Canada's Digital Collections, "The Underground Railroad Years: Canada in an International Arena" (http://epe.lac-bac.gc.ca/100/205/301/ic/cdc/E/Alphabet.asp), accessed July 2008. Alexander and Glaze, *Towards Freedom*, 53. Hill, *The Freedom-Seekers*, 18. Williams, *The Road to Now*, 25.
11 See Blais, "Un document inédit sur l'esclavage au Québec."
12 Sulte, "L'esclavage en Canada," 333.
13 Sulte, *Histoire des Canadiens-français*, 6:118 n4.
14 CWS, register, 5–6 September 1860, *R v. Archibald Brown*. RPM, Box 42, 21 August 1860. *Transcript*, 23 August and 8 September 1860.

CHAPTER ONE

1 *Morning Chronicle* (Quebec), 14 August 1847. See Appendix I/A, notice 5.
2 Viger and LaFontaine, *De l'esclavage en Canada* (hereafter *De l'esclavage*), ii. For Viger, see Jean-Claude Robert, "Jacques Viger."
3 Viger and LaFontaine, *De l'esclavage*, 1.
4 The relevant part of Garneau's text is quoted in Viger and LaFontaine, *De l'esclavage*, 10. For later amendments, see Garneau, *Histoire du Canada*, 8th ed., 4:286–7.
5 *Gazette*, 4 March 1790.
6 Lebrun, *Tableau statistique et politique des deux Canadas*, 125. See also Dunbar, *History of the Rise and Decline of Commercial Slavery in America*, 243–7; Stouffer, *The Light of Nature and the Law of God*, 8; Trudel, *Deux siècles d'esclavage au Québec* (hereafter *Deux siècles d'esclavage*), 341–3; Viger and LaFontaine, *De l'esclavage*, 9–12; Winks, *The Blacks in Canada*, 19–20. "There are thousands of persons in Canada who would be ... astounded if told that slavery existed in Canada for more than a century; and yet such is the fact," a Toronto newspaper, cited in Dunbar, said in reporting the findings of Viger and LaFontaine. Stouffer notes that when the anti-slavery Toronto *Globe* stated in 1849 that "slavery never had an existence in Canada," no one challenged the assertion. As the editor of the *Provincial Freeman* in Canada West in 1853, the former American slave Samuel Ringgold Ward observed: "The fact that this is a British Province, and that slavery has no existence on British soil – the fact that this soil never was polluted by slavery – and the fact that since the ever memorable Somerset decision, the slave of another country became a freeman by touching our soil – place us in relations of antagonism to slavery" ("Relations of Canada to American slavery," *Provincial Freeman*, 24 March 1853). Former slaves, their children, and others knew better. See, for example, chapter 2 n31, or the "Interesting Obituary" in the *Colored American* (New York), 13 October 1838).
7 SLCC, *Pierre, a mulatto v. Choteau [sic], Thérèse Cerré*, November 1840, no. 192, 1–6, and *Pierre, a mulatto v. Chouteau, Gabriel*, November 1842, no. 125, 1–2; *Mary Charlotte, a woman of color v. Gabriel Chouteau*, November 1843, no. 13, 1–2; *Chouteau, Louis, a man*

of color v. Chouteau, Gabriel, April 1844, no. 51, 1–2; *Paul, Michel v. Gabriel Paul*, April 1844, no. 151, 1.

8 Stock would have left Montreal no earlier than August 1791. He spent the month of July recruiting men for his western trading expedition (BANQ, notary L. Chaboillez, Engagements, nos 735–8, 8–9 July 1791, and nos 743–51, 18–27 July 1791). As to the accounts of Rose working for Étienne Campion, it is possible that this was another Rose, and that the witnesses remembered the name rather than the person. Campion did own a black slave named Rose at this time: she gave birth at Montreal on 22 August 1793 to a daughter named Julie. Campion, who died on 23 December 1795, mentioned no slaves in his will, nor was there any reference to slaves in the inventory or sale of his estate (BANQ, register of Notre-Dame Church, 22 August 1793 and 26 December 1795; notary J.G. Delisle, no. 2077, 19 December 1795; no. 2084, 11 January 1796, and no. 2091, 21 January 1796).

9 Copies of the bills of sale from Todd to Didier and from Didier to Auguste Chouteau were filed with the Circuit Court of St Louis on 24 September 1840. See SLCC, *Pierre v. Thérèse Cerré Choteau*, November 1840, no. 192, 9–11 and 12–14. For Auguste Chouteau, see Foley and Rice, *The First Chouteaus;* for his and his family's views on slavery, and their dealings with slaves, see pages 28, 42, 43, 99–100, 114, 191–2, 196, 201. At his death on 24 February 1829, Chouteau left fifty slaves. The date of Rose's death is not known. For Andrew Todd, see Rice, *The First Chouteaus*, 53–4, 75, 77–8, and J.I. Cooper, *James McGill of Montreal*, 37–9.

10 SLCC, *Pierre v. Gabriel Chouteau*, November 1842, no. 125, 61–2; *Louis Chouteau v. Gabriel S. Chouteau*, April 1844, no. 51, 22, 32; *Paul, Michel v. Paul, Adolph, Administrator*, April 1845, no. 143, 3.

11 For the final decision in Charlotte's case, see SLCC, *Mary Charlotte v. Gabriel Chouteau*, November 1843, no. 13, 305, judgment of the Supreme Court of Missouri, 9 December 1862. For published accounts of the cases, see Catterall, *Judicial Cases Concerning American Slavery*, 5:111–13, 162–3, 174, 194–5, 203–5, 216–17, 340–4; by the same author, "Some Antecedents of the Dred Scott Case," 61–2; Frazier, *Runaway and Freed Missouri Slaves*, 51–2; Anonymous, "Slavery in Lower Canada," *The Lower Canada Jurist*, 3 (1860):257–68; *The Liberator*, 25 March 1859. The famous case of *Dred Scott v. Sandford*, launched in the Circuit Court of St Louis in 1846, was decided by the US Supreme Court on 6 March 1857. See Fehrenbacher, *The Dred Scott Case*.

12 For the evidence taken at Montreal, see SLCC, *Pierre v. Gabriel Chouteau*, November 1842, no. 125, 57–146, and *Mary Charlotte v. Gabriel Chouteau*, November 1843, no. 13, 145–372. UMCB, QI/165, "Proceedings of a 'Commission rogatoire' of the State of Missouri respecting Slavery in Canada, and Notes by Justice Reid on the Subject." Depositions in the first case were taken in April–May 1846. The only witness examined before the second commission, it seems, was Justice William Badgley, on 5 February 1859. For the judges' testimony, see Appendix II.

13 SLCC, *Pierre v. Gabriel Chouteau*, November 1842, no. 125, 180–3. *Mary Charlotte v. Gabriel Chouteau*, November 1843, no. 13, 62.

14 SLCC, *Pierre v. Gabriel Chouteau*, November 1842, no. 125, 35–6, 177–9, 201–202; *Mary Charlotte v. Gabriel Chouteau*, November 1843, no. 13, 57–8, 64. On the Cerré and Panet families, see Faribault-Beauregard, *La vie aux Illinois au XVIIIe siècle : Souvenirs inédits de Marie-Anne Cerré*, and P.-G. Roy, *La famille Panet*, particularly 175–8.

15 SLCC, *Mary Charlotte v. Gabriel Chouteau*, November 1843, no. 13, 63. See note 21, below. One wonders why the black voyageurs would have bothered to state that they were free if there were no question about it.
16 SLCC, *Pierre v. Gabriel Chouteau*, November 1842, no. 125, 183–4; *Mary Charlotte v. Gabriel Chouteau*, November 1843, no. 13, 63–4.
17 SLCC, *Pierre v. Gabriel Chouteau*, November 1842, no. 125, 179–80.
18 SLCC, *Mary Charlotte v. Gabriel Chouteau*, November 1843, no. 13, 60–1; *Pierre v. Gabriel Chouteau*, November 1842, no. 125, 188.
19 SLCC, *Pierre v. Gabriel Chouteau*, November 1842, no. 125, 17–8; *Mary Charlotte v. Gabriel Chouteau*, November 1843, no. 13, 17–20.
20 Four Claus slaves – Nicholas, Tom, Peter, and Maria – were listed in the summer of 1781 in the "Return of Negroes & Negroe Wench's brought into the Province by Parties under the Command and Direction of Lieut. Colo. Sir John Johnson Bart.," reproduced in Appendix III. For Campbell's slaves, see chapter 3. For Campbell and Claus, see Leighton, "John Campbell" and "Christian Daniel Claus."
21 This slave was probably the same person mentioned by Michel Marly, who testified in 1845 that although he had never heard of slaves in Canada, he had known "a slave of St George who was free, a voyager, a mulatto." Le Compte Dupré had had at least one black slave, a male who died on Christmas Day 1774 at the age of about twenty-three (BANQ, register of Notre-Dame Church, 26 December 1774. SLCC, *Mary Charlotte v. Gabriel Chouteau*, November 1843, no. 13, 60–1. For Le Compte Dupré, see P.-G. Roy, *La Famille Le Compte Dupré*, 41–6).
22 SLCC, *Pierre v. Gabriel Chouteau*, November 1842, no. 125, 193–5; *Mary Charlotte v. Gabriel Chouteau*, November 1843, no. 13, 66–7. Claus died in 1787, when Smith would have been about sixteen.
23 She was said to be seventeen when she married Tison, a widower, in January 1785 (BANQ, register of Notre-Dame Church, 17 January 1785).
24 SLCC, *Pierre v. Gabriel Chouteau*, November 1842, no. 125, 149–53, 195–202; *Mary Charlotte v. Gabriel Chouteau*, November 1843, no. 13, 67–9.
25 Berlinguet owned at least one other slave, as a Pierre Pagé demanded £1 from him in September 1793 for taking his "négresse" to Quebec the previous fall (CCP, *Pierre Pagé v. Joseph Berlinguet*, 14 September 1793).
26 SLCC, *Pierre v. Gabriel Chouteau*, November 1842, no. 125, 37–8, 150–1, 196–9, 201.
27 SLCC, *Pierre v. Gabriel Chouteau*, November 1842, no. 125, 115–17. BANQ, register of Notre-Dame Church, 2 May 1798 and 22 July 1800. HDM, admission registers, Book C, 18 April 1780. If Adélaïde Chaboillez spoke of the slaves as belonging to her mother rather than to her parents, it was probably because her father spent most of his time in fur-trade country. In addition to the slaves whom she named, it is known that her father bought a sixteen-year-old mulatto named Pierre at Montreal in 1793 from hairdresser Jean Regot for 200 Spanish dollars, merchant Joseph Frobisher acting as proxy for Charles Chaboillez in this transaction. Adélaïde Chaboillez's mother died on 29 April 1798. An inventory of the common property of Adélaïde's parents as of that date listed no slaves (BANQ, notary J.G. Beek, no. 1250, 20 June 1798; notary P. Lukin Sr, no. 233, 11 July 1793). Edward Pollard owned at least two black slaves. One called Marie lingered for six months in the Hôtel-Dieu before she died there on 24 April 1788

at the reputed age of twenty-seven. Pollard died less than two months later, on 13 June. At his death, he had a nine-year-old mulatto slave named Tim, who was perhaps Marie's son (BANQ, register of Notre-Dame Church, 25 April 1788; register of Christ Church, 15 June 1788; notary J.G. Beek, no. 419, 30 June 1788. HDM registers, Book E, 25 October 1787).

28 SLCC, *Pierre v. Gabriel Chouteau*, November 1842, no. 125, 118–21. For her father's slave, see Appendix I/A, notice 65.
29 Viger and LaFontaine, *De l'esclavage*, ii.
30 SLCC, *Pierre v. Gabriel Chouteau*, November 1842, no. 125, 122–4. BANQ, HDQ admission registers, 22 December 1790, 1 January 1791, 26 September and 1 October 1794, 3 October 1796. Grant's parents were David Alexander Grant, captain in the 84th Regiment, and Marie Charles Joseph Le Moyne de Longueuil, baronne de Longueuil. The Lanaudière slave could also have been the unnamed male mentioned on page 128. On the Lanaudière slaves, see Imbeault, *Les Tarieu de Lanaudière*, 148–50. William Smith's slaves included Leeds Blair (alias Austin Blair, Ostend), his wife Charlotte, and their daughter Alicia. Charlotte Blair died in 1801. In January 1804, the widowed Blair, no longer a slave but servant of Lieutenant Henry Mordaunt Gage Vigoureux of the Royal Engineers, married Diana Moulton. In 1817, at the governor's request, he was placed in the Hôpital-Général at Quebec. The governor's secretary wrote to the Superior of the Grey Nuns, who ran that hospice: "I am directed by His Excellency the Govr. in Chief to request that you will receive into the General Hospital Austin Blair, a Negro, who from infirmity is unable to earn his subsistence." He died there in his sixties on 3 June 1818 (BANQ, register of Quebec Anglican Church, 12 December 1790, 26 January 1804, 4 June 1818; register of St Andrew's Presbyterian Church, Quebec, 25 February 1795, 20 March 1801. LAC RG7 G15 C, Lower Canada Civil Secretary's Letter Books, 24:325, L. Montizambert to Superior of the General Hospital, 11 August 1817).
31 The only known slave who might possibly correspond to this one is Marie, identified at her death on 23 July 1787 as the roughly forty-year-old "négresse" of a Mr Lacroix (BANQ, register of Notre-Dame Church, 24 July 1787).
32 BANQ, notary J.G. Delisle, no. 2280, 13 September 1796. LAC, RG4 B45, Declarations of Aliens, Lower Canada 1794–1811, 100–2. SLCC, *Pierre v. Gabriel Chouteau*, November 1842, no. 125, 125–7. *Gazette*, 21 February 1793 (see Appendix I/A, notice 82). The Declarations of Aliens, transcribed by S.A. Bartley, have been published by the Vermont Genealogical Society (Routier's declaration of 15 July 1794 is found on pages 23–4). The slave-owner identified here as Dumignault was called "Dumieaux" when his slave Jean Charper died at the Hôtel-Dieu in 1788, and "du Milleau" at the death of his slave Marie Josephte, wife of Henry Fortune, in 1794 (BANQ, register of Notre-Dame Church, 8 July 1788 and 10 March 1794).
33 SLCC, *Pierre v. Gabriel Chouteau*, November 1842, no. 125, 116, 120, 124, 126.
34 Their opinions are reproduced in Appendix II.
35 *Édits et Ordonnances*, 2:67–8, "Ordonnance Rendue au sujet des Nègres et des Sauvages appellés Panis," 13 April 1709, and 2:105, 308–9, "Ordonnance Concernant l'affranchissement des Esclaves," 1 September 1736.
36 Kennedy, *Documents of the Canadian Constitution, 1759–1915*, 13. Presumably the captured slaves were to be restored to their British owners, but the case of Estiennette, taken as a baby with her parents at Saratoga, NY, in December 1745, illustrates the kind of difficulties that

could arise. As the slave of Geneviève Gamelin, she applied to the court in 1761 to be allowed to return to the American colonies, claiming that she must be considered a British subject and therefore free under the terms of the capitulation. Did she come under the terms of the capitulation? Did that document cover prisoners taken at any time, or just in the most recent war? Did anyone know to whom Estiennette had belonged at Saratoga sixteen years earlier? Were those owners still alive? Would they want her back? The court heard the case and left it to the governor to decide her fate. There seems to be no further record of the case (BANQ, TL12, Chambre des milices, Registres des procès-verbaux d'audience en appel – 28 octobre 1760– 26 avril 1764, 6 June 1761, f. 77)

37 *Great Britain, Statutes at Large*, 30 Geo. III (1790), c. 27.
38 See Trudel, *Deux siècles d'esclavage*, 146–7. Winks, *The Blacks in Canada*, 6–7. A study of the reading habits of the nobility in New France found that, although the ordinances of King Louis XIV were among the most common reading materials, no copy of the ordinance known as the Code noir was found in any estate inventory (M. Robert, "Le livre et la lecture dans la noblesse canadienne 1670–1764," 19).
39 SLCC, *Pierre v. Gabriel Chouteau*, November 1842, no. 125, 74.
40 For a recent reappraisal of the Somerset case, see Van Cleve, "*Somerset's Case* and its Antecedents in Imperial Perspective." See also Blumrosen and Blumrosen, *Slave Nation;* Gerzina, *Black London*, 116, 131–2, 122, 128; Higginbotham, *In the Matter of Color*, 311–68; Nadelhaft, "The Somersett case and slavery"; Shyllon, *Black Slaves in Britain;* Wiecek, *The Sources of Antislavery Constitutionalism in America, 1760–1848*, 20–39; Wise, *Though the Heavens May Fall*.
41 Wise, in *Though the Heavens May Fall*, 193–7, says that Mansfield's ruling "profoundly influenced the development of American slave law. Its moral weight and the reputation of its author ensured that *Somerset* haters and lovers both would agree that it stood for three propositions: Natural law rejected slavery, English common law prohibited it, and only positive local law supported it. ... As a result, judges North and South absorbed *Somerset* into their common law and either freed slaves or didn't, depending on whether positive law creating slavery existed in their states."
42 Cited in Shyllon, *Black Slaves in Britain*, 109. See also Appendix I to the online edition of Van Cleve, "*Somerset's Case* and its Antecedents in Imperial Perspective," at www.historycooperative.org/journals/lhr/24.3/cleve.html; Wise, *Though the Heavens May Fall*, 175–85.
43 SLCC, *Mary Charlotte v. Gabriel Chouteau*, November 1843, no. 13, 162–3. On the correspondence between the authorities in New France and Paris on this subject, see Trudel, *Deux siècles d'esclavage*, 32–47.
44 See Trudel, *Deux siècles d'esclavage*, 34–5.
45 Viger and LaFontaine, *De l'esclavage*, 2.
46 The foreword to *De l'esclavage* (page ii) states that Viger had communicated the fruits of his researches to Badgley and to lawyers in Missouri. Viger died on 12 December 1858, less than two months before Badgley gave his testimony.
47 SLCC, *Mary Charlotte v. Gabriel Chouteau*, November 1843, no. 13, 170–1.
48 Anonymous, *Canadian Letters: Description of a Tour Thro' the Provinces of Lower and Upper Canada, in the Course of the Years 1792 and '93*, 59.

49 Boyer, *Les crimes et les châtiments*, 218–39. Lachance, *Juger et punir en Nouvelle-France*, 173–81 and, "Mathieu Léveillé." Trudel, *Dictionnaire*, 175–6.

50 On 6 September 1760, Charles, "nègre de m. de Vaudreuil," and his wife Marie Anne Victoire, "négresse," had a son, Adrien, baptized the same day. This was two days before Vaudreuil surrendered New France to the British forces under General Jeffrey Amherst at Montreal. Vaudreuil took another slave, Jean Baptiste *dit* Canon, a native of the Gold Coast, to France with him after the Conquest. In 1769, Quebec tavern keeper Miles Prentice, former provost marshal (sheriff) at Quebec, offered for sale three slaves, including a twenty-five year old "Negro Woman" who had formerly belonged to Governor James Murray, and her nine-month-old son. Gage owned a slave named Benjamin who was baptized at Montreal in May 1762. The record did not give his age (BANQ, register of Notre Dame Church, 6 September 1760, register of Garrison Anglican Church, 11 May 1762. *Quebec Gazette*, 23 February and 15 June 1769. Boulle, *Race et esclavage dans la France de l'Ancien Régime*, 178. Trudel, *Dictionnaire*, 161. For Prentice's slaves, see Appendix I/A, notice 9. For Murray's views on slavery, see Winks, *The Blacks in Canada*, 26).

51 See Appendix I/A, notices 26 and 27, and n32.

52 Gray owned the slave Sylvia (alias Sylvia Gray), whom he had bought at an auction of the bankrupt estate of tailor James Perry *circa* 1777. Perry had bought her on 27 August 1773 from Garret Van Vliet of Kinderhook, NY, for £60 New York currency. At the time, she was said to be twenty-four. Her age was given as forty-five at her death on 9 December 1787 (BANQ, register of Christ Church, 10 December 1787. HDM, admission registers, Book E, 3 December 1785, 17 November 1787. Riddell, "Further Notes on Slavery in Canada," 26–7). In February 1798, when François Dumoulin, seigneur of Courval, near Trois-Rivières, ceded a nineteen-year-old slave named Julie to his mother-in-law, Charlotte Dumont, widow Laframboise, in payment of a debt, he stated that he had bought her at a public sale held by Gray. The date of this sale is unspecified, but it was before 1790: on 2 January that year, Julie was identified as a fifteen-year-old *"Negresse de Mr Dumoulin"* when she was admitted to the Hôtel-Dieu (BANQ, notary J.G. Delisle, no. 2574, 5 February 1798. HDM, admission registers, Book E, 2 January 1790). For the third slave, Thomas, see chapter 4.

53 Members of the first Legislative Assembly who are known to have owned slaves were Pierre-Amable Debonne, Michel Eustache Gaspard Alain Chartier de Lotbinière, Antoine Juchereau Duchesnay, Georges Hyppolite Le Compte Dupré, Pierre Guerout, William Grant, Jacob Jordan, Joseph-Hubert Lacroix, François Antoine Larocque (he died before he could take his seat), John Lees, Robert Lester, David Lynd, James McGill, Matthew Macnider, François Malhiot, Louis Olivier, Joseph Papineau, and John Young.

54 SLCC, *Pierre v. Gabriel Chouteau*, November 1842, no. 125, 79. Reid certainly had known Montrealers who were slave-owners, but, as difficult as it may be to credit, he might not have known that they owned slaves. For example, he was one of four men whom merchant James McGill, the owner of several slaves over the years, named in his will in 1811 to be trustees of the land and funds he bequeathed for the creation of what became McGill University (MUA, RG4, C438, no. 11060, copy of will of James McGill, 8 January 1811). Another slave-owner whom Reid knew owned slaves in the West Indies but not in Canada. In 1806, Eliza Smith, mother of James Murray, seigneur of Argenteuil, made out her will as she was about to leave

for the Bahamas, naming Reid and Dr Charles Blake, a former slave-owner, as trustees of her estate. Her properties consisted of "three Plantations, one whereof in the Caoicas [Caicos?], with Twenty five Negroes & more, another on Cat Island and the last at Abiko [Abaco]." Two years later, she wrote to Reid from New Providence that she intended to return to Montreal as soon as she had sold her property in the Bahamas (BANQ, notary P. Lukin Sr, no. 2858, 30 April 1803, no. 2861, 2 May 1803, and no. 3791, 9 June 1806. UMCB, U/11070, Eliza Smith to James Reid, 24 April 1808).

55 SLCC, *Pierre v. Gabriel Chouteau*, November 1842, no. 125, 78. In a draft of his written replies to the commission, Reid wrote: "I enclose my answers to the Interrogations which I have made as concise as possible but leave it with you to get them copied fair. What I have said in answer to the [word illegible] Interrogs. may in some respects be considered unnecessary, but what is too much may be retrenched – & if there be any error let it be corrected" (UMCB, Q1/165).

56 SLCC, *Pierre v. Gabriel Chouteau*, November 1842, no. 125, 73. For Robin, see chapter 2.

57 SLCC, *Pierre v. Gabriel Chouteau*, November 1842, no. 125, 86.

58 Trudel, in *Dictionnaire*, 208, and *Deux siècles d'esclavage*, 304, mentions a slave named Philis who ran away from a Sorel woman named Sawer in 1798.

59 SLCC, *Pierre v. Gabriel Chouteau*, November 1842, no. 125, 92–3.

60 SLCC, *Mary Charlotte v. Gabriel Chouteau*, November 1843, no. 13, 186–91, 233–60.

61 Trudel, *Deux siècles d'esclavage*, 103–4.

62 BANQ, TL12, Chambre des milices de Montréal, Registre d'audiences 1760–64, 27 September 1763, ff. 18–19; TL10, Registre des jugements en appel au commandant Thomas Gage, 6 décembre 1760 au 10 août 1764, 15 October 1763, 237.

63 BANQ, TL11, Conseil militaire, Registre d'appels 1761–1764, 20 July 1762 (the same record is found in TL279, Conseil militaire du district de Montréal, Plumitif des appels 20 janvier 1762 au 21 octobre 1763, f. 66), and 20 April 1763 (also in TL279, ff. 70–1); TL 279, Conseil militaire du district de Montréal, Plumitif des appels 20 janvier 1762 au 21 octobre 1763, 20 May 1763, f. 71. Doutre and Lareau, in *Droit civil*, 2:538, mistake Levy for a Mr de Léry and presents the case as an application by a master for permission to sell his slave outside the judicial district, when it was André who sought to alert the authorities that Levy was trying to sell him before the court had ruled on his petition. Shortly after André filed his suit, Levy sold a Panis to fur-trade merchant Chapman Abraham (BANQ, notary A. Souste, 17 September 1762).

64 He was probably the fugitive slave identified in 1767 as Andrew. See Appendix I/A, notice 4.

65 SLCC, *Mary Charlotte v. Gabriel Chouteau*, November 1843, no. 13, 190. Badgley seems to have considered Quebec slavery akin to the "near slavery" or "slavish servitude" that had existed in England. See Van Cleve, "*Somerset's Case* and Its Antecedents in Imperial Perspective."

66 Panet died at Montreal in 1812, and Ogden and Monk in England respectively in 1824 and 1826.

67 *Édits et Ordonnances*, 399–402, 464–76, 553–4. "Déclaration du Roi au sujet des Tuteurs," 15 December 1721 (specifically Art. 4); "Lettres Patentes du Roi, en forme d'Édit, concernant le Commerce étranger aux Isles et Colonies de l'Amérique," October 1727 (notably Title I, Articles 11 and 13–16; Titles II and III; and Title V, Articles 5 and 6); and "Arrêt du Conseil d'Etat du Roi, portant que les Nègres qui se sauvent des Colonies des ennemis, aux Colonies Françoises, appartiennent à sa Majesté," 25 July 1745.

68 SLCC, *Mary Charlotte v. Gabriel Chouteau*, November 1843, no. 13, 171.
69 CQS register, 10 April 1766. See Fyson, *Magistrates, Police, and People*, 24–5.
70 CQS register, 17 December 1767.
71 BANQ, P345, Château de Ramezay Collection, Numismatic and Antiquarian Society of Montreal, D-1, document 185. CQS register, 30 April 1781 and 9 April 1782. *Quebec Gazette*, 17 May 1781.
72 CQS register, 9 April 1782, 16 April 1784, 26 May 1785, 21 April and 22 July 1786, 8 May 1787, 26 July 1788, 19 May and 17 November 1789, 27 April 1791, 15 April 1794, 12 January and 16 July 1795, 19 January and 16 July 1796, 19 January 1797, 19 July 1799. *Quebec Gazette*, 22 May 1783, 16 June 1785, 11 May 1786, 17 May 1787.
73 Badgley had earned the thanks of black refugees and abolitionists in 1847 when, as attorney general for Canada East, he had assured them that a fugitive slave named Isaac Brown would not be surrendered to Maryland slave-catchers who were on his trail (see *Liberator*, 15 October 1847; Prince, "The case of Isaac Brown," 28–9). Of Gale, it was said at his death that "[o]f late years his heart has been most deeply interested in the freedom of the slave. He could not speak with patience of any compromise with slavery and waxed indignant in denunciation of all who in any way aided, abetted, or even countenanced it" (*Gazette*, 17 April 1865). For Gale's sentiments on, and contributions to, the anti-slavery struggle in the United States at the time of the Civil War, see items on the annual National Anti-Slavery Subscription anniversaries in the *Liberator* (Boston), 15 February 1861, 14 February 1862, 20 February 1863, 19 February 1864, 3 March 1865, as well as "More encouraging words," 16 January 1863, and "The late Judge Gale of Montreal," 28 April 1865. From his first donation of $50 in 1861, Gale's contributions mounted year by year; shortly before his death in 1865, he gave $500.
74 SLCC, *Mary Charlotte v. Gabriel Chouteau*, November 1843, no. 13, 181.
75 See chapter 9.
76 Ward, *Autobiography*, 146–7.

CHAPTER TWO

1 For this slave, see Beaugrand-Champagne, *Le procès de Marie-Josèphe-Angélique*, and Cooper, *The Hanging of Angélique*. The plaque was stolen in 2006 and is thought to have been melted down for its metal content. The text read:

In this International Year to Commemorate the Struggle against Slavery and its Abolition, this plaque is dedicated to the memory of the black slave Marie-Josèphe-Angélique, iconic figure of slavery in Quebec, who was accused of arson, tried, hanged, then burned at the stake at Montreal in 1734, her ashes cast to the winds. Lest we forget, and to remind us that slavery was practised here until its abolition in 1833, this plaque is presented to the City of Montreal by the government of Quebec this 23 February 2004 [translation].

2 *Gazette*, 25 July 1833. *Vindicator*, 6 August 1833.
3 The names appear to have been written as heard. Jarrad Banks, as he wrote his name, is identified as Gerard Banks. Peter Dago, who could not write, is recorded as P. Dogo. As for "Anthony Ingston," his name was more properly Hinksman or some variation thereof (Hinckman,

Hingsman, Hinsman, Hinxman, Inksman, or Kinckman). "Jacob Abadillard" was Jacob Abdella, whose name of Arabic origin (meaning slave, or servant, of God) changed at every writing: Abdala, Abdalah, Abdalha, Abdalla, Abdallah, Abdally, Abdeler, Abdeley, Abdello, Abdallah *dit* Bisornon, Abdelad Bisornon, Abdelin, Abdellah *dit* Bissernon, Abdelloy, Adna, Bissernet Abdeloy, Bisorno Abdella, Dabdala, Obdelay, etc. John Broome's name, often written without the final E, was sometimes turned into "Brown." The initial of the second name on the list, G. Grant, should be J, for Jacob.

4 Gay, in *Les Noirs du Québec 1629–1900*, 128, turns this press release of 1833 into a petition of 1832 to the British parliament for the emancipation of blacks in Canada as well as in the West Indies. It has Alexander Grant giving a speech on 19 August 1834 "pour célébrer l' 'abolition totale', cette année, de l'esclavage dans tout le Canada" (to celebrate the "total abolition" that year of slavery throughout Canada). Grant gave his speech on 1 August 1834 and said not a word about slavery in Canada. The text of his speech, published in the Montreal *Gazette* of 19 August 1834, is reproduced in Mackey, *Black Then*, 196–9.
5 W.L. Mackenzie, *Sketches of Canada and the United States*, 349.
6 *Statutes of the United Kingdom*, 3 & 4 William IV (1833), c. 73.
7 Black Torontonians celebrated "the anniversary of the West Indian Emancipation as a gala day" in 1852 (*Gazette*, 6 August 1852). Two years later, at a meeting to organize yet another gala, they "[r]esolved, that we celebrate that glorious event which took place in the Year of our Lord 1834, when the British Nation did honour to itself and justice to 800,000 of her coloured subjects in the West Indies." Accordingly, an Upper Canadian newspaper reported that "[t]he Colored population of Toronto had a great gathering on the first of August, to celebrate the emancipation of the negroes in the West Indian Islands" (*Provincial Freeman*, 29 July and 12 August 1854). In 1856, "the colored inhabitants of Brantford held a meeting to celebrate the Anniversary of the Abolition of Slavery in the West indies," a Montreal newspaper reported (*Pilot*, 9 August 1856). In Montreal itself in 1861, "[o]n the first of August, – a day ever memorable in the annals of human freedom, – services were held in this city, morning and evening, partly commemorative of the emancipation of 800,000 slaves in the British West Indies, on 1st August 1834, but chiefly to pray for the emancipation of the four millions of slaves now held in bondage in the United States" (*Witness*, 7 August 1861). "To-day being the Anniversary of Negro Emancipation in the British West India Islands, the colored residents of this city purpose to celebrate the day," another newspaper announced in 1862 (*Transcript*, 1 August 1862). Likening the emancipation of 1 August 1834 to the deliverance of the Jews from Egypt, a Montreal paper observed in 1862 that "it is only reasonable and right that the African race should observe, all over the world, the first of August as the anniversary of the deliverance from long and cruel bondage of their brethren in the West India Islands" (*Witness*, 2 August 1862).
8 The law stipulated that the commissioners responsible for awarding compensation "shall proceed to apportion the said Sum into Nineteen different Shares, which shall be respectively assigned to the several *British* Colonies, or Possessions herein-after mentioned; (that is to say,) the *Bermuda Islands,* the *Bahama Islands, Jamaica, Honduras,* the *Virgin Islands, Antigua, Montserrat, Nevis, Saint Christopher's, Dominica, Barbadoes, Grenada, Saint Vincent's, Tobago, Saint Lucia, Trinidad, British Guiana,* the *Cape of Good Hope,* and *Mauritius*" (*Statutes of the United Kingdom*, 3 & 4 William IV, c. 73, Section 45).

9 *Gazette*, 19 August 1834. See also *Gazette*, 2 August 1834.
10 SLCC, *Pierre v. Gabriel Chouteau*, November 1842, no. 125, 141–4. Regarding Elliot, see n16, below.
11 Riddell, "An International Complication between Illinois and Canada Arising out of Slavery," 125. The text of the Executive Council's report of 18 June 1829 is also found in Riddell's *The Slave in Canada*, 314–15. In pushing for an agreement with Britain on the return of fugitive slaves in 1826, US Secretary of State Henry Clay anticipated that Britain might argue that it had nothing to gain from such a pact, "there being no corresponding class of persons, in her North American Continental dominions." He instructed the American envoy to London to reply that whatever advantage Americans drew from such an agreement would be more than offset by Britain's gain from a similar proposed agreement for the return of deserting soldiers and sailors (Clay, *Papers of Henry Clay*, 5:472. Howe, *The Refugees from Slavery in Canada West*, 12–14. See also Lindsay, "Diplomatic relations between the United States and Great Britain bearing on the return of negro slaves, 1783–1828").
12 Lord, *Memoir of the Rev. Joseph Stibbs Christmas*, 152.
13 *Liberator* (Boston), 20 October 1837. Christie and Dumond, *George Bourne and "The Book and Slavery Irreconcilable,"* 82–3. Mayer, *All on Fire*, 69–70. Christie and Dumond's book reproduces Bourne's tract on pages 103–206.
14 *Gazette*, 10 May 1823.
15 Trudel, in *Deux siècles d'esclavage*, 109–10, reports the claim made in extreme old age by a white man born in 1819 that, as a very young child on a visit to Montreal with his mother, he had seen a full-fledged slave market ("un marché aux esclaves en règle"), where a black man, aged and sick, had offered himself for sale to his mother. A desperate or drunken man may have proposed himself to a passerby in this way, but the idea that a slave market operated in Montreal in the nineteenth century is preposterous. The odd slave had been sold in the market in the eighteenth century, but there was never such a trade that slavery needed its own market – and where ailing old slaves offered themselves for sale.
16 Barrister William Elliot of Sandwich (Windsor, Ont.), a witness before the rogatory commission of 1846 on the Missouri slave cases, did testify as to the existence of slavery after 1800, but in Upper Canada. "At the time I came to Canada [1802], I found slavery in existence there, and it continued there to my knowledge until 1812," he said. His cousin, Colonel Matthew Elliot of Amherstburg, superintendent of Indian affairs, owned several slaves, blacks and Panis. In 1802, acting on behalf of his cousin, William Elliot had tracked down and sold one of his slaves who had run away to Pennsylvania; and at his marriage in 1804, he said, Colonel Elliot had given him a Panis slave as a wedding present. Thomas McKee, also of Amherstburg, a subordinate to Colonel Elliot, had seven or eight slaves on his farm (SLCC, *Pierre v. Gabriel Chouteau*, November 1842, no. 125, 141–4).
17 A visiting Jamaican named James Drummond complained at Quebec in 1816 of the desertion on 29 July of his servant/slave Robert (CQS-Q, no. 71406, 29 July 1816). This might be seen as an attempt to reclaim a runaway slave, as it surely was on Drummond's part, but he was careful not to state his purpose in those terms. Although Robert was his slave in Jamaica, he said, for the purposes of this trip he had engaged Robert as a servant, and it was of Robert as a thieving, absconding servant that he complained. It does not appear that Robert, then in custody, was formally charged, but we do not know whether he was simply freed or told to return to his

master. Some evidence of the absence of slavery at Quebec by this time may be seen in the remarks made by a tart-tongued visitor in 1811: "The Canadian ladies are certainly as fond of ease as the West India ladies; – the only difference is, the former employ free squalid Canadians; the latter Negro slaves, who altho' equally ignorant, are certainly more cleanly in their habits than the former" (Cockloft, *Cursory Observations, Made in Quebec, Province of Lower-Canada, in the Year 1811*, 25).

18 LAC, RG1 E1, Journals of the Legislative Council of Quebec, 109, Minute Book D (17 August 1775–20 February 1786), 285. From the suspension of Chief Justice Peter Livius in 1778 to the appointment of William Smith in 1786, the function of chief justice was placed in a commission consisting of Mabane, Thomas Dunn, and Jenkins Williams.

19 LAC, RG14 A1, Records of the Legislative Council of Quebec to 1791, 4, File 1786–1787, Reports on police & commerce, "Report – Merchants of Montreal on Commerce and Police, 23 January 1787," 29.

20 BANQ, notary L. Chaboillez, no. 3676, 14 September 1799. *Gazette*, 22 January and 20 August 1798. For the text of the newspaper notices, see Appendix I/A, notices 92 and 93.

21 BANQ, notary B. Faribault, 29 March 1787.

22 LAC, RG1 E1, Journals of the Legislative Council of Quebec, 109, Minute Book D (17 August 1775–20 February 1786), 285; Minute Book E (15 January 1787–30 April 1789), 3–4.

23 LAC, RG4 B6, Legislative Council records, ordinances and working papers, 18, File 1787.

24 Of the gradual-emancipation laws adopted between 1780 and 1804 by the states of Connecticut, New Jersey, New York, Pennsylvania, and Rhode Island, historian David Brion Davis has written: "Since only future generations were freed ... and since the children of slaves were compelled to work for their mothers' owners until the children were in their twenties, the owners in effect received handsome compensation for the 'loss' of this form of property" (Davis, *Inhuman Bondage*, 152–3).

25 LAC, RG14 A1, Records of the Legislative Council of Quebec to 1791, 4, File 1786–1787, Reports on police & Commerce, circular letter to Montreal magistrates and merchants, 13 November 1786; follow-up letter to the committee of Montreal merchants, 8 December 1786; and "Report – Merchants of Montreal on Commerce and Police, 23 January 1787," 29. The signatories of the merchants' report were Jacob Jordan, James McGill, Pierre Guy, Benjamin Frobisher, Maurice Blondeau, Alexander Auldjo, Pierre Bouthillier, Richard Dobie, Joseph Périnault, John McKindlay, James Walker, and Thomas McCord. Blondeau, Jordan, McGill, Guy, and Périnault are known to have owned slaves.

26 LAC, RG1 E1, Journals of the Legislative Council of Quebec, 109, Minute Book E (15 January 1787–30 April 1789), 5, 74, 77–82. A table showing how each councillor voted in committee and in the council is found in LAC, RG4 B6, Records of the Quebec Legislative Council to 1791, 18, File 1787.

27 LAC, RG4 B6, Records of the Quebec Legislative Council, ordinances and working papers, 18, File 1787, copy of the dissent in Mabane's hand. This text, with minor differences, was recorded in LAC, RG1 E1, Journals of the Legislative Council of Quebec, 109, Minute Book E (15 January 1787–30 April 1789), 82, under the date 16 April 1787.

28 One slave who might have inspired Mabane's motion of April 1785 was Joseph Beaumenil (alias Joseph, Joseph Baumini, Joseph Beaumenais, Joseph Beauminet, Joseph Beaumini, Joseph Bominique, Joseph Dominique) of Quebec, then close to forty years old. On 9 February,

he asked the Court of Common Pleas to order notary J. Antoine Panet to provide him with a copy of the 1768 deed by which his then master, ship captain Antoine Cureux *dit* Saint-Germain, had sold him to merchant Michel Fortier. Saint-Germain and Fortier, brothers-in-law, were both dead, as was notary Jean-Claude Panet, Antoine Panet's father, who had drawn up the deed. "The aforesaid Joseph Bominique wishing, with good reason, to be apprised of the arrangements made between the said Messrs. St Germain & Fortier relative to himself, humbly requests that you order Mr A. Panet, notary of this city, to deliver to your petitioner a copy of the said deed, inasmuch as he is a party thereto, & the one most concerned by its contents [translation]." Panet gave Beaumenil a copy of the deed on 21 February. If Beaumenil had hoped to find there some key to his release, he was disappointed: all that the deed provided for was the sale of Beaumenil and another slightly younger slave named Michel to Fortier for a total of 4,000 schelins (about £165). Beaumenil, however, appears to have been freed within the next five years. He married a black woman named Marie Louise, by whom he had a daughter in 1790 (she died in May 1791 at the age of seven months) and a son who died at birth in 1795. After the death of his first wife, he was married again in 1799 to servant Marie Thérèse Laisné, daughter of a French-Canadian farming couple from St-Vallier (BANQ, notary J.C. Panet, 27 October 1768, with appended petition of 9 February 1785; register of Notre-Dame Church, Quebec, 28 September 1767, 9 October 1790, 9 May 1791, 12 January 1795, 16 April 1799).

29 Winks, *The Blacks in Canada*, 28.
30 *Édits et Ordonnances*, 2:105, 308–9, "Ordonnance Concernant l'affranchissement des Esclaves," 1 September 1736. Mention is made elsewhere in this book of some free blacks of prewar years, including Jean François Dominique *dit* Mentor who was freed at his master's death in 1748 and became a silversmith; Louis Antoine, who sold himself into slavery in 1761, then became free again at his master's death in 1769; Louise, who was dealing in tobacco in 1761 and successfully sued a customer for non-payment; Jacques César *dit* Jasmin and his wife Marie Élisabeth Charles, who were freed at their wedding in 1763; and Marianne Caploux and her son, Jean-Baptiste Quéry, of Sorel, freed by their master in 1765. There were others, like Joseph Hypolite and his wife, Marie Magdeleine, slaves who had become "neigres libres" by the time their son Louis was born in June 1760, three months before the military surrender of New France; Charles, a "nègre libre" in the spring of 1761 when he was sued by his former landlord for back rent; and Charles Larramée *dit* Latour who, after the death of his mistress, a widow named Latour, and according to her instructions, was freed by her heirs on 6 July 1770 (BANQ, notary P. Panet de Méru, no. 3505, 13 July 1770; register of Notre Dame Church, 26 June 1760; TL12, Chambre des milices, Registres des procès-verbaux d'audience en appel – 28 octobre 1760–26 avril 1764, 7 April 1761).
31 The claim was made in an obituary of Thomas York, who died at an advanced age at Cobourg, Canada West, on 11 March 1848: "We are informed that Mr York was born in Guinea, and was seized and sold as a slave in New York. At the breaking out of the Revolutionary war his master came into Canada, and Mr Y. was for several years held a slave in this Province. At the time Prince Wm. Henry was in Montreal, Mr Y. headed a number of colored persons who applied to the Prince to know if they were rightfully held in bondage. He replied they were not, and that he would represent their case to the King, his father, on his return; which he did,

though Mr Y. was held in slavery seven years longer. He was at one time a follower of Gen. Burgoyne's army" (*Pilot*, 25 March 1848, copied from the Cobourg *Provincialist*). There may be some truth to this story. Prince William did visit Montreal in September 1787 when he was serving with a Royal Navy. But the only Thomas York (alias York Thomas) found in the archival records of Montreal around this time was a free black man hired as a servant by New York Loyalist Phillip Peter Lansingh, a lieutenant in the 2nd Battalion, King's Royal Regiment of New York, in October 1781. He was rehired by Lansingh for another three years in July 1785, but his marriage in 1786 may have ended in his leaving Lansingh's service soon afterward. He and his bride, Margaret McCloud, were identified as "both Negroes" and said to have been "Married by leave of their respective Masters." They are believed to be the Thomas and Marguerite, the black parents of Marguerite, born on 24 October 1790, who lived just one month. As a widowed labourer of about forty in 1807, Thomas York married the twenty-year-old widow Flora Freeman (alias Mary Freeman, Sarah Trueman), by whom he had five children: Flora (born 1808), Sally (1809–1811), Thomas (born 1811), Eleanor (1814–1815), and Russell (1816). Nothing more has been found on this family at Montreal after their son Russell's death in November 1816 (BANQ, register of Christ Church, 22 January 1786; register of Notre-Dame Church, 20 and 23 November 1790; register of St Gabriel Presbyterian Church, 6 September 1807, 15 November 1816; notary J.G. Beek, no. 15, 31 October 1781, and Baux et protêts, 1:149, 15 July 1785).
32 Of the forty-three advertisements of slave sales that appeared in the newspapers, only one, in the *Quebec Gazette* of 21 August 1788, identified the slave by name. See Appendix I/A.
33 *Gazette*, 22 January 1798. The advertisement was published in two successive issues of the newspaper, on 22 and 29 January. The date of 18 January at the foot of the notice suggests that it was first posted as a handbill before being published in the first ensuing issue of the weekly newspaper on 22 January.
34 BANQ, notary N.B. Doucet, no. 9389, 16 January 1822; register of Quebec Anglican Church, 17 June and 30 December 1787; register of Christ Church, Montreal, 23 September 1823. POBR 2:23.
35 See BANQ, notary N.B. Doucet, no. 12216, will of Dominique Rousseau, 4 December 1824. See also Derome, "Dominique Rousseau."
36 Spring and summer were the favoured times for escapes, if the notices published in newspapers are any indication (see Appendix I/A). No court record survives of Charlotte's case; the only contemporary account is found in a petition of Montreal district slave-owners of 1 April 1799, presented to the Legislative Assembly of Lower Canada on 19 April. The English text of the petition is found in JALC 1799, 122–8, and the account of Charlotte's case on page 126. It is reproduced in Mackey, *Black Then*, 187–90. The French version of the petition was reproduced in Viger and LaFontaine, *De l'esclavage*, 29–33.
37 For Trim, see chapters 3 and 5. There is no doubt of his marriage to Charlotte, even if no official record has survived. It is possible that they were privately married, as in the case of Jacob Smith and Catherine Coll, outlined below. The earliest documentary evidence found of Charlotte's marriage to Trim is the baptismal record of Ann Ashley in September 1808, where "Charlotte Trimm" is recorded as a sponsor (BANQ, register of Christ Church, 25 September 1808).

38 Lambert, "James Monk." Stier, "Chief Justice Sir James Monk," xiv, 42–7.
39 JALC 1799, 126–7, Petition of Montreal-area slave-owners.
40 As with Charlotte, and probably for the same reason – that she appeared before Monk outside the regular quarterly sittings of the court – there is no record of Judith's case other than the reference to it in the slave-owners' petition of 1799 (JALC 1799, 126). On the point of a house of correction versus jail, see Riddell, "The Slave in Canada," 308–10. In 1799, at the March Term of the Court of King's Bench, the grand jury pressed the need for a house of correction. The necessary legislation was passed in the Assembly that spring, and a facility opened that year. See *Gazette*, 11 March 1799. Fyson, *Magistrates, Police, and People*, 29–31.
41 In the Court of Common Pleas in 1789, George Young testified that, as keeper of the jail, it was his duty to take custody of "all servants or slaves committed to the prison upon complaint of their masters to the civil authority" (Viger and LaFontaine, *De l'esclavage*, 46–7).
42 JALC 1799, 126–7.
43 BANQ, notary J.A. Gray, nos 73 and 74, 25 August 1797. KBCV, June Term 1798, *Jervis George Turner v. Thomas J. Sullivan*, deposition of Margery Campbell, 16 October 1798. Viger and LaFontaine, *De l'esclavage*, 55.
44 BANQ, notary J.G. Beek, no. 1186, 26 February 1798.
45 LAC, RG4, A1, Civil and Provincial Secretary Lower Canada, 1760–1840, 66:21153–5, "Memorial James Frazer Current of St Mary's near Montreal 13th March 1798 Respecting two Negroes."
46 KBCV, June Term 1798, no. 52, *Jervis George Turner v. Thomas J. Sullivan*. Viger and Lafontaine, *De l'esclavage*, 52–6. John Turner Sr had died on 3 January 1798 (BANQ, register of Christ Church, 5 January 1798).
47 BANQ, notary J. Papineau, no. 2701, 27 January 1798. KBCV, *André Winclefosse v. Nicholas Marchesseau & uxor*, no. 33, June Term 1798. The copy of the deed of sale in Papineau's records give the price as 400 livres, or roughly £16 10s; the copy filed in court correctly gives the price as 1,500 livres, or £62 10s, the sum that Winklefoss paid for Augustin.
48 *Gazette*, 27 August 1798. The notice, dated 12 August, was published in the newspaper of 20 and 27 August.
49 Quebec newspapers had stopped running such advertisements well before Montreal's only paper. In the *Quebec Gazette*, the last notice for the sale of a slave was dated 9 October 1793, and the last for an escaped slave was published on 22 May 1794.
50 Mary Martin was known under her successive married names as Mary Wiggans, Mary Jacobs, and Mary Smith. Even after she married Robert Smith in 1788, she was often called Mary Jacobs, up to her death on 5 February 1806 (BANQ, register of Christ Church, 27 July 1767 and 19 November 1788; notary J.A. Gray, no. 397, 11 October 1799; CT601, S1, Cour supérieure, Testaments olographes, no. 32, will of Mary Martin, 30 September 1801, probated 25 February 1806).
51 BANQ, notary J.G. Beek, no. 290, 4 December 1785.
52 CCP, *Mary Jacobs v. Donald Fisher & wife*, 1787–1788, contains a copy of the Fishers' deed of mortgage to Jacobs of 30 June 1787. The Fishers' acknowledgment, dated 30 June 1787, of the 1785 deed of sale of the two slaves is appended to the deed of sale. The lands mortgaged by the Fishers were Lot 24 (100 acres) in Township no. 1 (Charlottenburgh), sold to them on

NOTES TO PAGES 51–3

1 February 1787 by Duncan MacCarter, and Lot 40 and half of Lot 41 (500 acres total) of Township no. 1, second concession on the north side of the River aux Raisins, bought on 18 May 1787 from Daniel Wilkinson.
53 BANQ, notary J.G. Beek, no. 380, 29 February 1788. CCP, *Mary Jacobs v. Donald Fisher & Wife*, July Term 1788. *Gazette*, 29 November 1787, 1 January and 5 February 1789.
54 BANQ, notary L. Chaboillez, no. 160, 3 March 1789, no. 222, 11 September 1789, and no. 285, 6 March 1790. CCP, *Rosseter Hoyle v. Donald Fisher & Wife*, March Term 1788; *Mary Jacobs v. Donald Fisher & Wife*, July Term, 1788; *Rosseter Hoyle v. Donald Fisher & Wife*, July Term 1789. Viger and LaFontaine, *De l'esclavage*, 43.
55 CCP, May Term 1792, *Robert Smith & Mary his Wife v. Finlay Fisher*, plaintiffs' declaration, 24 May 1792. Fisher does not seem to have filed a reply to this complaint until the following 19 November.
56 CCP, May Term 1793, *Robert Smith & Wife v. Finlay Fisher*; court register, 14, 18, 22 and 31 May 1793.
57 For the rescue at Boston of a Virginia slave who fled to Montreal in 1851 and lived out his life there, see Collison, *Shadrach Minkins: From Fugitive Slave to Citizen*, especially chapters 7–8. The rescue at Detroit of Kentucky slaves Thomas and Lucy Blackburn, who went on to make their home at Toronto, is treated in Smardz Frost, *I've Got a Home in Glory Land*, chapter 8. See also von Frank, *The Trials of Anthony Burns*, concerning a Virginia slave who, arrested at Boston in 1854 and returned to slavery, ended his days as pastor of Zion Baptist Church at St Catharines, Ont., in 1862.
58 CCP, register, 18 and 22 May 1793.
59 BANQ, register of Christ Church, 24 February 1799.
60 LAC, MG19 A2, Jacobs-Ermatinger Estate fonds, 8:27A–27B.
61 LAC, MG19 A2, Jacobs-Ermatinger Estate fonds, 5:4, 61 and 62, Michael (Michel) Cornud to the widow Jacobs, 22 August 1786, Cornud to Dr Jean-Baptiste Rieutord, 29 July 1790, and Cornud to Dr and Mrs. Rieutord, 14 October 1790; 25:61, no. 3345, Joseph Vignau to Cornud, 25 September 1790; MG23 GII 3, Edward William Gray Papers, v. 4, Gray to Rieutord, 9 August 1790. Samuel Jacobs' widow married Trois-Rivières surgeon Jean-Baptiste Rieutord. Merchant Michel Cornud of Quebec and Sheriff Edward William Gray of Montreal were the executors of Jacobs' estate.
62 CQS, *Eden Johnston v. Diah*, deposition of Eden Johnston and arrest warrant for Diah, both 8 October 1794; court register, *Eden Johnston v. Diah a negro – his slave*, 14 October 1794. LAC, RG4 B45, Declarations of Aliens under the Alien Act, 34 Geo. III c. 5, Lower Canada, 1794–1811, f. 244, 23 September 1794. *The Times*, Quebec, 20 October 1794. These documents are reproduced in Mackey, *Black Then*, 203–05.
63 For Charles Blake's slaves, see note 44 above and Appendix III. In the mid-1780s, James Finlay had owned Peggy Finlay, of whom Jacques Viger wrote: "I saw two deeds of sale for the same negress, one of 9 June 1783 by Elias Smith to James Finlay, the other by Finlay to Patrick Langan of 14 May 1788, both for the sum of 50 pounds. Her name was given as Peg." The sale from Smith to Finlay, father-in-law and former fur-trading partner of John Gregory, took place on 9 June 1784, not 1783. In June 1783, Smith had not yet left New York for Montreal, as is evident from a memorial he addressed that August to Guy Carleton, then stationed at New

York as commander in chief of British forces in North America. Peggy Finlay died at Montreal on 22 June 1805 (BANQ, register of Christ Church, 24 June 1805. LAC, MG19 A3, Askin Family fonds, 33:10959–60; MG23 B21, Headquarters Papers of the British Army in America, 77, memorial of Elias Smith, 7 August 1783. POBR I:225. Viger and LaFontaine, *De l'esclavage*, 21–2). Alexander Henry had a black woman named Phillis Murray, allegedly forty-two, "living with" him in early 1797, probably as a slave. The slave Manuel Allen (name recorded as Mandaville Turner) and free blacks Caesar Johonnot and Margaret (Plauvier) Moore were the sponsors at her baptism (BANQ, register of Christ Church, 5 March 1797). For a 1778 slave transaction involving Henry, see Appendix I/A n25.

64 The record of this wedding of 17 October 1791 is found in no church register, but a certificate attesting to it from the Reverend John Young was filed in the Court of Common Pleas on 22 February 1792 (KBCV, October Term 1796, no. 2, *Jacob Smith v. Peter McFarlane*). For Jacob Smith, see chapter 3.

65 Mabon, a baker, married Sarah Stanley at Montreal in 1780. In 1806, the widowed Stanley married widower John Gerbrand Beek, a notary and surveyor of customs at the port of Montreal (BANQ, register of Christ Church, 15 October 1780, 17 May 1806; notary J.M. Mondelet, no. 3035, 17 May 1806).

66 KBCV, October Term 1796, no. 2, *Jacob Smith v. Peter McFarlane*. CCP, *Jacob Smith v. Peter McFarlane*, copy of judgment in appeal, 19 July 1793 (the text of this judgment, with minor variations, is reproduced in Viger and LaFontaine, *De l'esclavage*, 49–51). CQS, October Term 1793, complaint of Peter McFarlane, 5 September 1793; court register, *The King on the prosecution of Peter McFarlane v. Jacob Smith*, 7 November 1793.

67 BANQ, notary L. Chaboillez, no. 2919, 4 May 1798.

68 BANQ, notary J.G. Delisle, no. 880, 28 July 1794, and no. 2014, 18 August 1795; notary J.B. Planté, no. 1022, 7 September 1795; notary C. Stewart, 16 November 1795 and 17 June 1799. Beatson sold Sylvie to James Medcalfe, master of the brig *Maria*. For Jones's slave dealings, see Appendix III.

69 BANQ, register of Notre-Dame Church, 3 January 1790; notary L. Chaboillez, no. 3676, 14 September 1799.

70 *Journals of the Continental Congress*, 32:334–43, 13 July 1787, "An Ordinance for the government of the territory of the United States North West of the river Ohio," Article 6. Girardin, "Slavery in Detroit," 415. See also Anonymous, "Copies of papers in possession of the Historical Society, at Detroit: Opinions of Judge Woodward relative to the subject of slavery"; Riddell, "An International Complication between Illinois and Canada Arising out of Slavery," 123–4, and the same author's *The Slave in Canada*, 323–4. Campeau could argue that he had a right to keep slaves already in his possession, under Article 2 of Jay's Treaty, which provided that on the surrender to the United States of the British-held posts in American territory, "All settlers and traders, within the precincts or jurisdiction of the said posts, shall continue to enjoy, unmolested, all their property, of every kind, and shall be protected therein" (*American State Papers*, Series I: Foreign Relations, 1:520, "Treaty of Amity, Commerce, and Navigation, between His Britannic Majesty, and the United States of America, by their President, with the advice and consent of their Senate." Hartgrove, "Story of Marie L. Moore and Fannie M. Richards," 27.).

71 BANQ, notary L. Chaboillez, no. 1436, 15 June 1795, and nos 2564 and 2565, 31 August 1797. Berthelet had bought Sarah in 1795 for 600 livres from Joseph Louis Ainsse, a former Indian Department interpreter at Michilimackinac, who stated that he had himself bought her in 1788 from Alexis Rivard *dit* Maisonville of Detroit. Sarah was said to be about forty-five when Berthelet bought her, and still about forty-five two years later, when he set her "free."
72 KBCV, February Term 1800, *R v. James Fraser*. Viger and LaFontaine, *De l'esclavage*, 56–63. The only other King's Bench judge, James Walker, had died on 31 January.
73 BANQ, notary J.G. Beek, no. 874, 15 February 1794. *Quebec Gazette*, 27 February 1794.
74 *Great Britain, Statutes at Large*, 30 George III, 1790, c. 27, "An act for encouraging new settlers in his Majesty's colonies and plantations in America," Section 1.
75 *Gazette*, 20 August 1798.
76 Winks, *The Blacks in Canada*, 26.
77 LAC, RG4, A1, Quebec and Lower Canada: Correspondence received by Civil and Prov. Secretaries; records of the clerk of the Executive Council (1760–1840), 66:21153–55, "Memorial James Frazer Current of St Mary's near Montreal 13th March 1798 Respecting two Negroes."
78 The court's terse decision is found in KBCV, February Term 1800, *R v. James Fraser*. It was entered in evidence in SLCC, *Pierre v. Gabriel Chouteau*, November 1842, no. 125, 102, and *Mary Charlotte v. Gabriel Chouteau*, November 1843, no. 13, 259, and published in Viger and LaFontaine, *De l'esclavage*, 63.
79 JALC 1800, 18 April 1800, 154.
80 *Great Britain, Statutes at Large*, 5 Geo. II (1732), c. 7, "An Act for the more easy Recovery of Debts in His Majesty's Plantations and Colonies in America," and 37 Geo. III (1797), c. 119, "An Act to repeal so much of an act, made in the fifth year of the reign of his late majesty King George the Second, intituled, *An act for the more easy recovery of debts in his Majesty's plantations and colonies in America,* as makes negroes chattels for the payment of debts."
81 In 1792, the *Quebec Gazette* was rather sanguine about the imminent end of the international slave trade (Britain and the United States would not outlaw it until 1 January 1808) and a peculiar economic benefit that Lower Canada could expect to reap from this: the "almost certain advancement" of its maple sugar industry, from the decline of West Indian sugar production that was bound to follow the abolition of the slave trade (*Quebec Gazette*, 19 April 1792).
82 Stowe, *A Key to Uncle Tom's Cabin*, 71–2.
83 HP, MS21867:2–55. For another instance of Monk's detachment on the question of slavery, see Appendix I n25. It would be interesting to know how Monk had come by Charles, his "negro Srvt," who drowned at Quebec in 1786 at the reputed age of seventeen, and Prince Brown, "Negro Man," who died in Monk's service on 20 September 1812 (BANQ, register of Quebec Anglican Church, 25 June 1786; register of Christ Church, Montreal, 21 September 1812).
84 The details of the case are taken from KBCV, *John Dease v. Joseph Ainsse*, no. 65, October Term 1799. Dease died on 16 January 1801 (BANQ, register of Notre Dame Church, 19 January 1801); his executors, Sir John Johnson and Dr Robert Jones, carried on the lawsuit after his death.
85 LAC, MG23 GIII 26, Louis-Joseph Ainsse fonds, folders 89, 90. Lyons had bought Frank at Detroit the previous 21 June from fellow merchant Thomas Finchley for £200 New York currency (£125 Quebec currency). If the records are to be believed, he sold Frank to Ainsse a little

more than two weeks later at a considerable loss – "Twelve Hundred livres current Currency of Quebec equal to Eighty Pounds New York Cy.," or £50 Quebec currency. For Sarah, see note 71, above.

86 BANQ, notary L. Chaboillez, no. 2359, 10 March 1797.
87 An anti-slavery argument presented in the same year as Robin's case before the Supreme Court of New Brunswick, the "Ward Chipman Slavery Brief" in the Beaverbrook Collection of the Archives and Special Collections of the University of New Brunswick, is of considerable interest (accessed online in 2006–07 at www.lib.unb.ca/Texts/NBHistory/chipman/index.html). Equally interesting is the *Opinions of Several Gentlemen of the Law, on the Subject of Negro Servitude, in the Province of Nova-Scotia*, published in 1802 (online copy from the Special Collections department of the McPherson Library, University of Victoria, British Columbia, at http://gateway.uvic.ca/spcoll/digit/slavery_opinion/index.html). Both of these cases and broader issues of the legality of slavery are discussed in T.W. Smith, *The Slave in Canada*, 97–117, and Winks, *The Blacks in Canada*, 102–10.
88 BANQ, register of Christ Church, 31 May 1778. KBCV, June Term 1798, no. 52, *Jervis George Turner v. Thomas J. Sullivan. Quebec Gazette*, 22 June 1797. Perry, born to tailor James Perry and his wife, Amelia Lambe, on 10 May 1778, trained under the two lawyers who successively represented Jacob Smith in his suit against Peter McFarlane. He was not yet fourteen when he began his apprenticeship as a clerk to James Walker in April 1792. After the latter's appointment to the bench, Perry's apprenticeship was transferred in November 1796 to Stephen Sewell, who had himself trained in the law in New Brunswick in the office of Ward Chipman (BANQ, register of Christ Church, 18 February 1776, 31 May 1778; notary J.G. Delisle, no. 489, 11 April 1792, and no. 2316, 11 November 1796).
89 *JALC* 1800, 18 April 1800, Petition of Montreal slave-owners, 154.
90 *JALC* 1799, 19 April 1799, Petition of Montreal slave-owners, 122–8.
91 *JALC* 1800, 18 April 1800, Petition of Montreal slave-owners, 150–6. The manuscript petitions have not been found. As a result, we do not know how many slave-owners signed them and who they were. The English text of both petitions is reproduced in Mackey, *Black Then*, 187–93.
92 BANQ, notary J.P. Gauthier, no. 231, 15 September 1792. Papineau, father of the future Patriote leader Louis-Joseph Papineau, bought Prince, said to be about fifty-four, for 300 livres (£12 10s) from tailor Joseph Benoit *dit* L'hyvernois. The claim made by Gérard Parizeau (*La société canadienne-française au XIXe siècle*, 395) that Joseph Papineau could not abide the idea of human bondage and that he presented a petition for abolition to the Assembly is not supported by the evidence.
93 See Chiasson, "James Kerr."
94 Elias Smith had moved to Upper Canada by April 1801 when he swore the oaths of allegiance, declaring himself to be "now of the Township of Hope" (Oaths of Allegiance, Port Hope and Hope Township [1801–06], compiled by Phyllis H. White, accessed January 2008 at www.nhb.com/hunter/oaths.htm). In 1797, Smith's son, Elias Smith Jr, a distiller, hired at Montreal a free black man named Tymon Richards for one year as a "Servant or Workman either in the Province of Lower and Upper Canada," promising that on top of £20 plus room and board, he would "give to the said Tymon Richards at the expiration of the Said Year one Certificate gratis for Two hundred Acres of land in the Township of Hope provided he Settle on

the same and fulfil the Duties required by law" (BANQ, notary L. Chaboillez, no. 2286, 3 February 1797). The Oaths of Allegiance of Hope Township have "Simon Richards," a thirty-three-year-old black man, living in Hope Township in June 1801.
95 LAC, MG23 HII 13, Elias Smith fonds, Letter Book 1799–1800, Elias Smith to David Smith & Co., 29 March 1800. The law Smith spoke of was 37 Geo III (1797), c. 104, "An Act for regulating the shipping and carrying of Slaves in British Vessels from the Coast of Africa."
96 Ibid., Smith to John Grant, 27 March 1800.
97 Ibid., Smith to Frederick Petry, and Smith to Joseph Papineau, both 8 April 1800.
98 Cuthbert does not appear to have been a slave-owner, but his parents, James Cuthbert Sr and Catherine Cairns (d. 1785), were, as was his stepmother, Rebecca Stockton, his father's third wife (they were married in 1786). A "petite négresse" slightly more than one year old, belonging to James Cuthbert Sr, was buried at Berthier in March 1773. A "daughter of Mrs. Cuthbert's Black Girl," born about February 1790, was privately baptized four months later at Sorel. In the will that he drew up shortly before his death in September 1798, Cuthbert Sr stipulated that his "negro Wench named Margaret and her Children shall be deemed and considered to be the Property of the said Rebecca Stockton otherwise called Rebecca Cuthbert." Rebecca Stockton was the daughter of the late Judge John Stockton of the Court of Common Pleas in Somerset County, NJ (BANQ, register of Ste-Geneviève Church, Berthier, 3 March 1773; register of Christ Church, Sorel, 28 June 1790; CT601, S1, Cour supérieure, Testaments olographes, no. 23, will of James Cuthbert, 4 August 1798).
99 LAC, MG23 HII 13, Elias Smith fonds, Letter Book 1799–1800, Smith to Petry, 5 May 1800; Smith to James Robins, 27 July 1800. JALC 1800, 156, 158, 218, 222, 232–4, 242, 268.
100 BANQ, notary J. Papineau, no. 3069, 11 August 1800. Louis Joseph *did* Pompé was said to be five and a half years old at his baptism on 20 May 1786 at St-Michel Church, Vaudreuil.
101 JALC 1801, 54, 58, 72, 122 204, 234, 290. The committee chairman, merchant Francis Badgley, elected that summer in the East Ward of Montreal with Pierre-Louis Panet, was the father of William Badgley, the future judge.
102 BANQ, notary A. Dumas, 3 October 1792.
103 JALC 1792–93, 188, 314, 462, 540–2. One month later, on the day before he sold the seigneury of Argenteuil, Panet granted a lifetime lease there to Ben, a black resident. This suggests that Panet wanted to see Ben settled before the new seigneur took over. On 18 July 1786, Panet had acted as agent for his friend, Montrealer Joseph Quesnel, in the sale of Betsy, a "Femme Negre," to Quebec merchant Joseph Drapeau, who resold her four days later to merchant Mathew Macnider for £20 (BANQ, notary P.R. Gagnier, no. 952, 23 May 1793, and no. 953, 24 May 1793; notary P.L. Deschenaux, no. 855, 22 July 1786).
104 JALC 1803, 160, 188, 208–10.
105 JALC 1802, 104–8, 302, 340–2, 354–8, 360–4, 374. *Quebec Gazette*, 25 February, 1 April and 8 April 1802. On 19 February 1802, James McGill presented a petition from residents of Montreal calling for such a law. The bill was introduced on 19 March. Ten days later, the committee studying the bill reported that it was too late in the session for the measure to pass as it stood, "but as they are convinced of the necessity of certain regulations being made," they proposed that the Assembly adopt a general bill authorizing the magistrates of Montreal to act in the matter. A bill was introduced immediately, read twice that day, and adopted the next day, March

30. The Legislative Council approved the bill that same day, and it was given royal assent on 5 April as "An Act to empower the Justices of the Peace, to make for a limited time, Rules and Regulations for the Government of Apprentices and others." This example shows that the Assembly could act expeditiously when its members believed it necessary to do so. Servants and apprentices were a public concern – everyone had servants – whereas slaves were the particular concern of the few people who had invested in them.

106 White's advocacy of the measure blighted his political future. See Riddell, *The Life of John Graves Simcoe*, 192–3, 202 n11.
107 Anonymous, *Canadian Letters: Description of a Tour Thro' the Provinces of Lower and Upper Canada, in the Course of the Years 1792 and '93*, 59.
108 *Statutes of the Province of Upper Canada*, 33 Geo. III (1793), c. 7, "An Act to prevent further introduction of slaves, and to limit the term of contracts for servitude within this province."
109 Simcoe, *Correspondence of Lieut. Governor John Graves Simcoe*, 2:53, Simcoe to Colonial Secretary Henry Dundas, 16 September 1853.
110 Christie and Dumond, *George Bourne and 'The Book and Slavery Irreconcilable,'* 204. In urging immediate abolition in the British West Indies in 1824 – not by legislation but by a boycott of slave-produced sugar – the Quaker Elizabeth Heyrick denounced gradual abolition as the satanic "artifice of the slave holder," meant to gull opponents of slavery: "By converting the cry for *immediate*, into *gradual* emancipation, the prince of slave holders, 'transformed himself, with astonishing dexterity, into an angel of light,' – and thereby – 'deceived the very elect' " (Heyrick, *Immediate, Not Gradual, Abolition*, 9–20).
111 Askin, *The John Askin Papers*, 1: 476, D.W. Smith to John Askin, 25 June 1793.
112 Idem.
113 *Statutes of the Province of Upper Canada*, 33 Geo. III (1793), c. 7, "An Act to prevent further introduction of slaves, and to limit the term of contracts for servitude within this province."
114 Melish, in *Disowning Slavery*, 84, notes of the reaction to similar gradual-abolition measures elsewhere: "People of color did not celebrate gradual emancipation anywhere in New England. ... The reason seems clear: the statutes effectively preserved the status quo."
115 Riddell considered that the absence of legislation in Lower Canada had the same effect: "As Lower Canada passed no legislation on slavery, the extradition of fugitives was made impossible and Canada became therefore an asylum for the oppressed in the United States" (Riddell, *The Slave in Canada*, 313). Regarding Upper Canada's status as a place of refuge, an interesting exchange took place in 1819 between US Secretary of State John Quincy Adams and the British chargé d'affaires at Washington, Gibbs Crawfurd Antrobus. Adams inquired whether the owners of Tennessee slaves who had run away to Malden (Amherstburg), Upper Canada, could expect help from the government there to reclaim them. Antrobus replied that "the Legislature of His Majesty's Province of Upper Canada having adopted the Law of England as the Rule of decision in all questions relative to Property and Civil rights, the Negroes have, by their residence in Canada, become free, whatever may have been their former condition in this Country [the US], and should any attempt be made to infringe upon this right of freedom, these Negroes would have it in their power to compel the interference of the Courts of Law in His Majesty's Province of Upper Canada for their protection, and the Executive Government could in no manner restrain or direct the Judges in the Exercise of their duty" (Manning, *Diplomatic Correspondence of the United States*, 1: 294, 909–10).

116 *JAUC* 1793, 32, 33, 35–6, 38, 42. *JCUC* 1793, 25–8.
117 *Statutes of the Province of Upper Canada*, 33 Geo. III, c. 7, "An Act to prevent further introduction of slaves, and to limit the term of contracts for servitude within this province," Section I.
118 Riddell, *The Life of John Graves Simcoe*, 192–3, 202 n11. Winks, in *The Blacks in Canada*, 97–8, suggests that the bill "might not have been legal had anyone chosen to challenge it … however, in these years before the Colonial Laws Validity Act [1865], no one contested Upper Canada's power to limit slavery within its own borders, and by the time the Imperial Parliament clarified the status of contradictory colonial enactments, slavery was illegal throughout the Empire."
119 *JAUC* 1793, 42–3. *JCUC* 1793, 33.
120 Riddell, *The Slave in Canada*, 310.
121 *JAUC* 1798, 64, 67, 69–71, 74. *JCUC* 1798, 67–70. This move occurred under the administration of President Peter Russell, himself a slave-owner. The measure was entitled "a Bill to authorize and allow persons coming into this Province to settle to bring with them their Negro Slaves." The Assembly adopted the bill on 20 June 1798. Voting in favour were speaker Colonel John Macdonell, Richard Beasley, Benjamin Hardison, Christopher Robinson, Captain Thomas Fraser, Edward Jessup, Samuel Street, and Dr Solomon Jones; voting against were Solicitor-General Robert Isaac Dey Gray, David McGregor Rogers, John Cornwall, and Captain Richard Wilkinson. After debating and amending the Assembly's bill, the Legislative Council approved a motion that "said Bill be read a third time three months hence," which, as the session was to end in a few days, meant that the Council effectively killed it.
122 T.W. Smith, *The Slave in Canada*, 97. Winks, *The Blacks in Canada*, 102 n12. For Osgoode, see Audet, *Les juges en chef de la province de Québec 1764–1924*, 31–6; Hamilton, *Osgoode Hall*, 20–1; Mealing, "William Osgoode"; Read, *Lives of the Judges of Upper Canada*, 26; P.G. Roy, *Les juges de la province de Québec*, 401; Turcotte, *Le Conseil Législatif de Québec 1774–1933*, 57–8. As T.W. Smith opined, the legend stems from the confusion of Osgoode, chief justice of Lower Canada, with his contemporary, James Monk, chief justice for the Montreal District. In his 1960 study, *L'esclavage au Canada français*, Trudel attributes to Osgoode all of Monk's anti-slavery rulings of 1798–1800. The error went uncorrected in the second edition of his work, published in 2004 under the title *Deux siècles d'esclavage au Québec*.
123 The words are taken from identical nineteenth-century accounts in the anonymous *History of the County of Brant*, 36, and *History of the County of Welland*, 36–7:

> The second session of the Parliament of Upper Canada was memorable for the abolition, by a unanimous vote, of negro slavery. By the 47th article of the capitulation the French Canadians had been allowed to retain their slaves, and the poison of this ever-accursed traffic might have continued in full play all through Lower Canada, but for the introduction, through the settlement of Upper Canada, of the emancipating spirit of English law.
>
> Our Parliament, at a time when labour was priceless, when the forests had to be fought against for dear life, determined to make the free air of their forests more free, by 'An Act to Prevent the further Introduction of Slaves.' Such was the first utterance of the voice of our national life, ever hearafter to speak with no uncertain sound where the interests of freedom and humanity demand expression. …

The Lower Canadian Parliament refused to follow the noble example of the upper Canadian Parliament in abolishing slavery. This was, however, effected by a decision of Chief Justice Osgoode that slavery in any part of Canada was contrary to law.

124 Canniff, *History of the Settlement of Upper Canada*, 474. In speaking in 1884 at celebrations of the 100th anniversary of the settlement of Upper Canada, the writer William Kirby sacrificed accuracy and nuance in praising the Loyalists' role in ending slavery (see U.E. Loyalist Centennial Committee, *The Centennial of the Settlement of Upper Canada by the United Empire Loyalists*, 114–50):

The States which had rebelled in the name of Liberty and had declared all men to be free and equal, did in their new constitution solemnly sanction the institution of human slavery, and perpetuate it, seemingly, for ever! While the U.E. Loyalists of Upper Canada, in their first parliament, and on this spot, made sacred by that Act of eternal justice, did without a dissenting voice, and without a claim for compensation, declare slavery to be for ever abolished in this Province! All honour to the true freemen and their noble governor Simcoe, who won for Canada the glory of being the first country in the world which abolished slavery by an Act of the Legislature! – and they not only set free their slaves, but placed them on a civil and political equality with themselves. We are not a boastful people, or we might justly boast of having taken the lead of all the world in that great act of justice to humanity. So far was Upper Canada in advance of all other people at that time, on this momentous question.

In light of such glowing fictions, it is no wonder that we still come across references to the Upper Canadian law of 1793 as an abolition law pure and simple, and one that wiped out slavery not just in Upper Canada, but in Canada as a whole. The Canadian government's Heritage Department website (www.canadianheritage.gc.ca), consulted in December 2005, stated: "Slavery existed in Canada from 1628 until it was abolished in Upper Canada in 1793 and throughout the entire British empire in 1833." The website referred to the 1793 law as the Abolition Act, and said in a brief, warped explanation of its thrust that it "freed slaves aged 25 and over and made it illegal to bring slaves into Upper Canada."

125 Anonymous, "Assignment of a Slave (1824)." Canniff, *History of the Settlement of Upper Canada*, 576. Gourlay, *Statistical Account of Upper Canada*, 241. T.W. Smith, *The Slave in Canada*, 95. Yeigh, *Ontario's Parliament Buildings*, 141–2. Writing of Sir Adam Wilson, one-time mayor of Toronto and chief justice of the Ontario Court of Queen's Bench, lawyer James Cleland Hamilton, said: "From him I learned of probably the last negro slaves in the Province, a boy called Hank, and a girl, Sukey, who belonged to Mrs. O'Reilly, mother of the late Miles O'Reilly, Q.C., well known as a lawyer and Master in Chancery in the City of Hamilton. They were seen at the O'Reilly homestead shortly before August, 1834, when slavery was abolished in the British possessions by the Imperial Act" (Hamilton, *Osgoode Hall*, 162). It is highly improbable that Hank and Sukey were slaves in 1834; black residents of the area would not have tolerated it. At Kingston the year before, mere suspicion that the black servant of a visiting American family was a slave had sparked a near-riot (*Kingston Chronicle & Gazette*, 21 September 1833).

126 Riddell, *The Slave in Canada*, 313 n19. In this note, Riddell adds: "For example one hears of two of the three slaves whom Captain Allan brought with him into Upper Canada from New

Jersey running away to Montreal. The owner pursued them to Montreal and searched for them in vain for ten days."
127 Ouellet, *Éléments d'histoire sociale du Bas-Canada*, 213.
128 T.W. Smith, *The Slave in Canada*, 89.
129 Phoebe, bought in Albany in February 1784 by Daniel Jones and sold by him on 24 May to innkeeper Pierce Ryan of Quebec (see Appendix III), went by the name Phoebe Jones and Phoebe Ryan, then Phoebe Johnson after she married Benjamin Johnson, another of Ryan's slaves, on 11 April 1790. They had three children – Sarah in 1791, Pierre, who lived only six months, in 1792, and Jean Benjamin in 1793. Her husband died in 1793. She had a son out of wedlock who was baptized at Montreal in October 1801 under the name William Taylor; the sponsors included blacks John Fleming and Sarah (Johnson) Luke, another former resident of Quebec (BANQ, register of Christ Church, 4 October 1801; register of Notre-Dame Church, Quebec, 23 January and 14 August 1792, 7 June 1793; register of Quebec Anglican Church, 11 April 1790, 11 March 1791, 8 May 1793).
130 BANQ, register of Christ Church, 29 November 1802. François was called Joseph Frank at their wedding. See chapter 3.
131 BANQ, register of L'Annonciation Church, Oka, 19 June 1809.
132 BANQ, register of St Gabriel Presbyterian Church, 17 December 1799, 26 May 1806; register of Notre-Dame Church, 24 April 1807.
133 BANQ, register of Notre-Dame Church, 10 September 1796; register of Quebec Anglican Church, 18 November 1798; register of St-Antoine-de-Padoue Church, St-Antoine-sur-Richelieu, 16 March 1802.
134 *Quebec Gazette*, 14 July 1803.
135 *JALC* 1804, 16 March 1804.
136 Of 190 sometime Montreal-area owners of black slaves for whom some death record is known, the number of deaths per decade is as follows:

1760s	4
1770s	9
1780s	21
1790s	43
1800s	30
1810s	39
1820s	26
1830s	11
1840s	6

A Joseph Roy who died at Montreal in 1856 at age eighty-five may have been the Jos. Roy who had offered a slave for sale there in 1786 (see Appendix I/A, notice 56), which would make him the last surviving Montreal slave-owner and the only one who could have been called to testify before the 1846 rogatory commission in the Missouri freedom suit of *Pierre v. Gabriel S. Chouteau*, discussed in chapter 1. The only other surviving Montreal slave-owner in 1846 was John Shuter, but he was living in England, where he died in 1847 at age seventy-two (see chapter 3 n8).

137 BANQ, register of the Hôpital-Général chapel, 2 and 28 October 1801, and 6 July 1802. Other entries are for François Anovre (Hanover) and Marie Thérèse Zémire, who died respectively in July and December 1800, the former a sixty-year-old slave of fur trader Charles Chaboillez and his wife, Marguerite Larchevêque *dit* La Promenade, and the latter the twenty-nine-year-old slave of Benoite Gaëtan, the widow of painter François Malepart de Beaucourt, (BANQ, register of Notre-Dame Church, 22 July 1800, and register of the Hôpital-Général chapel, 16 December 1800). One entry refers to a boy, Urbain, who died in 1802, one of the child slaves whom Jean-Baptiste Routier had brought back to Quebec in 1792, as mentioned in chapter 1 (BANQ, register of Notre-Dame Church, 13 February 1802. See n142, below). The latest such entry, in the register of Notre-Dame Church on 18 July 1808, is of the baptism of sixty-five-year-old Marie Catherine, identified as a "Négresse" belonging to merchant Pierre Berthelot. For the seventh entry, see n138 below.

138 BANQ, notary N.B. Doucet, no. 5080, 9 April 1818; notary H. Griffin, 9 May 1814; register of Notre-Dame Church, 27 January 1806, 5 January 1838. HDM, admission registers, Book i, 21 December 1821. MUA, RG4, C438, no. 11060, will of James McGill, 8 January 1811 (also found in PROB 11/1559). Berthelot, *Le bon vieux temps*, 2e série, 35, 46. The story in the latter work concerning Jacques' slave status in the 1820s mentions that "L'esclave de M. Desrivières était considéré comme enfant de la maison" (Mr Desrivières's slave was counted a member of the family). McGill did not mention Jacques by name in his will. He may have been covered by the following clause: "I Give and bequeath a suit of Mourning to each of my Servants."

139 De Gaspé, *Les Anciens Canadiens*, 292–3, 406–7. See also the same author's *Mémoires*, 73, 199. Neilson, "Slavery in Old Canada," 39, says: "I remember well my grandmother's stories of her childhood; (she died in 1866, aged 86,) she always spoke affectionately of a devoted negro slave named Lilique (Angélique) originally from Guadaloupe [sic]; she had been many years in the family; she positively refused her freedom and died at Three Rivers about 1808 or 1810."

140 BANQ, notary F. Tetu, 6 March 1807. Gray's will, drafted in French, named his slave Neron Bartholomy. Variants of the name included Nero Batermy, Barthelemy Nero, Barthelemi Néron, and Berthelmi Nero. Hospitalized at the Hôtel-Dieu at Québec in 1817, he was identified in the admission records as Nero Batermy, the fifty-eight-year-old Boston-born son of Thomas and Catherine Batermy, and, on another hospital stay from 19 January to 27 April 1818, as Barthelemy Nero, a fifty-six-year-old Boston-born domestic servant, widower of Marie Chalifour. At their wedding in 1796, his wife's name was written Magdalen McGraw, but at the birth and death of their son Vital that same year, she was called Magdelène or Magdelaine Chalifou (BANQ, HDQ admission registers, 8 August 1817, 19 January, 1 February, 1 March and 1 April 1818; register of Notre-Dame Church, Quebec, 28 March, 19 June and 6 July 1796).

141 POBR I:223.

142 One of the last two slave patients was nine-year-old Lubin, "nègre de Routier," who entered the hospital on 26 December 1801 and left on 2 January 1802; this slave of Jean-Baptiste Routier died that February and was buried under the name Urbain. The other was Marie, "negresse de md beaucour," who was a patient 1–22 January 1802 (BANQ, register of Notre-Dame Church, 13 February 1802. HDM, admission registers, Book E, 26 December 1801, and Book

D, 1 January 1822). The one possible exception found to the 1802 cut-off was twelve-year-old Nacée (Nancy?), hospitalized in January 1813, and identified as a "negresse ... de mr megille" – another "pseudo-slave" of James McGill or simply a hired servant.
143 Buchanan, *The Bench and Bar of Lower Canada Down to 1850*, 40–1. T.W. Smith, *The Slave in Canada*, 96–7.
144 Riddell, *The Slave in Canada*, 313.
145 T.W. Smith, *The Slave in Canada*, 125.
146 For a denunciation of the enslavement of children under the guise of gradual abolition as enacted in New York, see Stewart, *A Far Cry From Freedom*.
147 BANQ, notary F.M. Pétrimoulx, no. 3165, 10 January 1802. The deed does not identify Henry McEvoy's master. The boy may have been a slave of one of the Byrnes. In that case, the indenture would have represented an effort by them to retain his services, implying a recognition that they could no longer hold him as a slave.
148 Oral tradition holds that black slaves were buried at "Nigger Rock," on the property once owned by Loyalist Philip Luke. Anthropologist Roland Viau, who looked into the matter in 1998 on behalf of Quebec's ministry of culture and communications, believed the tradition credible, and that Nigger Rock was the last resting place of Luke's slaves. Theorizing that six slaves owned by Luke's mother, a resident of Albany County, NY, came into Luke's possession after her death in 1794, Viau says (translation): "On the Luke property (and on how many others?), these black slaves – probably six in number to begin with, but whose number, through births and perhaps purchases, increased to ten, twelve, fifteen by the time slavery was abolished in the British colonies, including Canada, on 28 August 1833 – set up their cabins ... undoubtedly near the potash works and lime kilns" where they were employed (Viau, *Ceux de Nigger Rock*, 90–1). There is no evidence that Luke acquired his mother's slaves, that their numbers subsequently increased, that slaves built shanties on the Luke property or worked at potash-making in the area. Nigger Rock may be the burial site of free blacks who lived in the area in the nineteenth century, but history strongly suggests that it is no "slave cemetery."

CHAPTER THREE

1 BANQ, notary P. Lukin Sr, no. 1251, 27 July 1798. For Trim, see chapter 5.
2 In a deposition she gave in 1828 in a court case pitting Trim against neighbour Simon Clark, Guillet (written Gayet) said that she was forty years old, a native of St-Domingue, and that her parents were born in Africa. She had lived at Trim's "for fifteen years and left his service about eight years ago" (KBCV, *John Trim v. Simon Clark*, 1823, no. 162, deposition of Catherine Gayet, 28 September 1828). The name Guillet was written variously as Diette, Gaillete, Gayet, Gillet, Goyet, Guillette, Guiot, Guyette; besides these variations, she was also recorded under the names Catherine, Marie Catherine, or simply Marie; Catherine Cora or Curra; and under the married names of Catherine Abdallah or Abdelah and Catherine Wright.
3 BANQ, register of Christ Church, 25 September 1808, 5 August and 3 September 1821; register of Notre-Dame Church, 27 July 1821; notary N.B. Doucet, no. 5080, 9 April 1818. Charlotte's godchildren were Ann Ashley, born in 1808 to former ship steward Robert Ashley and his wife, Margaret Pearce; and Hero Alexander Richardson, born in 1821, the son of Hero Richardson, a black veteran of the War of 1812, and of Dinah (Diana, Dianna) Morrison, a

former servant of James McGill's widow, Charlotte Guillimin. Guillimin left £10 in her will to "Dianna Morrisson ma servante." Dinah Morrison died one week after giving birth to her son. The boy himself lived only six weeks.
4 BANQ, notary N.B. Doucet, no. 9389, 16 January 1822.
5 BANQ, register of Christ Church, 23 September 1823.
6 *JALC* 1799, 19 April 1799, petition of Montreal slave-owners. Trudel, *Dictionnaire*, 109.
7 BANQ, register of St Gabriel Presbyterian Church, 4 March 1798.
8 At some unknown date (but see n11, below), John Shuter, born 27 December 1774, married Sarah Smith, who was born at New York City on 18 December 1780. They moved to England in the second decade of the nineteenth century (from early 1818, various court proceedings in Montreal refer to him as a resident of Longport in Staffordshire, then of London); he died there in 1847, she in 1854. When he was apprenticed to merchant Jacob Schieffelin in April 1791, Shuter was identified as the son of Alexander and Elizabeth Bissett of Sorel. Alexander Bissett, a language teacher, had acquired a twelve-year-old black slave girl from local innkeeper Mrs Jean Paterson in November 1784. The girl belonged to Paterson's daughter, a gift from her uncle, Loyalist John Cobham. Ownership was transferred to Bissett in payment of a loan of £40 to Mr and Mrs Patterson from Elizabeth Shautter (*sic*), who had since become Mrs Bissett. The Bissetts were to return the slave girl to the Patersons when they paid back the £40. Shuter was not quite ten years old then. It appears from his name that he may have been born to Elizabeth Shautter before she married Bissett (she had perhaps been previously married to John Sutter, alias John Shooter, a baker, who was hired at Montreal in 1787 by fur-trader Andrew Todd to work for fifteen months out of Detroit: cf. BANQ, notary J.G. Beek, no. 258, 11 April 1787). John Shuter entered on his apprenticeship with Schieffelin when he was sixteen. He was supposed to remain with him until he reached the age of twenty-one, but Schieffelin, who had fought on the British side in the American Revolution, returned to live in New York City in 1794. Schieffelin was a friend of Elias Smith; his wife, Hannah Lawrence of New York, a Quaker with anti-slavery leanings, was a cousin of slave-owning John Doty, rector of Christ Church at Sorel, or of Doty's wife, Lydia Burling. Sometime after Schieffelin's departure, Shuter formed a partnership with James Badgely (Badgley), an association that was dissolved in October 1796, when he continued operating a shop on his own on St-Paul Street, selling crockery, porcelain and glassware (BANQ, notary B. Faribault, 18 November 1784; notary J.G. Beek, no. 702, articles of apprenticeship John Shuter to Jacob Schieffelin, 18 April 1791, with authorization of his parents 4 April 1791, and cancellation of apprenticeship on 30 May 1795, retroactive to 1 October 1794. A manuscript copy of Shuter's indenture, without the accompanying documents, is also found at the New York Public Library, Schieffelin Family Papers, Box 1, Folder 1. Also in the Schieffelin Family Papers, see Box 1, Folder 1, John B. Lawrence to Hannah Lawrence Schieffelin, 11 July 1793; Box 7A, folder 1, Hannah Lawrence Schieffelin to her parents John and Ann Lawrence, 4 January 1790. KBCV, no. 92, 1818, *John Shuter v. Cornelius Truesdell*. LAC, MG25 G444, Elias Smith Family fonds, "The Descendants of Elias Smith 'U.E. of Hope' [1736–1820]" by Joseph Smith, *circa* 1900, edited by Suzanne A. Jackson and Phyllis White, 1987; and "Elias Smith 1736–1820: Merchant from Montreal and Nominee of Hope Township," 1988, Phyllis H. White and Suzanne A. Jackson. *Gazette*, 24 October 1796. *Pilot*, 30 April 1847).
9 BANQ, register St Gabriel Presbyterian Church, 19 January 1799.

NOTES TO PAGES 80–2

10 BANQ, register of Christ Church, 29 October 1797.
11 BANQ, notary J.G. Beek, no. 1078, 3 September 1796. Two months after he bought a slave, Shuter bought a house on St-Paul Street. These purchases suggest a major change in his living arrangements; perhaps this was when he married (BANQ, notary P. Lukin Sr, no. 899, 24 November 1796. *Quebec Gazette*, 8 December 1796).
12 BANQ, notary J.G. Beek, no. 1079, 3 September 1796.
13 Manuel Allen entered into a similar arrangement, without a proxy, when he was sold to Thomas John Sullivan in 1797. He signed an agreement with Sullivan to work as a "covenant servant" for five years, at the end of which, provided that he had served Sullivan faithfully, he was to go free (BANQ, J.A. Gray, no. 74, 25 August 1797). It is doubtful that this contract by a slave had any legal validity. As we saw in chapter 2, Allen deserted Sullivan's service in March 1798, claiming to be free. Whether it was that he felt legally or personally bound by the articles of servitude, he seems to have returned to work for Sullivan as a servant once he was declared free by the court in 1799 (see chapter 5, n11).
14 BANQ, register of Christ Church, 29 April 1798. Their sponsors were Samuel Luke, a black man who moved to Montreal from Quebec, and Sarah Mandaville, i.e., Sarah Jackson, wife of Manuel Allen.
15 BANQ, register of Christ Church, 16 December 1798. The witnesses were blacks Isaac Newton and Caesar Scipio. Newton was a Montreal resident (see chapter 9), but there is no other record of Caesar Scipio's presence at Montreal, which suggests that he lived elsewhere. One possibility: Upper Canada. The following letter of 10 March 1868 was written in old age by Adiel Sherwood to William Canniff. Sherwood, the son of a Loyalist, served as sheriff of the Johnstown District of Upper Canada from 1829 to 1864. In his *History of the Settlement of Upper Canada* (575–6), Canniff gave what appears to be an edited version of Sherwood's letter; it makes no mention of a Scipio, but a version of the same letter found in Leavitt, *History of Leeds and Grenville*, 20–1, does:

> as regards slaves, I only recollect two or three who were settled in the District of Johnstown. One colored man, in particular, named Caesar Congo, was owned by Captain Justus Sherwood ... Captain Justus Sherwood came, with his family [from Montreal], in the same brigade of boats with my father [in 1784], and located two miles above Prescott. I recollect distinctly Caesar Congo, then a stout young man. He often took the late Mr Justice [Levius P.] Sherwood and myself [boys then] on his back, to assist us in walking, while the boats were being drawn up the rapids. The boys used to call Caesar, 'Scippio.' Caesar was sold to a half-pay officer, Mr [Elijah] Bottom, who settled about six miles above Prescott. After twenty years' service [one year, says the version in Canniff], Mr Bottom gave Caesar his freedom. Caesar then married a free colored woman, and settled in the Town of Brockville.

16 BANQ, notary J.A. Gray, nos 1138 and 1139, 11 May 1804.
17 KB, *R v. James Grant*, March Term 1815. In 1811, John Fleming was identified as a "Negro Servant" living in Ste-Anne Suburb in a house that he owned, rated at £10 annual value (LAC, RG4, B19, v. 1, "List of persons liable to serve as Jurors residing in the Town and Banlieu of Montreal – June 1811," f. 31).
18 POBR I:222.

19 BANQ, register of Notre-Dame Church, 18 November 1833. HDM, admission registers, Book O, 14 November 1833, and list of deaths 1831–34 at end of volume.
20 French-speaking Catholics in Quebec assumed the name Marie to be part of every female's name, so that Anne, Catherine, Charlotte, Élisabeth, Françoise, Julie, Louise, Madeleine, etc., will inevitably have been recorded at some time as Marie Anne or Marianne, Marie Catherine, Marie Charlotte or Marie Charles, Marie Élisabeth, etc. In some cases, their other names are dropped and they are called simply Marie. This was true for whites, but was all the more true for slaves.
21 HDM, admission registers, Book H, 13 February 1813.
22 RPQ, 1 (1813–23): ff. 17, 36, 100, 134, 140, 145, 155, 199, 207, 212, 216, 225, 239, 241, 261, 268; 2 (1823–37): ff. 70, 73, 75, 83, 88, 93, 95, 98, 102. LAC, RG4 B16, Quebec, Lower Canada and Canada East: (Civil Secretary) records of courts, v. 11, "Criminal Offences Taken from the Records of the Court of Kings Bench for the District of Quebec beginning in the Year 1765 and ending with the Year 1827 with Abstracts," 103.
23 BANQ, register of Christ Church, 8 August 1802, 11 May 1803, 22 April 1804, 20 July 1807 and 24 July 1808; register of Notre-Dame Church, 18 July 1813; notary H. Griffin, no. 1652, 28 November 1816. POBR 1:219. Trudel, *Dictionnaire*, 99. On the question of Rose's identity, see chapter 5, n 10. John Fleming and Moses Meyers had a falling out in 1806, when they accused each other of assault. A grand jury found no grounds to indict Fleming, but it did find a true bill against Meyers. John Trim was a witness for the prosecution. Meyers had to post a £20 recognizance to keep the peace (CQS register, October Term 1806, *R v. Moses Myers*, 21 and 25 October 1806, and *R v. John Fleming*, 22 October 1806; CQS, indictments of Fleming and Myers, scribbled note of Myers's recognizance).
24 BANQ, register of Christ Church, 23 October 1803. Maria Keeling was the daughter of Othello Keeling and Josette Christie. Her father's first name was variously recorded as A., Joller, Nicolas, Othello, Othellor, Pollock, Toller, Tollock, Tulla, Tuller, Tulloch, and Tullock; the family name as Kalings, Keelin, Keeling, Keelings, Kellings, Kennings, Kerlings, Kiling, Killings, Killins, and Kyling.
25 BANQ, register of Christ Church, 3 April 1805; register of St Gabriel Presbyterian Church, 12 November 1808, 13 September and 5 November 1809, 29 April, 11 July and 11 September 1811, and 26 July 1812. CQS, October Term 1804, complaint of Hanna Caesar, 26 September 1804. Pierson's sons James by Julia Johnson and Valentine by Mary Rusk were baptized together on 29 April 1811, their ages given as "about eight months each." Valentine died 10 July 1811, said to be about eleven months old; James was said to be about twelve months old when he died the following 10 September.
26 BANQ, notary J.A. Gray, no. 2251, 6 February 1809.
27 Trudel, *Dictionnaire*, 99, 100, 102, 106, 109, 165.
28 Trudel *Dictionnaire*, 99, lists as slaves Jacques Fleming's wife, Magdeleine Carmel, and their son Jacques, born in 1813. The son was never a slave. The mother? Perhaps. As for John Fleming's three children by his "wife" Rose, the *Dictionnaire* makes no mention of them.
29 BANQ, notary J.G. Beek, no. 453, 25 September 1788. Trudel, *Dictionnaire*, 202. The *Dictionnaire* lists Sarah as a slave at the village of St-Laurent, five or six kilometres northwest of Montreal, whereas the deed of sale says she was from the *faubourg St-Laurent*, the St-Laurent

Suburb, just outside the walls of Montreal. McGill's slave Louise, buried under the name Marie Louise, had formerly belonged to merchant Joseph Amable Trottier *dit* Desrivières. Desrivières's widow, Charlotte Guillimin, had married McGill on 2 December 1776. Charlotte Guillimin had been a sponsor at Marie Louise's baptism in 1771. Marie Louise was then said to be about six. In the summer of 1788, when she was a patient in the Hôtel-Dieu, she was identified as a twenty-seven-year-old "Négresse appartenant à Mr Méguil, Ecuier Juge à paix." She re-entered the hospital on 22 November and died there on 5 February 1789 (BANQ, register of Notre-Dame Church, 17 January 1771 and 6 February 1789. HDM, admission registers, Book E, 24 July and 22 November 1788).

30 Trudel, *Dictionnaire*, 108.
31 HDM, admission registers, Book F, 2 February 1798.
32 BANQ, register of Christ Church, 29 November 1802; register of Notre-Dame Church, 11 October 1803, 20 March and 4 November 1805, 4 May 1807, 25 April 1809. HDM, admission registers, Book G, 16 April 1809, and Book H, 4 September 1813. Trudel, *Dictionnaire*, 98.
33 The bilingual Joseph François may have been the bilingual slave François or Frank mentioned in chapter 2 as having left the service of John Dease in 1799.
34 Leighton, "John Campbell." J.J. Lefèvre, ed., "Inventaire des biens de Luc Lacorne de Saint-Luc," 31–5, gives a sketch of the St-Luc family. Marie-Anne, the oldest child of her father's first marriage, born 31 March 1744, married John Campbell in 1763. Geneviève Élisabeth, born 28 August 1748, married Charles-Louis Tarieu de Lanaudière on 10 April 1769. Marie Louise Charlotte, born 18 September 1750, married Georges Hippolyte Le Compte Dupré in 1769, but died on 25 January 1771. St-Luc had no children by his second wife. By his third, he had Marie Marguerite, born on 3 January 1775; she married Lieutenant John Lennox of the 60th Regiment on 8 March 1794, and secondly Jacques Viger on 17 November 1808. Marie-Anne, Geneviève Élisabeth and Marie Marguerite were St-Luc's only surviving children at his death on 1 October 1784 (BANQ, notary L. Chaboillez, no. 109, 27 September 1788).
35 BANQ, notary J. Papineau, no. 2516, 17 August 1796, no. 2551, 2 November 1796, and no. 2609, 8 July 1797. Christie held the seigneuries of Bleury, Lachenaie, Lacolle, Léry, Repentigny, and part of Noyan. He also owned an undetermined number of slaves. He acquired an Indian slave named Jacques in the fall of 1763. One of his black slaves was Bruce (see chapter 4). In early 1797, a black woman called Mary Campbell was "Living at his excellency General Christie" when she died of a fever at the reputed age of fifty-one. Robert Allen, identified at his death on 23 April 1801 as an eighteen-year-old "Mulatto late Servant to The Widow Mrs Christie," née Sarah Stevenson, was possibly also a one-time Christie slave, or the son of a Christie slave. When he and his mother, Margaret July, were baptized together in 1799, she was identified as Margaret Julia Christie, "a black Woman" about thirty-two years old. At Christie's death on 20 January 1799, a partial inventory of his estate listed a slave girl named Clarice, about eighteen years old, at the manor house of Lacolle on the New York border. Christie's wife, the daughter of a merchant of Albany, NY, died on 26 October 1803 at age sixty-six (BANQ, register of Christ Church, 6 February 1797, 23 January and 1 September 1799, 25 April 1801, 29 October 1803; notary P. Panet de Méru, 19 November 1763; notary J. Papineau, no. 2879, 7 February 1799. POBR 1:226. *Gazette*, 28 January 1799).
36 BANQ, register of Christ Church, 20 January 1785.

37 BANQ, register of Notre-Dame Church, 13 April 1785.
38 BANQ, register of Notre-Dame Church, 5 April 1786 and 2 April 1787.
39 BANQ, notary J. Papineau, no. 2655, 23 October 1797.
40 BANQ, register of Notre-Dame Church, 6 May 1795. HDM, admission registers, Book F, 31 March 1795. François had entered the Hôtel-Dieu on 31 March 1795.
41 BANQ, register of Notre-Dame Church, 13 April 1785; register of St-François-d'Assise Church, Longue-Pointe, 21 April 1787.
42 BANQ, register of Notre-Dame Church, 5 April 1786 and 10 October 1797. Marie Élisabeth, sometimes called Marie, was also the godmother of Jean-Baptiste, who was baptized at age five in 1774, a slave of Charles-François Tarieu de Lanaudière. Marie was said to be about forty-eight in late April 1786 when she was briefly hospitalized at the Hôtel-Dieu. She died there on 16 June 1793, identified as Marie Elizabeth, a sixty-year-old "femme négresse appartenant à madame veuve Saint Luc Lacorne" (BANQ, register of Notre-Dame Church, 23 June 1774, 28 April 1786, 18 June 1793. HDM, admission registers, Book E, 28 April 1786, 9 June 1793).
43 BANQ, register of Notre-Dame Church, 2 April 1787 and 24 June 1799. HDM, admission registers, Book F, 21 March 1799. Trudel, *Dictionnaire*, 111.
44 BANQ, register of Notre-Dame Church, 24 October 1788; register of St-François-d'Assise Church, Longue-Pointe, 29 May 1792.
45 BANQ, register of Notre-Dame Church, 21 October 1791.
46 BANQ, register of Notre-Dame Church, 22 November 1794.
47 BANQ, register of Notre-Dame Church, 11 March 1793; register of St-François-d'Assise Church, Longue-Pointe, 10 July 1793. This boy's mother was probably the Campbell slave who was called Marie when she was a patient at the Hôtel-Dieu 9 February – 28 March 1780 (HDM, admission registers, Book D, 9 February 1780).
48 BANQ, register of Notre-Dame Church, 29 May 1788.
49 BANQ, register of Notre-Dame Church, 22 April 1787, 26 May 1791. Trudel, *Dictionnaire*, 105.
50 BANQ, notary L. Chaboillez, no. 3676, 14 September 1799.
51 BANQ, register of Notre-Dame Church, 3 January 1790.
52 The adult Thomas (or Tomas), "negre de Mr Cambell," was twice registered as a patient at the Hôtel-Dieu in February-March 1792 (HDM, admission registers, Book E, 26 February and 19 March 1792).
53 KB-Q (Oyer & Terminer), March Term 1794, 1793: 365-B9, *R v. Thomas Grant*.
54 CQS, January Term 1794, Calendar of Prisoners, 13 January 1794; court register, January 1794, *R v. Reuben Thomas & Tom Grant*, 21 January 1794. KB-Q, March Term 1794, 1793: 365-B9, *R v. Thomas Grant*. Tom was jailed on 24 December 1793 for stealing various items, including firearms, three scalping knives, and two tomahawks, from Campbell's home (Campbell occupied a farm at Lachine, where the Indian Department was headquartered, and a house at Montreal) on 15 April and 20 September 1793. He readily admitted to stealing the goods from Campbell, whose service he had deserted three months earlier, running off to Quebec, from where he had been recently returned. He claimed that he had committed the thefts at the instigation of Reuben Thomas, another black Montrealer, whom he knew as Jupiter, and his "wife," Thérèse Maçon (Masson). Reuben Thomas was picked up and jailed on Christmas Day. The

list of prisoners in jail in January 1794 identified Tom as Thomas, alias Tom Grant. According to the court docket of 13 January, the case of *R v. Reuben Thomas & Tom Grant* was slated to proceed that month before the Court of Quarter Sessions, but the minutes of the court show that, on 21 January, *R v. Thomas a Negro* ended abruptly: "The Grand Jury having ignored the Bill, the Prisoner was discharged by proclamation." Through some confusion, Thomas Grant, "labourer," was indicted for grand larceny in the March 1794 term of the Court of Oyer & Terminer, for the same theft. Surviving court records do not indicate how far this case proceeded. There seem to have been no further proceedings against Reuben Thomas. The court docket for the October 1794 Term of the Court of Quarter Sessions shows that he was to be tried on a charge of assault and battery, for beating Thérèse Maçon (CQS, October Term 1794, court docket).

55 Charles-François Tarieu de Lanaudière and his wife, Louise Geneviève Deschamps de Boishébert, members of the colony's élite, had seven children, six of whom died within months of their birth (Imbeault, *Les Tarieu de Lanaudière*, 43–5). Much lower on the social scale, Jacob Smith and his mulatto wife, Catherine Coll, had one child per year at Quebec in 1798, 1799, 1800, and 1801, and not one lived into the next year (see n103, below). Carpenter Augustin Labadie and his wife, the mulatto Marie Angélique Price, had six children between 1800 and 1806, none of whom made it to the age of two years (see chapter 5). The six children of Jean-Baptiste L'Africain and Charlotte Bonga, and the five children of Richard Rogers and Asenath Myers all died young (see chapter 6).

56 BANQ, register of Notre-Dame Church, 12 September 1785.

57 BANQ, register of Notre-Dame Church, 10 September 1795.

58 BANQ, notary J. Delisle, no. 97, 13 March 1773.

59 BANQ, notary P. Panet de Méru, no. 4714, 2 August 1777.

60 For this case, see chapter 4.

61 HDM, admission registers, Book E, 25 May 1792 and 15 January 1793.

62 HDM, admission registers, Book E, 11 November 1795 and 14 March 1796.

63 HDM, admission registers, Book F, 25 November 1796. Cuff was an anglicized form of the West African day-name Kofi, for a male born on a Friday.

64 CQS, October Term 1794, "Cath. Vallet, Examen Volontaire," 21 May 1794. McCord Museum, P212, Court of Common Pleas, complaint of Joseph Roussin, 12 July 1794, and grand jury presentment to the Court of Quarter Sessions, July 1794. A modern-day writer identified Seabrook as "the sleazy keeper of a disorderly house" (Victoria M. Stewart, ed. *The Loyalists of Quebec*, 411).

65 BANQ, register of Notre-Dame Church, 17 December 1794, 10 April 1795.

66 CQS register, *R v. Mary Warren*, 28 April 1804. Another prosecution witness in the case was "Chloe, a Blackwoman." The accused was acquitted.

67 BANQ, notary J.A. Gray, no. 2744, 11 May 1810. It was to Seabrook, the butcher, that Gabriel Johonnot, son of black distiller Caesar Johonnot, was apprenticed in March 1807 (BANQ, notary J.A. Gray, no. 1775, 14 March 1807).

68 BANQ, register of Notre-Dame Church, 18 June 1821.

69 Trudel, *Dictionnaire*, 119, lists another slave of John Campbell named Sylvie as having been confirmed a Roman Catholic on 28 June 1795.

70 BANQ, notary J. Papineau, no. 2655, 23 October 1797.
71 Trudel identifies the following slaves as belonging to Campbell (page references to the *Dictionnaire* in parentheses): Geneviève, a Panise (61); François-Xavier and Marie, and their son François-Xavier (100); Jacques and Marguerite, and their son Jacques (103); Jean-François/Francis, Jeanne/Jane/Jane Harrison and their daughters Marie Marguerite and Marie Angélique, as well as Élisabeth, Jean-François's daughter by Geneviève (105–6); John (106); Josephe and her daughter Marie Josephe (109); Louise and her children François and Marie-Anne (111); Marie Angélique (112); Pierre Jean (116); Sylvie (119); Thomas (119–20). He does not list the boy François Josué, or Cuff and Violetta. Making no connection between the Campbell slave François-Xavier born at Montreal in March 1793 and the black boy of that name who died at Longue-Pointe in July at the age of four months, the *Dictionnaire* lists them as two persons, the latter as the son of unknown parents (38).
72 Trudel, *Deux siècles d'esclavage*, 96.
73 "Census of 1784," *Censuses of Canada, 1665 to 1871*, 4:74. A footnote in this report states that the census excluded the estimated 10,000 Loyalists – men, women and children – in the western part of the province, the future Upper Canada, but this appears to be an error. An undated memo by Haldimand, written in French, makes clear that he understood this census to cover all of Canada, i.e., all of the old Province of Quebec. Translated, it reads: "There were in Canada at the time that Gen. Amherst effected its conquest in 1760, according to the reports made to him, 76,122 souls in the entire Province of which 16,212 were fit for Militia duty. According to the census which I ordered to be taken toward the end of 1784, there were 113,012 Souls in the Province, so that by deducting the 76,122 souls present at the time of the Conquest, it will be found that in 24 years the Population increased by 36,890 Souls" (HP, MS21816:391). Riddell also understood the census to cover the extended territory: "The returns of the census of 1784 show that very many of the 212 slaves in the District of Montreal, which then extended from the Rivers St Maurice and Godfrey to the Detroit River *de jure* and to the Mississippi *de facto*, were the property of the United Empire Loyalists on the St Lawrence in territory which in 1791 became part of the new Province of Upper Canada" (Riddell, *The Slave in Canada*, 325). See also D.G. Simpson, *Under the North Star*, 144.
74 KB-Q, 1793: 365-B9, *R v. Thomas Grant*. HP, MS21826:33–8, "Return of Families of Loyalists Receiving Provisions out of the Different Magazines or Depots in the District of Montreal from the 25th of Octbr. To the 24th of Novembr. 1780 Inclusive," lists Johnson's slave as Jupiter Johnson, a member of Herkimer's Batteau Company at Coteau-du-Lac.
75 Trudel, *Dictionnaire*, xxi–xxii.
76 See the brief foreword (*Avant-propos*) in Trudel, *Dictionnaire*.
77 Trudel, *Dictionnaire*, xiv.
78 La Jonquière, *Chef d'escadre*, 149, reproduces a dispatch of 16 July 1750, concerning an exchange of captives with the New England colonies, in which the Marquis de La Jonquière, governor of New France, uses this saying twice in reference to black prisoners of war.
79 Neilson, "Slavery in Old Canada," 37–8. Viger and Lafontaine, *De l'esclavage*, 22.
80 Trudel, *Dictionnaire*, 91 and 95. The *Dictionnaire* lists Diah as an anonymous slave. For documents in his case, see Mackey, *Black Then*, 203–6. For Cesar, see BANQ, notary J.G. Delisle, no. 2332, 23 November 1796.

81 Trudel, *Dictionnaire*, 93.
82 Roquebrune, *Testament de mon enfance*, 23–4. See also 25–8, 34–6, 74–5, 135–8, 149–158.
83 Trudel *Dictionnaire*, 34.
84 Winks, *The Blacks in Canada*, 234; Fisher, *Legend of the Drinking Gourd*; Anonymous, *The Story of Oro*, 29–32; Wayne, "The Black Population of Canada West on the Eve of the American Civil War: A Reassessment Based on the Manuscript Census of 1861." For Nigger Rock, see chapter 2, n148.
85 The misplaced blacks are (*Dictionnaire* page references in parentheses): William Dowling (164); William Feeler, Nancy Bradshaw, Julie Fleming, Aaron Forsyth and Titus Fortune (165); Leonard Freeman and James Grant (166); John Baptist (170); Maria Kellings and Jean-Baptiste Lafricain (174); Murray (179); Abraham Peter (i.e., Peter Abraham) (180); Richard (182); Margaret Sinclair (183); William Taylor and Thomas (185); Henry Thompson, Eber Wedden and Charles Whitemore (186); and Aaron York (187). These twenty-one persons must be subtracted from the Quebec list, but we cannot simply add them to Montreal's because the *Dictionnaire* already lists some of them there, under the same name or a variant. Besides Julie Fleming, these are William Taylor (born free in 1801), listed under that name at Quebec and at Montreal (106); Henry Thompson at Quebec, listed at Montreal as William Thompson, although his name was always recorded there as Henry (120); Murray at Quebec listed twice at Montreal, under the names Murray Hall and Montreal (101, 114); and Jean-Baptiste Lafricain at Quebec counted as Jean-Baptiste-François at Montreal (105). On the other hand, some slaves listed at Montreal, such as Caleb (95), Ruth (118), and the anonymous female slave of the widow of Jacques Perrault (92), were slaves at Quebec, not at Montreal.
86 Trudel, *Dictionnaire*, 174.
87 Ibid., 186.
88 Contemporary records give the family name variously as Vailledanne, Walden, Waldin, Walding, Welden, Weldin, Welding, Weldon, Wellden, Welldone, Wildain, and Wolden; and Ebert's first name as Abraham, Eber, Hébert, Hubert, Ibre, Ybe, and Yvre. See Appendix I/A, notice 80.
89 BANQ, notary J.G. Beek, no. 523, 1 May 1789. *Gazette*, 11 October 1792. Ebert Weldin's brothers and sisters were Mary, born c. 1778; Elizabeth, b. 1780; and Elie, born c. 1785. See BANQ, notary J.G. Beek, no. 492, 2 February 1789, and no. 555, 21 July 1789; notary J.G. Delisle, no. 472, 13 March 1792.
90 Trudel, *Dictionnaire*, xi.
91 Ibid., 93, 98.
92 Ibid., 120.
93 Ibid., 95, 110. For Lamour, see chapter 5.
94 BANQ, register of St-Enfant-Jésus Church, Pointe-aux-Trembles, 8 December 1800; register of Notre-Dame Church, 27 January 1805. Trudel, *Dictionnaire*, 93, 99.
95 Trudel, *Dictionnaire*, 118. The three Roses were:
– *Rose I*, about twenty-nine, mother of Jeanne, about six, and Henri, about five, was sold with her son on 9 August 1790 by lawyer Pierre Mézière and his wife, Archange Campeau, to merchant Louis Moquin for 840 livres. Moquin paid 140 livres cash, and promised to pay the rest in kind, i.e., 80 cords of hardwood and 140 livres worth of merchandise. Mézière had bought

Rose from Martin Macevoy (McEvoy) on 6 April 1785 at an auction held by J.G. Beek. On 4 July 1794, Mézière sold Rose's daughter, Jeanne, renamed Marianne, to his son-in-law, merchant Adrien Berthelot, for 400 livres (BANQ, notary J.G. Delisle, 9 August 1790, and no. 872, 4 July 1794).

– *Rose II*, was a nursing (*nourrice*) black girl of fourteen or fifteen when she was sold on 27 March 1787 by Samuel Mix, trader at St-Jean, to tanner Louis Gauthier of the St-Laurent Suburb of Montreal for £40. Gauthier sold Rose to distiller John Lagord who, in turn, sold her to Sorel innkeeper and grocer William Mathews (or Matthews). On 9 November 1791, Mathews sold Rose, about 19, at auction to Montreal trader Lambert St-Omer for £38 5s (BANQ, notary J. Papineau, no. 825, 27 March 1787; notary J.B. Desève, no. 671, 9 November 1791; register of Notre-Dame Church, 31 May 1788. See Appendix I n59).

– *Rose III* was a slave of Lambert St-Omer, baptized Marie in 1787, at the age of about sixteen, but buried under the name Rose. She died at the Hôpital-Général of the Grey Nuns on 10 July 1791, at the age of about nineteen, four months before St-Omer bought Rose II, who was about the same age (BANQ, register of Notre-Dame Church, 26 June 1787; register of the Hôpital-Général chapel, 11 July 1791).

96 Trudel, *Dictionnaire*, 94, 157. Other variants of Ashley's name include John Robert Ashley, Robert Hasly, and "Joseph Astley (or Ashley)."

97 Ibid., 179. Robert Ashley and Margaret Pearce were married at Quebec in 1802. Their daughter Elizabeth was born there on 7 September 1804 (BANQ, register of Quebec Anglican Church, 22 July 1802, 30 September 1804).

98 For Margaret Ashley, see BANQ, register of Christ Church, 4 August 1816, 25 February 1818. Robert Ashley's wife, Margaret Pearce, was a sponsor at the baptisms of blacks Robert Jackson at Quebec in 1803, and Elizabeth McGuire at Montreal in 1804 (BANQ, register of Quebec Anglican Church, 3 April 1803; register of Christ Church, Montreal, 26 February 1804).

99 BANQ, register of Christ Church, 25 September 1808 and 4 November 1810.

100 Trudel, *Dictionnaire*, 162. BANQ, HDQ admission registers, 20 May, 1 June, 1 July, 1 August, 1 September 1817; register of HDQ chapel, 12 September 1817. Catherine Coll was identified as Catherine Smith, 51, the American-born wife of Jacob Coale when she entered the hospital on 20 May 1817. Her name was corrected to Catherine Coale in subsequent entries in the hospital register. She remained in the hospital until her death on 11 September. The Quebec slave named Catherine Smith, was said to be fifty-six and the property of a saddler named Lane at her baptism on 30 October 1796; eleven days later, on her admission to the Hôtel-Dieu, she was identified as a forty-six-year-old "Esse Clave de Mr Lind" (slave of Mr Lind), a native of Guinea and widow of William (BANQ, register of Quebec Anglican Church, 30 October 1796; HDQ admission registers, 10 November and 1 December 1796).

101 KBCV, October Term 1796, No. 2, *Jacob Smith v. Peter McFarlane*, depositions of Reverend John Young, Thomas Walker, Alexander Degrey and Marie-Françoise Bertrand, filed 7 October 1795.

102 BANQ, notary F. Tetu, 9 February 1800. LAC, RG1, L3L, Lower Canada Land Papers, 207:90716–19, 90728–30. Smith was perhaps the Jacob Smith from Quebec who unsuccessfully petitioned the government in 1797 for an inordinate grant of 1,200 acres in Chatham Township on the

Ottawa as a reward for his services in the 34th Regiment of Foot in the American War of Independence. While land board documents identified the 200 acres granted to Smith in 1789 as Lot 25 in Township 5 on the north side of the Ottawa, a list of titles that Richard Wragg filed with a notary in 1797 identified the 200 acres that he had acquired from Smith as Lot 31 in Township 3, in the second Concession on the south side of the Ottawa (BANQ, notary L. Chaboillez, no. 2607, 23 September 1797. LAC, RG1 L3L, Lower Canada Land Papers, 12:4232, 184:88159–60). The grant was conditional on Smith settling and clearing the land, but he notified the board in March 1794 that, unable to fulfill these conditions, "having had the Misfortune to loose one of his hands," he had sold his grant to Wragg. After moving to Quebec, Smith had occasion to confirm that he had sold the land to Wragg for unspecified *"considérations."*

103 BANQ, register of Quebec Anglican Church, 26 February and 14 August 1798, 4 August 1799, 16 April and 29 December 1800, 26 July and 26 December 1801. The sponsors at the baptism of the Smiths' first child, Catherine, were Johan Freell and Helena Poser (a Friedrich Hoffman was a witness at her burial); those at the baptism of their third child, Henry Charles, were John Harry Heineman, Charles Henwicker and Jean Chambers; and at the baptism of their last child, John, Hannah Chambers, Frederick Wilhelm and John Seybold were the sponsors.

104 BANQ, register of Saints-Anges Church, Lachine, 11 April and 15 May 1767. Her father, Charles, had been a witness at the wedding of Louis Antoine and Catherine Baraca in March 1761. Louis Antoine and the free black Joseph Hypolithe *dit* l'espiègle were witnesses at Charles' burial.

105 BANQ, notary J.T. Raymond, no. 656, 11 March 1787. Two weeks later, Baudain and Larocque agreed to annul this sale. Larocque handed back the slave, and Baudain reimbursed the 500 livres that Larocque had paid, plus 24 livres. There is no reason given for the cancellation or for the payment of the extra 24 livres (BANQ, notary J. Papineau, no. 814, 20 March 1787).

106 BANQ, notary P. Lukin Sr, no. 144, 13 August 1792; register of Christ Church, 25 March 1794. Daniel Steel was said to have been born in 1753.

107 CQS, October Term 1793, *R v. George Baron and Charlotte Prudhomme.* KB-Q, 1800:463-B12, *R v. Marie Charlotte Prudhomme. Quebec Herald,* 16 May 1791.

108 BANQ, register of Notre-Dame Church, 2 February 1822. HDM, admission registers, Book i, 1 January 1822.

109 Trudel, *Dictionnaire,* 110, lists a Joseph Lafricain as a sometime slave, citing as evidence a contract of 1807 by which he was hired as a carpenter by the fur-trading Michilimackinac Company. The contract says nothing about his being black. In fact, Joseph Tribot *dit* L'Africain was white, the son of master mason Jean-Baptiste Tribot *dit* L'Africain and Jeanne Sabatte (BANQ-M, notary L. Chaboillez, no. 3813, 11 December 1799, and Engagements, no. 7621, 13 February 1807).

110 Trudel, *Dictionnaire,* 115. For confusion over this name, see Appendix I n5.

111 Trudel, *Deux siècles d'esclavage,* 84–5.

112 Trudel, *Dictionnaire,* xvi.

113 Trudel, *Deux siècles d'esclavage,* 115.

114 HP, MS21735:371–2, Yohannes Decker to Governor Haldimand, 10 March 1784.

115 Trudel, *Deux siècles d'esclavage,* 166–7.

CHAPTER FOUR

1 The annals of the Ursulines record this unnamed "négresse de Mme. Grant" as a pupil at their convent in 1772. Mme Grant was Marie-Anne-Catherine Fleury Deschambault, dowager baroness of Longueuil, the widow of Baron Charles Jacques Le Moyne de Longueuil, remarried at Montreal in 1770 to Quebec merchant and politician William Grant (Mère St-Thomas, *Les Ursulines de Québec depuis leur établissement jusqu'à nos jours*, 3:213).
2 Sansom, *Travels in Lower Canada*, 77.
3 Jean-Claude Robert, *Atlas historique de Montréal*, 78. *Gazette*, 25 August 1806. Robert sets the population at about 9,000 in 1800. The *Gazette*, reproducing a "Sketch of Montreal in Lower Canada" from the *Boston Repository*, set the figure as of May 1806 at 9,568 (4,554 males and 5,014 females). By comparison, the population of the four largest US cities in 1800 – New York, Philadelphia, Baltimore and Boston – has been estimated respectively at 60,515, 41,220, 26,514 and 24,937 (Gibson, "Population of the 100 Largest Cities and Other Urban Places in the United States: 1790 to 1990," Table 3.)
4 Scadding, *Toronto of Old*, 292.
5 HDM, admission registers, Book C, 10 November 1780 and 15 June 1782. HP, MS21763:368–9, "Return of Negroes & Negroe Wench's brought into the Province under the Command and Direction of Lieut. Col. Sir John Johnson Bart." The record of the sale of Ignace Bourassa's estate in March 1779 mentions that, by mistake, "le lit du nègre" (the negro's bed) had been auctioned to a man named Roi, when it had already been sold, along with the negro and other effects, to Curatteau. Curatteau's name does not appear as a buyer in the record of the estate sale, which lists the buyer of the "nègre" as a man named "Dupéré." In Curatteau's correspondence, this name was written Duperet. This was a man who handled some of Curatteau's business affairs at this time (BANQ, notary P. Mézière, no. 2384, 1 March 1779. For Dupéré, see UMCB U3104, U3105, U3107, letters of Curatteau to François Baby of 22 August and 23 September 1779, and 22 September 1780).
6 HP, MS21822:349, John Doty to Robert Mathews, 15 September 1784.
7 BANQ, register of Notre-Dame Church, 2 September 1771, 29 November 1772.
8 BANQ, notary A. Foucher, no. 5466, 20 April 1784. Dianne appears to have become, perhaps through baptism, Marie Charle, or Charlotte for short. She was registered as the nameless "nôtre negresse" (our negress) about thirty years old, when she was admitted to the Hôtel-Dieu hospital for the first time in May 1785. The same age was given for her in the summer of 1788, when "notre négresse" was again a patient. Admitted to the hospital twice in 1789, "Charlotte negresse de Lhôtel Dieu" was said to be thirty-six. No age was given for "charlote négresse a La communauté" when she was a patient again in October 1794. She was registered as "Marie Charle negresse a gée de 30 ans de chez nous" when she stayed in hospital again from 28 December 1796 to 6 January 1797. Slightly more than a year later, she was "charle negresse de chez nous a gee de 40 ans," then "marie charle négrese de chez nous" when she entered the hospital for the last time on 21 April 1798. She died three days later. At her burial, the church record added another 20 years to her life, making her sixty years old (BANQ, register of Notre-Dame Church, 25 April 1798. HDM, admission registers, Book E, 23 May 1785, 11 July 1788, 18 and 29 September 1789, 4 October 1794; Book F, 28 December 1796, 1 April and 21 April 1798).

NOTES TO PAGES 110–15   457

9 HDM, admission registers, Book E, 5 August 1786. Faribault-Beauregard, *La Population des forts français*, 133. Trudel, *Dictionnaire*, 250, 394.
10 BANQ, register of St-Antoine-de-Padoue Church, St-Antoine-sur-Richelieu, 24 November 1786.
11 BANQ, notary F. Leguay Sr, no. 1861, 11 January 1787; register of St-Antoine-de-Padoue Church, St-Antoine-sur-Richelieu, 13 September 1789. Jean Baptiste *dit* Pompé is believed to be the Jean Baptiste Pomp (or Pompe) who married Marie Angélique William, daughter of the slave François William and his white wife, Élisabeth Mondina, at Beauport in 1808 and who died at Quebec in 1809 (BANQ, register of Notre-Dame-de-Miséricorde Church, Beauport, 29 February 1808; register of HDQ chapel, 29 April 1809).
12 BANQ, notary J.P. Gauthier, no. 449, 4 March 1795.
13 BANQ, notary P. Lukin Sr, no. 235, 27 July 1793, and no. 5298, 25 May 1814; notary J.G. Delisle, no. 878, 21 July 1794, and no. 2090, 16 January 1796.
14 BANQ, notary C. Michaud, 2 September 1796; notary A. Dumas, 9 September 1796. In English, the name of Thomas Lée, of Irish and French descent, was often written Thomas Lee.
15 Frost, *James McGill of Montreal*, 63–4. Concerning a slave advertisement published at Toronto in 1806, Henry Scadding reminded his late-nineteenth-century readers: "According to our ideas at the present moment, such an advertisement as this is shocking enough. But we must judge the words and deeds of men by the spirit of the age in which they lived and moved" (Scadding, *Toronto of Old*, 293).
16 Acting for distiller Thomas Corry of L'Assomption, McGill sold two black slaves, Caesar and Flora, to Montreal merchant Levy Solomon for £100 in 1784. In 1787, he was reimbursed by the government for the cost of four slaves (perhaps not blacks), bought for £33 each and given to Indians for four warriors they had lost in battle. One gets the impression that McGill could just as equably have built his fortune on trading in slaves as in furs, had slaves been as much in demand as animal skins. As one of his biographers remarked, "McGill was obviously ready to accept 'any commission for a commission' " (BANQ, notary J.G. Beek, no. 98, 10 December 1784. Audet, *Les Députés de Montréal*, 136. Frost, *James McGill of Montreal*, 63–4). For Daniel Jones, see Appendix III.
17 BANQ, notary J.P. Gauthier, no. 231, 15 September 1792.
18 BANQ, notary B. Faribault, 18 April 1787; register of Ste-Geneviève Church, Berthier, 20 February 1793. For Loubet's slave, see Appendix III, n5.
19 BANQ, notary B. Faribault, 29 March 1787 and 9 February 1789; notary F. Leguay Sr, no. 2083, 2 June 1788; register of Notre-Dame Church, 15 October 1789.
20 BANQ, notary B. Faribault, 29 March 1787, 9 June 1788, 9 February 1789; notary M.L. Desdevens de Glandons, 13 May 1797; register of Ste-Geneviève Church, Berthier, 13 September and 3 October 1792, 25 July and 24 October 1795, 30 June and 2 August 1797; register of Christ Church, Montreal, 14 April 1801. POBR 1:223. Mary McFarlane had previously been married to Hugh Ferries (Faries, Faris), a merchant and tavern-keeper, then to John McNamara, a fur-trade merchant who, at the time of his death on 29 September 1788, owned a farm at Berthier. In his will, McNamara had left her "all the Stock and Utensils of Husbandry, Furniture, Goods, Household Stuff, Silver Plate and Slaves in and about my House at Berthier." About two and a half years before his death at the age of thirty-seven, McNamara had bought the black slaves Mimy and Prince, both about thirty-five, for a total of £70 from Levi Allen,

brother of Vermont's famed Ethan Allen (BANQ, notary J.G. Beek, no. 148, 1 February 1786; register of St Gabriel Presbyterian Church, 1 October 1788; CT601, S1, Cour supérieure, Testaments olographes, no. 19, will of John McNamara, 27 February 1788, probated 17 October 1788).

21 BANQ, notary F. Leguay Sr, no. 2007, 18 September 1787.
22 BANQ, notary F. Leguay Sr, no. 2006, 7 September 1787.
23 BANQ, notary F. Leguay Sr, no. 2025, 3 November 1787. Viger and LaFontaine, *De l'esclavage*," 47–8. It is possible that Lagord sold only one slave to Poiré, but if that was the case, one is at a loss to explain the two deeds of sale two months apart.
24 BANQ, notary F. Leguay Sr, no. 2027, 17 November 1787; notary C. Stewart, 4 December 1787. This may be the same Harry who was convicted of theft at Quebec in 1790. In the Court of Quarter Sessions that opened on 13 April 1790, "Harry, a negro, for stealing hay, soap, and candles, [was] sentenced to be whipt in the Lower and Upper town Market places, 12 lashes in each, which has been put in execution" (*Quebec Herald*, 22 April 1790). Another newspaper identified Harry as the slave of John Munro and said that the whipping had taken place on 20 April (*Quebec Gazette*, 22 April 1790). John Munro was a merchant who had settled at Quebec in 1774. In the summer of 1801, he was to leave for the West Indies as the paymaster of the 3rd Battalion, 60th Regiment. He died in Grenada on 18 July 1803, at age forty-two (*Quebec Gazette*, 29 September 1803).
25 BANQ, notary J. Papineau, no. 825, 27 March 1787; notary J.B. Desève, no. 671, 9 November 1791; register of Notre-Dame Church, 31 May 1788.
26 Fur trader James Morrison worked a similar flip in 1789. See Appendix III.
27 BANQ, CT601 S1, Cour supérieure, Testaments olographes, no. 20, will of Jane Richardson, 22 November 1777, probated 24 June 1789. Her husband had died on 4 November 1777 (BANQ, register of Christ Church, 7 November 1777).
28 BANQ, notary J.B. Desève, no. 1434, 1 May 1798. In a study of slavery in the northern United States, Edgar McManus found that "Slaves belonging to estates undergoing probate were often hired out to provide income for the heirs and to free the executors and administrators of the burden of supervision" (McManus, *Black Bondage in the North*, 46–7).
29 This appears to have been the case for Manuel Allen in 1797 (see chapter 3, n13), and all the more so for Guillaume in 1798, bound out as a servant when the court rulings freeing Charlotte and Judith had spread alarm among the slave-owners and spurred the slaves Manuel Allen and Augustin to desert their masters. Some Upper Canadian slave-owners had had the same reaction at the prospect of gradual abolition in 1793 (see pages 83–4).
30 Hill, *The Freedom-Seekers*, 8–9.
31 Bruce's freedom may have been short-lived. A little more than two months later, the sheriff of Montreal offered a reward of £4 for the arrest of "a Negro man called *Bruce*, tall, well made, with a high Nose and very black complexion, about thirty-five years of age," wanted for a burglary committed on the night of 4–5 September, and "who has since absconded" (See Appendix I/A, notice 20). Bruce was arrested at Quebec the following winter, returned to Montreal, and tried under the name Thomas Bruce for felony and burglary at the March Term of the Court of King's Bench in 1788. He pleaded not guilty at his arraignment on 3 March, but was convicted at his trial on 5 March. On 10 March, he was sentenced to hang on 10 April, but there

is no trace of a confirmation of his execution or record of his death (UMCB, J2/129, "Docket Book of Judgments in Criminal Causes Recorded in the said Court [of King's Bench] from July 1777 to May 1784," Montreal, March Sessions 1778, 8).

32 BANQ, notary J.G. Beek, no. 1218, 1 June 1798, no. 1331, 23 July 1799, and no. 1638, 9 March 1802.

33 BANQ, notary J.A. Gray, 22 November 1796. The two slaves were sold together by John Turner Sr, who had also once owned Manuel Allen. Brooks was legally interdicted in 1805; his father was named his curator. He died in the Montreal General Hospital on 10 October 1829 at age 60 (BANQ, register of St Gabriel Presbyterian Church, 11 October 1829. *Gazette*, 27 May 1805).

34 BANQ, notary J. Papineau, no. 825, 27 March 1787; notary P. Lukin Sr, no. 143, 10 August 1792; register of St Gabriel Presbyterian Church, 2 October 1805. For Nero, see Appendix III. There was some doubt as to the seller's title to Kitts, as he was made to promise to pay a penalty of £50 sterling if the sale turned out to be illegal. In June 1793, Carbry sold Kitts, said to be 15 years and 10 months, to merchant James Holmes of St-Jean for £40 (BANQ, notary P. Lukin Sr, no. 229, 11 June 1793).

35 BANQ, notary P. Lukin Sr, no. 1099, 22 November 1797; notary J.A. Gray, no. 133, 27 November 1797. *Gazette*, 22 November 1787.

36 Upton, *The Loyal Whig*, 169. Winks, *The Blacks in Canada*, 26.

37 There appear to be no records of poisoning or sabotage, or suspected instances of such, by slaves. As for arson, other than the famous case of Marie Josèphe Angélique in Montreal in 1734, where it is doubtful that she set the fire for which she was hanged, we know of one slave at Montreal who was tried for arson and acquitted, and of two fires set by slaves at Quebec. The most destructive was set accidentally at Quebec in September 1796 by an eleven-year-old boy at play (see n50, below). In the other Quebec case, in December 1786, a slave named Dick set fire to a shed belonging to his master, Alexander Wilson, hoping that in the excitement over the blaze he would escape punishment for beating another man's servant. The only evidence against Dick was his own admission, and a jury acquitted him at his trial. In the Montreal case, Anne, "a Negro Girl," was arraigned in the Court of King's Bench on 8 September 1786 on a charge of house-burning. She pleaded not guilty, and at her trial the next day was acquitted and discharged. She may have been Marie Anne Catherine, the slave of Étienne Dubois Sr, who was about six years old at her baptism in 1779, which would have made her about thirteen in 1786 (BANQ, register of Notre-Dame Church, 25 November 1779. KB-Q, 1787: 286-B7, *R v. Dick*. LAC, RG4 B16, Quebec, Lower Canada and Canada East: [Civil Secretary] records of courts, v. 11, "Criminal Offences Taken from the Records of the Court of Kings Bench for the District of Quebec beginning with the Year 1765 and ending with the Year 1827 with Abstracts," 21. UMCB, J2/141, "Docket Book of Judgments in Criminal Causes and Records of Entries on Crim. prosecutions in the said Court [of King's Bench] from September Sessions 1784 to May Sessions 1789," Montreal, September Sessions 1786, 62, and Quebec, May Sessions 1787, 76).

38 *Quebec Gazette*, 24 January 1777. "E**" probably stands for "Eve."

39 CCP, *Casar Johonnot v. Philip Lansing*, 1789. HP, MS21818:160, Certificate recommending Philip P. Lansing to Governor Frederick Haldimand. Cruikshank and Watt, *The History and Master Roll of the King's Royal Regiment of New York*, 247. Johonnot sued Lansingh for pay-

ment of his meals and washing. In his statement of claim of 14 January 1789, he said that Lansingh "constantly during the said period had his suppers furnished to him at the same Table with the Plaintiff and his family." Johonnot won, but it was a pyrrhic victory: Lansingh had no seizable assets at Montreal. He held land in the Kingston area, where he died in November 1792 (BANQ, notary J.G. Beek, no. 234, 25 January 1787. Young, *The Parish Register of Kingston, Upper Canada, 1785–1811*, 155).

40 Johonnot is undoubtedly the "Cesar Jahomet" whose case Borthwick (*History of the Montreal Prison*, 234) cites from court proceedings in 1786:

On the 27th June, 1876 [sic], an assault case takes up the attention of the Court. Cesar Jahomet v. Private Skr. Campbell. The plaintiff declares that he was struck by Defendant, a soldier of the 34th Regiment. The defendant swears that he did not strike him and Thos. Fairly, a comrade, on oath, declares that "on taking water at the Fountain, at the Mountain, near the City, they saw a dog above them, at the stream, that they threw a stick at the dog, which happened to hit a Negro man, the plaintiff, who thereupon came down from the stream where the said dog was, and threatened said Fairly and the rest that he would and could fight any or either of them. That thereupon seeing himself and his comrades so threatened, he gave said plaintiff a blow and knocked him down." – Dismissed.

41 BANQ, notary J.G. Beek, no. 525, 5 May 1789; notary E.W. Gray, no. 65, 26 February 1789, and no. 80, 16 October 1794. From early 1789, the partners in the Montreal Distillery Co. were Todd, McGill & Co., Forsyth Richardson & Co., and King & McCord, each with a quarter interest, and merchants Jean-Baptiste Durocher of Montreal and Robert Lester of Quebec, each holding a one-eighth share. They hired Johonnot on a renewable two-year contract from 1 May 1789. The previous September, McGill, partner with Isaac Todd in Todd, McGill & Co., had bought the slave Sarah (alias Charlotte McGill). Lester owned two slaves – Sambo (alias Jean), who drowned in 1783 at the age of about eighteen, and Jean Baptiste (BANQ, register of Notre-Dame Church, Quebec, 18 May 1782, 20 May and 7 June 1783; notary J.G. Beek, no. 453, 25 September 1788; notary C. Stewart, 30 August 1781).

42 For Johonnot's hiring by Fortune and other aspects of his career, see chapter 5. The slave was "une Négresse nommée Louise ou Lisette," about twenty-five, whom François Latour of Detroit had obtained in the 1780s in an exchange with a Jean-Baptiste Meloche. Latour sold her for £40 New York currency (half payable in cash, half in kind) to Victor Baudain (Baudin, Beaudin) on 2 August 1789. That fall, Baudain, then a fur trader, later a butcher, sold her on approval at Montreal to soap merchant Louis Dufour *dit* Latour. Dufour paid Baudain 1,000 livres for her the following summer. Baudain certified that she was "free of infirmities having had the smallpox by inoculation." In the spring of 1792, Dufour sent her to Quebec to be auctioned by Burns & Woolsey (William Burns and John William Woolsey). On 9 May, at age 27 or so, she was sold to innkeeper Thomas Ferguson for £25. Ferguson kept her for less than one year before selling her to Fortune, on 29 January 1793. Sometime before 1801, she went free. At Montreal on 19 August 1801, under the names Lizette Louis and Lizette Lewis, she was hired by innkeeper Robert Walker of Kingston, Upper Canada, for one year, at £18 a year plus room and board (BANQ, notary J.G. Delisle, no. 218, 7 August 1790; notary P.L. Deschenaux,

no. 2830, 18 May 1792; notary C. Stewart, 29 January 1793; notary J.A. Gray, no. 664, 19 August 1801; Fonds Drouin, "Notaires de Détroit," 3:471–2, records of notary Guillaume Monforton, 2 August 1789).
43 BANQ, notary P. Panet, no. 1266, 24 March 1761; register of Notre-Dame Church, 17 March 1746.
44 BANQ, register of Saints-Anges Church, Lachine, 31 March 1761. The church record gave his age as twenty-five, the contract with Gaudet, twenty-one.
45 As a witness at the wedding of the slaves Marie Louise and Charles Dominique Loisi (or Lazie) on 23 September 1760, Louis Antoine was identified as Louis Antoine Gaudet, suggesting that he was in Gaudet's employ (BANQ, register of Notre-Dame Church, 23 September 1760).
46 BANQ, notary J.G. Beek, no. 696, 30 March 1791. CCP, *Josette Lajeunesse v. John Merckell*, November Term 1790. *Gazette*, 11 and 18 November 1790, 3 February 1791. Jean-Baptiste Gamelin, a seventeen-year-old apprentice of furrier, tanner, and shoemaker John Merckell, left his master on 8 November 1790, complaining of mistreatment. His mother took him back to Merckell's that evening. After she had left, Merckell stripped Gamelin, tied him to a post and thrashed him until his arm gave out, whereupon he ordered two other apprentices to carry on the whipping. Gamelin fainted under this torture. Merckell then rubbed brine into his wounds. The Court of Quarter Sessions happened to be sitting at the time. The grand jury, hearing of the incident, dispatched a bailiff the next day to collect the beaten youth, and on the basis of his account and the evidence etched into his lacerated body, indicted Merckell for assault. Merckell pleaded guilty that same day. A shoemaker, offended at a newspaper's identification of Merckell as a practitioner of that trade, suggested that the author of the "cruel flagellation" should properly have been identified as "John Merckell, furrier, Notre-Dame Street, no. 72." Merckell went bankrupt two months later. For another case of an apprentice who complained of mistreatment, though of much less barbarity, and the court's response, see CQS register, *James Forsyth v. James Poupart*, 18 and 30 April 1781.
47 This was the case of Reuben Chambers, outlined in chapter 9. Charles-Louis Tarieu de Lanaudière requested that his imprisoned slave be kept in chains, as we mention below, but this was at Quebec.
48 BANQ, register of St-Antoine-de-Pades Church, Longueuil, 5 February 1763. Jodoin and Vincent, *Histoire de Longueuil*, 246–8.
49 *Quebec Gazette*, 27 March 1788.
50 BANQ, register of Notre-Dame Church, Montreal, 1 October 1785; notary J.N. Pinguet, 16 September 1788. In September 1788, Guichaux sold this slave family for 2,200 livres to his brother-in-law, Executive Councillor Thomas Dunn of Quebec, a judge of the Court of Common Pleas and later administrator of the province, and his wife Henriette Guichaux. The separation of Michel Remy from his father and mother came eight years later when, in September 1796, the boy, who had just turned eleven, accidentally set fire to the straw in Dunn's stable while playing. The flames engulfed the stable, then spread to other buildings, including the convent of the Récollets priests, which was razed. As a punishment, Dunn sent Michel Remy off on a frigate then in port. It is not known whether he intended that the boy serve on board the ship or that he be sold abroad (E. Gagnon, *Le fort et le château Saint-Louis*, 145. LeMoine, *L'album du touriste*, 40. Elizabeth Simcoe, *Mrs. Simcoe's Diary*, 199–200).

51 BANQ, register of Saints-Anges Church, Lachine, 11 October 1766. Trudel, *Deux siècles d'esclavage*, 129, 141. Trudel, *Dictionnaire*, 336–7. We have not found the deed by which Louis Richard gave himself to Gaudet, but for another example of this kind of servitude, see BANQ, notary S. Sanguinet, no. 330, 18 July 1769, and notice in *Quebec Gazette*, 10 August 1769, both concerning labourer Jacques Dubois, who gave himself as a servant for life to Montreal merchant Pascal Pillet.

52 BANQ, register of Notre-Dame Church, 15 April 1767, 27 March, 24 May and 29 October 1769; register of Saints-Anges Church, Lachine, 24 August 1762, 17 March 1765, 12 July 1766; register of St-Joachim Church, Pointe-Claire, 3 February 1777. The children were Pierre Dominique, August 1762–1 February 1777, buried at Pointe-Claire under the name Pierre Dominique Niagas; Marie Catherine, 17 March 1765–11 July 1766; Jeanne, 15 April 1767–19 December 1769; and Marie Charlotte, 23 May 1769–28 October 1769. No record has been found of Louis Antoine's death. His wife, identified as the "Neigresse" Marie Catherine, died on 24 April 1780 at the age of thirty-four. Her mother, Marie Anne, died on 23 August 1777, at the age of about 80 (BANQ, register of Notre-Dame Church, 28 April 1780; register of Saints-Anges Church, Lachine, 24 August 1777).

53 BANQ, notary L. Miray, 16 March 1782 and 2 August 1783; register of Notre-Dame Church, Quebec, 5 August 1783. Élisabeth Mondina, born 5 August 1749 at L'Islet, below Quebec, was the daughter of Jacques Mondina *dit* Olivier, a Frenchman, and Canadian-born Marie Posé (BANQ, register of Notre-Dame-de-Bonsecours Church, L'Islet, 6 August 1749). Her children by François William (or Williams), all baptized at the church of Notre-Dame-de-Miséricorde in Beauport on the day they were born, were Marie Louise, 26 September 1783; François, 17 December 1785, who died at Loretteville on 2 March 1787; Jean-Baptiste, 15 June 1787; Marie Marguerite, 30 June 1788, who died the next day; and Marie Angélique, 10 December 1790. In his will of 24 December 1802, Juchereau Duchesnay stipulated: "I will and intend that my negro, François Williams, be not sold; but that as full freedom would be more harmful than helpful to him considering his age, I desire that he have but the freedom to choose a master from among my five children ... and that the one he chooses for a master be obliged to take good care of him both in sickness and health. I further give the same freedom to his wife and to her two daughters for the time they must remain with me or belong to me" (cited in Audet and Surveyer, *Les députés au premier Parlement du Bas-Canada, 1792–1796*, 1:168). Juchereau Duchesnay died in 1806, whereupon François William and his wife, although not their two surviving children, Marie Louise and Marie Angélique, went to work in the household of Duchesnay's daughter, Louise Françoise (1771–1841), wife of Gabriel Elzéar Taschereau, seigneur of Nouvelle-Beauce. François William and his wife died at Ste-Marie-de-Beauce, he in August 1836, at the reputed age of about eighty-five, and she ten years later, at ninety-seven (BANQ, register of Ste-Marie-de-Beauce Church, 5 August 1836 and 2 August 1846).

54 HDM, admission registers, Book C, 26 February 1781.

55 See Appendix III, letter of Brigadier General Allan Maclean to Major Robert Mathews, 5 July 1781, and Sir John Johnson's "Return of Negroes brought in Canada by Scouts, and Sold at Montreal," 1781.

56 CQS register, *Samuel Judah v. Jacob*, 10 April 1781.

57 See Stampp, *The Peculiar Institution*, 141–91. Genovese, *Roll, Jordan, Roll*, 25–49. "Without

the power to punish, which the state conferred upon the master, bondage could not have existed," Stampp says (171).
58 See Brown-Kubisch, *The Queen's Bush Settlement*, 3; Greaves, *The Negro in Canada*, 10–11; Stouffer, *The Light of Nature and the Law of God*, 10; Winks, *The Blacks in Canada*, 24–5.
59 That Judah was not above getting physical seems borne out by the fact that he was accused of assault at this time by fellow merchant Myer Michaels. Charges and countercharges flew involving several persons in a case that divided Montreal's small Jewish community. Judah was convicted on 20 April, but fined a minimal six pence plus costs. At the same time, he was accused of bastardy by a woman who claimed that he had fathered a boy born to her on 26 February. Judah formally denied paternity, but on 25 April, the same day on which he was sentenced for the assault against Michaels, the court ruled against him and ordered him to pay child support of 10s a week for as long as the mother continued to nurse the boy (CQS register, 10, 18, 20, 21, 23, and 25 April 1781).
60 BANQ, notary P. Panet de Méru, no. 2915, 8 February 1768; notary P. Mézière, no. 2383, 1 March 1779. UMCB, U5179 and U5180, Pierre Guy to François Baby, 1 and 5 October 1778.
61 UMCB, U6716, Charles-Louis Tarieu de Lanaudière to François Baby, 17 September 1776. This letter is quoted in Imbeault, *Les Tarieu de Lanaudière*, 149.
62 The conduct of William Brown of Quebec, publisher of the *Quebec Gazette*, offers an interesting illustration. In 1774, when he wanted to haul his runaway African-born slave, Joe, off a ship that was about to sail, he did not venture to collar Joe himself but paid a bailiff 7s 6d to seize him. Three years later, when Joe, about twenty years old, ran off and was again caught, Brown paid the public executioner five shillings to whip his errant slave in Quebec's market square. In both instances, Brown enlisted compliant officers of the law to do the dirty work (Neilson, "Slavery in Old Canada," 33).
63 See n45, above. Marie Louise, born at Quebec, was the widow of a slave named Joseph when she married Charles Dominique Loisi or Lazie in Montreal on 23 September 1760, fifteen days after the surrender of New France to the British. Both were slaves of the merchant Joseph Fleury Deschambault de la Gorgendière. The witnesses of record at their wedding were the free black Joseph Hyppolite; Louis Antoine, then still free, whose name was entered as Louis Antoine Gaudet; and Charles Vaudreuil, also called simply Charles or Charlot, slave of the Marquis de Vaudreuil, Deschambault's brother-in-law and, as governor-general of New France, the man who had signed the articles of capitulation on 8 September. The fate of Marie Louise's husband is unknown, but Marie Louise herself was still a slave of Deschambault at her death on 27 November 1778 at the reputed age of about sixty. It is possible that Deschambault had lent or hired her services to Haldimand at some time during the latter's first stay in Canada from 1760 to 1767, when he had served in various capacities at Montreal and Trois-Rivières. Haldimand had acted, among other things, as liaison officer with Vaudreuil in arranging the return to France of French troops and civil officials after the Conquest (BANQ, register of Notre-Dame Church, 23 September 1760, 29 November 1778. Trudel, *Dictionnaire*, 107. Sutherland, Tousignant and Dionne-Tousignant, "Sir Frederick Haldimand").
64 HP, MS21728:117, Sergeant James Orr to General Frederick Haldimand, 21 January 1767. Marry Lewis's pursuer was Luc de Lacorne St-Luc; the reference to the "Mr Walker Mercht. Affair" is to the notorious case of the Montreal merchant and magistrate Thomas Walker, who

had been the victim of a home invasion and assault by a group of masked men, most of them believed to be soldiers, in December 1764, for which St-Luc and five other men were arrested in November 1766.

65 "Justice Robertson" was Montreal magistrate Daniel Robertson, who had served in the 42nd Regiment of Foot during the Seven Years War, rising by purchase from surgeon's mate to lieutenant. He had taken part in the British capture of Montreal in 1760, and of Martinique and Cuba in 1762. Within that period, he had married the young widow Marie Louise Rhéaume in Canada, and in Martinique he had bought a slave, Hilaire Lamour, who was to remain with him for twenty-five years.

66 CQS register, *The King on the prosn [prosecution] of Col. John Campbell v. Violetta, a Negroe wench*, 11 July 1793. Borthwick, *History of the Montreal Prison*, 243–4. Borthwick erred in saying this case took place in 1792.

67 HP, MS21761:115, Brigadier General Allan Maclean to Major Robert Mathews, 5 July 1781. The text of MacLean's letter is reproduced in Appendix III.

68 See notice in *Quebec Gazette*, 9 September 1784.

69 Sylvia, a "Negroe Wench," twenty-four years old, "in Good health and free of faults," was sold by Garret Van Vliet of Kinderhook, NY, to tailor James Perry of Montreal for £60 New York currency on 27 August 1773. On Perry's going bankrupt in 1777, lawyer and notary Pierre Panet (succeeded in 1778 by lawyer and notary Simon Sanguinet) was appointed to liquidate his assets, and Sylvia, said to be about 28, was sold at auction to Sheriff Edward William Gray for £50. She was termed the "negresse a madame gré" (Margaret Oakes) when she was admitted to the Hôtel-Dieu hospital 3–8 December 1785, and the "Négresse a monsieur graye," said to be forty-five, when she entered the Hôtel-Dieu on 17 November 1787 and died there on 10 December (BANQ, register of Christ Church, 10 December 1787. HDM, admission registers, Book E, 3 December 1785, 17 November 1787. *Quebec Gazette*, 16 April 1778. Riddell, "Further Notes on Slavery in Canada," 26–7).

70 LAC, MG23 GII 3, Edward William Gray Papers, 3, Gray to Amos Hayton, 3 August 1786.

71 Ibid., 3, Gray to Hayton, 14 December 1786.

72 Ibid., 3, Gray to Hayton, 18 March 1787.

73 Ibid., 3, Gray to Hayton, 11 June 1787.

74 Ibid., 3, Gray to William Lindsay, 11 August 1787.

75 BANQ, notary J.G. Beek, no. 324, 18 October 1787. The protest identified Chloe Forsyth as the widow of a John Elliot, formerly of Delaware.

76 LAC, MG23 GII 3, Edward William Gray Papers, 3, Gray to Lindsay, 22 August 1787.

77 Ibid., 3, Gray to Hayton, 22 October 1787.

78 Ibid., 4, Gray to Hayton, 22 October 1788.

79 Ibid., 4, Gray to Hayton, 19 October 1790.

80 Ibid., 4, Gray to Lindsay, 27 December 1790.

81 Ibid., 4, Gray to Lindsay, 30 December 1790.

82 On the inherently contradictory notion of "human property," see Melish, *Disowning Slavery*, 25–7. An Illinois judge, sitting on a fugitive-slave case in 1851, released the fugitive, holding that a man could not be claimed at one and the same time as "a *person* owing service, and ... a chattel, liable to sale" (*Frederick Douglass' Paper*, Rochester, NY, 27 November 1851).

83 Questioned about the workings of the upcountry slave trade in 1801, Alexis Rivard *dit* Maisonville of Detroit, who stated "[t]hat he had traded in slaves but he no longer does so," was asked whether the traders observed any greater formality when dealing in slaves than when selling other goods: "He answers that some persons had deeds of sale drawn up, some did not" (KBCV, *John Dease v. Joseph Ainsse*, no. 65, October Term 1799).

84 BANQ, notary A. Foucher, no. 5597, 29 September 1784; register of Notre-Dame Church, 14 November 1788. For this slave, see pages 203–4. Viger's wife, who was twelve years older than him, had died in 1845 at age seventy (BANQ, register of Notre-Dame Church, 17 November 1808 and 29 May 1845).

CHAPTER FIVE

1 David Walker, *David Walker's Appeal*, 30. The English actor John Bernard, who spent the years 1797–1811 in the United States, wrote in a similar way about the handicap of the slave: "He is like a man whose legs have been bound from infancy, and who on reaching manhood, though his bonds are cut, cannot walk." The American abolitionist Samuel Ringgold Ward used the image of the deer in referring to fugitive slaves in Canada in the 1850s: "In various parts of Canada Yankees have settled, and for miles around them the poison of their pro-slavery influence is felt. Some of them do not scruple to make known their desire to see Canada a part of the Union, and thus brought under the control of the slave power, and made a park for slaveholders to hunt human deer in" (Bernard, *Retrospections of America*, 117. Ward, *Autobiography*, 138).

2 BANQ, notary F. Racicot, 25 May 1789, 12 May 1794. For Arakwente, see Delâge and Gilbert, "La justice coloniale britannique et les Amérindiens au Québec 1760–1820. I – En terres amérindiennes." Lefrançois, "Thomas Arakwenté."

3 BANQ, notary J.B.H. Deguire, no. 184, 29 November 1799; notary J. Papineau, no. 3069, 11 August 1800; register of St-Michel Church, Vaudreuil, 2 July 1787.

4 LAC, RG68, Registrar General, Commissions and Letters Patent, Province of Quebec, 1764–91, 1:316–18. The records are mum on how this Bruce, believed to be the Christie slave of that name mentioned in the previous chapter as having been banished from the province under pain of death in 1773, could have remained in Montreal or returned by 1777.

5 The identification of Thomas, alias Tom, as a slave of John Grant rests on the assertion in a private letter of David Ross, the lawyer appointed to represent him in this case. But as we saw in chapter 3, Thomas, or Tom Grant, accused of theft in 1793, had been mistakenly identified as a slave of Colonel John Campbell, because he was working for Campbell and had stolen from his house; Tom Grant claimed to be a servant of Campbell, but "the property of Duncan McKillock Lieut. in the 1st Regt. of foot." He may subsequently have been sold to Grant, or possibly Ross presumed that, because he was in Grant's service and because the theft took place in Grant's house, he was Grant's slave (KB-Q, 1793: 365-B9, *R v. Thomas Grant*. McCord Museum, McCord Papers, 1458:4, David Ross to Arthur Davidson, 9 March 1795).

6 CQS, January Term 1795, Calendar of Prisoners, 10 January 1795; April Term 1795, Calendar of Prisoners, 21 April 1795. LAC, RG4, B20, Quebec, Lower Canada and Canada: [Provincial Secretary and Registrar] Applications for pardons or clemency 1766–1858, 1:386–91; RG68, Registrar General, Commissions and Letters Patent, Province of Quebec, 1764–91; Condi-

tional Pardons, Lower Canada, 1792–1841, 1:63–5. McCord Museum, McCord Papers, 1458:4, David Ross to Arthur Davidson, 9 March 1795. *Quebec Gazette*, 26 March and 7 May 1795.
7 Most of the American slave states "recognized the justice of compensating owners for slaves executed for crimes" (Stampp, *The Peculiar Institution*, 199).
8 Outside of the Montreal area, the case of the Trois-Rivières slave Genni, or Jenny, is also suggestive. Her owner, Zachary Macaulay, manager of the Forges St-Maurice, north of Trois-Rivières, formally emancipated her on 2 August 1796 as she sat in jail (BANQ, notary J.B. Badeau, 15 March 1788; notary A.I. Badeau, 2 August 1796).
9 BANQ, notary B. Faribault, 10 February 1765, 8 and 9 August 1772, 26 February 1776; notary J.J. Jorand, 17 April, 6 August, and 7 August 1792; register of St-Pierre Church, Sorel, 10 August 1772, 16 April 1788, and 3 October 1792. See also notary Jorand deeds of 28 January, 4 February, and 26 July 1791, 11 October 1792, and 21 May 1793. Jean-Baptiste Quéry died at Sorel on 19 November 1815, his age given as sixty-nine (BANQ, register of St-Pierre Church, Sorel, 21 November 1815).
10 BANQ, notary J. Papineau, no. 1731, 14 October 1791; notary L. Chaboillez, no. 6842, 1 April 1805; register of Notre-Dame Church, 27 August 1799. It is possible that this Rose was the Rose or Rosina who, around this time, had become the mate of John Fleming and the mother of his three sons, born in 1802, 1804 and 1807 (see chapter 3).
11 That Manuel Allen returned to work for Thomas John Sullivan is suggested by the fact that both men moved to Pointe-aux-Trembles around the same time. Sullivan disposed of his Montreal coffee house in 1799 and opened a tavern at Pointe-aux-Trembles; the birth record of Allen's daughter Marie Hélène (alias Marie Anne) in 1800 shows that Allen was then a resident of that parish. Allen may have returned to Montreal by 1805, when his daughter was buried there (BANQ, register of St-Enfant-Jésus Church, Pointe-aux-Trembles, 8 December 1800; register of Notre-Dame Church, Montreal, 27 January 1805. *Gazette*, 4 March, 8 April, and 5 August 1799. *Spectateur canadien*, 31 July 1815).
12 KBCV, *John Trim v. Simon Clark*, 1823, no. 162, deposition of Catherine Gayet (Guillet), 23 September 1828. HDM, admission registers, Book R, 6 April 1838.
13 For Beaucourt, see Major-Frégeau, *La vie et l'oeuvre de François Malepart de Beaucourt*, and the same author's "François Malepart de Beaucourt." The identity of the model for his *Portrait d'une négresse* is a mystery. If she was one of the black slaves known to have belonged to his widow, then the only possibility is Marie-Thérèse Zémire, who was said to be twenty-five years old in April 1796, and twenty-nine at her death on 15 December 1800 (BANQ, register of the Hôpital-Général chapel, 16 December 1800. HDM, admission registers, Book E, 19 April 1796).
14 HDM, admission registers, Book G, 12 March 1801, and Book D, 1 January 1802.
15 BANQ, register of St Gabriel Presbyterian Church, 26 May 1806.
16 BANQ, register of Notre-Dame Church, 24 April 1807. Marie Catherine Wright lived only three months. William Wright and Catherine Guillet were to have five more children – William Jr, born in 1808, Catherine in 1810, Marie Charlotte in 1811, Andrew in 1812, and John in 1823. All but John died in infancy.
17 BANQ, register of Notre-Dame Church, 5 July 1810 and 18 May 1811.
18 BANQ, register of St Gabriel Presbyterian Church, 12 February 1825; register of Notre-Dame

Church, 16 October 1826. POBR 2:56, 12 February 1825. Abdella and Guillet had three children, none of whom lived past the age of two: Marguerite (1827–1829), Pierre (1829–1830) and Jacob (1833–1834).
19 CQS, July Term 1832, *R v. Jacob Abdallah and Catherine Curra.* RPM, Box 50, nos 1886 and 1887, 26 June 1832.
20 BANQ, notary P. Lacombe, no. 71, 5 July 1832. Gaëtan's husband, Gabriel Franchère Sr, had died on 16 May at age 83. Gaëtan herself died on 13 January 1844 (BANQ, register of Notre-Dame Church, 19 May 1832 and 16 January 1844).
21 BANQ, notary J.B. Houlé, no. 3491, 17 February 1855, and no. 3495, 19 February 1855.
22 BANQ, TL12, Chambre des milices de Montréal, Registre d'audiences 1760–64, f. 29, 28 October 1763.
23 BANQ, notary J.G. Beek, Baux et Protêts, 1:142, no. 1; notary J. Papineau, no. 3068, 9 August 1800; register of Notre-Dame Church, 30 April 1795. HDM, admission registers, Book E, 19 December 1795.
24 BANQ, notary J.G. Beek, Baux et Protêts, 1: 217, 218, 220. *Statutes of the United Kingdom*, 5th Geo II (1732), c. 7, "An act for the more easy recovery of debts in his Majesty's plantations and colonies in America." Hilaire Lamour was probably the "nègre de Mr. Robertson" at the American siege and capture of Saint-Jean in the fall of 1775; he would have followed his master into captivity (Foucher, *Le Journal du célèbre siège de Saint-Jean*, 21).
25 BANQ, notary C. Stewart, 7 October 1793. Sarah Allen was probably the Mrs Allen who advertised the opening in January 1790 of her school for "Young Ladies" in a part of Finlay Fisher's house. Her husband, Edward Allen, may have been the actor-manager of that name who, with William Moore and John Bentley, had brought their theatre company to Montreal and Quebec from the United States in 1786; Edward Allen had opened Allen's Hotel in Montreal in December 1787 (*Gazette*, 9 and 30 March 1786, 13 December 1787, 7 January 1790). The theatre company left Albany in February 1786, and arrived at Montreal at the end of February or beginning of March; practically every issue of the weekly *Gazette* from 9 March on carried reports of its activities, until 13 July, when it was reported that the company had left for Quebec. Further items recording the Allens' presence at Montreal are found in the *Gazette* of 26 February and 12 March 1789.
26 Salzberger and Turck, eds., *Reparations for Slavery*, 66. Congressman Thaddeus Stevens of Pennsylvania made the remark in the US House of Representatives, on 19 March 1867, as he argued in favour of confiscating lands in the Southern states in the wake of the Civil War and turning over 40-acre parcels to the recently freed slaves.
27 For Rubin Middleton, see Appendix III.
28 BANQ, notary J.G. Beek, no. 668, 13 November 1790; notary L. Chaboillez, no. 2607, 23 September 1797; register of Christ Church, 26 January 1783, 4 October 1802. HDM, admission registers, Book G, 14 July 1809. LAC, HP, MS21765/59–60, muster rolls for John Butler's company. Smy, *An Annotated Nominal Roll of Butler's Rangers*, 42, 56. U.E. Loyalist Centennial Committee, *The Centennial of the Settlement of Upper Canada by the United Empire Loyalists*, 287. Becket married a Mary Richardson at Montreal in January 1783. The Old Loyalist List identified him sketchily as "Negro. No description." His mother, Mary Wright, died a "pauper living at Petite Cote [Rosemont Blvd.] near Montreal" on 3 October 1802, at the re-

puted age of eighty-three. Becket was said to be fifty-eight when he died at the Hôtel-Dieu on 25 July 1809.

29 BANQ, register of St-Louis Church, Terrebonne, 23 February and 18 July 1783; register of Notre-Dame Church, Montreal, 23 and 29 September 1801; notary L. Chaboillez, no. 1755, 11 April 1796. CQS, April 1795, *R v. Mary Fundy*; court register, 25 April 1795. HDM, admission registers, Book E, 28 May 1792, 23 September 1801, and Book F, 19 September 1801. *Gazette*, 22 November 1787, 6 February 1797. Cruickshank and Watt, *The History and Master Roll of the King's Royal Regiment of New York*, 97, 103. Fraser, *Seventeenth Report of the Department of Public Records and Archives of Ontario*, 74, 76. Pringle, *Lunenburgh*, 403. Malcolm Robertson, "Black Loyalists of Glengarry," 23. Cruickshank and Watt do not list John Powell as a member of the KRRNY, unless he is the private of the 2nd Battalion enlisted on 12 November 1781 under the name Paul/Powlis/Poulus James. The Powells died within a week of each other at the Hôtel-Dieu in 1801, Elizabeth, in her early fifties, on 21 September, and "Jean Paoulle," said to be about fifty-six, on 28 or 29 September. When Mary Fundy was accused of theft by the Powells, she was identified as the wife of a labourer named Peter Fundy. She is believed to be the black woman Mary Campbell who was jailed, along with Jacob Simpson, a black man, on 29 January 1793 on charges of having stolen items from the house of Sir John Johnson. They were acquitted at their trial on 16 July 1793. Mary Campbell was arrested again the following year, this time identified as Mary Funder, alias Mary Campbell. In a letter of 24 March 1794, the governor's secretary wrote to Sheriff Gray: "Lord Dorchester directs me to inclose you a Petition of Mary Funder alias Mary Campbell, at present in the Gaol of Montreal, stating that she is near Childbirth, & praying to be released, if that is really the case, it might endanger her own & the Child's life to keep her in Confinement. His Lordship therefore desires that if you find her statement true, that you would discharge her, warning her to be more cautious in future." On 31 March, Gray reported that "she was found to be very big with child, tho it did not appear that she was so near her delivery as stated in her petition, but I thought proper to release her for fear of any accident happening to herself or the child by her being detained in the Goal, as she can at any time be re-apprehended in case it should be judged necessary to prosecute her for the offence with which she stands charged." It is not known what happened to the baby. In April 1798, it was the turn of "Mary Fundy, a negro woman," to lay a criminal charge. She accused an innkeeper of having assaulted her on 5 April, but when the case came to court, she "acknowledged satisfaction for the injury done her by the Defendant, and prayed leave to withdraw her complaint" (CQS, April and July terms 1793, *R v. Mary Campbell and Jacob Simpson*; April Term 1798, *R v. Francis Siebenhart*. LAC, RG7, GI5 C, Lower Canada, Civil Secretary's Letter Books 1788–1829, 2:40–1, Thomas Aston Coffin to Edward William Gray, 24 March 1794; MG23 GII 3, Edward William Gray Papers, v. 5, Gray to Coffin, 27 and 31 March 1794).

30 BANQ, register of Christ Church, 17 July 1787, 11 June 1794, 1 and 5 September 1799; register of Quebec Anglican Church, 23 August 1810; notary J.G. Beek, no. 438, 30 August 1788. It appears that George Crane was married twice, to Mary Belangé in 1787, and to Mary Johnson in 1794. It was Crane and Belangé who, in 1788, sold their land claim. The buyer was farmer David Campbell of Ste-Rose. Crane was identified at Montreal in 1799 as a soldier in the Canadian Volunteers.

31 BANQ, notary J. Papineau, no. 2070, 4 September 1793; notary J.B. Desève, no. 909, 16 April 1794, and no. 1057, 30 October 1795; register of the Hôpital-Général chapel, 14 August 1811 and 17 December 1822. *Herald*, 14 March 1812. Around the time of his wife's death, Hilaire Lamour was employed by a Mary Donnellan; when she dismissed him the following year, she identified him as William Lamour, "an elderly negro man," adding a non-sequitur: "This man is well known, having formerly lived some time at the Hospital of l'Hotel Dieu." He died at the Hôpital-Général on 15 December 1822, identified as an eighty-nine-year-old labourer. He and his wife had no children.

32 BANQ, notary J.G. Beek, no. 525, 5 May 1789. Egerton, "Quok Walker's Suit: Emancipation in the North," chapter 4 in *Death or Liberty*. Johonnot, "The Johonnot Family," 141. MacEacheren, "Emancipation of Slavery in Massachusetts," 303. The distillery company was launched in 1785 by Jean-Baptiste Durocher, Levy Solomon, George King, Thomas McCord, George McBeath, Norman McLeod, Samuel Birnie, Francis Winter, Matthew Lessey, John McNamara, and Alexander Hay. On 16 April 1785, they bought the distillery property in the heart of the city. In early 1789, the company was dissolved and immediately re-formed, with new owners Todd, McGill & Co., Forsyth Richardson & Co., King & McCord, Jean-Baptiste Durocher of Montreal, and Robert Lester of Quebec. The distillery advertised its rum in the *Gazette* of 10 February 1791. In June 1794, after a fire severely damaged the distillery buildings, the two lots on which they stood were sold at auction for £166 13s 4d. The company itself was dissolved the following December.

33 BANQ, notary A. Foucher, no. 7262, 14 April 1794.

34 BANQ, notary J.G. Delisle, no. 936, 31 December 1794, and no. 2361, 30 January 1797.

35 UMCB, C3/170, report by François Papineau of the survey of the property of Cesar Johannot, 25 August 1797.

36 BANQ, notary J.G. Delisle, no. 2493, 7 September 1797.

37 BANQ, notary J. Papineau, no. 2694, 11 January 1798.

38 BANQ, notary P. Lukin Sr, no. 1127, 23 January 1798, and no. 1166, 26 February 1798. See also notary J.A. Gray, no. 1326, 4 March 1805. The distillery of Levy Solomon & Co. at Cornwall may have been the one that had been put up for sale in 1796 under the name Warffe's Distillery (*Quebec Gazette*, 12 May 1796).

39 BANQ, notary P. Lukin Sr, no. 1287, 9 October 1798.

40 BANQ, register of Christ Church, Sorel, 9 June 1800. CCP, "Executions issued out of the Court of Common Pleas 1789–1801," *Robert Jones v. Caesar Johannot*, 7 and 14 November 1799. KBCV, October Term 1799, no. 133, *Robert Jones v. Caesar Johannot*, and June Term 1800, no. 77, *Robert Jones v. Caesar Johannot and J.M. Auguste Roux & al. Opposants*. LAC, RG4, B17, Quebec and Lower Canada: [Civil Secretary], Lawsuits, v. 17, file 17, *Robert Jones v. César Johannot*, 1799. *Quebec Gazette*, 21 November 1799.

41 BANQ, notary Louis Chaboillez, no. 1366, 27 March 1795; notary P. Lukin Sr, no. 747, 21 April 1796.

42 BANQ, notary P. Lukin Sr, no. 1251, 27 July 1798. The deed of sale identified Trim and Margaret Moore as "Nègre et Négresse," which has led to their being mistaken for husband and wife. It is not clear why Margaret Moore was the buyer of record, rather than her husband, who was still living: he acted as sponsor at the baptism of John Fleming's son, John, in 1802

and died in the house on St-Augustin Street in February 1803 at the reputed age of 42. The witnesses at his burial were Trim and Joseph Pierson (BANQ, register of Christ Church, 6 February 1803. POBR 1:224. Trudel, *Dictionnaire*, 120).
43 BANQ, notary L. Chaboillez, no. 8233, 18 April 1808, and no. 8387, 30 September 1808; notary J. Desautels, no. 1570, 21 April 1815. LAC, RG 4, B19, Assessments for the Year 1813, Montreal, 1:48. See also BANQ, notary L. Huguet-Latour, no. 1280, 13 November 1816. *Gazette*, 7 May 1810. *Canadian Biographical Dictionary: Quebec and Maritime Provinces*, 158. In 1819, Trim's address was given as 23 McGill Street (Doige, *Montreal Directory*, 1819 ed., 177). The property lies on the east side of McGill Street, at the head of St-Maurice Street.
44 BANQ, notary L. Chaboillez, no. 3532, 17 May 1799.
45 BANQ, notary T. Barron, no. 1540, 19 April 1809; no. 2438, 30 September 1814; no. 2594, 2 May 1815.
46 BANQ, notary N.B. Doucet, no. 5406, 25 July 1818; notary H. Griffin, no. 6210, 26 January 1826; register of Christ Church, 23 September 1823, 9 October 1825, 2 April 1826; register of Notre-Dame Church, 9 May 1827, 10 August 1829. TC, 20 December 1825, no. 636.
47 BANQ, notary P. Ritchot, no. 1863, 10 July 1827, and no. 2468, 2 September 1829; notary F.M.T. Chevalier de Lorimier, no. 542, 19 September 1832. KBCV, *J.D. Lacroix v. Isaac Taylor et al.*, and *Henri Vallotte v. Isaac Taylor et al.*, 1849, nos 1910 and 1409, declaration and exhibits of Henri Vallotte.
48 BANQ, notary G.D. Arnoldi, no. 623, 7 December 1829; notary P. Lukin Jr, no. 2343, 16 November 1831. In the end, Kurczyn alone acted as executor.
49 BANQ, notary J.A. Gray, nos 1138 and 1139, 11 May 1804.
50 Outside Montreal, several blacks secured seigneurial lands in this period, by grant from a seigneur or by purchase from the previous occupants. The seigneury of Argenteuil, on the Ottawa River, is particularly striking in this regard. On 23 May 1793, Pierre-Louis Panet granted to the "Nègre" Ben a life lease (*bail à vie*) of a plot on the west side of the North River (*rivière du Nord*), within the seigneurial domain. This was the day before Panet sold the seigneury to Patrick Murray, major of the 2nd Battalion, 60th Regiment, and former commander at Detroit. In return for his lease, Ben was to act as a gatekeeper and maintain the road running by the property, and to pay the seigneur roughly two bushels of merchantable grain or corn per year (BANQ, notary P.R. Gagnier, no. 952, 23 May 1793, no. 953, 24 May 1793). A black man who obtained land from Patrick Murray around this time was Hyacinthe, a farmer (see Appendix I/B, notice 4). Gad Way, identified as "a person of Color, late from the United States," bought Lots 20 and 21, on the "East side of the East settlement," in November 1803 from farmer Lansing Warren for 50 "silver Spanish Mill'd Dollars." In a second transaction five days later, naval officer James Murray, who had purchased the seigneury from his father, Patrick Murray, the previous 30 April, granted Way, "a person of Color residing at said place," Lot 9, Prince Edward Street, in the Village of St Andrew's (St-André-d'Argenteuil). That property was 90 feet wide by 2 arpents deep. Way was to pay the seigneur one Spanish dollar, or 5 shillings, each year on St Martin's Day, 11 November (BANQ, notary P. Lukin Sr, no. 2858, 30 April 1803, no. 3111, 23 November 1803, and no. 3125, 28 November 1803). Joseph Freeman, "an Affrican late from Boston," bought Lot 10 in the Côte-du-Midi from farmer John Doxteder on 13 November 1804. That same day, Doxteder sold the lot next to it, no. 11, to Edward Thompson,

"an Affricain late from Albany." Both lots measured 3 arpents by 30, and in both cases, the purchase price was not in money but in labour: Freeman was to clear four or five acres of Doxteder's land and prepare it for seeding and cultivation by the following 1 May, and Thompson undertook to cut down the wood on eight acres of Doxteder's lands (BANQ, notary P. Lukin Sr, nos 3380 and 3381, 13 November 1804). One week later, on 21 November, Patrick Murray, acting for his absent son, granted Lot 2 in the Côte-du-Midi to Benjamin Robertson (alias Jacques Robertson, Jacques Robinson, James Robinson, Benjamin Rorberson) for an annual payment of one Spanish dollar and three bushels of merchantable grain or corn. Robertson sold his property, "bounded in front by the Rivière Rouge Lots, in the rear by the Bay [of Carillon] concession lots," in 1822, but his extended family remained in the area for many years, engaging in farming and other pursuits. One of his granddaughters, Emelie Robertson (alias Emilia Robeson, Amelia Robinson), born in 1838 to Joseph Robertson and Eugénie Villeneuve of St Andrew's, married the fugitive Virginia slave Edmond Albert Turner in Montreal in December 1862. Their children, Mary Elisabeth and twins Jane and Margaret, were born at St Andrew's, respectively on 15 September 1863 and in Christmas Week 1864 (BANQ, notary P. Lukin Sr, no. 3404, 21 November 1804; notary C.L. Nolin, no. 797, 21 June 1822; register of St-André Church, Argenteuil, 30 September 1838, 25 December 1864; register of Église évangélique française, Montreal, 24 December 1862; register of St John's Presbyterian Church, Montreal, 11 September 1864). Emelie Robertson's younger half-sister, Marguerite Robertson, born in 1854 to Joseph Robertson and his second wife, Esther Papineau, of Beech Ridge (Coteau-du-Hêtre), St Andrew's Parish, married Montreal barber Michael Speck, a widower, in 1872. Speck's first wife, Sarah Elizabeth Jones, was the daughter of barber William Francis Jones and Ann Queen, free blacks from Maryland who had moved to Montreal around 1850 (BANQ, register of St-André Church, Argenteuil, 11 June 1854; register of St-Joseph Street Methodist Church, Montreal, 18 March 1872; register of Erskine Presbyterian Church, Montreal, 24 April 1866).

51 See BANQ, notary L. Chaboillez, no. 6399, 10 April 1804; notary J.A. Gray, no. 1006, 31 October 1803.

52 BANQ, notary L. Chaboillez, no. 9477, 1 October 1810. Stockbird was identified in the deed of sale as a "Nègre demeurant au fief Nazareth." Nothing else is known about him. His property consisted of half of a lot, measuring 108 feet, 10 inches, by 90 feet, on Prince Street at the corner of Gabriel Street.

53 BANQ, notary J.A. Gray, no. 1367, 24 May 1805; notary H. Griffin, no. 1652, 28 November 1816. KBCV, June Term 1816, no. 254, *Thomas McCord v. John Fleming*. *Quebec Gazette*, 8 August 1816.

54 BANQ, notary A. Jobin, no. 1947, 4 July 1820; register of St Gabriel Presbyterian Church, 26 May 1806 and 31 August 1815; CT601 S1, Cour supérieure, Testaments olographes, no. 70, will of James Dunlop, 7 May 1810, probated 5 September 1815. KBCV, *John Trim v. Simon Clark*, 1823, no. 162, deposition of Catherine Gayet (Guillet), 23 September 1828. At his baptism in 1799, Wright was identified simply as William, "a Negroe belonging to James Dunlop of Montreal Esq." Then in 1802, he was William Dunlop when he acted as proxy for John Trim as a sponsor at the baptism of John Fleming's son John (BANQ, register of St Gabriel Presbyterian Church, 17 December 1799; register of Christ Church, 8 August 1802).

55 BANQ, notary A. Jobin, no. 1949, 4 July 1820.
56 BANQ, notary A. Jobin, no. 1933, 26 June 1820, and no. 1938, 30 June 1820.
57 BANQ, register of St Andrew's Presbyterian Church, 16 October 1823; register of St Gabriel Presbyterian Church, 12 February 1825; register of Notre-Dame Church, 16 October 1826; register of St-Jean-Baptiste Church, Quebec, 17 November 1862; notary J.B. Houlé, no. 3491, 17 February 1855, and no. 3495, 19 February 1855. POBR 2:56.
58 BANQ, notary J. Desautels, no. 4888, 8 June 1820; notary N.B. Doucet, no. 20608, 22 June 1833; register of Christ Church, 30 July 1834.
59 Variants of his name included Volantin, Volemten, Volemtin, Vollantin, Vollintin, Volomtin and Volumten.
60 BANQ, notary J.M. Mondelet, no. 2365, 2 February 1803, and no. 2530, 10 October 1803. *Gazette*, 7 February 1803.
61 BANQ, notary J.M. Mondelet, no. 2707, 15 June 1804, and no. 2727, 23 July 1804.
62 BANQ, notary J.M. Mondelet, no. 2781, 9 October 1804, and no. 2956, 7 October 1805.
63 KBCV, June Term 1805, no. 37, *Augustin Labadie & uxor v. Alexandre Volemtin*, and no. 95, *John Freer v. Augustin Labadie*.
64 KBCV, June Term 1805, no. 37, *Augustin Labadie & uxor v. Alexandre Volemtin & uxor*, plea by the defendants, 5 June 1805.
65 Ibid., "Rapport de Louis Guy & Louis Chaboillez," 16 October 1805. A draft of this report is found in UMCB, C3/203.
66 BANQ, notary L. Guy, 7 December 1805.
67 BANQ, notary J.M. Mondelet, no. 3099, 17 October 1806; notary L. Guy, 16 March 1808; notary G.D. Arnoldi, no. 615, 24 November 1829.
68 BANQ, notary T. Barron, no. 969, 2 November 1805. UMCB, A5/515, notice of sale of Labadie property to be read by public crier at the church door, 13 December 1807, and report of the crier, bailiff Andrew Kollmeyer, 20 December 1807; C2/304, power of attorney from Augustin Labadie to Louis Guy, 23 February 1808, and receipt of Gabriel Cotté to "Jean Bte Labadie," 29 September 1808.
69 KBCV, February Term 1809, no. 121, *Elizabeth Perras v. Augustin Labadie*. UMCB, C2/304, various receipts by the widow Cotté to Threer and Labadie, note of Joseph Quesnel to Louis Guy, 20 June 1809, and receipt from bailiff Andrew Kollmeyer to Louis Guy, dated 10 November 1809, for the cost of three cryings at the church door and adjudication of Labadie property; D/110, letter of Joseph Quesnel to Louis Guy, 22 August 1809.
70 BANQ, register of St Gabriel Presbyterian Church, 5 October 1800. HDM, admission registers, Book S, 5 February 1842. No witnesses were recorded at the wedding of Alexander Smith and Catharine Fletcher, who were identified summarily on the occasion as "a Negroe man" and "a Negroe woman," both "of age."
71 BANQ, register St-Antoine-de-Padoue Church, St-Antoine-sur-Richelieu, 18 September 1798. She was identified as "presse ... né dans Les colonnie" (Presse, born in the American colonies) when she was admitted to the Hôtel-Dieu hospital in 1807 (HDM, admission registers, Book G, 10 April 1807).
72 BANQ, register of Notre-Dame Church, 25 November 1799.
73 BANQ, register of Notre-Dame Church, 25 January 1793. On the Houldin family, see chapter 7.

74 UMCB, C2/304, receipt by the widow Cotté to John Threer for payment by Jean-Baptiste (*sic*) Labadie, 8 August 1807.
75 Augustin Labadie was again misidentified as Jean-Baptiste Labadie in a receipt from the representative of the widow Cotté of 29 September 1808 (see above, n68), but he was not then termed a "nègre." That payment was made in Labadie's name by notary Louis Guy after the Labadies had left Montreal.
76 BANQ, register of Notre-Dame Church, 4 October 1800, 23 September, 24 September and 5 October 1801, 13 August and 2 November 1802, 30 July and 3 September 1803, 26 August 1804, 16 November 1805, 24 September and 19 November 1806, 23 December 1807.
77 BANQ, register of Notre-Dame Church, 14 September 1801, 8 February 1804.
78 BANQ, register of Notre-Dame Church, 18 July and 18 December 1803, 4 November 1805.
79 UMCB, C2/304, account of Augustin Labadie with lawyer Joseph Bédard, 4 November 1807.
80 Valentine was a witness at the baptisms of Thomas Fleming, John Fleming's son, in 1807, Ann Ashley in 1808, and Hero Alexander Richardson in 1821; the weddings of Thomas York and Flora Freeman in 1807, Peter Abraham and Mary Rusk in 1815, and Joseph Francis and Anne York in 1822; and the burials of Marie Jones (alias Marie-Félicité Coudrin), daughter of Narcisse Coudrin and Mary Violet Jones, in 1815, and of William Feeler in 1828. Valentine Pierson, the son born to Joseph Pierson and Mary Rusk in 1810 and who died in 1811, was probably named for Alexander Valentine. Under the name Catherine Volantin, Valentine's wife was the sponsor, with Narcisse Coudrin, at the baptism of Étienne L'Africain, the son of Jean Baptiste L'Africain and Charlotte Bonga, in 1807.
81 BANQ, notary G.D. Arnoldi, no. 615, 24 November 1829, no. 616, 26 November 1829; register of Christ Church, 20 November 1829. POBR 2:159. The inventory of Valentine's property is one of two documents that list the contents of a black Montreal household of that time; the other is the inventory of John Trim's estate in 1833 (BANQ, notary P. Lukin Jr, no. 2759, 8 February 1833).
82 BANQ, notary G.D. Arnoldi, no. 2051, 5 November 1833, no. 3344, 5 April 1834; notary L. Marteau, no. 951, 4 March 1831; notary J.H. Jobin, no. 199, 1 May 1834; register of Notre-Dame Church, 30 January 1843. HDM, admission registers, Book S, 5 February 1842. In a similar case at Quebec, the black cooper Jean (alias Jacques) Barthélemy and his Montreal-born wife, Ursule Démet, both in their fifties, had ceded their stone house on Sault-au-Matelot Street to merchant George Arnold in 1824 in return for an annual payment of £60 (to be reduced to £36 should one of them die), reserving the right to live on the second floor, with rights to the attic, part of the cellar and the yard, and a small shed for their chickens. In September 1836, the widowed Barthélemy ceded full use of the premises to Arnold for an additional payment of £10 (BANQ, notary A. Campbell, no. 3668, 27 October 1824, with addendum of 28 September 1836).
83 BANQ, notary H. Griffin, no. 8420, 14 September 1829; register of St Gabriel Presbyterian Church, 8 August 1815.
84 Archives de la Ville de Montréal, VM2, yearly assessment rolls, 1847 to 1853. BANQ, register of Christ Church, 6 April 1841. LAC, RG31-C-1, 1842 census, manuscript returns, Canada East, Montreal, St-Laurent Ward, St-Constant Street, f. 1350, no. 11. POBR 3:181. *Gazette*, 9 July 1852. CD 1842–43, 1844–45, 1845–46, 1849, 1850 and 1852. Bertrand, *Histoire de Montréal*, 2:175–6. Linteau, *Brève histoire de Montréal*, 72. The census of January 1861 found Mary

Ann Drummond living with expatriate American blacks Joseph Ash and his wife, Lucinda Steve (or Steele), in the east-side St-Jacques Ward. She was said to be fifty-nine, yet she had supposedly been of the age of majority (twenty-one or older) when she married in 1815, which would have made her at least sixty-six by 1861. The 1871 census was probably closer to the truth when it gave her age as seventy-seven, although it erred in identifying her as American-born. At that time, she was a resident of the Ladies' Benevolent Institution on Berthelet (Ontario) Street, where she died of "senility" on 18 February 1876. She was buried in the institution's plot in Mount Royal Cemetery (BANQ, register of Christ Church, 19 February 1876. LAC, RG31-C-1, 1861 census, manuscript returns, Canada East, Montreal, St-Jacques Ward, f. 7656; 1871 census, manuscript returns, Province of Quebec, Montreal, St-Laurent Ward, 106/C6:51, no. 10. Mount Royal Cemetery, Grave G-402).

85 BANQ, notary P.R. Gagnier, no. 3500, 21 February 1801; notary L. Chaboillez, no. 5105, 17 February 1802; notary J.A. Berthelot, no. 1797, 28 March 1820; register of St-Eustache Church, St-Eustache, 5 November 1827, 24 September 1829. HDM, admission registers, Book K, 29 May 1826. LAC, RG31-C-1, 1831 census, manuscript returns, Lower Canada, St-Eustache, Côte-St-Jean, f. 1892. Other forms of his name recorded included Démarois, Desmarais, Demarin, Démarins, Desmarins, and Desmarois. He was identified as a sixty-seven-year-old "neigre de la rivière du Chaine" (St-Eustache) when he was admitted to hospital at Montreal in 1826, but at his wedding at St-Eustache in 1827, he was identified as a Montrealer, the widower of Angélique Lavallée *dit* Jolibois. He died at St-Eustache on 22 September 1829, aged about seventy-eight. He and Filiatrault had two children, Joseph and Angélique, before they married. They legitimized the children at their wedding. Their son is believed to have been the boy christened Joseph (no family name) at St-François-de-Sales Church on Île Jésus (Laval) on 12 March 1802. The date and place of birth of Angélique are unknown, but she was said to be of the age of majority when she married Louis Dufour of Ste-Scholastique at St-Eustache on 24 October 1836, meaning that she was born at the latest in 1815.

86 CQS, April 1795, *R v. Mary Fundy*; court register, *R v. Mary Fundy*, 25 April 1795.

87 CQS, *R v. Peter Dego, Titus Fortune and [blank] Freeman*, complaint of John N. Smith, dated 6 September 1819, bundled with documents of July 1820. Doige, *Montreal Directory*, 1819 ed., 81, 98.

88 CQS, May 1818, *R v. William Meikins Nation & Warren Glawson*, deposition of Ace Gabriel, 9 April 1818. For Dago and his mother, see chapter 7, n16.

89 KB, March 1820, *R v. Warren Gawson, George Binks and Richard Jackson*.

90 CQS, March 1833, *R v. Jacob Abdallah and Peter Peterson*, affidavit of James Sampson, 15 March 1833.

91 KB, November 1814, *R v. James Grant*, deposition of John Fleming and examination of James Grant, both 28 November 1814.

92 CQS, July Term 1816, *Madeleine Fleming (also written Marguerite Fleming) v. Jany Graves (also written Jane Grames)*, Fleming's complaint 1 May, Graham's bond 2 May. Jane Graham's name was recorded variously as Jane Garret, Mrs Jane Gearish, Jane Grahams, Jennie Graham, Jane Graims, Jane Grames, Jany Graves, and Jane Grimes. When Fleming's wife gave her notice to move out on 1 May 1816, Graham allegedly threw a fit, tossed a cudgel (*casse-tête*) at her, took up a gun and was only prevented from shooting at her by the interpo-

sition of Henry Garish (Henry Garrett), Graham's husband. Graham was arrested several times for assault or threats, and for disorderliness. In November 1820, for instance, at least her fourth arrest that year, she and three other women were jailed on charges of being "loose idle women and public prostitutes and with having no fixed place of residence or any visible means of subsistance, and if suffered to go at large that there would be great danger of their perishing upon the public streets for want of sustenance." In May 1821, she was committed to jail as "a loose idle woman and Public Prostitute" (KB, July 1821, Calendar of the House of Correction, 10 July 1821. LAC, RG4, B21, Lower Canada and Canada East Gaol Calendars and Prison Returns, 3:1450, 1460).

93 Doige, *Montreal Directory*, 1819 ed., 140, 143. Perrault, *Montréal en 1825*, 286.

94 BANQ, register of Christ Church, 15 April 1832; register of Zion Congregational Church, 15 January 1855; TL19, S41, Box 13009, Poll Book, Montreal West Ward, 1834, under date 10 November. LAC, RG31-C-1, 1842 census, manuscript returns, Canada East, Montreal, St-Laurent Ward, St-Constant Street, f. 1350, nos 10 and 11. CD 1842–3, 1843–4, 1844–5, 1845–6, 1847, 1849, 1850 and 1852.

95 CQS, October 1830, *R v. Jacob Abdallah*, deposition of Peter Dago, 30 September 1830. LAC, MG24, B173, James Reid Papers, Criminal Cases, 3, *R v. Henry Johnson*, 27 October 1821, testimony of Mary Abraham. Perrault, *Montréal en 1825*, 315.

96 BANQ, register of Christ Church, 6 February 1803; register of St Gabriel Presbyterian Church, 9 September 1827. POBR 1:224, 2:115. Margaret Plauvier died on 8 September 1827, say the church records. The cemetery record says she died on 15 September.

97 KBCV, 1823, no. 162, *John Trim v. Simon Clark*, deposition of Abraham Low, 15 May 1829. Low stated that he had lived at Trim's during the War of 1812; it must have been at the end of the war, because from December 1812 to 4 November 1814 he had served in the militia in the Quebec District (LAC, RG9 1A7, Adjutant-General's Office, Lower Canada fonds, Militia Lists, War of 1812, vols 3, 13 and 14).

98 BANQ, register of St Gabriel Presbyterian Church, 4 November 1815, 3 May 1829; register of St Paul's Presbyterian Church, 22 June 1833; notary J. Desautels, no. 719, 19 October 1813. KBCV, 1823, no. 162, *John Trim v. Simon Clark*, deposition of Robert Moore, 18 May 1829.

99 BANQ, register of Notre-Dame Church, 7 January and 30 June 1823, 16 October 1826. KBCV, 1823, no. 162, *John Trim v. Simon Clark*, deposition of Jacob Abdella, 12 June 1824. HDM, admission registers, Book P, 31 December 1831, and Book Q, 29 November 1839.

100 BANQ, notary L. Chaboillez, no. 7077, 22 August 1805. With interest at the going rate of six per cent, Reid's debt would have amounted to £233 4s by August 1806. As Reid gave Trim a new note for precisely that sum in September 1806, payable in a year's time, it appears that this second note was not for a new debt but an extension of the 1805 one (BANQ, notary L. Chaboillez, no. 7586, 2 September 1806).

101 KBCV, *John Trim v. Simon Clark*, 1823, no. 162, deposition of Joseph Routier, 7 December 1824.

102 BANQ, TL19, S41, Box 13007, Poll Book, County of Montreal, August 1827, under date 9 August.

103 A grand jury in April 1830 deplored "the practice of issuing warrants for the apprehension of persons complained against without instituting further enquiry than that contained in the

examination on oath of the complainant." As a remedy, the grand jury proposed a procedure similar to today's preliminary inquiries to determine the validity of an accusation. This, they believed, would do away with the "expensive, irritating and vexatious mode of proceeding by what is commonly called *a Cross bill*," where the accused would respond to a charge by filing a countercharge against his accuser, a tit-for-tat practice that was common, particularly in assault cases. It would also help to ensure that "the liberty of His Majesty's Subjects would not be endangered by the complaints of persons making their depositions under the excitement of passion, a circumstance which has often heretofore occurred" (CQS register, April Sessions 1830, grand jury presentment, 30 April).

104 CQS, October Term 1810, *R v. Hazen Cross. Gazette*, 8 October 1810. The Crosses were Trim's neighbours. Innkeeper Thomas Cross had taken a five-year lease on Simon Clark's property in 1809 (BANQ, notary J.A. Gray, no. 2353, 14 April 1809).

105 CQS, Trim's deposition of 11 November 1813, and the Finch recognizances, 12 November 1813, filed with documents of July Term 1815.

106 CQS, *John Trim v. Richard Thompson*, complaint by Trim, 6 November 1818, Thompson recognizance, 7 November 1818.

107 CQS, Trim complaint, 16 May 1820. The intruder is not named.

108 CQS, *John Trim v. Jane Wilson*, 2 September 1823.

109 BANQ, register of Christ Church, 9 October 1825.

110 KB, Administrative Documents, "Calendrier de la prison commune du district de Montréal octobre 1823–avril 1827," calendars of August–September, 1 October, 1 November, 1 December 1825, 90, 94, 99 and 102–6. CQS, *John Trim v. Tally Reny Valentine*, Trim complaint, 13 August 1825.

111 BANQ, notary H. Griffin, no. 6210, 26 January 1826; register of Christ Church, 2 April 1826. TC, no. 636, 20 December 1825, "Fleurie Deniger, Tutelle ad hoc." Deniger being a minor of about seventeen, her stepfather petitioned the court for the appointment of a tutor, or guardian, to assist her in setting the terms of her marriage contract. Merchant Joseph Shuter was appointed. The only previous marriage contract entered into by Montreal blacks was that of shoemaker Narcisse Coudrin and Mary Violet Jones in 1807 (BANQ, notary J.M. Cadieux, no. 79, 2 May 1807).

112 CQS, *John Trim v. Robert Moore*, October 1830, Trim affidavits, 18 and 29 October 1830, Moore recognizances 24 December 1830 and 22 February 1831. KB, September 1831, *R v. Robert Moore and Jacob Grant*, Trim affidavit, 3 September 1831. Jacob Grant and James Rollings acted as Moore's sureties when he posted his bond in December 1830; for his bond of February 1831, the sureties were Rollings and notary George Dorland Arnoldi.

113 BANQ, notary P. Lukin Jr, no. 2343, 16 November 1831, appended codicil of 9 February 1832.

114 CQS, July Term 1832, *R v. Jacob Abdallah & Catherine Curra, his wife;* court register, 12, 13, 14, 17 July 1832. RPM, Box 50, nos 1886–1887, 26 June 1832.

115 CQS, Deposition of *John Trim v. Jacob Julian and Catherine Guerin*, 1 November 1832, *R v. Jacob Julian & wife*, recognizance of Jacob Julian, 2 November 1832.

116 BANQ, register of Christ Church, 28 January 1833. POBR 2:355.

117 BANQ, register of St Gabriel Presbyterian Church, 1 February 1820; register of St Paul's Presbyterian Church, 22 June 1833; notary D.L. St-Omer, no. 18, 10 July 1837. TC, no. 794, 2 July 1833.

NOTES TO PAGES 162–4

118 BANQ, register of Notre-Dame Church, 30 November 1836, 19 September 1838 and 9 February 1839. CQS, *R v. Robert Moore*, complaint of Flavie Denaigé (*sic*), 23 October 1838.
119 BANQ, register of St Paul's Presbyterian Church, 30 May 1839; register of Notre-Dame Church, 17 November 1839.
120 BANQ, register of St Paul's Presbyterian Church, 2 July 1842. LAC, RG31-C-1, 1842 census, manuscript returns, Canada East, Montreal, Queen's Ward, Janvier Street, f. 1414, no. 23; 1871 census, manuscript returns, Quebec, Montreal, Ste-Anne Ward, 106/A1:18, no. 17. Hornby, *Black Islanders*, 53 and 74, n35.
121 BANQ, notary L.S. Martin, no. 2268, 14 July 1843. TC, no. 317, 14 July 1843. Mary Ann Trim was married on 10 April 1841 to Virginia-born Thomas Brooks, identified on the occasion as a tavern-keeper, although he had been denied a tavern licence (his lease on a property at the waterfront Pointe-à-Callière gave his occupation as keeper of a boarding house). The church record stated that Mary Ann was of the age of majority; in fact, she had just turned sixteen (BANQ, register of St Paul's Presbyterian Church, 10 April 1841; notary J.H. Jobin, no. 2361, 13 April 1840. CWS, "Certificats et cautionnements des aubergistes et listes des aubergistes certifiés, ... 1839–1841," Box 174, "List of Applications for Tavern Licences unfavorably reported upon by the Committee for the year 1840"; Box 173, "Report of Committee on tavern licences," 30 January 1840, and "Reconsideration of licences," 20 July 1840; the record of 20 January 1841 indicates no application by Brooks for a tavern licence that year).
122 BANQ, register of Notre-Dame Church, 14 February 1843. She married a French-Canadian, Wilbrod Séguin (BANQ, register of Notre-Dame Church, 29 October 1860).
123 BANQ, register of Notre-Dame Church, 26 November 1860. LAC, RG31-C-1, 1861 census, manuscript returns, Canada East, Montreal, St-Antoine Ward, 70 St-Antoine Street, f. 5114. Deniger was buried under the name Flavie Dagenais.
124 One of Trim's great-grandsons, William Isaac Taylor, served in the Canadian Expeditionary Force in World War I in No. 2 Construction Battalion, a black unit whose story is told in Ruck, *The Black Battalion (1916–1920)*. A grandson of Trim's daughter Henriette, he enlisted on 16 September 1916, identified as an unmarried man of forty-three, a plasterer by trade, of 1067 St-Jacques Street. As his next of kin, he named his forty-two-year-old cousin, Charles J. Tinsley, grandson of Charlotte Trim (LAC, RG 150, Accession 1992-93/166, Box 9555 – 42, regimental number 931266, Taylor, William Isaac).
125 See BANQ, notary G.D. Arnoldi, no. 623, 7 December 1829. In this first will, Trim left his estate to his children "share and share alike," adding as an afterthought that he was "desirous should he beget sons with his present wife, that the eldest have unto himself his Watch chain[,] Seals and Key, and that his wearing apparel be divided amongst them equally."

CHAPTER SIX

1 Merchant tailor Muir's interest in the welfare of black Montrealers may have been sharpened by an incident the previous year, when George Johnson had stolen a pair of flannel underwear from a clothesline in his yard. Johnson, a black man, one of the floating world of drunks, vagabonds, and prostitutes who were in and out of jail in the 1820s and 1830s, was convicted of petty larceny and sentenced to three months in the house of correction (LAC, MG24, B173, James Reid Papers, Criminal Cases, 5, *R v. George Johnson*, 7 March 1826. See also RPM, 30 April 1829, Box 50, no. 587. CQS, affidavits of watchman Charles Coulombe, 20 November

1832 and 24 November 1833, of Constable Alexis Bellaire, 4 December 1832, and of Constable Henri Hébert, 2 August 1833). Twenty-five-year-old Dwight Plimpton Janes, a native of St Alban's, Vt, and partner at this time with his brother Lewis in L. M. Janes & Co., grocers, would play a key part in the *Amistad* affair as a resident of Connecticut in 1839 (Jones, *Mutiny on the Amistad*, 35–6, 85, 120–1. Susan M. Stanley, "The Montrealer who helped free the Amistad slaves," *Gazette*, 4 January 1998, C3).

2 APC, Box 167, A121, American Presbyterian Sunday School Society (hereafter APSSS) Minutes, 1826–27, 81, 83; Box 168, A70, APSSS Reports & Correspondence, 1827, "Report of the Committee appointed to form a School for the Coloured population, 4th March 1827"; Box 168, A71, APSSS Reports & Correspondence, 1828, Second Annual Report, 4; Box 168, A72, APSSS Reports & Correspondence, 1829, annual report for 1828, 2.

3 Thomas C. Buchanan, *Black Life on the Mississippi*. Stenberg, "An Unknown Factor?" 65–6.

4 CQ3, *R v. Washington Williams*, voluntary statement of Washington Williams, 29 April 1841. Bonnycastle, *The Canadas in 1841*, 1:136.

5 BANQ, register of Christ Church, 9 November 1819. *Herald*, 8 March 1817. Sinclair had been sponsor at the baptism of Maria Keeling (1803–1805), daughter of Othello Keeling, a black man who in 1799 had been a resident of Ste-Anne, Fief Bellevue, as a slave or servant of fiefholder John Gregory (BANQ, register of Christ Church, 23 October 1803; register of Ste-Anne-du-Bout-de-l'Île Church, 11 November 1799).

6 Some payments entered in the Molson cash journal in the summer of 1810 suggest that other blacks may have worked briefly on the boat: "Joseph in full of 1 mo wages on Stmbt – £1 10," and "Black Jack on board the Steam Boat – £1 5s." Single-named Joseph may have been black or an Indian; Black Jack would seem to have been a black man. Both names appear only once in the Molson records (MA, v. 46, Journal 1808–10, entries under dates 18 June and 9 July 1810).

7 MA, v. 46, Journal 1808–10, entries under dates 1 and 29 July 1809. L'Africain was down on the books as John African. On 29 July, builder Andrew White, who was later to work as a contractor on the Rideau Canal, was paid £67 for the cabin work on the boat.

8 At his baptism, he was identified as Jean Baptiste François, about fourteen years old, "garçon nègre appartenant à Madame veuve beaucour." At his wedding in 1801, he was Jean Beaucour dit l'Africain, a twenty-year-old "Nègre libre" (BANQ, register of Notre-Dame Church, 14 April 1796, 14 September 1801. For Beaucourt, see Major-Frégeau, *La vie et l'oeuvre de François Malepart de Beaucourt*, 30–1).

9 At his wedding in 1802, he was identified as twenty-six-year-old "John Robert Ashley, Steward of the Brig *Hope*, now lying in this Harbour." At his daughter Elizabeth's baptism, he was identified as "a Negroe, of the City of Quebec, late Steward on board the Ship *Adeona*" (BANQ, register of Quebec Anglican Church, 22 July 1802, 30 September 1804).

10 HDM, admission registers, Book G, 7 February 1809; Book i, 10 October 1820. The only hint of Rogers's origins is found in that second hospital record, where he is identified as Richard Rooders, a thirty-six-year-old "Neigre Natif du haut Canada."

11 BANQ, register of Notre-Dame Church, 14 September 1801. Faribault-Beauregard, *La Population des forts français d'Amérique (XVIIIe siècle)*, 1:122, 133. Their children were François-Xavier (1803), a second François-Xavier (1804–1806), Marie Jeanne (1805–1806), Étienne (1807–1808), Marie Rosalie (1809–1811), and Charlotte (1814–1823).

12 The children were Sarah (1809–1810), George (1814–1817), Amanda (1816–1819), Henry (1819), and Annie (1820).
13 BANQ, register of Quebec Anglican Church, 22 July 1802. Their children were Elizabeth (Betsy) (b. 1804), Ann (b. 1808), Thomas (b. 1810) and Margaret (1815–1818). A Moses Ashley seems connected to the family, but it is not clear what his relationship was to Robert Ashley – a son, a nephew? Jacob Abdella accused him and Peter Dago of assault in 1830, and he was a witness at the wedding of Thomas Ashley and Ann Porter in 1834 (BANQ, register of St Paul's Presbyterian Church, 23 December 1834. CQS, October 1830, *Jacob Abdella v. Peter Dago and Moses Ashley*, deposition of Jacob Abdella, 30 September 1830).
14 BANQ, notary Peter Lukin Sr, no. 4414, 29 December 1809.
15 Franchère, *Journal of a Voyage on the North West Coast of North America*, 47–9.
16 MURB, MS405, Thomas Storrow Brown fonds, Folder 4, "Journal of Thomas Storrow Brown 1838," entry under date 23 September 1838.
17 Bolster, *Black Jacks*, 81–2, 167–9. See also pages 33 and 35. From the 1830s, blacks in New York had their "Stewards and Cooks Marine Benevolent Society" (*Colored American*, 28 September 1839 and 15 August 1840).
18 MA, v. 46, Journal 1808–10, entries under the dates on which payments were made.
19 MA, v. 47, Journal 1809–10, entries under dates 16 October, 10 and 15 November 1809. John Trim was also a Molson customer, making eight purchases of "small beer" in 1809 and 1810 – one-eighth of a hogshead each time, at 3s 4d each – perhaps in his capacity of "trader," for purposes of retail sale (MA, v. 46, Journal 1808–10, entries under dates 7 and 24 January, 13 February, 1 March, 19 April and 29 October 1809, and 21 March 1810).
20 MA, v. 46, Journal 1808–10, entries under the respective payment dates. Hunter, *Molson*, 332–3. "A 'cambouse,' probably an on-deck cookhouse, was added for the second season, in addition to a mast and sail for auxiliary power," Hunter says. "Cambouse" was a variant of "caboose"; before the railway age, the word referred to a cookhouse on the deck of merchant ships.
21 MA, v. 46, Journal 1808–10, entries of 18 and 27 June, 10 July, 1, 3, 14, 15, and 25 August, 8, 18 and 19 September, 2, 13 and 29 October, 2 November 1810; v. 47, Journal 1809–10, entries of 10 July, 3 and 14 August, 8, 18 and 19 September, 2, 13 and 29 October 1810; v. 48, Account Book 1809–11, ff. 20, 21, 248, and 279.
22 MA, v. 46, Journal 1808–1810 and v. 47, Journal 1809–10, payments entered under their respective dates; v. 48, Account Book 1809–11, ff. 248, 279.
23 BANQ, register of Notre-Dame Church, 22 November 1815.
24 BANQ, register of Christ Church, 24 January 1818. CQS, *Robert Ashley v. Alexander Todd*, Ashley complaint and Todd recognizance, both 17 November 1817. Within a year, his widow apparently married Leonard Freeman, a "labourer," by whom she had one last child, named Leonard like his father. The boy was said to be seven months old at his baptism in July 1820, and sixteen months old at his death on 1 June 1821. The witnesses at his burial were his stepsister Betsy Ashley, William Wright and Tulloch (Othello) Keeling. As Margaret Freeman, Margaret Pearce consented to her daughter Ann Ashley's marriage to John Patten in 1832, and was a sponsor at the baptism of her granddaughter, Elizabeth Sampson, in 1833 (BANQ, register of St Gabriel Presbyterian Church, 29 July 1820, 3 June 1821; register of St James Methodist Church, 11 October 1832; register of Christ Church, 3 April 1833).

25 BANQ, register of St John's Anglican Church, St-Jean-sur-Richelieu, 3 and 5 March 1817.
26 Doige, *Montreal Directory*, 1819 ed., 125, lists Richard Rogers, labourer, at 44 St-Maurice Street.
27 BANQ, register of St Gabriel Presbyterian Church, 4 November 1820. CQS, July Term 1820, *Ephraim Goodsell v. Richard Rodgers*, 8 July 1820. HDM, admission registers, Book i, 10 October 1820.
28 BANQ, register of St Andrew's Presbyterian Church, Montreal, 25 July 1824. MURB, MS475, St Lawrence Steamboat Co., v. 28, *Quebec* manifest, 7 September 1826; v. 88, page 14. A James Sampson, "free coloured man," was listed in June 1816 by the secretary of the colony of Demerara (part of Guyana) among those people who were on the point of leaving the colony (*Demerary & Essequebo Royal Gazette*, 1, 8, 15, 22, and 29 June 1816, accessed online November 2007 at www.vc.id.au/edg/).
29 BANQ, register of Christ Church, 4 August 1816; register of St Gabriel Presbyterian Church, 26 October 1816. MURB, MS475, St Lawrence Steamboat Co., v. 28, manifest, 3 May, 7 and 22 September, and 3 October 1826; v. 88, *Quebec* Wages Book, 13, 14, 16.
30 BANQ, register of St Gabriel Presbyterian Church, 2 April 1828; register of St Paul's Presbyterian Church, 20 September 1831.
31 BANQ, notary G.D. Arnoldi, no. 615, 24 November 1829, and no. 616, 26 November 1829.
32 BANQ, TL19 S41, Box 13009, Poll Book, Montreal West Ward election, October–November 1834, under date 30 October. LAC, RG31-C-1, 1831 census, manuscript returns, Lower Canada, Montreal, v. 13, Part 2, f. 80.
33 BANQ, register of St James Methodist Church, 11 October 1832. MURB, MS475, St Lawrence Steamboat Co., v. 67, *John Molson* manifest, 24 August 1832; v. 69, *John Molson* manifest, 25 June 1833; v. 84, Wages Book 1832–35, 11 October and 5 December 1832, 5 and 27 August, 14 and 25 September, 30 October, and 21 November 1833.
34 *Gazette*, 25 July 1833, 2 and 19 August 1834. *Vindicator*, 6 August 1833, 29 July 1834. See pages 36–8.
35 BANQ, St James Protestant Episcopal Church, Trois-Rivières, 26 June 1835. MURB, MS475, St Lawrence Steamboat Co., v. 67, *John Molson* manifest, 24 August 1832; v. 69, *John Molson* manifest, 25 June 1833; v. 75, *Canada* manifest, 26 April 1835; v. 68, *John Bull* manifest, 13 June 1835; v. 84, Wages Book 1832–35, 30 May and 24 July 1835. There is no later record of the presence of the Ashleys at Montreal.
36 MURB, MS475, St Lawrence Steamboat Co., v. 71, *Canada* manifest, 21 April 1834; v. 84, Wages Book 1832–35, 24 June, 29 July, 9 September, 4 October, and 12 November 1833, 27 June, 29 July, 9 September and 17 October 1834.
37 BANQ, register of Christ Church, 14 March 1833, 2 August and 28 December 1834, 19 May 1840. MURB, MS475, St Lawrence Steamboat Co., v. 84, Wages Book 1832–35, 29 July 1834. POBR 3:150. The census of 1861 found Broome's widow living at the home of her daughter, Sarah, who was married to Virginia-born John Wilson, a brickmaker. She was enumerated as the widow Jane Broons, fifty-seven, a native of Bermuda, "coloured." She died 24 August 1866, at the reputed age of sixty-four (BANQ, register of Christ Church, 14 December 1854; register of St John the Evangelist Anglican Church, 26 August 1866. LAC, RG31-C-1, 1861 census, manuscript returns, Canada East, Montreal, St-Louis Ward, f. 12620).

38 BANQ, notary H. Griffin, no. 5654, 22 March 1825; register of Christ Church, 4 November 1810. CQS, April term 1818, *R v. William Meikins Nation and Warren Glawson*, depositions of Richard Thompson, 16 April, and Ace Gabriel, 19 April. HDM, admission registers, Register No. 3, 1855–65, 1 June 1859, p. 462. MURB, MS475, St Lawrence Steamboat Co., v. 35, *Waterloo* manifest, 13 April 1828.
39 *Gazette*, 2 August 1834.
40 For an overview of early black churches in Upper Canada, see D. Simpson, *Under the North Star*, 21–68.
41 APC, Box 166, file A29, Minutes of Session 1823–47, p. 14; Box 180, A279, "Historic Roll" of church members 1823–1932, no. 66, Hester James.
42 Mention has already been made of Dwight P. Janes' abolitionist work and of the anti-slavery convictions of the church's first pastor, Joseph Stibbs Christmas (1824–28). The second pastor, George William Perkins, who married a daughter of steamboat owner Horace Dickinson in 1831, returned to Connecticut in 1839 and was an active member of the American and Foreign Anti-Slavery Society, the Liberty Party, and of anti-slavery religious bodies, as well as a contributor to an anthology of abolitionist essays (BANQ, register of St Andrew's Presbyterian Church, 7 September 1831. *Frederick Douglass' Paper*, 25 September, 9 October and 11 December 1851, 24 December 1852, 22 April 1853. *National Era*, 20 May 1847, 5 October 1848, 21 November 1850, 9 October 1851. Perkins, *Scriptural Missions* and *Remarks on Mr Stuart's Book "Conscience and the Constitution."*). Another member of the church who merits attention is Massachusetts-born Jacob Bigelow, the founding secretary of the American Presbyterian Society of Montreal, brother-in-law of Horace Dickinson, and a resident of the city circa 1809 to 1835. Bigelow probably moved to Montreal as an employee of Tappan & Sewall, the dry goods business operated by Americans Arthur Tappan and Henry Devereux Sewall from 1809 to 1812. Tappan and his brother, Lewis, later played leading roles in the American antislavery movement. Bigelow, whose father presided over anti-slavery societies in Connecticut and later in Indiana, was a key figure in the Underground Railroad at Washington, DC in the 1840s and 1850s (*Liberator*, 11 April 1835, 11 January 1839. Harrold, *Subversives: Antislavery Community in Washington, D.C., 1828–1865*, 96–7, 106–7, 134–5, 203–24. Mackey, *Steamboat Connections: Montreal to Upper Canada, 1816–1843*, 63–4, 70, 75–6, 107–8, 267).
43 MURB, MS475, St Lawrence Steamboat Co., v. 84, Wages Book 1832–35, 24 October 1834. RPQ, 1838–43, 3:34, 2 October 1838.
44 CQS, October 1830, *Jacob Abdella v. Peter Dago and Thomas Ashby* (sic), Abdella complaints, Dago and Ashley recognizances, all 2 August 1830.
45 CQS, October 1830, *Jacob Abdella v. Peter Dago and Moses Ashley*, Abdella complaint, Dago deposition, both 30 September 1830; Abdella recognizance 1 October, Dago recognizance 8 October. Robert Jackson, born at Quebec on 27 February 1801, was the third of eight children – the oldest boy – of Robert Jackson and Catherine Stephens. Margaret Pearce (Ashley) was a sponsor at the baptism of his brother, Joseph Jackson, in April 1803. Robert moved to Montreal in the 1820s, it seems, and died there on 3 October 1845 (BANQ, register of Quebec Anglican Church, 8 March 1801 and 3 April 1803; register of Notre-Dame Church, Montreal, 4 October 1845. HDM, admission registers, Book T, "Registre des Etrangers 1843–49," 5 August 1845).

46 CQS, March 1833, *R v. Jacob Abdallah and Peter Peterson*, affidavits of James Sampson and Thomas Brown English, both 15 March 1833.
47 KBCV, 1823, no. 162, *John Trim v. Simon Clark*, deposition of Robert Moore, 18 May 1829. MURB, MS475, St Lawrence Steamboat Co., v. 40, *Waterloo* manifest, 21 April 1829; v. 71, *Canada* manifest, 12 August 1834; v. 84, Wages Book 1832–35, 15 July, 1 August, 2 and 29 September 1834.
48 CQS, *R v. Joseph Brisebois*, Williams deposition, 23 July 1831. MURB, MS475, St Lawrence Steamboat Co., v. 28, *Quebec* manifest, and v. 71 and 75, *Canada* manifests; v. 84, Wages Book 1832–25, 17 June, 18 July, 29 August, 3 and 18 October, 2 December 1833; 3 and 24 June, 24 July, 25 August, 17 September, 6 December 1834; v. 88, *Quebec* Wages Book for 1826, 13.
49 MURB, MS475, St Lawrence Steamboat Co., v. 28, *Quebec* manifest, 3 October 1826; v. 88, *Quebec* Wages Book for 1826, 16; v. 84, Wages Book 1832–35, 20 September 1834.
50 HDM, admission registers, Book Q, 15 January 1835. RPQ, 1823–37, 2:27.
51 RPQ, 1813–23, 1:82.
52 BANQ, register of St Gabriel Presbyterian Church, 3 September 1822; register of Notre-Dame Church, 25 September 1823, 31 October 1826, 23 February 1827, 11 August 1827. CQS, October 1826, *Sarah York v. John Cross*, complaint of Sarah York, 18 September 1826; November 1827, *Catharine Guyette v. Sally York*, Guillet's complaint, 30 October, York's recognizance, 14 November.
53 CQS, *R v. Sarah Pierre*, affidavit of Robert Moore, 13 August 1838.
54 *Transcript*, 24 July 1838.
55 BANQ, register of Crescent Street Presbyterian Church, 6 October 1871. CQS, *R v. Sarah York*, affidavit of Robert Anderson, 25 February 1840. Mount Royal Cemetery, grave G-450. Sarah York died on 5 October 1871, her age given as 90, which seems an exaggeration; she was probably closer to 70.
56 BANQ, register of Christ Church, Sorel, 14 April 1834. A Charles Williams was a member of the crew of the steamer *Chambly* in 1831 (MURB, MS475, *Chambly* manifest, 8 September 1831).
57 MURB, MS475, St Lawrence Steamboat Co., v. 79, *John Bull* manifest, 6 October 1837; v. 80, *Canada* manifest, 10 May and 5 November 1837.
58 MURB, MS475, St Lawrence Steamboat Co., vols. 68, 79, 80, manifests; vol. 84, Wages Book 1832–35, 16 August, 4 September, 8 and 26 October 1832.
59 BANQ, notary G. Cauchy, no. 31, 4 July 1840. CQS, *R v. Prince Phillips*, Phillips statement, 10 November 1838, and recognizance, 20 November 1838; *Prince Phillips v. John J. Collins*, Phillips affidavit, 20 July 1840; court register, *R v. Prince Phillips*, 19 January 1839. MURB, MS475, St Lawrence Steamboat Co., v. 79, *John Bull* manifest, 26 September 1837. RPM, 1835–38, Box 56, no. 968, 10 November 1838.
60 CQS, *R v. Joseph Brisebois*, deposition of Robert Williams, 23 July 1831; *R v. Alexander Courtney*, affidavit of Jacob Grant, 24 October 1836, Courtney recognizance, 31 October 1836. MURB, MS475, St Lawrence Steamboat Co., v. 78, *Canada* manifest, 8 July and 16 November 1836.
61 LAC, MG24 B173, James Reid Papers, Criminal Cases, 1, *R v. John Forrest*, 8 September 1810. In reporting his arrest, the *Gazette*, 3 September 1810, gave his name as John Forster. Forrest,

who had worked on the building of the *Vermont*, the first steamer on Lake Champlain, appears to have begun working on the *Accommodation* in June or July 1810. He was paid £2 on 1 August, 5 shillings on account on 14 August, and £4 7s on 24 August, the balance of his wages for one month and fourteen days. He rejoined the boat after his acquittal on the theft charge, and was paid off on 2 October, receiving £3 2s (MA, v. 46, Journal 1808–10, entries under respective dates). Nothing in the records suggests that John Forrest, alias Jack Forest, was other than white, but it is possible that he was the "Nègre" Jacques Foret, whose daughter Christine died on 3 December 1817 (BANQ, register of Notre Dame Church, 9 December 1817). He could also be the John Forester who acted as a witness at the wedding of blacks Morris Thompson, a foundry worker, and Susan Sinclair in 1825 (BANQ, register of St Gabriel Presbyterian Church, 10 October 1825). John Forrester, founder, died on 6 March 1831 at age 48 (POBR 2:191).

62 MURB, MS405, Thomas Storrow Brown fonds, Folder 4, "Journal of Thomas Storrow Brown 1838," entry under date 23 September 1838.
63 MURB, MS255, Charles Kadwell fonds, v. 1, "Notes, &c. during a Trip from Montreal to Upper Canada, From the 3rd to the 18th August, 1838," under date 6 August 1838.
64 Ibid., under date 17 August 1838.
65 Chauveau, *De Québec à Montréal, 1850*, 105.
66 MURB, MS475, St Lawrence Steamboat Co., v. 66, *John Molson* manifest. Paola Brown is believed to have been the "Mr P. Brown," listed as passenger no. 17 on the trip down to Quebec on 5 September 1832. He paid a fare of 10s. For Brown, see Brown-Kubisch, *The Queen's Bush Settlement*, 25–9, 194; McCullough, "Paola Brown, the Town Crier"; Mackey, *Black Then*, 76–84, 194–96; and Weaver, "Paola Brown."
67 *Voice of the Fugitive*, 5 November 1851. The letter is reproduced, with annotations, in Peter Ripley, ed., *The Black Abolitionist Papers*, 2:177–81.
68 Ward, *Autobiography*, 136.
69 Widower Brown's marriage contract with widow Hester Livingston Strong of St Augustine, Fla., mentioned that her property consisted of "her Wearing apparel, Jewelry, and paraphernalia real property and Slaves." The 1850 US census recorded her in October 1850 as a thirty-two-year-old native of England and the owner of three slaves, all female, aged fifty-five, ten, and two. She died at Montreal on 12 March 1885. During his stay in St Augustine in the first half of the 1840s, Brown was involved in Democratic Party politics and, for forty-two days in 1841, he acted as an agent of the US War Department on a mission to Tampa to try to persuade the Seminole to leave their lands and relocate west of the Mississippi. By the time he submitted his account, and those of the five men who had accompanied him on this mission, the Democratic administration of President Martin Van Buren had given way to the Whigs under President William Henry Harrison, and Brown experienced difficulty in getting paid. The Florida delegate to Congress wrote to one of Brown's companions: "The difficulty in relation to your claim, and that of the delegation generally is a charge that you all went down there [to Tampa] to claim negroes, rather than to do service in the purposes of your commission" (BANQ, register of Christ Church, 16 March 1885. MURB, MS405, T.S. Brown fonds, Folder 9, J.R. Poinsett to Brown, 18 January 1841; same to same, "private," 18 January 1841; John Bell to Brown, 11 March and 12 May 1841; Brown to Bell, 24 May 1841; D. Levy to Mateo Solana, 5 August 1841; Folder 10, Brown's account to the US War Department for services rendered in

1841, and notary Thomas Robert Jobson, no. 5176, marriage contract of T. S. Brown and Hester Livingston Strong, 2 June 1860. United States census, 1850, manuscript returns, Florida, St John's County, St Augustine, schedule of free inhabitants, 407, and slave schedule, 893. *Gazette*, 23 March 1841).

70 The census of January 1861 listed Selina Simmons as the only "coloured" person in the Brown household at 6 Près de Ville Place, on Lagauchetière Street. She was said to be seventeen, single and a native of Florida (LAC, RG31-C-1, 1861 census, manuscript returns, Canada East, Montreal, St-Laurent Ward, f. 9987. Montreal city directory, 1860–1).

71 G. H. Wilson, "The Application of Steam to St Lawrence Valley Navigation, 1809–1840," 12.

CHAPTER SEVEN

1 CQS, January 1818, *Robert Ashley v. Alexander Todd*, complaint of Robert Ashley, 17 November 1817.

2 KB-Q (Oyer & Terminer), March 1794, *R v. Thomas Grant*, 1793: 365-B9.

3 BANQ, register of Notre-Dame Church, 18 September 1804; register of St Gabriel Presbyterian Church, 7 November 1809.

4 BANQ, register of Notre-Dame Church, 31 December 1800.

5 BANQ, notary L. Huguet-Latour, no. 1280, 13 November 1816; notary T. Bedouin, no. 1358, 24 October 1821; notary H. Griffin, no. 3984, 13 November 1821; register of Christ Church, 9 October 1825. Doige, *Montreal Directory*, 1820 ed., 138. An 1816 protest from the owner of a lot adjacent to Trim's on McGill Street contains the earliest known reference to Trim as a *marchand*. In earlier references, he is always a "negro" or a "gardener." Doige's directory for 1820 gives his occupation as "curer of hams." A protest from neighbour Simon Clark in 1821 refers to him as a "curer of meat." In his reply, Trim calls himself a "trader." At the baptism of his first child, Mary Ann, in 1825, he was termed a "dry salter."

6 BANQ, notary N.B. Doucet, no. 11617, 10 April 1824. Doige, *Montreal Directory*, 1820 ed., 120. Perrault, *Montréal en 1825*, 199. Pruyn's name, pronounced Prine, was usually recorded by others as Prime, but he always wrote it Pruyn. His lease was for land in the St-Louis Suburb, but the census of 1825 placed him in the neighbouring Quebec (Ste-Marie) Suburb.

7 BANQ, notary T. Barron, no. 2049, 16 March 1812. For Pierson's death, see chapter 9, and Mackey, *Black Then*, 50–4. "Pierson" is the spelling that Pierson used in signing his name.

8 HDM, admission registers, Book i, 9 November 1818 and 14 April 1819. LAC, MG24 B173, James Reid Papers, Criminal Cases, 3, *R v. George Binks and Richard Jackson*, 15 May 1820. Porteous said that, after leaving him, Jackson had gone to work for Mr Bleury, believed to be the young lawyer, Clément-Charles Sabrevois de Bleury.

9 CQS, January Sessions 1832, *R v. William Murphy et al.* (filed with documents of April Sessions); court register, 13, 14, 16, 17 January 1832. LAC, MG24, B173, James Reid Papers, Criminal Cases, 6, *R v. Joseph Lavigne*, 6 September 1831. RPM, Box 50, August 1826–July 1834, no. 1648, 9 January 1832. We do not know the name of Jackson's first wife. As a widower in 1835, he married Martha Curtis Hyers, the fifteen-year-old daughter of blacks John Hyers and Catherine Salter. He died on 12 February 1839 (BANQ, register of First Baptist Church, 5 August 1835; register of Christ Church, 13 February 1839. POBR 3:122).

10 BANQ, Garrison of Quebec Anglican Church, 10 January 1824; Trinity Anglican Church, Mon-

treal, 17 March 1869; notary B. Durant, no. 197, 2 July 1866; notary W.F. Scott, 7 February 1824, 14 and 15 August 1826. LAC, RG4 B28, Lower Canada Marriage Bonds 1779–1858, v. 32, no. 524, 8 January 1824. MRCR, Grave F-208. *Gazette*, 8 January 1859, 16 and 18 March 1869. J. I. Cooper, *History of St George's Lodge No. 10 Q.R.*, 37, 47, 129. There is no known record of William Wright's birth. His obituary, headed "An old Mason gone," says he was born at Halifax on 2 August 1804, whereas his tombstone says 4 August 1804. He was identified as a clerk in the Adjutant General's Department at Quebec at the birth of his son William in 1827, as second clerk at the birth of his daughter Henrietta in 1831, as chief clerk at the birth of his son Henry Blake in 1839, and then as chief or first clerk at the birth at Montreal of his daughters Sarah Miller, Mary Jane, and Susan Caroline between 1841 and 1851. A daughter, Mary Ann, born at Quebec in 1834, died at Montreal in March 1841; a son, George Charles, born at Quebec in 1836, died at Montreal in 1839. In addition, cemetery records show that a son named Frederick M., born at Montreal before the mid-1850s, died in infancy (BANQ, register of Garrison of Quebec Anglican Church, 15 July 1827, 13 November 1831, 18 May 1839; register of Christ Church, Montreal, 20 August 1839, 12 March 1841; register of Garrison Anglican Church, Montreal, 31 October 1841, 30 December 1847, 6 April 1851. MRCR, Grave F-208).

11 BANQ, register of Garrison of Quebec Anglican Church, 15 July 1827, 18 May 1839; notary I. J. Gibb, no. 6562, 2 May 1843; notary T. B. Doucet, no. 10835, 10 February 1857. LAC, RG31-C-1, 1861 census, manuscript returns, Canada East, Montreal, St-Louis Ward, f. 11314; 1881 census, manuscript returns, Quebec, Montreal, St-Laurent Ward, 90/i7:80; 1901 census, manuscript returns, Quebec, Montreal, St-Laurent Ward, 177/A29:10. MRCR Grave F-208. MU, Osler Library, circular of William Wright, "being a candidate for the vacancy in the medical staff of the Montreal General Hospital," 28 August 1852. *Montreal Star*, 17 April 1908. *Pilot*, 8 May 1848, 1 January 1850, 7 May 1860. *Transcript*, 21 February 1850. *Montreal Medical Journal*, 37, no. 5 (May 1908): 365–8. *Medical Chronicle or Montreal Monthly Journal of Medicine & Surgery.* Borthwick, *History of the Diocese of Montreal, 1850–1910*, 138. Hanaway and Cruess, *McGill Medicine, Volume I*, 56–7. MacDermot, *A History of the Montreal General Hospital*, 64–5. Wright and Dr Duncan McCallum launched *The Medical Chronicle or Montreal Monthly Journal of Medicine & Surgery* in June 1853. After four years, they sold the journal to their printer (see note to subscribers in v. 4, no. 12, May 1857, 470), but they remained the editors through its nearly six years of publication (to 1859).

12 *Montreal Star*, 22 December 1882; 8, 9, 10, 17 January 1883.
13 BANQ, notary A. Foucher, no. 5892, 16 November 1785.
14 CQS, November 1791, complaint of Henry Loedel, 23 November 1791.
15 Archives de la ville de Montréal, VM35, Fonds des juges de paix de Montréal, D7, Procès-verbaux 4 (1818–21):110. BANQ, notary T. Bedouin, no. 523, 21 November 1818. CQS register, January 1818, grand jury presentment, 19 January; April 1818, "Rules and Regulations Respecting the Watch of the City of Montreal," 24 April. LAC, RG7 G15C, Lower Canada, Civil Secretary's Letter Books 1788–1829, 25:125, A. W. Cochran to Police Magistrates in Montreal, 9 May 1818. *Provincial Statutes of Lower Canada*, 58 Geo III (1818), c. 2, "An Act to provide more effectually for the security of the Cities of Quebec and Montreal, by establishing a Watch and Night Lights in the said Cities, etc."
16 One of Dago's acquaintances stated in the spring of 1818 that during the previous winter "Dego

lighted the Lamps and gave [William Meikins] Nation his board for assisting him" (CQS, *R v. William Meikins Nation & Warren Glawson*, deposition of Ace Gabriel, 9 April 1818). Dago is believed to be the man who, identified as Peter Day, was one of the five "transient Blackamoors or Negroes" arrested after crossing the border at St-Armand in March 1810 and sent to the Montreal jail, charged with stealing eight hams, a horn, and a pleasure sleigh from Joshua Hilyard of Plattsburgh, NY, on 17 March. Peter Day, identified as a New York–born black man, was a patient at the Hôtel-Dieu 26 September–5 October that year. That July, a thirty-six-year-old American-born black woman identified as Nadine Day, believed to be his mother, had spent a week in the same hospital. Various sources, including his death record in 1868, suggest that Dago was born ca 1792–94 (BANQ, register of Notre-Dame Church, 18 August 1868. HDM, admission registers, Book H, women's ward, 31 July 1810, and men's ward, 26 October 1810. LAC, MG23 GIII3, Ruiter Family fonds, v. 2, "Miscellaneous 1787–1813," ff. 744–745; RG31-C-1, 1861 census, manuscript returns, Canada East, Montreal, St-Jacques Ward, f. 7284).

17 BANQ, register of Christ Church, 24 October 1823. For Glossen, see chapter 9.
18 CQS, July 1830, *R v. Thomas Cockburn and John Simpson*, deposition of High Constable Adelphe Delisle, 5 May 1830; March 1838, *R v. Richard Jackson et al.*, and *R v. William Murphy et al.*, affidavits of Charles and Alexander M. Delisle, 24 March 1838. CWS, register, 17 April 1832, *Benjamin Delisle v. Daniel Todd*, and 5 August 1834, *Benjamin Delisle v. Joseph Dufaux*.
19 *Quebec Gazette*, 30 November 1775.
20 KB-Q, 1781:199-B4, deposition of Jean-Baptiste St-Germain.
21 The account book of Philipsburg merchant and innkeeper Philip Ruiter for 1799–1800, lent to the Missisquoi Historical Society in 2007 by Phyllis Montgomery and Robert Galbraith, shows (p. 45) that in September 1799 "Morris the blackman" owed Ruiter £5 15s 1½d for drinks, board, and other items, and that he paid off part of his debt by working for Ruiter for sixteen days, at a wage calculated at the rate of $6 a month, or 20 cents a day. Of the various amounts Morris owed Ruiter, by far the greatest was $13 (£3 5s) for a fiddle (plus 2s 6d for two fiddle strings). This purchase strongly suggests that "Morris the blackman" was the man recorded seventeen years later at the baptism of his son Zephaniah, about two years old, as the late Morris Emery, a mulatto musician of Caldwell's Manor, husband of Hannah Caesar, also a mulatto (BANQ, register of St Gabriel Presbyterian Church, 8 September 1816). Caldwell's Manor, the former seigneury of Foucault, today the area of Clarenceville, lay across Missisquoi Bay from St-Armand.
22 CQS, April Term 1816, complaint of Stephen Rogers, 7 February 1816. Perhaps Rogers had also played the fiddle at a New Year's Eve party at Montreal in 1804 when he was assaulted by Joseph Pierson. Joseph Frank (alias Joseph François) and Jean-Baptiste L'Africain each posted a £5 bond to guarantee that Pierson would show up for his trial (CQS, January 1805, *Stephen Rogers v. Joseph Pearson*, arrest warrant bearing Pierson's recognizance, 2 January 1805).
23 KB (Oyer & Terminer), October Term 1821, *R v. Joseph Leclair*. LAC, MG24, B173, James Reid Papers, Criminal Cases, 3, *R v. Joseph Leclaire*, 30 October 1821. *Herald*, 25 August 1821. *Spectateur canadien*, 25 August 1821.
24 BANQ, register of Christ Church, 4 May 1834 and 21 November 1846. CQS, April Term 1841,

R v. Abraham Low, affidavit of Louis Day, 28 April 1841. POBR 4:67. The church records say Low died on 19 December 1846; it was really 19 November.
25 The advertisement was published in the *Canadian Spectator* of Friday, 13 August 1824, and (in English) in the French-language *Spectateur canadien* the next day.
26 For Brown, see McAllister, *White People Do Not Know How to Behave at Entertainments Designed for Ladies & Gentlemen of Colour;* Thompson, *A Documentary History of the African Theatre;* and White, *Stories of Freedom in Black New York*, 68–116.
27 Turnbull had previously kept an inn and commanded a schooner in the West Indies trade. See BANQ, register of St Gabriel Presbyterian Church, 1 August 1820, 30 July 1822. *Herald*, 11 June 1814, 27 July 1816, 15 February 1817.
28 APC, Box 168, A70, APSSS Reports & Correspondence, "Report of the Committee appointed to form a School for the Coloured population, 4th March 1827." The committee found that "3 of them could read fluently, that 4 could read tolerably and that the rest could read little and some of them none at all."
29 *Canadian Courant*, 10 July, and 14 and 21 August 1824. *Gazette*, 10 July 1824.
30 BANQ, register of Notre-Dame Church, 15 February 1816. HDM, admission registers, Book H, 23 August 1815, 24 January 1816. Pierre Alex died at the Hôtel-Dieu on 11 February 1816.
31 HDM, admission registers, Book i, 4 March, 30 May and 30 July 1820, 5 March, 5 May and 29 May 1821, 22 August 1822; Book K, 17 June 1823. James Noël was said to be in his thirties. He may have been the man identified a decade earlier as Amédée Noël, a twenty-one-year-old "domestique" from St-Domingue (HDM, admission registers, Book H, 25 May 1811).
32 CQS, *R v William Johnson & al.*, deposition of Jean François, 29 September 1835. On his arrival at Montreal, he was identified as a labourer when he complained that he had been robbed. CD 1842–43 and 1843–44 listed him as John Francis, cook, a resident of St-Constant Street, near Mignonne Street (he was a tenant of Mary Ann Drummond). He died in the Montreal General Hospital on 14 January 1855, identified as John François St Elistan, 65, "labourer, a Native of St Domingo." Cemetery records gave his name as John Francis, and his age as 66 (BANQ, register of Zion Congregational Church, 15 January 1855. POBR 5:336. CD 1842–43 to 1855).
33 David Bristow was first recorded at Montreal in September 1840 when he married Cecilia Farley, the widow of Alexander Grant (CC, 14 September 1840). In June 1846, as David Bristol, cook, he took in as an apprentice "tailoress" Mary Ann Johnson, one of three children of a runaway Virginia slave named Henry Johnson. The deed of apprenticeship offers no explanation as to how a cook was qualified to teach tailoring (BANQ, notary J.H. Isaacson, 29 June 1846).
34 BANQ, register of American Presbyterian Church, 24 March 1840. LAC, RG4 B28, Lower Canada Marriage Bonds 1779–1858, v. 40-A, no. 2681, 24 May 1840. RPM, Box 51, 12 April 1856; Box 59, no. 424, 12 April and 19 May 1856.
35 BANQ, notary J.G. Beek, no. 523, 1 May 1789. For Weldin, see chapter 10, and Appendix 1 n 60.
36 BANQ, notary J.G. Beek, no. 1872, 17 September 1805; register of Notre-Dame Church, 4 May 1807; register of St Gabriel Presbyterian Church, 3 April 1811. The name was also recorded as Antoine Coudrain, Narcisse Coudray, and "Narcisse Coutrain alias Antoine." He and his wife were the first black Montrealers to sign a marriage contract. The contract was in French,

a language that Mary Violet Jones, a native of Leicester, Mass., did not understand; Joseph François acted as an interpreter for her on this occasion. François was also a sponsor at the baptism of their only child, Marie Félicité Coudrin, in January 1808. Marie Félicité is believed to be the seven-year-old Marie Jones, "a mulatto girl living in Dr [Benjamin] Green's family," who died on 14 February 1815. John Trim and Alexander Valentine were the witnesses at her burial (BANQ, notary J.M. Cadieux, no. 79, 2 May 1807; register of Notre-Dame Church, 9 January 1808; register of St Gabriel Presbyterian Church, 15 February 1815).

37 BANQ, register of Ste-Anne-de-la-Pocatière Church, 15 September 1791; register of Notre-Dame Church, Montreal, 14 August 1825. HDM, admission registers, Book i, 24 December 1816, 17 February and 6 May 1822. Catherine Barbe was a sixteen-year-old "negresse" at her baptism at Ste-Anne-de-la-Pocatière in 1791, the name Barbe perhaps taken from the first name of her mistress, Barbara Boyton Smith, the wife of seigneur Laughlin Smith, a former sergeant of the Fraser Highlanders. She was admitted to the Hôtel-Dieu in Montreal in the winter of 1816–17, registered as Catherine Babberine, forty-one, "native de guienne dans les Iles," widow of George Croon. As a patient in 1822, her son was identified as shoemaker James Croni, a twenty-seven-year-old native of Ste-Anne-du-Sud, son of George Croni and Catherine, "négresse." Catherine Barbe, said to be a charwoman of about sixty-one at her death 12 August 1825, was buried under the name Catherine Barbary.

38 BANQ, register of Christ Church, 1 August 1819; notary J.A. Labadie, no. 3558, 16 July 1834. TC, no. 513B, 11 July 1834.

39 CQS, May 1831, *R v. Betsy Thompson*, recognizance of 6 May 1831. The sureties for Betsy Thompson were John Trim and shoemaker Thomas Smyth.

40 *Gazette*, 21 February 1793. See chapter 1.

41 BANQ, register of Quebec Anglican Church, 13 August 1820; register of St Gabriel Presbyterian Church, 22 March 1826; register of Christ Church, 1 September 1830.

42 BANQ, notary P. Lukin Jr, no. 1095, 29 April 1826; notary R. O'Keeffe, no. 401, 2 September 1826, and no. 681½, 20 March 1828. LAC, RG31-C-1, 1831 census, manuscript returns, Lower Canada, Montreal, v. 13, Part 2, f. 78, St-Paul Street. *Canadian Courant*, 21 July 1830.

43 BANQ, notary I.J. Gibb, no. 924, 9 March 1837, and no. 2130, 10 May 1838; notary E. Guy, no. 1350, 23 March 1837, and nos 2260 and 2262, 6 March 1839; notary W.S. Hunter, no. 17, 10 October 1835; notary J.H. Jobin, no. 756, 10 March 1836; register of Christ Church, 22 August 1838. *Canadian Courant*, 21 July 1830. *Herald*, 27 December 1836. *Transcript*, 18 April 1839.

44 BANQ, register of Christ Church, 14 December 1835. CQS, June 1834, *Alexander Grant v. Hisun Loney and Thornton Taylor*. For Grantham, see chapter 10. He was identified as a barber on 5 June 1834 when he and John Patten acted as sureties for barbers Loney and Taylor, whom Grant had accused of assault.

45 BANQ, notary E. Guy, no. 2877, 2 May 1840, and no. 3960, 14 March 1842; notary A. Montreuil, no. 119, 12 January 1844; notary D.E. Papineau, no. 1222, 28 October 1844, and no. 1247, 8 November 1844. CD 1842–3 and 1843–4 give Smith's address as 111 Notre-Dame Street. After his marriage in 1843 to Louisa Martin, an Irishwoman born in England, he moved to a shop next to the Anglican Cathedral. His rent that year – £105 per year, raised to £116 the next year – and his advertising indicate that he operated in high style (BANQ, register of St

Paul's Presbyterian Church, 3 April 1843; notary E. Guy, no. 5934, 10 February 1844, no. 5937, 12 February 1844, no. 6763, 26 May 1845, no. 7018, 28 August 1845. *Gazette*, 21 May 1844).

46 BANQ, register of St Paul's Presbyterian Church, 14 February and 2 December 1834; register of Notre-Dame Church, 23 March 1835. POBR 3:144. *Freedom's Journal* (New York), 18 May 1827. Molliston is believed to be the New York City resident "Sol. Moleston," who, with partner John Robinson, advertised as "Tailors and Clothes Dressers" in *Freedom's Journal*, the first black-owned newspaper, published at New York in 1827–29. A postscript to their ad indicated that his wife ran a boarding house. In Montreal, Molliston, as a widower, married Irish widow Bridget (Biddy) Conway in 1834. He was said to be forty-four at his death on 23 January 1840.

47 BANQ, notary W.S. Hunter, no. 347, 4 May 1837; notary J.A. Labadie, no. 7271, 24 February 1842; register of Christ Church, 20 May 1854. LAC, RG31-C-1, 1842 Census, manuscript returns, Canada East, Montreal, West Ward, St-Paul Street, f. 1301, no. 7. Gordon was listed in CD 1842 to 1847.

48 BANQ, notary L.C. Danré de Blanzy, no. 2376, 4 March 1745, and no. 3978, 22 April 1749; notary J.B. Decharnay, 23 July 1756; register of the Hôpital-Général chapel, Montreal, 10 May 1773.

49 BANQ, notary N.B. Doucet, no. 12134, 6 November 1824.

50 BANQ, register of St Andrew's Presbyterian Church, 16 October 1823; notary J. Belle, no. 3166, 11 December 1839. TC, no. 798, 10 December 1839. For John Wright, see chapter 10.

51 CD 1842–43 lists him as C. Jiles, tailor, St-Dominique Street near Vitré Street (Viger Avenue); CD 1843–44 and 1844–45 place him on St Charles Borromée Street near Craig (Clark near St-Antoine). His name is absent from subsequent editions. In 1843, he married Chloe Pierce, the widow of hairdresser William Goodrich. The marriage record gives his name as Cupid Giles, but he signed Cubit Giles (BANQ, register of St James Methodist Church, 11 January 1843).

52 BANQ, register of St Gabriel Presbyterian Church, 2 September 1806. Dolphin's name was written Dofen.

53 BANQ, register of Notre-Dame Church, 14 July 1809. HDM, admission registers, Box G, 29 June 1809.

54 BANQ, register of St Gabriel Presbyterian Church, 31 August 1812, 20 January 1813.

55 BANQ, register of St Gabriel Presbyterian Church, 6 June, 8 June, and 14 September 1813.

56 BANQ, register of St Gabriel Presbyterian Church, 22 July 1812. While Lydia Dolphin was said to be thirty at her wedding, now she was supposedly twenty-six.

57 BANQ, notary P. Lukin Sr, nos 5126 and 5127, 16 February 1813. There is no record of their parents having lived at Montreal. A hospital record of 1818 identified Dolphin as the twenty-nine-year-old son of John Dolfin and Sally Heart, a native of [Siout?]" (HDM, admission registers, Book H, 13 February 1818).

58 BANQ, notary P. Lukin Sr, 5230, 11 April 1814; register of St Gabriel Presbyterian Church, 8 June and 14 September 1813, 5 January 1819. Stansfeld hired Thomson at $9 a month, plus lodging and firewood.

59 BANQ, register of St Gabriel Presbyterian Church, 26 November 1815; notary H. Griffin, no. 1661, 16 December 1816. KB, September Term 1815, *R v. James Douglas*, depositions of

Joseph Pierson, 9 March 1815, and Sgt. John Kennedy, 13 March 1815. CQS, *John Dorfin (sic) v. William Appleby and Messey Appleby*, and *William Appleby v. John Dolfin*, both 12 February 1818, recognizance of Appleby and his wife, Massy Lamplow, 13 February 1818. HDM, admission registers, Book H, 13 February 1818.

60 BANQ, register of St Gabriel Presbyterian Church, 4 March 1798, 19 January 1799; register of Christ Church, 8 August 1802, 22 April 1804, 20 July 1807; register of Notre-Dame Church, 18 July 1813; notary J.A. Gray, no. 2251, 6 February 1809; notary H. Griffin, no. 1652, 28 November 1816. CQS, July Term 1816, *Madeleine Fleming v. Jany Graves* (also written *Marguerite Fleming v. Jane Grames*), Fleming's complaint, 1 May, Graham's bond, 2 May; July Term 1820, *R v. Magdeleine Flemming* (also written *R v. Several Prostitutes*), affidavits of John Elliot, Joseph Hill and Patrick Graham, 8 May, Magdeleine Flemming's recognizance 12 May, Pierre Moreau's recognizance 16 May. In that last case, Thomas Cockburn and Jacob Simpson acted as sureties for Magdeleine Flemming.

61 BANQ, register of St Gabriel Presbyterian Church, 5 March 1807. Ann Garner appears to have been the "femme de couleur, âgée d'environ quatre-vingt-quatorze ans, épouse de Rodgers" (woman of colour, about ninety-four years old, wife of Rodgers) who was baptized under the name Marie Elizabeth Rogers in 1842 at the Roman Catholic parish church of Ste-Mélanie-d'Ailleboust. The age appears to be an exaggeration. Her sponsor was Louise Amélie Panet, daughter of the late Judge Pierre-Louis Panet and Marie Anne Cerré (BANQ, register of Ste-Mélanie-d'Ailleboust Church, 17 March 1842).

62 BANQ, register of St Gabriel Presbyterian Church, 21 August 1819.

63 The possibility that Cato Giles had been a slave is suggested in the will of Loyalist Jacob Best of St-Armand, dated 14 September 1794, in which Best stated: "Also I give my Nigro Cato, full and free liberty to Live with any of my Own Children, Or with any of my Grant Children, to keep his Own wearing Aparel, and what Ever he Owns, without, he, or She, with whom Soever, of Own, or Grant Child, Cato Chuses to live, paying no mony for Cato, but in Case Cato will not Stay with One of my Own or Grant Children, Cato is to find a Master to Buy him, and the Money is to be Devited Equealy among my Children" (BANQ, notary L. Chaboillez, no. 1340, 11 March 1795).

64 BANQ, register of St Gabriel Presbyterian Church, 6 December 1819. LAC, MG30-C100, George A. Montgomery fonds, "Philip Ruiter Account and rent books, 1778–1834," folder 2, Account book 1797–98, pp. 9, 10, 17, 19, 34, 41, 43, 50, 64, 74, 76, 83, 88; Account book 1810–12, ff. 99, 105, 127. There are similar entries for "Cato" in a Ruiter account book of 1799–1800 lent to the Missisquoi Historical Society in 2007 by Montgomery descendant Phyllis Montgomery and her husband.

65 BANQ, register of Notre-Dame Church, 7 March, 17 May, 4 July and 28 July 1820. HDM, admission registers, Book J, 22 May, 10 June, 17 June and 9 July 1820.

66 BANQ, notary P. Lukin Sr, no. 4336, 17 July 1809, and no. 4414, 29 December 1809.

67 BANQ, notary J.A. Gray, nos 1274 and 1275, 29 December 1804.

68 Of the American fur trade from the late eighteenth century onward, Kenneth Porter wrote: "Any picture of the racial aspects of the fur trade of that period which omits the Negro is so incomplete as to give a false impression, for representatives of that race were to be found in all three groups connected with the trade" (Porter, "Negroes and the Fur Trade," 423). The three groups Porter referred to were the entrepreneurs and clerks, voyageurs, and hunters. Other

than the well-known Sir James Douglas (1803–1877), a man of mixed race of Scottish and West Indian origin who rose from apprenticeship in the North West Company to become a chief factor of the Hudson's Bay Company, then governor of Vancouver Island and the colony of British Columbia, it does not seem that blacks in the fur trade under the British made it to the rank of entrepreneurs and clerks.

69 Podruchny, *Making the Voyageur World*, 15.
70 BANQ, notary F. Simonnet, 1 April 1777.
71 HDM, admission registers, Book F, 24 January, 3 June and 12 August 1797, and, in the same book, "Registre pour la Salle des hommes nombre des morts depuis Le 14 novembre [1795]." PRDH, records of St-Joachim Church, Pointe-Claire, 7 October 1785, burial of anonymous month-old son of Cannon and his wife Lognon. Peter Canon and his wife, Marie Louise Loignon, had six other known children: François, alias Pierre, who lived only nine months in 1783; Jean Joseph, alias Pierre, who died at one month in 1784; François, who lived seven and a half months in 1787; Marie Amable, born in 1788; Marie Louise, born in 1791; and Claude, born in 1797. Peter Canon, said to be fifty, died at Montreal on 16 October 1797. His widow may have remarried. When she died in 1823, she was said to be the sixty-year-old widow of a man named Jacob, who was otherwise unknown (BANQ, register of Notre-Dame Church, 27 May and 20 December 1783, 4 June and 7 July 1784, 14 January and 23 August 1787, 16 December 1788, 24 March 1791, 25 March and 17 October 1797, 26 April 1823).
72 BANQ, notary J.G. Delisle, Engagements, 8 April 1794. Another slave hired in a similar way was Thome (Tom?), a "Nègre" of the Chevalier Charles de Labruère de Boucherville. With his master's consent, he was hired by fur trader Jean-Baptiste Berthelot in May 1799 to travel to Michilimackinac and to winter around the Mississippi ("dépendances du misissipi"). He was to be given blankets, some cloth, a necklace and a pair of ox-hide shoes, and to be paid 400 livres one month after his return. Unlike Constant, he was not promised his freedom (BANQ, notary J.P. Gauthier, no. 1128, 6 May 1799).
73 BANQ, notary L. Chaboillez, Engagements, no. 6397, 15 November 1803, and no. 7940, 25 January 1808. A witness at the wedding of Joseph François and Charlotte Cavilhe (alias Charlotte McGill) in 1802 and at the funeral of farmer Robert Boston's wife, Betsy Thomson, in 1813, Dowling was married at Montreal in 1817 to the widow Elizabeth Franklin, six years after the birth of their daughter, Louisa. He was said to be fifty at his wedding, but sixty-six at his death three years later (BANQ, register of Christ Church, 29 November 1802; register of St Gabriel Presbyterian Church, 6 March 1811, 20 January 1813, 31 March 1817, 10 October 1820).
74 HDM, admission registers, Box G, 7 August 1806.
75 BANQ, register of St Gabriel Presbyterian Church, 8 February and 28 June 1813, 13 January 1814; register of Hôpital-Général chapel, 13 June 1818. For the children of this family, see chapter 10.
76 BANQ, register of Notre-Dame Church, ND, 14 September 1801; register of St Gabriel Presbyterian Church, 9 June 1806. HDM, admission registers, Book F, 22 June 1798. Faribault-Beauregard, *La Population des forts français d'Amérique*, 1:122, 133, 171. Armour and Widder, *At the Crossroads*, 191. Rosalie Bonga is believed to have been the "Rosalie domestique negre" of John Fraser, judge of the Court of King's Bench and member of the Legislative Council, who was owed nine francs in wages at Fraser's death on 5 December 1795 (BANQ, notary J. Papineau,

11 February 1796; register of Notre-Dame Church, 8 December 1795).
77 Henry, *The Journal of Alexander Henry*, 1:126. See also Coues, *New Light on the Early History of the Greater Northwest*, 1:49–50, 52, 159–60; Henry, *The Journal of Alexander Henry*, 1:42, 150, 184.
78 BANQ, register of Notre-Dame Church, 4 November 1804; notary J.M. Mondelet, no. 2815, 12 November 1804, no. 2821, 16 November 1804, and no. 3092, 30 September 1806. TC, 10 November 1804. Coues, ed., *New Light on the Early History of the Great Northwest*, 1:276. Once the expenses and his debts were cleared, each of Étienne Bonga's three siblings was entitled to receive 1,288 livres 3 sols. Charges related to the curatorship reduced Pierre's share by twenty-five livres.
79 BANQ, register of St Gabriel Presbyterian Church, 18 August 1810, 11 November 1811; notary J.G. Beek, no. 2140, 30 April 1812, and no. 2162, 8 May 1813; notary H. Griffin, no. 962, 6 May 1815; notary P. Lacombe, no. 31, 13 January 1832. TC, 1 February 1812, 1 October 1812. Coues, ed., *New Light on the Early History of the Great Northwest*, 3:926. Katz, *The Black West*, 28–30. Porter, "Negroes and the Fur Trade," 424–6. Spangler, *The Negro in Minnesota*, 18–19. In a letter he wrote in old age, George Bonga offered some information and speculation about his early days and his family background (Bonga, "Letters of George Bonga," 53–4):

As to My self, I was born, somewhere near where Duluth now is ... pretty near 70 Years ago [ca 1804], at that time there was great rivalrie, between the 2 fur Companys the old North west & the Hudson Bay Co. My father was in the employ of the former [blank space] there head quarters was at Fort William Lake Superior. I left there when I was a little boy, as I have no recollection, of the place & went to School in Montreal. as there was no one, to take any particular interest about me, I did not get as good an education, as I might have had. ... I have always been sorry, that I did not ask my father while living, if he knew where he immigrate from. I am now inclined to think, that they must have come, from the new State of Missouri, as he did not Speak any thing but french. I presume at that time, Very few inhabited that out Skirts State, Iowa, Illinois, & Michigan except those connected with the fur trade. the North west company had, what was Styled, the South west Division [blank space] that division had its head quarters at MacKinac. My grand father & his family of 5 or 6 children, might have been taken Prisoners by the Ind.s & Sold to the Indn traders. that is the only way I can guess at it. I understood my father to say, that all his fathers family came to MacKinac, this I am certain of, for I had one Uncle & 2 Aunts, who went to Montreal with the Ind traders.

At this writing (July 2008), information on George Bonga and his descendants can be found online at www.ojibwe.info/.
80 BANQ, register of St Gabriel Presbyterian Church, 4 February 1811. George Simpson, *Journal of Occurrences in the Athabasca Department*, 112.
81 George Simpson, *Journal of Occurrences in the Athabasca Department*, 290. Rich, *Hudson's Bay Company*, 2:381.
82 BANQ, register of St-François-Xavier Church, Sault-St-Louis (Kahnawake), 23 May 1842; reg-

ister of St-Joseph Church, Huntingdon, 5 July 1880. CQS, January 1825, *Joseph Morrin v. Joseph Thompson*; October 1852, *R v. Andrew Smith*, deposition of Joseph Thompson, 4 September 1852. *Canadian Gleaner* (Huntingdon), 6 March 1873, 8 July 1880. When Thompson was charged with assaulting Joseph Morrin (or Morin) in 1825, Peter Dago and Abraham Low acted as his sureties.
83 UMCB, U5881-2, James Hughes to Colonel Duncan Napier, 28 March 1836.
84 *Quebec Gazette*, 19 September 1771. See Appendix I/A, notice 16.
85 CCP, *Caesar Hunkin v. Charles Bennet*, 13 November 1793.
86 BANQ, notary J.A. Gray, Engagements, 24 April 1804.
87 BANQ, notary J.A. Gray, Engagements, 22 March 1809; register of St Gabriel Presbyterian Church, 7 November 1809. The log of the Montreal prison in 1833 identified Cockburn as having come from Ireland and described him as forty years old, 5' 5" tall, of a black complexion, with black hair and eyes. He was jailed then with several others, including Catherine Salter, the widow of lamplighter John Hyers, and her daughter Martha Hyers, on charges of keeping a bawdy house (RPM, Box 50, nos 3557–64, 6 August 1833, and no. 3559 in the descriptions at the back of the volume).
88 BANQ, notary J.A. Gray, Engagements, 5 May 1809.
89 CQS-Q, no. 182185, deposition of Samuel Hough, 8 June 1827; RPQ, 1823–37, 2:57. Garret was indicted for assault on a constable in the execution of his duty, and held from 8 June to 13 July under the name Henry Gerrat.
90 BANQ, register of St Gabriel Presbyterian Church, 26 July 1816. U.E. Loyalist Centennial Committee, *The Centennial of the Settlement of Upper Canada by the United Empire Loyalists, 1784–1884*, 308. Captain Bird of the 8th Regiment had led an expedition into Kentucky in the spring of 1780, where, in June, he and his men and their Indian allies had captured two forts and taken several prisoners, including several black slaves. The whites were marched to Detroit, then to Montreal, where they were held prisoner. The slaves were sold at Detroit. Bird kept Esther, one of the slaves for himself, then in 1784, he gave "said Wench and her male Child to William Lee in consideration of having cleared for me sixteen acres of land" (BANQ, Fonds Drouin, "Notaires de Détroit," 4:74–6, notary Guillaume Monforton, "Capt. Bird to Wm. Lee a Negroe free," 29 June 1791. HP, MS21877:98, Memorial of Agnes LaForce, 6 January 1781. Riddell, *The Life of William Dummer Powell*, 26–30.)
91 HDM, admission registers, Book F, 22 June 1794. LAC, RG4 B45, Declarations of Aliens, Lower Canada 1794–1811, p. 82.
92 *Quebec Gazette*, 24 November 1803, 1 March 1804. Squires, *The 104th Regiment of Foot*, 31–45. Half the regiment was raised in Canada, Squires says (83). In March 1797, the King's Own Infantry, stationed at Montreal, advertised for "two or three good Musicians." The 98th Regiment at Quebec called for "two smart Boys" to join its band in 1807 (*Quebec Gazette*, 23 March 1797, 24 December 1807).
93 BANQ, notary F.M. Pétrimoulx, no. 3165, 10 January 1802. Squires, *The 104th Regiment of Foot*, 54, 221. From Squires' roll of the New Brunswick regiment 1803–17 (Appendix B, 196–240), the names of the blacks who were transferred to the York Rangers would have been John Davis, Moses Diamond, Tobias Francis, Abraham Gordon, Henry McEvoy, Charles Prince, Richard Purce, Thomas Robinson, William Swain, and James Thomas.

94 Squires, *The 104th regiment of Foot*, 54, 66. See also Summers and Chartrand, *Military Uniforms in Canada*, 63–65.
95 Lieutenant A.W. Playfair, quoted in Squires, *The 104th Regiment of Foot*, 127–8. Further glancing evidence of a black drummer in the regiment is found in the records of the Quebec jail, which show that on 13 November 1815 a James Millins was committed to prison "Charged with suspicions of having offered through the medium of a black drummer of the 104th Regiment, a single snapple bridle for sale, of the getting of which he renders a suspicious account" (RPQ, 1813–23, 1:15).
96 BANQ, register of Christ Church, 8 March 1786; register of Notre-Dame Church, 14 November 1788, 26 August 1791, 25 January 1793, and 10 November 1794. Houldin's name is given here as he signed it at the baptism of three of his children; at the baptism of the fourth child, he wrote it Huldin. Squires, *The 104th Regiment of Foot*, 214, identifies him as Richard Holden. At the burial of his wife, he was identified in French as the late Richard Ogden. Other records give his first name as Ridchard or Richet, and the family name as Aldelne, Alden, Aldenne, Bouldin, Golden, Holaday, Holding, Hollady, Hordan, Horiday, Horriday, Ocden, Ocdene, Ocdette, and Odimne. He might be the Richard Holden who was sued for a debt of 18s 9d in 1786, and who successfully sued a James Reed for 30s due for house rent. As it happens, two years later, Reed successfully sued Caesar Johonnot for £3 17s 1d (BANQ, register of Notre-Dame Church, 24 April 1819. CCP, register, *Mary Campbell v. Richard Holden*, 30 June 1786, and *Richard Holden v. James Reed*, 10 and 17 November 1786; *James Reed v. Cesar Johonnet*, 11 October 1788).
97 BANQ, register of Notre-Dame Church, 24 April 1819. Squires, *The 104th Regiment of Foot*, 169, 214. Squires says that thirty-six men of the regiment were transferred to the Royal Veterans in November 1814, most of them members of the two companies that had been stationed at Cape Breton and Prince Edward Island.
98 BANQ, register of Notre-Dame Church, 14 November 1788 and 24 April 1819; notary A. Foucher, no. 5597, 29 September 1784.
99 BANQ, register of Notre-Dame Church, 26 August 1791 and 25 January 1792.
100 Squires, *The 104th Regiment of Foot*, 244. Variations in the writing of Andrew Holiday's name included André Alledy, Andrew Alledy, André Holedai, Andrew Holyday, and André Oldé. It is possible that Holiday and Marie Anne Houldin were married at Fredericton, New Brunswick, where the regiment was headquartered. Recruits from North America and from the British Isles were sent there. The Houldins probably were among the recruits from Canada who reached Fredericton in early July 1805: "160 fine, tall-looking men of all nations, and have with them fourteen women and children," the commander's wife noted. Holiday may already have been there, or he may have been among the thirty-four men recruited in Scotland who arrived at Fredericton on 20 September that year. His daughter by Marie Anne Houldin was born at Montreal nine months later, on 25 June 1806 (BANQ, register of Notre-Dame Church, 26 June and 8 July 1806. Squires, *The 104th Regiment of Foot*, 40–1).
101 HDM, admission registers, Book H, 4 January 1814, 6 February 1815; Book V, 12 July 1848; Register No. 1 (1850–63), 14 and 24 December 1850, 11 February 1851. LAC, RG1, L3L, Lower Canada Land Papers, 107:52644–8. Squires, *The 104th Regiment of Foot*, 214. Euphrosine Houldin married white widower Martin Parent, a carter, in January 1820. They had at least

seven children, between 1821 and 1834. The youngest of them, a boy, as well as her husband, died in July 1834 during a cholera outbreak. Euphrosine, apparently still living in 1847, had died by the fall of 1850 (BANQ, register of Notre-Dame Church, 31 January 1820, 23 February 1821, 23 July 1822, 20 January 1825, 10 September 1826, 2 April 1829, 6 September 1830, 4 January, 23 and 26 July 1834, 14 October 1850; register of Hôpital-Général chapel, 2 March 1838; register of St-Martin Church, Île Jésus, 18 February 1800. HDM, admission registers, Book H, 5 June 1813, 14 November 1814; Book I, 8 September 1818, 8 May and 26 October 1819; Book L, 7 February 1824; Book M, 20 July and 9 August 1847).

102 BANQ, register of Quebec Anglican Church, 9 September 1812; register of Christ Church, Sorel, 3 December 1812. Hill, *The Freedom-Seekers*, 64. Squires, *The 104th Regiment of Foot*, 208. On blacks in Oro Township, see W. Allen Fisher's booklet, *Legend of the Drinking Gourd*. Falkner's wife was Elizabeth Mathews (Mathus, Matthus). They were married at Montreal in 1801, John Trim and Joseph François acting as witnesses. Falkner, whose name was recorded as Charles Falkendow, was said to be twenty-six, his bride twenty-three. Charles Falkendow himself was a witness that year at the burial of Nancy Buckley, the black "servant" of tailor Benaiah Gibb. Two years later, as Charles Faulkner, he acted as a witness at the burial of John Fleming (buried as William Fleming), the son of John Fleming (BANQ, register of Christ Church, 14 April and 9 November 1801, 11 May 1803. POBR 1:224).

103 BANQ, register of Christ Church, 1 December 1819. HDM, admission registers, Book i, 19 November 1819, and list of deaths in the hospital 1819–23 at the back of the volume. Squires, *The 104th Regiment of Foot*, 202. There are traces of other black members of this regiment found in other Quebec localities. Private John Closs, "a man of colour" who had enlisted on 13 April 1809, was quartered at Trois-Rivières in 1815–16. He and his wife, Harriet, had a daughter there in December 1815 who lived only a few weeks. He was discharged on 29 May 1816 (BANQ, register of St James Protestant Episcopal Church, Trois-Rivières, 14 and 17 January 1816. Squires, *The 104th Regiment of Foot*, 202). Peter Cole, who had served as a private from 22 August 1808 to 20 May 1816, was arrested at Quebec in the fall of 1816 for deserting from the ship *Charlotte*. He was wanted on a warrant for stealing an ox the previous August, a charge of which he was acquitted in the Court of King's Bench in March 1817. He was jailed from 30 October 1816 to 29 March 1817 (RPQ 1813–23, 1:37. LAC, RG4 B16, Quebec, Lower Canada and Canada East: [Civil Secretary] records of courts, v. 11, "Criminal Offences Taken from the Records of the Court of Kings Bench for the District of Quebec beginning in the Year 1765 and ending with the Year 1827 with Abstracts," 118. Squires, *The 104th Regiment of Foot*, 203).

104 BANQ, register of St Gabriel Presbyterian Church, 27 August 1819; register of St-Pierre Church, Sorel, 30 October 1827, 9 August and 2 September 1828; TL19 S41, Box 13011, Poll Book, Warwick County, 29 July–3 August 1824. LAC, RG1, L3L, Lower Canada Land Papers, 3:1025–6, 209:98000–8. Othello Keeling (name written Tullock Keelings) was a witness at Zamphier's wedding. When Zamphier's wife was arrested in 1821 for passing counterfeit $5 bills of the Bank of Montreal, she claimed that Peter Dago had given her the bills and told her to use them to buy goods from specific businessmen. She said that she had given Dago the change that she had received on her purchases. Dago denied having anything to do with this business. Charlotte Meunier was charged with two counts of obtaining money and goods under false pretenses, but on 4 May the grand jury of the Court of Oyer & Terminer returned an indictment

on only one charge, to which she pleaded not guilty. The next day, she was brought up on a bench warrant and committed to jail, but the registers contain no explanation for this proceeding. She was tried on 7 May and acquitted (KB, January 1821, *R v. Charlotte Meunier* and *R v. John Murray*, Charlotte Meunier, Arthur Smith and Joseph Millaire; court register, Court of Oyer & Terminer, May 1821, *R v. Charlotte Munier*, 29, 33, 41, 44–6).

105 BANQ, register of Notre-Dame Church, 22 August 1813.
106 BANQ, register of St Gabriel Presbyterian Church, 4 September 1814. Twice married and father of five children by Tibby Prejumier, the first of his two wives, William Feeler was to die in July 1828 under circumstances that warranted an inquest; the inquest record is missing, however, and all that is known is a report of the verdict – that he died "by the visitation of God," i.e., suddenly but without marks of violence (BANQ, register of St Gabriel Presbyterian Church, 23 February 1807, 4 September 1814, 23 October 1819, 14 July 1828 KB, Oyer & Terminer, register, August–September 1828, p. 4, report of coroner's inquests, no. 685, William Feller. POBR 2:129).
107 BANQ, register of Quebec Anglican Church, 23 May 1816. CQS register, 19 January 1811. HDM, admission registers, Book G, 23 April 1806. A list of the men enrolled in the Voltigeurs as of 24 May 1812 names a John Williams as having joined the corps on 27 April. A month later, John Williams was listed as a private in Captain Michel-Louis Juchereau Duchesnay's company at Fort Chambly (LAC, RG9 IA7, Militia and Defence Pre-Confederation Records, Adjutant General's Office, Lower Canada, Militia Muster Rolls, v. 1).
108 BANQ, notary P. Lukin Sr, no. 5075, 10 December 1812.
109 BANQ, notary P. Lukin Sr, no. 5083, 28 December 1812. LAC, RG9 IA7, Militia and Defence Pre-Confederation Records, Adjutant General's Office, Lower Canada, Militia Muster Rolls, v. 1. List of Canadian Voltigeurs – National Historic Park of the Battle of Châteauguay, Allan's Corners, Que., 55.
110 LAC, RG9 IA7, Militia and Defence Pre-Confederation Records, Adjutant General's Office, Lower Canada, Militia Muster Rolls, v. 1, Captain Charles Taché's company, 24 October, 24 November, 24 December 1814, 24 February and 24 March 1815.
111 BANQ, notary J. Blackwood, no. 906, 8 September 1845. BANQ-Q, E21, S64, SS4, Ministère des terres et forêts, Lower Canada Militia Claims, nos 10038–9. KBCV, 1823, no. 162, *John Trim v. Simon Clark*, deposition of Abraham Low, 15 May 1829. LAC, RG9 IA7, Militia and Defence Pre-Confederation Records, Adjutant General's Office, Lower Canada, Militia Muster Rolls, vols 3, 13 and 14.
112 BANQ, register of St Andrew's Presbyterian Church, Quebec, 6 December 1814. CQS-Q, no. 9414, 25 March 1815, recognizance of Gabriel Janot. LAC, RG9, IA7, Militia and Defence Pre-Confederation Records, Adjutant General's Office, Lower Canada, Militia Muster Rolls, vols 6–7. At his wedding, Gabriel Johonnot was identified as Gabriel Jeanneau, about twenty-two, a militiaman in the 1st Batt., Select Embodied Militia. His wife was identified as seventeen-year-old Magdalene Maréchal.
113 BANQ, notary L. Huguet Latour, no. 922, 30 May 1814. LAC, RG19 IA7, Militia and Defence Pre-Confederation Records, Adjutant General's Office, Lower Canada, Militia Muster Rolls, vols 6–7, 1st Battalion, Select Embodied Militia. Nothing much is known of Richardson after the war. He married at Montreal in 1820 and had a son the following year, but both his wife and son died shortly after the boy's birth (see chapter 3 n3). He appears to have remarried, moved

to Quebec, and to have died by 1827, as a woman named Ann Richardson, "widow of the late Hero Richardson" and a resident of Quebec, was married there in September 1827 to a Thomas Williams Sparock (BANQ, register of Quebec Anglican Church, 20 September 1827).

114 BANQ, notary J. Desautels, no. 1334, 16 January 1815. Robert Ashley and Hero Richardson were the witnesses at Williams' wedding to Esther Thompson in 1816 (BANQ, register of St Gabriel Presbyterian Church, 26 October 1816).

115 BANQ, notary H. Griffin, no. 2616, 20 April 1819; notary T. Barron, nos 3573 and 3574, 6 May 1820. LAC, RG9 IA7, Militia and Defence Pre-Confederation Records, Adjutant General's Office, Lower Canada, Militia Muster Rolls, v. 1, muster roll of Capt. John F. Mackay's company, 24 February 1814. Ogilvy died on the job at Amherstburg, Upper Canada, on 28 September. His successor, Anthony Barclay, rehired Thomas Williams in May 1820, at the same wage of £3 10s a month.

116 BANQ, register of Notre-Dame Church, 8 May 1797; notary P. Lukin Sr, no. 4942, 5 May 1812.

117 LAC, RG9 IA7, Militia and Defence Pre-Confederation Records, Adjutant General's Office, Lower Canada, Militia Muster Rolls, v. 1.

118 Crozier (Croger, Croser, and Crozer) was the only witness called for the defence at Pierson's trial on 16 January 1805 for assaulting black farmer Stephen Rogers on New Year's Eve. Pierson was convicted and fined 5s plus costs. The following April, Crozier was a witness at the burial of Pierson's son by Julia Johnson, Joseph Jr (BANQ, register of Christ Church, 3 April 1805. CQS register, January Term 1805, *R v. Joseph Pearson*, 15–16 January).

119 BANQ, notary P. Lukin Sr, no. 5001, 21 May 1812. LAC, RG9 IA7, Militia and Defence Pre-Confederation Records, Adjutant General's Office, Lower Canada, Militia Muster Rolls, v. 1.

120 LAC, RG9, IA7, Militia and Defence Pre-Confederation Records, Adjutant General's Office, vols 1, 5, 6, and 7. Thomas served in various companies of the 1st Battalion, Select Embodied Militia. According to the muster roll and pay list of 24 March 1813, volunteer William Thomas was counted from 11 March 1813 as part of the "new levy" attached to Captain Godfroy de Tonnancour's company. From 25 March to 24 April, he was a bugler in Captain Samuel Mackay's company (muster roll of 24 April), then from 25 April, bugler of Captain Philippe Panet's (muster roll of 24 May). He was stationed at Kingston with Panet's company that summer, and on the Châteauguay River in Lower Canada in October at the time of the crucial battle there (muster rolls of 24 July, 24 August, 24 September, 24 October, 24 November). From 25 July 1814 until his discharge on 28 March 1815, he served in the company of Captain Olivier Fleury de la Gorgendière, first as a private, then as one of the "Drummers, Bugles, or Fifers" (muster rolls Panet's company 24 July 1814; de la Gorgendière's company, 24 August, 24 September, 24 October, 24 November and 24 December 1814, 24 January, 24 February, 8 March, and 28 March 1815). A William Thomas, labourer, was recorded as living at 5 St-Ignace Street in the Quebec Suburb in 1819. He is believed to be the man of that name who was a witness in the early 1820s at the weddings of blacks Joseph Francis and Anne York, and Joseph Pierre and Sarah York, and at the baptism of Abraham Low's son, Jacob Low. In 1825, Montrealer William Thomas was hired by Hyland Millen to go work at Hubbard's Bay (Millen's Bay), NY, a lumbering area (BANQ, register of St Gabriel Presbyterian Church, 17 April and 3 September 1822; register of Christ Church, 18 September 1825; notary J.M. Mondelet, 21 April 1825. Doige, *Montreal Directory*, 1819 ed., 176).

121 BANQ, register of Notre-Dame Church, 7 November 1815.

122 BANQ, register of St Gabriel Presbyterian Church, 9 June 1806 and 24 April 1807.
123 BANQ, register of Notre-Dame Church, 17 September 1815; register of St Gabriel Presbyterian Church, 24 April 1807, 16 May and 6 September 1819. Eliza lived only five months.
124 BANQ, register of Notre-Dame Church, 7 November 1815; register of St Gabriel Presbyterian Church, 19 November 1816.
125 A sixth child, a boy, died at birth on 26 August 1822 (BANQ, register of Notre-Dame Church, 27 August 1822).
126 RPM, Box 50 (August 1826–July 1834).
127 BANQ, TL12, Chambre des milices de Montréal, Registre des procès verbaux d'audiences, 1761–62, f. 29, 17 November 1761; TL10, Registre des jugements en appel au commandant Thomas Gage, 6 décembre 1760 au 10 août 1764, 67–8, 3 December 1761. Louise's claim against a widow Lorange for payment of a rather steep 396 livres (about £16 10s) for 8¼ pounds of tobacco was rejected by the militia tribunal, as was Lorange's counterclaim that Louise's slave husband owed her 60 livres for washing. Louise appealed to Commander Thomas Gage, who ordered Lorange to pay her 6 livres per pound (for a total of just over £2). From the appeal ruling, it appears that Louise's husband was, or had been, a slave of Jean-Baptiste-Grégoire Martel, king's storekeeper under the French régime, and that Louise was or had been Martel's servant. In throwing out Lorange's counterclaim, Gage observed that the master of a slave was responsible for his maintenance, washing included.
128 CQS, October Term 1810, *R v. Joseph Pierson*, complaint of Mary Rusk, 16 June 1810.
129 KB (Oyer & Terminer), *R v. Henry Johnson*, depositions of Guillet et al., 5 July and 8 September 1821; court register, *R v. Henry Johnson*, 26–7 October and 12 November 1821. KBCV, *John Trim v. Simon Clark*, 1823, no. 162, deposition of Catherine Gayet (sic), 23 September 1828. LAC, MG24, B173, James Reid Papers, Criminal Cases, 3, *R v. Henry Johnson*, 27 October 1821.
130 BANQ, notary H. Griffin, no. 8420, 14 September 1829.
131 BANQ, register of Christ Church, 23 December 1832. CQS, *Benjamin Hart v. Isabella Lowe*, Hart affidavit, 23 October 1846; *R v. Augustus Tully*, Hart deposition, 16 November 1846; court register, *R v. Augustus Tully*, 13 and 16 January 1847. A search was made of the Low home in St-Laurent Suburb but nothing was found. Low and Elizabeth Pruyn (alias Isabella Prime) had six children, all boys: Joseph (1834–1835), John (b. 1835), William (1837), Thomas (b. 1838), Richard (1842), and an unnamed boy who died at birth or soon after and who was buried on 8 July 1844. Low had had three children – Esther Ann (1823–1896), Jacob (b. 1825) and Abraham (1827–1831) – by his first wife, Julia Runnel (alias Julia Rennolds, Julianna Reynolds, Julian Runalles, Julian Runi), formerly of Quebec, whom he had married at Montreal in 1821.
132 CQS, January Sessions 1796, *R v. Mary Lapierre*, deposition of Catherine Damour (sic), 27 November 1795, voluntary statements of Marie Lapierre, 27–8 November 1795; court register, 12–13 January 1796. In the case of Marie Lapierre, Hilaire Lamour was identified as William D'amour.
133 BANQ, register of Notre-Dame Church, 25 November 1799.
134 BANQ, register of Notre-Dame Church, 4 May 1807.
135 CQS, *R v. Catherine Baird*, Hoyle affidavit, 10 September 1832, two rejected indictments of Catherine Baird, both 22 October 1832; court register, *R v. Catherine Baird*, 25 and 26 October 1832.

136 BANQ, notary J.A. Gray, no. 2275, 24 February 1809. TC, 22 February 1809. "Vagueness in general about the origins of children of color rendered them subject to simply materializing into service," historian Joan Pope Melish remarked about similar cases in New England (Melish, *Disowning Slavery*, 91–2).
137 See Appendix I/A, notices 94 and 94b.
138 BANQ, notary A. Jobin, no. 1371, 14 December 1818. TC, no. 128, 24 March 1818. CQS, *Cornelius Chatfield v. Caroline*, 15 December 1818; October Term 1819, complaint of Marie Sicard, 28 August 1819. The following August, a white servant of Chatfield's complained that he had whipped her. Chatfield, who lived at 57 St-Paul Street and had his store at 25 McGill, seems to have later moved to Hamilton, Canada West (Doige, *Montreal Directory*, 1819 ed., 73. *Pilot*, 12 June 1845).
139 On prostitution at Montreal at this time, see Poutanen, "'To Indulge Their Carnal Appetites'": Prostitution in Early Nineteenth-Century Montreal, 1810–1842."
140 See chapter 3.
141 BANQ, register of Notre-Dame Church, Quebec, 18 February 1817. BANQ-Q, TL31, S26, S1, Coroner's Inquests 1765–1818, 17 February 1817, no. 3; RPQ, 1:36.
142 BANQ, register of St Gabriel Presbyterian Church, 28 February 1820; register of First Baptist Church, 5 August 1835; register of Christ Church, 13 February 1839; register of Notre-Dame Church, 26 November 1841; TL32, S26, SS1, Coroner's inquests, 1841, no. 421, Martha Hyers, 25 November 1841; TL32, S37, Journal of the Watch Committee of the West Ward of Montreal (22 November 1836–25 April 1837), 20 April 1837. CQS, *R v. Martha Hyres*, deposition of Constable Robert Burrell, 30 July 1839, and indictment, 3 October 1839; *R v. Martha Hyers*, affidavit of Jane Ferguson, 7 November 1839, and indictment 15 January 1840; summary proceedings before police magistrate, 19 February, 22 March, 7 July, 7 August, 4 September, 22 October and 22 December 1840; 24 February, 26 April, 19 May and 27 July 1841; court register, 30 October 1839. KB, July 1833, *R v. Martha Hyers*, affidavit of William Murphy, 27 July 1833. LAC, MG24, B173, James Reid Papers, Criminal Cases, 7, *R v. Martha Hyers*, 14 August 1833. RPM, Box 50 (August 1826–July 1834), no. 3564, 6 August 1833; Box 56 (1835–38), no. 355, 21 April 1837, and Literacy List at end of volume, no. 82; Box 54 (January 1839–August 1843), no. 3, 2 January 1839; no. 101, 2 February 1839; no. 281, 4 April 1839; no. 874, 6 June 1839; no. 1380, 2 October 1839; no. 1527, 7 November 1839; no. 1412, 22 December 1840; no. 274, 24 February 1841; no. 458, 26 April 1841; no. 521, 19 May 1841; no. 809, 27 July 1841; no. 963, 9 October 1841; no. 1034, 23 October 1841. See also Mackey, *Black Then*, 107–11, 199–200. Variations in the spelling of her family name included Airs, Ayers, Harris, Hayers, Heyers, Hiers, Hyas, Hyears, Hyrs, and Hyres.
143 BANQ, register of St Gabriel Presbyterian Church, 3 March 1811; register of Quebec Anglican Church, 8 November 1838. BANQ-Q, TL31, S26, SS1, Coroner's inquests, 1838, no. 62. CQS, affidavits of *Thomas Cockburn and John Simpson v. Joseph Lavigne, Ann Lapsley, Nancy Feeler and Miss Matha*, 27 July 1832; affidavit of watchman *Charles Coulombe v. George Johnson et al.*, 24 January 1833; affidavit of *Constable Henri Hébert v. Eliza Martin & others*, 10 August 1833; affidavit of *Constable Julien Martineau v. Julie Détouin, Nancy Feeler, Jane Wallace, Jane Bell, Bridget Carthy and Ann Riley*, 22 January 1834; affidavit of *High Constable Benjamin Delisle v. Nancy Feeler & al.*, 30 May 1834. RPM, August 1826–July 1834, Box 50,

no. 1939, 27 July 1832; no. 3195, 24 January 1833; no. 3331, 1 May 1833; no. 3578, 10 August 1833; no. 3796, 4 December 1833; no. 3874, 22 January 1834; no. 4052, 29 May 1834; no. 5038, 28 July 1834; Box 55, no. 51, 5 September 1834. RPQ, 2 (1823–37): 293, 303, 310, 316, 321, 324, 331, 338, 345, 350, 355, 361, 369, 379, 386; 3 (1838–43): 4, 8, 16, 21, 32. Nancy Feeler's name was variously recorded as Ann(e) or Nancy Feelan, Feeler, Feelers, Feler, Field, Fielders, Fielders, Fielding, Filler, and Fuller.

144 Prostitution was one element in a notorious crimping racket that fed on the growth of Quebec as a shipbuilding centre. The city produced many ships, but virtually no seamen. To recruit crews to sail the ships to their British buyers, crimps induced incoming seamen to desert, promising them higher wages. They would conceal the deserters in waterfront shebeens and "boarding houses" until the ship they were to man was ready to sail, all the while plying them with drink and prostitutes. In the end, the deserters would get the higher wages promised them, only to find that the money went to pay the tab for their lodging and dissipation. There are several references to this racket in the records of the Legislative Assembly of Lower Canada from the 1820s on and in the records of the Legislative Assembly of the Province of Canada after 1840. See, for instance, *Appendix to the Eighth Volume of the Journals of the Legislative Assembly of the Province of Canada*, 1849, Appendix WW. For an earlier description of the practice, see Cockloft, *Cursory Observations*, 16–18.

145 BANQ, notary T. Bedouin, no. 523, 21 November 1818. The watchmen's contracts are found in the same notary's records, nos 533–48, all 9 December 1818. The first watchmen, hired in May 1818, had also been paid three shillings a night (see notary T. Bedouin, nos 398–415, 4 May 1818, no. 421, 9 May 1818, and no. 423, 12 May 1818). By the end of February 1819, 174 lamps had been installed. The magistrates governing the city had resolved to install another 502, but in the spring of 1824 there were only 276 in the city and suburbs (Archives de la ville de Montréal, Fonds des juges de paix de Montréal, VM35, D7, Procès-verbaux, 4:141–2; VM1, Rapports et dossiers divers, 1796–1840, "Requête d'E. d'Aubreville re éclairage de la Ville," 10 April 1824).

146 BANQ, notary N.B. Doucet, nos 12134 and 12135, 6 November 1824.

147 BANQ, notary J. Belle, no. 3166, 11 December 1839, and no. 5755, 18 May 1843.

148 The contracts are found in the records of Quebec notary Archibald Campbell at the BANQ. Nero Bartholomy's is no. 2521, 24 April 1821. The others are no. 2519, 23 April 1821; nos 2520, 2522, and 2523 of 24 April; nos 2525, 2526, 2527 and 2528 of 27 April; nos 2531, 2533 and 2534 of 30 April; nos 2546 and 2547 of 7 May.

149 The northern posts and the Bay, without further precision, were given as the destination in Nero Bartholomy's contract (BANQ, notary A. Campbell, no. 2521, 24 April 1821). The contract of seaman Richard Harris mentions no destination but stipulates that he was to serve "for and during the term of a Trip in the Sloop Reward to commence 1 May next and end on the unloading of the Sloop Reward in the Port of Quebec" (BANQ, notary A. Campbell, no. 2533, 30 April 1821).

150 He was said to be fifty-eight in August 1817 when he was hospitalized for two weeks, and fifty-six in January 1818 when he returned to the hospital for three and a half months. (BANQ, HDQ admission registers, 8 August 1817, 19 January, 1 February, 1 March, and 1 April 1818).

CHAPTER EIGHT

1 SLCC, *Mary Charlotte v. Gabriel Chouteau*, November 1843, no. 13, 181.
2 Sections 20–24 of the Constitutional Act 1791 spelled out who had the right to vote and who did not. For the text of those articles, see Kennedy, *Documents of the Canadian Constitution 1759–1915*, 211–2.
3 J.I. Cooper, *James McGill of Montreal*, 97.
4 BANQ, TL19, S41, Box 13007, Poll Book, Montreal East Ward, 1827, under date 10 August, entry for Josette St-Antoine. On the subject of women voters, see Garner, *The Franchise and Politics in British North America 1755–1867*, 155–9, and Picard, "Les femmes et le vote au Bas-Canada de 1792 à 1849." In 1834, Patriote leader Louis-Joseph Papineau expressed the view that "It is ridiculous and highly distasteful to see women dragged along to the hustings by their husbands, or girls by their fathers, often against their will. The public interest, decency and the modesty of the fair sex demand an end to these scandalous occurrences" (*Minerve*, 3 February 1834).
5 Picard, "Les femmes et le vote au Bas-Canada de 1792 à 1849," 21–2, 35–6, 57–9, 63, 66.
6 JALC 1820–21, 30 December 1820. *Appendix to the XXXth volume JALC*, 1821, Appendix W; JALC 1821–22, 31 December 1822. JALC 1823, 10 January 1823, *Appendix to the XXXIInd volume JALC*, 1823, Appendix H, "Election Expenses," itemized in "Account of the Contingent Expenses of the Civil Government of Lower-Canada, incurred between the 11th October 1821 and the 10th October 1822, and of the Regular Annual Charges from the 1st November 1821 to the 31st October 1822."
7 *Appendix to the XXXth volume JALC*, 1821, Appendix W, testimony of boardinghouse-keeper Guy Mills, 30 January, notary Théophile Lemay, agent for Joseph Franchère, 2 February; and trader Levi Kemp, 5 February. The list of unqualified electors that Mills produced is appended to the report as sub-appendix W-B.
8 *Appendix to the XXXth volume JALC*, 1821, Appendix W, testimony of Allan Hungerford, 6 February.
9 See chapter 7, n21.
10 BANQ, notary L. Lalanne, 16 February 1822. Billings must have acquired other land because, when he voted in the Missisquoi County election on 25 November 1829, he was identified as a yeoman proprietor of St-Armand. The poll books also still exist for the Missisquoi County elections of 1834 and 1841, showing that he voted on 7 November 1834 at Frelighsburg, and on 18 March 1841, in the elections for the first parliament of the united Province of Canada, as a farmer of St-Armand (BANQ, TL19, S41, Box 13005, Poll Books, Missisquoi County, 23 November–1 December 1829, 3–22 November 1834, 15–25 March 1841).
11 Murray Hall was possibly the "Montreal, Negro, aged 27 years" named in a "Return of Loyalists at Carleton Island" of 26 November 1783. He first surfaced in Montreal around the turn of the century as the husband of Christie (alias Christine), a native of the Bay of Quinte, and father of Elizabeth, the latter said to have been born on 18 October 1802. At her baptism in Montreal on 10 June 1804, the same day as her mother's, Elizabeth Hall's parents were identified as "Murry Hall a Black man and Christie his Wife." At Christie's death on 8 March 1807 at the age of about twenty, however, and at Elizabeth's own death on 22 December that year, Murry Hall's name was written Montreal. In 1817, said to be about sixty years old, he married

Margaret July (alias Peggy Christie, Elizabeth Hall, Margaret Julia Christie, Margaret Murray), the widow of William Wily, who was said to be fifty. She was still said to be fifty at her death on 14 December 1822 (BANQ, register of Christ Church, 10 June 1804, 9 March and 23 December 1807, 16 December 1822; register of St Gabriel Presbyterian Church, 17 March 1817. HDM, admission registers, Book G, 4 February 1807. POBR 1:218, 219. Burleigh, *Tales of Amherst Island*, 21).

12 BANQ, TL19, S41, Box 13007, Poll Book, Montreal East Ward, 1820. The entries for the black voters are as follows: Jacob Simpson, f. 11; Thomas Cockburn, f. 12; Peter Dago, William Filler and Warren Glossen, f. 14; John Hyres, f. 15; Murray Hall and Richard Thompson, f. 19; Isaac Newton, f. 21; Jacob Grant, f. 25. One other black man may have voted: the William Thomas identified as a labourer and a tenant in the Quebec Suburb who voted on 15 March (f. 22), may be the black man of that name active in Montreal in the early 1820s. See chapter 7, n120.

13 Had the election been held a few weeks later, Dago could not have cast his vote. Within a week of the poll closing, he was charged with "stealing in a dwelling house to the value of 40s." He was convicted of a reduced charge of petty larceny and sentenced on 20 May to three months in jail (KB/Oyer & Terminer, register, May 1820, *R v. Peter Dago*, 12, 15, and 20 May. LAC, MG24, B173, James Reid Papers, Criminal Cases, 3, *R v. Peter Dago*, 15 May 1820. *Spectateur canadien*, 27 May 1820). One witness called by the prosecution in Dago's case was Cockburn, his neighbour on St Nicholas Tolentine (St-Timothée) Street. Cockburn was accused that March of operating a brothel in his home. He apparently had to post a recognizance of £10 to keep the peace and show up in court on 21 April, but his recognizance is unsigned by anyone, and it is not clear that he was prosecuted (CQS, April Term 1820, *R v. Thomas Cockburn and others*). Glossen, for his part, was accused, with George Binks and Richard Jackson, of stealing chickens, a rooster, and half a cord of wood, worth a total of £1 12s, on the night of 14 March. The case went to court on 9 May, but the grand jury found no bill against Glossen (KB, March 1820, *R v. Warren Gawson, George Binks and Richard Jackson*, depositions of 15, 16 March; court register, Court of Oyer and Terminer, May 1820, *R v. Warren Gawson, George Binks and Richard Jackson*, 9, 10, 15, and 20 May).

14 William Thomas (see n 12), like Feeler and Glossen, cast a single vote, for Molson.

15 Nelson, *Écrits d'un patriote 1812–1842*, 166.

16 Cited in Landon, "Social Conditions among the Negroes in Upper Canada before 1865," 153. See also Landon, *Western Ontario and the American Frontier*, 171–2. St. G. Walker, *A History of Blacks in Canada*, 170–1.

17 A note on US Independence Day printed in the *Vindicator*, 4 July 1834, is one of the milder samples of this needling: "A number of Americans at the Sault au Recollet commenced at an early hour this morning, firing a Salute in honor of the day, and the Steamer *Canadian Patriot*, we perceive, has hoisted her colours in celebration of this Festival, so dear to the heart of every friend to 'The Rights of Man'"

18 Worshipping the American system, Papineau found Southern slavery distressing but scorned anti-slavery agitators because they provoked the South and threatened the union. He blamed the scourge of slavery on Britain's having imposed it on the American colonists in the first place. If, on the eve of the Civil War, the problem had become nearly insoluble, it was because

NOTES TO PAGES 226–7

in the United States black slaves, "better treated than by other peoples, had multiplied more than anywhere else, and their numbers had grown so great, that there is no longer any possibility of compensating their owners" in any abolition scheme (Papineau, *Lettres à divers correspondants*, 2:214–15, 231; see also ibid. 1:450, 571; 2:83, 250.

19 David Walker, *Walker's Appeal*, 61.
20 Wallace Brown noted that "on the subject of race relations it should be stressed that the loss of America, and in particular the loss of the South, facilitated the ending of slavery, throughout the British Empire in 1833, while, ironically, the country dedicated to the principles of the Declaration of Independence required a civil war to accomplish the same ends" (Brown, *The Good Americans*, 256). In a similar vein, David Brion Davis wrote: "To plunge for a moment into the realm of the hypothetical: In 1860 and 1861, Virginia and the Upper South in general were very slow in following the Deep South in seceding from the Union ... In many ways the slaveholding states were not truly united. Therefore, one can only wonder what the United States might have been like if Georgia and South Carolina had joined the Caribbean colonies in *not* rebelling in the 1770s and in remaining part of the British Empire. This would surely have deepened the difficulties for British abolitionists but might possibly have saved the United States from a Civil War" (Davis, *Inhuman Bondage*, 155).
21 The Annexation Association of Montreal published its manifesto in October 1849. James Grantham was the only black Montrealer to join opponents of annexation in signing a protest against the manifesto. In January 1850, in publishing the text of the Fugitive Slave Bill introduced in the US Senate by James M. Mason of Virginia, the *Pilot* newspaper used it as an argument against the annexationists: "A fugitive slave from Georgia [Richard Bastard] arrived in Montreal a few days ago. He is free now, and no one can touch him. Canada is a refuge for the bondman. But Canada annexed will be no refuge. Will Britons consent to it?" Earlier that month, when John Trim's McGill Street property was sold by the sheriff to pay off a judgment against Trim's estate (the buyer was Olivier Berthelet), it fetched £1,100. The *Gazette* and the *Transcript* cited this sale to rebut charges by the annexationists that, in contrast to the booming United States, all was "ruin and decay" in Canada: "This merely shows that the value of property, where really and not *fictitiously* valuable, is very much what it has been, and what it ought to be" (BANQ, notary D.E. Papineau, no. 5303½, 3 February 1876, no. 5304, 5 February 1876, and no. 5307, 8 February 1876. KBCV, 1849, nos 1910 and 1409, *J.D. Lacroix v. Isaac Taylor et al.*, and *Henri Vallotte v. Isaac Taylor et al. Gazette*, 9 January 1850. *Pilot*, 20 October 1849, 22 and 26 January 1850). In a speech he gave on the condition of blacks in Canada in Abington, Mass., in 1854, Toronto Unitarian minister Charles H.A. Dall said of annexation that "the thing had not been talked of since the passage of the Fugitive Slave Law. That act was looked upon as an insuperable barrier to the annexation of the two countries. ... Of course the colored people deprecated the idea of annexation to the United States" (*Liberator* [Boston], 4 August 1854. See also Landon, *Western Ontario and the American Frontier*, 202. Donald G. Simpson, *Under the North Star*, 74).
22 See St. G. Walker, *A History of Blacks in Canada*, 170–1.
23 "Prospectus of the British American Journal of Liberty," *Colored American* (New York), 22 June 1839. It does not appear that this journal ever got off the ground. For Gallego, see Donald G. Simpson, *Under the North Star*, 206–7.

24 BANQ, TL19, S41, Box 13007, Poll Book, Montreal East Ward, 1824, under date 5 August.
25 BANQ, TL19, S41, Box 13009, Poll Book, Montreal West Ward, 1824. No blacks voted in the Montreal county election, either.
26 BANQ, TL19, S41, Box 13009, Poll book, Montreal West Ward, 1827, under dates 11, 14 and 15 August.
27 Abdella was a property owner through his wife.
28 BANQ, TL19 S41, Box 13007, Poll book, County of Montreal, 1827, under dates 8 and 9 August. A plumper was a single vote cast for one candidate when the voter was entitled to vote for two or more. By plumping for a candidate, the voter indicated a preference for that candidate above all others.
29 BANQ, TL19 S41, Box 13007, Poll book, Montreal East Ward, 1832, under date 4 April. Olivier Berthelet (1798–1872) was a son of Pierre Berthelet (1746–1830).
30 BANQ, TL19 S41, Box 13009, Poll book, Montreal West Ward, 1832, ff. 1, 3, 4, and 5; register of Notre-Dame Church, 18 July 1832.
31 *Gazette*, 23 October 1834.
32 *Gazette*, 23 October 1834. *L'Ami du peuple*, 25 October 1834. *Minerve*, 23 October 1834. *Vindicator*, 24 October 1834.
33 *Gazette*, 23 October 1834.
34 *Liberator* (Boston), 27 September 1834.
35 *Gazette*, 19 August 1834.
36 *Canadian Courant*, 8 September, 6 October, and 17 November 1832. *Montreal Gazette*, 4 October 1832. *Quebec Gazette*, 17 and 21 September 1832. Brown married a Catherine Lloyd at Montreal during his visit, on 27 October; Alexander Grant and Jarrad Banks acted as witnesses (BANQ, register of St Andrew's Presbyterian Church, 27 October 1832. *Canadian Courant*, 7 November 1832).
37 *Gazette*, 25 July 1833. *Vindicator*, 6 August 1833.
38 *Vindicator*, 16 May 1834.
39 BANQ, TL19, S41, Box 13009, Poll Book, Montreal West Ward, 1834, under dates 30 and 31 October.
40 For reports of mob activity and the actions of the local authorities, see BANQ, TL32, S38, register of Special Sessions of the Peace, 26 June 1833–25 November 1842, 34–67.
41 BANQ, TL19, S41, Box 13009, Poll Book, Montreal West Ward, 1834, under dates 5 and 10 November.
42 BANQ, TL19, S41, Box 13007, Poll Book, Montreal East Ward, 1834, under date 10 November.
43 CQS, *R v. Robert Jackson*, Patrick Brennan's deposition and Robert Jackson's recognizance, both 26 November 1834; court register, *R v. Robert Jackson*, 17 January 1835.
44 *Vindicator*, 15 July 1836.
45 BANQ, TL36, S1, SS11, Court of Weekly Sessions, register, *Benjamin Delisle v. Peter Daigo*, 27 August 1840, and *Alexander Comeau v. Peter Daigo*, 1 December 1840. CQS, *R v. Peter Dego, Titus Fortune, [Leonard] Freeman*, affidavit of John N. Smith, 6 September 1819 (filed with documents of July 1819); *R v. Peter Dago et al.*, affidavit of Charles St-Sauveur, 31 December 1835; *R v. Peter Daigo et al.*, affidavit of 5 February 1838, recognizances of 5, 6, 8, 15 Feb-

ruary, indictment of Peter Daigo et al., 21 April; *R v. Peter Daigo et al.*, joint affidavit of Robert Burrell, Jos. Racette and Thomas Webb, 8 November 1839, Dago recognizance 11 November, indictment 10 January 1840, recognizances, 27 and 31 July 1840; *R v. Peter Daigo*, affidavit of William Collins, 3 March 1840; *R v. Peter Daigo*, affidavit of Thomas Dillon, 9 December 1840, and Dago recognizance, 10 December; court register, 27 April 1838; 13, 14, 18 January, 21, 30 April, 13, 18 July, 23, 27 October 1840. KB, *R v. Peter Dago*, affidavits of Mehitabel Woodbury, 23 March 1820, and Richard Hart, 27 March, and statement by Dago, 27 March; court register (Oyer & Terminer), 12, 15 and 20 May 1820; January 1821, *R v. Charlotte Meunier* and *R v. John Murray, Charlotte Meunier, Arthur Smith, Joseph Millaire*; court register (Oyer & Terminer), *R v. Charlotte Munier*, 4, 5 and 7 May 1821. LAC, MG24, B173, James Reid Papers, criminal cases, 3, *R v. Peter Dago*, 15 May 1820. RPM, Box 50, no. 679, 26 November 1826; Box 56, no. 160, 5 February 1838; Box 54, no. 886, 24 September 1840, and no. 1355, 10 December 1840.

46 Lewis, *Crisis in North America*, 3. See Mackey, *Black Then*, 120–6.
47 Besides posting bail for blacks accused of offences on several occasions, Dago took in young Washington Williams for a few days in March 1841 when the latter was between jobs, and in April 1845 he signed as a guarantor for Jacob Low, Abraham Low's nineteen-year-old son, who had been hired by the Hudson's Bay Company and given an advance on his wages, that Low would abide by the terms of his engagement (BANQ, notary J. Dubreuil, no. 549, 24 March 1845. CQS, *R v. Washington Williams*, voluntary examination of Williams, 29 April 1841). For another instance of Dago's benevolence to a black in difficulty, see Mackey, *Black Then*, 129–34.
48 BANQ, register of Notre-Dame Church, 18 August 1868. HDM, admission registers, Register 1867–72, St Patrice Ward, f. 125. At his death from pneumonia in the Hôtel-Dieu, he was identified as Peter Vago, a seventy-six-year-old native of New York.

CHAPTER NINE

1 LAC, RG4 B19, Montreal – Lists of Jurors 1811–35, 1:20, 31, 48 and 1A:34, 51, 55, 63, 66, 73.
2 LAC, RG4 B19, Montreal – Lists of Jurors 1811–35, v. 6, "Liste additionnelle des petits Jurés de la Cour du Banc du Roi et d'oyer et terminer pour l'année 1833."
3 The experience of tobacconist John Scott in 1864 gives some idea of the negative reaction of some whites to the presence of a black man on a jury. Scott, who had fled slavery in Richmond, Va., in 1857, was among the panel of prospective jurors summoned for 2 April 1864 in the March Term of the Court of Queen's Bench. He was a jury candidate for the 4 April trial before Justice Charles Mondelet of a man accused of counterfeiting charges. A newspaper reported on the jury selection:

Richard Sheils, a juror, when his name was called, came before the Court and said he had objections to sitting in the jury-box with the preceding witness, John Scott, who is a colored man.

Judge Mondelet indignantly ordered him to take his seat, and further said that he ought to be ashamed of himself, for objecting to sit with a man who was created by the Being who created himself.

Mr Johnson, Q.C. [defence counsel], said the juror although a poor man was entitled to his opinion, and the liberty of expressing it.

Judge Mondelet said that he would not tolerate such an objection, this was a free country, and the law recognized no distinction between men on the ground of colour.

Mr Johnson said there could be but little freedom in a country where the bench cannot tolerate the free expression of opinion.

Judge Mondelet said Mr Johnson knew well that the objection made by the juror was one which could not be sustained by the law.

The Juror with anything but an amiable look at the colored man, took his seat beside him, and was reminded by the Court that he would have to conduct himself with propriety in the jury room towards the juror Scott.

The fears of the Court on that score were removed, and the tender sensibilities of the member of the superior race were spared the shock of contact or communion with a member of the detested black race, by Mr Devlin [another defence lawyer], who came to the rescue by challenging the Juror Scott.

As it turned out, on 9 April, Sheils (or Shields) and Scott sat together on the jury that determined the insanity of a woman accused of murder. On 13 April, both were on the panel for the trial of a man accused of embezzlement, but Sheils was challenged by the Crown, and Scott by the defence, so that neither served (QB, March Term 1864, Precept, Schedule A, "Petit Jurors," 2 April 1864, juror no. 24; court register, March Term 1864, *R v. John Ashley Payne*, 4 April, *R v. Josephine Achin*, 9 April, and *R v. John Taylor Standring*, 13 April. *Herald*, 5 April 1864. For reports of similar incidents in the courts of Canada West, see the *National Era* [Washington, DC], 29 May 1851, *Voice of the Fugitive* [Windsor, Ont.], 21 May 1851, and *Transcript*, 30 April 1863).

4 Fyson, *Magistrates, Police, and People*, 302–8.
5 On Quebec aboriginals and justice, see Delâge and Gilbert, "La justice coloniale britannique et les Amérindiens au Québec. I – En terres amérindiennes," and "II – En territoire colonial."
6 The idea of blacks as torturers and executioners has a long history. "From the twelfth to the mid-fourteenth century, the iconography of western European churches became stocked with the images of unmistakable black Africans as torturers, tempters, and executioners, often in scenes of the Passion of Christ," American historian David Brion Davis wrote. Davis also noted that the Dutch, who ruled New Amsterdam, New York, until 1664, "used slaves as the executioners of white criminals." In writing of the mutilations prescribed for fugitive slaves under Louisiana's *Code noir*, in force for eighty years from 1724, Harriet Frazier wrote: "As for actual lopping of bondpersons' ears and apparently slicing their tendons, thereby disabling the fugitives, these grisly tasks were left to the public hangman, usually a black prisoner on probation." On the Canadian front, James Cleland Hamilton wrote in 1904 of an early-day public whipping of two convicts at Toronto, under the watchful eye of the sheriff, by "Black Joe," a former army drummer: "The coloured man has been connected with the law, as appears by the records at Osgoode Hall, from the early day when the town, as Little York, enjoyed the luxuries of a town pump, a whipping post and pillory." A "negro hangman" dispatched wife murderer Michael Vincent at Hamilton, Upper Canada, on 8 September 1828. The following January, in an incident known as the "Hamilton outrage," unknown protestors against the de-

tention of Reform journalist Francis Collins hanged an effigy of Lieutenant-Governor Sir John Colborne near the courthouse in Hamilton, with the inscription: "Francis Collins avenged! Executed at Hamilton on Thursday, the 29th of January, 1829, Sir John Colborne, K.C.B., his body left for dissection by the negroes of the place. So perish all upholders of 'British Feelings.' N.B. Sir Peregrine Maitland having absconded, poor Sir John had to suffer." In disparaging Niagara District Sheriff Alexander Hamilton for having carried out the execution of a participant in the Rebellion of 1838, William Lyon Mackenzie observed that Hamilton had "hanged and quartered him after every negro in the country had refused $1000 to perform the terrible work." When Marie Anne Crispin and J.B. Desforges were hanged for murder at Montreal on 25 June 1858, "[t]he executioner enlisted for the occasion – we having no public functionary of that sort – was a negro undergoing imprisonment for some petty offence. As his fee, he received thirty dollars and his liberty, and made off for parts unknown on obtaining the latter." On 29 December 1868, at London, Ontario, a black hangman executed Thomas Jones, convicted of murdering his own niece (*Canadian News*, London, 21 July 1858. *Mackenzie's British, Irish, and Canadian Gazette*, New York, 2 March 1839. Anonymous, *History of the County of Middlesex, Canada*, 122, 124. Anonymous, *Procès et exécution de Marie Anne Crispin et de J.B. Desforges*, 31. Ancaster Township Historical Society, *Ancaster's Heritage: A History of Ancaster Township*, 42. Davis, *Inhuman Bondage*, 59, 129. Frazier, *Runaway and Freed Missouri Slaves*, 27. Frazier, *Slavery and Crime in Missouri, 1773–1865*, 18. J.C. Hamilton, *Osgoode Hall*, 128. See also Scadding, *Toronto of Old*, 42, 176).

7 For public executioners in Quebec under French rule, see Lachance, *Le bourreau au Canada sous le régime français*.

8 LAC, MG1-CIIA, Correspondance générale; Canada, 50:493, Maurepas to Governor Charles de Beauharnois and Intendant Claude Thomas Dupuy, 18 May 1728, 51:41–2, Beauharnois and Intendant Gilles Hocquart to Maurepas, 25 October 1729; 52:83, Beauharnois and Hocquart to Maurepas, 15 October 1730.

9 LAC, MG1-CIIA, Correspondance générale; Canada, 56:38, Maurepas to Beauharnois and Hocquart, 17 April 1731; 55:81, Beauharnois and Hocquart to Maurepas, 12 October 1731; 58:247, précis of letter from Hocquart, 5 January 1733; 60:47, Hocquart to Maurepas, 3 October 1733; 79:344–5, Hocquart to Maurepas, 9 October 1743. Boyer, *Les crimes et les châtiments*, 218–39. Lachance, *Juger et punir en Nouvelle-France*, 173–81. Trudel, *Dictionnaire*, 175–6.

10 Lachance, *Le bourreau au Canada sous le régime français*, 75, 78, 79–81.

11 LAC, MG1-G2, 186:437–438, Conseil supérieur de Louisbourg, "Extrait des Registres du Conseil Supérieur de la Martinique." The original documents are in France's Centre des archives d'outre-mer.

12 LAC, MG23 GII 3, Edward William Gray Papers, v. 1, Gray to Major Skene, 3 October 1767.

13 LAC, MG23 GII 3, Edward William Gray Papers, v. 1, Gray to James Goldfrap, 14 September, 12 October, 19 October 1767; Gray to unnamed correspondent (either Goldfrap or Quebec Sheriff Jacob Rowe), 25 January 1768; Gray to Goldfrap, 27 June 1768; Gray to Jacob Rowe, 20 August 1768; Gray to Hugh Finlay, 11 September 1768.

14 Boyer, *Les crimes et les châtiments*, 233. Riddell, *Michigan Under British Rule*, 49–51, 414.

15 De Gaspé, *Les Anciens Canadiens*, 360.

16 LAC, RG68, Registrar General, Commissions and Letters Patent, Province of Quebec, 1764–91, 3:41–42. UMCB, J2/141, KB, Docket Book, September 1784–May 1789, Quebec, May Term

1785, 36. *Quebec Gazette*, 16 June 1785. P.-G. Roy, *A travers Les anciens Canadiens de Philippe Aubert de Gaspé*, 133–4. Webb had been convicted of stealing £7 10s worth of goods from the shop of merchant William Gill on 11 March 1785.

17 Trudel, *Dictionnaire*, 160.

18 KB-Q, 1781:199-B4, deposition of Jean-Baptiste St-Germain, and 1781:209-A, calendar of prisoners in the Quebec Jail on 30 April 1781. According to St-Germain, Bob "and a woman who passes for his wife" had dropped by the house of St-Germain's mother on 2 January to wish her a happy New Year. "After compliments passed and some short conversation the said Bob proposed to the Deponent's Mother and the rest of the Company present to Drink a Dram together, upon which Bob's Wife took a Bottle of Rum from under her Cloak, which they drank; the Negro Bob, then went out staid a Short time and returned with another bottle of Rum, which they drank also. Bob then declared they must have more Rum, and asked for a Quart Mug, which they gave him. he went out staid about six or seven minutes and returned with the Quart Mug full of Rum."

19 *Quebec Gazette*, 19 November 1789.

20 BANQ, register of Notre-Dame Church, Quebec, 7 February 1796. KB-Q, 1789:319-B8, *R v. Robert Lane*. One piece of evidence tending to reinforce the theory that Bob, the rum drinker, and Robert Lane were the same man is the record of the inquest into the sudden death at the jail on 21 November 1783 of Margaret Lane, who may have been Bob's companion – the "woman who passes for his wife" mentioned in note 18, above. It appears that she lived at the jail, without being an inmate. She had just returned to the jail after being sent out on an errand when she dropped dead at the door. A witness testified that "for Some days past She & her husband has drank pretty freely & deponent Believes that they have Eat very Little" (BANQ-Q, TL31, S26, SS1, Coroner's Inquests, 1783, no. 28, 22 November 1783).

21 SLCC, *Mary Charlotte, a woman of color, v. Gabriel Chouteau*, November 1843, no. 13, 57–8, testimony of Paschal Léon Cerré, 21 May 1845. This could be the executioner who died in 1789, as Sheriff Gray reported to the government secretary that September: "[T]he late Executioner having died during the sitting of the Court of King's Bench, by the permission of His Majesty's Chief Justice and with the consent of the Attorney General I have engaged one Samuel Reeves, a Prisoner confined for Petty Larceny to serve in the Capacity and in consequence thereof the Attorney General at my request declined prosecuting him until his Lordships pleasure shall be known. Wherefore humbly request that His Lordship will be pleased to grant the said Samuel Reeves His Majesty's pardon for the said offence in consideration of his having undertaken to discharge that duty." Reeves was an Irishman in his thirties, a soldier who had been drummed out of the 34th Regiment (LAC, MG23 GII 3, Edward William Gray Papers, v. 4, Gray to Henry Motz, 21 September 1789. *Gazette*, 10 July 1788).

22 BANQ, register of Notre-Dame Church, Montreal, 16 June 1798. Burns was identified as George Born at the baptism of his daughter, Marie Joseph. His wife was Josephe Dubreuil, the daughter of François Dubreuil and Brigitte Henry, born at Chambly on the Richelieu River in 1777. Two months before the birth of their daughter, Burns and his wife, as well as her brother, François Dubreuil Jr, each received $5 from Dubreuil Sr to renounce all claims to the estate of his late wife (Brigitte Henry had died in 1780). There seems to be no record of Burns' marriage, and his background is a mystery. There was a George Burns, master wheelwright, at Chambly

in the early 1780s. If this was our man, then he was considerably older than his wife. A "George Burn & Sarah, Negroes, were Married by leave the 10th Jany" 1787 at Montreal. If this was our man, then he may have been a slave at that time, and Josephe Dubreuil would have been his second wife (BANQ, register of St-Joseph Church, Chambly, 31 March 1777, 27 January 1780; register of Christ Church, Montreal, 10 January 1787; notary A. Grisé, no. 1834, 30 August 1780, and no. 2133, 18 September 1781; notary P. Lukin Sr, no. 1202, 10 April 1798).

23 BANQ, register of Notre-Dame Church, Quebec, 29 November 1804; register of Quebec Anglican Church, 12 September 1798. It is not clear when Burns and his family moved to Quebec. De Gaspé speaks of a hangman named Ward who executed David McLane, the Rhode Island merchant hanged for treason at Quebec on 21 July 1797. This was possibly the executioner who died in September 1798 and was buried under the name Thomas Wall (De Gaspé, *Les Anciens Canadiens*, 360. Landmann, *Adventures and Recollections*, 1:319–26).

24 *RAPQ* 1948–49, "Dénombrements de Québec," 167. De Gaspé, *Mémoires*, 47–8. The parish census identified him as "George, nègre boureau."

25 BANQ, register of Quebec Anglican Church, 12 October 1806.

26 BANQ, register of St-Joseph Church, Trois-Rivières, 2 June 1817. LAC, RG7 G15 C, Civil Secretary's Letter Books, 24:165, A.W. Cochran to the Chief Justice, 26 February 1817; 24:167, Cochran to Advocate General George Pyke, 28 February 1817; 24:176–7, Cochran to Sheriff of Quebec, 14 March 1817; RG68, Registrar General, Commission for Special Court Pardons, Lower Canada, 2:273–9.

27 Hodges, ed., *Black Loyalist Directory*, 189–190. A Benjamin Field, private in the 26th Regiment, was recorded at Quebec in the 1780s, but he died in 1796 (BANQ, register of Quebec Anglican Church, 3 August 1788, 16 June 1796).

28 BANQ, register of Notre-Dame Church, 17 and 27 December 1808, 17 June 1810; register of St Gabriel Presbyterian Church, 26 February 1808. *Spectateur canadien*, 6 May 1816. Field's wife was identified at different times as Mary Anna Johnson, Maria Jansonn and, at her death, Marie Anne Thompson.

29 An earlier Montreal hangman had much the same reputation. In April 1798, a grand jury had complained of the presence of prostitutes conducting their business near the city ramparts, charging that "one Francis Carron the Common hangman harbours a number of these disorderly Women and keeps a very disorderly house" (CQS, April Sessions 1798, Grand Jury presentment, 30 April 1798).

30 CQS, "Calendar of the House of Correction 21st October 1819"; July Term 1820, *R v. Several disorderly women*, affidavit of François Lecompte, 10 May 1820. KB, Administrative Documents, "Calendrier de la prison commune du district de Montréal, octobre 1823–avril 1827," jail calendar of 1 October 1823, p. 1. Benjamin Field is listed as an inmate in every monthly calendar of prisoners to 1 October 1824.

31 Ermatinger, nephew of Edward William Gray, had succeeded his uncle as sheriff of the Montreal District after the latter's death on 22 December 1810.

32 CQS, April Term 1825, *R v. Benjamin Field*. KB, Administrative Documents, "Calendrier de la prison commune du district de Montréal, octobre 1823–avril 1827," calendar of May 1825, p 77. RPM, Box 50, August 1826–July 1834, no. 59. HDM, admission registers, Book K, 24 June 1826.

33 CQS register, grand jury presentment, 19 July 1823.
34 *Spectateur canadien*, 25 May 1822. The attrition rate among hangmen could be high. At Quebec, four died between 1798 and 1811, one by his own hand. After Thomas Wall and George Burns, who died respectively in 1798 and 1806 (see nn22, 23 and 25, above), Burns' successor, identified by the coroner as John Jacob Kazeau, and by the church at his burial as François Caiseau, killed himself in his room at the jail on 28 May 1810; his successor, Andrew Berryhill, died in his apartments at the jail on 22 May 1811, of a lung inflammation (BANQ, register of Notre-Dame Church, Quebec, 29 May 1810; register of St Andrew's Presbyterian Church, Quebec, 24 May 1811. BANQ-Q, TL31, S26, SS1, Coroner's inquests, 23 May 1811, no. 3. *Quebec Gazette*, 31 May 1810.
35 LAC, MG24 B173, James Reid Papers, Criminal Cases, 4, *R v. Jean Baptiste Verdon, Benjamin Augé, Jean Baptiste Delinelle*, 9 September 1825; RG4, B20, Quebec, Lower Canada and Canada: [Provincial Secretary and Registrar] Applications for pardons or clemency 1766–1858, 11:3918–33, James Reid to A.W. Cochran, 5 October 1825, particularly pages 3922–3.
36 *JALC*, Appendices to vols 17–36, "Abstracts of warrants" for the payment of the government's civil expenditures, itemized payments to Sheriff E.W. Gray and his successor, F.W. Ermatinger. In a letter to Provincial Secretary Herman Witsius Ryland in 1816, Ermatinger stated that "the only annual allowances made to me by His Majesty are £100 Stg. Salary as Sheriff and £27 Stg. for a public executioner" (LAC, MG23 GII 3, Edward William Gray Papers, v. 6, 1792–1826, Ermatinger to H.W. Ryland, 17 September 1816).
37 LAC, MG23 GII 3, Edward William Gray Papers, v. 2, Gray to unidentified correspondent, 15 November 1784.
38 LAC, MG23 GII 3, Edward William Gray Papers, v. 3, Gray to Jenkins Williams (April 1786).
39 See Greenwood and Boissery, *Uncertain Justice*, 15–17. *The Canadian Magazine and Literary Repository*, no. III (September 1823), 1:283.
40 CQS register, *R v. Geo. a Nagre & W. March and Eleonor March*, 6 May 1765; *R v. Geo. a Negroe*, 22 July 1765.
41 CQS register, *The King at the Prosecution of Antoine Chattelin v. Cesar a Negro Man*, 10, 19 and 23 April 1781, 11 November 1783, 15 April, 13 July, and 12 October 1784.
42 LAC, RG4 B16, Quebec, Lower Canada and Canada East: [Civil Secretary] records of courts, v. 11 "Criminal Offences Taken from the Records of the Court of Kings Bench for the District of Quebec beginning with the Year 1765 and ending with the Year 1827 with Abstracts," p 18. UMCB, J2/141, KB, Docket Book, September 1784–May 1789, Quebec, May Sessions 1786, 55.
43 BANQ, notary C. Stewart, 20 October 1786. Newton was hired as a domestic servant by James Frost, harbour master of Quebec, from 24 October 1786 to 1 May 1787, for $3 a month and "sufficient Provision." He could have lived at Frost's, but it appears that he declined. Frost agreed "[t]hat in the Evening when the affairs of His [Frost's] Family are finished to allow the said Isaac Newton to go home to his Family He always returning early in the morning to his work as a Servant."
44 CQS, Calendar of Prisoners, 10 January 1795, 21 April 1795. LAC, MG23 GII 3, Edward William Gray Papers, v. 6, Gray to Sewell, 5 October 1795; RG4 B20, Quebec, Lower Canada and Canada: [Provincial Secretary and Registrar] Applications for pardons or clemency 1766–1858, 1:399–405; RG7, G15, C, Lower Canada, Civil Secretary's Letter Books 1788–1829,

NOTES TO PAGES 247–50 511

3:59–60, H.W. Ryland to Chief Justice Monk, 3 September 1795; RG68, Registrar General, Commissions and Letters Patent, Province of Quebec, 1764–91; Conditional Pardons, Lower Canada, 1792–1841, 1:67–8. *Quebec Gazette*, 26 March 1795. Newton was spared the branding, but Dorchester's speed in ordering a pardon was not matched by those responsible for its formal drafting. The approved document itself was not issued until 26 October.

45 CQS, *R v. Isaac Newton*, indictment 22 April 1816, depositions of Léonard Dutelle and François Collin, 15 February 1816; court register, 23 and 26 April 1816.

46 KB, Administrative Documents, "Calendrier de la prison commune du district de Montréal, octobre 1823–avril 1827," 29, 32, 36, 39. CQS register, 19 July 1824, order of the court discharging several prisoners, including Isaac Newton and his wife, whom the grand jury had declined to indict. Two months after his release from jail, Newton, identified as a fifty-two-year-old "Negre journalier" born in England, was a patient for ten days at the Hôtel-Dieu. In 1825, he and his wife, Amelia (alias Mary, Milly), were recorded as neighbours of Jacob Simpson in the Quebec Suburb. When he died in the Montreal General Hospital on 14 December that year, he was said to be sixty-eight. Milly Newton was identified as a native of Africa, seventy years old, when she was hospitalized in February–March 1827. She was said to be sixty-five at her death in the Montreal General Hospital on 15 May that year. Both were buried in the Protestant Poor Ground (BANQ, register of Christ Church, 16 December 1825 and 16 May 1827. HDM, admission registers, Book K, 16 September 1824, and Book L, 21 February 1827. POBR 2:78 and 106. Perrault, *Montréal en 1825*, 171).

47 KB, November 1814, *R v. James Grant*; court register, March Term 1815, *R v. James Grant*, 3 and 6 March 1815.

48 One other black Montrealer, American-born Robert Ellis (alias Black Bob), suffered the death penalty, but at Quebec, in 1827. See chapter 10.

49 LAC, RG68, Registrar General, Commissions and Letters Patent, Province of Quebec, 1764–91; Conditional Pardons, Lower Canada, 1792–1841, 1:63–5 and 316–18.

50 BANQ-Q, TL5, Pièces judiciaires et notariales détachées, D4286, court order of 18 February 1778 transferring custody of Thomas Bruce from the sheriff of the Quebec District to the sheriff of the Montreal District. UMCB, J2/129, KB, Docket Book, 1777–84, Montreal, March Term 1778, 8. *Quebec Gazette*, 18 September 1777.

51 LAC, RG4, B20, Quebec, Lower Canada and Canada: [Provincial Secretary and Registrar] Applications for pardons or clemency 1766–1858, 24:10760–81.

52 For another infanticide prosecution, at Quebec in 1799, see BANQ-Q, TL31, S26, SS1, Coroner's Inquests 1765–1818, 1 February 1799, no. 49. KB-Q, 1799:449-B12, March Term 1799, *R v. Mary Ann a Black Woman*.

53 LAC, MG23 GII 3, Edward William Gray Papers, v. 6, Ermatinger to John Richardson, 7 January 1824. Richardson was chairman of the committee.

54 LAC, MG24 B173, James Reid Papers, Criminal Cases, 4, *R v. Reuben Chambers*, 5 March 1824.

55 LAC, RG4 B20, Quebec, Lower Canada and Canada: [Provincial Secretary and Registrar] Applications for pardons or clemency 1766–1858, 11:4255–67; RG68, Registrar General, Conditional Pardons, Lower Canada, 5:482–9. See also Borthwick, *History of the Montreal Prisons*, 47.

56 KB, February–April 1818, "Nos. 2 & 3, Dominus Rex v. Wm Meikins Nation, Wyman Virginia and Warren Glawson, for Stealing a quantity of Leather from Geo. Forsyth, & against

Oliver Berthelet for having purchased the Same Knowing it to be Stolen," copies of three receipts from Nation to Berthelet for payment of leather purchases, dated 26 and 31 January and 3 February 1818; *R v. Wyman Virginia and R v. Weyman Virginia and Warren Glossen*, indictments, 21 February; deposition of George Forsyth, 30 March; depositions of George S. Knowers, Amable Gaudrie, and George Forsyth, 1 April; depositions of Alonzo Bangs and Amable Gaudrie, 2 April; depositions of Michel Landry, Daniel Ward Eager and Levi Mower, 6 April; examination of Wyman Virginia and William Meikins Nation, 7 April; court register (Oyer & Terminer), May 1818, *R v. Weyman Virginia*, 9, 11, and 12 May. CQS, May 1818, "Dom Rex v. Wm Meikins Nation & Warren Glawson for Stealing Butter & Cheese at James McDouall & Co., & agt. Warren Glawson as an Accomplice with said Meikins Nation and Wyman Virginia in Stealing the Leather, Vide Case No. 2 & 3 [refers to theft of leather from George Forsyth]," depositions of Daniel Ward Eager and Ace Gabriel, 9 April 1818, examination of Warren Glawson, 13 April, and deposition of Richard Thompson, 16 April 1818. *Spectateur canadien*, 23 May 1818. Wyman and William C. Virginia were brothers of Luther Virginia, "a youngerly colored man of intemperate and dishonest habits," a former Vermonter living on the Canadian side of the border near Highgate, Vt., who was hanged for murder at St Alban's, Vt., on 14 January 1820 (see Hemenway, *The Vermont Historical Gazetteer*, 2:298)

57 KB, January 1819, *R v. John Bowman and Warren Glossen*; court register, 9 March 1819.

58 CQS, July Term 1819, *R v. Warren Gaussen alias Glasford Warren*, indictment of Warren Gaussen alias Glasford Warren, 10 July 1819; court register, 14, 16, 17, and 19 July. *Spectateur canadien*, 31 July 1819.

59 CQS, *John Baptist v. Glasson Warren*, John Baptist deposition, 23 August 1819.

60 KB, March 1820, *R v. Warren Gawson, George Binks and Richard Jackson*, deposition of Charlotte Robidou, 15 March; depositions of Louis Pasquine and Rufus Bodford, and examination of Gawson, Binks and Jackson, 16 March; court register (Oyer & Terminer), May 1820, 9, 10, 15, and 20 May.

61 KB, January 1823, *R v. Warren Glossen & al.*, witness recognizances of Samuel Crane, Isaac Hitchcock, John Price, John Skelton, and Benjamin Thatcher, 11 January; court register, August–September 1823, *R v. Warren Glossen, Peter Johnson, Jean Bte Bowman, Joseph Yager, and Jean Bte Albert*, 28 August, 1, 2, 5, and 10 September. LAC, RG7 G15 C, Lower Canada, Civil Secretary's Letter Books 1788–1829, 32:261, A.W. Cochran to F.W. Ermatinger, 21 October 1823. *Canadian Courant*, 11 and 15 January, 1 February, 1 March, 5 April, 13 September, 25 October, and 8 November 1823; *Gazette*, 10 and 17 January, 13 September, 25 October 1823; *Herald*, 13 September, 25 October, 8 November 1823; *Spectateur canadien*, 25 October 1823. Peter Johnson was probably the man of that name who was a witness at the burial of Julia Murray, the one-year-old daughter of black labourer Philip Murray and his wife, Christian Dingwall, at Montreal in April 1819. Neither the court records nor newspapers reports of the 1823 case identified him as black, but on his transfer to the house of correction at Quebec on 23 November 1823, the records there made him a thirty-two-year-old American-born man of a "black" complexion. Sentenced to five years' imprisonment, he served only about one year and a half before being discharged on 12 April 1825 (BANQ, register of St Gabriel Presbyterian Church, 29 March 1818, 23 April 1819. RPQ, 2:24).

62 Variations of his name include Manuel Firmin, Emanuelle Firmain, Manuel Firman, Manuelle Firmand, Emanuel Firmin, Emmanuel Firmin, Manuel Freeman, and Manuel Philman.
63 CQS-Q, no. 10597, *R v. Manuel Firman*, 21 January 1820. RPQ, 1813–23, 1:102, 28 May 1818. Delâge and Gilbert, "La justice coloniale britannique et les Amérindiens au Québec 1760–1820. I – En terres amérindiennes," 72.
64 KB, November 1820, *R v. Manuel Firmin*, depositions of Frederick Diganard, Francis Metzler, Charles Bond, 6 November, and examination of Firmin, 9 November; court register (Oyer & Terminer), 9 and 15 November.
65 KB, March 1821, *R v. Manuel Firmin & others*, depositions of Michel Munro, Donald Shearer, and James Stacks, 3 March 1821; letter of Donald Shearer to Solicitor General Charles Montizambert, 18 April 1821; calendar of prisoners in the house of correction, 10 July 1821; court register (Oyer & Terminer), *R v. James Kelly, Manuel Firmin, Voltus Deselbi, Tobias Burke and John Whiteman*, 5 and 14 May, and 7 and 12 November 1821. The calendar of prisoners identified Firmin as a native of South America.
66 KB, register (Oyer & Terminer), May 1822, *R v. Manuel Firmin*, 8 and 17 May.
67 BANQ, notary J.B. Badeau, 15 December 1826. The dating of Firmin's move to Trois-Rivières in 1822 is based on a statement made by his wife in February 1831 that, by the summer of 1830, he had been living there for nine years. See LAC, RG4, B20, Quebec, Lower Canada and Canada: [Provincial Secretary and Registrar] Applications for pardons or clemency 1766–1858, 17:7070–7, Petition of Marie Maclode, 23 February 1831, in particular f. 7074.
68 LAC, RG4, B20, Quebec, Lower Canada and Canada: [Provincial Secretary and Registrar] Applications for pardons or clemency 1766–1858, 17:7043–8, 7054–77.
69 KB, August 1833, depositions of Marcel Brunette, 23 August, and Louis Deguire *dit* Desroziers and Emanuelle Firmain, both 26 August; recognizance of all three to give evidence, 26 August 1833.
70 KB, registers, *R v. Emanuel Firmin*, 3, 4, 5 and 10 March 1834. LAC, MG24, B173, James Reid Papers, Criminal Cases, 7, *R v. Emanuel Firmin*, 5 March 1834.
71 LAC, RG4, B20, Quebec, Lower Canada and Canada: [Provincial Secretary and Registrar] Applications for pardons or clemency, 1766–1858, 17:7061–9; RG68, Registrar General, Conditional Pardons, Lower Canada, 1792–1841, 9:49–57, 95–101.
72 BANQ, TL32, S26, SS1, Coroner's Inquests, 1826, Inquisition on view of the body of Thomas Halbert, 18 August 1826. KB, *R v. Collins*, August 1826, depositions of William Doley, William Dunn, John Nixon, Mary (Brunelle) Parker, and Dr John Hill Roe, all 18 August, and surgeon T. Walker, 19 August; court register, *R v. William Collins and James Laing*, 2, 6 and 9 September 1826. LAC, MG24, B173, James Reid Papers, Criminal Cases, 5, *R v. William Collins and James Laing*, 6 September 1826. The prosecution witness Mary Brunelle and her husband, Willard Parker, had both been sentenced to six months in the house of correction in 1822 for keeping a disorderly house (CQS register, *R v. Willard Parker and Marie Brunelle*, 29–30 October 1822).
73 KB, register, February Term 1827, *R v. Alexandre Johanet*, 24 and 26 February, and 10 March. RPM, Box 50, no. 644, 7 October 1826. LAC, MG24 B173, James Reid Papers, Criminal Cases, 5, *R v. Alexander Johannet*, 26 February 1827.

74 KB, May 1818, *R v. Edward Sidney, James Healy, William Meikins Nation, Tobias Burke, Edmund Burke*; court register, *R v. Edward Sidney, James Healey, William Meakins Nation, Daniel Burns, Tobias Burke and Edmund Burke*, 2 September 1818.
75 For Middleton, see chapter 5 and Appendix III.
76 CQS, October Term 1820, *R v. François Aumier*, 19 September.
77 KB, August 1821, *R v. Joseph Leclair*, "Copy of Enquest & affidavit on the body of Ths. Perks," 15 August, examination of Jos. Leclair, 22 August; court register (Oyer & Terminer), 29–30 October 1821. LAC, MG24 B173, James Reid Papers, Criminal Cases, 3, *R v. Joseph Leclaire*, 30 October 1821. *Herald*, 25 August 1821. *Spectateur canadien*, 25 August and 17 November 1821. The day before his trial for murder, Leclerc had been convicted of stealing money from a guest at an inn at Soulanges on 31 July, for which he was sentenced on 10 November to receive 39 lashes and to serve three months at hard labour in the house of correction (KB–Oyer & Terminer, July 1821, *R v Joseph Leclair*, depositions of Benjamin Schermerhorn, 31 July and 4 August, deposition of Philologus Culver, 4 August; court register, 27 and 29 October, and 10 November 1821. *Spectateur canadien*, 17 November 1821.)
78 BANQ, TL32, S26, coroner's inquest, Joseph Pierson, 10 March 1815. KB, September Term 1815, *R v. James Douglas*, various depositions of March 1815, and indictment of 1 September; court register, 7 and 9 September. See Mackey, *Black Then*, 50–4.
79 KB, March 1815, *R v. James Douglas*, depositions of Joseph Pierson, 9 March, and of Sgt. John Kennedy, 13 March.
80 CQS register, *R v. William Thompson*, 30 October 1815. KB, *R v. William Thompson*, deposition and bond of Thomas Webster, 29 September 1815 (the bond is filed under September 1815, the deposition under February 1816). KB–Oyer & Terminer, March Term 1816, *R v. William Thompson*, indictment of 20 March 1816. LAC, RG4 B21, Lower Canada and Canada East Gaol Calendars and Prison Returns, 1:398, "Calendar of prisoners in the Montreal jail, October 1815." Webster's death on 15 July 1816 would have proved a major obstacle to further prosecution.
81 CQS, *Hanna Ceasar v. Joseph Pearson & Julia Flemming*, complaint of Hanna Ceasar, 26 September 1804; January Sessions, 1805, *R v. Joseph Pearson*, deposition of Stephen Rogers and recognizance of Joseph Pearson, both 2 January, indictment of 10 January; court register, 15–16 January.
82 CQS, *François Cati v. Joseph Pearson*, deposition of François Cati and arrest warrant for Joseph Pearson, 24 February 1807, Pierson recognizance, 26 February 1807.
83 CQS, October Term, *R v. Joseph Pierson*, complaint of Mary Rusk, arrest warrant and recognizance of Joseph Pearson, all 16 June 1810. William Feeler was one of Pierson's sureties, posting a £5 bond. Pierson and Rusk had married on 13 September 1809. Their son was said to be about eight months old at his baptism on 29 April 1811, and eleven months old at his death the following 10 July, meaning that he would have been born in August 1810 (BANQ, register of St Gabriel Presbyterian Church, 13 September 1809, 29 April and 11 July 1811).
84 Their daughter, Sarah Anne Pierson, was born on 13 May 1812 (BANQ, register of St Gabriel Presbyterian Church, 26 July 1812).
85 BANQ, register of St Gabriel Presbyterian Church, 2 October 1815. Mary Abram was a sponsor at the baptisms of William Thomson, son of farmer Henry Thomson and his wife Phillis, in 1817, and of John Wright, the son of William Wright and Catherine Guillet in 1823 (BANQ,

register of St Gabriel Presbyterian Church, 25 May 1817; register of St Andrew's Presbyterian Church, 16 October 1823).

86 Like Jacques Viger's wife, Porteous's wife, Anne Mompesson, was to have inherited a slave as a young girl. In his will of 8 October 1793, her father, John Mompesson, formerly a captain in the 8th (King's) Regiment, stated: "I give and bequeath to my daughter Ann Mompesson, my Negro wench called Isabell." His daughter was then ten years old. It appears, however, that Isabell was no longer in Mompesson's possession at his death on 30 July 1799, as no slaves were recorded in the inventory of his estate (BANQ, notary J.A. Gray, no. 372, 13 August 1799, and no. 493, 31 May 1800; register of Notre-Dame Church, 30 August 1788; register of Christ Church, 10 February 1816).

87 KB–Oyer & Terminer, 1821, *R v. Henry Johnson*, depositions of Catherine Guillet and Joseph Picard, 5 July, examination of Henry Johnson, 8 September, indictment of 25 October; court register (Oyer & Terminer), October Term 1821, 26–27 October and 12 November. LAC, MG24 B173, James Reid Papers, Criminal Cases, 3, *R v. Henry Johnson*, 27 October 1821.

88 CQS, *R v. Luke Stewart*, Low affidavit, Stewart recognizance, both 22 July 1840. That same year, Low himself was sentenced to fifteen days' hard labour on a charge of being "disorderly." This stemmed from two attacks that he made on Jane Wilson, the widow of John Broome, specifically his second attack on her on the night of 21 September. In June, she had accused Low of abusing her and threatening her. He had had to post a bond of £20 to keep the peace for six months, with two securities of £10 each provided by Peter Dago and Washington Williams. Low was at her again that September. She ran into a room of her house and closed the door to protect herself; he tried to break it down, and "he did further swear, scream [...] and call her all manner of gross and abusive names," she said. She said that Low was a man of "drunken and violent habits and when intoxicated is a dangerous person." A note on the affidavit says that Low was tried and convicted on 23 September and sentenced to fifteen days' imprisonment at hard labour. This seems to be confirmed by the prison records, but the records of the Court of Quarter Sessions have him posting a recognizance of £20 – with Robert Gordon and Thomas Brooks as his sureties – on 26 September to keep the peace for six months (CQS, *R v. Abraham Low*, Wilson affidavits of 9 June and 22 September 1840, Low recognizances, 9 June and 26 September 1840. RPM, Box 54, no. 882, 23 September 1840, and Box 56, Literacy List at end of volume, no. 868). The following year, Low was twice accused of assault with intent to murder, the second time for stabbing Peter Dago in the face with a penknife. On the first charge, Low was acquitted when the victim failed to show up to testify; in the second, he pleaded guilty to a lesser charge of simple assault and was sentenced to only two days in the house of correction (CQS, *R v. Abraham Low*, affidavit of Louis Day and Low recognizance, 28 April 1841, indictment of 29 April and Low recognizance of 6 May; court register, 29 April, 10 and 13 July; *R v. Abraham Low*, affidavit of Peter Daigo, 25 July 1841, indictment filed 22 October; court register, 22 October. RPM, Box 54, no. 1030, 22 October 1841).

89 APC, Box 166, A29, "Minutes of Session 1823–47," 13 April 1823 and October 1823 (no day specified), pp. 6–7. The Gelston family seems to have come to Canada from New York State.

90 *Vindicator*, 15 July 1836.

91 CQS, *Ebenezer Marvin v. Betsey Freeman*, affidavit of Ann Gelston, 13 June 1836.

92 *Vindicator*, 15 July 1836.

93 KBCV, June Term 1836, *On petition of Alexander Grant for a Writ of Habeas Corpus*, affidavit and petition of Alexander Grant, 13 June; motion filed by Charles-Ovide Perrault and order of the court, both 14 June, subscribed to Grant's petition of 13 June. Hardware merchant Cyrus Brewster was misidentified in the court records as Silas Brewster. See Appendix IV.

94 CQS, *R v. Daniel Arnoldi*, affidavit of A. Grant and recognizance of Daniel Arnoldi, both 14 June 1836; indictment of Arnoldi, 11 July 1836 (filed 12 July). See the account of these cases in Fyson, *Magistrates, Police, and People*, 304–8.

95 KBCV, June Term 1836, *On Petition of Alexander Grant*, certificate of High Constable Benjamin Delisle, 14 June. *Minerve*, 16 June 1836. *Vindicator*, 14 June 1836.

96 KBCV, June Term 1836, *On Petition of Alexander Grant*, return of Mrs Marvin (Ann Gelston) to writ of habeas corpus, 14 June 1836.

97 KBCV, June Term 1836, *On Petition of Alexander Grant*, short untitled document recording the decision of the court. *Gazette*, 16 June 1836. *Minerve*, 16 June 1836. *Vindicator*, 17 June 1836.

98 CQS, July Sessions 1836, register, *R v. Daniel Arnoldi Esq.*, 19 July. *Minerve*, 25 July 1836. *Vindicator*, 19 July 1836. In correspondence with the government at Quebec, Arnoldi mounted a defence of his actions that was successful insofar as it kept him from being permanently removed from the ranks of the magistracy, but not before he had been suspended and rebuked by the Governor, Lord Gosford (LAC, RG4 C2, Provincial Secretary's Office, Correspondence: Canada East/Lower Canada, Civil Secretary's Letter Books 1829–41, 16:152, Civil secretary to Daniel Arnoldi, 9 September 1836). On hearing of Arnoldi's reinstatement, the *Vindicator* commented on how odd it was that "being found guilty of an assault ... and being fined by the Bench in consequence, does not disqualify, in the opinion of our Executive, from being a Magistrate, or render a person unworthy of being on the Commission of the Peace" (*Vindicator*, 4 November 1836. See also *Minerve*, 19 September and 3 November 1836).

99 *Minerve*, 8 September 1836.

100 *Vindicator*, 15 July 1836.

101 In July 1833, when Grant was keenly following the progress of the bill to abolish slavery in the British West Indies, Montreal newspapers reported the death of O'Callaghan's brother, Eugene, a Catholic priest who had been serving as "assistant protector of slaves for the 3rd district of the colony of St Lucia" (*Minerve*, 4 July 1833).

102 BANQ, register of Notre-Dame Church, 24 September 1809. *Mackenzie's European and Canadian Gazette*, New York, 25 May 1839. David, *Les Patriotes de 1837–1838*, 175–84. Séguin, *Le mouvement insurrectionnel dans la presqu'île de Vaudreuil 1837–1838*, 135. Audet, "Le Barreau et la Révolte de 1837," 87, 89–91. DeCelles, "Lettres de 1835 et de 1836." Fabre Surveyer, "Charles-Ovide Perrault (1809–1837)." Perrault died on 24 November 1837.

103 *Gazette*, 25 and 30 November 1837. *Transcript*, 28 and 30 November 1837. Miller, "Charles Dewey Day." Day's father, druggist Ithamar Hubbell Day, had gone into business with Samuel Folger Gelston and Frederick Benjamin Gelston in 1815, operating a drugs and commission business under the name Day & Gelston & Co. and a hardware business called F.B. Gelston & Co. Frederick Gelston died at Montreal on 31 December 1818. Samuel Gelston, after leaving Montreal, remained in touch with Ithamar Day, as witness a power of attorney of February 1825 by which Gelston, then living in Penfield, NY, gave Day authority to sell a tract of land that he owned at St-Armand (BANQ, register of St Gabriel Presbyterian Church, 3 January 1819; notary G.D. Arnoldi, 8 August 1827. *Spectateur canadien*, 31 July 1815).

104 On Arnoldi's political travails, see Janson, "Daniel Arnoldi."
105 *Vindicator*, 15 July 1836.
106 David, *Les Patriotes de 1837–1838*, 177.
107 Lesage, *Le Collège des médecins et chirurgiens de la province de Québec 1847–1947*, 68–72.
108 BANQ, register of Christ Church, 22 August 1838. *L'Ami du peuple*, 22 August 1838. Brief reports of Grant's death also appeared in the *Gazette* and the *Transcript* of 21 August.

CHAPTER TEN

1 BANQ, notary J.G. Beek, no. 1872, 17 September 1805; notary J.M. Cadieux, no. 58, 2 April 1807, and no. 173, 21 December 1807. In his marriage contract of 2 May 1807, Coudrin was called Narcisse Coutrain, the adult son of Marchenois, deceased, and his wife, Félicité Bagnerisse, who was out of the province. At his wedding two days later, he was Narcisse Coudray, son of Marcellin Coudray and Félicité Bagnielis from New Orleans. Before moving to Montreal, he may have lived at Quebec, where we find several references in 1804–06 to a black woman called Phillis Bagnell, a name that appears to be an English version of his mother's. In the spring of 1804, she was identified as the wife of Private Sampson Bagnell of the 41st Regiment of Foot, and mother of a young girl, Jane Bagnell, who lived only one week. In October 1805, she was a sponsor at the baptism of Anne Brooks, the daughter of blacks Thomas Brooks and Hannah Perkins. In July 1806, Phillis Bagnell was accused of compound larceny for stealing £25 10s from a dwelling. The indictment identified her as the wife of Sampson Bagnell, "late of the same parish of Quebec Labourer." Her examination before a Justice of the Peace shows some of the connections between blacks at Quebec:

[O]n Tuesday the eighth Day of July, she came to Quebec to get six Dollars from Betsy Brown but she found her gone up the Country and in Coming up Pallace Street, she met Henry a Servant to Major De Salaberry[,] that she borrowed eight Dollars from the said Henry[.] she went to Mrs Murpheys and bought eight Yards of Cotton at 2.3 per yard[,] a pair of Stockings for five Shillings[,] a Shawl for seven Shillings and six pence[,] and she paid Mrs Murphy one Pound one shilling and nine Pence which she owed her[.] and she got five Dollars from Robt. Ashley. Sally Luke is Witness[.] She was taken sick at Mrs Mathers and her little Girl went home with her[.] she said she had no other money[,] only that which she got from Henry and Robert Ashley[.] after she came home she gave John Taylor a crown to get a Pint of Rum which was drank.

We know no more of the woman called Betsy Brown, who was probably black. De Salaberry's servant, Henry, was the African-born Henry Victor who had arrived at Quebec from the West Indies in the service of Charles de Salaberry, then captain in the 60th Regiment. Robert Ashley was the ship steward who would move to Montreal and work on the *Accommodation* in 1809–10. Sally Luke was Sally Johnson, the widow of Samuel Luke and mother of Samuel Jr (see chapter 4). The Mrs Mathers whose little girl accompanied Phillis Bagnell back to her home may have been a black woman, perhaps related to Joseph Mathurst, "a man of colour" who died at the Quebec Emigrant Hospital in January 1824, or to the Woolsey Mathers who was a witness at the burial of another "man of colour," seaman Joseph McIntyre, that same year. John Taylor had been identified in 1786 as "A black Servt to Mr Jenkins, in ye Country," and at his baptism in April 1791 as John, "an indented Negroe servant to Mr George Jenkins," a butcher. Phillis Bagnell was acquitted of the charge of larceny at the September Term of the Court of King's Bench (BANQ, register of Quebec Anglican Church, 4 November 1786, between 3 and 10 April 1791, 28 May and 4 June 1804, 20 October 1805, 28 January and 19 September 1824; register of Notre-Dame Church, Quebec, 2 April 1806. KB-Q, 1806-560-B16, *R v. Phillis Bagnell*. LAC, RG4 B16, Quebec, Lower Canada and Canada East: [Civil Secretary] records of courts, v. 11, "Criminal Offences Taken from the Records of the Court of Kings Bench for the District of Quebec beginning in the Year 1765 and ending with the Year 1827 with Abstracts," p. 60).

2 BANQ, notary P. Lukin Jr, no. 3059, 31 October 1833; notary E. Guy, no. 1496, 19 July 1837; CWS, register, 23 June 1835, *Alexander Grant v. Alexander McPherson*, 144. CQS, *Alex. Grant v. Alex. McPherson*, Grant affidavit, 25 June 1835; *R v. Alexander Grant et al.*, Whalon affidavit and recognizances of Cecilia Farley and Alexander Grant, all 12 February 1838. *Transcript*, 13 February 1838. Grant hired a James Lawlor in 1836, but the deed of his hiring, dated 22 June 1836, no. 867 in the records of notary J.H. Jobin, is missing.

3 BANQ, notary J.A. Labadie, no. 7332, 4 April 1842; notary E. Guy, no. 4633, 11 August 1842. Smith filed a complaint against his first apprentice, Gosselin, for desertion in January 1844, but a doctor certified that the boy was too sick to work (CQS, Smith affidavit, 11 January 1844, and certificate of Dr Benjamin Berthelet, 18 January 1844). The 1861 census recorded three teenage apprentices in Smith's household: Theodore Cloutier had been indentured to him for five years in 1857, at the age of fourteen; Elizabeth Murphy for four years from June 1859, at age fifteen; and Augustin Daigneau for five years in November 1860, at age fifteen. Daigneau's apprenticeship ended before term, on 31 August 1863 (BANQ, notary J. Belle, no. 16779, 14 November 1857, no. 18661, 12 May 1860, and no. 19024, 26 November 1860. LAC, RG31-C-1, 1861 census, manuscript returns, Canada East, Montreal, Centre Ward, f. 54). Smith hired his last apprentice, Louis Duquette, for five years in May 1873; a few months earlier, he had hired two English-speaking apprentices, brother and sister Edward and Margaret MacKay, both minors, for four years (BANQ, notary B. Durand, no. 623, 24 September 1872, and no. 724, 1 May 1873).

4 For a sample of his scheming, which cost one of John Trim's daughters her inheritance, see Mackey, *Black Then*, 129–34.

5 BANQ, register of Christ Church, 14 December 1835; notary J. Blackwood, no. 650, 19 April 1836, and no. 718, 30 September 1836; notary J.A. Labadie, no. 4911, 17 January 1837. Grantham is believed to have been the unmarried adult male native of the United Kingdom who was recorded in the household of Alexander Grant in the census of 1831 (LAC, RG31-C-1, 1831 census, manuscript returns, Lower Canada, Montreal, St-Paul Street, v. 13, Part 2, f. 80). Grant and Grantham were certainly well acquainted. When Grant accused two men of threatening and assaulting him in his house in 1834, Grantham, identified as a barber, and shoemaker John Patten acted as sureties for the two accused when they had to post bail (CQS, *Alexander Grant v. Hisun Loney and Thornton Taylor*, affidavit and recognizances of 5 June 1834). Grant was a witness at Grantham's wedding in 1835, and Grantham was a defence witness at Grant's trial for riot in September 1836 (see chapter 9 and Appendix IV).

6 BANQ, notary P. Beaudry, no. 483, 20 May 1839. CWS, register, *James Grantham v. Joseph Champagne*, 23 July 1839.

7 BANQ, notary E. Guy, no. 3442, 19 April 1841; notary A. Montreuil, no. 1, 4 May 1841, and no. 3, 15 May 1841; notary G. Busby, no. 99, 1 April 1843; notary J. Blackwood, no. 874, 20 June 1845, no. 898, 19 August 1845, and no. 901, 27 August 1845; register of St Luke's Anglican Church, 19 June 1861. *Pilot*, 18 June 1861.
8 CQS, *James Grantham v. Thomas Panton*, Grantham affidavits, 9 and 16 May 1838.
9 CQS, *R v. Celia Farley*, Farley recognizance, 22 November 1838.
10 CQS, *R v. François Berthiaume*, affidavit of Constable Théophile Foisy, 29 July 1839, Grantham affidavit, 30 July, Berthiaume recognizance, 3 August, and indictment of 3 October 1839.
11 CQS, *R v. Cawthorn*, Grantham and Paquette affidavits and Cawthorn recognizance, all 24 July 1840. Grantham would later lease a flat to Cawthorn in Ste-Marie Ward (BANQ, notary A. D'Amour, no. 1720, 15 April 1856, and no. 2067, 1 April 1857).
12 Julie was said to be fourteen months old at her baptism in January 1838, and Rebecca seventeen months old when she was baptized in June 1840 (BANQ, register of Notre-Dame Church, 10 January 1838; register of the Hôpital-Général chapel, 27 June 1840).
13 BANQ, TP10, S2, SS2, SSS1, Circuit Court, no. 2164, 1843, *James Grantham v. Charles Blake Radenhurst*.
14 CQS, *R v. Prince Philips*, Phillips' statement 10 November 1838, recognizance 20 November; court register, 19 January 1839. RPM, 1835–38, Box 56, no. 968, 10 November 1838.
15 BANQ, notary G. Cauchy, no. 31, 4 July 1840. CQS, *Prince Phillips v. John T. Collins*, Phillips affidavit 20 July 1840.
16 BANQ, notary L.C. Danré de Blanzy, no. 2376, 4 March 1745.
17 BANQ, notary L.C. Danré de Blanzy, no. 3978, 22 April 1749; notary J.B. Decharnay, 23 July 1756; register of the Hôpital-Général chapel, Montreal, 10 May 1773. P.-G. Roy, "La vente des esclaves par actes notariés sous les régimes français et anglais," 119–20. For Delezenne, see Derome, "Ignace-François Delezenne." Delezenne later owned an Indian slave named Marie-Anne (BANQ, notary S. Sanguinet, 15 November 1766).
18 BANQ, notary J.B. Desève, no. 817, 30 March 1793. Becket and Mary Richardson had married in 1783 (BANQ, register of Christ Church, 26 January 1783).
19 BANQ, register of Notre-Dame Church, 8 and 10 March 1794; register of Christ Church, 11 July 1794.
20 McCord Museum, P212, Court of Common Pleas, deposition of Marianne Denoyer, 16 June 1794; bond of Peter Backet, 17 June 1794. Becket had to post a £20 bond to keep the peace and show up in court when required.
21 BANQ, notary P. Lukin Sr, no. 2205, 11 May 1801; notary L. Chaboillez, no. 6809, 8 March 1805.
22 BANQ, register of Notre-Dame Church, 30 June 1804; notary J.A. Gray, Engagements, 24 April 1804, and no. 1646, 10 September 1806; notary P. Lukin Sr, nos 3267 and 3268, 28 May 1804. The only information that has come to light concerning Joseph's birth comes from his death record, when he was said to be two months old; hence, he was born about 29 April 1804.
23 BANQ, notary J.A. Gray, no. 1775, 14 March 1807; notary L. Chaboillez, no. 8725, 2 June 1809. HDM, admission registers, Book H, 9 March 1811.
24 The family name was spelled many different ways in the records of the time. Besides Wily, it appears as Wallé, Waylay, Weelly, Wheyley, Whilie, Whylie, Wiely, Willie, Willy, Wyley, and Wyllie.

25 BANQ, register of Christ Church, 3 March 1805, register of Notre-Dame Church, 30 August 1809; notary J.A. Gray, no. 2437, 3 August 1809; notary H. Griffin, no. 1011, 9 June 1815. HDM, admission registers, Book G, 20 April, 7 June and 25 July 1809. *Spectateur canadien*, 31 July 1815.
26 BANQ, notary P. Lukin Sr, no. 5221, 22 July 1813.
27 BANQ, register of St Gabriel Presbyterian Church, 26 and 29 June 1813.
28 BANQ, notary H. Griffin, no. 1071, 24 July 1815; register of St Gabriel Presbyterian Church, 13 January 1814; register of Hôpital-Général chapel, 13 June 1818. TC, no. 398, 18 July 1815.
29 BANQ, register of Christ Church, 1 August 1819, and 2 August 1834; register of St Gabriel Presbyterian Church, 1 March 1819, 11 January 1820; notary J.A. Labadie, no. 3558, 16 July 1834. TC, no. 513B, 11 July 1834.
30 See Appendix I, n60.
31 BANQ, notary J.G. Beek, no. 492, 2 February 1789; register of Christ Church, 21 September 1789.
32 BANQ, notary J.G. Beek, no. 523, 1 May 1789. Cruikshank and Watt, *The King's Royal Regiment of New York*, 265. Tieple is written in the latter as Teeple and Tipple.
33 BANQ, notary J.G. Beek, no. 555, 21 July 1789.
34 For the text of the notice, see Appendix I/A, notice 80.
35 BANQ, notary P.R. Gagnier, no. 977, 6 July 1793; register of Ste-Rose-de-Lima Church, Île Jésus (Laval), 15 July 1793.
36 See chapter 2, n121.
37 BANQ, notary J.G. Delisle, no. 472, 13 March 1792.
38 BANQ, register of St Andrew's Presbyterian Church, 16 October 1823; notary J. Belle, no. 3166, 11 December 1839. TC, no. 798, 10 December 1839.
39 BANQ, notary J.B. Houlé, no. 913, 23 September 1848, and no. 925, 28 October 1848; notary E. Lafleur, no. 282, 6 April 1853. CD, 1854.
40 The advertisement is found in the unnumbered green pages at the beginning of the Quebec city directory. Wright's address, "St John Street, without," refers to the part of St-Jean Street that stood outside the walls of the Upper Town. Similar, but smaller, advertisements appeared in Quebec directories for 1857–58 and 1858–59, as well as in French-language newspapers in 1856–58. See the *Courrier du Canada*, 2 February 1856, 11 March 1857, and successive issues to 14 May 1858, and the *Journal de Québec*, 28 February 1857.
41 BANQ, register of St Andrew's Presbyterian Church, 16 October 1823. LAC, RG31-C-1, 1861 census, manuscript returns, Canada East, Quebec, St-Jean Ward, f. 5338.
42 BANQ, register of Notre-Dame Church, Quebec, 2 October 1865; register of St-Jean-Baptiste Church, Quebec, 17 November 1862 and 2 April 1866; notary C. Tessier, no. 2232, 2 October 1865. Quebec city directories listed him at 10 Ste-Claire Street in the St Jean Suburb in 1860–61; at the corner of Ste-Claire and Latourelle streets in 1861–62 and 1862–63, and at 29 Latourelle in 1863–64 and 1864–65. There seem to be no later listings for him. His wife had married her first husband, herbalist-grocer Lazare Trudel, in 1860; she was identified on that occasion as Marie Anne Perrin, adult daughter of François Perrin and Louise Mongrain. Trudel died in 1864 (BANQ, register of St-Roch Church, Quebec, 16 April 1860 and 21 June 1864).
43 Ward, *Autobiography*, 150.
44 Ibid., 151.

45 The *Gazette*, 3 August 1841, reprinted a report from the *Cobourg Star* on a vicious attack carried out the previous 13 June in Cobourg, Canada West, on a newly married black grocer and his wife, a white servant.
46 Trudel, *Deux siècles d'esclavage*, 284. Trudel devotes chapter 11 of his book (279–94) to this subject under the title "Les Canadiens ont-ils du sang d'esclaves?" i.e., "Do French Canadians have slave blood?"
47 BANQ, register of Notre-Dame Church, 2 January 1832. CQS, January Term 1794, calendar of prisoners, and October Term 1794, court docket. KB-Q, 1793: 365-B9, *R v. Thomas Grant*.
48 BANQ, register of St Gabriel Presbyterian Church, 7 November 1809.
49 HDM, admission registers, Book E, 6 May 1802.
50 BANQ, register of Notre-Dame Church, 2 May 1870.
51 BANQ, register of St Gabriel Presbyterian Church, 6 October 1821, 5 April 1822.
52 BANQ, register of Christ Church, 6 February 1797.
53 BANQ, notary N.B. Doucet, no. 5080, 9 April 1818; notary P. Lukin Sr, no. 1166, 26 February 1798.
54 BANQ, register of Christ Church, 11 January 1789; register of Notre-Dame Church, 30 August 1795, 16 February 1796, 26 November 1797, and 31 December 1800. There appears to be no birth record for Ruth or Gabriel Johonnot; judging from later references to Gabriel's age, he would have been born in the second half of 1792.
55 BANQ, register of Notre-Dame Church, 24 July and 25 October 1803, 15 January 1804.
56 BANQ, notary J.A. Gray, no. 1775, 14 March 1807; notary L. Chaboillez, no. 8725, 2 June 1809.
57 BANQ, register of Notre-Dame Church, 9 March 1806, 24 January 1807, 7 March 1809, 22 May, 1813. CQS, *Marguerite Loiselle v. François Houle*, complaint of 28 July 1817; *Marguerite Loiselle v. Emmanuel d'Aubreville*, complaint and D'Aubreville's bond to keep the peace, both 19 September 1818; court register, 30 October 1818.
58 HDM, admission registers, Book H, 22 October 1810, 9 March 1811. *Gazette*, 5 November 1810.
59 A Marie Marguerite Campbell Loiselle was married at Quebec on 9 June 1790, but she was the daughter of a Scottish father, John Campbell, and a Canadian mother, Marguerite Campbell Loiselle. This is the only instance of the names Campbell and Loiselle being so closely linked. Perhaps Johonnot's wife, Margaret, had some connection to these Campbell Loiselles.
60 CQS, *François Houle v. Gabriel Johonnot*, Houle deposition 26 September 1815, Johonnot bond, 27 September 1815; *Catherine Janot v. François Houle*, complaint of 12 November 1818.
61 KB, Administrative Documents, Calendars of the Montreal jail, October 1823–April 1827, pp 7, 12, 16, 18, 101, 103, 108, 111, 118, 133, 136, 165. CQS, *Paul Jos. Lacroix v. François Houle*, 2 August 1817, and *Henry Forrest v. François Houle*, 24 May 1819, both filed with documents of July 1821; arrest warrant for François Houle on the accusation of Benjamin Schiller, 23 October 1825. RPM, Box 50, August 1826–July 1834, no. 473, 12 June 1826, no. 759, 31 March 1827. LAC, MG24, B173, James Reid Papers, Criminal Cases, 4, 9 September 1825, *R v. Jean-Baptiste Verdon, Benjamin Augé and Jean-Baptiste Delinelle*.
62 CQS, *R v. Alexis Jonneau*, recognizance, 23 September 1817; *R v. Alexander Janneau alias Alexander Hoole*, deposition of John Roy, 26 December 1817, and indictment of 20 January

1818; *R v. Alexander Johannet*, indictment, 21 April 1821; court register, 12, 13, 14, and 19 January 1818; 11, 13, and 19 January; and 26, 27, and 30 April 1821. KB, May 1819, *R v. Alexandre Johonnot*, deposition of Richard Thompson, 22 May 1819; court register (Oyer & Terminer), *R v. Alexandre Johonnot*, 3, 4, and 11 November 1819, and *R v. Alexander Jeannot*, 9, 11 and 20 May 1822; KB, Administrative Documents, calendars of the Montreal jail, October 1823–April 1827, p 68. LAC, MG24, B173, James Reid Papers, Criminal Cases, 3, *R v. Alexander Johonnot*, 4 November 1819, and *R v. Alexander Jeannot*, 11 May 1822. *Spectateur canadien*, 13 November 1819, 25 May 1822.

63 KB, February–March 1824, *R v. Robert Ellis*, depositions of Martin Cheney, William Murphy and Sophia Houle, 13 March 1823; court register, 8 and 9 March 1824.

64 KB, Administrative Documents, calendars of the Montreal jail, October 1823–April 1827; court register, 9 September 1826. RPM, Box 50, August 1826–July 1834, no. 381, 1 March 1826. *Canadian Courant*, 7 August 1824. *Gazette*, 25 September and 2 October 1824.

65 The details of this case are drawn from Anonymous, *The Trial, Defence, &c. of William Ross*, and from: BANQ, register of Quebec Anglican Church, 21 April 1827. *Minerve*, 13 November 1826. *Quebec Mercury*, 30 September; 3, 17, and 24 October; 14 November 1826, 31 March, 3, 7, 21; and 24 April 1827. J.-Edmond Roy, *Histoire de la seigneurie de Lauzon*, 5:221–39. Pierre-George Roy, *Toutes petites choses du régime anglais*, 226–9.

66 *Quebec Mercury*, 17 October 1826.

67 *Quebec Mercury*, 21 April 1827.

68 KB, register, February Term 1827, *R v. Alexandre Johanet*, 24 and 26 February and 10 March. RPM, Box 50, no. 644, 7 October 1826. LAC, MG24, B173, James Reid Papers, Criminal Cases, 5, *R v. Alexander Johannet*, 26 February 1827.

69 BANQ, notary P. Ritchot, no. 2025, 12 February 1828; register of Christ Church, 22 July 1832. CQS, *R v. Guillaume Laverdure et al.*, joint deposition of Bénoni Leclaire and Joseph Donegani, 2 May 1831, recognizances 4 May 1831. RPM, Box 50, no. 488, 2 March 1829. LAC, RG31-C-1, 1831 census, manuscript returns, Lower Canada, Montreal, College Street, v. 13, Part 2, f. 70. *Gazette*, 25 July 1833. For the text of the resolutions and the names of the signatories, see page 37.

70 *Transcript*, 18 February 1864. Anonymous, *Miscegenation*, 29–32. S. Kaplan, "The Miscegenation Issue in the Election of 1864." See also articles on miscegenation, reprinted from British publications and from the New York *World*, in the *Gazette*, 9 and 30 March and 18 April 1864. The anonymous *Miscegenation* pamphlet of 1864 was later attributed to the journalists David G. Croly and George Wakeman.

71 Dickinson, *A Sermon, Delivered in the Second Congregational Church, Norwich, On the fourth of July, 1834*, 30.

72 *Herald*, 21 July 1821.

73 *Gazette*, 25 July 1821.

74 *Spectateur canadien*, 4 August 1821.

75 BANQ, register of Notre-Dame Church, LaPrairie, 9 and 10 July 1821.

76 See, for instance, the writings of Dr Josiah Clark Nott, in particular, Part I of J.C. Nott and G.R. Gliddon, *Types of Mankind: or, Ethnological Researches, Based upon the Ancient Monuments, Paintings, Sculptures and Crania of Races, and upon their Natural, Geographical, Philologi-*

cal and Biblical History, 7th edition, Philadelphia and London, Lippincott, Grambo & Co., and Trübner & Co., 1855, and the article "Negro – Nature and destiny of," in J.D.B. DeBow, *The Industrial Resources, etc., of the Southern and Western States*, New Orleans, The office of DeBow's Review, 1852, 2:308–310 (both accessed online, 2007, at http://quod.lib.umich.edu:8o/m/moa/. See also "Discovery of a tribe of Men with Tails," *British American Journal of Medical & Physical Science*, 5, no. 6 (October 1849): 163–4. For modern views of these matters, see Jean-Dominique Penel, *Homo caudatus – Les hommes à queue d'Afrique Centrale: un avatar de l'imaginaire occidental*, Louvain, Belgium, Peeters Publishers, 1982; and Peter Rigby, *African Images: Racism and the End of Anthropology*, Oxford, England, Berg Publishers, 1996.

CHAPTER ELEVEN

1 *Transcript*, 5 August 1863 and 5 July 1864. *Witness*, 5 August 1863.
2 BANQ, notary L.C. Danré de Blanzy, 22 April 1749.
3 BANQ, register of Saints-Anges Church, Lachine, 15 May 1767.
4 BANQ, register of Notre-Dame Church, 11 July 1767. He was said to be the slave of a man named De Berge.
5 BANQ, register of Notre-Dame Church, 24 May and 29 October 1769.
6 BANQ, register of Notre-Dame Church, 19 September 1770.
7 BANQ, register of the Hôpital-Général chapel, Quebec, 3 January 1778.
8 BANQ, register of St-Michel Church, Vaudreuil, 24 July 1779.
9 BANQ, notary A. Foucher, no. 5466, 20 April 1784.
10 BANQ, register of St-Antoine-de-Padoue Church, St-Antoine-sur-Richelieu, 13 September 1789.
11 BANQ, register of Ste-Geneviève Church, Berthier, 20 February 1793. One witness at her baptism was a woman identified as Marie-Joseph Pouget-Mailloux, which suggests that Marie Joseph Elizabeth was the fifteen-year-old slave who had been sold to the Misses Joseph and Amable Pouget in 1787 under the name Bellai (BANQ, notary B. Faribault, 18 April 1787).
12 BANQ, notary A. Foucher, no. 7262, 14 April 1794.
13 BANQ, register of Ste-Élisabeth Church, seigneury of d'Ailleboust, 24 February 1815.
14 BANQ, register of St-Antoine-de-Padoue Church, St-Antoine-sur-Richelieu, 30 September 1823. As a young girl, this woman may have been the slave of François Corbin, major of the militia and captain of batteaux at Sorel. A black slave of Corbin was identified as Angélique Anne, fourteen years old, at her baptism there in 1789. Corbin died in 1798 (BANQ, register of St-Pierre Church, Sorel, 28 March 1789, 27 September 1798).
15 See Melish, *Disowning Slavery*, 3–4: " 'Race', as an embodied category of difference and a constructed aspect of identity, is not imposed by one group upon another, nor is it a construction by one group of its own identity in opposition to the 'other'; rather it is a product of an ongoing dialogue between dominated [dominating?] and subordinated peoples. 'Racial' identifications therefore function as tools of both domination and resistance." Genovese's *Roll, Jordan, Roll* opens with the observation: "The question of nationality – of 'identity' – has stalked Afro-American history from its colonial beginnings, when the expression 'a nation within a nation' was already being heard."

16 Debate over the desirability of separate institutions has been a constant of black life in Canada. Of blacks in Upper Canada, a commentator observed in 1841 "that separate schools, and separate churches should be established among them, is bad policy, and in a short or a long run will be of ruinous tendency to all concerned. Whenever we [US blacks] have adopted a principle, or sanctioned a measure, which, either directly or indirectly, went to the support, or in the defence of any separate organization among us, it has always been in view of the deepest necessity; when law, common consent and usage, all combined, as in our country, to deprive us of some absolutely needful privilege, or to prevent our moral and religious improvement. But such is not the case in Canada." An interesting instance of black resistance to the establishment of a black church occurred in British Columbia in 1893. When the African Methodist Episcopal Church of the United States dispatched a clergyman to erect churches there, he reported: "Victoria is our most difficult point, the colored people don't believe in having a colored church." In Vancouver, a black resident warned him: "We belong to the white churches and a black church will not do any good and the man who attempts to organize a colored church here will suffer, for we will starve him out, so my friend you will do well to leave because we want no black church nor color line here" (*Christian Recorder*, Philadelphia, 18 May, 13 July 1893. *Colored American*, New York, 6 February, 13 March 1841).

17 Drew, *The Refugee: or the Narratives of Fugitive Slaves in Canada*, 38, narrative of Reverend Alexander Hemsley.

18 *Pilot*, 15 January 1859. This item, published under the heading "Negro Wit," was undoubtedly taken from an American publication, but in choosing to publish it with no comment the editors of the Montreal newspaper no doubt believed that it would touch a funny bone – and a nerve – among readers.

19 HP, MS21843:7, "Prisoners taken at Cherry Valley & sent back the 18th Novr. 1778, for whom an Equal Number is to be Returned."

20 John Durang, *The Memoir of John Durang*, 83.

21 *Quebec Gazette*, 24 January 1777 and 14 July 1803.

22 QB, September 1844, *R v. Jane Broom*.

23 According to his gravestone in Quebec's Mount Hermon Cemetery (Lot 0-218), and the cemetery's own records, Dunscomb was born 24 December 1808 and died 16 December 1891. His father, John Dunscomb, a Bermuda merchant trading to Newfoundland, moved to Newfoundland, where he was appointed an aide-de-camp to Governor Sir Thomas Cochrane in 1825. It is not known when John William Dunscomb settled in Montreal. He played an active role in the business life of Montreal from his twenties. Newspapers of the day contain several references to him as a director of the City Bank from 1835, as a member of the board of the Montreal Cab Co. in 1842, as deputy master of Trinity House from February 1843 and treasurer of the Montreal Board of Trade that year, as well as manager and director of the Canadian branch of the National Loan Fund Life Assurance and Deferred Annuity Society of London. His principal interest was his wholesale grocery business, which he operated with partners Joseph William Leaycraft and Jeremiah Leaycraft, under the name J.W. Dunscomb & Co. at Montreal, and J.W. Leaycraft, Dunscomb & Co. at Quebec. Jeremiah Leaycraft withdrew from the firm on 1 January 1841, to be replaced by Donald Lord McDougall. The company went bankrupt in the spring of 1843. Dunscomb continued in business for some time afterward and then entered government service, becoming commissioner of customs at Montreal and later col-

lector of customs at Quebec. He was appointed to the Montreal city council in 1840, a position he resigned on 1 July 1841. In the first general election after the union of Lower and Upper Canada in February 1841, he ran as a Tory at Beauharnois in February–March, defeating reformer Jacob DeWitt by a vote of 245 to 79. A propos of his connections with the West Indies, in 1838 he and his company acted as agents for a James Kavanagh of Port of Spain, Trinidad, and in 1843 he held a power of attorney from Sir William Crisp Hood Burnaby of Bermuda. On 26 April 1840, at St George's, Hanover Square, London, he married Caroline Birch Durnford, daughter of Major General Elias Walker Durnford, who had been commander of the Royal Engineers in Canada, stationed at Quebec, from 1816 to 1831, and previously commander of that corps in Newfoundland. They had a daughter, Caroline Durnford Dunscomb, born on 12 February 1841 (BANQ, notary I.J. Gibb, no. 1618, 6 October 1837, no. 2243, 20 June 1838; notary H. Griffin, no. 19905, 18 July 1843; register of Trinity Anglican church, 20 March 1841; Registre d'inhumation du Mount Hermon Cemetery, 1848–1904, consulted online at www.banq.qc.ca. *Montreal Gazette*, 1 November 1836; 27 February, 2, 10, and 18 March, 13 May and 8 June 1841; 7 April, 3 May, and 8 June 1842; 14 and 21 February, 15 May, and 13 June 1843. *Newfoundlander*, St John's, 25 June 1840. *Quebec Mercury*, 28 May 1840. *Montreal Transcript*, 25 April 1839. Bertrand, *Histoire de Montréal*, 2:141).

24 BANQ, notary H. Griffin, no. 17645, 4 March 1841. *Gazette*, 13 May 1841. Leaycraft returned to Montreal in June 1843 to marry Agnes Jane Griffin, daughter of notary Henry Griffin (BANQ, register of Christ Church, 15 June 1843. *Gazette*, 17 June 1843).

25 *Gazette*, 10 June 1841. Jamaica Archives, *Laws of Jamaica 1837–42*, 3 Victoria, c. 63, "An act to encourage immigration." See also the open letter by Edmund A. Grattan, British vice-consul at Boston and immigration agent for Jamaica at that port, published in the *Liberator*, Boston, 20 August 1841.

26 CO 137/324, no. 101, report of David Ewart to Hugh W. Austin, secretary of Sir Henry Barkly, governor of Jamaica, 31 July 1854, enclosed in Barkly to Sir George Grey, 22 September 1854 (hereafter David Ewart's Report). David Ewart became Jamaica's agent-general of immigration in 1848. A John Beattie was in St Catharines, Canada West, in October 1841 seeking emigrants for Dunscomb (D.G. Simpson, *Under the North Star*, 197).

27 Jamaica Archives, *Votes of the Assembly 1841–42*, Appendix 4, "Report on Immigration," by John Ewart, agent-general of immigrants, 30 September 1841.

28 *Canadien* (Quebec), 12 October 1842. *Gazette*, 12 and 13 October 1842.

29 *Gazette*, 14 October 1842.

30 David Ewart's Report.

31 David Ewart's Report. Farrell, "Schemes for the Transplanting of Refugee American Negroes from Upper Canada in the 1840s." Ripley, *The Black Abolitionist Papers*, 2:93, n14. Turner, "Thomas Rolph." The immigration figures for 1841–44 are taken from David Ewart's Report.

32 Cited in David Ewart's Report. Dunscomb had advertised his services as immigration agent for Jamaica in the Montreal city directory for 1844–45. The advertisement appeared one last time on the last page of the directory for 1845–46. In subsequent years, efforts were made to institute other programs of assisted immigration to Jamaica (see *Pilot*, 1 March 1851, 5 September 1859; *Provincial Freeman*, Toronto, 1 July 1854; Sires, "Sir Henry Barkly and the Labor Problem in Jamaica, 1853–1856").

33 *Gazette*, 15 October 1840. *Liberator*, Boston, 9 October 1840. On a similar scheme promot-

ing the immigration of African-Americans to British Guiana, see *Liberator*, 31 January, 7, 14, and 21 February, 10 and 17 April, 1 May, 2 and 16 October 1840, 30 July 1841. The *National Era*, Washington, of 5 August 1858 contains interesting views on labour in the West Indies and ways of attracting immigrant workers, in a letter from Francis Hincks, governor of Barbados, formerly co-premier of the Canadas and founder of the Montreal newspaper *The Pilot*. See also D.G. Simpson, *Under the North Star*, 142–4, 207.

34 On Rolf's efforts, see Stouffer, *The Light of Nature and the Law of God*, 58–66.
35 Sanderson, ed., *The Arthur Papers*, 3:232, Arthur to Sydenham, 4 January 1841.
36 Ibid., 3:248, Sydenham to Arthur, 16 January 1841.
37 Martin, "British Officials and Their Attitudes to the Negro Community in Canada, 1833–1861," 84.
38 BANQ, register of Christ Church, 19 May 1840; register of Notre-Dame Church, 23 April 1840. POBR 3:144 and 150. Broome, who died at the Montreal General Hospital, was buried under the name John Brown.
39 BANQ, TL32, S26, coroner's inquests, no. 328, Adam Cockburn, 14 February 1841, and no. 421, Martha Hyers, 25 November 1841; register of Christ Church, 6 April 1841; register of Notre-Dame Church, 26 November 1841. POBR 3:181.
40 BANQ, register of Christ Church, 13 July, 12 and 24 October 1842; register of Notre-Dame Church, 25 November 1842. HDM, admission registers, Book S, 22 April 1842. Brigitte Lafortune had been a patient at the Hôtel-Dieu as early as 1810, and was identified at that time as the twenty-three-year-old daughter of François Lafortune and Madeleine Constantin (HDM, admission registers, Book H, 19 June 1810, 16 November 1811).
41 BANQ, register of Christ Church, 6 December 1841; register of Notre-Dame Church, 30 January and 6 April 1843.
42 BANQ, register of Christ Church, 21 December (read November) 1846; notary J. Dubreuil, no. 549, 24 March 1845. POBR 3:304 and 4:67. The cemetery record of his burial identified Abraham Low as A. Lance, "Colrd man." The church record misdated his death and burial by a month, making it December when it was in fact November.
43 BANQ, register of Notre-Dame Church, 4 October 1845; register of Trinity Anglican Church, 26 August 1845. CQS, October Term 1845, *R v. William Murphy*, 18 August. HDM, admission registers, Book T, "Registre des Étrangers 1843–49," 22 April 1844, 20 May and 5 August 1845. RPM, Box 53, no. 749, 18 August 1845. In October 1839, accused of stealing a coat from an officer of the 71st Regiment, Murphy claimed in his defence that he had been so drunk that he had no idea what he had done (CQS, *R v. William Murphy*, indictment and related affidavits, 3 October 1839).
44 QB, August Term 1845, coroner's inquest reports, no. 973, William Murphy.
45 The armed Rebellions of 1837–38 slowed the flow of immigrants generally, including runaway American slaves. James Curry, a slave from North Carolina who had paused in his flight with Quakers in Philadelphia, had resolved to leave for Canada shortly after Christmas 1837. "But the situation of that country at that time was such, that my friends thought it not best for me to go immediately, and advised me to come into the State of Massachusetts, as the safest place for me until the difficulties in Canada were passed away" (*Liberator*, Boston, 10 January 1840).
46 BANQ, register of American Presbyterian Church, 24 May 1863; register of Christ Church, 14

September 1840; register of St Paul's Presbyterian Church, 10 April 1841, 2 July 1842; register of Wesleyan Methodist Church, Quebec, 20 November 1843; register of Zion Congregational Church, 5 June 1846 and 25 September 1848; register of Notre-Dame Church, 17 February 1863; notary J.B. Houlé, no. 2366, 26 July 1853, and no. 4048, 2 October 1855; notary E. McIntosh, nos 797, 805, 814, and 862, 13, 16, and 18 March and 12 April 1858, nos 4582 and 4653, 11 and 23 April 1863; notary T.B. Doucet, nos 19248 and 19763, 24 January and 6 May 1863; TL32, S26, SSI, Coroner's inquests, Inquest on the body of Nancy Feron Meads, 16 February 1863. HDM, admission registers, Book R, 6 September and 9 October 1837. LAC, RG4 B28, Lower Canada Marriage Bonds 1779–1858, v. 41-A, no. 68, 20 November 1843. RPQ, 1838–43, 3:120. TC, nos 99, 140, and 167, 28 March, 27 April, and 28 May 1863. *Transcript*, 18 February 1863.

47 *Liberator*, Boston, 28 May 1841. Hileman, "Dwight Janes, Conscience of the Amistad," and "The Amistad's Unsung Hero," *The Day*, New London, Conn., 5 October 1997; "A City Divided" and "A Church Divided," *The Day*, 6 October 1997. Jones, *Mutiny on the Amistad*, 200. Osagie, *The Amistad Revolt*, 13. S.M. Stanley, "The Montrealer who helped free the Amistad slaves," *Gazette*, 4 January 1998, C3. In a letter to the editor of the New York newspaper the *Emancipator*, John Dougall, publisher of the Montreal *Witness* and a commission merchant, wrote: "I am happy to inform you that the boy Antonio, of Amistad celebrity, came in here safely, two or three days ago, and is consequently beyond the reach of all the slaveholders in the world. He is for the present in my employment, and I will endeavor to give him some education" (*Emancipator*, New York, 6 May 1841). Dougall's friend, Dwight Janes, and his wife, Jane Winthrop Allyn, who were married at Montreal in 1828, moved to the whaling port of New London, Conn., her native town, in the mid-1830s. New London was where the American authorities took the *Amistad* after seizing her off Long Island, NY, on 27 August 1839. Janes, then a member of the American Anti-slavery Society, went on board on 30 August and discovered the illegal nature of the cargo. In 1840, he returned to Montreal, where he operated as a grocery and flour merchant and, in the 1870s, as the agent of the Whitehall Transportation Co. He died at Montreal on 26 December 1878 (BANQ, register of St Gabriel Presbyterian Church, 6 March 1828; register of American Presbyterian Church, 28 December 1878. CD 1842–43 to 1879–80. *Liberator*, Boston, 24 May 1839, 17 January 1840. *Witness*, 28 December 1878).

48 Perkins spent thirteen years in Meriden, "courting great unpopularity by earnest work as an Abolitionist" (Lighthall, *A Short History of the American Presbyterian Church of Montreal*, 11). See also chapter 6 n42.

49 LAC, RG31-C-1, 1842 census, manuscript returns, Canada East, Montreal, West Ward, Pointe à Callière, f. 1305, no. 2; East Ward, St-Vincent Street, f. 1336, no. 7.

50 LAC, RG31-C-1, 1842 census, manuscript returns, Canada East, Montreal, St-Laurent Ward, Vitré Street, f. 1380, no. 6. BANQ, register of Notre-Dame Church, 16 August 1843, 17 June 1850, 18 September 1851. This may have been the house in Sentenne's Court, off Vitré Street, for which Dago failed to pay his assessment of 1s 3d for the year 1844 and was taken to court by the city; in the same case he was charged for failing to pay 15s in tax for two dogs and 5s for statute labour (BANQ, TL36 S1 SSI 1, Court of Weekly Sessions, Box 276, p. 85, *The Mayor, Aldermen and Citizens of the City of Montreal v. Peter Dago*, 2 April 1845).

51 BANQ, register of Crescent Street Presbyterian Church, 6 October 1871. CQS, November 1827,

Catharine Guyette v. Sally York, Guillet's complaint, 30 October, York's recognizance, 14 November. LAC, RG31-C-1, 1842 Census, manuscript returns, Canada East, Montreal, St-Laurent Ward, St-Charles-Borromée Street, f. 1365, no. 13.

52 A good example is the American-born resident of St-Antoine Ward enumerated in the census of January 1861 as H. Pleasant, and named variously in the course of his life at Montreal as Benjamin Herbert, Benjamin Hobart, Benjamin Hobert, Benjamin Hubbert, Benjamin Robert, Pleasant Hibbard, Pleasant Hubbard, and Pleasant Hubbert. A native of St Louis, Mo., he married Mary Sewell, a white Irishwoman, in 1862, fathered three sons, and died in the Protestant House of Industry and Refuge on 25 September 1900, supposedly at age 72. He was buried in the House of Industry's plot in Mount Royal Cemetery. In the census of April–May 1881, he and his family were enumerated twice in St-Laurent Ward. As Benjamin Hibbard, forty-five years old, he was an American-born labourer of "African" origin (i.e., black); as Benjamin Hubbard, fifty, he was an American-born labourer of "English" origin (i.e., white). The Hibbard children were said to be all Quebec-born, of African origin and Wesleyan Methodists: Frederick, eighteen, a turner; Henry, fourteen, a printer; and John, eleven, an apprentice. As Hubbards, the boys were all of English origin and Anglican: Frederick was a nineteen-year-old American-born labourer, Henry a fifteen-year-old Quebec-born painter, and Quebec-born John, twelve, was in school. The one member of the family whose identification did not shift from one enumeration to the other was their mother – Mary, forty, Irish-born and of "Irish" origin, a Roman Catholic (BANQ, register of Erskine Presbyterian Church, 7 October 1862. LAC, RG31-C-1, 1861 census, manuscript returns, Canada East, Montreal, St-Antoine Ward, f. 4788; 1881 census, manuscript returns, Quebec, Montreal, St-Laurent Ward, 90/i4:83 and 109. Mount Royal Cemetery records, Grave G-400. *Gazette*, 24 January 1861. *Pilot*, 24 January 1861).

53 If American slave-owners told scare stories about Canada to keep their slaves from running there, American blacks who settled in Ontario could be quite negative about Quebec, a land of long "cheerless winters," in the view of freeborn Delaware native Mary Ann Shadd. In urging US blacks to move to Ontario, where she had settled and where she would found and publish the *Provincial Freeman* newspaper from 1853 to 1857, Shadd wrote in a pamphlet: "Canada East ... is not so well-suited to a variety of pursuits as the more western part of the Province. The surface is generally uneven, and in many parts mountainous; its more northern location subjects the inhabitants to extremely cold, cheerless winters, and short but warm summers. The land is of good quality, and vegetation is of rapid growth, but the general healthiness of the country is inferior to some of the other districts. ... Population (which is principally French) is confined chiefly to the valley of the St Lawrence and the country contiguous." She characterized that French population as having a strong affinity for "Yankees," and being therefore "predisposed ... to deal roughly" with blacks, with this saving grace that "in the main benevolence and a sense of justice are elements in their character" (Shadd, *A Plea for Emigration*, 45–6, 49, 86–7. For slave-owners' scare stories, see Blassingame, *Slave Testimony*, 401, 405–6, 410).

54 American abolitionist Samuel Gridley Howe, sent to Canada West during the Civil War to report on the condition of blacks there, wrote: "If slavery is utterly abolished in the United States, no more colored people will emigrate to Canada; and most of those now there will soon leave

it. There can be no doubt about this. Among hundreds who spoke about it, only one dissented from the strong expression of desire to 'go home.' In their belief, too, they agreed with Rev. Mr Kinnard, one of their clergy, who said to us, 'if freedom is established in the United States, there will be one great black streak, reaching from here to the uttermost parts of the South." Though he spoke of "Canada," Howe's observations were based solely on his soundings in southwestern Ontario (Howe, *The Refugees from Slavery in Canada West*, 28). On this subject of a post-war exodus of Canadian blacks to the United States, see Wayne, "The Black Population of Canada West on the Eve of the American Civil War," 62.

55 Stouffer, *The Light of Nature and the Law of God*, 43–57.

APPENDIX I

1 Not all sales and escapes were the subject of a notice. Although the last advertisement of a slave for sale was published in January 1798, the last actual sale, unadvertised, took place on 14 September 1799. Also, a few issues of these newspapers have not survived, meaning that a few other notices might have been published of which there is no record.
2 UMCB, J2/141, KB, Court Docket, Quebec, May Sessions 1787, 75.
3 Neilson, "Slavery in Old Canada," 41. Winks, *The Blacks in Canada*, 110. The notices with logos were published in the *Quebec Mercury* of 28 January 1820; 4, 15, 22, 25 August and 5 September 1820; 18 and 25 May; and 1 and 5 June 1821.
4 *Gazette*, 24 June 1778. Elgersman, *Unyielding Spirits*, 81. Trudel, *Dictionnaire*, 92. The notice was published, in French only, in Mesplet's weekly *Gazette du commerce et littéraire*. Elgersman appears to have relied on a reference to it in Riddell, *The Slave in Canada*, 277. Riddell did not specify whether the slave was Indian or black. He gave the source as the first issue of the newspaper, published on 3 June 1778, leading readers to suppose that the escape had taken place on 14 May instead of 14 June.
5 *Quebec Gazette*, 20 July 1769. A. Cooper, *The Hanging of Angélique*, 85. Gay, *Les Noirs du Québec*, 109. Neilson, "Slavery in Old Canada," 35. Trudel, *Dictionnaire*, 115. Cooper's version of the notice reads as follows:

Joseph Negrie, a young man of about 22 years of age, of brown complexion, slim made, 5 feet 3 inches high, small legs, speaks French and English tolerably well, ran away in the night between 7th and 8th instant ... The public is desired not to employ the said Negrie, and all captains of vessels who may take him on board are forewarned from carrying him out of the province, as they will be pursued to the utmost rigour of the law. Whoever shall discover said Negrie is desired to inform his master, Peter Du Calvet, esquire of Montréal.

It leaves out at least two key elements. The first dropped passage stated that Negrié spoke French, as well as passable English "though French by Birth," or, as the French-language version of the notice stated, "Français de nation." The second indicated that Negrié had fled from Ducalvet "with whom he was engaged," – in French, *engagé*, i.e., indentured, or hired under contract. Neilson's transcription of the notice omitted the same crucial phrases. The persistent confusion over Negrié probably stems from the combination of his suggestive name and the logo of a running figure that illustrated this notice.

6 *Quebec Gazette*, 27 June 1765. Gay, *Les Noirs du Québec*, 98.
7 *Quebec Gazette*, 25 February 1768. There were also, at least until the end of the 1760s, the "donnés," destitute or improvident whites who gave themselves for life to a master in return for the bare necessities. See chapter 4, n51.
8 *Quebec Gazette*, 24 November 1766.
9 In printer William Brown, Winks (*The Blacks in Canada*, 100) detected a sort of conversion to anti-slavery from the fact that Brown "appears to have held no slaves after 1789" and that his newspaper then began publishing various items that depicted slavery in a negative light. Jason Silverman (*Unwelcome Guests*, 10), citing secondary sources, stated that Brown "had emancipated his slaves" by 1789. Brown did nothing of the kind; he held no slaves after 1789 for the simple reason that he died that year. He left a slave as part of his estate (see n28 below). If there was a conversion at the newspaper, it was owing to his death and the new generation that took over in the persons of his nephews, especially John Neilson, who was only sixteen when, under the guardianship of the Reverend Alexander Spark, a Presbyterian minister who acted as managing editor, he inherited the paper in 1793. But we must beware of seeing in the reproduction of anti-slavery matter from foreign sources a reflection of the convictions of newspaper owners, as Jean-Paul de Lagrave strains to do in his biography of Mesplet (see *Voltaire's Man in America*, 87, 282–5). In September 1789, as Samuel Neilson published long accounts of British debates on the international slave trade and of abolition agitation in France, he also printed a notice of the escape of a slave named Joe, alias Cuff (see notice 70); under his watch, the newspaper published a half-dozen more notices of slave escapes and slave sales. Only two such notices (nos 86 and 87) were published under John Neilson's tenure, the last in May 1794. In the case of Mesplet, his original prospectus in 1778 pledged that his paper would offer, among other advantages, the "conveniency of advertising for lost effects, Slaves deserted from their Masters," etc. Later, while his *Montreal Gazette* also published foreign items with an anti-slavery tone (see the lyrics to "The Negro's Complaint" in the *Gazette* of 11 June 1789; reports on abolition efforts in France in the issues of 20 August and 10 September 1789; the letter on "Negroes" published on 10 December that year; a report from Paris on Haitian claims to a seat in France's National Assembly in the paper of 3 June 1790; and "A Negro Love Elegy" in the paper of 10 January 1793), it continued to advertise slaves for sale throughout Mesplet's tenure.
10 The dates given are for the original publication of a notice, which may have been republished in successive issues of the paper. Thus, the last advertisement of a slave for sale in the *Montreal Gazette*, originally published in the issue of 22 January 1798, was repeated in the next issue, on 29 January.
11 The fact that Drummond spoke little English and no French suggests that he was a recent arrival from overseas. His master, John McCord, immigrated from Ireland to Canada at the time of the Conquest and settled at Quebec. He was the father of Montreal businessman and magistrate Thomas McCord, the leading director of the Montreal Distillery Company. (See chapter 4. See also Fyson and Young, "Origins, Wealth and Work," *The McCord Family*, 26–53).
12 Merchant Isaac Werden, coroner for the Quebec District in the mid-1760s, was living in Dominica by mid-1776, employed as a surveyor by land commissioner William Hewitt (BANQ, notary J.A. Panet, 13 March 1779. *Quebec Gazette*, 19 July 1764, 28 February 1765. BRH, 8:78,

147. See also Anonymous, *Pioneer Life on the Bay of Quinte*, 875–84. The Library of Congress in Washington, DC, holds copies of several of Werden's Dominican survey maps from 1776. Some of his letters and accounts are found in the William Hewitt Papers at the University of London). Mary Wiggans was the woman mentioned in chapter 2 under the name Mary Jacobs, née Martin, the Montreal shopkeeper who went to court to recover the slave Jenny from schoolmaster Finlay Fisher (see BANQ, register of Christ Church, Montreal, 27 July 1767 and 19 November 1788; notary J.A. Gray, no. 397, 11 October 1799). The pistole, one of several types of coin in circulation, was a gold coin worth four Spanish dollars or half a Johannes, often called a "half Jo."

13 It is possible that Brouce, who ran away from John Grant but was owned by Lieutenant-Colonel Gabriel Christie of the 60th (Royal American) Regiment, then deputy quartermaster general, was the same Bruce, alias Brous, mentioned in chapter 8, who was banished from the province in 1773. In the French version of this notice, David Elves is called David Alves, which appears to be the correct spelling.

14 Andrew seems to be the slave mentioned in chapter 1 who, under the name André, petitioned the Militia Tribunal in 1762 to set him free from his then master, merchant Gershon Levy.

15 Joseph Howard was a Montreal fur-trader, and merchant Henry Boone of Quebec had formerly been clerk of the market at Montreal. Crofton, who lived in the market place, had published a similar promise of reward in 1764 for a runaway white servant – "a High-Dutcher, named Catherine Elizabeth Renoe, about 20 Years of Age, sworthy-Complexion, short Stature, inclined to Fat, speaks good English and a little French" (*Quebec Gazette*, 26 July 1764).

16 As mentioned in chapter 1, this notice was brought to the public's attention in 1847 in a letter to the editor of the Quebec *Morning Chronicle* of 14 August 1847. The notice was republished several times after this first appeared in the *Quebec Gazette*.

17 Will might be the man identified at his death at Quebec's Hôpital-Général on 23 December 1768 as Joseph, the roughly fifty-year-old black slave of an English merchant identified (in French) only by his last name, "Levi." Merchant Eleazar Levy lived at Montreal in the early 1760s, then at Quebec from late 1764 or early 1765. He appears to have been the owner of a brig in 1768. He moved to New York in the early 1770s (BANQ, HDQ admission registers, 24 December 1768. Lees, *Journal of J.L., of Quebec, Merchant*, 8. Godfrey and Godfrey, *Search Out the Land*, 97–100, 284).

18 The English version of this notice had Dick escaping from his master, William Grant of St-Roch, a suburb of Quebec, on Thursday, dressed in a blue short coat; the French version said that he had escaped on Sunday in a red coat. Grant, who died in 1805, was a privy councillor and legislative councillor under the Quebec Act of 1774, and was elected three times to the Legislative Assembly of Lower Canada as member for the Upper Town of Quebec. His slave could be the black man named Dick who was in Quebec when the Americans under General Richard Montgomery attacked the town on 31 December 1775. Montgomery was killed in the attack. By one account, after his death, one of his bags was opened before some of his officers and its contents sold or given away, a pair of wool stockings going to Dick. At the end of 1786, "Dick a negro man of Quebec," labourer, was accused of arson and tried in the Court of King's Bench (on this case, see chapter 4, n37). A man identified simply as "Dique, *negre*" entered the Hôtel-Dieu on 30 July 1802; there is no further record of Dique's hospital stay, but a "Charles, *Negre*"

was recorded as having been discharged on 26 August – when there was no record of him being admitted. It is possible that "Dique" and "Charles" were the same man (BANQ, HDQ admission registers, 30 July and 1 August 1802. LAC, RG4 B16, Quebec, Lower Canada and Canada East: [Civil Secretary] records of courts, v. 11, "Criminal Offences Taken from the Records of the Court of Kings Bench for the District of Quebec beginning with the Year 1765 and ending with the Year 1827 with Abstracts," 21. *Quebec Mercury*, 7 October 1805. J.I. Cooper, *James McGill of Montreal*, 16–22. Faucher de Saint-Maurice, *Notes pour servir à l'histoire du Général Richard Montgomery*, 74. Roberts, "William Grant").

19 Tavern-keeper Miles Prentice, formerly provost marshal of the Quebec District, was unsuccessful in selling his three slaves privately. As a result, in June, he put them up for auction (notice 11). "Prenties" is the same man who offered a reward for his runaway slave Jacob in 1778 (notice 25). Prentice died at Quebec in June 1787 at age sixty (BANQ, register of Quebec Anglican Church, 11 June 1787. For Prentice's family and background, see BANQ, notary P.L. Deschenaux, no. 1411, 17 September 1787, and J. Ross Robertson, *Landmarks of Toronto*, 2:742).

20 This John Ferguson was either the man of that name who was assistant commissary at Oswegatchie (Ogdensburg, NY) at his death on 13 February 1778, or more probably the John Ferguson who served as quartermaster of the Royal Rangers during the American War of Independence and who died at Montreal on 26 August 1809, age seventy (BANQ, register of St Gabriel Presbyterian Church, 27 August 1809. *Quebec Gazette*, 30 April 1778).

21 Judging by his age and vaunted cooking skills, this was probably the same adult male slave that Miles Prentice had sought to sell privately in February and then put up for auction in June (notices 9 and 11). He was again up for sale in 1770 (notice 14).

22 Susannah's masters are not clearly identified. On the basis of this notice, Trudel (*Dictionnaire*, 119, 319, 330) makes her the Montreal slave of merchants Richard Dobie and Joseph Frobisher, but it seems more likely that she was the slave of someone at Quebec. Had she been the slave of Dobie and Frobisher, the notice would normally have been dated at Montreal, not Quebec.

23 Jacques Perras was a grain and flour merchant. In the fall of 1783, when two consecutive years of business losses had left him deeply in debt, he assigned his assets, including "My Negro whom I estimate at £40," to his creditors. On 28 June 1784, seeing that the trustees of his estate had not yet disposed of his slave, his furniture, or his sloop, he asked for the return of these "three articles that are absolutely necessary to him." His slave was undoubtedly the black "domestique" listed in an inventory of Perras' estate in 1786 as George, about twenty-two years old (BANQ, notary P.L. Deschenaux, no. 238, 3 November 1783, and no. 391, 28 June 1784; notary A. Dumas, 8 March 1786).

24 Johnston & Purss, active in the West Indies trade, were later the owners of the slave Bett, who is the subject of notices 57 and 58.

25 Irish-born William Gilliland was a New York City merchant who, in 1765, moved to the shores of Lake Champlain, where he founded the settlement of Willsborough (Willsboro), NY. He was associated at the time with John McCord of Quebec (notice 1) in a fisheries venture at Gaspé, and with other businessmen in Quebec, as the trade of Lake Champlain was then carried on mainly with Montreal and Quebec. When the American Revolution broke out, he sided with the Americans (Watson, *Pioneer History of the Champlain Valley*, 95, 125, and 137). Ire-

land is believed to be the Gilliland slave whom Montreal merchant Alexander Henry the Elder seized and sought to sell seven years after this 1771 escape. In a memorial of 5 October 1778 to Governor Haldimand (HP, MS21877:17–8), Henry explained:

Sometime ago, I obtained a Judgment in the Court of Common Pleas, against one Gilliland in the [American] Colonies, who owes me a pretty considerable sum of money. hearing that a Negro of his had deserted from him and was Lurking in this Province, I obtained an Execution upon that Judgment, & got the negro apprehended, who is still in Goal. Genl. Powel, who then commanded here, sent to Mr Gray the Sheriff, desiring him to postpone the Sale of the Negroe untill such time as that your Excey. should be made acquainted with the matter. Mr Gray has since informed me that he mentioned the affair to you when here, who Likewise ordered him to postpone the Sale untill you should have confer'd with the Attorney Genl [James Monk]. The Attorney Genl. has since this, through the Channel of one of my friends at Quebec, informed me that he had spoken to your Excy. and that it was your Excys. intention that the Civil Law should take its course, by which I conceive your Excy. will no longer impede the Sale. but as Mr Gray does not think this a Sufficient authority for him to sell the Negroe, I must beg the favour of your Excy. to signify your intention to him, as there is Some Gentlemen here from the upper Countries, whom, I presume, will give more for him than any Person resident here, and as they are now on their return home is the reason of my present application to your Excy. in order that if it is Your Excys. will & Pleasure that the Negroe Shall be sold, that it may be done before the departure of these Gentlemen.

26 Jean Orillat, a wealthy French-born fur-trade merchant who committed suicide in May 1779, had several black slaves whose names are known. The only one who might fit the description given in this notice is Cesar, the roughly nineteen-year-old black slave whom Orillat had bought on 25 August 1773 from Garret Van Vliet of New York. At the same time, Van Vliet had sold to Orillat a three-year-old boy named Jacques, for a total price of 210 Spanish dollars (BANQ, notary P. Panet de Méru, no. 4086, 25 August 1773). As for other Orillat slaves, in March 1771, for 2,400 schelins, he had bought an entire five-member family from Jacob Thomas of New York State. The family consisted of a man named Thom, the only one of the five who was identified by name, who was said to be 30 to 34 years old. The others were Thom's wife, about thirty; a daughter, about four; and two sons, about age three and one. Thom's wife was probably the invalid woman who died at the Hôpital-Général in Montreal in 1802, identified as Marie Louise Jeanne Thomme, a roughly sixty-year-old black woman born in Guinea, the widow of Thomas Allen (which would mean that Thom was Thomas Allen) and formerly a slave of Orillat. It is likely that she was the woman identified as Marie Joseph, the sixty-year-old "négrèse" of Orillat's widow, Thérèse Amable Viger, when she was admitted to hospital in June 1799. The Orillat slave Marie Anne, who died on 30 December 1775 at the age of about eleven, was probably Thom's daughter. Another Orillat slave, a boy called Dominique who died 4 March 1776 at the reputed age of three, was probably one of Thom's sons. An anonymous male slave of Orillat who died on 26 December 1773 may have been Thom's other son, or Thom himself; no age was given for him. On the same day in March 1771 that he had bought Thom's family, Orillat had given Jacob Thomas 700 schelins, plus a grey mare and its colt, in payment for Jeannette, another black slave, whom he had had in his possession since the pre-

vious September. At his death in 1779, Orillat owned four slaves: Neptune, about sixty; Jeannette, about forty-five; and Fortune and Jacques, two male slaves whose ages were not stated in the inventory of Orillat's estate. If Jacques was the boy of that name whom Orillat had bought in August 1773, then he would have been about nine years old. Neptune and Jeannette were each valued at 400 livres, Fortune at 600, and Jacques at 500. That August, at the auction sale of the estate, Orillat's son-in-law, Alexis Réaume (Rhéaume), bought Neptune for 320 livres and Jeannette for 300. Fortune and Jacques were not part of this sale. Fortune may have been the twenty-five-year-old slave of that name who, the following year, escaped at Carleton Island (notice 34). Jacques probably was the slave of that name who was recorded in 1788 as belonging to Pierre Panet (also called Pierre Méru Panet, Pierre Panet de Méru), the former Montreal notary who had become a judge of the Prerogative Court and of the Court of Common Pleas at Quebec. Panet had been Orillat's notary for twenty years, and his son, Pierre-Louis Panet, the future judge of the Montreal Court of King's Bench, spent the summer of 1783 at the home of Orillat's widow to settle estate matters (BANQ, notary P. Mézière, no. 2416, 19 July 1779, and no. 2421, 9 August 1779; notary P. Panet, no. 3616, 12 March 1771; register of the Hôpital-Général chapel, 2 and 28 October 1801, 6 July 1802; register of Notre-Dame Church, Montreal, 27 December 1773, 31 December 1775, 5 March 1776; register of Notre-Dame Church, Quebec, 16 April 1788. BANQ -Q, TL31, S26, SS1, Coroner's inquests 1765–1818, inquest into the death of Jean Orillat, 30 May 1779. HDM, admission registers, Book F, 16 June 1799. Dumais, "Pierre Panet"; Morel, "Pierre-Louis Panet"; Igartua, "Jean Orillat").

27 Lowcanes' name may hint at his origins. This English name, for a slave who spoke no English but good French, suggests that it might be an English pronunciation of Léogane, from the name of a town in St-Domingue. Lowcanes' English master, William Gill, was a merchant and ship captain who had settled at Quebec before the American War of Independence. He married there in 1771. In his lifetime, Gill had at least one other slave. In December 1788, almost two years after his death in England in February 1787, his widow, Mary Cawley, sold their slave Rebecca, about 25, and her 10-month-old daughter, Peggy, to Elizabeth Wilkinson of Yamachiche, seigneuress of Dumontier, Frédéric, Grand Pré, and Grosbois Ouest. Mother and daughter were still Wilkinson's slaves when the latter died in 1794. In her will, Wilkinson stipulated that her slaves were to go to Adélaïde Conradine Gugy, niece of the late Conrad Gugy, who had been Wilkinson's companion or lover. It was Conrad Gugy, a former military officer and secretary of General Frederick Haldimand when the latter had been governor of Trois-Rivières, who, at his death in 1786, had left Wilkinson a lifetime interest in the four seigneuries named above (BANQ, notary A.I. Badeau, 19 March 1794; notary J.B. Badeau, 17 August 1789; notary P.L. Deschenaux, no. 1334, 30 June 1787; notary C. Stewart, 13 December 1788. Bellemare, *Les bases de l'histoire d'Yamachiche 1703–1903*, 76–100, 284–91, 395–402).

28 Joe, a slave of printer William Brown, for whom he worked as a pressman, made many escape attempts. Five were the subject of notices in the *Quebec Gazette* between 1777 and 1786 (nos 21, 22, 28, 30, 54–55). There were others before this. Both Trudel and the author of the article on Joe in the *DCB* mistook him for the slave named Joe, alias Cuff, who ran away at Quebec in August 1789 (notice 70). Brown's slave is believed to have been the "Negro Man" who was still in Brown's possession at the latter's death in March 1789. In an application to the Court of Prerogatives on 21 April 1789 for permission to liquidate the estate, the trustees stated

that "part of said Estate consists of a Negro Man, Press, Types and Sundry Printing Utensils with various articles of Stationary and Household Furniture." With the court's authorization, the trustees announced that the auction sale of Brown's estate would begin on 24 April and continue until everything was sold. It is believed that merchant Peter Stuart, one of the three trustees of the estate, acquired Brown's slave and that Joe was the "Joseph" who, at his death in January 1790, was identified as Stuart's "Negro man servant" (BANQ, register of St Andrew's Presbyterian Church, Quebec, 15 January 1790. LAC, MG24 BI, Neilson Collection, Brown & Gilmore records, 47, file 3, Letterbook of the William Brown Estate 1789–90, p 6. *Quebec Gazette*, 23 April 1789. Thérèse P. Lemay, "Joe." Trudel, *Dictionnaire*, 171–3).

29 Auctioneer Samuel Morin was probably not the owner of this slave, but an agent acting for the seller.

30 James Finlay Sr and John Gregory were partners in a fur-trading firm based in Montreal. Captain Simeon Covell served in Lieutenant-Colonel John Peters' Queen's Loyal Rangers in the American War of Independence. In the summer of 1781, when a rumour was spread at Quebec that Connecticut-born Peters had enlisted a "Negro," Peters wrote to Governor Haldimand's secretary denying that he had done so: "the Man that did engage the Negro is a Soldier & in the Engineers Employ, Timber Cutter ... It is not Negroes that I would inlist or Except [accept] of" (HP, MS21821:262, Col. John Peters to Robert Mathews, 19 July 1781).

31 For Prentice, see nn19 and 21 above.

32 Butcher George Hipps had bought Bell at auction from a ship captain called Thomas Venture. Note that in this notice of Bell's second escape in less than three months, Hipps offered no reward for her return. Two weeks later, on 14 November 1778, he sold her to Lieutenant-Governor Hector Theophilus Cramahé for £50. She was identified then as a mulatto called Isabella or Bell, about fifteen years old. The following 20 April, Cramahé sold the girl, then about sixteen, to Quebec harbour master Captain Peter Napier for £45. Napier, grandfather of the Upper Canadian politician Sir Allan Napier McNabb, died on 9 February 1782. On 6 February 1783, his widow, Sarah, sold Bell, identified as "a Certain Molatto Woman Known by the name and Appellation of Isabella Grant," to Quebec merchants Francis Daniel and Richard Dalton for £52 10s (BANQ, notary J.A. Panet, 14 November 1778, and 20 April 1779; notary C. Stewart, 6 February 1783; register of Quebec Anglican Church, 13 February 1782. Pierre-George Roy, "La vente des esclaves," 120–1).

33 Ishmaël ran away from merchant John Turner Sr at least three times in ten years, his age always given as thirty-five or thirty-six in the notices of his escapes. Turner owned several other slaves. On 18 February 1785, he paid £32 10s "and one gray Horse" to Elijah Cooper of Williamstown, Mass., for Josiah Cutan (alias Josiah or Joseph, Cotton or Cutten), a roughly twenty-two-year-old slave he resold for £50 on 29 March to Montreal merchant David Rankin. Josiah Cuttan was later owned by various masters at Detroit, the last being merchant John Askin, who bought him on 16 May 1792 when Cutan was in jail accused of burglary. He was tried and convicted at a Court of Oyer & Terminer at Detroit the following 7 September, and sentenced to hang. In November 1796, Turner sold Jacqho, a "Negro Man," about thirty-six, and a "Negro Woman" named Rose, about twenty-five, to tavern-keeper John Brooks, of the Quebec Suburb, for £100 and £50 respectively. In the legal dispute over the status of runaway slave Manuel Allen in 1798 (see chapter 2), Jervis George Turner and his wife stated that they

had acquired Allen from John Turner Sr, Jervis Turner's father (BANQ, notary J.A. Gray, 22 November 1796, and no. 73, 25 August 1797. *JALC*, 19 April 1799. Askin, *The John Askin Papers*, 1: 284–8, 410–11. Hill, *The Freedom-Seekers*, 91–2. Riddell, *Michigan Under British Rule*, 347–55, 456, 457).

34 A detailed inventory of tailor Hugh Ritchie's home in June 1780 ended with these items found in the stable: "a black Stallion, a Cow, Two Calashes mounted, a Cart mounted, a Cart Harness, a Harness for the Calash, a Negro boy about the age of [blank]." The "Negro boy" was probably Nemo (BANQ, notary C. Stewart, 11 June 1780).

35 Fortune may have been the slave of that name formerly owned by Montreal merchant Jean Orillat. See n26, above.

36 For Nero, see Appendix III.

37 The owner of these two women was Ralph Gray, who was also the owner of the slave Nero Bartholomy (see chapters 4 and 7).

38 It seems that Charles fled down river, toward the Gulf of St Lawrence. In a letter of 2 August 1783 to his cousin, Captain John Inglis of HMS *Pandora*, Quebec notary Charles Stewart asked: "May I also entreat you'll be so obliging as to Remember to cause enquiry about that Negroe Boy of Mr Gerouts who has run away. it is imagined He has got amongst the Troops. when you are at Bic will surely hear of him." Guerout was elected to the first parliament of Lower Canada as the member for Richelieu County (HP, MS21735:175. For Guerout, see obituary in *Gazette*, 24 June 1830; Dever, "Pierre Guerout"; E. Fabre-Surveyer, *The First Parliamentary Elections in Lower Canada*, 15).

39 No name, no age, no origin, no description of her abilities – this slave for sale was probably Guadeloupe-born Catherine (alias Catiche, Catherine Martin), mother of Alexis (notice 59). Mother and son had been slaves of the prosperous merchant Jacques Perrault, husband of Louise Charlotte Boucher de Boucherville. Perrault had paid 1,275 livres for Catherine in February 1755. After his death in 1775, his widow bought Catherine and her mulatto son, Alexis, for £66 3s 4d at the auction of her husband's estate. Catherine was then said to be about fifty years old, and Alexis about eighteen. Yet only five years earlier Catherine Martin had been identified as a thirty-year-old "Negraisse de chez M. perrault" when she was admitted to Quebec's Hôtel-Dieu. She was back in the hospital from 1 December 1772 to 4 January 1773, still a slave of Perrault's. She was a "naigresse Libre" when she was again a patient at the Hôtel-Dieu 6–28 January 1799 (Mrs Perrault had died in 1792). She was also said then to be the widow of Alexis Thomas. Her age was given as sixty-five, but when she returned to the hospital in 1800 (23 November–15 December), she was said to be seventy-two. She re-entered the hospital one last time on 20 April 1801, remaining there until her death on 31 March 1802 (BANQ, notary M.A. Berthelot Dartigny, no. 391 bis, 8 September 1777, and no. 392 bis, 15 September 1777; HDQ admission register, 2 March, 1 April 1770; 1 December 1772, 1 January 1773, 23 November and 1 December 1800, 20 April 1801, and every succeeding month until March 1802; HDQ register of interments, 1 April 1802. *BRH*, 8:33–6. Mathieu, "Un négociant de Québec à l'époque de la Conquête: Jacques Perrault l'aîné").

40 Tight and his wife, Ruth, who was to escape in 1789 (notice 69), were both slaves of baker John Saul. They were brought into the country by Loyalist Daniel Jones, who had bought them at Albany, NY, on 14 November 1783. Jones sold them to Saul on 25 May 1784 for a total of

NOTES TO PAGE 327

£88. Tite, as his name was written in the deed of sale, was said to be about twenty-five in 1784, and Ruth about twenty-one (BANQ, notary P.L. Deschenaux, no. 359, 25 May 1784).

41 Snow's master, René Hippolyte Laforce, a ship captain trading to the West Indies who had previously served as a French naval officer on Lake Ontario, then as a commander in the British service there, did not publish a separate notice for his slave.

42 The identity of this slave is unknown. In offering her for sale, Swiss-born merchant Michel Cornud might have been acting as an intermediary, as he did a few years later with another slave. Cornud is known to have owned one male slave, a "Negroe boy" named Jack whom he had bought from James Thompson, master of the ship *Minerva*, in 1782. Jack was then said to be about fourteen. As co-executor with Montreal Sheriff Edward William Gray of the estate of merchant Samuel Jacobs of St-Denis and Quebec, Cornud was involved in transactions regarding the disposal of a female slave, possibly the "Negro Girl" named Jenny whom Samuel Jacobs had bought from Hyam Myers of New York City for £64 New York currency on 9 September 1761. Jacobs, formerly of Nova Scotia, had settled in Quebec shortly after 1760. He died at Quebec on 3 August 1786. Cornud then wrote to Jacobs' companion (they were not formally married), Marie Josette Audet *dit* Lapointe, that he was sending her some of her late husband's effects, "& la Negresse de Madlle. Marianne" (the black female slave of her daughter, Marianne Jacobs). Jacobs' widow married Trois-Rivières surgeon Jean-Baptiste Rieutord. In 1790, Dr and Mrs Rieutord wished to get rid of their slave. Cornud wrote to Rieutord suggesting that he turn her over to one of Jacobs' two married daughters. That September, Joseph Vignau of Boucherville, husband of Jacobs' daughter Marie Geneviève, wrote to Cornud that he was willing to take the "negresse," but that the Rieutords needed Cornud's written consent to transfer her. Cornud readily obliged (BANQ, notary C. Stewart, 15 August 1782; register of Quebec Anglican Church, 5 August 1786. LAC, MG19 A2, Jacobs-Ermatinger Estate fonds, 8:27A and 27B, deed of sale by Hyam Myers to Samuel Jacobs of the negro girl Jenny; 8:27C, Myers to Jacobs, 28 September 1761; 5:4, Michael Cornud to the widow Jacobs, 22 August 1786; 5:61, Cornud to Rieutord, 29 July 1790; 25:61, Joseph Vignau to Cornud, 25 September 1790; 5:62, Cornud to Dr and Mrs Rieutord, 14 October 1790; MG23 GII 3, Edward William Gray Papers, 4, Gray to Rieutord, 9 August 1790).

43 This unnamed black girl might be Lucie, an indentured black servant. On 3 January 1785, a little more than two months after this notice appeared, the unexpired time of Lucie's indenture was sold by Quebec tavern-keeper John Reed to bread-baker Melchior Poncet for £8. But the deed stated that Lucie's indenture was to expire on 26 May 1787, not in seven or eight years, the term stated in the notice. The deed mentions that Lucie's indenture had been transferred to Reed by a William Dempsey, but it gives no date for that transfer, and no details as to when Lucie was first indentured. (The transfer took place before notary David Algeo, whose records have not survived.) Lucie is believed to be the "Naigresse Libre" of that name who was a patient at the Hôtel-Dieu from 10 February 1793 until her death there on 22 May (BANQ, notary P.L. Deschenaux, no. 489, 3 January 1785; HDQ admission registers, 10 February, 1 March, 1 April, 1 May 1793).

44 William Roxburgh served as an intermediary in this transaction. Carpenter Charles Bordwine, formerly of the King's Works in New York City, was the owner of the three slaves mentioned in the notice but left unnamed – Grace; her three-year-old daughter, Maria; and a thirteen-year-

old boy named George. On 25 August 1785, Bordwine sold "Gresse," her daughter, and the boy for a total of £80 to David Lynd, coroner and clerk of the courts in the Quebec District. "Gresse," who was later to go by the name Grace Lynd, and her daughter went for a combined price of £48 10s, and George for 30 guineas. David Lynd died in June 1802. When Grace Lynd was baptized a year later, she was identified as "a negro woman lately Servant to Mrs Lynd [Jane Henry]" (BANQ, notary M.A. Berthelot Dartigny, no. 1727, 25 August 1785; register of St Andrew's Presbyterian Church, Quebec, 1 July 1802, 5 June 1803. For Roxburgh, see BANQ, register of St Andrew's Presbyterian Church, Quebec, 31 May 1818, and Aubert de Gaspé, *Mémoires*, 523–9).

45 Elizabeth McNiell (*sic*), née Savage, was the widow of baker Archibald McNeill, a Loyalist who had fled Boston in 1776. A calendar of prisoners in the Quebec jail in the summer of 1780 listed another McNeill slave, "John a Nagor Man," as having been committed the previous 6 March "for Misbehaving to his Master Mr Archibald McNiel." Archibald McNeill was killed by a Malecite Indian in the summer of 1784 (KB-Q, 1780:196A, calendar of prisoners in Quebec jail, 11 July 1780. Delâge and Gilbert, "La justice coloniale britannique et les Amérindiens au Québec 1760–1820. I – En territoire colonial," 107–8. For the McNeill family, see BANQ, notary C. Stewart, 10 June 1789. Maas, *Divided Hearts: Massachusetts Loyalists 1765–1790*, 104. Stark, *The Loyalists of Massachusetts*, 125, 132, 135, 137).

46 Thomas Brooks, married to a woman called Elizabeth, fled the service of Dr Robert Maghlin Guthrie just two months before the birth of their daughter, Marguerite. He was probably the unnamed slave in Guthrie's possession who had been claimed in 1781 by Private Nicholas Schuyler of Butler's Rangers, the Loyalist corps to which Guthrie was attached during the American War of Independence (see Appendix III). In the late 1780s, the Irish-born Guthrie, who had property and connections at Quebec, lived at L'Assomption, northeast of Montreal. He died there on 18 February 1789. While Tom Brooks seems to have escaped from Guthrie at Quebec, this notice did not appear in the *Quebec Gazette*, the one newspaper then published there, but in the *Montreal Gazette* (BANQ, register of Quebec Anglican Church, 20 November 1785; register of Christ Church, Montreal, 20 February 1789. For Guthrie, see also BANQ, notary P.L. Deschenaux, no. 1920, 2 February 1789; notary J.G. Beek, no. 536, 23 May 1789. *Quebec Gazette*, 25 June 1789. *Montreal Gazette*, 8 October 1789. Pringle, *Lunenburgh*, 365).

47 This same advertisement, with slight modification, was also published in the *Montreal Gazette*, 11 May 1786.

48 As with the black female slave she offered for sale in 1784 (notice 46), Mrs Perrault was chary of description, as though she expected everyone to recognize Alexis without further identification than his name. This "negro" Alexis was the "mulatto" son of Catherine, bought in 1755 by merchant Jacques Perrault and, after Perrault's death, bought by his widow, Louise Charlotte Boucher de Boucherville, at the auction of her husband's estate. Mrs Perrault paid £66 13s 4d for Catherine and Alexis on 22 September 1778. Alexis was then said to be about eighteen (see n39, above).

49 The unnamed slave couple were Jeanne and Salé (John and Sally), slaves of the Reverend Jacques Guichaux, the parish priest of Ste-Famille on Île d'Orléans. For this slave couple and their son, Michel Remy, see chapter 4. Guichaux died 2 May 1790 at the age of about thirty-five (BANQ, register of the Hôpital-Général, Québec, 4 May 1790).

50 Merchant Mathew Macnider, brother and partner of John Macnider, bought Caleb on 26 June 1786 from carpenter William Mackenzie for £35. The deed of sale identified Caleb as a native of Guinea, about thirty years old. Mackenzie himself had bought Caleb from James Davidson, captain of the brig *Ceres* on 13 July 1783. A month after he bought Caleb, Mathew Macnider purchased a slave named Betsy from Quebec merchant Joseph Drapeau for £20. Drapeau had acquired her only four days earlier from Montrealer Joseph Quesnel, a merchant and an early Canadian poet and playwright; Pierre-Louis Panet, then clerk of the Court of Common Pleas at Quebec and later a judge of the Court of King's Bench at Montreal, acted for his friend Quesnel in the transaction. It might be a simple coincidence, but one week after Caleb ran off in April 1788, a slave of a "Mr Macnider" called "Thiquelle" was admitted to the hospital for what turned out to be a stay of almost five months (BANQ, notary P.L. Deschenaux, no. 814, 26 June 1786, and no. 855, 22 July 1786; HDQ admission registers, 20 April, 1 May, 1 June, 1 July, 1 August, 1 September 1788). The Macniders were in-laws of James Johnston of Johnston & Purss (notices 15 and 57).

51 This Ben might be the black male of that name to whom Judge Pierre-Louis Panet would grant a life lease on land in the seigneury of Argenteuil in 1793. See chapter 5, n50.

52 John Sargent, owner of the *Lucy*, was a Loyalist from Salem, Mass. who, after the American War of Independence, settled at Barrington, NS, where he prospered as a merchant and shipowner (Maas, *Divided Hearts: Massachusetts Loyalists 1765–1790*, 132. Marion Robertson, "John Sargent." Stark, *Loyalists of Massachusetts*, 131, 138).

53 "Fee-man" appears to be a misprint for "free-man."

54 Caesar's owner, Jean-Baptiste Bouchette, was a mariner and merchant who rose to command the Provincial Marine on Lake Ontario, thanks to his skills in seamanship and the services he had rendered to Sir Guy Carleton (Lord Dorchester) during the American invasion of Quebec in 1775. It was his daughter, Marie Angélique, who testified in 1846, before the rogatory commission in Montreal in the case pitting the Missouri children of the slave Rose against the heirs of Auguste Chouteau (see chapter 1), that "about the year 1790 I remember that my father sold a slave called Caesar, at public auction, at Quebec."

55 Joseph François Perrault's selling of a slave girl in 1789 does not quite jibe with the view of him presented in an 1882 book on his life. In 1772, he and his mother and siblings had sailed from Quebec to New Orleans to join his father, who was in business there. They were shipwrecked at St-Domingue and later put in to Havana for repairs. "The slave trade in its most repulsive form was carried on here and at San Domingo, and Mr Perrault had frequent opportunities of seeing shiploads of Africans, in every state of mental and physical wretchedness, landed at these islands, for the vile and mercenary objects of selfish planters and heartless men-stealers. These sights in after life formed subjects of frequent thought, which evidenced itself in sympathy with the poor oppressed bondsmen" (Bender, *Old and New Canada, 1753–1844*, 27). In 1789, Perrault, who was later to be dubbed the "father of education for the Canadian people" for his philanthropic efforts to establish non-sectarian schools and vocational training facilities for boys and girls, was a retail merchant in Montreal, where he lived from 1781 to 1795 after working for his father's fur-trade business in St Louis, Mo. In 1790, he began studying law under lawyer Pierre Mézière. In 1795, he was appointed clerk of the peace and prothonotary of the Court of King's Bench at Quebec, where he spent the rest

of his long life (see Joseph-François Perrault, *Biographie de Joseph François Perrault*. P.-B. Casgrain, *La vie de Joseph-François Perrault*, reproduces the autobiography at pp 31–59).

56 For Ruth and her husband, Tight (or Tite), see n40, above. It is odd that Saul waited until December to publish this offer of a reward for his slave who had fled in the spring.

57 This notice appeared only once, in French. Joe, alias Cuff, a slave of militia captain Alexis Rivard *dit* Maisonville of Detroit, has been confused with printer William Brown's slave Joe (see n28, above). Brown was dead by this time. Joe, alias Cuff, was soon recaptured, and sold on 19 September. The French-language deed of sale, identifying him as "Joe ou Cof," stated that Maisonville had acquired him from a merchant at the Niagara Portage named Stedman. Acting as Maisonville's agent for the sale of Joe at Quebec was Detroiter François Deruisseau *dit* Bellecour. Bellecour sold Joe for £20 to Quebec merchant Christopher Kilby Allicocke (BANQ, notary P.L Descheneaux, no. 2135, 19 September 1789).

58 Judah Joseph was a Jewish merchant at Berthier.

59 The slave whom Gray advertised for sale on 2 November as a woman of about twenty-five may have been Rose, a slave elsewhere said to be about nineteen, whom he sold at auction a few days later. As a young nursing woman of fourteen or fifteen, Rose had been sold for £40 in March 1787 by trader Samuel Mix of St-Jean to tanner Louis Gauthier of the St-Laurent Suburb of Montreal. Mix promised to take back the girl and refund Gauthier's money "if the said girl now sold were found to have such a marked fault be it of humour or temperament of which the said purchaser could not correct her within six months." If Rose was a *nourrice* (wet nurse) in March 1787, then she was probably the mother of one-year-old Jean Baptiste, the Gauthier slave who was recorded as dying at the Hôtel-Dieu in April 1788. Gauthier sold Rose to John Lagord who, in turn, sold her to Sorel innkeeper William Mathews, formerly of Montreal. Mathews sold her on 9 November 1791 to Montreal trader Lambert St-Omer for £38 5s, "amount of the adjudication made by Mr Jonathan Abraham Gray, auctioneer of this city." Mathews was eager to be rid of Rose, then said to be about nineteen, because she had stolen from him. This explains the last line in Gray's advertisement: "She will be disposed of on very moderate terms." In October, Mathews had charged that a Sorel woman, Catherine Black, alias Boyle, did "falsely subtilly and unlawfully solicit incite and persuade one Rose, servant of the said William Mathews ... secretly and clandestinely to take and embezil diverse goods and chattles of him the said William Matthews." Mathews died at Montreal on 19 December 1823 at age 80 (BANQ, notary J.B. Desève, no. 671, 9 November 1791; notary J. Papineau, no. 825, 27 March 1787; register of Notre-Dame Church, 31 May 1788; register of St Andrew's Presbyterian Church, 22 December 1823. CCP, February Term 1792, *Catherine Boyle v. William Mathews*).

60 This is the only reference found that identifies Ebert Weldin, or any member of his family, as a mulatto. Born to "yeoman" James Weldin and his wife Anna, supposedly on 13 February 1773, he was apprenticed to shoemaker John Tieple of Sault-au-Récollet on 1 May 1789 and was to serve with Tieple until he turned twenty-one. Despite his flight in 1792, Weldin learned the shoemaker's trade, set up in business and, around 1795, married a woman named Marie Larose (alias Marie Chauret, Marie Saurette *dit* Larose, Rosalie Sorette, Marie Rosalie Soret-Larose). They had five children between 1796 and 1804. Sometime between 1800 and 1802 they may have lived at Quebec, where their daughter Sophie was born in March 1802; she

died at Montreal that September. Some time after the birth of their fifth child, Édouard, in 1804, Weldin's wife died. The widower married Julie Lemoine in 1810. They had at least one child, in 1816. The one time when the records reveal a rather indirect association between Weldin and a black person was in August 1821, when Jacob Simpson (see notice 84, and n63, below), under the name John Simpson, was arrested with two white men – François Sauret *dit* Larose and André Boileau, godfather of Édouard Weldin – for keeping a disorderly house on St-Paul Street. Eber Welding (*sic*) was one of two guarantors of Boileau's bail. Black Montrealers Thomas Cockburn and William Freeland (Feeler) acted as sureties for Simpson. The only other known connection between the Weldin family and black Montrealers concerns Ebert Weldin's sister, Mary. In 1810, her husband, carpenter Paul Descary, sold a property in the Ste-Anne Suburb to Thomas Stockbird, "Nègre demeurant au fief Nazareth" (BANQ, register of Christ Church, 21 September 1789 and 20 April 1800; register of Notre-Dame Church, Montreal, 4 September 1802, 3 February 1804; register of Notre-Dame Church, Quebec, 20 March 1802; register of St Gabriel Presbyterian Church, 17 June 1810; notary J.G. Beek, no. 492, 2 February 1789, and no. 523, 1 May 1789; notary L. Chaboillez, no. 9477, 1 October 1810. CQS, July 1821, *R v André Boileau, John Simpson and François Sauret dit François Larose*. KBCV, *John Trim v. Simon Clark*, 1823, no. 162, deposition of Marie Weldon, 6 May 1830).

61 This notice refers to Jean Louis, the slave sold by starchmaker Jean-Baptiste Routier to Solicitor-General Louis Charles Foucher. See chapter 1.
62 The French version of this notice identified the seller by his full name, Thomas McMurray. He was a Montreal merchant who died on 27 November 1796 at age fifty-six (BANQ, register of Christ Church, 28 November 1796).
63 This notice ran in several successive issues of the weekly newspaper, but Jacob Simpson was mentioned only the first time it was published because he was caught and jailed again on 16 May. He had been jailed the previous 29 January, along with a black woman named Mary Campbell, accused of stealing items from the home and farm of Sir John Johnson at St Mary's Current, where Campbell and Simpson lived. Rather confusingly, the records refer to him as Jacob Simpson and Jacob Smith. The court register consistently referred to him as Smith, but the indictment named him Simpson, as did the jail record; the title page of his statement to police called him Jacob Smith, but in the statement itself he was named Jacob Simpson. He and Campbell were arraigned on 25 April 1793, but the absence of a prosecution witness delayed their trial until July. On 16 July, both were acquitted. In later life, Jacob Simpson was also called Jacques Simpson and John Simpson (CQS, April and July terms 1793, *R v. Jacob Simpson and Mary Campbell;* court register, *R v. Jacob Smith and Mary Campbell*, 24, 25, 27 April and 16 July 1793. KB-Q, 1793:372A, calendar of prisoners in Montreal jail, 1 June 1793. *Montreal Gazette*, 16 May 1793. *Quebec Gazette*, 16 May 1793).
64 Welsh-born Azariah Pritchard was a Connecticut Loyalist who served in the British intelligence service during the American War of Independence, as captain of the King's Rangers. After the war, he and other Loyalists sought to settle on Missisquoi Bay, on Lake Champlain, but he was persuaded instead to lead a group of refugees to the Gaspé (see Victoria Stewart, ed., *The Loyalists of Quebec*, 56, 63, 105. Mimeault, "Azariah Pritchard").
65 The slave advertised by the partnership of tailors Benaiah Gibb and Thomas Prior might be Catherine, a "Négresse appartenant à Monsieur Gible tailleur" (a Negress belonging to Mr

Gibb, tailor), who died in the Hôtel-Dieu on 21 February 1797 at the age of about fifteen (BANQ, register of Notre-Dame Church, 22 February 1797. HDM, admission registers, Book F, 28 January 1797).

66 On this prison break, see LAC, MG23 GII 3, Edward William Gray Papers, v. 6, Gray to Herman Witsius Ryland, 17 November 1796.

67 This was the last published advertisement offering a slave for sale. It is believed to refer to Charlotte, the slave of Jane Cook. See chapters 2 and 3.

68 This was the last published notice about a fugitive slave. See chapter 2.

69 For Eve's engagement by merchant Baruch Berold Levy, see chapter 5. The French version of this notice highlights the $5 reward, gives Eve's height and describes her as "bienfaite" (well made) besides mentioning her smallpox scars; does not identify Polley by his full name, and offers a reward for Eve's return, but promises no indemnification for expenses incurred. The English notice, in its physical description, says only that Eve was black and had smallpox scars; it does give William Polley's full name, promises the reimbursement of any expenses incurred, and warns that anyone who so much as trusts Eve will be prosecuted, while the French notice threatens prosecution for anyone who shelters her.

70 This case is intriguing, not only because the identity of the "negroe Man" and the cause of his death remain unknown, but also because the inquest itself created a stir. The inquest records are not to be found, but as the protest by the members of the grand jury states, the body was found on the shore of Wolfe's Cove (L'Anse-aux-Foulons) on 9 April 1765. The inquest was held before Coroner Williams Conyngham in the house of a Michael Miller at the cove. Lawyer Conyngham, who was clerk of the peace and the first coroner of the Quebec District, was in league with merchants opposed to the government of General James Murray. Historian A.L. Burt referred to Conyngham as a "rascally lawyer ... whose career in Canada was short and far from sweet." Hilda Neatby termed him "an incorrigible mischief-maker." At the time of the inquest, he was particularly obnoxious to the government because his alleged machinations had frustrated attempts to bring to trial that March certain army officers and others accused of assaulting Montreal magistrate Thomas Walker. Something occurred during the inquest that gave the government the pretext that it needed to dismiss Conyngham as coroner and to bar him from ever practising law in the colony's courts. The fact that he summoned Executive Councillor Adam Mabane to appear as a witness at the inquest might have been viewed as a rather insolent gambit. (Attorney-General George Suckling, already upset by the "intrigues" of Conyngham in the Walker case, later complained that Conyngham had launched a "frivolous prosecution against me before the Chief Justice for assaults in chastising My Servant.") Conyngham was dismissed as coroner and, on 22 April, the Executive Council appointed Isaac Werden as his successor. Conyngham petitioned the authorities to be readmitted to the bar, supported by his allies among the merchants, who called on the government to state clearly the cause of his dismissal and to give him a chance to clear his name. On 25 June, however, Provincial Secretary James Goldfrap issued this categorical statement:

WHEREAS it has been industriously propagated, That Mr Williams Conyngham, who at the unanimous Request of His Majesty's Council, has been dismiss'd from acting as an Attorney or Advocate in any of the King's Courts of Judicature within this Province, will again be admitted to practice : It is necessary to inform the Public, and all Persons who may have Business in his Hands, That such Admission can never take Place, and that therefore they may regulate themselves accordingly.

Conyngham left for England that fall, perhaps to plead his case in London. He returned to Quebec the following spring, reaching the waters off Île-aux-Coudres on 23 May. The wind was too strong for a pilot to board and take the ship in to Quebec. Impatient to reach the city, Conyngham and other passengers got into the ship's yawl, with two seamen, intending to row ashore. The boat capsized and everyone on board drowned. Without alluding to the controversy that had swirled around him, the *Quebec Gazette* said:

Mr Conyngham, tho he had resided here but about a Year, had gain'd many Friends, was look'd upon as an able and diligent Man in his Profession, had important Affairs of several principal Persons here in his Hands, who must be great sufferers by his untimely Death, and leaves besides a poor helpless Orphan, of about 8 or 9 Years old, at Hernden School, a boy of promising Expectations, depriv'd now of both his Parents, his Mother having died here about 7 or 8 Months past.

(LAC, RG4 A1, Quebec and Lower Canada: Correspondence received by Civil and Prov. Secretaries; records of the clerk of the Executive Council, 1760–1840, 12:4693; RG1 E1, Quebec, Lower Canada, Upper Canada, and Canada: Executive Council, State Minutes and Submissions, B:45–51. *Quebec Gazette*, 4 October 1764; 3 January, 28 February, 23 May, 27 June, 1 August and 12 September 1765; 29 May 1766. Audet, *Les juges en chef de la province de Québec 1764–1924*, 10. Burt, *The Old Province of Quebec*, 1:100–3, 107. Neatby, *Quebec: The Revolutionary Age, 1760–1791*, 37).

71 This notice concerns Charity (Charety, Charité) a "Neigresse disant Etre de Condition Libre" (a Negress who claims she is free), who was about twenty-six when she bound herself for ten years as a servant to innkeeper John McIntyre and his wife, Sophia Murchison, of Soulanges in July 1798, for five shillings a year plus room and board and clothing. In March 1799, the *Montreal Gazette* reported that, in the Court of King's Bench, "Charité, a Negro woman, was tried for compound larceny, and acquitted for want of evidence." The records of the case no longer exist and we would know no more about it were it not for this notice by Michael Vankoughnet, a former soldier of the KRRNY and head of one of the leading Loyalist families at Cornwall, Upper Canada. The first time the newspaper ran the testimonial, it omitted Vankoughnet's name; the second time, it gave his name as Michael V. Koughner (BANQ, notary J. Gabrion, no. 10, 14 July 1798. *Montreal Gazette*, 18 March, 26 August, and 9 September 1799).

72 For Caesar Johonnot and this property, see chapter 5.

73 Hyacinthe's land in Argenteuil consisted of eighteen acres, part of Lot no. 19 on the east side of the rivière du Nord. He sold it to farmer James Bailey in the fall of 1800 for "eighteen Silver Spanish Milld Dollars." Hyacinthe said he held the land by a deed "which he declares to have obtained from Patrick Murray Esquire Seigneur and proprietor [since May 1793] of the

said Seigneurie of Argenteuil, but which he unfortunately lost by conflagration, a Copy whereof is nevertheless in the possession of the sd. Seigneur" (BANQ, notary P. Lukin Sr, no. 2022, 17 November 1800). Hyacinthe is believed to have gone on to farm in the area of St-Eustache.

74 Alexander Volumten is one of several variants of the name of Alexander Valentine. The seller's name was Étienne Roy, not, as stated in the notice, Étienne Roland. This notice, seeking to establish that a property was clear of mortgages or liens, was typical of those published before the establishment of land registry offices. For this transaction, see chapter 5.

75 This notice omits any mention of a reward for the capture of the deserters. The captain seems only to want his boat back.

76 This advertisement is reproduced for its incidental mention of John Trim. The reference to the adjacent property of the Jesuits is a mistake; the land had belonged to the Récollets order.

77 This is one of two known instances when Hilaire Lamour was called William. See chapter 5.

78 Few women in Canada would have risked a trip across the Atlantic in 1803 except out of necessity. This was no time for the grand tour. Much of Europe had been at war with France since 1793. The Treaty of Amiens in March 1802 provided a year's respite, when British tourism and travelling on the continent resumed. But that ended in May 1803 when Britain declared war on France; Europe became once again a battlefield, until Napoleon's final defeat at Waterloo on 18 June 1815.

79 For William Alexander Brown and the African Theatre, see chapter 7.

80 This is the earliest evidence found of Alexander Grant's presence at Montreal.

APPENDIX II

1 SLCC, *Pierre v. Gabriel Chouteau*, November 1842, no. 125, 68–80. Reid, then about seventy-six years old, was examined at his home. It may be indicative of the state of his mind and his health that he made out his will a week later. He died on 19 January 1848 (BANQ, CT601, S1, Cour supérieure, Testaments olographes, no. 499, will of James Reid, 16 April 1846, probated 1 February 1848).

2 SLCC, *Pierre v. Gabriel Chouteau*, November 1842, no. 125, 80–93. Gale was examined at the Montreal courthouse. On the same day that he testified, Samuel Wentworth Monk, joint prothonotary of the Court of Queen's Bench, filed in evidence copies of court records pertaining to the habeas corpus case of the slave Robin, alias Robert, heard in February 1800 (ibid., 94–104).

3 SLCC, *Mary Charlotte v. Gabriel Chouteau*, November 1843, no. 13, 151–91. Badgley submitted his answers in writing. Succeeding pages (193–372) contain copies of documents he cited in his testimony, including excerpts of Jacques Raudot's intendant's commission of 1 January 1705 and his ordinance of 1709, and sundry court records 1788–1800 corresponding to documents published in Viger and LaFontaine's *De l'esclavage en Canada*. John Joseph Caldwell Abbott, counsel for Chouteau, was Badgley's law partner in the firm of Badgley & Abbott and succeeded him as dean of the McGill Law Faculty in 1855, a post he held until 1880. He became Canada's third prime minister (1891–92).

4 Pownall held the posts of provincial secretary and registrar from 1775 to 1807. In his undated certificate, he observed that "on a general search through the French registers no Confirmation of the foregoing [Raudot's ordinance] is to be found" (SLCC, *Mary Charlotte v. Gabriel Chouteau*, November 1843, no. 13, 194–5).

5 Badgley was obviously unaware of Adam Mabane's abolition bill, debated and defeated in the Legislative Council in 1787, as he was of the last stab at legislation in 1803. See chapter 2.

APPENDIX III

1 Jacob Thomas made several slave-trading trips to Montreal, but other Americans also made the odd foray into Quebec for this purpose. In August 1773, for example, Garret Van Vliet of Kinderhook, NY, travelled to Montreal, where he sold four slaves. On 25 August, he sold Cesar, about nineteen years old, and Jacques, about three, to merchant Jean Orillat for a total of 210 Spanish dollars. Two days later, he sold the "Negroe Wench" Sylvia, age twenty-four, to tailor James Perry for £60 in New York currency. On 2 September, he sold a "Négresse mulâtre" named Suzanne, also twenty-four, to butcher André Roy, who resold her four days later to trader Jean Dumoulin (BANQ, notary P. Panet de Méru, no. 4086, 25 August 1773, and no. 4090, 6 September 1773. Riddell, "Further Notes on Slavery in Canada," 26–7).
2 BANQ, notary P. Panet de Méru, no. 3616, 12 March 1771. For more on this family and on Orillat's other slaves, see Appendix I, n26.
3 LAC, MG23 GIII 5, James Morrison Fonds, 410.
4 CCP, *Thomas Barron v. Jacob Thomas*, filed 21 June 1774.
5 Reference is made to this sale in a deed of 1777 by which Panet sold Marie for £50 to merchant Philippe Loubet *dit* Toulouse. As a patient at the Hôtel-Dieu 1–13 August 1785, Marie was identified as twenty-eight-year-old "marie Lanné négresse apartenant a monsieur loubete." In hospital again 1–12 April 1787, she was not identified by name but simply as "la negresse de monsieur Loubete," age thirty. At the end of that month, her master fled the country to escape his creditors. He later returned, and died at St-Denis on 15 February 1810. Marie's fate is difficult to determine. It is possible that she was the woman identified in 1806 as Mary Louisa Dooly, a forty-four-year-old American-born "negress" who was a patient at the Hôtel-Dieu from 31 May to 15 June. The same woman was there again from 14 to 23 August that year, this time identified as forty-four-year-old American-born Marie Louise Donay, daughter of Donay and Jenny Donay. On 24 November 1807, she re-entered the hospital for six days under the name Marie Louise Dulanay, "negresse," fifty years old, a native of the American colonies. A year later, on 2 November, she was registered as Marie de Launai, about fifty years old, an unmarried "Négrése." Ten years later, the "Negrêse" Marie Delonois, the sixty-year-old American-born daughter of Jane and Tode, was a patient at the Hôtel-Dieu for fifty-one days from 14 July 1818 (BANQ, notary S. Sanguinet, no. 1135, 1 December 1777; register of St Denis Church, St-Denis-sur-Richelieu, 17 February 1810. CCP, *Marie Louise Dalpech* dit *Parizeau v. Philippe Loubet, her husband*, 1787. See also CCP, *James McGill and John Grant v. Philippe Loubet*, 1787. HDM, admission registers, Book E, 1 August 1785 and 1 April 1787; Book G, 31 May and 14 August 1806, 24 November 1807, 2 November 1808; Book i, 14 July 1818).
6 Some slave traffic may have gone on in the Niagara region. Colonel John Clark, born in 1783, who grew up in that area, wrote in 1860 at age 77: "After the Declaration of Independence, drovers used to come in with droves of horses, cattle, sheep and negroes, for the use of the troops, forts, and settlers in Canada, and my father purchased his four negroes" (Clark, "Memoirs of Colonel John Clark, of Port Dalhousie, C.W.," 187. Canniff, *History of the Settlement of Upper Canada*, 575).
7 HP, MS21774:23–4, Claus to Governor Haldimand, 30 December 1779.

8 HP, MS21843:181, "Return of the Persons Names, who Came in from the Colonies in the Month of July 1781," no date; MS21874:248, "Memorial of William Parker," 16 March 1782. The two black men brought in by Parker on 7 July 1781 were recorded on their arrival as Peter Hales and Thomas, both of Schenectady, NY. Thomas was a twenty-one-year-old "Negro belonging to ye Revd. Mr Stewart," i.e., John Stuart, missionary of the Anglican Society for the Propagation of the Gospel in the Mohawk Valley, who was based at Montreal 1781–85, then moved to Kingston. Thomas was probably the slave of whom Stuart, on being authorized to leave Schenectady for Canada in exchange for an American prisoner held by the British, wrote that "my negroes being personal property I take with me, one of which being a young man and capable of bearing arms I have given £100 security, to send back a white prisoner in his stead." Peter Hales was identified as a thirty-year-old slave of "James Ellis, a Rebel at Schenectady," probably a reference to Scottish-born James Ellice, not a rebel but a member of the trading firm Phyn, Ellice & Co., who had stayed behind at Schenectady to mind the company's and his family's considerable interests in trade and lands while his older brothers Alexander and Robert left to set up branches of the firm in London and Montreal respectively. Both of Parker's black refugees were said to have enlisted in Sir John Johnson's corps, but Parker complained at Montreal the following March that, while the sixteen whites whom he had brought from the Mohawk Valley had joined Johnson's regiment, "the Negroes have not, altho' they came ... on that Condition; they are in this Town at present." Cruickshank and Watt, in *The History and Master Roll of the King's Royal Regiment of New York*, list no black man named Thomas (Talman, *Loyalist Narratives from Upper Canada*, 339, letter of Reverend John Stuart to Reverend William White, 17 April 1781).

9 See Egerton, *Death or Liberty*, chapter 3, "The Transformation of Colonel Tye." Quarles, *The Negro in the American Revolution*, chapter 2, "Lord Dunmore's Ethiopian Regiment," and chapter 7, "The British and the Blacks." Ellen Gibson Wilson, *The Loyal Blacks*, 21–9.

10 HP, MS21843:5-6, "Return of the Rebel Prisoners at Quebec the 10th of July 1778."

11 HP, MS21877:19, "Petition of Joseph King a Negro," 17 October 1778.

12 HP, MS21877:2227, "Memorial of Rathass Coffee," 27 October 1778; MS21793:18, General Henry Watson Powell to Haldimand, 9 October 1778.

13 HP, MS21774:88 and 23–4, Haldimand to Claus, 13 December 1779, and Claus to Haldimand, 30 December 1779.

14 HP, MS21843:339, "List of the names of Rebel Prisonners brought at St John's mentioning the time they arrived & in What Corps Enld." Afua Cooper, "Acts of Resistance," 9–13. Cruickshank, "The Administration of Lieut.-Governor Simcoe Viewed in his Official Correspondence," 292. Riddell, *The Life of John Graves Simcoe*, 192–3. Smy, *An Annotated Nominal Roll of Butler's Rangers 1777–1784*, 123. The list of "rebel prisoners" is undated, but all the "prisoners" named in it arrived at St-Jean between 15 and 25 May.

15 HP, MS21818:156–7, Johnson to Haldimand, 3 June 1780. The officers named by Johnson were his brother-in-law Daniel Claus of the Indian Department, and his cousin, Colonel Guy Johnson.

16 HP, MS21819:105, Haldimand to Johnson, 6 June 1780. Lieutenant-Colonel Campbell was John Campbell, superintendent of the Indian Department.

17 HP, MS21818:158, Johnson to Haldimand, 12 June 1780.

18 HP, MS21818:155, Mathews to Campbell, 24 July 1780; MS21819:111, Mathews to Johnson, 24 July 1780.
19 HP, MS21771:225, Campbell to Mathews, 10 August 1780, and MS21818:155, "Return of negroes taken by Sir J. Johnson's party in May 1780."
20 This was probably merchant Pierre Gamelin, and the slave sold to him was probably one called Stevens. In May 1785, while Gamelin was in London on business, his representatives, Jacob Jordan and Dr Henry Loedel, entrusted Stevens to fur trader Augustin Dubuc (or Dubuque), who was off to the Illinois country, with instructions to sell him for the best possible price. This was just days after Adam Mabane had given notice of his intention to bring in a bill to abolish slavery. Dubuc sold Stevens for 900 livres but went bankrupt before Gamelin was paid. Gamelin sought to recover the 900 livres as a preferred creditor when some of Dubuc's furs were seized at Michilimackinac (CCP, *Pierre Gamelin v. Augustin Dubuc*, undated statement of claim by Gamelin).
21 McCord Museum, Montreal, M17609, John Porteous Papers. The unnamed slave here referred to is believed to be Betty, listed as no. 6 in the "Return of Negroes & Negroe Wench's brought into the Province by Parties under the Command and Direction of Lieut. Colo. Sir John Johnson Bart." The man identified by Hewit as captain Tyranes Collins is identified as Francis Collins in a "List of Rebell Prisoners brought to Montreal 31st October 1780" (HP, MS21843:113–114). John Howell, identified by Hewit as belonging to the Indian Department, was also Sergeant-Major of the KRRNY (Canniff, *History of the Settlement of Upper Canada*, 105–6. Cruickshank and Watt, *The History and Master Roll of the King's Royal Regiment of New York*, 237).
22 Conrad Gugy, a seigneur, justice of the peace and former officer in the 60th Regiment, had been secretary to Haldimand in 1763–64 when the latter was military governor of Trois-Rivières. Gugy had later acquired four seigneuries west of Trois-Rivières, among them Grosbois Ouest, on which he established and supervised a Loyalist refugee camp. See Bellemare, *Les bases de l'histoire d'Yamachiche 1703–1903*, 76–100. Douville, "Conrad Gugy."
23 HP, MS21761:115. That Jacob and the Isaac to whom Maclean refers were the same man becomes clear if we compare the details about Isaac in Maclean's letter, the record of Jacob's trial for assaulting Samuel Judah (CQS register, *Samuel Judah v. Jacob*, 10 April 1781), and the information about Jacob in Johnson's "Return of Negroes brought in Canada by Scouts, and Sold at Montreal" (HP, MS21763:368–9). Johnson's report lists no Isaac, but has Jacob and a nameless "Negroe Wench," both captured at the home of Colonel James Gordon in Balls Town (Ballston) in October 1780. Jacob and the "Wench" were sold to Judah for a total of £84, the return says. This was equivalent to 80 guineas, which, Maclean's letter tells us, was the price that Judah paid "Mr Langdale" (Patrick Langan) for Isaac and his wife in November 1780. In April 1781, Jacob was tried for assaulting Judah. Maclean phrases it differently: "in the spring Isaac obtained a hearing before the Justice's ..." The court record shows that Jacob was not sentenced for assault – the court declined passing sentence on Isaac, said Maclean – but he was held in custody until he could provide bail. Maclean informs us that he put up bail for Isaac and urged him to go to Quebec, where he would be safer, which is where Johnson's report places Jacob in the summer of 1781. For Maclean, see G.F.G. Stanley, "Allan Maclean."

24 HP, MS21773:211, Haldimand to Campbell, 16 July 1781; MS21774:206, Haldimand to Claus, 16 July 1781; MS21819:202, Haldimand to Johnson, 16 July 1781.
25 HP, MS21761:136.
26 Roger later asked to be allowed to remain in Canada. See n65, below.
27 The original consists of a table of nine columns. In the list reproduced here, blank spaces have been eliminated, so that, for example, if no remarks were made about a person, the "Remarks" heading is dropped. The two columns headed respectively "Property of Loyalists" and "Rebel Property" have been folded into one, "Loyalist or Rebel property."
28 HP, MS21763:368–9. This is the heading on the document, but the title on a cover sheet reads: "Return of Negroes brought in Canada by Scouts, and Sold at Montreal."
29 This is the woman to whom Brigadier General Maclean referred as the wife of "Isaac," in his letter of 5 July 1781 to Robert Mathews, reproduced on pages 567–8.
30 See n21, above.
31 Samuel Anderson, the master of the late Jack and of Diana (no. 9), settled "on the 1,200 acres of land granted to him near Cornwall" after the war. He may still have had Diana with him then, although, as mentioned later, her former American master, Adam Fonda, sought to have her sold in 1784 to pay off a debt. Anderson later became the first judge of the District and Surrogate Courts for the Eastern District of Upper Canada (Macdonell, *Sketches Illustrating the Early Settlement and History of Glengarry in Canada*, 73–5. Pringle, *Lunenburgh*, 202–4).
32 Combwood's master was Captain Justus Sherwood of the Queen's Loyal Rangers, head of the intelligence service during the war. Combwood died at Montreal on 9 December 1786 (BANQ, register of Christ Church, 10 December 1786).
33 Captain Johan Joost Herkimer received land in the District of Mecklenburgh (Midland District), at what is now Kingston, after the war. He died there in August 1795. See Casey, "Early Slavery in the Midland district," 14–15. James C. Hamilton, "The African in Canada," 368. Daniel G. Hill, *The Freedom-Seekers*, 208. W.D. Reid, "Johan Jost Herkimer, U.E., and his family." A.H. Young, ed., *The Parish Register of Kingston, Upper Canada, 1785–1811*, 155.
34 Johnson sold or gave Tanae to William Byrne, who was a captain in his KRRNY during the war and later his land agent. In July 1793, Byrne gave this "Negro Boy commonly called Tanno," then said to be sixteen, as well as a twenty-eight-year-old black woman named Rose to his adoptive son, Philip, as a wedding present (BANQ, notary P. Lukin Sr, No. 235, 27 July 1793, and letter of William Byrne to Thomas Finchley, 5 March 1793, attached to notary P. Lukin Sr, no. 5298, 25 May 1814).
35 Viger and LaFontaine, *De l'esclavage*, 22–4.
36 See Appendix I/A, notice 35.
37 CCP, *John Mittleberger v. Patrick Langan*, 1788–89; Writs issued out of the Court of Common Pleas 1786–93, Item 49, *John Mittleberger v. Patrick Langan*, summons of 5 July 1788.
38 The testimony is taken from Viger and LaFontaine, *De l'esclavage*, 45–7.
39 CCP, *John Mittleberger v. Patrick Langan*, 1788–89. Viger and LaFontaine, *De l'esclavage*, 47.
40 Viger and LaFontaine, *De l'esclavage*, 22. Munro's deposition of 16 July 1788 is also reproduced in Neilson, "Slavery in Old Canada," 37–8, where it is misdated 16 July 1780 (before the Ballston raid had taken place). For Munro's accounts of that raid, see HP, MS21821:154–6

and 167–8, Munro to Haldimand, 25 October 1780, and Munro to Major Richard B. Lernoult, 20 November 1780. These two documents have been published in Cruickshank and Watt, *The History and Master Roll of The King's Royal Regiment of New York*, 55–9.
41 Dublin appears to be the Private John Dublin of Munro's company who is recorded as having enlisted on 16 October 1780. Munro's attack on Ballston took place that night (Cruickshank and Watt, *The History and Master Roll of The King's Royal Regiment of New York*, 207).
42 BANQ, notary F. Leguay Sr, no. 543, 12 June 1780.
43 KB-Q1781:203-B4, *R v. Rubin Middleton*, deposition of Eleanor Caldwell, and 1781:209A, calendar of prisoners in the Montreal jail, and minutes of the Court of King's Bench at Montreal, September Term, 1781, *R v. Rubin Middleton*.
44 HP, MS21843:211, petition of Rubin Middleton, 26 November 1781.
45 HP, MS21721:180, Robert Mathews to E.W. Gray, 17 December 1781.
46 HP, MS21819:231, Mathews to Robert Leake, 17 December 1781; MS21814:309, Mathews to William Twiss, 17 December 1781; MS21818:300, Leake to Mathews, 24 December 1781. Cruikshank and Watt, *The History and Master Roll of The King's Royal Regiment of New York*, 257. "Settlements and Surveys," *Report on Canadian Archives*, 1891, 16. U.E. Loyalist Centennial Committee, *The Centennial of the Settlement of Upper Canada by the United Empire Loyalists*, 211. Cruikshank and Watt have Middleton born in the American colonies in 1760, standing 5 feet, 6 inches tall, and enlisting in the regiment on 20 December 1780, which is one year too early; Middleton is credited with four years' service when in fact he served three. The Old Loyalist List identified him as discharged soldier Robert Middleton, a resident of Marysburgh, receiving provisions at Kingston in 1786.
47 For Claus's slaves, see chapter 1.
48 HP, MS848:100, Robert Mathews to Lieutenant Jacob Maurer, 6 July 1780; MS21823:45 and 47, Haldimand to Major Daniel McAlpine, 6 July 1780, and McAlpine to Mathews, 9 July 1780; MS21819:135, Mathews to Major John Ross, 4 September 1780. W.D. Reid, "Johan Jost Herkimer, U.E., and his Family."
49 HP, MS21821:109, Herkimer to Mathews, 30 August 1780; MS21823:63, Mathews to Herkimer, 4 September 1780.
50 HP, MS21848:104, Mathews to Maurer, 18 September 1780. It appears that through most of its life the company consisted of twenty-nine men: one captain (Herkimer), paid eight shillings a day; one lieutenant, four shillings; one ensign, three shillings; three senior and three junior foremen, paid respectively eight pence and 6 pence; and twenty "common workmen," at four pence a day (HP, MS21848:151, Mathews to Maurer, 3 May 1781; MS21753:7, 75–6, 111, 129–30, pay records for batteaumen from 22 December 1782 to 24 December 1783).
51 HP, MS21848:110 and 112, Maurer to Mathews, 9 October 1780, and Mathews to Maurer, 12 October 1780; MS21788:110, Mathews to Herkimer, 12 October 1780.
52 HP, MS21848:118–119, Maurer to Mathews, 30 October 1780.
53 HP, MS21826:33–38, "Return of Families of Loyalists Receiving Provisions out of the Different Magazines or Depots in the District of Montreal from the 25th of Octbr. To the 24th of Novembr. 1780 Inclusive."
54 HP, MS21822:100, Butler to Conyn, 13 September 1783.

55 HP, MS21814:301–3, Twiss to Haldimand, 3 December 1781.
56 HP, MS21814:305, Haldimand to Twiss, 6 December 1781.
57 HP, MS21848:350–1, Maurer to Mathews, 22 September 1783, and MS21848:354, Mathews to Maurer, 6 October 1783; MS21765:346, Butler to Mathews, 3 November 1783. In February 1784, Mathews sent Maurer a pass for Conyn "and such Negros as are really his," communicating Haldimand's wish that in the case of the black slaves claimed by masters at Niagara, Herkimer should send them by the first opportunity (HP, MS21723:19–20, Mathews to Maurer, 2 February 1784).
58 HP, MS21765:209, Petition of Niclos Schylor, 13 March 1781.
59 See Appendix I/A, notice 53.
60 HP, MS21775:160–161, Johnson to Haldimand, 8 September 1783.
61 HP, MS21819:280, Mathews to Johnson, 6 October 1783.
62 HP, MS21735:371–2, Yohannes Decker to Haldimand, 10 March 1784.
63 HP, MS21822:336, Alexander Campbell to Mathews, 16 August 1784. For another similar case, see Appendix I/A, notice 16 and n25.
64 HP, MS21758:272–3, Robertson to Captain Dietrich Brehme, 29 October 1783. On the origin of the Bongas, see chapter 7 n79.
65 HP, MS21843:299, "Return of Prisoners who have requested leave to remain in the Province," 3 November 1782; MS21877:269, "Memorial from Plato a Negroe," 16 July 1783. Roger's name appeared on the above prisoners' list as Roger Vansoke, with the explanation: "taken at Fort George now living with Lt. Johnson, says that he was to have his Freedom for serving so long, & that his time is very near out."
66 HP, MS21843:317 and 336, "Return of Rebel Prisoners, Montreal District," 22 December 1782, and "Return of Rebel Prisoners in & about Montreal," undated.
67 HP, MS21825:242, DeLancey to Mathews, 17 May 1784.
68 HP, MS21723:111, Mathews to DeLancey, 24 May 1784; MS21775:293–4, Johnson to Haldimand, 27 May 1784.
69 LAC, RG1 L3, Upper Canada Executive Council, Land Petitions, v. 285, L5:21, report of Surveyor General David W. Smith and related documents on petition of several inhabitants of Lancaster. Fraser, *Seventeenth Report of the Department of Public Records and Archives of Ontario (1928)*, 73–6. Pringle, *Lunenburgh*, 403. Malcolm Robertson, "Black Loyalists of Glengarry," 23–4. Ross, *Lancaster*, 12–13, 89. In records of the settlement of discharged soldiers and Loyalists, published in the *Report on Canadian Archives, 1891* ("Settlements and Surveys," pp. 1–35), Pruyn is listed in September 1784 as Cato Trine at the Seigneury of Sorel (p. 17), and in October as Catto Prince at Point Mullie (Mouillée) (p. 7), which is in Lancaster Township. Tanse, former slave of Adam Fonda, is believed to be the black settler on Lot 14, 2nd Concession, identified by Pringle and Ross as James Fonda, and by Robertson as Thomas Fonda. The records of grants of Crown lands found in the Ontario Archives report cited above, p. 14, have James Fonda on Lot 14, 2nd Concession, and Thomas Fonda holding half (100 acres) of Lot 14, 3rd Concession. For John Powell, another black landholder in Lancaster, see chapter 5.
70 BANQ, notary P.L. Deschenaux, no. 357, 24 May 1784, and no. 359, 25 May 1784; notary J.G. Delisle, no. 880, 28 July 1794; register of Christ Church, 15 June 1784. Queen's University

Archives, Kingston, Ont., Jones Family Fonds, 2239, Series III, Legal Documents, Box 4, Folder 35 (1783–98), photocopy of deed of sale of a black girl from Daniel Jones to Solomon Jones, 30 August 1788, the original of which is in Ontario Heritage Foundation, Homewood Museum, Maitland, Ont., accession no. 986.15.9. (Homewood was Solomon Jones' home.) *Quebec Gazette*, 11 December 1777. Carter-Edwards, "Solomon Jones." Leavitt, *History of Leeds and Grenville*, 188, 197. MacPherson, *Matters of Loyalty*, 18–19, 31. For Sylvie, see chapter 2; for Tite and Ruth, see Appendix I/A, notices 48 and 69.

71 Note from McAdam to Morrison annexed to the deed of sale for Sarah, BANQ, notary J.G. Beek, no. 109, 9 March 1785.
72 LAC, MG23 GIII I 5, James Morrison Fonds, 502, Morrison to Hugh McAdam, 10 March 1785.
73 BANQ, notary J.G. Beek, nos 539 and 540, 6 June 1789.
74 Although Beek practised as a notary for more than forty years (1781–1822), he was not identified as such in his will or at his death on 3 December 1822. He identified himself in his will as "Surveyor and Principal Officer of His Majesty's Customs." His obituary notice said: "At 2 o'clock yesterday [6 December], the remains of the late John Gerbrand Beek, Esq. aged 84 years, were attended to the grave by a respectable concourse of citizens. Mr Beek was a native of Amsterdam, and for the last forty years was Surveyor of His Majesty's Customs here; he came to Canada soon after the conquest, where he remained ever since and uniformly supported the character of a true Christian, an affectionate husband, a tender parent and sincere friend" (BANQ, CT601, S1, Cour supérieure, Testaments olographes, no. 112, will of John Gerbrand Beek, 8 December 1812, probated 31 May 1823. *Gazette*, 7 December 1822.).
75 BANQ, notary J.G. Beek, Baux et protêts, 1:142.
76 Ibid., 1:142–3.
77 HDM, admission registers, Book E, 30 September 1791.
78 BANQ, notary J.G. Beek, Baux et protêts, 1:142, no. 1.
79 BANQ, notary J. Papineau, no. 3068, 9 August 1800; register of Notre Dame Church, 30 April 1795.
80 BANQ, register of Christ Church, 17 May 1799; notary J.G. Beek, no. 1186, 26 February 1798; notary F. Leguay Sr, no. 1441, 4 April 1785. HDM, admission registers, Book F, 7 February and 16 March 1799. Sarah was buried under the name Sarah Tobias, the thirty-eight-year-old "servant" of Charles Blake. Toby Tobias was a witness at her burial.
81 BANQ, notary J.G. Beek, no. 148, 1 February 1786.
82 BANQ, notary J.G. Delisle, 9 August 1790 and no. 872, 4 July 1794. There is no record of the 1785 sale of Rose to Mézière in Beek's papers. The sale must have included her daughter, who was christened Marie Anne in April 1785, and identified at the time as a "negresse," about thirteen months old, belonging to Mézière and his wife, Archange Campeau (BANQ, register of Notre-Dame Church, 12 April 1785).
83 WO, Class 71, 87:173–8, as cited on the website of the On-Line Institute for Advanced Loyalist Studies, www.royalprovincial.com/index.htm (accessed November 2006).
84 BANQ, notary J.G. Beek, no. 232, 11 January 1787; register of Saints-Anges Church, Lachine, 27 December 1793. This may be the Paul who was a patient at the Hôtel-Dieu in 1808, identified as a thirty-five-year-old mulatto born at Philadelphia (HDM, admission registers, Book G, 16 November 1808).

85 BANQ, notary J.P. Gauthier, no. 231, 15 September 1792. This is the deed of sale for Prince by Joseph Benoit *dit* L'Hyvernois to Joseph Papineau, which recites the chain of titles to the slave.
86 BANQ, register of Christ Church, 22 August 1788.
87 As mentioned on p. 23, Gabriel Cerré of St Louis took six slaves to Montreal for sale in 1796, but found no takers. The day of the slave drovers had passed.

APPENDIX IV

1 The text of the indictment was found among unsorted papers at the Centre de pré-archivage of the BANQ. If it has since been transferred to the archives, it would be filed with other Court of King's Bench indictments in TL19, S1, SS38. The cover sheet identifies it as indictment no. 33, and bears this summary of the case: "Filed 1 Septr./plea not Guilty/trial for 6 Septr./7 Septr. trial had/acquitted."
2 "Silas" Brewster was Cyrus Brewster, at one time the treasurer of the American Presbyterian Society of Montreal and husband of Ann Tappan (d. 1835), niece of the American anti-slavery stalwarts Arthur and Lewis Tappan. Cyrus and his brother, William, partners in a hardware business, both testified for the defence (BANQ, register of St Paul's Presbyterian Church, 7 June 1835; notary N.B. Doucet, no. 26097, 23 May 1839. Lighthall, *A Short History of the American Presbyterian Church of Montreal*, 38. Tappan, *Memoir of Mrs. Sarah Tappan*, 139–40).
3 KB, register, 7 September 1836.
4 The testimony given here consists of the trial notes of Chief Justice Reid, LAC, MG24 B173, James Reid Papers, Criminal Cases, 8, *R v. Alexander Grant, George Nixon and Moses Powell Wormley*, Wednesday, 7 September 1836. Frequent abbreviations are: Ag^t (against), D^t (defendant), K^s (knows), q^h (which), w^h (with), W^s (witness), and X^d (cross-examined).
5 The name is properly Alexandre Maurice Delisle.
6 This midnight serenade might seem like the work of louts, but there was a point to belting out this British patriotic song outside the home of people of American origin, as the Dwights were. In the context of the Betsy Freeman affair, its refrain – "Rule Britannia!/Britannia rules the waves/Britons never, never, never shall be slaves" – echoed the abolitionist message that while slavery had been abolished in Britain's colonies in 1834, it endured in the United States. On this occasion, *Rule Britannia* was a protest song.
7 John Craig appears to have taken over the premises formerly occupied by barber James Rollings. See chapter 5.
8 Cecilia (Farley) Grant was Alexander Grant's wife. We can only speculate as to the reason for this overlined entry.
9 William Fuller's name is given as William Pollock in the court register.
10 He is called Edward Twaddle in the court register.
11 KB, register, 7 September 1836.

Sources

MANUSCRIPT SOURCES
Archives de la Ville de Montréal
VM2 City assessment rolls (begin in 1847)
VM35 Fonds des Juges de paix de Montréal

Bibliothèque et Archives nationales du Québec, Montreal
Church registers, Montreal

84th Regiment Presbyterian
American Presbyterian
Christ Church (Anglican)
Crescent Street Presbyterian
Erskine Presbyterian
First Baptist
Garrison Anglican
General Hospital (Anglican chapel)
Hôpital-Général des Soeurs de la Charité (RC)
Notre-Dame (RC)

Primitive Methodist
St Andrew's Presbyterian
St Gabriel Street Presbyterian
St James Street Methodist
St Joseph Street Methodist Church
St John's Presbyterian
St Luke's Anglican
St Paul's Presbyterian
Trinity Anglican
Zion Congregational

Church registers outside Montreal
Cap-St-Ignace (RC)
Christ Church, Sorel (Anglican)
Garrison of Quebec Anglican

Hôtel-Dieu chapel, Quebec (RC)
Hôpital-Général, Quebec (RC)
L'Annonciation d'Oka (RC)
L'Immaculée-Conception, Trois-Rivières (RC)
Notre-Dame, LaPrairie (RC)
Notre-Dame, Quebec (RC)
Notre-Dame-de Bonsecours, L'Islet (RC)
Notre-Dame-de-Miséricorde, Beauport (RC)
Quebec Anglican Church
St-Ambroise de la Jeune Lorette (RC)
St-André d'Argenteuil (RC)
St Andrew's Presbyterian, Quebec
Ste-Anne-du-Bout-de-l'Ile (RC)
St-Antoine-de-Pades, Longueuil (RC)
St-Antoine-de-Padoue, St-Antoine-sur-Richelieu (RC)
St-Enfant-Jésus, Pointe-aux-Trembles (RC)
St-Eustache, St-Eustache (RC)
St-François-d'Assise, Longue Pointe (RC)
St-François-de-Sales, Île Jésus (Laval) (RC)
St-François-Xavier, Sault-St-Louis (RC)
St-François-Xavier, Verchères (RC)
St-Gabriel, St-Gabriel-de-Brandon (RC)
St James Protestant Episcopal, Trois-Rivières (Anglican)
St-Jean-Baptiste, Quebec (RC)
St-Joachim, Pointe-Claire (RC)
St-Jean-François-Regis, St-Regis (RC)
St John's Anglican Church, St-Jean-sur-Richelieu
St-Joseph, Chambly (RC)
St-Joseph, Pointe-Lévy (RC)
St-Joseph, Trois-Rivières (RC)
St-Louis, Terrebonne (RC)
St-Michel, Vaudreuil (RC)
St-Nicolas (RC)
St Paul's Anglican, Lachine
St-Pierre, Sorel (RC)
St-Pierre-du-Portage, L'Assomption (RC)
St-Roch, Quebec (RC)
St-Thomas-de-la-Pointe-à-la-Caille, Montmagny (RC)
Ste-Anne, Varennes (RC)
Ste-Anne-de-la-Pocatière (RC)
Ste-Elizabeth, seigneurie d'Autray (RC)
Ste-Famille, Boucherville (RC)
Ste-Geneviève, Berthierville (RC)

SOURCES 555

Ste-Madeleine, Rigaud (RC)
Ste-Marie-de-Beauce (RC)
Ste-Mélanie D'Ailleboust (RC)
Ste-Rose-de-Lima, Laval (RC)
Saints-Anges, Lachine (RC)
Wesleyan Methodist Church, Quebec

Court records
CC601, S1 Cour supérieure, tutelles et curatelles (guardianships and curatorships)
CT601, S1 Cour supérieure, Testaments olographes, 1658–1971
TL10 Registre des jugements en appel au commandant Thomas Gage, 6 décembre 1760 au 10 août 1764
TL11 Conseil militaire – Registre d'appels 20 novembre 1761 au 20 juillet 1764 (also TL279 Conseil militaire du district de Montréal – Plumitif des appels, 20 janvier 1762 au 21 octobre 1763)
TL12 Chambre des milices, 1760–1764
TL16 Court of Common Pleas
TL19, S1 Court of King's (or Queen's) Bench, criminal side, to 1849, and Court of Oyer & Terminer.
TL19, S4 Court of King's (Queen's) Bench, civil side.
TL32, S1 Court of General Quarter Sessions of the Peace
TL32, S26 Coroner's inquests
TL32, S37 Journal of the Watch Committee of the West Ward of Montreal, 22 November 1836–25 April 1837
TL32, S38 Tavern Licences (Box 173 contains a volume listing cases in the Court of Weekly Sessions January 1832–February 1834 and November 1837–July 1839, as well as the register of the Special Sessions of the Peace, 26 June 1833–25 November 1842)
TL36, S1 Court of Special and Weekly Sessions of the Peace (see also TL32, S38)

Election records
TL19, S41 Poll books – Lower Canada elections

Hospital records
Hôtel-Dieu, Quebec, admissions

Notarial records
A. Adhémar, C. Ainslie, G.D. Arnoldi, J. Aussem, A.I. Badeau, J.B. Badeau, A.E. Bardy, T. Barron, P. Beaudry, P.J. Beaudry, R. Beaufield, L. Bédard, T. Bedouin, J.G. Beek, J. Belle, J.A. Berthelot, M.A. Berthelot-Dartigny, L.T. Besserer, J. Blackwood, I.G. Bourassa, G. Busby, G.H.Z. Cadieux, J.M. Cadieux, A. Campbell, G. Cauchy, L. Chaboillez, M. Charest, F.M.T. Chevalier de Lorimier, E. Clément, W.N. Crawford, L.C. Danré de Blanzy, J.B. Decharnay, J.B.H. Deguire, J. Delisle, J.G. Delisle, J. Desautels, P.L. Deschenaux, M.L. Desdevens Deglandon, C. Desève, J.B. Desève, N.B. Doucet, T.B. Doucet, J. Dubreuil, A. Dumas, B. Farib-

ault, J.E. Faribault, A. Foucher, J. Gabrion, P.R. Gagnier, J.P. Gauthier, I.J. Gibb, E.W. Gray, J.A. Gray, H. Griffin, A. Grisé, E. Guy, L. Guy, G. Hodiesne, J.B. Houlé, J.H. Isaacson, L. Huguet-Latour, W.S. Hunter, C. Huot, A. Jobin, J.H. Jobin, John Jones, J.J. Jorand, J.A. Labadie, P. Lacombe, L.R. Lacoste, L. Lalanne, H. Lappare, F. Leguay Sr, P. Lukin Sr, P. Lukin Jr, E. McIntosh, L. Marteau, L.S. Martin, P. Mathieu, A.N. Mathon, P. Mézière, C. Michaud, L. Miray, J.M. Mondelet, A. Montreuil, L.A. Moreau, C.L. Nolin, R. O'Keeffe, J.A. Panet, J.C. Panet, P. Panet de Méru, D.E. Papineau, J. Papineau, F.M. Pétrimoulx, J.N. Pinguet, C.D. Planté, J.B. Planté, F. Racicot, F.X. Racicot, J.T. Raymond, P. Ritchot, D.L. St. Omer, S. Sanguinet Jr, W.F. Scott, A. Souste, F. Simonet, Charles Stewart, C.A. Terroux, C. Tessier, F. Tetu, T. Vuattier

Prison records
E17, S1, SS1 Registre de prison, Montréal

Other records at BANQ
P345 Château de Ramezay Collection/Numismatic and Antiquarian Society of Montreal
P603, S2, SS14 United Church Records, American Presbyterian Church, Montreal

Bibliothèque et Archives nationales du Québec, Quebec
E17 Registre de la prison de Québec (online database at www.banq.qc.ca/portal/dt/genealogie/genealogie.jsp)
E21, S64, SS4 Ministère des terres et forêts, Lower Canada Militia Claims, 1812–14
TL15 Court of Common Pleas
TL18, S1, SS1 Court of King's Bench
TL31, S1, SS1 Court of General Quarter Sessions of the Peace
TL31, S26, SS1 Coroner's inquests

Hôtel-Dieu, Montreal
Admission registers 1780–1870

Jamaica Archives
Laws of Jamaica, 1837–42
Votes of the Assembly, 1841–42

Library and Archives Canada
MG19 A2 Jacobs Ermatinger Estate series
MG19 A3 Askin Family fonds
MG21 Add. Mss. 21661–21892 Haldimand Papers
MG23 B21 Headquarters Papers of the British Army in America
MG23 GII 3 Edward William Gray Papers
MG23 GII 17 Robert Prescott fonds
MG23 GIII 5 James Morrison fonds
MG23 GIII 18 Labadie Family fonds

MG23 GIII 26 Louis Joseph Ainsse fonds
MG23 HII 13 Elias Smith fonds
MG24 B1 Neilson Collection
MG24 B173 James Reid Papers
MG25 G444 Elias Smith Family fonds
MG28 III 57 Molson Archives
MG30 C100 George A. Montgomery fonds
MG55/23-No. 51 Notes and copies of documents dealing with slavery 1664–1800
RG1 E1 Quebec, Lower Canada, Upper Canada, Canada: Executive Council Minute Books
RG1 L3 Upper Canada and Canada; land committee, Petitions
RG1 L3L Lower Canada Land Papers
RG1 L7 List of United Empire Loyalists
RG4 A1 Quebec and Lower Canada: Correspondence received by Civil and Prov. Secretaries; records of the clerk of the Executive Council (1760–1840)
RG4 B6 Ordinances and related legislative records of the Council, 1764–1775, and Legislative Council, 1775–1791 (of the old Province of Quebec)
RG4 B16 Quebec, Lower Canada and Canada East: [Civil Secretary], records of Courts
RG4 B17 Quebec and Lower Canada: [Civil Secretary] Lawsuits
RG4 B18 Lower Canada, Canada East: [Civil Secretary] Records relating to the administration of justice
RG4 B19 Montreal – Lists of Jurors 1811–1835
RG4 B20 Quebec, Lower Canada and Canada: [Provincial Secretary and Registrar] Applications for pardons or clemency 1766–1858
RG4 B28 Lower Canada Marriage Bonds 1779–1858
RG4 B45 Declarations of Aliens, Lower Canada, 1794–1811
RG4 C1 Provincial Secretary's Office, Canada East
RG4 C2 Provincial Secretary's Office, Correspondence: Canada East (Lower Canada, Civil Secretary's Letter Books 1829–1841)
RG7 G15, C Lower Canada, Civil Secretary's Letter Books 1788–1829
RG9 I-A-7 Adjutant-General's Office, Lower Canada fonds, militia lists, 1776–1846
RG14 A1 Ordinances and related legislative records of the Council, 1764–1775, and Legislative Council, 1775–1791
RG31 C1 Lower Canada and Canada East Census Returns 1825–1861; Canadian census returns for 1871, 1881, 1891, and 1901
RG68 Registrar General, Commissions and Letters Patent, Province of Quebec, 1764–1791; Conditional Pardons, Lower Canada, 1792–1841

McCord Museum of Canadian History, Montreal
C202 Collection of legal documents
P195 Badgley Papers
P197 McCord Family Papers
M17609 John Porteous Papers
P212 Court of Common Pleas

McGill University, Department of Rare Books and Manuscripts
MS 255 Charles Kadwell fonds 1832–38
MS 405 Thomas Storrow Brown fonds
MS 475 St Lawrence Steamboat Co. papers

Mount Royal Cemetery
Mount Royal Cemetery records
Protestant Old Burial Ground records

New York Public Library
Schieffelin Family Papers

Private collection
Philip Ruiter Ledgers, 1799–1811, property of Phyllis Montgomery and Robert Galbraith, on temporary loan to the Missisquoi Historical Society, Stanbridge East, Que., in 2007

Queen's University Archives, Kingston, Ont.
Jones Family Fonds
Miscellaneous Collection

St Louis, Missouri, Circuit Court
Circuit Court Case Files, Office of the Circuit Clerk, St Louis, Missouri State Archives, accessed online at http://stlcourtrecords.wustl.edu in 2006–2008

Université de Montréal
Projet de recherche en démographie historique (PRDH), online at
   www.genealogie.umontreal.ca/en/
P0058 Collection Louis-François-Georges Baby in the university's Division des archives

University of New Brunswick, Archives and special collections, Beaverbrook Collection
Ward Chipman Slavery Brief. Accessed online, fall 2007, at
www.lib.unb.ca/Texts/NBHistory/chipman/index.html

PRINTED SOURCES
Newspapers, Serials, and Directories, Montreal
Ami du Peuple
British American Journal of Medical & Physical Science
Canadian Courant
Canadian Magazine and Literary Repository
Canadian Spectator
City (Lovell's) directories
Commercial Advertiser
Gazette

Herald
Medical Chronicle or Montreal Monthly Journal of Medicine & Surgery
Minerve
Montreal Medical Journal
Montreal (Daily) Star
Morning Courier
Pilot
Spectateur canadien
Transcript
Vindicator
Witness

Newspapers, Serials, and Directories Outside Montreal
Boston Gazette
Brockville Gazette, Brockville, Ont.
Canadian Gleaner, Huntingdon, Que.
Canadian News, London, Eng.
Le Canadien, Quebec
Christian Recorder, Philadelphia, Pa.
Colored American, New York, NY
Courrier du Canada, Quebec
Le Courier de Québec ou Héraut François, Quebec
The Day, New London, Conn.
Demerary & Essequebo Royal Gazette, Demerara (Guyana)
Emancipator, New York, NY
Frederick Douglass' Paper, Rochester, NY
Freedom's Journal, New York, NY
Gazette des Trois-Rivières
Journal de Québec
Kingston Chronicle & Gazette, Kingston, Ont.
Liberator, Boston
Mackenzie's Gazette, New York, NY
Morning Chronicle, Quebec
National Era, Washington, DC
Newfoundlander, St John's, NL
Provincial Freeman, Windsor, Toronto and Chatham, Ont.
Quebec city directories
Quebec Gazette
Quebec Mercury
The Times/Le Cours du tems, Quebec
Herald, Quebec
Voice of the Fugitive, Windsor, Ont.

LEGISLATIVE DOCUMENTS

American State Papers, Series I: Foreign Relations, v. 1, 1789–1797. Washington: Gales and Seaton, 1832.
Great Britain, Statutes at Large
Journals of the Continental Congress 1774–1789
Journals of the House of Assembly of Lower Canada
Journals of the House of Assembly of Upper Canada
Journals of the Legislative Assembly of the Province of Canada
Journals of the Legislative Council of Upper Canada
Journals of the Legislative Council of Quebec
Provincial Statutes of Lower Canada
Statutes of the Province of Upper Canada
Statutes of the United Kingdom

BOOKS, JOURNALS, AND OTHER PUBLISHED SOURCES

Anonymous. *The Canadian Biographical Dictionary and Portrait Gallery of Eminent and Self-made Men: Quebec and the Maritime Provinces Volume*. New York and Toronto: American Biographical Publishing Co., 1881.
– *Canadian Letters: Description of a Tour Thro' the Provinces of Lower and Upper Canada in the Course of the Years 1792 and '93*. Reprinted from *Canadian Antiquarian and Numismatic Journal* 9, 3rd series, nos 3–4 (July–October 1912), for Thomas O'Leary by C.A. Marchand, 1914.
– *Census of the Canadas 1860–61*. 2 vols. Quebec: S.B. Foote, printer, 1863–64.
– *Censuses of Canada, 1665–1871*. Vol. 4. Ottawa: I.B. Taylor, printer, 1876.
– "Copies of papers in possession of the Historical Society, at Detroit: Opinions of Judge [A.B.] Woodward relative to the subject of slavery." *Michigan Pioneer Collections* 12 (1887): 511–22.
– *Édits et ordonnances royaux*. I – *Édits, Ordonnances Royaux, et Arrêts du Conseil d'État du Roi, Concernant le Canada*; II – *Ordonnances des Intendants et Arrêts portant règlements du Conseil supérieur de Québec. Avec les Commissions des Gouverneurs et Intendants, et des Officiers Civils et de Justice servant en Canada*. Quebec: P.E. Desbarats, 1803–06. Reprint, Ste-Eulalie, Que.: Éditions du Chardonnet, 1991.
– *Friendly spies on the Northern tour, 1815–1837: The Sketches of Henry Byam Martin* [exhibition catalogue]. Ottawa: Public Archives of Canada, 1981.
– *The History of the County of Brant, Ontario*. Toronto: Warner, Beers & Co., 1883.
– *History of the County of Middlesex, Canada*. Toronto and London: W.A. and C.L. Goodspeed, 1889.
– *The History of the County of Welland, Ontario, Its Past and Present*. Welland, Ont.: Welland Tribune Printing House, 1887.
– *Miscegenation: The Theory of the Blending of the Races, Applied to the American White Man and Negro* (attributed to David G. Croly and George Wakeman). New York: H. Dexter, Hamilton & Co., 1864. Reprint, Upper Saddle River, NJ: Literature House, 1970.
– *Opinions of Several Gentlemen of the Law, on the Subject of Negro Servitude, in the Province*

of Nova-Scotia. Saint John, NB: John Ryan, printer, 1802. Copy from Special Collections department, McPherson Library, University of Victoria, BC, accessed Fall 2007 at http://gateway.uvic.ca/spcoll/digit/slavery_opinion/index.html.
– *Pioneer Life on the Bay of Quinte*. Toronto: Rolph & Clark, 1904. Reprint, Milton, Ont.: Global Heritage Press, 1999.
– *Procès et exécution de Marie Anne Crispin et de J.B. Desforges, accusés du meurtre de Catherine Prévost, épouse d'Antoine Desforges, trouvés coupables et condamnés à être pendus, le 25 juin 1858*. Montreal: Sénécal, Daniel et compagnie, 1858.
– "Settlements and Surveys." *Report on Canadian Archives*, 1891. Douglas Brymner, editor. Ottawa: Queen's Printer, 1892.
– "Slavery in Canada. As It Existed Under English Rule Up Till the Present Century." *Montreal Gazette*, 27 April 1886, 7.
– "Slavery in Lower Canada." *The Lower Canada Jurist* 3 (1860): 257–68.
– *The Story of Oro*. Barrie, Ont.: Historical Committee of Oro Township, 1972.
– *The trial, defence, &c. of William Ross: who was executed, together with Robert Ellis, J.B. Monarque & W. Johnson, at Quebec, in April last, for a burglary and robbery committed at the house of Messire Masse, cure of Pointe Levi, on the night of the 29th September 1826*. Quebec: Neilson & Cowan, 1827.
– "Assignment of a Slave (1824)." *Lennox and Addington Historical Society: Papers and Records* 2 (1910): 41–2.
Alexander, Ken, and Avis Glaze. *Towards Freedom: The African-Canadian Experience*. Toronto: Umbrella Press, 1996.
Ancaster Township Historical Society. *Ancaster's Heritage: A History of Ancaster Township*. Ancaster, Ont.: The Society, 1973
Armour, David A. "Daniel Robertson." *DCB* 5:714–16.
Armour, David A., and K.R. Widder. *At The Crossroads: Michilimackinac During The American Revolution*. Mackinac Island, Mich.: Mackinac Island State Park Commission, 1978.
Askin, John. *The John Askin Papers*. Edited by Milo M. Quaife. 2 vols. Detroit: Detroit Library Commission, 1928.
Atherton, W.H. *Montreal from 1535 to 1914*. 3 vols. Montreal: S.J. Clarke Publishing Co., 1914.
Audet, Francis J. "Le Barreau et la Révolte de 1837." *Mémoires et Comptes Rendus de la Société Royale du Canada*, 3e série, 31 (1937), Section 1: 85–96.
– *Les Députés de Montréal (ville et comtés) 1792–1867*. Montreal: Éditions des Dix, 1943.
– *Les juges en chef de la province de Québec 1764–1924*. Quebec: L'Action Sociale, 1927.
Audet, F.J., and E. Fabre Surveyer. *Les députés au premier Parlement du Bas-Canada (1792–1796)*. Montreal: Éditions des Dix, 1946.
Bartley, S.A., transcriber. "Declarations of Aliens, Lower Canada, 1794–1811." *Vermont Genealogy* 11, nos 1–2 (January–April 2006), Special Publication no. 12 of the Vermont Genealogical Society.
Beaugrand-Champagne, D. *Le procès de Marie-Joseph-Angélique*. Montreal: Libre Expression, 2004.
Bédard, T.P. *Histoire de cinquante ans (1791–1841): Annales parlementaires et politiques du Bas-Canada depuis la Constitution jusqu'à l'Union*. Quebec: Léger Brousseau, 1869.

Bellemare, R. *Les bases de l'histoire d'Yamachiche 1703–1903*. Montreal: C.O. Beauchemin & Fils, 1903.

Bender, Louis Prosper. *Old and New Canada, 1753–1844: Historic Scenes and Social Pictures, or the Life of Joseph-François Perrault*. Montreal: Dawson Brothers, 1882.

Bernard, John. *Retrospections of America 1797–1811*. New York: Harper & Brothers, 1887.

Berthelot, H. *Montréal: Le bon vieux temps*. Montreal: Librairie Beauchemin, 1916.

Bertley, Leo W. *Canada and its People of African Descent*. Pierrefonds, Que.: Bilongo Publishers, 1977.

Bertrand, Camille. *Histoire de Montréal*. 2 vols. Montreal: Beauchemin-Plon/Frères des écoles chrétiennes, 1935–1942.

Blais, Christian. "Un document inédit sur l'esclavage au Québec." *Bulletin de la Bibliothèque de l'Assemblée nationale* 35, nos 3–4 (October 2006): 11–15.

Blanchard, Claude. "La pratique testamentaire à Montréal (1777–1825)." *Cahiers de Thémis*, no. 1, January 1972.

Blassingame, John W., editor. *Slave Testimony: Two Centuries of Letters, Speeches, Interviews and Autobiographies*. Baton Rouge, La.: Louisiana State University Press, 1977.

Blumrosen, A.W., and R.G. Blumrosen. *Slave Nation: How Slavery United the Colonies & Sparked the American Revolution*. Napierville, Ill.: Sourcebooks, Inc., 2005.

Bolster, W. Jeffrey. *Black Jacks: African American Seamen in the Age of Sail*. Cambridge, Mass.: Harvard University Press, 1997.

Bonga, George. "Letters of George Bonga." *JNH* 12, no. 1 (January 1927): 41–54.

Bonnycastle, Richard H. *The Canadas in 1841*. 2 vols. London: Henry Colburn, 1841.

Borthwick, J.D. *From Darkness to Light: History of the Eight Prisons which Have Been, or Are Now, in Montreal, from A.D. 1760 to A.D. 1907 – "Civil and Military."* Montreal: Gazette Printing Co., 1907.

– *History of the Diocese of Montreal, 1850–1910*. Montreal: John Lovell & Son, 1910.

– *History of the Montreal Prison from A.D. 1784 to A.D. 1886*. Montreal: A. Periard, 1886.

Bosworth, Newton. *Hochelaga Depicta; or, The History and Present State of the Island and City of Montreal*. Montreal: William Greig, 1839.

Boulle, Pierre H. *Race et esclavage dans la France de l'Ancien Régime*. Paris: Perrin, 2007.

Boyer, Raymond. *Les crimes et les châtiments au Canada français du XVIIe au XXe Siècle*. Montreal: Cercle du Livre de France, 1966.

Brown, Paola. *Address Intended to be Delivered in the City Hall, Hamilton, February 7, 1851, on the Subject of Slavery*. Hamilton: Printed for the Author, 1851.

Brown, Wallace. *The Good Americans: The Loyalists in the American Revolution*. New York: William Morrow and Co., 1969.

Brown-Kubisch, L. *The Queen's Bush Settlement: Black Pioneers 1839–1865*. Toronto: Natural Heritage Books, 2004.

Buchanan, A.W. Patrick. *The Bench and Bar of Lower Canada Down to 1850*. Montreal: Burton's Ltd., 1925.

Buchanan, Thomas C. *Black Life on the Mississippi: Slaves, Free Blacks and the Western Steamboat World*. Chapel Hill, NC: University of North Carolina Press, 2004.

Burger, Baudoin. *L'activité théâtrale au Québec (1765–1825)*. Montreal: Éditions Parti pris, 1974.

Burleigh, H.C. *Tales of Amherst Island.* Kingston, Ont.: Printed by Brown & Martin, 1980.
Burt, A.L. *The Old Province of Quebec.* 2 vols. Toronto and Minneapolis: Ryerson Press and University of Minnesota Press, 1933. Reprint, Toronto: McClelland & Stewart, 1968.
Canniff, W. *History of the Settlement of Upper Canada (Ontario), with Special Reference to the Bay Quinte.* Toronto: Dudley & Burns, 1869.
Carter-Edwards, Dennis. "Solomon Jones." *DCB* 6: 363–5.
Casey, Thomas W. "Early Slavery in the Midland District." *Lennox and Addington Historical Society: Papers and Records* 4 (1912): 12–21.
Casgrain, P.-B. *La vie de Joseph-François Perrault, surnommé le père de l'éducation du peuple canadien.* Quebec: C. Darveau, 1898.
Catterall, H.T., ed. *Judicial Cases Concerning American Slavery and the Negro, with additions by James J. Hayden.* Vol. 5. Washington, DC: Carnegie Institution of Washington, 1937.
– "Some Antecedents of the Dred Scott Case." *American Historical Review* 30, no. 1 (Oct. 1924): 56–71.
Chauveau, P.J.O. *De Québec à Montréal : Journal de la seconde session, 1846, suivi de Sept jours aux États-Unis.* Edited by Georges Aubin. Quebec: Éditions Nota bene, 2003.
Chiasson, Paulette M. "James Kerr." *DCB* 7: 464–6.
Christie, J.W., and Dwight L. Dumond. *George Bourne and "The Book and Slavery Irreconcilable."* Wilmington, Del., and Philadelphia, Pa.: Historical Society of Delaware/Presbyterian Historical Society, 1969.
Clark, John. "Memoirs of Colonel John Clark, of Port Dalhousie, C.W." *Ontario Historical Society Papers and Records* 7 (1906): 157–93.
Clay, Henry. *The Papers of Henry Clay.* Edited by James F. Hopkins and Mary W.M. Hargreaves. Vol. 5. Lexington, Ky.: University Press of Kentucky, 1973.
Cockloft, Jeremy the Elder (pseud). *Cursory Observations, Made in Quebec, Province of Lower-Canada, In the Year 1811.* Bermuda: printed for the author by Edmund Ward, King's Printer, n.d. (repr. Toronto: Oxford University Press, 1960).
Collison, Gary. *Shadrach Minkins: From Fugitive Slave to Citizen.* Cambridge, Mass.: Harvard University Press, 1997.
Cooper, Afua. *The Hanging of Angélique: The Untold Story of Canadian Slavery and the Burning of Old Montreal.* Toronto: HarperCollins, 2006.
– "Acts of Resistance: Black Men and Women Engage Slavery in Upper Canada, 1793–1803." *Ontario History* 99, no. 1 (spring 2007): 5–17.
Cooper, J. Irwin. *History of St George's Lodge No. 10 Q.R., 1829–1954.* Montreal: n.p., n.d.
– *James McGill of Montreal: Citizen of the Atlantic World.* Ottawa: Borealis, 2003.
Coues, Elliott, ed. *New Light on the Early History of the Greater Northwest: The Manuscript Journals of Alexander Henry, Fur Trader of the Northwest Company, and of David Thompson, Official Geographer and Explorer of the same Company, 1799–1814.* 3 vols. New York: Francis P. Harper, 1897.
Cruikshank, E.A. "The Administration of Lieut.-Governor Simcoe, Viewed in his Official Correspondence." *Transactions of the Canadian Institute* 2 (1891): 284–98.
– *The Settlement of the United Empire Loyalists on the Upper St. Lawrence and Bay of Quinte in 1784: A Documentary Record.* Toronto: Ontario Historical Society, 1934. Reprint, Milton, Ont.: Global Heritage Press, 2007.

Cruikshank, E.A., and Gavin K. Watt, *The History and Master Roll of the King's Royal Regiment of New York.* Campbellville, Ont.: Global Heritage Press, 2006.

David, L.O. *Les Patriotes de 1837–1838.* 1884. Reprint, Montreal: Jacques Frenette, 1981.

Davis, David Brion. *Inhuman Bondage: The Rise and Fall of Slavery in the New World.* New York: Oxford University Press, 2006.

DeCelles, A.D. "Lettres de 1835 et 1836." *Mémoires et Comptes Rendus de la Société Royale du Canada*, 3e série, 7 (1913): 169–79.

De Gaspé, P.A. *Les Anciens Canadiens.* Quebec: Desbarats and Derbyshire, 1863.

– *Mémoires.* Ottawa: G.E. Desbarats, 1866.

Delâge, Denis, and Étienne Gilbert. "La justice coloniale britannique et les Amérindiens au Québec 1760–1820. I – En terres amérindiennes" and "II – En territoire colonial." *Recherches amérindiennes au Québec* 32, no. 1 (2002): 63–82, and 32, no. 2 (2002): 107–17.

De Lagrave, J.-P. *Voltaire's Man in America.* Montreal and Toronto: Robert Davies Multimedia Publishing, 1997.

Derome, Robert. "Ignace-François Delezenne." DCB 4: 204–7.

– "Dominique Rousseau." DCB 6: 663–7

Dever, Alan. "Pierre Guerout." DCB 6: 305–6.

Dickinson, James Taylor. *A Sermon, Delivered in the Second Congregational Church, Norwich, On the fourth of July, 1834, at the request of the Anti-Slavery Society of Norwich & Vicinity.* Norwich, Conn.: Norwich Anti-Slavery Society, 1834.

Doige, Thomas. *The Montreal Directory &c.: An Alphabetical List of the Merchants, Traders and Housekeepers Residing in Montreal.* First and second editions. Montreal: James Lane, 1819, 1820.

Doutre, Gonzalve, and Edmond Lareau. *Le Droit civil canadien suivant l'ordre établi par les codes, précédé d'une Histoire générale du droit canadien.* 2 vols. Montreal: Alphonse Doutre, 1872.

Douville, Raymond. *Aaron Hart : Récit historique.* Trois-Rivières: Éditions du Bien Public, 1938.

– "Conrad Gugy." DCB 4: 316–17.

Drew, Benjamin. *The Refugee: or the Narratives of Fugitive Slaves in Canada.* Boston: John P. Jewett and Co., 1856. Reprint: Toronto: Prospero Books, 2000.

Dumais, Raymond. "Pierre Panet." DCB 5: 652–3.

Dunbar, Edward E. *History of the Rise and Decline of Commercial Slavery in America.* New York: Carleton, 1863.

Durang, John. *The Memoir of John Durang, American Actor, 1785–1816.* Edited by Alan S. Downer. Pittsburgh: University of Pittsburgh Press, 1966.

Egerton, Douglas R. *Death or Liberty: African Americans and Revolutionary America.* New York: Oxford University Press, 2009.

Elgersman, M.G. *Unyielding Spirits: Black Women and Slavery in Early Canada and Jamaica.* New York: Garland Publishing, 1999.

Ellice, Katherine Jane. *The Diary of Jane Ellice.* Edited by Patricia Godsell. Ottawa: Oberon Press, 1975

Extian-Babiuk, Tamara. " 'To be sold: a Negro Wench' – Slave Ads of the *Montreal Gazette* 1785–1805." Unpublished MA thesis, McGill University, 2006.

Fabre-Surveyer, E. "Charles-Ovide Perrault (1809–1837)." *Mémoires et Comptes Rendus de la Société Royale du Canada*, 3e série, 31 (1937), Section 1: 151–64.
– *The First Parliamentary Elections in Lower Canada.* Quebec: Louis Carrier, 1927.
– "Pierre Berthelet and His Family (in Canada and in the United States)." *Transactions of the Royal Society of Canada*, 3rd series, 37 (1943), Section 2: 57–76.
Faribault-Beauregard, M. *La Population des forts français d'Amérique (XVIIIe siècle).* 2 vols. Montreal: Éditions Bergeron, 1982.
– *La vie aux Illinois au XVIIIe siècle : Souvenirs inédits de Marie-Anne Cerré.* Montreal: Société de recherche historique Archiv-Histo, 1987.
Farrell, John K.A. "Schemes for the Transplanting of Refugee American Negroes from Upper Canada in the 1840's." *Ontario History* 52, no. 4 (1960): 245–9.
Faucher de Saint-Maurice, N.H.E. *Notes pour servir à l'histoire du Général Richard Montgomery.* Montreal: Imprimerie Eusèbe Sénécal & fils, 1893.
Fecteau, J.-M. *Un Nouvel ordre des choses : la pauvreté, le crime, et l'état au Québec de la fin du XVIIIe siècle à 1840.* Montreal: VLB éditeur, 1989.
Fehrenbacher, Don E. *The Dred Scott Case: Its Significance in American Law and Politics.* New York: Oxford University Press, 1978.
Fisher, W. Allen. *Legend of the Drinking Gourd.* Barrie, Ont.: W.A. and M.W. Fisher, 1973.
Foley, W.E., and C.D. Rice. *The First Chouteaus: River Barons of Early St Louis.* Urbana, Ill.: University of Illinois Press, 1983.
Franchère, Gabriel. *Journal of a Voyage on the North West Coast of North America during the Years 1811, 1812, 1813 and 1814.* Toronto: Champlain Society, 1969.
Foucher, Antoine. *Le Journal du célèbre siège de Saint-Jean.* Saint-Jean-sur-Richelieu, Que.: Le Canada Français, n.d.
Fraser, Alexander. *Seventeenth Report of the Department of Public Records and Archives of Ontario (1928).* Toronto: King's Printer, 1929.
Frazier, Harriet C. *Runaway and Freed Missouri Slaves and Those Who Helped Them, 1763–1865.* Jefferson, NC: McFarland & Co., 2004.
– *Slavery and Crime in Missouri, 1773–1865.* Jefferson, NC: McFarland & Co., 2001.
Frost, Stanley B. *James McGill of Montreal.* Montreal and Kingston: McGill-Queen's University Press, 1995.
Fyson, Donald. *Magistrates, Police, and People: Everyday Criminal Justice in Quebec and Lower Canada, 1764–1837.* Toronto: University of Toronto Press / Osgoode Society for Canadian Legal History, 2006.
Fyson, Donald, and Brian Young. "Origins, Wealth and Work." In *The McCord Family: A Passionate Vision* [exhibition catalogue], edited by Pamela Miller, 26–53. Montreal: McCord Museum, 1992.
Gagnon, Ernest. *Le fort et le château Saint-Louis (Québec) : Étude archéologique et historique.* Montreal: Librairie Beauchemin, 1925.
Garneau, F.X. *Histoire du Canada*, 8th ed. 9 vols. Montreal: Éditions de l'Arbre, 1944–46.
Garner, John. *The Franchise and Politics in British North America 1755–1867.* Toronto: University of Toronto Press, 1969.
Garrison, W.F., and F.J. Garrison. *William Lloyd Garrison 1805–1879: The Story of His Life Told by His Children.* New York: The Century Co., 1885.

Gay, Daniel. "Des empreintes noires sur la neige blanche: Les Noirs au Québec (1750–1900)." Rapport final au Conseil québécois de la recherche sociale, 1988.
– *Les Noirs du Québec 1629–1900*. Sillery, Que.: Éditions du Septentrion, 1904.
Genovese, Eugene D. *Roll, Jordan, Roll: The World the Slaves Made.* New York: Vintage Books, 1976.
Gerzina, Gretchen H. *Black London: Life Before Emancipation.* New Brunswick, NJ: Rutgers University Press, 1995.
Gibson, Campbell. "Population of the 100 Largest Cities and other Urban Places in the United States: 1790 to 1990." Washington, US Census Bureau, Population Division Working Paper no. 27, June 1998. Available at www.census.gov/population/www/documentation/twps0027.html.
Girardin, J.A. "Slavery in Detroit." *Michigan Pioneer Collections* 1 (1874–75): 415–17.
Goddard, Jane Bennett. *Hans Waltimeyer.* Cobourg, Ont.: J.B. Goddard, 1980.
Godfrey, Sheldon J., and Judith C. Godfrey. *Search Out the Land: The Jews and the Growth of Equality in British Colonial America, 1740–1867.* Montreal and Kingston: McGill-Queen's University Press, 1995.
Gooding, Alfred. "Records of the South Church of Portsmouth, N.H." *New England Historical and Genealogical Register* 81 (1927): 419–53.
Gourlay, Robert. *Statistical Account of Upper Canada: Compiled with a view to a grand system of emigration.* London: Simpkin & Marshall, 1822
Greaves, Ida. *The Negro in Canada.* Orillia, Ont.: McGill University Economic Studies, no. 16, 1930.
Greenwood, F. Murray, and Beverley Boissery. *Uncertain Justice: Canadian Women and Capital Punishment, 1754–1953.* Toronto: Dundurn Press, 2000.
Guitard, Michelle. *Histoire sociale des miliciens de la bataille de la Châteauguay.* Ottawa: Parks Canada, National Historic Sites and Parks Branch, 1983.
Hamilton, James C. *Osgoode Hall: Reminiscences of the Bench and Bar.* Toronto: The Carswell Co., 1904.
– "The African in Canada." *Proceedings of the American Association for the Advancement of Science* 38 (1889): 364–70.
– "The Maroons of Jamaica and Nova Scotia." *Proceedings of the Canadian Institute*, 1890.
– "The Panis: An Historical Outline of Canadian Indian Slavery." *Proceedings of the Canadian Institute*, New Series 1, Part 1, no. 1 (1897): 19–27.
Hanaway, J., and R. Cruess. *McGill Medicine, Volume I: The First Half Century 1829–1885.* Montreal-Kingston: McGill-Queen's University Press, 1996.
Harrold, Stanley. *Subversives: Antislavery Community in Washington, D.C., 1828–1865.* Baton Rouge, La.: Louisiana State University Press, 2003.
Hartgrove, W.B. "Story of Marie L. Moore and Fannie M. Richards." *JNH* 1, no. 1 (January 1916): 23–33.
– "The Negro Soldier in the American Revolution." *JNH* 1, no. 2 (April 1916): 110–31.
Hemenway, Abby M., ed. *The Vermont Historical Gazetteer.* 5 vols. Burlington and Brandon, Vt., and Claremont, NH, 1867–91.
Henry, Alexander. *The Journal of Alexander Henry the Younger, 1799–1814.* Edited by Barry Gough. 2 vols. Toronto: Champlain Society, 1988.

Heyrick, Elizabeth. *Immediate, Not Gradual, Abolition; or, An Inquiry into the Shortest, Safest, and Most Effectual Means of Getting Rid of West Indian Slavery.* London: Knight and Bagster, printers, 1824.

Higginbotham, A.L. Jr. *In the Matter of Color – Race & The American Legal Process: The Colonial Period.* New York: Oxford University Press, 1980.

– *Shades of Freedom: Racial Politics and Presumptions of the American Legal Process.* New York: Oxford University Press, 1998.

Hileman, Maria. "Dwight Janes, Conscience of the Amistad" and "The Amistad's Unsung Hero." *The Day*, New London, Conn., 5 October 1997; "A City Divided" and "A Church Divided," in the same newspaper, 6 October 1997.

Hill, Daniel G. *The Freedom-Seekers: Blacks in Early Canada.* Agincourt, Ont.: The Book Society of Canada Ltd., 1981.

Hodges, Graham Russell, ed. *The Black Loyalist Directory: African Americans in Exile After the American Revolution.* New York: Garland Publishing, 1996.

Hornby, Jim. *Black Islanders: Prince Edward Island's Historical Black Community.* Charlottetown, PEI: Institute of Island Studies, 1991.

Howe, S.G. *The Refugees from Slavery in Canada West: Report to the Freedmen's Inquiry Commission 1864:* Boston: Wright & Potter, 1864. Reprint, New York: Arno Press/New York Times, 1969.

Hunter, Douglas. *Molson: The Birth of a Business Empire.* Toronto: Penguin Books, 2001.

Imbeault, Sophie. *Les Tarieu de Lanaudière: Une famille noble après la Conquête 1760–1791.* Sillery, Que.: Éditions du Septentrion, 2004.

Igartua, José E. "Jean Orillat." *DCB* 4: 591–3.

Israel, Wilfrid E. "The Montreal Negro Community." Unpublished MA thesis, McGill University, 1928.

Janson, Gilles. "Daniel Arnoldi." *DCB* 7: 27–9.

Jean-Baptiste (F.A. Baillargé). *Mgr Bourget: Ça et là.* Montreal: Cadieux & Derome, 1881.

Jodoin, A., and J.L. Vincent. *Histoire de Longueuil et de la famille De Longueuil.* Montreal: Gebhardt-Berthiaume, 1889.

Johonnot, Andrew. "The Johonnot Family." *New England Historical and Genealogical Register* 6 (1852): 357–366, and 7 (1853): 141–4.

Jones, Howard. *Mutiny on the Amistad.* New York: Oxford University Press, 1987. Rev. paperback ed. 1988.

Kaplan, Sydney. "The Miscegenation Issue in the Election of 1864." *JNH* 34, no. 3 (July 1949): 274–343.

Katz, W. Loren. *The Black West: A Documentary and Pictorial History of the African American Role in the Westward Expansion of the United States.* New York: Ethrac Publications/Simon & Schuster, 1996.

Kennedy, W.P.M. *Documents of the Canadian Constitution 1759–1915.* Toronto: Oxford University Press, 1918.

Lachance, André. *Le bourreau au Canada sous le régime français.* Quebec: Société historique de Québec, Cahiers d'Histoire 18, 1966.

– *La justice criminelle du roi au Canada au XVIIIe siècle: Tribunaux et officiers.* Quebec: Presses de l'université Laval, 1978.

– *Juger et punir en Nouvelle-France: Chroniques de la vie quotidienne au XVIIIe siècle.* Montreal: Libre Expression, 2000.
– "Mathieu Léveillé." *DCB* 3: 398–9.
La Jonquière, Marquis de. *Le Chef d'escadre M. de La Jonquière gouverneur général de la Nouvelle-France et le Canada de 1749 à 1752.* Paris: Garnier Frères, 1896.
Lambert, James H. "James Monk." *DCB* 6: 511–15.
Landmann, George T. *Adventures and Recollections of Colonel Landmann, Late of the Corps or Royal Engineers.* 2 vols. London: Colburn & Co., 1852.
Landon, Fred. *Western Ontario and the American Frontier.* Toronto: McClelland & Stewart, Carleton Library Series, 1967.
– "Canadian Negroes and the Rebellion of 1837." *JNH* 7, no. 4 (October 1922): 377–9.
– "Social Conditions among the Negroes in Upper Canada before 1865." *Ontario Historical Society Papers and Records* 22 (1925): 144–61.
Lapalice, O.M.H. "Les esclaves noirs à Montréal sous l'Ancien Régime." *Canadian Antiquarian and Numismatic Journal,* 3rd Series, 12, no. 3 (July 1915): 136–58.
Lawson, Philip. *The Imperial Challenge: Quebec and Britain in the Age of the American Revolution.* Montreal and Kingston: McGill-Queen's University Press, 1989.
Leavitt, T.W.H. *History of Leeds and Grenville, Ontario, from 1749 to 1879.* Brockville, Ont.: Recorder Press, 1879. Reprint Belleville, Ont.: Mika Publishing, 1986.
Lebrun, Isidore. *Tableau statistique et politique des deux Canadas.* Paris: Treuttel et Weurtz, 1833.
Lees, John. *Journal of J.L., of Quebec, Merchant.* Detroit: Society of Colonial Wars of the State of Michigan, 1911.
Lefèvre, J.J., ed. "Inventaire des biens de Luc Lacorne de Saint-Luc." *RAPQ* 1947–48, 31–70.
Lefrançois, Alexandre. "Thomas Arakwenté: promoteur de la modernité dans la communauté iroquoise du Sault Saint-Louis (1791–1820)." *Revue d'éthique et de théologie morale,* Supplement, 228 (March 2004): 357–78.
Leighton, Douglas. "John Campbell." *DCB* 4: 129–31.
– "Christian Daniel Claus." *DCB* 4: 154–5.
Lemay, Thérèse P. "Joe." *DCB* 4: 392–3.
LeMoine, James M. *L'album du Touriste – Archéologie, histoire, littérature-sport : Québec.* Quebec: printed by Augustin Côté et cie., 1872.
– *Picturesque Quebec: A Sequel to Quebec Past and Present.* Montreal: Dawson Brothers, 1882.
– "Le premier gouverneur anglais de Québec – le général James Murray 1759–1766." *Mémoires de la Société royale du Canada* 8 (1890), Section 1: 73–90.
Lesage, Albert. *Le Collège des médecins et chirurgiens de la Province de Québec, 1847– 1947.* Montreal: The College, 1947.
Lewis, Israel. *Crisis in North America: Slavery, War, Balance of Power and Oregon.* Montreal: Harrison Printer, 1846.
Lighthall, G.R. *A Short History of the American Presbyterian Church of Montreal, 1823–1923.* Montreal: The Herald Press, 1923.
Lindsay, A.G. "Diplomatic Relations between the United States and Great Britain Bearing on the Return of Negro Slaves, 1783–1828." *JNH* 5, no. 4 (October 1920): 391–419.

Linteau, Paul-André. *Brève histoire de Montréal*. Montreal: Éditions du Boréal, 2nd ed., 2007.
Long, David E. *The Jewel of Liberty: Abraham Lincoln's Re-election and the End of Slavery*. New York: Da Capo Press, 1997.
Lord, E. *Memoir of the Rev. Joseph Stibbs Christmas*. Montreal: John Lovell, 1868.
Maas, David E., comp. *Divided Hearts: Massachusetts Loyalists, 1765–1790. A Biographical Directory*. Boston: Society of Colonial Wars/New England Historic Genealogical Society, 1980.
McAllister, Marvin. *White People Do Not Know How to Behave at Entertainments Designed for Ladies & Gentlemen of Colour*. Chapel Hill, NC: University of North Carolina Press, 2003.
McCullough, Charles R. "Paola Brown, the Town Crier." *Hamilton Spectator*, 30 January and 6 February 1937.
MacDermot, H.E. *A History of The Montreal General Hospital*. Montreal: The Montreal General Hospital, 1950.
Macdonell, J.A. *Sketches Illustrating the Early Settlement and History of Glengarry in Canada*. Montreal: Wm. Foster, Brown & Co., 1893.
MacEacheren, E. "Emancipation of Slavery in Massachusetts: A Reexamination 1770– 1790." *JNH* 55, no. 4 (October 1970): 289–306.
Mackenzie, W.L. *Sketches of Canada and the United States*. London: Effingham Wilson, 1833.
Mackey, F. *Black Then: Blacks and Montreal, 1780s–1880s*. Montreal and Kingston: McGill-Queen's University Press, 2004.
– *Steamboat Connections: Montreal to Upper Canada, 1816–1843*. Montreal and Kingston: McGill-Queen's University Press, 2000.
MacLean, Jill. *Jean Pierre Roma of the Company of the East of Isle St. Jean*. Prince Edward Island Heritage Foundation, 1977. Reprint, Charlottetown, PEI: Acorn Press, 2005.
McManus, E.J. *A History of Negro Slavery in New York*. Syracuse, NY: Syracuse University Press, 1966.
– *Black Bondage in the North*. Syracuse, NY: Syracuse University Press, 1973.
MacPherson, Ian. *Matters of Loyalty: The Buells of Brockville, 1830–1850*. Belleville, Ont.: Mika Publishing Co., 1981.
Major-Frégeau, Madeleine. *La vie et l'oeuvre de François Malepart de Beaucourt (1740–1794)*. Quebec: Ministère des affaires culturelles, 1979.
– "François Malepart de Beaucourt." *DCB* 4: 507–9.
Manning, William R. *Diplomatic Correspondence of the United States: Canadian Relations 1784–1860*. Vol. 1. Washington: Carnegie Endowment for International Peace, 1940.
Martin, Ged. "British Officials and their Attitudes to the Negro Community in Canada, 1833–1861." *Ontario History* 66, no. 2 (June 1974): 79–88.
Masson, L.R. *Les Bourgeois de la Compagnie du Nord-Ouest*. 2 vols. Quebec: A. Coté et cie, 1889–90.
Mathieu, "Un négociant de Québec à l'époque de la Conquête: Jacques Perrault l'aîné." *RAPQ* 48 (1970): 27–82.
Mayer, Henry. *All on Fire: William Lloyd Garrison and the Abolition of Slavery*. New York: St Martin's Press, 1998.
Mealing, S.R. "William Osgoode." *DCB* 6: 557–60.

Melish, Joanne Pope. *Disowning Slavery: Gradual Emancipation and "Race" in New England, 1780–1860.* Ithaca, NY: Cornell University Press, 1998.

Miller, Carman. "Charles Dewey Day." *DCB* 11: 237–9.

Mimeault, Mario. "Azariah Pritchard." *DCB* 6: 616.

Morel, André. "Pierre-Louis Panet." *DCB* 5: 653–5.

Myers, Norma. *Reconstructing the Black Past: Blacks in Britain 1780–1830.* London: Frank Cass, 1996.

Nadelhaft, J. "The Somersett Case and Slavery: Myth, Reality, and Repercussions." *JNH* 51, no. 3 (July 1966): 193–208.

Neatby, Hilda. *Quebec: The Revolutionary Age, 1760–1791.* Toronto: McClelland & Stewart, 1966.

Neilson, Hubert. "Slavery in Old Canada – Before and After the Conquest." *Transactions of the Literary and Historical Society of Quebec* 26 (1901): 19–45.

Nelson, Wolfred. *Écrits d'un patriote 1812–1842.* Georges Aubin, editor. Montreal: Comeau & Nadeau, 1998.

Osagie, Iyunolu Folayan. *The Amistad Revolt: Memory, Slavery, and the Politics of Identity in the United States and Sierra Leone.* Athens, Ga.: University of Georgia Press, 2000.

Ouellet, Fernand. *Éléments d'histoire sociale du Bas-Canada.* Montreal: Hurtubise HMH, 1972.

Papineau, Louis-Joseph. *Lettres à divers correspondants. Tome I: 1810–1845; Tome II: 1845–1871.* Edited by Georges Aubin and Renée Blanche. Montreal: Varia, 2006.

Parizeau, Gérard. *La société canadienne française au XIXe siècle.* Montreal: Fides, 1975.

Peabody, Sue. *"There Are No Slaves in France": The Political Culture of Race and Slavery in the Ancien Régime.* New York: Oxford University Press, 1996.

Pease, W.H., and J. Pease. *Black Utopia: Negro Communal Experiments in America.* Madison, Wisc.: State Historical Society of Wisconsin, 1963.

G.W. Perkins. *Remarks on Mr Stuart's Book "Conscience and the Constitution," at a meeting in Guildford, August 1, 1850, Commemorative of Emancipation in the West Indies.* West Meriden, Conn.: Hinman's Print, 1850.

– *Scriptural Missions. A Sermon, Preached by the Rev. G.W. Perkins, at the Annual Meeting of the American Missionary Association, at Hartford, September 26, 1848.* New York: American Missionary Association, 1848.

Perrault, Claude. *Montréal en 1825.* Montreal: Groupe d'études Gen-Histo Inc., 1977.

Perrault, Joseph-François. *Biographie de Joseph François Perrault, protonotaire de la Cour du banc du roi pour le district de Quebec, écrite par lui-même, à l'âge de quatre-vingts ans, sans lunettes, à la suggestion du Lord Aylmer, gouverneur en chef du bas-Canada,* Quebec: Thomas Cary, 1834.

Picard, Nathalie. "Les femmes et le vote au Bas-Canada de 1792 à 1849." Unpublished MA thesis, Université de Montréal, 1992.

Pilarczyk, Ian C. " 'Too Well Used by His Master': Judicial Enforcement of Servants' Rights in Montreal, 1830–1845." *McGill Law Journal* 46, no. 2 (2001): 491–529.

– "The Law of Servants and the Servants of Law: Enforcing Masters' Rights in Montreal, 1830–1845." *McGill Law Journal* 46, no. 3 (2001): 779–836.

Podruchny, Carolyn. *Making the Voyageur World: Travelers and Traders in the North American Fur Trade.* Toronto: University of Toronto Press, 2006.

Porter, Kenneth W. "Negroes and the Fur Trade." *Minnesota History* 15, no. 4 (December 1934): 421–33.
Poutanen, M.A. " 'To Indulge Their Carnal Appetites': Prostitution in Early Nineteenth-Century Montreal, 1810–1842." Unpublished PhD thesis, Université de Montréal, 1997.
Prince, Bryan. "The case of Isaac Brown: fugitive slave." *Ontario History* 99, no. 1 (spring 2007): 18–30.
Pringle, J.F. *Lunenburgh or the Old Eastern District.* Cornwall, Ont.: Standard Printing House, 1890. Reprint, Belleville, Ont.: Mika Publishing Co., 1980.
Quarles, Benjamin. *The Negro in the American Revolution.* New York: W.W. Norton & Co., 1973.
Read, D.B. *The Lives of the Judges of Upper Canada and Ontario, From 1791 to the Present Time.* Toronto: Rowsell & Hutchison, 1888.
Reid, W.D. "Johan Jost Herkimer, U.E., and his Family." *Ontario Historical Society Papers and Records* 31 (1936): 215–27.
Rich, E.E. *Hudson's Bay Company 1670–1870.* 3 vols. Toronto: McClelland & Stewart, 1960.
Riddell, W.R. *The Life of William Dummer Powell: First Judge at Detroit and Fifth Chief Justice of Upper Canada.* Lansing, Mich.: Michigan Historical Commission, 1924.
– *The Life of John Graves Simcoe, First Lieutenant-Governor of the Province of Upper Canada 1792–96.* Toronto: McClelland & Stewart, 1926.
– *Michigan Under British Rule: Law and Law Courts, 1760–1796.* Lansing, Mich.: Michigan Historical Commission, 1926.
– *The Slave in Canada.* JNH 5, no. 3 (July 1920): 261–377.
– "The Slave in Upper Canada." JNH 4, no. 4 (October 1919): 373–95.
– "Notes on Slavery in Canada." JNH 4, no. 4 (October 1919): 396–411.
– "Notes on the Slave in Nouvelle-France." JNH 8, no. 3 (July 1923): 316–30.
– "Further Notes on Slavery in Canada." JNH 9, no. 1 (January 1924): 26–33.
– "Method of Abolition of Slavery in England, Scotland and Upper Canada Compared." *Ontario Historical Society Papers and Records* 27 (1931): 511–13.
– "An International Complication between Illinois and Canada Arising out of Slavery." *Journal of the Illinois State Historical Society* 25 (April 1932–January 1933): 123–6.
Ripley, John. "Shakespeare on the Montreal Stage 1805–1826." *Theatre History in Canada* 3, no. 2 (Spring 1982): 3–20.
Ripley, Peter, ed. *The Black Abolitionist Papers. I – The British Isles, 1830–1865;* and *II – Canada, 1830–1865.* Chapel Hill, NC: University of North Carolina Press, 1985, 1986.
Robert, Jean-Claude. *Atlas Historique de Montréal.* Montreal: Art Global/Libre Expression, 1994.
– "Jacques Viger." *DCB* 8: 909–13.
Robert, Mario. "Le livre et la lecture dans la noblesse canadienne 1670–1764." *Revue d'histoire de l'Amérique française*, 56, no. 1 (summer 2002): 4–27.
Roberts, David. "William Grant." *DCB* 5: 367–76.
Robertson, J. Ross. *Landmarks of Toronto.* 6 vols. Toronto: J. Ross Robertson, 1894–1914.
Robertson, Malcolm. "Black Loyalists of Glengarry." *Glengarry Life* 33 (1994): 21–4.
Robertson, Marion. "John Sargent." *DCB* 6: 682–3.
Roquebrune, Robert de. *Testament de mon enfance.* Montreal: Fides, 1958.

Ross, Ewan. *Lancaster Township and Village.* Ste-Anne-de-Bellevue, Que.: Imprimerie cooperative Harpell, 1982.

Roy, J.-Edmond. *Histoire de la seigneurie de Lauzon.* Vols 3 and 5. Lévis: Mercier & cie, 1900 and 1904.

Roy, Pierre-Georges. *A travers Les anciens Canadiens de Philippe Aubert de Gaspé.* Montreal: G. Ducharme, 1943.

– *A travers Les Mémoires de Philippe Aubert de Gaspé.* Montreal: G. Ducharme, 1943.

– *La Famille Le Compte Dupré.* Lévis, Que., n.p., 1941.

– *La Famille Panet.* Lévis, Que.: J.A.K. Laflamme, printer, 1906.

– *Les Juges de la province de Québec.* Quebec: Imprimeur du Roi, 1933.

– *Toutes petites choses du régime anglais*, 1ère série. Quebec: Éditions Garneau, 1946.

– "La vente des esclaves par actes notariés sous les régimes français et anglais." RAPQ 1921–1922: 109–23.

Ruck, Calvin W. *The Black Battalion (1916–1920): Canada's best kept military secret.* Halifax: Nimbus, 1987.

Rushforth, Brett. " 'A Little Flesh We Offer You': The Origins of Indian Slavery in New France." *William and Mary Quarterly* 60, no, 4 (October 2003): 777–808.

Saint-Thomas, Mère. *Les Ursulines de Québec depuis leur établissement jusqu'à nos jours.* Vol. 3. Quebec: C. Darveau, 1866.

Salzberger, Ronald P., and Mary C. Turck. *Reparations for Slavery: A Reader.* Lanham, Md.: Rowman & Littlefield, 2004.

Sanderson, Charles R., ed. *The Arthur Papers, Being the Papers mainly Confidential, Private, and Demi-Official, of Sir George Arthur, Last Lieutenant-Governor of Upper Canada, in the Manuscript Collection of the Toronto Public Libraries.* Toronto: Toronto Public Librairies/University of Toronto Press, 1943–59.

Sansom, Joseph. *Travels in Lower Canada, with the Author's Recollections of the Soil, and Aspect; the Morals, Habits, and Religious Institutions, of That Country.* London: Printed for Sir Richard Phillips, 1820.

Scadding, Henry. *Toronto of Old: Collections and Recollections Illustrative of the Early Settlement and Social Life of the Capital of Ontario.* Toronto: Adam, Stevenson & Co., 1873.

Séguin, Robert-Lionel. "L'esclavage dans la presqu'île." BRH 55, nos 4–6 (1949): 91–4; nos 7–9: 168.

– *Le mouvement insurrectionnel dans la presqu'île de Vaudreuil 1837–1838.* Montreal: Librairie Ducharme, 1955.

Shadd, Mary Ann. *A Plea for Emigration.* Detroit: George W. Pattison Printing, 1852. Reprint, edited by Richard Almonte. Toronto: Mercury Press, 1998.

Shyllon, F.O. *Black Slaves in Britain.* London: Oxford University Press, 1974.

Silverman, Jason H. *Unwelcome Guests: Canada West's Response to American Fugitive Slaves, 1800–1865.* New York: Associated Faculty Press, 1985.

Simcoe, Elizabeth. *Mrs. Simcoe's Diary.* Edited by Mary Q. Innis. Toronto: Macmillan Canada, 1965.

Simcoe, J.G. *The Correspondence of Lieut. Governor John Graves Simcoe.* Edited by E.A. Cruikshank. 5 vols. Toronto: Ontario Historical Society, 1924.

Simpson, Donald G. *Under the North Star: Black Communities in Upper Canada Before Confederation (1867)*. Trenton, NJ: Africa World Press, 2005.

Simpson, George. *Journal of Occurrences in the Athabasca Department, 1820 and 1821, and Report*. Edited by E.E. Rich. Toronto: Champlain Society, 1938.

Sires, Ronald V. "Sir Henry Barkly and the Labor Problem in Jamaica, 1853–1856." *JNH* 25, no. 2 (April 1940): 216–35.

Smardz Frost, Karolyn. *I've Got a Home in Glory Land: A Lost Tale of The Underground Railroad*. Toronto: Thomas Allen Publishers, 2007.

Smith, T. Watson. *The Slave in Canada*. Collections of the Nova Scotia Historical Society, 1896–98, 10 (1899): 1–161.

Smy, William A. *An Annotated Nominal Roll of Butler's Rangers 1777–1784 with Documentary Sources*. Welland, Ont.: Friends of the Loyalist Collection at Brock University, 2004.

Spangler, Earl. *The Negro in Minnesota*. Minneapolis, Minn.: T.S. Denison & Co., 1961.

Squires, W. Austin. *The 104th Regiment of Foot (The New Brunswick Regiment) 1803–1817*. Fredericton, NB: Brunswick Press, 1962.

Stampp, Kenneth M. *The Peculiar Institution: Slavery in the Ante-Bellum South*. New York: Alfred A. Knopf, 1956.

Stanley, G.F.G. "Allan Maclean." *DCB* 4: 503–4.

Stanley, Susan M. "The Montrealer who helped free the Amistad slaves." *Gazette*, 4 January 1998, C3.

Stark, James H. *The Loyalists of Massachusetts and the Other Side of the American Revolution*. Boston: James H. Stark, 1910.

Stenberg, Richard K. "An Unknown Factor? : The Role of African-Americans at Fort Union." *Museum of the Fur Trade Quarterly* 43, no. 3–4 (fall–winter 2007): 64–8.

Stewart, L. Lloyd. *A Far Cry From Freedom: Gradual Abolition (1799–1827) – New York State's Crime Against Humanity*. Bloomington, Ind.: Author House, 2006.

Stewart, Victoria M., ed. *The Loyalists of Quebec, 1774–1825: A Forgotten History*. Montreal: Price-Patterson Ltd., 1989.

Stier, Wendela F. "Chief Justice Sir James Monk, Monkville in Montreal, and some Related Neo-Palladian Revival Architecture in Early Lower Canada and Nova Scotia." Unpublished MA thesis, Concordia University, 1990.

Still, William. *The Underground Railroad*. Philadelphia: Porter and Coates, 1872. Reprint, New York: Arno Press / New York Times, 1968.

Stouffer, Allen P. *The Light of Nature and the Law of God: Antislavery in Ontario 1833–1877*. Montreal and Kingston: McGill-Queen's University Press, 1992.

Stowe, H. Beecher. *A Key to Uncle Tom's Cabin*. Boston: John P. Jewett & Co., 1853.

Sulte, Benjamin. *Histoire des Canadiens-français, 1608–1880*. 8 vols. Montreal: Wilson & Cie/Société de publication historique du Canada, 1882–84.

– "L'esclavage en Canada." *Revue canadienne* 61 (1911): 315–34.

Summers, Jack L., and René Chartrand. *Military Uniforms in Canada 1665–1970*. Ottawa: Canadian War Museum, Historical Publication no. 16, 1981.

Sutherland, S.R.J, P. Tousignant and M. Dionne-Tousignant, "Sir Frederick Haldimand." *DCB* 5: 887–904.

Talman, James J. *Loyalist Narratives from Upper Canada.* Toronto: Champlain Society, 1946.

Tappan, Lewis. *The Life of Arthur Tappan.* New York: Hurd and Houghton, 1871. Reprint, Westport, Conn.: Negro Universities Press, 1970.

– *Memoir of Mrs. Sarah Tappan Taken in Part From the Home Missionary Magazine of November 1828, and Printed for Distribution Among Her Descendants.* New York: West & Trow, printers, 1834.

Thompson, George A. Jr. *A Documentary History of the African Theatre.* Evanston, Ill.: Northwestern University Press, 1998.

Thomson, Colin A. *Blacks in Deep Snow: Black Pioneers in Canada.* Don Mills, Ont.: J.M. Dent & Sons, 1979.

Trudel, Marcel. *Deux siècles d'esclavage au Québec.* Montreal: Hurtubise HMH, 2004.

– *Dictionnaire des Esclaves et de leurs Propriétaires au Canada Français.* 2nd ed. Montreal: Hurtubise HMH, 1994.

– *L'Esclavage au Canada français.* Quebec: Presses Universitaires Laval, 1960.

– *Mythes et réalités dans l'histoire du Québec.* Montreal: Hurtubise HMH, 2001.

Turcotte, Gustave. *Le Conseil Législatif de Québec 1774–1933.* Beauceville, Que.: L'Éclaireur, 1933.

Turner, Wesley B. "Thomas Rolph." *DCB* 8: 764–5.

U.E. Loyalist Centennial Committee. *The Centennial of the Settlement of Upper Canada by the United Empire Loyalists, 1784–1884.* Toronto: Hunter and Rose, 1885.

Upton, L.F.S. *The Loyal Whig: William Smith of New York & Quebec.* Toronto: University of Toronto Press, 1969.

Van Cleve, George. "Somerset's Case and Its Antecedents in Imperial Perspective." *Law and History Review* 24, no. 3 (Fall 2006): 601–45.

Viau, Roland. *Ceux de Nigger Rock: Enquête sur un cas d'esclavage des Noirs dans le Québec ancien.* Montreal: Libre Expression, 2003.

Viger, Jacques. *Règne militaire en Canada, ou administration judiciaire de ce pays par les Anglais du 8 septembre 1760 au 10 août 1764.* Montreal: Mémoires de la Société historique de Montréal, no. 5, La Minerve, 1870.

Viger, Jacques and L.H. LaFontaine. *De l'Esclavage en Canada.* Montreal: Mémoires et documents relatifs à l'histoire du Canada, nos 1 and 2, La Société historique de Montréal, 1859.

Von Frank, Albert J. *The Trials of Anthony Burns: Freedom and Slavery in Emerson's Boston.* Cambridge, Mass.: Harvard University Press, 1998.

Walker, Charles I. "The Northwest during the Revolution." *Michigan Pioneer Collections* 3 (1903): 12–36.

Walker, David, *David Walker's Appeal To the Coloured Citizens of the World, but in particular, and very expressly, to those of the United States of America.* 3rd and final edition of 1830. Baltimore: Black Classic Press, 1993.

Walker, J.W. St. G. *A History of Blacks in Canada: A Study Guide.* Hull, Que.: Minister of State for Multiculturalism, 1980.

Wallot, J.-P. *Intrigues françaises et américaines au Canada 1800–1802.* Montreal: Éditions Leméac, 1965.

Ward, Samuel R. *Autobiography of a Fugitive Negro: His Anti-Slavery Labours in the United States, Canada, & England.* London: John Snow, 1855.

Watson, Winslow C. *Pioneer History of the Champlain Valley; Being An Account of the Settlement of the Town of Willsborough by William Gilliland, Together with His Journal and Other Papers, and a Memoir, and Historical and Illustrative Notes.* Albany, NY: J. Munsell, 1863.

Wayne, Michael. "The Black Population of Canada West on the Eve of the American Civil War: A Reassessment Based on the Manuscript Census of 1861." In *A Nation of Immigrants: Women, Workers, and Communities in Canadian History, 1840s–1960s,* edited by Franca Iacovetta. Toronto: University of Toronto Press, 1998.

Weaver, John C. "Paola Brown." *DCB* 8: 105.

White, John. "The Diary of John White." Edited by William Colgate. *Ontario History* 47 no. 4 (1955): 147–70.

White, Shane. *Somewhat More Independent: The End of Slavery in New York City, 1770–1810.* Athens, Ga.: University of Georgia Press, 1991.

– *Stories of Freedom in Black New York.* Cambridge, Mass.: Harvard University Press, 2002.

Wiecek, William M. *The Sources of Antislavery Constitutionalism in America, 1760–1848.* Ithaca, NY: Cornell University Press, 1977.

Williams, Dorothy W. *Blacks in Montreal 1628–1986: An Urban Demography.* Cowansville, Que.: Les Éditions Yvon Blais, 1989.

– *The Road to Now: A History of Blacks in Montreal.* Montreal: Véhicule Press, 1997.

Wilson, Ellen Gibson. *The Loyal Blacks.* New York: Capricorn Books / G.P. Putnam's Sons, 1976.

Wilson, G.H. "The Application of Steam to St Lawrence Valley Navigation, 1809–1840." Unpublished MA thesis, McGill University, 1961.

Winks, Robin W. *The Blacks in Canada; A History.* 2nd ed. Montreal and Kingston: McGill-Queen's University Press, 1997.

Wise, Steven M. *Though the Heavens May Fall: The Landmark Trial That Led to the End of Human Slavery.* Cambridge, Mass.: Merloyd Lawrence/Da Capo, 2005.

Wyatt-Brown, B. *Lewis Tappan and the Evangelical War Against Slavery.* Cleveland, Ohio: The Press of Case Western Reserve University, 1969.

Yeigh, Frank. *Ontario's Parliament Buildings; or, A Century of Legislation, 1792–1892.* Toronto: Williamson Book Co., 1893.

Young, A.H., editor. *The Parish Register of Kingston, Upper Canada, 1785–1811.* Kingston, Ont.: British Whig Publishing Co., 1921.

INFORMATION ON ILLUSTRATIONS

Daniel Jones' monument, Oakland Cemetery, Brockville, Ont. Author's photograph | 5
For sale: a boy. *Quebec Gazette*, 18 June 1767 | 16
Map of Montreal in 1761. BANQ, G/3454/M65S1/1914/G67 CAR | 19
Market Place, Montreal, 1790, by Paul Sandby, attributed to George Heriot.
   LAC, C-151295 | 21
Judge James Reid. Pierre-George Roy, *Les juges de la province de Québec* | 25
Judge Samuel Gale. McCord Museum. I-1835.1 | 25
Judge William Badgley. McCord Museum. II-42658.7 | 25
Governor-General Michaëlle Jean and Montreal Mayor Gérald Tremblay before plaque
   honouring the slave Marie Joseph Angélique. Archives de la Ville de Montréal.
   VM94-0604071000-img0024 | 37
Excerpt from a report by the merchants and magistrates of Montreal urging an end to slave
   imports. LAC, RG14 A1, Records of the Legislative Council of Quebec to 1791, 4, File
   1786–1787, Reports on police & Commerce, "Report – Merchants of Montreal on
   Commerce and Police, 23 January 1787," 29 | 42
Adam Mabane. Pierre-George Roy, *Les juges de la province de Québec*, 328 | 42
Adam Mabane's abolition bill, 1787. LAC, RG4 B6, Legislative Council records, ordinances
   and working papers, 18, File 1787 | 43
Place d'Armes, 1829, watercolour by James Pattison Cockburn. LAC, C-150711 | 57
Judge James Monk, miniature, artist unknown. McCord Museum. M22340 | 61
Montreal in 1803. Bosworth, *Hochelaga Depicta*, 1839 | 83
James McGill, miniature by William Berczy, ca 1805–1811. McCord Museum. M1150 | 86
Marguerite Boucher de Boucherville, artist unknown. McCord Museum. M22337 | 90

Luc de Lacorne St-Luc, miniature, artist unknown. McCord Museum. M22334 | 93

Cachenoga [Caughnawaga] Indians, by Dudley Baxter, 1818. Musée national des beaux-arts du Québec, Quebec. 56.176 | 102

Various notices concerning slave sales and fugitives (*Quebec Herald*, 9 February 1789; *Quebec Gazette*, 9 February 1767; *Quebec Gazette*, 27 October 1768; *Quebec Herald*, 4 November 1790; *Quebec Herald*, 14 December 1789) | 104–5

"The land of the free & the home of the brave." Slave market, Charleston, SC, 4 March 1833. Sketch by Captain Henry Byam Martin. LAC, C-115001 | 109

Hôtel-Dieu, Montreal, 1829, by James Pattison Cockburn. LAC, C-150712 | 111

Front page of *Quebec Herald*, 22 April 1790 | 113

Marguerite de Lacorne St-Luc, ca 1790, artist unknown. McCord Museum. M 22338 | 134

Portrait d'une négresse, ca 1786, by François Malepart de Beaucourt. McCord Museum. M 12067 | 141

Caesar Johonnot's lot, 1797. Université de Montréal, division des Archives, Collection Louis François Georges Baby, P0058/C3, 170 | 145

Plan of the City of Montreal, 1823 [detail], by A. Bourne and C. Robinson. BANQ, G/3454/M65/1823/R63 CAR | 146

Montreal, Quebec Gate, ca 1793, watercolour by George Heriot. National Gallery of Canada. No. 16676. Photo © National Gallery of Canada | 148

Artist's sketch of William Wright's house, 1820. Courtesy of Robert Lemire | 151

American Presbyterian Church. Bosworth, *Hochelaga Depicta*, 1839 | 165

Horace Dickinson's McGill Street property 1824–26. BANQ, notary L. Huguet-Latour, no. 1851, 30 March 1824 | 166

Black waiter on *British America*, 1838, by James Hope-Wallace. LAC, C-150585 | 166

View of Montreal from St Helen's Island, 1830, by Robert Auchmuty Sproule. LAC, C-002642 | 171

Steam Boat Wharf, Montreal, ca 1837, by James Duncan. LAC, C-041069 | 173

Paddleboat, 1818, by Dudley Baxter. Musée national des beaux-arts du Québec, Quebec, 56.177 | 181

"Portrait: William Wright, MD, LRCS, Professor of Materia Medica," 1928 copy of a photograph taken ca 1850s when he was a young man. McGill University Archives, Photo Collection, PR008103 | 187

Dr William Wright, photograph taken in the 1870s or 1880s. McCord Museum. II-63408 | 187

Wright family grave in Mount Royal Cemetery, Montreal. Ann Carroll | 188

Minuets of the Canadians, by George Heriot, 1807. LAC, C-252 | 190

Notice of the flight of the slave Lowcanes. *Quebec Gazette*, 30 November 1775 | 190

Table d'hôte in the Catskills, 1838, by Katherine Jane Ellice. LAC, C-013388 | 193

George Bonga, 1870, photograph by Charles A. Zimmerman. Minnesota Historical Society, negative 94486 | 200

Stephen Bonga, ca 1870, photograph by William D. Baldwin. Minnesota Historical Society, negative 93216 | 201

INFORMATION ON ILLUSTRATIONS 579

Pioneer of 104th (New Brunswick) Regiment, by R.J. Marrion. Beaverbrook Collection of War Art, Canadian War Museum. CWM95-06383 | 204

Black drummer of the 7th Regiment of Foot (Royal Fusiliers) in 1787, copied by Lucien Rousselot in 1954 from a manuscript in the Cabinet des Estampes, Bibliothèque Nationale, Paris. Anne S.K. Brown Military Collection, Brown University, Providence, RI | 205

Canadian voyageurs walking a canoe up a rapid. Currier & Ives print after W. H. Bartlett. LAC, C-008373 | 216

Election scene, by Joseph Légaré. Musée de la civilisation du Québec, Collection du Séminaire de Québec, no. 1991.79. Photo by Pierre Soulard | 220

Capture of Navy Island, 1838 [detail], anonymous American caricature. McCord Museum, P195, A/2-22.1 | 225

Ste-Anne Market. Bosworth, *Hochelaga Depicta*, 1839 | 230

Map of Montreal, 1834 [detail], by André Jobin. BANQ, G/3454/M65/1834/J63 CAR | 233

The Montreal Jail. Borthwick, *From Darkness to Light: History of the Eight Prisons Which Have Been, or Are Now, in Montreal* | 244

[two images] "Looking south[west] from the citadel, Montreal, Lower Canada," 1824. Artist unknown. LAC, William H. Coverdale Collection, C-40084 and C-40092 | 256

The courthouse. Bosworth, *Hochelaga Depicta*, 1839 | 261

"A real scene in Montreal," by Henry Alken. LAC, C-987 | 267

Marguerite Eulalie Thompson and son Maxime Clément around 1890. Courtesy of Patricia Clement Wood | 282

Sir Charles Metcalfe opening parliament in Montreal, 1845, by Andrew Morris. LAC, C-000315 | 298

The Burning of Parliament in Montreal, 1849, by Joseph Légaré. McCord Museum, M11588 | 299

Dwight P. Janes. McCord Museum, I-35214.1 | 303

Notice of the flight of Joseph Negrié. *Quebec Gazette*, 20 July 1769 | 311

Sir John Johnson, artist unknown. McCord Museum, M17590 | 383

Notice of the flight of the slave Nero. *Quebec Gazette*, 4 October 1781 | 396

INDEX

A separate index of slaves follows.

Abdella, Jacob, 37, 140, 151, 158, 161, 162, 175–6, 177, 178, 191, 227–8, 232–3, 234–4, 275–6, 288, 429n3; his family, 151, 158, 275, 467n18
Accommodation. See Steamboats
Africa, 9, 59, 64, 74, 79, 106, 112, 113, 224, 229, 293–4, 309, 319, 320, 321, 322, 328, 361, 367
African Theatre, 189–91, 344
Ainsse, Joseph Louis, 60–2
Albany (NY), 55, 80, 81, 118, 185, 191, 201, 254, 323, 326, 402, 403, 404, 405
Alex, Pierre, 192
Allen, Levi, 405, 457n20
Allen, Sarah, 142
Allicocke, Christopher Kilby, 540n57
American Presbyterian Church, 39, 164–5, 175, 260, 294, 302–3
Amistad case (US), 302–3
Anderson, Joseph, 404–5
Anderson, Samuel, 384, 389, 402
Annexation movement, 226, 503n21

Antonio (*Amistad* slave), 302
Arakwente, Thomas, 137
Archambeau, Jean, 88–9, 92
Argenteuil, 248–50, 341, 470n50
Arnoldi, Daniel, 156, 260–5, 301, 413
Arnoldi, George Dorland, 156, 476n112
Arthur, Sir George, 300
Askin, John, 535n33
Ashley, Ann, 100, 173–4, 288, 433n37, 445n3, 473n80
Ashley, Elizabeth, 99, 157–8, 172, 454n97, 479n24,
Ashley, Margaret, 99–100, 172
Ashley, Moses, 176, 479n13
Ashley, Thomas, 100, 174, 175–6, 479n13
Aylmer, Matthew Whitworth–Aylmer, Lord, 253

Baby, François, 128
Badgley, Francis, 65, 439n101
Badgley, James, 446n8
Badgley, William, 24–5, 27–35, 51, 60, 76, 218, 439n101
Bagnell, Phillis, 517n1

Bahamas, 58, 426n54, 429n8,
Baird, Edward, 211, 288
Balis, James, 114
Ballston (NY), 97, 126, 378, 384–5, 388, 394–5, 549n41
Baltimore (Md.), 205, 302, 456n3
Banks, Jarrad, 37, 428n3, 504n36
Barbados, 158, 173, 174, 192, 232, 302, 429n8
Barber-hairdressers, 23, 36, 119, 161, 173, 183, 185, 191–4, 227, 232, 268–9, 281, 283, 334, 344, 414, 471n50
Barney, Joseph, 54, 406
Baudin, Victor, 101, 460n42
Bay of Quinte (Ont.), 142, 202, 272, 501n11
Beatson, Patrick, 55
Beaubain, Charles, 404
Beaubin, Mr, 402
Beaucourt, François Malepart de, 72, 140–1, 168, 275
Beauport, 74, 125, 207, 213, 278, 457n11
Becket, Peter, 143–4, 149, 157, 202; his family, 271, 279
Becket, William, 271, 279
Beek, John Gerbrand, 132, 404–6, 551n74
Beleau, Anthony, 243–4
Bell, Mathew, 162
Bellecour, François Deruisseau *dit*, 540n57
Bellet, François Jr, 111
Berlinguet, Joseph, 20–1, 24, 119
Bermuda, 58, 158, 174, 250, 254, 297, 303, 429n8
Berthelet, Nicolas, 55–6, 403
Berthelet, Olivier, 228, 503n21, 512n56
Berthelet, Pierre, 56, 62, 444n137, 504n29
Berthelot, Adrien, 454n95
Berthelot, Jean-Baptiste, 491n72
Berthier (Berthierville), 40, 114, 189, 204, 206, 218, 255, 258, 280, 282, 293, 308, 334, 420n8, 439n98, 457n20, 540n58,
Best, Jacob, 490n63
Bibb, Henry, 181–2
Binks, George, 157, 251

Blais, Desanges, 280, 282
Blake, Charles, 49, 53, 405, 427n54
Blaney, Mary, 49, 378
Blondeau, Angélique, widow Cotté, 152
Blondeau, Maurice, 431n25
Bonga, Blanche, 198–9
Bonga, Étienne (son of Pierre), 198–9, 201
Bonga, George, 198–200, 492n79
Bonga, Jean-Baptiste, 198–9
Bordwine, Charles, 537n44
Boston (Mass.), 9, 26, 97, 122, 145, 185, 206, 211, 224, 435n57, 444n140, 456n3, 470n50, 538n45
Boston, Robert, 194–5, 491n73
Boston, Robert Hunter, 194
Boucher de Boucherville, Louise Charlotte, 536n39, 538n48
Boucher de Boucherville, Marguerite, 55, 88, 90–1, 135
Boucher de Laperrière, François, 137
Boucher de Niverville, Joseph, 253
Boucherville, 53, 137, 537n42
Bouchette, Jean-Baptiste, 22, 539n54
Bouchette, Joseph, 21, 207
Bouchette, Marie Angélique, 22–4
Bouchette, Robert Shore Milnes, 22, 35, 345, 347, 350, 353
Bourassa, Ignace, 110
Bourne, George, 39–40, 68
Bowen, Edward, 253, 288
Bowen, William, 390
Brennan, Patrick, 232, 409
Brewster, Cyrus, 409, 411, 413, 414
Brewster, William, 409–10, 413–4
Bristow, David, 192, 276, 302
British Columbia, 11, 491n68, 524n16
British Conquest, 6–7, 16, 30, 33, 66, 127, 218, 270, 351,
British Indian Department, 7, 20, 24, 55, 60, 110, 200, 382, 385, 387, 397, 402, 450n54
Brockville, Ont., 5, 55, 144, 275, 403, 447n15
Brooks, John (Montreal), 119, 535n33

Brooks, John (Quebec), 326
Brooks, Thomas (Montreal), 302, 515n88
Brooks, Thomas (Quebec), 517n1
Broome, John, 37, 158, 160, 174, 177, 232, 234–5, 296, 300, 304
Broome, Sarah, 174, 303, 480n37
Brown, Archibald, 14
Brown, Paola, 180, 231
Brown, Sarah, 196
Brown, Thomas Storrow, 168–9, 178, 182
Brown, William Alexander, 189–91
Bruce, John, 161
Butler, John, 383, 390, 398, 400, 401
Butler's Rangers, 143, 382, 383, 384, 389, 390, 400, 401
Byrne, Philip, 77, 110, 203, 548n34
Byrne, William, 77, 110, 203, 548n34
Bytown (Ottawa), 172, 174, 192

Cady, Elijah, 405
Caesar, Hannah, widow Morris Emery, 221
Cairns, Mary, 439n98
Cameron & McMillan, 202
Campbell, Alexander, 402
Campbell, John, 20, 55, 73, 87–95, 101, 118, 122, 135, 184, 296, 384, 386–7, 402
Campbell, Margaret, 197, 278, 284–9
Campbell, Mary. *See* Mary Fundy.
Campbell, Private Skr., 460n40
Campbell, William, 405
Campeau, Joseph, 55–6, 90, 135
Campion, Étienne, 17, 73, 422n8
Canada Steamboat and Mail Coach Co., 178, 179
Canadian Courant & Montreal Advertiser, 313
Canniff, William, 71
Canon, Peter, 197, 198; his family, 279, 491n71
Capitulation of 1760, 24, 63, 121, 346–7, 348, 352, 355, 356, 368–372, 374, 380, 425n36, 441n123, 463n63
Carbry, Daniel, 119

Carleton Island (NY), 308, 323, 501n111
Carmel, Magdeleine, 84, 195
Caroline (servant), 211
Carpenter, James, 162, 283, 302
Cartier, Sir George-Étienne, 154, 293
Cartier, Jacques, 154, 293
Cartier, Marie Geneviève, 154
Catin, Thérèse, 30–1
Caughnawaga. *See* Kahnawake.
Cerré, Gabriel, 17–8, 23, 552n87
Cerré, Marie-Anne, 18, 490n61
Cerré, Paschal Léon, 18, 32, 241
Cerré, Thérèse, 17
Cesar (free black man), 97
Chaboillez, Adélaïde, 21–3
Chaboillez, Charles, 21–2, 118
Chaboillez, Louis, 72, 153
Chaboillez, Marie-Marguerite, 118
Chambers, Reuben, 248–50, 255
Chambly, 77, 128, 280, 383, 394
Charland, Louis, 155
Charlotte (Missouri slave), 17, 345, 357
Chase, Walter, 272
Chatfield, Cornelius, 211
Chaussegros de Léry, Gaspard, 45
Chauveau, Pierre-Joseph-Olivier, 179–80, 182, 277
Cherrier, Perrine, 155
Cholera, 173, 174, 228, 274, 283, 288, 495n101
Chouteau, Auguste, 17–8, 32
Chouteau, Gabriel Sylvestre, 17, 19–22, 34–5
Chouteau, Louis (Missouri slave), 17
Christie, Gabriel, 73, 87, 117–8, 137, 285, 315, 449n35
Christmas, Joseph Stibbs, 39–40
Clark, George, 196, 273
Clark, Isaac Winslow, 168
Clark, Simon, 159, 274
Clark, William, 208, 274
Clarke, Henry, 205
Claus, Daniel, 20, 118, 76–80, 87–8, 89, 398

Clément, Félix, 280, 282
Clinton, Sir Henry, 386
Closs, John, 495n103
Cockburn, Thomas, 184, 188–9, 202, 206–7, 222–3, 236, 284, 300, 301, 304, 490n60, 541n60
Code noir, 24, 40, 360, 362–3, 375
Coffin, Marie Catherine Eulalie, 162, 281
Coffin, Paul, 162, 281
Cohran, Colonel, 61
Cole, Peter, 495n103
Collins, William, 251–2, 254–5
Colombeau, Joseph, 197
Committee of merchants and magistrates (1787), 44–5, 51
Community forming, 38, 157, 158, 175, 176, 226–7, 235, 291, 292–4. *See also* Betsy Freeman
Congregation of Notre Dame, 110
Connecticut, 55, 97, 272, 289, 302, 481n42
Constitutional Act (1791), 12, 30, 66, 218–9, 350, 377
Consultation Committee of Coloured People of Montreal, 235
Conway, Bridget, 281
Conyn, John, 384–5, 387, 400–1
Conyngham, Williams, 340
Cook, George, 47, 79–80
Cook, Jane, 47–8, 55, 79–80, 99, 119, 140
Cooks, 17, 23, 84, 100, 157, 165, 167, 168–9, 172–8, 184, 185, 191–2, 199, 206, 208, 210, 213, 215–17, 254, 280, 301, 317, 320, 327, 332, 333, 336, 337
Coopers, 275, 279, 399
Cornwall, Ont., 50, 147, 179, 340, 548n31
Corps of Canadian Voltigeurs, 195, 206–8
Corrigan, Bartholomew, 272
Côte-St-Antoine (Westmount), 119, 144
Côte-Ste-Catherine (Outremont), 148–9, 197
Coteau-du-Lac, 189, 257, 340, 391, 398–401
Coudrin, Marie Félicité, 473n80, 488n36
Coudrin, Narcisse, 155, 192, 211, 267–8
Coursol, Charles J., 14
Covell, Simeon, 320

Craig, John, 410, 414
Cramahé, Hector-Theophilus, 28, 535n32
Crane, George, 144, 194
Crawford, Glasgow, 199–200
Crofton, James, 315
Croni, James, 192
Cross, John, 177
Crowell, Catharine, 192, 273–4
Crozier, George, 208
Cuba, 240, 302, 382, 464n65
Cuisy, Marguerite, 154
Curatteau, Jean Baptiste, 110
Curtin, Caroline, 302
Curtin, John, 302
Curtis, Isaac, and family 196
Cuthbert, James Jr, 64–6
Cuthbert, James Sr, 439n98

Dago, Peter, 37, 157–8, 175–6, 186–8, 222–3, 235, 255, 287, 295, 302–3, 493n82, 495n104, 515n88; his family, 283
D'Ailleboust (seigneury), 189, 195, 293
Dalhousie, George Ramsay, Lord, 250
Dalton, Piers, 178
D'Aubreville, Emmanuel, 186–8, 206, 250, 286
David, David, 130–3
David Smith & Co., 64
Davidson, Arthur, 152–4, 156
Day, Charles Dewey, 262, 264–5
Day, Nadine, 157, 283
De Bleury, Clément-Charles Sabrevois, 228, 484n8
De Bonne, Pierre Amable, 66, 405, 426n53
De Gaspé, Philippe Aubert, 74, 137, 240–2
De Hertel, Daniel, 250
De Labruère de Boucherville, Charles, 491n72
De Longueuil, Marie Anne Catherine Fleury Deschambault, dowager baroness, 122, 456n1
De Longueuil, Marie Charles Joseph Le Moyne de Longueuil, baroness, 424n30
De Lorimier, Guillaume Chevalier, 397

De Lotbinière, Michel Eustache Gaspard Alain Chartier, 65, 72, 137, 139, 278
De St Remy, E.L., 226
De Salaberry, Charles-Michel d'Irumberry, 195, 517n1
Dease, John, 60–2
Dejean, Philippe, 240
DeLancey, Stephen, 403
Delezenne, Ignace, 271
Delisle, Alexandre Maurice, 409, 413
Delisle, Benjamin, 261–3, 409, 412–3,
Delisle, David Chabrand, 110, 384, 388
Deniger, Fleurie, 8–9, 149, 158–62, 277, 278, 281, 283; her parents, 281; stepfather, 160
Denoyer, Marie, 271, 279
Descary, Paul, 150, 541n60
Deseronto, John, 385
Desrivières, François, 74
Desrivières, Joseph Amable Trottier *dit,* 449n29
Desrivières Beaubien, Eutache Ignace Trottier *dit,* 99
Desrosiers, Louis Deguire *dit,* 253–4
Detroit, 55–6, 61, 90, 96, 101, 106, 110, 202, 240, 309, 329, 370, 446n8, 460n42, 493n90, 535n33, 540n57
DeWitt, Jabez Dean, 273
DeWitt, Jacob, 150, 525n23
Diah (fugitive NY slave), 31, 32, 53–4, 97
Dickinson, Horace, 165–6, 289
Dickinson, James Taylor, 289
Didier, Pierre Joseph, 17
Diller, Scholastique, 283, 303
Dillon, Richard, 57, 119
Dolphin, John, 194–5, 202, 206, 257–8
Domestic service, 19–20, 77, 101, 117, 118, 124, 136, 152, 167, 168, 183, 184, 185, 198, 202, 208, 210–1, 246, 258, 266, 271, 272, 273
"Donnés," 123, 530n7
Donnellan, John, 228–9, 232
Donnellan, Mary, 343, 469n31
Door, John, 272

Dorchester, Guy Carleton, Lord, 41, 138, 247, 468n29, 539n54
Doty, John, 110, 253, 446n8
Douglas, Sir James, 491n68
Dowling, William, 197–8, 453n85
Downing, Mary, 158
Dred Scott case (US), 17
Drummond, James, 430n17
Drummond, Mary Ann, 156–8, 160, 172, 210, 228, 300
Dubois, Étienne Sr, 459n37
Dublin (American captive), 97
Dubreuil, Josephe, 279–80
Dubuque, Augustin, 128, 547n20
Ducalvet, Pierre, 311–2
Dufaux, Joseph, 114–5
Dufort, Antoine Badel *dit,* 145, 197
Dufour, Louis, 281, 474n85
Dufresne, Romain, 18
Dumignault, Pierre, 23
Dumoulin, François, 426n52
Dunlop, James, 72, 140, 150–1
Dunn, Thomas, 128, 431n18, 461n50,
Dunoyer, François, 139–40
Dunscomb, John William, 297–300
Durang, John, 295–6
Duvernay, Ludger, 264–5
Dwight, James Adams, 252, 260, 262–3, 409–15
Dyers and scourers, 36, 188, 192, 228, 283

Edwards, Abraham, 242
8th (King's) Regt., 195, 202, 257–8, 280, 394, 515n86
84th (Royal Highland Emigrants) Regt., 142, 144, 402, 424n30
Elections: Bedford County, 219–23; at Berthier (Warwick County), 206; Montreal, 227–35; Montreal County, 159, 227, 234
Elliot, William, 39, 430n16
Ellis, Robert, 287–8
Emery, Morris, 189, 221; his family, 486n21
Emigration schemes, 9, 297–300, 528n54

English, Thomas Brown, 176, 232
Ennuel, Joseph, 290–1
Ennuel, Magdelaine, 290–1
Entrepreneurship, 162–3, 184–5
Ermatinger, Frederick William, 243, 249
Etherington, Thomas, 338
Eve (servant), 211, 339–40

Falkner, Charles, 115, 205
Farley, Cecilia (Celia), 193, 260, 268, 269, 302, 552n8
Farmers, 194–6, 220, 272, 275, 280, 282
Fearson, Marie, 155
Feeler, Mary, 206
Feeler, Nancy, 212
Feeler, William, 206, 212, 222–3, 234, 255–7, 453n85, 473n80, 496n106, 514n83, 541n60
Ferguson, John, 316
Feron, Nancy, 302
Ferris, Mary Ann, 269–70, 281, 283
Fidler, Thomas, 196
Field, Benjamin, 243–5, 251, 255, 259
Field, Joseph, 243
Field, Mary, 243–4
53rd Regt., 130, 385
Filteau, Joseph, 110, 123
Finlay, Hugh, 44
Finlay, James, 53, 320, 435n63; Finlay & Gregory, 320
Firmin, Manuel, 251–5
Fisher, Donald, 30, 50–3, 378
Fisher, Elizabeth (Mrs), 50–3, 378
Fisher, Finlay, 51–3, 54, 65, 142–3
Fleming, John (son of slave John Fleming), 84
Fleming, John (soldier), 81
Fleming, Mary (Mrs), 81
Fleming, Moses Alexander, 84
Fleming, Thomas, 84
Fleming, William, 80, 82, 84–5
Fleury de la Gorgendière, Marie Thomas, 311
Florida, 29, 129, 168–9, 178, 182
Fonda, Adam, 389, 391, 402

Fonda, Jelles, 389, 391, 401, 403
Fontaine, Michel, 19
Forrest, John, 178
Forsyth, Chloe, 131
Forsyth, George, 250
Forsyth, William, 149–50
Fortennéter, Geneviève, 155
Fortune, William, 120–1, 147
Fortune, William Brusler, 192, 273
Foucher, Louis-Charles, 22–4
Franchère, Gabriel, 140
Franchère, Gabriel Jr, 168
Franchère, Jean-Baptiste, 140
Franchère, Julie Victoire, 140
François, hangman at Louisbourg, 239
François, Jean, 158, 192
François, Joseph Jr, 85–6
François, Pierre Augustin, 85–6
Franklin, Elizabeth, 272, 491n73
Franklin, Mary Ann, 272
Franks, John, 93
Fraser, John, 73, 101, 491n76
Frazer, James, 49, 50, 56–9, 62–3, 69, 119
Freedom certificates, 8, 271, 420n8
Freeman, Betsy, 260–5, 294, 408–415.
Freeman, Joseph, 470n50
Freeman, Leonard, 157, 453n85, 479n24
Frobisher, Joseph, 423n27, 532n22
Fugitive Slave Act (US), 35, 180, 226, 276
Fullman, Elisha, 114, 406
Fur trade: abettor of slavery, 17, 21–2, 23, 24, 31, 45, 49–50, 54–5, 110, 111–12, 117, 128, 152, 196–7, 202, 457n16; black voyageurs, 18–9, 197–201, 212, 213–17, 301, 423n21, 490n68

Gabriel, Ace, 157, 268
Gaëtan, Benoîte, 140, 168
Gage, Thomas, 28, 141,
Gale, Samuel, 24–35, 40, 60, 76, 350–7, 408, 413, 428n73
Gallego, Peter, 226–7, 299
Gamelin, Pierre, 384
Gardeners, 184, 196

Garner, Ann, 195, 293, 490n61
Garneau, François-Xavier, 16
Garret, Henry, 202, 243, 248
Gaspar, Charles, and family, 279
Gaspard, John Baptiste, and family, 206
Gatien, Marie Josephte, 49–50
Gaudet, Dominique, 121–4, 133–4
Gauthier, Louis, 116, 119, 454n95, 540n59
Gelston, Ann, 260–4, 410–1
Gent, Joseph, 115
Gibb, Benaiah, 100, 115, 337, 541n65; Gibb & Prior, 337
Giles, Catharine, 195
Giles, Cubit, 194
Gill, William, 319
Gilliland, William, 318
Glossen, Warren, 157, 186–8, 222–3, 234, 248, 250–1, 255, 266, 287
Goffre, Joseph, 94
Goodrich, William, 173, 192, 489n51
Goodsell, Ephraim, 172
Gordon, Adam Ann, 151
Gordon, James, 126, 378, 385, 388, 394–5
Gordon, Robert, 193–4, 269
Gosford, Archibald Acheson, Lord, 254
Graham, Jane, 158, 243
Grant, Alexander, 3–4, 36–8, 76, 174, 176, 192, 228–35, 237, 260–5, 268–9, 283, 288, 291, 295, 296, 302, 344, 408–15
Grant, Charles William, 22–3, 149
Grant, David Alexander, 335, 424n30
Grant, Harry, 203
Grant, Jacob, 37 (and 429n3), 156, 158, 161, 172, 178, 210, 222, 228, 232, 235, 236, 300
Grant, James, 158, 248, 251
Grant, James Charles, 227, 248
Grant, John, 64, 137, 246,
Grant, William, 44, 316, 335, 426n53, 456n1
Grantham, James, 193, 269–70, 281, 283, 410, 415, 503n21
Gray, Edward William, 29, 81, 116, 130–4, 239–40, 245, 319, 341, 397–8, 509n31
Gray, Jonathan Abraham, 81, 116, 334

Gray, Ralph, 74–5, 213, 309, 324
Gregory, John, 23, 54, 152, 320, 388,
Green, Benjamin, 258, 488n36
Green, Edward, 272
Greene, Louis, 37
Griffin, Mary, 150,
Guadeloupe, 144, 444n139, 536n39
Guerout, Pierre, 55, 325
Gugy, Adélaïde Conradine, 534n27
Gugy, Conrad, 386, 534n27
Guichaux, Jacques, 123, 461n50
Guillimin, Charlotte, 74, 285, 446n3, 449n29
Guinea, 47, 79, 309, 318, 320, 362–3, 432n31, 454n100, 533n26, 539n50
Guthrie, Robert Maghlin, 328, 401
Guy, Louis, 153–4
Guy, Pierre, 127–8, 431n25

Hagar, Benjamin, 267
Haiti (St-Domingue), 6, 23, 37, 79, 100–1, 106, 121, 125, 140, 158, 192, 359, 360, 363, 530n9, 534n27, 539n55
Haldimand, Frederick, 60, 110, 128–9, 130, 239, 382–6, 395, 397–8, 401–3, 452n73, 463n63
Halifax (NS), 72, 119, 186, 188, 252, 284
Hall, Elias, 115
Hamilton, Henry, 240
Hangmen, 28, 237–45, 506n6
Hart, Benjamin, 130
Hay, Alexander, 93, 137, 469n32
Hays, Barrak, 116
Hayton, Amos, 130–3
Hazen, Moses, 318
Hébert, Joseph, 405
Henry, "nègre métis," 101
Henry, Alexander, the elder, 53, 436n63, 533n25
Henry, Alexander, the younger, 198
Henry, William, 339
Herkimer, Johan Joost, 394, 398–402
Herkimer's Batteau Company, 391, 398–402, 452n74

Hewit, Randal, 385
Hincks, Francis, 526n33
Hinksman, Anthony, 37, 287–8, 428n3
Hipps, George, 321
Hocquart, Gilles, 24, 32, 46, 63, 238–9, 346, 348, 354, 368
Holiday, Andrew, 204, 280
Holiday, Marie Louise, 280
Holmes, James, 137, 459n34
Hooffstetter, Charles Frederick, 151
Hôpital-Général (Montreal), 99, 145, 233, 273, 301, 302, 454n95, 469n31, 533n26
Hôpital-Général (Quebec), 424n30, 531n17
Hotel, restaurant and tavern workers, 49, 57, 116, 117, 119, 144, 167, 172, 175, 178, 180, 183, 184–5, 191, 193, 198, 254, 256–7, 266, 270, 301, 302, 340, 403, 443n129, 460n42, 543n71
Hôtel-Dieu (Montreal), 75, 82, 83, 88, 93, 110, 111, 126, 140, 150, 168, 177, 196, 198, 205, 233, 273, 284, 286, 293, 343, 405, 423n27, 424n31, 449n29, 450n42, 464n69, 468n28 and n29, 487n30, 505n48, 540n59, 542n65, 545n5
Hôtel-Dieu (Quebec), 22, 536n39, 537n43
Houldin, Marie Anne, 155, 204, 280
Houldin, Marie Euphrosine, 204; her family, 280–1, 494n101
Houldin, Richard and family, 203–4, 280
Houle, François, 197, 250–1, 255, 285–6, 289
Houle, Sophie, 286, 287
Howard, Joseph, 23, 117, 315
Howell, John, 385
Hoyle, Rosseter, 51, 333, 378
Hubbard, Benjamin, 528n52
Hubbard, Peter, 404–5, 406
Hudson's Bay Co., 11, 197, 199, 215, 301, 491n68, 492n79
Hughes, James (Indian Dept.), 200
Hughes, James (Town Major), 93
Hull, Henry, 405
Hungerford, Allan, 220

Hunkings, Caesar, 8, 115, 201, 280
Hunter, Mary Ann, 194
Huntingdon, 200
Hyers, John, 186, 211, 222–3, 234, 284
Hyers, Martha Curtis, 211–2, 300–1

Île Dupas, 40, 114
Île Jésus (Laval), 98, 110, 275, 281, 287, 474n85
Illinois, 19, 39, 49, 55, 61, 464n82, 492n79, 547n20
Indians, 7, 8, 9, 13, 19, 27, 32, 44, 56, 68, 80, 101, 102, 105, 106, 129, 197, 200, 219, 224, 237, 278, 346, 361, 364, 365, 366, 382, 383–4, 387–8, 394, 395, 402, 457n16. *See also* Mohawks, Panis
Integration, 159, 178, 235, 294–5

Jackson, Richard, 157, 185, 188–9, 212, 251, 301
Jackson, Robert, 158, 176, 233, 301
Jacobs, Marianne, 53, 537n42
Jacobs, Marie Geneviève, 53, 537n42
Jacobs, Mary (née Martin), 30, 50–3, 119, 143, 434n50, 531n12
Jacobs, Phillip, 53
Jacobs, Samuel, 53
Jacques, Jean, 101–2
Jamaica, 4, 26, 65, 86, 156, 322, 374, 429n8, 430n17. *See also* Emigration schemes
James (son of Elizabeth Franklin), 272
James, Hester, 175
Janes, Dwight Plimpton, 164–5, 302–3
Jay, Castor, 202–3, 206, 272
Jay's Treaty (1794), 56
Jean Jacques, 101–3
Jessup, Edward, 421n8, 441n121
Johnson, George, 477n1
Johnson, Henry (thief), 259
Johnson, Henry (fugitive Virginia slave), 487n33
Johnson, Jean-Baptiste, 272

Johnson, Sir John, 44–5, 60, 77, 87, 96, 110, 143–4, 203, 383–403, 437n84, 468n29, 541n63
Johnson, Mary Anna, 509n28
Johnson, Peter, 251
Johnson, Tobias, 272
Johnston, Eden, 53
Johonnot, Alexander, 252, 255, 285, 286–8
Johonnot, Caesar, 9, 97, 120–1, 145–7, 149, 150, 157, 184, 185, 197, 207, 250, 255, 278, 284–6, 289, 293, 295, 341, 494n96
Johonnot, Catherine, 197, 285–8
Johonnot, Gabriel, 207, 272–3, 285–6
Johonnot, Zachary, 9, 145
Joinville, Charlotte, 115
Joinville, Pierre Fafard *dit,* 40–1, 46, 114–15
Jolibois, Angélique Lavallée *dit,* 279, 474n85
Jones, Daniel, 5, 55, 113–14, 275, 403, 406–7, 443n129, 536n40
Jones, John, 275
Jones, Mary Violet, 155, 192, 211, 473n80
Jones, Robert, 146–7, 341, 437n84
Jones, Solomon, 275, 403, 441n121
Jordan, Jacob, 73, 384, 387, 426n53, 431n25, 547n20
Joseph (son of Elizabeth Franklin), 272
Joseph, Judah, 334
Juchereau Duchesnay, Antoine, 125, 426n53, 462n53
Judah, Samuel, 126–7, 130–4, 385–6, 388, 394
Jury duty, 34–5, 143, 231–2, 234, 236–7, 245, 263

Kadwell, Charles, 179–80, 182
Kahnawake, 91, 102, 137, 199–200, 283
Keeling, Maria, 84, 98, 478n5
Kelly, Mr (steamboat purser), 181–2
Kerr, James, 57, 63–4, 288
King's Royal Regiment of New York, 110, 120, 126, 143, 144, 274, 382, 383–4, 389–94, 397, 543n71

Kingston, Ont., 143, 165, 181, 442n125, 460n39 and n42, 497n120, 546n8, 548n33, 549n46
Kuhn, Jacob, 247, 335, 336, 338
Kurczyn, Nicholaus Peter Mathias, 150, 162

Labadie, Augustin, 152–6, 159, 168, 211, 280, 284
Labadie, Louis Jacques Augustin, 155, 280
"Labourers," 75, 100, 160, 168, 175, 176, 184, 189, 192, 199, 210, 222, 241, 242, 264
Lachine, 64, 87, 91, 101, 110, 121, 181, 251, 293, 384, 403, 406
Lacroix, Janvier Domptail, 22–3, 29, 59
Lacroix, Joseph–Hubert, 22
LaFontaine, Louis–Hippolyte, 10, 15, 34, 35
Lafortune, Brigitte, 300–1
L'Africain, François-Xavier, 155
Lagord, John, 40–1, 46, 114–6
Laisné, Marie Thérèse, 279, 432n28
Lake Champlain, 172, 181, 201, 239, 308, 318, 370, 483, 541n64,
Lake Ontario, 167, 179, 398
Lake Township. *See* Lancaster, Ont.
Lalanne, Léon, 221
L'Ami du peuple, 265
La Minerve, 264
Lamothe, Joseph, 110–11
Lamplighters, 186–8, 212, 222, 250
Lancaster, Ont., 144, 403
Langan, Patrick, 7, 126, 378, 384–6, 389, 394–5, 435n63
Lansingh, Phillip Peter, 120, 433n31
Lapensée, Jean Roy *dit,* 49
Lapierre, Marie, 210
Lapointe, Marie Josette Audet *dit,* 53
LaPrairie, 172, 290, 405
La Promenade, Marguerite Larchevêque *dit,* 21, 23, 73, 444n137
La Promenade, Paul Larchevêque *dit,* 100
Larivière, Pierre, 18
Larocque, François, 101, 426n53

Lasselle, Jacques, 56
L'Assomption, 95, 97–8, 101, 327, 402
Latour, François, 460n42
Latour, Louis Dufour *dit*, 460n42
Laval. *See* Île Jésus.
Le Compte Dupré, Georges Hyppolite, 20, 73, 426n53, 449n34
Le Favori (ship), 279
Le Noir, Gilles, 238
Les Anciens Canadiens, 74, 240
Les Cèdres, 87
Leake, Robert, 398
Leaycraft, Jeremiah, 297, 524n23
Lebrun, Isidore, 17, 35
Lee, Silvia, 202
Lée, Thomas, 111, 311
Lee, William, 202
Lees, John, 426n53
Lennox, Penelope, 273
Lepailleur, Charles, 404, 405
Lester, Robert, 120, 426n53, 460n41, 469n32
Levy, Baruch Berold, 211
Levy, Gershon, 31
Lewis, George, 202
L'hyvernois, Joseph Benoit *dit*, 114
Liberator, 224
Lincoln, Abraham, 17, 289
Lindsay, William, 65, 130–3
Literacy, 38, 143, 148, 168, 191, 196, 215, 267, 269, 274, 275
Lloyd, Catherine, 504n36
Loedel, Henry, 188, 547n20
Loignon, Marie Louise, 279
London, 14, 36, 38, 40, 133, 168, 199, 305
Longue-Pointe, 55, 88, 89, 92, 95, 270
Lorette, 252
Loubet, Philippe, 114, 545n5
Louis XIV, 27
Louisbourg, 238–9
Louisiana, 12, 14, 18, 24, 49, 359, 361–3, 368, 374, 375, 506n6
Love, Captain, 130–1

Low, Abraham, 37, 158, 176, 189, 207, 210, 212, 259, 301, 493n82, 515n88
Low, Jacob, 301, 497n120, 498n131, 505n47
Low, John, 301, 498n131
Low, Richard, 301
Loyalists, 5, 12, 28, 34, 44, 48, 49, 55, 57, 63, 66–7, 69, 73, 77, 87, 100, 110, 113, 117, 120, 140, 143–4, 150, 202, 224, 271, 274, 279, 325, 382–403, 406, 421n8, 433n31, 442n124, 445n148, 446n8, 447n15, 452n73, 490n63, 538n45, 539n52, 541n64, 543n71
Luke, Samuel Jr, 118
Lukin, Peter Sr, 147
Lusignan, Charles, 54
Lynd, David, 426n53, 538n44
Lyons, George, 62

M.A.J., "a woman of colour," 73, 296
Mabane, Adam, 40–6, 48, 60, 62, 65, 68, 69, 76, 78, 110, 542n70, 545n5, 547n20
Mabon, Andrew, 54, 406
McAdam, Hugh, 404–5, 406–7
McArty, Mary, 202, 284, 304
Macaulay, Zachary, 466n8
Macloude, Thomas, 198
Macomb, William, 61
McCord, John, 314, 318
McCord, Thomas, 51–2, 53, 129, 150, 202, 243, 259, 318, 343, 431n25, 469n32, 530n11
McEvoy, Martin, 114, 405–6
McFarlane, Peter, 54, 60, 100, 115, 122
McGill, James, 4–5, 23, 72, 74, 85–6, 112, 113, 120, 197, 285
McGill, Peter, 194, 213, 227
McGill University, 4, 24, 186
McGillivray, Simon Jr, 199
McGinn, George, 402
Mackenzie, Sir Alexander, 196, 197, 198
Mackenzie, James, 213–5
Mackenzie, Roderick, 198

INDEX 591

Mackenzie, William Lyon, 38, 224, 226, 228
McKillock, Duncan, 91
McKinstry, David, 405–6
Maclean, Allan, 130, 133, 378, 385–7, 394–5
McLeod, Archibald Norman, 199
McLeod, Marie, 253
McMurray, Thomas, 323, 336
McNeill, Archibald, 538n45
McNeill, Elizabeth (Mrs), 327–8, 538n45
McPherson, Alexander, 3, 268
McTavish, Simon, 118, 184, 197, 279;
   McTavish, Frobisher & Co., 198
Maisonville, Alexis Rivard *dit*, 61, 465n83, 540n57
Malhiot, François, 426n53
Mansfield, William Murray, Lord, 26, 48, 60, 117, 369, 371, 373
Marchesseau, Nicolas, 49–50
Marie Charlotte, daughter of Louis Antoine, 124, 293, 462n52
Marly, Michel, 19, 423n21
Marmora Iron Works (Ont.), 194, 213
Marriage: contracts, 139, 160–1, 487n36; interracial, 8–9, 14, 72, 125–6, 139, 159–60, 204, 266, 276–91, 303; slaves, 32, 84–5, 87–8, 122–4, 125–6
Martin, Jeanie, 284, 304
Martinique, 28, 139, 142, 238–9
Marvin, Ebenezer, 260
Marysburgh Township (Ont.), 143, 398
Maryland, 154, 181, 205, 210, 280, 302, 303, 315, 428n73, 456n3, 471n50
Massachusetts, 61, 106, 138, 209, 211, 376, 382, 481n42, 488n36, 526n45, 535n33.
   See also Boston
Masson, François, 285
Masson, Thérèse, 284
Mathews, Robert, 130, 384–6, 397–8, 401–3
Mathews, William, 116, 540n59
Maurepas, Jean Frédéric Phélypeaux, comte de, 238
Maurer, Jacob, 399, 401–2

Mayson, Catherine, 152–6, 158, 301, 302
Meads, Charles, 302
Medical Chronicle or Montreal Monthly Journal of Medicine & Surgery, 186
Meloche, Simon, 110–11
Melvin & Burns, 331
Ménard, Pierre, 19
Mesplet, Fleury, 6–7, 530n9
Metcalfe, Sir Charles Theophilus, 297–8
Meunier, Charlotte, 206, 495n104
Meyers, Moses, 84
Mézière, Pierre, 73, 405–6, 453n95,
Michaels, Myer, 117, 330
Michigan, 55, 56, 95, 492n79. *See also* Detroit, Michilimackinac
Michilimackinac, 17, 60–2, 106, 110, 142, 168, 197–8, 402
Michilimackinac Company, 198, 455n109
Middleton, Rubin, 143, 157, 255, 397–8, 403
Military: abettors of slavery, 24, 47, 49, 68, 80, 81, 91, 110, 111, 116, 119, 126, 142, 202, 382–401, 402, 424n30, 449n35, 515n86, 531n13, 541n64; black soldiers and militiamen, 101, 126, 130, 143–4, 195, 202–9, 212, 234, 237, 255, 257–9, 280, 397–8
Minnesota, 55, 198–200, 492n79
Mississippi River, 11, 17, 18, 19, 55, 167,
Missouri, 13, 15–18, 20, 34, 35, 39, 87, 241, 345, 443n136, 492n79. *See also* St Louis
Mittleberger, John, 119, 378, 388, 394–6
Mix, Samuel, 110, 116
Mohawks, 7, 102, 126, 137, 199, 283, 378, 383, 384–5, 388–90, 393–4, 397
Mohawk Valley (NY), 44, 87, 383, 398, 403, 546n8
Molliston, Solomon, 193, 281, 300
Molson, John, 167–8, 170, 172, 222–3. *See also* Steamboats, St Lawrence Steamboat Co.
Mompesson, John, 515n86
Mondina, Élisabeth, 125–6, 178, 457n11

Monk, James, 32, 48–9, 54, 57, 60–1, 71, 72, 75–6, 80, 247, 353, 379, 533n25
Montreal Distillery Co., 120, 184, 469n32
Montreal Gazette, 16, 40, 47, 228–32, 290–1, 312–3
Montreal General Hospital, 174, 485n11, 487n32, 511n46
Montreal Herald, 231, 290–1
Moore, Henry, 99, 148, 158, 186, 197, 469n42
Moore, Margaret, 161, 162
Moore, Robert, 158, 161–2, 176, 177
Moquin, Louis, 453n95
Moreau, Rose, 279
Morning Chronicle, 15, 35
Morrison, Charles, 61–2
Morrison, Diana, 445n3
Morrison, James, 75, 98
Moses, Dorcas, 206, 211
Moss, Jonathan, 274
Muir, Ebenezer, 164–5
Munro, John (Loyalist), 384, 395–7
Munro, John (Quebec merchant), 458n24
Murphy, William, 185, 188–9, 228, 301
Murray, General James, 28, 119, 316, 370, 371, 542n70
Murray, James, seigneur of Argenteuil, 426n54, 470n50
Murray, Patrick, seigneur of Argenteuil, 470n50, 543n73
Musicians, 189–90, 195, 212, 221, 257
Myers, Asenath, 168
Myers, Hyam, 53

Nafrechoux, Dominique, 270–1
Nairne, John, 93
Nation, William Meikins, 157, 250, 255
"Nation nègre," 101, 110, 209, 292–5
Negrié, Joseph, 311–2
Neilson, John, 312, 530n9
Neilson, Samuel, 312, 530n9
Nelson, Robert, 224, 227, 228, 257
Nelson, Wolfred, 224

New Brunswick, 11, 12, 201, 203–5, 280, 438n87 and n88
New Brunswick Regt. of Fencible Infantry (104th), 203–5, 280
New France, 7, 9, 11, 12, 16, 24–8, 32–3, 36, 46, 66, 97, 101, 121, 150, 238–9, 312, 345–80
New Hampshire, 8, 54, 114, 406
New Jersey, 32, 57, 243, 431n24, 439n98, 442n126
New Richmond, 308, 337
New York City, 22, 36, 53, 57, 63–4, 106, 116, 130, 168, 169, 179–80, 189–91, 193, 201, 209, 243, 289, 300, 325, 344, 379
New York State, 29, 44, 51, 55, 93, 100, 106, 114, 117, 120, 144, 178, 179, 180, 188, 200, 201, 207, 234, 239, 248, 260, 265, 281, 283, 295, 308, 309, 326, 381, 382, 384, 402, 404, 405, 406, 407, 545n1. *See also* Albany, Ballston, Mohawk Valley, New York City, Plattsburgh, Schenectady, Whitehall, Willsboro
Newfoundland, 11, 524n23
Newton, Isaac, 196, 222–3, 246–8, 252, 273
Newton, Amelia (Mrs), 511n46
Niagara, 143, 174, 179, 382, 383, 384, 390, 394, 395, 400, 401
Nigger Rock, 78, 98
Nixon, George, 193, 260, 262–3, 268, 408–415
Noël, James, 192
North Carolina, 13, 260, 262, 408
North West Co., 54, 118, 197, 198–201, 213–5,
Northrop, Moses, 273, 285
Northwest Ordinance (US), 55–6
Nova Scotia, 10, 11, 12, 48, 57, 58, 189, 243, 257, 299–300, 305, 376, 379, 438n87. *See also* Halifax
No. 4 African School, 164–6, 175, 191, 289, 302

O'Callaghan, Edmund Bailey, 264–5

Ogden, Isaac, 32, 57, 353, 379
Ogilvy, John, 208
Olivier, Louis, 114–15, 426n53
Ontario (Upper Canada, Canada West), 11–12, 29, 50–1, 63, 66, 73, 76, 87, 98, 106, 114, 143–4, 147, 167, 175, 176–7, 180, 194, 195, 201, 202, 205, 206, 213, 224, 275, 276–7, 297–300, 304–5.
O'Reilly, Caroline, 192
Orillat, Jean, 74, 318, 381
Oro Township (Ont.), 98, 205
Osgoode, William, 10, 67, 70–1
Ottawa River, 100, 121, 144, 147, 172, 195, 200, 202, 272
Ottawa Steamboat Co., 165

Panet, Jean Antoine, 16
Panet, Pierre, 293, 381, 464n69, 534n26
Panet, Pierre-Louis, 18, 32, 57, 65–6, 341, 439n101 and n103, 490n61, 534n26
Panis, 7, 21–2, 24, 27–8, 30, 34, 72, 87–8, 92, 94, 95–6, 98, 101, 110, 123, 238, 311, 346–7, 248, 351–2, 354–5, 357, 364–9, 370, 372, 374–5, 380, 427n63, 430n16,
Papineau, Joseph, 63–5, 114, 135
Papineau, Louis-Joseph, 223, 225, 227, 228, 232–3, 264
Parker, Alvin, 273
Parker, Charles, 273
Parker, Susannah, 273
Parker, Thomas, 198, 273
Parker, William, 273
Patten, John, 173–4, 177, 183, 192, 232, 234, 288, 488n44
Paul, Michel (Missouri slave), 17
Payant, Peter, 19
Payet, Louis, 72, 110–11, 154, 293
Peak, Samuel, 397
Pécaudy de Contrecoeur, Marie Charles, 137
Périnault, Joseph, 93, 431n25
Perkins, George William, 302, 481n42
Perkins, Hannah, 517n1
Perks, Thomas, 189, 257

Perras, Elizabeth, widow Cavilhe, 154
Perrault, Charles Ovide, 262, 264–5, 413
Perrault, Joseph François, 331
Perrault, Widow. *See* Louise Charlotte Boucher de Boucherville
Perry, Alexander, 57, 62–3
Perry, James, 438n88, 464n69
Perth (Ont.), 206
Petitions of Montreal slave-owners, 59, 63–64, 73, 80, 135
Petry, Frederick, 64
Philadelphia, (Pa.), 23, 61, 130–1, 134, 143, 194, 224, 273, 279, 295, 312, 334, 406, 456n3, 551n84
Philipsburg, 195, 221
Phillips, Prince, 170, 178, 183
Pierce, Chloe, 192, 489n51
Pierre (Missouri slave), 17, 345, 350
Pierre, Joseph, 172, 176–7, 304
Pierson, Joseph, 84, 98, 158, 184–5, 191, 208, 210, 256–9; his family, 84
Pierson, Valentine, 84, 259
Platt, Nathaniel, 53
Plattsburgh (NY), 53, 97, 188
Plauvier, Margaret, 99, 148–9, 158, 436n63
Pointe-Fortune, 120, 147
Pointe-aux-Trembles, 75, 466n11
Pointe-Claire, 227, 462n52, 491n71
Pointe-Lévy, 287–8
Poiré, Joseph, 115–16, 378
Pollard, Edward, 21
Population, 12, 73–4, 109, 175, 228, 234, 302, 304–5, 456n3, 528n53; censuses, 4, 96, 302–4. *See also* Slave population
Port Hope (Ont.), 63
Porteous, Charles, 185
Pothier, Toussaint, 197
Pouget, Misses Amable and Josephte, 114
Poupard, James, 91
Powell, Elizabeth (Mrs), 144, 157
Powell, John, 144, 157, 202; his family, 144
Powis, Thomas, 119, 144
Pownall, George, 44, 366

Prairie du Chien (Wis.), 17
Prejumier, Tibby, 206, 212
Prentice, Miles, 316, 320,
Prescott (Ont.), 179, 202, 421n8
Prescott, Robert, 49, 58
Prince Edward Island, 11–12, 57, 69, 162, 283, 302
Pritchard, Azariah, 337
Prostitution, 94, 103, 128, 140, 161, 185, 188–9, 195, 211–12, 235, 243, 247, 251, 288, 300, 301, 500n144, 509n29
Prudhomme, Marie Charlotte, 101
Pruyn, Eliza, 209
Pruyn, Jane, 209
Pruyn, John, 184, 198, 209, 284
Pruyn, John Jr, 209
Pruyn, Marie Elizabeth, 209, 210, 301
Pruyn, William, 209
Pseudo-slavery, 72, 74–5

Quebec Act (1774), 26, 41, 347, 349, 352, 355–6, 374
Quebec Herald, 313
Quebec Mercury, 310, 313, 314
Queen, Samuel, 302
Quesnel, Joseph (attorney), 154
Quesnel, Joseph (poet and merchant), 539n50

Rafter, Margaret, 47, 79–80
Raftsmen, 184, 200–2, 206, 272
Raudot, Jacques, 24–8, 32, 63, 346, 348, 354–5, 365–8
Rebellions of 1837–38, 6, 168, 224–5, 264, 300
Regot, Jean, 423n27
Reid, James, 24–35, 39, 59, 60, 76, 117, 159, 263, 345–50
Rhéaume, Alexis, 534n26
Rhéaume, Charles, 30–1
Richards, Tymon, 438n94
Richardson, Hero, 207, 445n3
Richardson, Jane (Mrs), 117

Richardson, Mary, 271, 279
Richelieu River, 87, 139, 154, 172, 201
Riddell, William Renwick, 10, 70, 71, 76
Ritchie, Anne, 74–5
Robert (Jamaican slave), 430 n17
Robertson, Benjamin, 471n50
Robertson, Emelie, 471n50
Robertson, Daniel, 30, 129, 142, 198, 402
Rogers, Richard, 167–8, 170–2, 178, 182, 196; his family, 168, 479n12
Rogers, Stephen, 189, 195, 258, 293, 490n61
Rollings, James, 161, 192, 227–8
Rolph, Thomas, 300
Ross, David, 153–4, 465n5
Ross, John, 399
Rousseau, Dominique, 47
Routier, Jean-Baptiste, 23–4
Roxburgh, William, 327
Roy, Joseph, 329, 443n136
Roy, Pierre, 141–2, 405
Royal Engineers, 398, 399, 400, 424n30, 525n23
Royal Proclamation (1763), 26, 347, 348–9, 352, 355, 371–2, 374, 377
Ruette d'Auteuil de Monceaux, Charles, 31
Ruiter, Phillip, 195–6, 486n21
Runnel, Julia, 498n131
Rusk, Mary, 84, 158, 210, 258–9, 473n80
Russell, John, 37
Ryan, Pierce, 403, 443n129

St Andrew's (St-André-d'Argenteuil), 195, 248, 249, 471n50
St-Antoine-sur-Richelieu, 19, 72, 110, 154, 293
St-Armand, 78, 189, 195, 219, 221
St Augustine Society, 292
St-Denis-sur-Richelieu, 55, 224, 264
St-Eustache, 53, 156, 195, 275, 281, 544n73
St-Jean-Port-Joli, 74
St-Jean-sur-Richelieu (St John's), 110, 114, 116, 137, 172, 239, 253, 318, 332, 382

St Lawrence Steamboat Co., 165, 178
St Louis, Mo., 13, 16–22, 24, 29, 402
St Louis, Angélique Filiatrault *dit*, 156, 281
St-Luc, Luc de Lacorne, 55, 88, 90, 92, 93, 128–9, 134, 135, 203, 403
St-Luc, Marguerite de Lacorne, 134, 135, 203–4
St-Luc, Marie Anne de Lacorne, 55, 87–95, 135
St-Michel (on Montreal Island), 194–5, 196,
St-Omer, Lambert, 116, 454n95
Saint-Ours, Paul Roch de, 45
St Patrick's Society, 228, 292
Ste-Anne Market, 193–4, 230, 298
Ste-Anne-de-Bellevue, 152
Ste-Anne-de-Mascouche, 280
Ste-Anne-du-Sud (Ste-Anne-de-la-Pocatière), 192
Ste-Famille, Île d'Orléans, 123
Salter, Catherine, 211, 284, 288, 493n87
Sambo, one-time Virginia slave, 97–8
Sampson, James, 157–8, 172–3, 176, 183
Saul, John, 327, 332, 403
Sault-au-Récollet, 98, 274, 335
Schenectady (NY), 110, 200, 272, 283, 389, 546n8
Schylor, Niclos, 401
Scott, John, 505n3
Seabrook, James, 94, 272, 285
Seigneurial lands, 82, 150, 470n50, 534n27, 543n73, 547n22
Selkirk, Thomas Douglas, Lord, 199
"Servants," 3–4, 8, 13, 19, 20, 23, 26, 33–4, 44, 56, 66, 67, 72, 74, 80, 81, 91, 103, 111, 117–18, 121, 143, 184–5, 195–6, 210, 260–3
Settlement, 180, 231, 304–5; Land grants, 100, 143–4, 203, 204, 205–6, 207, 403; Montreal – cohabitation, 157–8; Montreal – landowners, 143, 144–157, 227; Montreal – tenants, 143, 157–8, 222–3, 227; Ottawa Valley, 100, 147, 272
Shaw, Angus, 199, 201

Shaw, Joseph, 37, 193
Sherbrooke, Sir John Coape, 242
Sherwood, Justus, 384, 389, 447n15, 548n32
Shields, John, 178
Shoemakers, 192, 267–8, 274–5
Shuter, John, 80–5, 150
Shuter, Joseph, 149–50, 161
Simcoe, John Graves, 28, 32, 67–9, 70, 76
Simmons, Selina, 182
Simon ("Free Negroe"), 390, 394
Simpson, George, 199,
Simpson, Jacob, 207, 222, 236, 284, 301, 336, 468n29, 490n60, 511n46, 541n60
Simpson, John (Quebec trader), 116
Sinclair, Margaret, 167, 191, 210, 453n85
Sinclair, Patrick, 402
Singer, James, 110
60th (Royal American) Regt., 47, 80, 81, 94, 119, 202, 449n34, 458n24, 470n50, 517n1, 531n13, 547n22
Skene, Philip, 239–40, 382
Sketchley & Freeman, 324–5
Slave discipline, 20, 48–9, 50, 108, 119–20, 122, 126–30, 136–8
Slave escapes, 40, 46–50, 56–62, 119–20, 138, and Appendix I
Slave manumissions, 9, 23, 24, 32, 33, 46, 56, 72, 74, 81, 82, 97, 121, 122, 124, 137–43, 271
Slave origins, 58, 73, 106, 116–17, 197, 202, 301–2, 304, 309, 381–407
Slave laws: Britain, 24, 29, 35–8, 58, 59, 64, 68–70, 75–8, 142, 349–50, 353–4, 355–6, 376; Ontario, 28, 29, 38–9, 58, 66–9, 71, 76, 135, 350, 356–7, 375–378; Quebec, 24–35, 38–9, 40–6, 58, 64–6, 69–71, 76–7, 347, 352, 356–7, 375. *See also* Capitulation of 1760, *Code noir*, Gilles Hocquart, Jacques Raudot, *Quebec Act*.
Slave population, 13, 27, 46, 95–7, 103–6, 107, 109, 116–17, 119
Slave trade: public sales, 22, 23, 29, 47, 55,

109, 116, 317, 324–5, 326, 331, 334–5, 430n15; traders and drovers, 4–5, 18, 23, 61, 101, 113–17, 134, 197, 380–1, 403–7, 465n83, 545n1 and n6

Slavery: a convenience, 46, 111–12, 118–19, 121, 133; a fact of life, 6, 23, 24, 60, 107, 109, 113, 135; its invisibility, 8, 12, 16–17, 18–19, 23, 24, 29, 108–9, 112–21, 134–5

Smith, Antoine, 19–20
Smith, David (David Smith & Co.), 63–4
Smith, David William, 68
Smith, Elias, 48, 63–5, 80–3, 247, 435n63
Smith, Elias Jr, 438n94
Smith, Eliza, 426n54
Smith, Jacob, 54, 65, 100, 123, 144, 278–9, 284, 379; his family, 279
Smith, James, 193, 269; his family, 283
Smith, John, 275
Smith, Laughlin, 192
Smith, Thomas H., 37, 192
Smith, William, 22, 29, 44, 119
Snetzsinger, Matthew, 385
Snider, Thomas, and family, 280
Société d'histoire de Montréal, 14
Société St-Jean-Baptiste, 265, 292
Soeurs Hospitalières de Saint-Joseph, 110
Solomon, Ezekiel, 197
Solomon, Levy Sr, 330
Solomon, Levy Jr, 147, 271; Levy Solomon & Co., 147
Somerset, James, 26, 48, 60, 117
Sorel, 30, 110, 116, 139, 147, 178, 205, 206, 251, 253–4
South America, 251
South Carolina, 58, 109, 120, 162, 376
Spectateur canadien, 290
Spencer, Hazelton, 67
Spencer, William, 335–6
Stansfeld, David, 195
Steamboats, 164–78, 180, 182, 183, 191–2, 196, 210, 212, 235, 270, 281, 301, 304
Steel, Daniel, 101

Stewart, Charles (Somerset's master), 26
Stewart Charles (Quebec notary), 536n38
Stock, John, 17, 111, 119
Stockbird, Thomas, 150, 157
Stockton, Rebecca, 439n98
Stowe, Harriet Beecher, 59–60
Strong, Hester Livingston, 483n69
Sullivan, Thomas John, 49, 63, 119, 447n13
Sulpician priests, 110, 150, 152
Sydenham, George Poulett Thompson, Lord, 249, 300

Tabeau, Jean-Baptiste, 197
Taffe, Henry, 118; his family, 279
Tappan, Ann, 552n2
Tappan, Arthur, 209, 481n42, 552n2
Tarieu de Lanaudière, Charles-François, 450n42, 451n55
Tarieu de Lanaudière, Charles-Louis, 22, 128, 449n34, 461n47
Taylor, Isaac, 302
Taylor, John, 303
Terrebonne, 144, 280
Thomas, Jacob, 381, 403–4
Thomas, Reuben. *See* Slaves: Jupiter.
Thomas, William, 208, 502n12 and n14
Thompson, Cornelius, 174
Thompson, Edward, 470n50
Thompson, Esther, 172
Thompson, Joseph, 200; his family, 283
Thompson, Marguerite Eulalie, 280, 282
Thompson, Morris, 194, 213, 483n61
Thompson, Richard, 157, 160, 174–5, 191, 222–3, 227, 268
Thompson, William, 255, 257–8; his family, 280, 282
Thomson, Betsy, 194, 491n73
Thomson, Henry, and family, 194–5, 514n85
Thomson, Prince, 186
Tieple, John, 274–5, 335
Tinsley, Thomas, 283
Tison, Marianne, 20–1, 87

Todd, Andrew, 17
Todd, Isaac, 17, 460n41
Toronto, 179, 180, 182, 226, 229, 281, 299, 304, 421n6, 429n7, 435n57, 457n15, 503n21, 506n6
Torrance, John, 165
Tracey, Daniel, 228
Treaty of Ghent (1814), 207–8
Treaty of Paris (1763), 7, 346, 351, 355, 370–1
Treaty of Paris (1783), 376, 403
Trim, Charlotte, 149, 281; her family, 283, 477n124
Trim, Henriette, 149, 281, 302, 477n124
Trim, Mary Ann Shuter, 149, 160–1, 162, 281, 302
Trinidad. *See* Emigration schemes
Trois-Rivières, 44, 96, 174, 242, 251, 253, 254, 287, 308, 333,
Trudel, Marcel, 9, 13, 80, 95–8, 103–7, 241, 278
Turnbull, John Duplessis, 189, 191, 344
Turner, Edmond Albert, 471n50
Turner, Jervis George, 49, 63, 378
Turner, John Sr, 49, 321–2, 326, 331, 434n46, 535n33
Twiss, William, 386, 398, 400–1

Union of the Canadas (1841), 6, 15, 297, 305, 356
Upper Canada Anti-Slavery Society, 304
Upper Canada Line (stages and steamers), 165, 166, 178, 289
Ursuline nuns, 108

Valentine, Alexander, 84, 152–6, 157, 159, 160, 173, 227, 234, 235, 236, 301
Valentine, Tally Reny, 160
Vankoughnet, Michael, 340, 543n71
Van Vliet, Garret, 426n52, 533n26, 545n1
Vaudreuil, Pierre Rigaud de Vaudreuil-Cavagnial, marquis de, 28, 370–1, 463n63
Vaudreuil (seigneury), 65, 137

Vermont, 78, 138, 189, 195, 196, 201, 202, 219, 224, 250, 264, 303, 382, 405, 406, 483n61, 512n56
Viger, Jacques, 10, 15–16, 22, 27, 34, 35, 134, 135, 155, 203, 232
Vignau, Joseph, 53, 537n42
Vincent, Nicolas, 252
Vindicator, 228, 231–2, 263–4
Virginia, 26, 39, 45, 97, 150, 197, 279, 364, 373, 376, 435n57, 471n50, 477n21, 480n37, 487n33, 503n20
Virginia, Luther, 512n56
Virginia, Stephen, 299
Virginia, William C., 250
Virginia, Wyman, 250
Voice of the Fugitive, 181
Voting rights, 34–5, 143, 218–20, 222, 232, 375

Wages, 125, 145, 147, 151, 169–72, 173–4, 175, 176, 186, 188, 196, 197–8, 201–2, 207, 208, 212–17, 245, 271, 272, 275, 460n42, 478n6, 486n21, 483n61, 491n76, 497n115, 543n71; slaves' wages, 118, 197, 399, 400–1
Walker, David, 136, 225–6
Walker, James, 53, 54, 65, 437n72
Walker, Robert, 460n42
Walton, Mary Ann Stewart, 115, 457n20
Ward, Samuel Ringgold, 35 (and 428n76), 180–1, 276–7, 289
Ward, William, 405, 406
Wars: Napoleonic Wars, 55, 69–70, 169, 200, 202; Seven Years War, 6, 118, 142, 239, 425n36; US Civil War, 11, 17, 97, 143, 182; US War of Independence, 29, 34, 45, 46, 47, 97, 100, 106, 110, 117, 126, 144, 202, 205, 239, 271, 274, 295, 376, 381–407; War of 1812, 35, 169, 172, 184, 194, 202–9, 257–9
Washerwoman, unnamed, 97
Way, Gad, 470n50
Webb, Alexander, 240–1

Webster, Thomas, 258
Weldin, Ebert, 98–9, 192, 274–5, 335
Weldin, Elie, 275
Weldin, Elizabeth, 274
Weldin, James, 98; his family, 274–5
Weldin, Mary, 274
Werden, Isaac, 314
West Indies, 27, 28, 32–3, 36, 37–8, 47, 64, 103, 106, 108, 117, 119, 128, 138, 140, 141, 168, 175, 202, 225, 297, 301, 304, 324, 346, 359–67, 374, 375, 376. *See also* Bahamas, Barbados, Bermuda, Jamaica, Emigration schemes
Westphall, George, 119
White, John, 67
Whitehall (NY), 239, 382
Whiting & Crane, 251
Wiley, Ann, 240
Wily, Isaac Newton, 273
Wily, William, 273
William IV, 38, 46
Williams, Charles, 178
Williams, Elizabeth, 249, 255
Williams, George, 196
Williams, John, 206, 208
Williams, Maria, 206, 211
Williams, Mauger, 161, 178
Williams, Patty, 198, 273
Williams, Robert, 158, 172, 176, 178, 208, 288
Williams, Sente, 158
Williams, Thomas, 208
Williams, Washington, 167, 183, 301, 302, 505n47, 515n88
Williamson, Jacques, 208; his family, 280
Willsboro (NY), 308, 318
Wilson, Jane, 158, 160, 174, 296, 297, 300, 303–4
Winklefoss, Andrew, 49–50
Women's work, 167, 210–12
Woolford, David, 192
Woolsey, John William, 55, 460n42
Wormley, Moses Powell, 262–3, 408–15

Wragg, Richard, 100, 144
Wright, Henrietta, 186
Wright, Henry Blake, 186
Wright, John, 151–2, 194, 213, 275–6, 277, 284; his family, 276, 284
Wright, Marie Catherine, 140, 466n16
Wright, Marie Charlotte, 140, 466n16
Wright, Mary, 143–4, 279
Wright, William, clerk, 186–8, 284
Wright, Dr William, 186–8, 284

Yeoman, Elisha, 114, 406
York, Sally, wife of James Grant, 158, 248
York, Sarah, wife of Joseph Pierre, 177, 304
York Rangers, 203
Young, Rev. John (Montreal), 54
Young, John (Quebec), 72, 426n53

Zamphier, Peter, 205–6, 218

SLAVES

The names of slaves are followed, in parentheses, by a brief indication of their owners' identity (U stands for "owner uncertain" or "owner unknown"). The other listings are of American slaves captured in wartime (W) or persons who, it is thought, might have been slaves in Quebec at one time but whose slave status is unconfirmed (?).

Abraham (W), 403
Abraham (J. Johnson), 392
Abraham, Peter (?), 259, 453n85, 473n80
Adrien (M. de Vaudreuil), 426n50
Allen, Manuel (T.J. Sullivan), 49–50, 59, 60, 62–3, 78, 80, 99, 119, 140, 436n63, 447n13
Ambroise, Marianne (Lacorne de St-Luc), 203–4, 280
André/Andrew (G. Levy), 31, 315
Angélique (H. Neilson's ancestors), 444n139

Angélique Anne (F. Corbin), 293, 523n14
Anne (P. Roy), 141–2, 405
Anne, accused of arson (U) 459n37
Ashley, Robert (?), 99–100, 167–76, 182, 517n1
Augustin (N. Marchesseau), 49–50, 60, 62, 78

Baid (?), 279
Baine, John (?), 184
Baraca, Catherine (D. Gaudet), 121–4, 293, 462n52
Baraca, Marie Anne (Mrs), (D. Gaudet), 123–4
Baraca, Pierre (D. Gaudet), 123–4
Barbe, Catherine (L. Smith), 192
Baron, George (?), 101
Barthélemy, Jean (?), 279, 473n82; his family, 279
Bartholomy, Nero (R. Gray), 75, 213–17
Beaumenil, Joseph (M. Fortier), 279, 431n28
Bell (G. Hipps), 8, 321
Bell (C. Beaubain), 404
Bellai (Misses Pouget), 114
Ben (M. Michaels), 330
Benjamin (T. Gage), 426n50
Bett (Johnston & Purss), 308–9, 329
Betty (J. Gregory), 388
Betty (J. Johnson), 393
Billings, Justus (?), 219–21
Blair, Alicia (W. Smith), 424n30
Blair, Charlotte (W. Smith), 424n30
Blair, Leeds (W. Smith), 424n30
Bonga, Charlotte (D. Robertson), 155, 168, 198–9
Bonga, Étienne, son of Jean (D. Robertson), 198
Bonga, Jean (D. Robertson), 142, 198, 402, 492n79
Bonga, Jeanne or Jeannette (D. Robertson), 142, 155, 198, 402
Bonga, Pierre (D. Robertson), 198–200

Bonga, Rosalie (D. Robertson), 110, 184, 198–9, 209
Brooks, Tom (R.M. Guthrie), 328, 401
Brown, Betsy (?), 517n1
Brown, Jean (J. Poiré), 116, 378
Bruce (G. Christie), 117–18, 137–8, 248, 315, 319, 531n13
Bulkley, Mary (L. Olivier), 114–15, 124–5
Burns, George (?), 241–2, 279–80

Caesar (J.-B. Bouchette), 22, 23, 308, 331
Caesar (L. Solomon), 457n16
Caesar Scipio (J. Sherwood), 447n15
Caesar, Hanna (?), 84, 258
Caleb (M. and J. Macnider), 330, 453n85
Campbell, Mary (G. Christie), 285
Canon, Jean Baptiste *dit* (M. de Vaudreuil), 426n50
Caploux, Marianne (F. Dunoyer), 139, 432n30
Carib Indian (J.-B. Routier), 23
Cash (H. Ritchie), 323
Catharine (J. Grant), 389–90
Catherine (L. Payet), 110
Catherine, wife Lamour (D. Robertson), 99, 142, 145, 210
Catherine (B. Gibb), 337, 541n65
Cato (T. Barron), 381–2
Cesar (J. Morrison), 381
Cesar, accused of assault (U), 246
César/Antoine, a Panis (L. Payet) 110
Charity (?), 543n71
Charles (M. de Vaudreuil), 101, 463n63
Charles (D.C. Delisle), 110
Charles (P. Guerout), 325
Charles, Marie Elisabeth (de Longueuil), 122
Charlotte (J. Cook), 47–8, 49, 50, 60, 62, 63, 72, 75, 78, 79–80, 99, 140, 149, 151, 159, 160, 161, 277
Charlotte (L. Olivier), 115
Charper, Jean (P. Dumignault), 424n31
Christie, Josette (J. Gregory), 448n24

Christie, Peggy/Margaret July (U), 273, 449n35, 501n11
Clarice (G. Christie), 449n35
Cloe (J. Joseph), 334
Coffee, Rathass (W), 239–40, 382–3
Coll, Catherine (P. McFarlane), 54, 60, 100, 123, 278, 279
Combwood (J. Sherwood), 389
Conine, John (J. Conyn), 400
Constant (P. Fortier), 197–8
Cuff (J. Campbell), 92–4
Cutan, Josiah (J. Turner Sr), 535n33
Cynda/Jenny (J. Lagord), 40–1, 114–15

Darlington, John (?), 197
Demarin, Joseph François (?), 156–7, 195, 278; his family, 279, 281
Denise (administrators of New France), 239
Diana (S. Anderson), 389, 402
Dianne/Charlotte (nuns of Hôtel–Dieu), 110, 293
Dick (W. Grant), 105, 316
Dick (P. Larchevêque *dit* La Promenade), 406
Drummond (J. McCord), 314

E**, a "sable" female (?), 120, 296
Élisabeth (J. Campbell), 87, 88, 89, 91, 92
Élisabeth (P. Panet), 293
Elizabeth (S. Jones), 403
Emilia/Amelia Fleming (E. Smith), 80–5, 211
Estiennette (G. Gamelin), 424n36
Étienne Paul (Congregation of Notre Dame), 110

Fanny (W.A. Grant), 22
Fary (J. Johnson), 392, 400
Ferland, Jacques (?), and family, 155
Finlay, Peggy (J. Finlay), 435n63
Fleming, John/John Gray (J. Shuter), 80–5, 150, 158, 159, 195, 248, 443n129, 466n10
Flora (Desrivières Beaubien), 405
Flora (L. Solomon), 457n16

Fonda, Jack (W), 391, 400, 402
Fonda, Jack Jr (W), 391, 400, 402
Fonda, Tanse (W), 391, 400
Fortennéter, Jean/John Fortunator (?), 155
Fortune (J. Orillat), 534n26
Fortune (U), 323
Fortune, Henry (P. Dumignault), 424n31
Fortune, Titus (?), 157, 273
François (J. Campbell), 87–92, 95, 101, 122,
François Jr (J. Campbell), 87–9, 91, 95
François (L. Payet), 110
François, Joseph/Joseph Frank (?), 85–6, 155, 486n22, 488n36, 491n73, 495n102
François Josué (J. Campbell), 88–9, 91
François Xavier (J. Campbell), 89–92
Frank (J. Johnson), 391, 400
Frank/François (J.L. Ainsse), 56, 60–2, 78, 449n33
Fraser (P. Guy), 127–8
Fundy, Mary (?), 144, 157

Geneviève (C.L. Tarieu de Lanaudière), 22
Geneviève (L. Olivier), 115
Grace (D. Lynd), 537n44
"George a Negroe" (?) 246
George (D. Lynd), 537n44
Giles, Cato (U), 195–6
Giles, Hannah (U), 196
Grandison, Charles (W), 394
Grant, Tom/Thomas (D. McKillock), 91, 137–8, 184
Guillaume (J. Howard), 117
Guillet, Catherine (Beaucourt), 79, 140, 150–2, 157, 158, 161, 162, 177, 194, 210, 259, 268, 275–6, 284, 304; her children, 140, 466n16 and n18

Hagar (J. Johnson), 393
Hall, Murray/Montreal (?), 222–3, 234, 453n85, 501n11
Hank (Mrs O'Reilly), 442n125
Hannah (W. Lindsay), 65
Hanover (C. Chaboillez), 21–2

Harry/Michel Henry (de Lotbinière), 137, 139
Harry (B. Hays), 116
Henry (V. Baudin), 101
Hyacinthe, a farmer (?), 341, 470n50
Hypolite, Joseph (U) 432n30

Ireland, fugitive New York slave, 318
Isaac/Charles (A. Pritchard), 337
Isabell (J. Mompesson), 515n86
Ishmaël (J. Turner Sr), 309, 321-2, 326, 331

Jack (S. Anderson), 383, 389, 394
Jack (Finlay & Gregory), 320
Jack (W. Grant), 335
Jack (J. Johnson), 392
Jack/Jacques (C. Chaboillez), 21-2
Jack/Jacques (F. Boucher de Laperrière), 137
Jack/Jacques (J. McGill), 74
Jackson, Sarah (?), 80, 447n14; her children, 99
Jacob (M. Prentice), 320-1
Jacob/Isaac (S. Judah), 126-7, 130, 133-4, 385-6, 388, 394
Jacob (J. Johnson), 392
Jacobs, Jenny (M. Jacobs), 53
Jacqho (J. Brooks), 119
Jacque (J. Campbell), 89-90
Jacque Jr (J. Campbell), 89-90, 91
Jacques (J. Orillat), 533n26, 545n1
Jacques Michel (de Lotbinière), 293
Jane (J. Johnson), 393
Jane (J. Frazer), 50, 339
Jane, associate of Charlotte Prudhomme (?), 101
Jarvis, Elizabeth (?), 194
Jasmin, Jacques César *dit* (I. Bourassa), 122, 432n30
Jean Baptiste (L. Gauthier), 116, 540n59
Jean Baptiste (L. Olivier), 115
Jean Baptiste (C.-F. Tarieu de Lanaudière), 450n42

Jean Baptiste (R. Lester), 41
Jean Louis (L.C. Foucher), 22-3, 541n61
Jeanne/Geneviève, a Panis (J. Campbell), 87-92, 101, 122
Jeanne/John (T. Dunn), 123, 538n49
Jeanne/Jeannette (J. Orillat), 381, 533n26
Jenny (Z. Macaulay), 466n8
Joe (W. Brown), 308, 309, 313, 319, 320, 321, 322, 328-9, 463n62
Joe/Cuff (Maisonville), 332
John (A. McNeill), 538n45
Johnson, Benjamin (P. Ryan), 443n129
Johnson, Sarah, wife of Samuel Luke (U), 118, 443n129, 517n1
Joseph (J. Hébert), 405
Jude (J. Johnson), 393
Judith/Julia Johnson (E. Smith), 48-9, 50, 57, 60, 62, 63, 75, 78, 79-85, 98, 99, 103, 122, 195, 211, 258-9, 296
Julie (É. Campion), 442n8
Julie (F. Dumoulin), 426n52
Jupiter (J. Johnson), 96, 284, 400, 450n54

Keeling, Othello (U), 152, 158, 448n24, 478n5, 479n24, 495n104
King, Joseph (W), 382
Kitts (D. Carbry), 119

L'Africain, Jean-Baptiste (Beaucourt), 72, 155, 167-8, 170, 172, 182, 198, 451n55, 453n85, 473n80, 486n22
Lamour, Hilaire (D. Robertson), 99, 142, 144-5, 149, 150, 197
Lane, Margaret (Mrs) (?), 508n20
Lane, Robert (Bob, hangman at Quebec) (?), 240-1
Latour, Charles Larramée *dit* (widow Latour), 432n30
Ledy (G. Westphall), 119
Le Jeune, Olivier (various owners), 27
Léveillé, Mathieu (administrators of New France), 238-9
Lisette (de Gaspé), 74, 137

Louis Antoine (D. Gaudet), 121–5, 128, 133–4, 293; his family, 462n52
Louise, tobacco seller (U), 432n30
Louise/Lisette Lewis (W. Fortune), 121
Long, George (W), 382
Louison (C. Chaboillez), 21
Lowcanes (W. Gill), 189–90, 319
Luke, Samuel (?), 118, 447n14
Lydia (J. Frazer), 8, 50, 57–9

McEvoy, Henry (U), 77, 203–4
Margaret and children (J. Cuthbert Sr), 439n98
Marguerite (J. Campbell), 89–90, 91
Maria (D. Claus), 20, 394
Maria (D. Lynd), 537n44
Marie (P. Loubet), 545n5
Marie (E. Pollard), 423n27
Marie (Mr Lacroix), 424n31
Marie, Panis at Lachine (U), 101
Marie/Manon (T. Catin), 30–1, 101, 140–1
Marie Angélique, 1788–92 (J. Campbell), 88–9, 91
Marie Angélique, ca 1781–95, (J. Campbell), 92, 95
Marie Anne (J. Campbell), 87–8, 90, 91
Marie Anne Catherine (É. Dubois), 459n37
Marie Anne Victoire (M. de Vaudreuil), 426n50
Marie Catherine (P. Berthelet), 444n137
Marie Elizabeth (Lacorne St–Luc), 88
Marie Josephe (J. Campbell), 89, 91
Marie Josephte (P. Dumignault), 424n31
Marie Josèphe Angélique (Poulin de Francheville), 36–7, 238
Marie Julie (L. Chaboillez), 72
Marie Louise (J. McGill), 85
Marie Magdeleine (U), 432n30
Marie Magdelene, died age 11 (U), 101
Marie Marguerite (J. Campbell), 89–90, 91
Marie Thérèse Zémire (Beaucourt), 444n137, 466n13

Marry Lewis/Marie Louise (U), 128–9
Martin, Peter (J. Butler), 383
Mentor, François Dominique *dit* (D. Nafrechoux), 194, 270–1, 293
Michel (M. Fortier), 432n28
Michel Remy (T. Dunn), 123
Mimi (J. McNamara), 457n20
Mink (J.J. Herkimer), 391, 400
Mongo (J.-B. Hervieux), 246

Nemo (H. Ritchie), 323
Neptune (J. Orillat), 534n26
Nero (J. Mittleberger), 119, 323, 378, 388, 394–6
Newport (W), 382
Nicholas (D. Claus), 393

Pearce, Margaret (?), 99–100, 168, 445n3, 479n24
Pegg (A. Fisher), 405
Peter (D. Claus), 394
Phillis, at Sorel (Sawer), 30
Phillis (J. Johnson), 393
Phoebe/Phoebe Johnson (P. Ryan), 72, 97, 443n129
Pierre (I. Delezenne), 271
Pierre Jean/John (J. Campbell), 92, 94
Pierre (C. Chaboillez), 423n27
Plato (W), 402–3
Pompé, Jean-Baptiste (L. Payet), 110
Pompé, Louis Joseph *dit* (de Lotbinière), 65, 72, 278
Pompey (Johnston & Purss), 309, 317
Pompey (Mr Beaubain), 402
Pratt, Caesar (A. Bradt), 400–1
Price, Marie Angélique (?), 154–5, 210, 280
Prince (J. Papineau), 114, 135
Prince (J. McNamara), 405, 457n20
Pruyn, Cato (W), 391, 400, 403
Puro, Pascal (J. Sargent), 331

Quéry, Jean-Baptiste (F. Dunoyer), 139

INDEX 603

Quéry, Jean-Baptiste Jr (F. Dunoyer), 139, 432n30
Richard (R. Hoyle), 333
Robin (J. Frazer), 29, 30, 32, 40, 50, 56–60, 62–3, 65, 75–6, 78, 119
Rose (J. Stock), 17–24, 27, 35, 39, 40, 87, 111, 119
Rose (P. Mézière), 405–6, 453n95
Rose (W. Mathews), 116, 119, 454n95
Rose (L. St-Omer), 454n95
Rose (L. Payet) 1793–96, 110–1
Rose (J. Brooks), 119, 535n33
Rose (É. Campion), 422n8
Rose (M.-L. Testard de Montigny), 139
Rose/Rosina, partner of John Fleming (?), 84
Ruth (J. Saul), 332, 403, 453n85, 536n40
Ruth Jane (D. Fisher), 50–3, 119, 378

Salé (T. Dunn), 123, 538 n49
Sambo/Jean (R. Lester), 460n41
Saunders, Lydia (G. Westphall), 119
Sam (J. Johnson), 392, 394
Sampson (Mr Dumont), 75
Sarah (P. Berthelet), 56, 61–2
Sarah (J. McGill), 72, 85–6, 103
Sarah (C. Lepailleur), 404
Sarah (C. Blake), 99
Sibilla (A. Fisher), 405
Smart, Antoine (North West Co.), 54–5, 56
Smith, Catherine (Mr Lane), 100
Snow (R.H. Laforce), 326–7
Stevens (P. Gamelin), 547n20
Sukey (Mrs O'Reilly), 442n125
Susannah (U), 317
Susanne (L. Parent), 293
Suzanne (J. Dumoulin), 545n1
Sylvia (E.W. Gray), 130
Sylvia (W. Lindsay), 65
Sylvie (P. Beatson), 55–6, 403
Sylvie Jane (U), 50–3, 119, 378

Tanno (J. Johnson), 110, 392

Thomas. *See Tom Grant*.
Thomas (J. Campbell), 55–6, 90–1, 95, 135
Thomas, a Panis (D.A. Grant), 22
Thomas (S. Judah), 126, 130–4
Thomas (J. Stuart), 546n8
Thome (C. de Labruère de Boucherville), 491n72
Thomme, Marie Louise Jeanne (J. Orillat), 73–4, 533n26
Thompson, Jonathan (S. Fraser), 322
Tight (J. Saul), 327, 403
Tim (E. Pollard), 424n27
Toby (C. Blake), 405, 551n80
Tom (D. Claus), 393, 423n20
Tom (J. Fraser), 101
Tom (J. Johnson), 392
Tom (J. Jordan), 387
Tom (P. Langan), 389
Trim, John (S. Allen), 9, 48, 79, 99, 140, 142–3, 144, 148–52, 156, 157–63, 164, 165–6, 176, 178, 184–5, 186, 188, 197, 207, 210, 218, 227–8, 233–5, 236, 268, 273, 274, 277–8, 281, 283, 295, 342, 448n23, 471n54, 473n81, 479n19, 488n36, 495n102, 503n21,

Unidentified:
"Black lady" at Louiseville (?), 296
Boy, age 2 (P. de Bonne), 405
Boy, age 9 (J. Grant) 405
Female (M.-A. Cerré), 18
Female (J. Berlinguet), 423n25
Female (J.-H. Lacroix), 22
Lydia Saunders' son (G. Westphall), 119
Male (G.H. Le Compte Dupré), 20
Male (J.-B. Curatteau), 110
Male (J. Lagord), 115–16
Male (W. Sutherland), 394
"Negro Wench" from New York (U), 325
"Petite négresse" (J. Cuthbert), 439n98
Runaway male (J. Orillat), 318
Slaves (2) (Jane Richardson), 117

Slaves (2) of (Rev. S. Belknap) (w), 295
Son of Sarah and Toby (C. Blake), 405
Wife of Jacob (S. Judah), 126, 130, 385–6, 388
Urbain (J.-B. Routier), 444 n137

Vansoke, Roger (w), 387, 402
Violetta (J. Campbell), 92–4, 129–30

Will (E. Levy), 315
William (J. Johnson), 400
William (Mr McDonell, Quebec), 385
William, François (A. Juchereau Duchesnay), 125–6
Williams (D.A. Grant), 22
Williams, Henry (J. Young), 72
Wright, William (J. Dunlop), 72, 140, 150–2, 156, 157, 158, 259, 275, 284, 479n24

York, Thomas (u), 433n31
Young, Mary (?), 420n7